Sex, Politics, and Putin

POLITICAL LEGITIMACY
IN RUSSIA

VALERIE SPERLING

OXFORD
UNIVERSITY PRESS

Oxford University Press is a department of the University of Oxford.
It furthers the University's objective of excellence in research, scholarship,
and education by publishing worldwide.

Oxford New York
Auckland Cape Town Dar es Salaam Hong Kong Karachi
Kuala Lumpur Madrid Melbourne Mexico City Nairobi
New Delhi Shanghai Taipei Toronto

With offices in
Argentina Austria Brazil Chile Czech Republic France Greece
Guatemala Hungary Italy Japan Poland Portugal Singapore
South Korea Switzerland Thailand Turkey Ukraine Vietnam

Oxford is a registered trade mark of Oxford University Press
in the UK and certain other countries.

Published in the United States of America by
Oxford University Press
198 Madison Avenue, New York, NY 10016

© Oxford University Press 2015

Library of Congress Cataloging-in-Publication Data
Sperling, Valerie.
 Sex, politics, and Putin : political legitimacy in Russia / Valerie Sperling.
  p. cm. — (Oxford studies in culture and politics)
 Includes bibliographical references and index.
 ISBN 978-0-19-932434-7 (hardcover : alk. paper) — ISBN 978-0-19-932435-4 (pbk. : alk. paper)
 1. Sexism in political culture—Russia (Federation) 2. Political participation—Russia (Federation)
 3. Sex role—Political aspects—Russia (Federation) 4. Women—Political activity—Russia (Federation)
 5. Russia (Federation)—Politics and government—1991– I. Title.
 JN6699.A15S676 2015
 322.40947—dc23
                    2014012792

9 8 7 6 5 4 3 2

Printed in the United States of America on acid-free paper

Contents

Acknowledgments

The "village" that it took to write this book spans two continents. Within its borders lie several generous institutions and numerous individuals who helped bring this project to fruition. First, the institutions. The Francis A. Harrington Public Affairs Fund at Clark University paid my way to Russia in June 2011 to interview pro- and anti-Putin political activists. My second research trip (June 2012) enabled me to connect with Russian feminist activists; it was supported by a fellowship from the International Research & Exchanges Board with funds provided by the US Department of State through the Title VIII Program, neither of which is responsible for the views expressed herein. The Davis Center for Russian and Eurasian Studies at Harvard University provided me with a Faculty Associateship while I was writing the book.

And now, the people. Nataliya Kun helped me dust off my Russian and translate my interview questions before my research trips. I translated the opaque parts of the interviews with her help as well as that of Sasha Zolotukhina White and Mariia Zolotukhina. Responsibility for any errors lies with me. Russian gender sociologist Irina Kosterina led me to information on the new wave of feminist groups organizing in Moscow. I am also grateful to Elena Zdravomyslova and Anna Temkina at the European University of St. Petersburg, who helped me connect with feminist activists in that city.

Critical to the writing of this book was a productive group of people who made sure that my inbox was constantly bulging with relevant citations to instances of gender norms in the Russian news: Mischa Gabowitsch, Julia Ioffe, Valentina Konstantinova, Nataliya Kun, Jussi Lassila, Peter Rutland, Tivur Shaginurov, Brian Taylor, and Elizabeth Wood. I am grateful to everyone who took the time to be interviewed for this project and to the Zolotukhina/White family, who housed, fed, and welcomed me as one of their own for two summers in a row. Credit for the book's title goes to Loren Graham, who, bent on simplicity, suggested "Sex, Politics, and Putin," after hearing several of my tortuous attempts at a title.

I thank the Oxford Studies in Culture and Politics Series co-editors, Clifford Bob, for listening to me talk about my project over a lunch of sushi pulled off a conveyor belt in Seattle and then encouraging me to submit a proposal to the series, and Jim Jasper, for his uplifting endorsement upon reading that proposal: "This is actually an extremely interesting topic. In fact more interesting than the author makes it out to be." James Cook, sociology editor at OUP, and his assistant, Peter Worger, carefully shepherded the manuscript from point A to point P (for "published"). Copy editor Alina Larson politely jettisoned a megabyte of superfluous commas and repaired other infelicities. The book's anonymous reviewers sharpened my thinking. Conor O'Dwyer and Doug Blum also offered clear formulations of some of my blurry ideas. I am particularly grateful to Helena Goscilo for sharing with me a wealth of smart comments and her passion for the subject.

I am beyond grateful to Sam Diener. Sam, my partner in life, love, and learning, has now borne the burden of helping me create three books. Sam also did the parenting for both of us when I was off researching in Russia (and when I was back at home, writing). Our now ten-year-old, Sasha, has probably come to think of me as a disembodied voice behind a closed home-office door—albeit a disembodied voice who loves him very much.

For two consecutive summers, as a seven- and then eight-year-old, Sasha tolerated several weeks of temporary momlessness during my trips to Russia. In an attempt to get him interested in the process of data collection, I asked each of my interviewees three questions of Sasha's choosing. He has not yet analyzed the resulting data (being too busy playing soccer and memorizing the horsepower of a wide variety of sports cars), but I offer here a smattering of that data for curious readers. Sasha's questions were: What's your favorite color? What's your favorite sport? What do you like to do? My own cursory analysis suggests no correlation between color preferences and ideology—or even gender. Answers to the second and third questions implied that, with few exceptions, activists of all stripes enjoyed sports and that they rarely had much time in which to do things for fun. But some managed to read, ride trolley-buses in the rain, play soccer, rollerblade, dance hip-hop, and even raise giant African snails.

These snails, conveniently, have no permanent biological sex (each one possesses both male and female reproductive equipment), making it impossible to gender their appearance, behavior, and social obligations (if snails have these) as masculine or feminine. In this, they differ enormously from most people. The absence of gender that can be read onto them and hence the absence of gender-based discrimination is nothing short of enviable. Gender norms—our stereotypical assumptions about the meanings of masculinity and femininity—govern so much of the way that we understand the world around us, often unconsciously. This book, I hope, by making explicit the ways in which gender norms are employed to convince people that politicians and political perspectives are legitimate or illegitimate will help raise our consciousness about this particular form of political manipulation and the reinforcement of sexism and heterosexism on which it relies.

Permissions

An earlier version of Chapter 3 was published as "Nashi Devushki: Gender and Political Activism in Putin's and Medvedev's Russia," in *Post-Soviet Affairs*, Volume 28, Issue 2 (2012), pp. 232–261 (see http://www.tandfonline.com/loi/rpsa). I thank the publisher for giving me permission to use that material here.

A section of Chapter 6 was published as "Feminist Perspectives on Pussy Riot" in *Nationalities Papers*, Volume 42, Issue 4 (2014), pp. 591–603 (see http://www.tandfonline.com/cnap). I thank the publisher for giving me permission to use that material here.

Notes on Transliteration

I have used a modified Library of Congress system for transliteration. Diacritical marks appear in the notes and bibliography, but largely have been omitted from the text so as not to distract readers. Thus, "Tatiana" in the text becomes "Tat'iana" in the notes. Diacriticals in the text remain in occasional transliterated phrases that serve to clarify my translations. Finally, well-known names are rendered in their familiar transliterated form (for example, Navalny rather than Naval'nyi, and Yabloko rather than Iabloko). I have also retained Russians' spelling of their own names in English on their blogs and elsewhere (for example, Ilya rather than Il'ia Varlamov; Yashin rather than Iashin; Nataliya rather than Natal'ia).

Sex, Politics, and Putin

1

The Power of Sex: Culture, Gender, and Political Legitimacy

In October 2010, as a gift for Prime Minister Vladimir Putin's birthday, twelve female students and alumni of Moscow State University's prestigious journalism department published a calendar featuring pin-up photographs of themselves looking as if they had walked out of a Victoria's Secret catalog. Offering witty, sexualized quips, each young woman suggested herself as a potential lover for the prime minister. "You put the forest fires out, but I'm still burning," smiled a fifth-year student illustrating the month of March.[1] The following summer, in the run-up to the election campaign for the lower house of Russia's parliament, the Duma, a series of video clips appeared on the Web, each featuring attractive young women in various stages of undress, proclaiming their support for Putin and President Dmitrii Medvedev. While the women of "Putin's Army" tore off their tank tops and promised to "Rip something—or someone—for Putin," the "Medvedev Girls" stripped down to their bikinis in a Moscow square in support of the president's new policy opposing public beer drinking.[2]

Russian politics was rife with images reinforcing the masculinity of the regime's leadership, not only those reflecting Putin's endless series of macho acts (riding a Harley Davidson with a Russian motorcycle gang, shooting a Siberian tiger, flying a firefighting helicopter to quell the forest fires that choked Moscow in summer 2010, etc.), but also images emphasizing attractive young women's support for the regime as it strove to remain

---

[1] Kristina Potupchik, "Devushki zhurfaka MGU razdelis' dlia Putina," October 6, 2010, http://krispotupchik.livejournal.com/92592.html.
[2] "Porvu za Putina!" [video], July 13, 2011, http://www.youtube.com/watch?v=1Easr8WTwxs; Alina Lobzina, "Stripping for Beer and Medvedev," *The Moscow News*, August 4, 2011, http://themoscownews.com/politics/20110804/188898817.html.

in power.[3] In response, opposition activists held actions suggesting that young women should refuse to sleep with Putin supporters[4] and made efforts to undermine Putin's macho image, referring to him as "botox" to feminize him.[5] Meanwhile, pro- and anti-Putin activists alike hurled homophobic slurs at their male political opponents. Pro-Putin youth claimed (without evidence) that liberal opposition leader Boris Nemtsov had been on the receiving end of homosexual rape in jail,[6] and anti-Kremlin activists made banners stating, "Putin is a faggot."[7]

What was going on here? While Russian political culture had long featured patriarchal elements, this stress on sexualization and politicized gender norms (i.e., gender stereotypes about masculinity and femininity that are taught, recognized, and respected within a given culture, though not universally so) seemed striking. Why were overtly gendered political rhetoric and action being employed so dramatically in the new Russia? What circumstances drive—or obstruct—the use of gender norms in politics in general? And what are the ramifications of using gender norms as a tool of political and organizational legitimation?

Sex, Politics, and Putin examines the use of gender norms in Russian political discourse, asking how and why activists on both sides of the Kremlin (pro- and anti-regime) have chosen to wield concepts of femininity, masculinity, and homophobia (heteronormativity) as tools in their political organizing efforts. I argue that in Russia political actors incorporated gender norms in their authority-building "toolboxes" because of the accessibility and resonance of these aspects of cultural identity at elite and mass levels alike. They also did so because of particular features of the Russian historical, economic, political, and cultural landscape, as well as the country's international position in the post-Cold War era.

---

[3] "Vladimir Putin Rides Harley-Davidson with Russian Biker Gang (VIDEO)," *Huffington Post*, August 30, 2011, http://www.huffingtonpost.com/2011/08/30/putin-motorcycle-russia_n_941963. html; Nabi Abduliaev, "Bears and Mammoth Bones Keep Putin on TV," *The Moscow Times*, August 27, 2010, http://www.themoscowtimes.com/news/article/bears-and-mammoth-bones-keep-putin-on-tv/413788.html; "Putin Saves TV Crew from Siberian Tiger," Reuters, September 2, 2008, http://www.reuters.com/article/2008/09/02/us-putin-tiger-idUSLV19939720080902.

[4] "V Moskve proshla aktsiia 'S putinistami ne spim!,'" February 14, 2009. http://www.grani.ru/Politics/Russia/activism/m.147569.html.

[5] Luke Harding, "Vladimir Putin Question and Answer Session in Russia—Live Updates," *The Guardian*, December 15, 2011, http://www.guardian.co.uk/world/blog/2011/dec/15/vladimir-putin-question-and-answer-session-in-russia-live.

[6] Molodezhnoe Patrioticheskoe Dvizhenie STAL', "'Stal'' pomozhet Nemtsovu preodolet' posledstviia nasiliia," January 7, 2011, http://bit.ly/1lCVq2u.

[7] "Delo o rastiazhke 'Putin – pidaras': Avtor foto khochet predstat' pered sudom," April 13, 2011, http://grani.ru/Society/Media/Freepress/m.187737.html.

In the contemporary Russian case, the Kremlin deployed a legitimation strategy that included stressing Putin's machismo—a strategy that bled over into popular cultural productions of the same ilk. This evoked a similarly gendered response from those opposed to the Putin-centered regime. The resulting political interactions have included homophobic discourse along with competing claims to femininity and masculinity both by regime supporters and detractors.

Legitimacy is at stake in any political system. Regime incumbents (and their supporters) rely on a variety of culturally familiar norms as they endeavor to present believable arguments to justify their ongoing power position. If their authority and power are widely accepted and sufficiently influential groups support their political viewpoints, then the incumbent's position is accepted as legitimate. Power-seekers (the incumbent's "opposition") use similar means to argue for their own political authority. Regime opponents seek legitimation; they want increased authority, more widespread support for their political positions, and to unseat the political (and possibly ideological) status quo.

Political legitimation is not exclusively about gender, of course. Economic policy, family values, military might, and national-patriotic pride, for example, also work their way into discussions and evaluations of political legitimacy and the right to rule. Here, too, however, gender norms often come into play— particularly with regard to nationalism and how "the nation" is constructed with the aid of ideas about femininity and masculinity.[8]

Nor is machismo the sole legitimation strategy being employed by the Putin-centered regime. The regime has also stressed the country's increased standard of living and Russia's resurgent assertion of power in the former Soviet states, among other achievements. It is also not a sufficient strategy for ongoing popularity. By the start of Putin's third presidential term in 2012, pundits had concluded that Putin needed more than his decisive, macho image to maintain or regain the citizenry's support in the face of ongoing problems such as corruption and inadequate housing, which have plagued the country.[9]

---

[8] Nira Yuval-Davis, *Gender and Nation* (London: Sage Publications, 1997). The gendering of Russian nationalist discourse constitutes a good example. Oleg Riabov has traced the ways in which one widespread and highly gendered construct, "Mother Russia," was used as a discursive tool of regime legitimation, particularly in wartime, in the twentieth century. See Oleg Riabov, *"Rossiia matushka": Natsionalizm, gender i voina v Rossii XX veka* (Stuttgart: *ibidem*-Verlag, 2007). Also, on the (de)construction of gender norms and national identity in Soviet and post-Soviet Russia, see Helena Goscilo and Andrea Lanoux, eds., *Gender and National Identity in Twentieth-Century Russian Culture* (DeKalb: Northern Illinois University Press, 2006).

[9] Steve Gutterman, "Putin Needs More Than Rhetoric to Win over Weary Nation," Reuters, December 12, 2012, http://uk.reuters.com/article/2012/12/12/uk-russia-putin-idUKBRE8BB00L20121212.

Their opinion, however, did not stanch the flow of machismo or of feminine endorsement of the man at the top of the regime.

What can the Russian case tell us about the circumstances under which such political dynamics arise? Part of the explanation may be individual. Putin—given his career trajectory and his lifestyle preferences for avoiding alcohol and embracing physical fitness—was well suited to be framed as a macho strongman who could reverse Russia's waning power and oversee the country's resurgence. But a larger part of the explanation goes beyond the Russian case and is rooted in a widespread, if not universal, phenomenon: *the cultural framing of masculinity under patriarchy makes the assertion of masculinity a vehicle for power.* Misogyny, which underlies patriarchal ideology, reduces women and femininity to a lower level of status and power than men and masculinity. Traditional masculinity therefore enables male political leaders (and some female ones as well) to assert their power over others who can be identified or characterized as traditionally feminine. Political actors in contests over power, then, can readily adopt the use of gender norms—including machismo, homophobia, and gay-baiting—as a legitimation tool. Regimes in power and their opponents seeking to gain power make strategic use of gender norms to highlight their masculinity and to justify the power that they have or seek.

This book, then, concerns the power of gender norms and sexualization as a means of political legitimation. However, political actors—both inside and outside a regime—can only make strategic use of these norms when they are deployed against a backdrop of patriarchy and sexism at the mass level and when the public use of those norms is not likely to be arrested by a strong feminist movement or other cultural force objecting to misogyny itself. The strength and perceived effectiveness of gender norms wielded rhetorically against opponents is such that—in the Russian case—even political liberals who might be expected to embrace anti-sexist or gay-friendly views exploit the use of this tool. The availability of a sexist and misogynist cultural idiom and the absence of a sizeable Russian feminist movement make the use of gender norms and the sexualization of politics possible in a way that it would not be in a community where overt sexism was no longer seen as acceptable in the political realm.

This study suggests three main insights. First, a close examination of the Russian case helps explain the use of gender norms as part of a legitimation strategy employed by regimes in power and by their political opponents. Regimes of varied political stripes (from democracies to single-party autocracies) have provided fertile ground for the tactical use of gender norms as a means of justifying and challenging power. By focusing analytically on a constellation of political, economic, historical, cultural, and international factors facilitating the foregrounding of gender norms in Russian politics, *Sex, Politics, and Putin* provides a multifaceted model for understanding the use of such legitimation strategies elsewhere. Taken together, similar studies in other states should reveal more general principles regarding the reasons why gender norms are invoked as a means of political legitimation.

Second, I argue that to use gender norms as a legitimation strategy requires widespread acceptance of gender stereotypes, and a patriarchal culture that privileges maleness and masculinity over femaleness and femininity. Using the Russian case as an illustration, I show that pro-Kremlin and opposition activists alike are affected by and situated in entrenched understandings about gender (perceived masculinity and femininity) that they reproduce—and challenge—to varying degrees, as individuals and as organizations. Because both liberal and pro-Kremlin youth organizations, for example, use ideas about gender in their activism in a fairly straightforward fashion (asserting their traditional masculinity and femininity and contending that their opponents' masculinity and femininity are deviant in some way), to some degree these political opponents are trapped in the same paradigm. Although their political positions sharply diverge, both sides use patriarchal culture in similar ways as an instrument of self-legitimation. While they use gender norms to legitimate their political perspectives (and to attempt to invalidate those of their opponents), they may be largely unaware of gender-based discrimination within Russian society and within their own organizations. In part this occurs because patriarchy normalizes sexism, thereby making sexist comments, a discriminatory or unequal division of labor, and all but the most blatant instances of misogyny seem the norm and hence unremarkable or invisible. Patriarchy is sustained, in this sense, by the very lack of awareness that it produces and encourages.[10]

Because of their critique of patriarchy as a system, feminist groups are more able than other political actors to recognize and object to sex-based discrimination and to identify it in settings across the political spectrum. Likewise, feminist movements endanger any legitimation strategy that relies on gender norms by questioning and criticizing the sexist hierarchy of values on which that strategy is based. Using young Russian feminists' analysis of the Russian case, I show how sexism and homophobia penetrate Russia's political arena. Because they bring patriarchy to the foreground and criticize it, feminists enable a radical critique of the Russian regime and the implicit roots of its power in claims about machismo.

It is worth noting that, just as political actors (outside of a feminist analysis) may be largely unaware of sexism and patriarchal culture, they may also use sexist rhetoric and homophobia in their political activism with varying

---

[10] I thank Mikaela Luttrell-Rowland for this point.

degrees of intentionality. To some extent, the choice to wield gender norms to devalue opponents and recruit adherents is conscious and, to some extent, unconscious—particularly for people whose interpretative toolboxes lack a feminist analysis. Generally speaking, our choices are constrained by the dominant paradigms of discourse and action in which we are immersed. Social movement groups and political actors cannot help but engage gender norms in their actions and speech, whether they do it on purpose or not. It is, of course, possible to employ these norms intentionally. Members of the Russian punk collective, Pussy Riot, were familiar enough with the feminist study of patriarchy to write lyrics that would consciously aim to distance Putin from his macho image by painting him as a scared little boy who "peed his pants" when confronted with protesters in late 2011. It is not a given, however, that the young women photographed for the pro-Putin birthday calendar—or the men who published it—were thinking, "We can strengthen Putin's image as a heterosexual man by putting out this calendar of nubile women who declare their sexual interest in him!" Whether the use of gender norms is conscious or unconscious, it is still inescapably a part of the context in which legitimation strategies are chosen.

Third, understanding the gender dynamics of regime legitimation (and the legitimation strategies of civil society organizations) is important for the study of democratization. The more we can learn about the links between gender dynamics and political legitimation strategies, the more complete our picture will be of how power reproduces itself—and about how power can be contested—in Russia and elsewhere.

In the remainder of this chapter, I set out the fundamental concepts underlying the study—gender, the social construction of gender, and the use of gender norms as tools of political legitimation—and describe the global context in which gender norms and sexualization have appeared in a variety of polities spread across time and geographical space.

Gender: Masculinity and Femininity

Political activism always occurs along an ideological spectrum.[11] Notions of gender and sexuality, sexism and homophobia, too, are woven into each society's fabric and emerge into the political realm, sometimes as propagandistic weapons. Accordingly, political actors wrangle over the ownership and attribution

[11] See, for example, Rebecca Klatch, *A Generation Divided: The New Left, the New Right, and the 1960s* (Berkeley: University of California Press, 1999).

of masculinity and femininity and over the masculine strength and power of the (male) leaders on their respective sides of the political spectrum.

This gendered political drama reinscribes patriarchy—the dominance of perceived masculinity over femininity and the relative empowerment of men versus women. Patriarchal societies, generally speaking, privilege maleness over femaleness, men over women, and masculinity over femininity while re-pressing or devaluing people of either sex who come across as atypically gen-dered (i.e., men who come across as "too" feminine and women who come across as "too" masculine). A patriarchal hierarchy of gender typically situates men seen to possess what R. W. Connell called "hegemonic masculinity"—the form of masculinity that is "culturally exalted" in a given time and place[12]—at the top. Men to whom some lesser form of masculinity is attributed (such as gay men) are relegated to locations lower down on the pyramid, as they become more easily conflated with women (which is to say identifiable as female, fem-inine, and less powerful).[13] Hegemonic masculinity, further, is defined as the "pattern" of practices[14] and ideas of masculinity that are not merely widespread or even dominant in a particular society at a particular time but that justify and legitimate "a hierarchical *relationship* between men and women and among men."[15] In short, hegemonic masculinity reinforces patriarchy; it validates and rationalizes a hierarchy wherein men and masculinity are seen as superior and valued more highly than femininity and those who are said to embody it.[16]

While few "exemplars" embody this apex of hegemonic masculinity, such as sports icons, movie stars, or even politicians, those who symbolize it wield au-thority and reinforce it as a "socially dominant" or "socially admired" form of masculinity.[17] The content of hegemonic masculinity (i.e., the practices be-lieved to characterize manliness at any given historical moment) varies geo-graphically and can change over time. James Messerschmidt and R. W. Con-nell therefore suggest that hegemonic masculinities be distinguished from

---

[12] R. W. Connell, *Masculinities*, 2nd ed. (Cambridge: Polity Press, 2005), 77.

[13] For a clearly laid out analysis of four paradigms for understanding gender and masculinity, see Michael Addis and Geoffrey Cohane, "Social Scientific Paradigms of Masculinity and Their Im-plications for Research and Practice in Men's Mental Health," *Journal of Clinical Psychology* 61, no. 6 (June 2005): 633–647. The paradigm that I adopt here is labeled the "feminist perspective," which takes the view that a person's gender is socially learned and socially constructed and is in-timately tied to the power relations in any given society.

[14] R. W. Connell and James W. Messerschmidt, "Hegemonic Masculinity: Rethinking the Con-cept," *Gender & Society* 19 (2005): 832.

[15] James Messerschmidt, *Hegemonic Masculinities and Camouflaged Politics: Unmasking the Bush Dynasty and Its War against Iraq* (Boulder, CO: Paradigm Publishers, 2010), 159.

[16] Ibid., 161.

[17] Connell and Messerschmidt, "Hegemonic Masculinity: Rethinking the Concept," 846, 849.

each other and analyzed locally, regionally, and globally. Hegemonic masculinity at the "regional" (countrywide, cultural) level is of interest in discussions about masculinity and politics. It influences the cultural understandings of masculinity within the societal groupings that collectively constitute that region. As Connell and Messerschmidt write, "Regional hegemonic masculinity shapes a society-wide sense of masculine reality and, therefore, operates in the cultural domain as on-hand material to be actualized, altered, or challenged through practice in a range of different local circumstances. A regional hegemonic masculinity, then, provides a cultural framework that may be materialized in daily practices and interactions."[18] This book examines the ways that Connell and Messerschmidt's regional-level gender norms have been used in Russian politics as means of authority-building and the impact that this has had on the political system.

Femininity is never "hegemonic" in this sense, as it is always defined in the context of patriarchy, that is, "constructed in the context of the overall subordination of women to men." Traditional femininity, or what Connell calls "emphasized" femininity, does not contest this subordination and "is oriented to accommodating the interests and desires of men."[19] As Mimi Schippers suggests, women who resist male dominance or adopt the characteristics of hegemonic masculinity embody "pariah femininities" that undermine or threaten the patriarchal order.[20] Such "pariahs" examined in this book include Russia's feminists, who resist patriarchy and the gender norms on which it rests.

Whereas the practices and characteristics identified with femininity and masculinity vary by time and place, femininity is always defined as lesser within the parameters set by patriarchal culture (though it is certainly reinforced by women as well as men). Likewise, masculinity is largely conferred upon men by one another; it cannot be perceived in isolation from its public performance (i.e., as it is practiced) and the garnering of other men's approval and acknowledgement.[21] Any given man's masculinity is further confirmed by the perceived attractiveness (or traditional femininity) of the women who proclaim themselves attached to the man in question. Actions like the "Putin's Army" video and the pro-Putin birthday calendar illustrate this point in high relief.

---

[18] Ibid., 849–850.

[19] Mimi Schippers, "Recovering the Feminine Other: Masculinity, Femininity, and Gender Hegemony," *Theory and Society* 36 (2007): 85–106, citing R. W. Connell, *Gender and Power: Society, the Person, and Sexual Politics* (Cambridge: Polity, 1987), 184–185, 187.

[20] Schippers, "Recovering the Feminine Other," p. 95.

[21] I.V. Kosterina, "Konstrukty i praktiki maskulinnosti v provintsial'nom gorode: Gabitus 'normal'nykh patsanov,'" *Zhurnal sotsiologii i sotsial'noi antropologii* 4, no. 11 (2008): 123.

Gender—our perceptions of masculinity and femininity—pertains to politics as much as to any other sphere of human interaction. In political life, gender is enacted and wielded in contests over power and policy, in forms we could refer to as "politicized masculinity" and "politicized femininity." Given the dominance of patriarchal culture that lauds machismo for men and rewards traditional (non-subversive) femininities for women (and punishes the reverse), political actors can employ gendered statements and symbols when trying to bolster their own political positions and undermine those of their opponents.[22] These authority-building strategies are designed to legitimate the actor and undercut opponents. Political actors of all kinds (including social movements, political organizations, and politicians) attempt to shape their rhetoric and actions to take advantage of cultural understandings and "frames" that resonate with the population.[23] These include gendered frames relying on masculinity, femininity, and homophobia. As Italian theorist Antonio Gramsci explains, hegemonic ideas (such as those about how women and men are supposed to look, behave, and interact) are powerful and typically get reinforced by political authorities and citizens alike.[24]

The Social Construction and Performance of Gender

A person's gender—that is, his or her perceived masculinity or femininity—is socially learned and socially constructed. As Kimmel and Messner write, echoing Simone de Beauvoir, "We may be born males or females, but we become men and women in a cultural context."[25] Children, teens, and adults receive cues about what kinds of behaviors, emotional expressions, and economic, social, and political roles are appropriately masculine and feminine. These understandings become routinized and accepted as "normal." Violations

---

[22] Individual women attempting to reach the heights of political power under patriarchy may find that endorsing traditional gender roles while adopting a style of traditionally aggressive machismo makes for an effective combination, enabling voters to overcome reluctance about placing a woman in such a high post (examples include Margaret Thatcher and Indira Gandhi).

[23] "Framing" is one of the core concepts in social movement theory, helping to explain how social movement actors shape their messages to most effectively gain supporters. See Erving Goffman, *Frame Analysis: An Essay on the Organization of Experience* (New York: Harper Colophon Books, 1974); Todd Gitlin, *The Whole World Is Watching: Mass Media in the Making and Unmaking of the New Left* (Berkeley: University of California Press, 1981); David A. Snow and Robert D. Benford, "Ideology, Frame Resonance and Participant Mobilization," *International Social Movement Research* 1, no. 1 (1988): 197–218.

[24] Anne Showstack Sassoon, *Gramsci's Politics*, 2nd ed. (Minneapolis: University of Minnesota Press, 1988).

[25] M. S. Kimmel and M. A. Messner, *Men's Lives*, 4th ed. (Boston: Allyn and Bacon, 1998).

of expected gender roles are noticed, giving rise to confusion and curiosity (e.g., when a person's sex cannot easily be determined from the social cues that she or he expresses via hair, visage, voice, and clothes), or dismay and violence (as occurs with hate crimes against transgendered people). While *sex* is conveniently regarded as being biological, *gender* is socially constructed and is what we witness on a daily basis in public.[26]

In making a distinction between biological sex (male and female) and socially constructed gender (the attributes or characteristics that we associate with maleness and femaleness), I follow feminist theorist Carol Cohn:

> I use the term *gender* to refer to the constellation of meanings that a given culture assigns to biological sex differences. But more than that, I use gender to refer to a symbolic system, a central organizing discourse of culture, one that not only shapes how we experience and understand ourselves as men and women, but that also interweaves with other discourses and shapes them—and therefore shapes other aspects of our world.[27]

People perceive the world through gender lenses, overtly and unconsciously assigning masculine or feminine characteristics to people, activities, behaviors, jobs, beliefs, and even foods (e.g., barbecuing meat—masculine; making and eating salad—feminine). Cohn continues:

> In this symbolic system, human characteristics are dichotomized, divided into pairs of polar opposites that are supposedly mutually exclusive: mind is opposed to body; culture to nature; thought to feeling; logic to intuition; objectivity to subjectivity; aggression to passivity; confrontation to accommodation; abstraction to particularity; public to private; political to personal, ad nauseam. In each case, the first term of the "opposites" is associated with male, the second with female. And in each case, our society values the first over the second.[28]

---

[26] Some theorists argue that biological sex, too, is a construction, since there is quite a broad spectrum of variety in genitalia and chromosomal combinations as well as in levels of the "sex hormones" testosterone and estrogen found within the category "women" or "men." See Anne Fausto-Sterling, "The Five Sexes, Revisited," *Sciences* 40, no. 4 (August 2000): 18–23.

[27] Carol Cohn, "Wars, Wimps, and Women," in *Gendering War Talk*, eds. Miriam Cooke and Angela Woolacott (Princeton, NJ: Princeton University Press, 1993), 228.

[28] Ibid., 229.

Cohn readily acknowledges that this is a "symbolic" system, rather than a mandate, but notes that even while actual people do not neatly "fit these gender 'ideals,'" men and women are still subject to that system's precepts. "Whether we want to or not," argues Cohn, "we see ourselves and others against its templates, we interpret our own and others' actions against it."[29] Like Connell and Messerschmidt in their discussion of hegemonic masculinity, Cohn notes that gender systems "vary by race, class, ethnicity, locale, sexuality, nationality, and other factors."[30]

Feminist theorist Judith Butler captured the notion that "gender" was not the reflection of some "internal essence," but rather that it is "performative"— that it is "manifested through a sustained set of acts, posited through the gendered stylization of the body."[31] In other words, gender is not unconsciously exhibited, but is *performed* by each individual. A person's gender performance can also be arranged by others. Newborns in the United States, for instance, are often bundled into pink or blue onesies with the intention of broadcasting the baby's sex. This performance—what Candace West and Don Zimmerman call "doing gender"—takes place through interactions in a social context that recognizes the cues put forth to indicate whether a person wishes to be perceived as male or female. As West and Zimmerman put it, "Gender activities emerge from and bolster claims to membership in a sex category."[32]

As a person's gender does not automatically derive from biological sex, it must be continually reasserted. Simply being male or female does not make a person masculine or feminine. As such, it is widely understood, if unstated, that the bearer of masculinity is always insecure, since masculinity can be lost (replaced by femininity and its attendant loss of status and power). In that regard, writes cultural historian George Chauncey, "Manhood . . . was not simply a quality that resulted naturally and inevitably from one's sex" but rather

---

[29] Ibid.

[30] Ibid., 230.

[31] Judith Butler, *Gender Trouble: Feminism and the Subversion of Identity* (New York: Routledge, 2006), xv.

[32] Candace West and Don H. Zimmerman, "Doing Gender," *Gender & Society* 1, no. 2 (June 1987): 127. For a straightforward discussion of this idea, illustrated with examples of how women in the US military make choices about their clothes, their activities (such as what sports they play), and various other aspects of their behavior to "manage how they are perceived by those around them" to try to achieve the desired balance of masculinity and femininity in how they come across, see Melissa S. Herbert, *Camouflage Isn't Only for Combat: Gender, Sexuality, and Women in the Military* (New York: New York University Press, 1998), 113. Christine Williams similarly shows how male nurses and women in the Marines maintain and even stress their respective masculinity and femininity while working in positions atypical for their gender. See Christine L. Williams, *Gender Differences at Work: Women and Men in Nontraditional Occupations* (Berkeley: University of California Press, 1989).

was perpetually in danger of being questioned, and its possessor constantly at risk of being labeled as "unmanly, a mollycoddle, a sissy, even a pansy."[33] Masculinity is "an ongoing performance" in Butler's sense, a set of practices always in the process of iteration.[34]

The US gun-making company Bushmaster epitomized this phenomenon with their "man card" campaign, initiated in 2010. The company provided a website where visitors could answer a set of questions determining their manhood status (e.g., whether they consume tofu or intentionally watch figure skating, which are presumably "feminine" traits) and then—if the questions had been answered correctly—be issued a "Man Card," valid for one year.[35] Site visitors could also revoke their friends' Man Cards. Given the cultural association between firearms and masculinity, buying a Bushmaster rifle, of course, enabled the purchaser to get his "man card reissued," according to Bushmaster ads made infamous in the wake of the Sandy Hook elementary school slaughter carried out by Bushmaster rifle-bearing Adam Lanza in late 2012.[36]

Gender Norms and Political Legitimation: Political Performances under Patriarchy

Regarding gender as a performance enables us to see that we are all acting out our gender identities—our masculinity and femininity—all the time; they are not just a permanent outgrowth of our biological sex. This is true for political actors as much—or more, perhaps—as for anyone else. Incumbent politicians and their opponents have to constantly prove, demonstrate, and reinforce their perceived gender identity—a matter with which their image-makers are intimately concerned. In Russia, as elsewhere, hegemonic ideas about gender are invoked and played out in the political realm, as political actors and their opponents vie for popular support. Putin's variety of macho stunts can be read as an ongoing effort to assert political masculinity in this way.

[33] George Chauncey, *Gay New York: Gender, Urban Culture, and the Making of the Gay Male World, 1890–1940* (New York: Basic Books, 1994), 80.
[34] Ibid.
[35] Adam Seitz-Wald, "Assault Rifle Company Issues 'Man Cards,'" December 17, 2012, http://www.salon.com/2012/12/17/bushmasters_horrible_ad_campaign/; "Proof of Your Manhood: The Man Card from Bushmaster," May 7, 2010, http://www.ammoland.com/2010/05/bushmaster-man-card/#axzz2zjW6C3lv.
[36] Hamilton Nolan, "Bushmaster Firearms, Your Man Card Is Revoked," December 18, 2012, http://gawker.com/5969150/bushmaster-firearms-your-man-card-is-revoked.

The very familiarity of gender norms in any given social context enables them to be utilized easily as "a primary way of signifying relationships of power."[37] Our ideas about how men and women are "supposed" to look, feel, and behave (including in relation to one another) are perceived as "very obvious and understandable, and therefore, legitimate."[38] This facilitates the use of gender norms as tools of political legitimation; they do not need to be explained to the public. In that light, as Russian social scientists Tatiana Riabova and Oleg Riabov put it, "Gender discourse acts as a resource of the regime (resursa vlasti) in various forms, one of which is the use of models of masculinity and femininity, with the goal of legitimating that regime." From this perspective, they suggest, "Putin's popularity derives from his embodiment of hegemonic masculinity."[39]

Gender is one of the most readily available and recognizable aspects of identity, which is one of the reasons that it functions well as an authority-building strategy in the political arena. Gendered (typically patriarchal) frames are thus used implicitly and explicitly by regimes, pro-regime activists, and oppositionists to support their own positions and undermine those of their opponents. In short, political actors employ widely familiar cultural notions of masculinity, femininity, and homophobia (heteronormativity) as political tools in their performance of legitimacy. They market these ideas to bolster their own political stances (e.g., liberal or conservative, pro- or anti-Putin) and policy positions (e.g., pro- or anti-abortion, for or against military conscription) among the populace.

In the quest for legitimacy and political authority, political actors engage in all kinds of "performances" with the intention of winning the audience of attentive citizens over to their side. Regarding "formally democratic societies," cultural sociologist Jeffrey Alexander writes, "Gaining power depends on the outcome of struggles for symbolic domination in the civil sphere."[40] All politics, in that sense, is a performance aimed at accruing legitimacy (in order to rely less on forceful coercion).[41] When political actors make claims about opponents, they hope those claims will be received as facts, whereas in reality these are largely "performative statements" that attempt "less to [describe] the world" than to "bring that world into being in the imaginations of their listeners."[42] Politicians also seek to convince their audience that an improved world

---

[37] T. B. Riabova and O. V. Riabov, "Nastoiashchii muzhchina Rossiiskoi politiki? (K voprosu o gendernom diskurse kak resurse vlasti)," *POLIS: Politicheskie Issledovaniia*, 5 (2010): 49, citing Joan W. Scott, "Gender: A Useful Category of Historical Analysis," *American Historical Review* 91, no. 5 (December 1986): 1067.

[38] Ibid., 49, citing Blom, 2000, p. 6.

[39] Ibid., 60; translation is mine.

[40] Jeffrey Alexander, *Performance and Power* (Malden, MA: Polity, 2011), 107.

[41] Ibid., 1, 89.

[42] Ibid., 102.

will result—or has resulted—from their rule, making that rule legitimate. To that end, as Alexander shows, political actors use cultural understandings to bolster their power in democratic polities, but they also do so in authoritarian regimes. Alexander cites work by Diana Taylor describing the military dictatorship that ruled Argentina in the late 1970s and early 1980s "in terms of [the junta's] performance of masculinity and aggression."[43] The Argentine generals who took over the country put their militarized masculinity on display, orchestrating a campaign of "disappearances" of thousands of citizens deemed threatening to the regime and applying a brutal cascade of rape and torture within the regime's detention centers. A dissident movement, the Mothers of the Plaza de Mayo, insisting on the return of their abducted children, responded to the dictatorship's inhumanity with a "counter-performance" highlighting their own traditional gender authority as mothers. Rather than contesting the masculinity of the junta (e.g., by accusing the generals of weakness), the Mothers used their gender performance (relying on a traditional femininity based in motherhood) to accrue value for their political position as opponents of the regime. In so doing, Taylor argues, the Mothers contributed to the junta's eventual collapse.[44] Successful "counter-performances . . . can undermine confidence and shatter legitimacy."[45]

Even in authoritarian regimes political actors make an effort to use cultural understandings to garner at least some legitimacy. To that end, they may turn to the most "apolitical" and widespread understandings—like gender norms—that tie into national status concerns. For instance, the Argentine generals adopted a tough, militarized, masculinized performance, arguing that their military discipline and ruthless suppression of the internal left-wing enemy would benefit the nation on the whole. As we will see in the next chapter, Putin's assertion of machismo likewise tied the country's fate to his own; with a masculine Putin in power, Russia would no longer be kicked around and disrespected on the international scene. Putin's regime emphasized his masculine toughness as a way to convince the population that they were safe under his rule and that instability would result from "weakening" the regime through protests or the election of someone other than Putin.[46] As authoritarianism grew during

---

[43] Ibid., 89, citing Diana Taylor, *Disappearing Acts: Spectacles of Gender and Nationalism in Argentina's "Dirty War"* (Durham, NC: Duke University Press, 1997). A similar movement in the Soviet Union, starting in the late 1980s, helped mobilize public opinion against the war in Afghanistan and later against the war in Chechnya in the mid-1990s. See Amy Caiazza, *Mothers and Soldiers: Gender, Citizenship, and Civil Society in Contemporary Russia* (New York: Routledge, 2002).

[44] Alexander, *Performance and Power*, 89.

[45] Ibid., 4.

[46] Messerschmidt similarly refers to George W. Bush portraying himself as the "hegemonic masculine heroic protector." See Messerschmidt, *Hegemonic Masculinities and Camouflaged Politics*, 112.

the Putin era, one of the steady sources of authority-building for the regime remained a focus on Putin's machismo.[47] Yet if machismo is a source of support for a political actor or organization, it can be partially undermined by portrayals of the leader as weak and effeminate. Reframing Putin's "objective" masculinity through parody or by directly contradicting it, opposition activists attempted to undermine the certainty of Putin's ongoing rule. By introducing an alternative narrative questioning Putin's machismo, the liberal opposition made political change appear less implausible.

In his essay about "iconic power and performativity," Alexander explains that "iconic objects can exert a powerful social force." Yet when they "perform" for an audience, iconic objects project meanings that may or may not be received as intended. Indeed, critics can actively disrupt an icon's envisioned meaning.[48] Alexander's essay is largely about material objects, but his analysis could be extended to human beings who are put forth as political icons. Russia's Putin, as a human icon radiating machismo (and its attendant representation of national strength and revival), projected a "meaning" that was appreciated by his supporters and derided by his political critics. Machismo, embedded in a political icon, can go a long way in power, but the icon ostensibly embodying that machismo is subject to critique on its own terms. Putin's critics sought to embed in the national imagination the notion that perhaps Putin was *not* macho, but was instead effeminate and, as such, not worthy of his political position. As Alexander puts it, "Skeptical audiences are the key to causing the performances of institutional power to fail."[49] Counterperformances like those by the Argentine Mothers and skeptics like Putin's liberal political opponents can lead the public to question a regime.

But beyond the political arena in which one iconic gender norm is set up in opposition to another (Argentine generals vs. mothers) or where one political grouping tries to undermine another's gender status (arguing for Putin as "sex symbol" or Putin as "fag"), another audience—namely, feminists—may reject the very foundation on which the icon rests: traditional, reified gender norms. Political actors may try to legitimate themselves on the basis of masculinity, as Putin has done, in part by building an iconography of masculine feats and feminine support. But for those citizens who successfully step outside of the gender-normative paradigm, the entire basis for the icon's power—machismo itself—is scorned as an invalid or irrelevant basis for political legitimacy. The trick then

---

[47] Elizabeth Wood, "The New Facade of Autocracy: Vladimir Putin and Hypermasculinity, 1999 to the Present" (Keynote Speech, Modern European Lunch, American Historical Association, January 2011).

[48] Alexander, *Performance and Power*, 206–207.

[49] Ibid., 91.

to undermining the icon's political authority is to recruit other citizens to step outside of the cultural paradigm and recognize its oppressive power.

According to Alexander, democracy creates a space for "counter-performances always to be made."[50] They are made in dictatorships as well, such as the efforts of the Mothers in Argentina to set their own feminine gender authority against that of the masculine junta. But—perhaps especially in nondemocratic polities—the broad societal acceptance of gender norms and their strict enforcement in policy (and, in the Russian case, by such regime-supporting institutions as the Russian Orthodox Church), create an environment in which a deeper counter-performance—critiquing political actors who use machismo to help justify their rule—is made far more difficult. That kind of counterperformance is relegated to a narrow band of feminists who are actively trying to overturn the existing patriarchal cultural understandings that are mobilized in the service of political legitimation. It is inconvenient for political actors operating within the traditional paradigm to be confronted by a movement that intends to eliminate the paradigm altogether, as feminism does. Actors across the spectrum prefer instead to attempt to perform—repeatedly—in a way that reinforces sexism and paints a negative picture of feminism as undesirable, unhealthy, and threatening to the nation itself.

Gender Norms and the Politics of Topping

Plying machismo as a means of political legitimation is a widespread phenomenon both historically and geographically. Yet machismo itself cannot be understood in isolation from the misogyny on which it relies. Manly men, in short, can only be manly by contrast to women. In an early example of identifying the link between gender and political legitimation, Virginia Woolf's essay, "Three Guineas," explains that patriarchal leaders (including Hitler, Mussolini, and the male leaders of the Anglican Church) appeal to the notion of manliness—and the division of life into the "world of men and the world of women"—as a means of legitimating their own rule.[51]

Homophobia is likewise rooted in misogyny, the perceived inferiority of women relative to men. Undermining a political opponent's masculinity by

---

[50] Ibid.

[51] Virginia Woolf, *Three Guineas* (Adelaide, Australia: University of Adelaide, 2014, originally published 1938), http://ebooks.adelaide.edu.au/w/woolf/virginia/w91tg/index.html; see Part 3 in particular, ft. 31. This aspect of Woolf's essay is usefully summarized in Sharon Macdonald, Pat Holden, and Shirley Ardener, eds., *Images of Women in Peace and War* (Madison: University of Wisconsin Press, 1987), 217–221.

implying his nontraditional sexual orientation is tantamount to stating that the man in question is more female than male and hence inferior. Such an implication is anathema to the vast majority of men under patriarchy, a social, cultural, and political system that values men and the attributes of masculinity over women and the feminine qualities stereotypically affiliated with them. Denigrating men by likening them to women is the essence of homophobic slurs, a widespread phenomenon from schoolyards to high politics.

While the familiar binary of homosexuality and heterosexuality is a mid-twentieth-century innovation of the middle class, describing sexual practices as "masculine" or "feminine" (appropriate to men and women, respectively) is a longer-standing way to categorize people and identify their relative status and power.[52] The dual notions of "topping" (a way to describe traditionally male or "insertive" sexual practices) and "bottoming" (the receptive or penetrated position traditionally affiliated with women) predate homo- and heterosexuality as concepts but likewise draw on misogyny for their meaning. George Chauncey, describing the evolution of gay life in New York in the first half of the twentieth century, explains that traditionally masculine men ("tops") who had sex with "fairies" (whom we would more commonly now term as drag queens or preoperative male-to-female transsexuals with an exaggeratedly feminine presentation) were commonly perceived as having "normal" sexuality, while their male partners (who offered "receptive" sexual practices such as anal sex and fellatio—practices seen to lower the status of their provider) were regarded as perverse.[53] Topping—the physical act of sexual penetration—"symbolized one man's power over another." For men who "topped," engaging in sex with effeminate men confirmed their masculinity rather than undermining it.[54]

In his multivolume history of sexuality, Michel Foucault points out that in classical Greek culture penetrative sexual interaction, like social interaction, implied a "polarity that opposed activity and passivity" and thus described a "relationship between a superior and a subordinate, an individual who dominates and one who is dominated, one who commands and one who complies, one who vanquishes and one who is vanquished." The "valorized" position in each of these relationships corresponded to the "active" partner, the penetrator.[55] Importantly, regarding sex between two males, there was no shame in

---

[52] Chauncey, *Gay New York*, 113, 117.

[53] Ibid., 85.

[54] Ibid., 81. This binary and status-laden division of sexual labor (penetrator/penetratee) is not the only metaphor for describing sexual interaction or even penetration. Other metaphors reverse the concept of penetration (i.e., envelopment) or simply stress shared pleasure.

[55] Michel Foucault, *The Use of Pleasure: The History of Sexuality*, vol. 2 (New York: Vintage, 1990), 215.

being the passive partner, typically a young male in the Greek context, as long as he did not come to internalize and enjoy "the role of [being a] pleasure object for others" (a position that presumably caused no such cognitive dissonance for women, given their "permanently unequal" social status).[56] This latter situation could disqualify such men—once they had reached adulthood—from political service; for an adult man, playing and actively adopting the "inferior and humiliating position of a pleasure object for others" was painted as "morally and politically incompatible with civic responsibilities and the exercise of political power."[57] In short, it was acceptable for boys but not grown men to be "bottoms." This understanding of sexual interactions between men provides some historical-social grounding for the use of rhetorical topping in political contests in the contemporary period. Attacking a political opponent's manliness (turning him into a "bottom") represented success for the traditionally masculine "top" by confirming his masculinity in the interaction.

Masculinity enters the public sphere in myriad guises and contexts, often in tandem with homophobia. When boys on the playground needle each other with the insult, "You throw like a girl!" or with the closely related moniker, "Fag!," they are, in effect, staking out the territory of their masculine identity by labeling other boys with misogynist and homophobic appellations.[58] School administrators in the United States occasionally reinforce the idea that homosexuality is humiliating, such as when a public high school principal in Arizona in 2012 punished two male students for fighting by having them hold hands in public for an hour while other students teased them.[59] Likewise, politicians commonly endeavor to best their opponents by coming across as more masculine, whether by asserting their own macho qualities or attempting to reveal their opponents' "bottomness" or relative insufficiency in manliness (and to avoid being tagged in that way themselves). Even when they take the form of specifically homophobic slurs, such assertions of dominance are rooted in misogyny.

Topping is a feature of international as well as domestic political contests. Cohn provides graphic examples from the Gulf War of the early 1990s, where various representations of the United States "topped" (or, more accurately, raped) Iraq's dictator, Saddam Hussein:

[56] Ibid., 216, 219.

[57] Ibid., 219.

[58] C. J. Pascoe, *Dude, You're a Fag: Masculinity and Sexuality in High School* (Berkeley University of California Press, 2007), 5.

[59] The students were offered suspension as an alternative punishment. See Sam Meier, "Gay Dad Defends AZ Principal Who Punished Male Students by Making Them Hold Hands," December 4, 2012, http://www.policymic.com/articles/20108/gay-dad-defends-az-principal-who-punished-male-students-by-making-them-hold-hands.

American derision of Saddam Hussein included bumper stickers that read "Saddam, Bend Over." American soldiers reported that the "U.S.A." stenciled on their uniforms stood for "Up Saddam's Ass." A widely reprinted cartoon . . . depicted Saddam bowing down in the Islamic posture of prayer, with a huge U.S. missile, approximately five times the size of the prostrate figure, about to penetrate his upraised bottom. Over and over, defeat for the Iraqis was portrayed as humiliating anal penetration by the more powerful and manly United States.[60]

Just as conflicts within a political community may draw on masculinity, interstate "political struggles can be interpreted as competition between masculinities" where the heads of state personify their countries and compete in relation to each other.[61] As we shall see in the next chapter, charges of effeminacy against international opponents were featured in some of Russia's foreign policy interactions; these were part and parcel of Putin's effort to portray himself and his country as a quintessential "top."

Politicizing Sexualization and Gender Norms in a Global Context

Although it may seem unusually overt, the use of gender norms and sexualization as tools of legitimation and delegitimation in Russia's political realm under Putin is far from unique. This section offers examples from a geographically and politically diverse set of states exhibiting the politicization of gender norms and sexualization, suggesting that the Russian case is more typical than not. I regard *Sex, Politics, and Putin* as contributing to a "comparative politics of gender" approach, which political scientist Aili Mari Tripp defines as research that regards gender "as central to political processes and institutions" and is interested in "understanding how masculinities and femininities interact with organizations, institutions and processes." Research under the comparative politics of gender rubric is designed to reveal how political, economic, social, cultural, and international institutions "are organized to maintain systematic gender-based inequalities and power relationships through norms and logics of domination" and examines how these "inequalities and forms of domination evolve, how they are maintained, and how they are dismantled."[62] This book's exploration of the

---

[60] Cohn, "Wars, Wimps, and Women," 236.
[61] Riabova and Riabov, "Nastoiashchii muzhchina Rossiiskoi politiki?," 50, drawing on Cohn, "Wars, Wimps, and Women," 239–241; translation is mine.
[62] Aili Mari Tripp, "Toward a Comparative Politics of Gender Research in Which Women Matter," *Perspectives on Politics* 8, no. 1 (March 2010): 192.

Russian case should shed light on the mechanisms by which patriarchal gender norms function as part of political legitimation strategies in other countries.

Masculinity is always in play in politics, perhaps especially when there is even a modicum of political competition. This has been the case in democratic states, in nominal democracies, and in outright authoritarian or single-party regimes. Variations on the assertion of masculinity in politics are nearly endless. Political contests in the United States have featured Ronald Reagan's promises to be tough on the Soviet "bear," and George H. W. Bush's suffering the "wimp factor" when he was told his ticket would benefit from adding some machismo in the form of Jeane Kirkpatrick.[63] Implications that a male politician lacks sufficient manliness can be traced further back in US political history; Thomas Jefferson was reportedly criticized for his "timidity" and whimsicality, while Andrew Jackson withstood charges of feminine behavior, being labeled as "Miss Nancy" and "Aunt Fancy."[64] Female politicians do not exist outside this trend, as witnessed by the attribution of machismo (and hence credibility) to women like Margaret Thatcher and Golda Meir, and the questions raised about whether women in general are "strong enough" (read: manly enough) to lead adequately.

But political masculinity does not remain static over time. In 1992, for example, Bill Clinton, lacking the sports-and-military-service background traditional in US presidential candidates' resumes, survived misogynist attacks labeling him as "she" and as "squishy" (the sexualized opposite of "hard" perhaps?), suggesting that by the early 1990s in the United States the demands on political candidates to exhibit traditional masculine credentials were either shifting or flexible enough to incorporate male emotionality and an aversion to war.[65] As Wahl-Jorgensen notes, "At a deeper level, American culture may have become increasingly receptive to the idea that potent masculinity capable of violence can coexist with pacifism, a concern for the environment, and the ability to cry."[66] Along with his draft-evading, feminist-wife-boasting, sensitive-new-age-man persona, however, Clinton's portrayal in the media during the 1992 campaign included more traditional elements of masculinity, such as frequent use of "the sports metaphor" and evidence that he enjoyed Hillary's occasional forays

[63] Messerschmidt, *Hegemonic Masculinities and Camouflaged Politics*, 1, citing B. Curtis, "The Wimp Factor," *American Heritage Magazine* 40, no. 7 (1989): 1–6; and M. Duffy and D. Goodgame, *Marching in Place: The Status Quo Presidency of George Bush* (New York: Simon and Schuster, 1992).

[64] Karin Wahl-Jorgensen, "Constructing Masculinities in U.S. Presidential Campaigns: The Case of 1992," in *Gender, Politics, and Communication*, eds. Annabelle Sreberny and Liesbet Van Zoonen (Cresskill, NJ: Hampton Press, 2000), 55.

[65] Ibid., 56, 66. In 2012, neither presidential candidate from the major parties had served in the military.

[66] Ibid., 66.

into the territory of cookie-baking. This depiction thus reassured the public that although Clinton might not fit the traditional presidential-masculine mold entirely, he shared enough of its previous occupants' masculine attributes to be electable.[67]

Battles over political masculinity also entail competition over symbolic manifestations of manliness. On the figurative level, in 2004, US presidential candidate John Kerry was teased by Republicans for his high-end road bike, which paled against George W. Bush's "more manly Trek mountain bike."[68] Eight years later the Internet buzzed over an indirect physical competition between the bare-chested photos of Barack Obama and a workout photo shoot in *Time* magazine featuring Republican vice-presidential candidate Paul Ryan, with commentators arguing over which man had the "better" body (in 2008, similar discussions had occurred when racy photos of Obama and Putin were released).[69] After George W. Bush's "Mission Accomplished" speech in May 2003, which was made aboard a US aircraft carrier and prematurely proclaimed an end to major military operations in Iraq, women reportedly made calls to G. Gordon Liddy's talk show to exclaim about "what a stud" the president was. Bush had worn a flight suit with a parachute harness, the straps of which caused a "noticeable bulge in the president's crotch"; debate ensued as to whether or not the president's handlers had engaged in "sock stuffing" to gain whatever symbolic masculine advantage could be conferred in that fashion.[70] Politicians of varied political persuasions have demonstrated physical proof of their masculine fortitude in a range of public-relations stunts. China's Communist Party Chairman Mao Zedong famously sought to exhibit his virility by swimming the Yangtse River (accompanied by a fully dressed military detachment) at age 72, while Chilean dictator Augusto Pinochet—like Putin, a martial arts practitioner—was in the habit of breaking bricks in public.[71]

[67] Ibid., 59, 68, 56.

[68] Andrew Leonard, "John Kerry: The Road Bike Warrior," September 3, 2008, http://www.salon.com/2008/09/03/john_kerry_road_rider/.

[69] "Obama vs. Putin—Shirtless," December 24, 2008, http://rt.com/news/prime-time/obama-vs-putin-shirtless/.

[70] William Conley Harris, *Queer Externalities: Hazardous Encounters in American Culture* (New York: SUNY Press, 2009), 84; Maureen Farrell, "George W. Kowalski?: Bush's Macho Facade Goes Limp," September 23, 2003, http://www.buzzflash.com/farrell/03/09/23.html.

[71] Roger Hudson, "The Great Helmsman Goes Swimming," *History Today* 62, no. 5 (2012), http://www.historytoday.com/roger-hudson/great-helmsman-goes-swimming; James F. Smith, "But Chilean Leader Slips in Polls: Combative Gen. Pinochet: Defeat Is Not in His Blood," *Los Angeles Times*, October 4, 1988, http://articles.latimes.com/1988-10-04/news/mn-3481_1_augusto-pinochet.

Claiming the most attractive women for one's own side (and putting down the physical beauty of opponents' female supporters) adds another angle to the use of gender norms in political contests. Russian activists in the Putin era have accused their opposing camps of lacking attractive women.[72] Likewise, in Italy's 2008 election campaign, Prime Minister Silvio Berlusconi reportedly stated that right-wing women politicians outdid the left on the criterion of female beauty, adding that leftists had "no taste—even in women."[73] In 2010, Julius Malema, a popular political figure and leader of the youth wing of the African National Congress (the governing party in South Africa), attacked the femininity of Patricia de Lille, the female leader of a rival party, saying that she "doesn't look like a married woman. There's no normal man who can marry Patricia. If Patricia has got a husband, that husband must divorce Patricia and come and look for well-mannered and beautiful women in the ANC."[74]

The demonstration of women's political approbation constitutes another aspect of political masculinity and the competitive use of gender norms in the political realm. Making the Putin public-relations machine appear relatively tame by comparison, Italian Prime Minister Silvio Berlusconi asserted his masculine vitality in part by throwing lavish "bunga-bunga" parties that featured attractive young women as his guests, ostensibly testifying to Berlusconi's power and manliness. (Presaging Berlusconi's twenty-first-century "bunga-bunga" parties, Chairman Mao hosted weekly ballroom-dancing soirees in the 1950s featuring attractive young women who danced with him and who would also disappear behind closed doors with him, one at a time.)[75] Confronted with multiple accusations of infidelity, Berlusconi reportedly responded with a homophobic remark intended to highlight his "correct" sexual orientation: "It's better to love beautiful women than to be gay."[76] Ultimately, however, Berlusconi's sexualization of politics (probably more a matter of his own preoccupation with sex than a political tactic *per se*) deteriorated into embarrassment and infamy when he was accused of having sex with a minor, the erotic dancer known as Ruby the Heart Stealer—an

---

[72] Valerie Sperling, "Nashi Devushki: Gender and Political Youth Activism in Putin's and Medvedev's Russia," *Post-Soviet Affairs* 28, no. 2 (June 2012): 247.

[73] Quoted in "The Most Macho Leaders in History," October 7, 2012, http://msn.lockeroom.com.my/features/2012/10/the-most-macho-leaders-in-history#.UH7NaIXd7io.

[74] Quoted in David Smith, "South African Court Finds ANC's Julius Malema Guilty of Hate Speech," *The Guardian*, March 15, 2010, http://www.guardian.co.uk/world/2010/mar/15/anc-julius-malema-guilty-hate-speech.

[75] Zhisui Li, *The Private Life of Chairman Mao* (New York: Random House, 1996), 93–95.

[76] Cited in Ol'ga Samofalova, "Samye gromkie seks-skandaly 2010 goda," December 20, 2010, http://www.rb.ru/topstory/entertainment/2010/12/20/090147.html; translation is mine.

allegation that Berlusconi's friend Putin reportedly said stemmed from "envy."[77] Berlusconi's opponents labeled his regime a "whoreocracy" and bordello state.[78]

The final years of the Russian empire provide a peculiar historical parallel to the sexual excesses in modern Italy's "court," as Maurizio Viroli refers to Italy's political center under Berlusconi. The Russian royal family's close "spiritual" advisor, Grigorii Rasputin, was a charismatic figure who, in addition to promising Tsar Nicholas II and his wife, Alexandra, that he could cure their son's hemophilia, was also known for using "his powers of seduction to attract female admirers, whom he lured into sensual excesses." This behavior redounded negatively on the tsar's own standing, "reminding the court and the public of the moral vacuum at the center of the autocratic state."[79] As was the case in Berlusconi's Italy, behavior that could symbolize virility and manliness and provide regime legitimation instead went overboard and undermined regime legitimacy by appearing excessive and therefore deviant.

A more successful method of representing male politicians' masculine image by publicizing the feminine attractiveness of their political supporters includes a campaign tactic embraced by the political party of Boyko Borisov, the sometime mayor of Sofia, Bulgaria. In 2009, Borisov's political vehicle, the Citizens for the European Development of Bulgaria (GERB), sponsored a campaign rally featuring bikini-clad female dancers and free drinks at a poolside bar in the capital.[80] Marilyn Monroe's birthday song for John F. Kennedy in 1962 and the Moscow State University women's birthday calendar for Putin are variants of this sexualization of women's political support. These tactics might become more prevalent in election campaign periods,

---

[77] After being indicted in February 2011 for having paid a minor for sex, Berlusconi's political fortunes seemed to decline dramatically. For example, in September of that year, his popularity rating descended to an all-time low of 24 percent, and he resigned in November 2011, facing severe criticism over Italy's economic situation. None of Berlusconi's previous encounters with the legal system—including multiple indictments on corruption charges—appeared to have had a lasting impact on his political career. See Lyubov Pronina and Henry Meyer, "Putin Says Berlusconi Sex Allegations 'Made Out of Envy,'" Bloomberg, September 16, 2011, http://www.bloomberg.com/news/2011-09-16/putin-says-berlusconi-sex-allegations-made-out-of-envy-1-.html; Michael Day, "Former Italian Prime Minister Silvio Berlusconi Sentenced to a Year in Jail for Tax Fraud," *The Independent*, October 26, 2012, http://www.independent.co.uk/news/world/europe/former-italian-prime-minister-silvio-berlusconi-sentenced-to-a-year-in-jail-for-tax-fraud-8228441.html.

[78] Maurizio Viroli, *The Liberty of Servants: Berlusconi's Italy* (Princeton, NJ: Princeton University Press, 2010), xvi.

[79] Laura Engelstein, *The Keys to Happiness: Sex and the Search for Modernity in Fin-de-Siecle Russia* (Ithaca, NY: Cornell University Press, 1994), 421.

[80] Kristen Ghodsee, "Electioneering on the Rocks," http://www.tol.org/client/article/20667-electioneering-on-the-rocks.html?print, accessed September 22, 2012.

but they are grounded in sexism and patriarchy that predate the election context.

A variant of women's political sexualization—women's semi-nude campaign efforts on behalf of male politicians—is women politicians' semi-nude campaign efforts on their own behalves. This, by contrast to male politicians' displays of machismo and of sexualized female support, is a rare occurrence. In September 2007, the Polish "Women's Party," a new entity on the political scene, published a visual advertisement featuring seven women candidates for Poland's October 2007 parliamentary elections. The women were pictured nude, holding a Women's Party poster with the party's catchphrase, "Poland is a woman," and the slogan: "Everything for the future . . . and nothing to hide."[81] The party failed even to gain a single parliamentary seat.

In a similar development on a different continent, Mexico's 2012 congressional elections produced no seat for Natalia Juarez, a candidate for a left-wing party who had posed on a campaign poster naked from the waist up with six of her female party comrades (they covered their breasts with their right arms, raising their left arms in gestures of victory).[82] Women's sexualization in the political realm may be more likely to backfire when women are the subjects of the campaign. Women offering their bodies in support of a male subject constitutes a political service that points above all to the man's qualifications (his strength, his desirability). But offering their own bodies as a means to substantiate their right to rule seems, under patriarchy's rules, to merely reinscribe the notion that women are primarily sex objects, not capable, desirable, worthy politicians in their own right.

While consenting women's bodies can be the territory on which political competition is enacted, some political contests featuring masculinity in the form of homophobic denunciations can have more dire consequences. One Malaysian politician, condemned to prison after being accused of homosexuality by the incumbent president in 1998, spent the next six years behind bars, only to be charged anew with sodomy in 2008 when his party achieved unexpected success in a national election.[83]

---

[81] "The Body Politic: Women's Party Bares All on Election Poster," September 26, 2007, http://www.spiegel.de/international/europe/the-body-politic-women-s-party-bares-all-on-election-poster-a-508030.html.

[82] Philip Caulfield, "Mexican Congressional Candidate Appears in Topless Billboard," *NY Daily News*, May 22, 2012, http://www.nydailynews.com/news/world/mexican-congressional-candidate-appears-topless-billboard-article-1.1082514; Juarez's party, the PRD, failed to win any seats in her state, Jalisco. See "Election Resources on the Internet: Federal Elections in Mexico," Election Resources, 2012, http://www.electionresources.org/mx/deputies.php?election=2012&state=14.

[83] Kate Hodal, "Anwar Ibrahim's Moment of Truth Looms," *The Guardian*, July 10, 2012, http://www.guardian.co.uk/world/2012/jul/11/anwar-ibrahim-moment-truth-looms.

The examples that I have presented here are illustrative and by no means exhaustive. They serve only to demonstrate that making use of gender norms politically is not uncommon. Thus, while one could read about Putin's macho antics and wonder, "Why is this happening in Russia at this time? And why are these tactics not in evidence all the time and everywhere?," even a superficial scan of readily accessible news sources suggests that this discourse and these tactics are, in fact, in evidence in many places and at many times. More specifically, such tactics are enabled—and indeed can only arise and thrive—under patriarchy and misogyny, themselves near universal conditions. Putin's Russia is not exceptional in this regard. Instances where political actors bring to bear masculinity, femininity, sexualization, and homophobia as political legitimation tools occur in a wide range of political contexts: in semi-authoritarian regimes like contemporary Russia's, in more authoritarian regimes like China's, and in democratically inclined regimes like those in Western Europe and the United States. It is patriarchy, not political regime type, that produces the use of gender norms as instruments of political authority-building.

A significant body of anthropological-sociological-feminist research has documented a wide variety of masculinities exhibited in social, economic, and political life.[84] The plethora of local, regional (country-level), and global types of hegemonic masculinity[85] and the huge variety of means and methods used to assert masculine and feminine norms in politics dictate against trying to craft a universal theory to explain how, when, and why the use of gender norms and homophobia arises in the political arena (beyond, that is, the feminist insight that their use is predicated on and takes advantage of the existence of patriarchy and misogyny). Instead, this book uses the ascendance of such tactics in Russian politics under Putin as an in-depth case exploring the use of gender norms to a particular end, namely, political authority-building by regime incumbents and their opponents.

Much of the extant scholarly analysis of masculinity in politics concerns machismo and war: masculinity as a key element in political leaders' discourses justifying war (and thereby demonstrating their legitimacy as manly leaders);[86]

---

[84] For a discussion of the literature on masculinity studies, specifically looking at studies of "hegemonic masculinity" see Connell and Messerschmidt, "Hegemonic Masculinity: Rethinking the Concept"; on masculinity in multinational corporations, see J. Elias, "Hegemonic Masculinities, the Multinational Corporation, and the Developmental State: Constructing Gender in 'Progressive' Firms," *Men and Masculinities* 10, no. 4 (2008): 405–421, cited in Messerschmidt, *Hegemonic Masculinities and Camouflaged Politics*, 166.

[85] Connell and Messerschmidt, "Hegemonic Masculinity," 849.

[86] Messerschmidt, *Hegemonic Masculinities and Camouflaged Politics*; Kristin L. Hoganson, *Fighting for American Manhood: How Gender Politics Provoked the Spanish-American and Philippine-American Wars* (New Haven, CT: Yale University Press, 1998).

attachment to masculinity as an obstacle to nuclear disarmament and as a driver for war;[87] the attempt to prove presidential masculinity by engaging in war;[88] the linkage of manliness and militarism and the glorification of both by political leaders endorsing war;[89] the rhetorical use of masculinity to support both pro- and anti-war stances;[90] loss in war driving a national "remasculinization";[91] and so on. There is, however, relatively less academic discussion of the ways in which machismo and gender norms are wielded more broadly as a means of political regime legitimation beyond election campaigning.[92] And very little academic work has appeared on gendered discourses and tactics in the context of contemporary Russian politics.[93] This book helps to fill that gap. It also helps to lay the groundwork for further investigation of how gender norms are used by political actors to legitimate their authority, and the risks that such a strategy entails for gender equality and for democracy more broadly, both inside and outside of Russia.

Synopsis of the Study

While gender norms have been used as tools of political legitimation in many states and circumstances, Chapter 2, *Putin the Sex Back in Politics: Gender Norms, Sexualization, and Political Legitimation in Russia*, puts the spotlight on

[87] John Stoltenberg, *Refusing to Be a Man: Essays on Sex and Justice* (New York: Penguin Books, 1989), 77–89; Cohn, "Wars, Wimps, and Women."

[88] Alexander Deconde, *Presidential Machismo: Executive Authority, Military Intervention, and Foreign Relations* (Boston: Northeastern University Press, 1999)

[89] Sybil Oldfield, "The Dubious Legacy of Bismarck and von Treitschke," in *Women against the Iron Fist: Alternatives to Militarism 1900–1989*, by Sybil Oldfield (Cambridge, MA: Basil Blackwell, 1989), 3–17.

[90] Myra Marx Ferree and Wendy Christensen, "Cowboy of the World? Gendered Discourse in the Iraq War Debate," *Qualitative Sociology* 31, no. 3 (2008), 287–306.

[91] Susan Jeffords, *The Remasculinization of America: Gender and the Vietnam War* (Bloomington: Indiana University Press, 1989).

[92] On masculinity as a characteristic of the US presidency and a requirement for its would-be occupants, see Janis L. Edwards, "Visualizing Presidential Imperatives: Masculinity as an Interpretive Frame in Editorial Cartoons, 1988–2008," in *Gender and Political Communication in America: Rhetoric, Representation, and Display*, ed. Janis L. Edwards (Lanham, MD: Lexington Books, 2009), 233–250; on the construction of masculinity in press coverage of US presidential campaigning, see Wahl-Jorgensen, "Constructing Masculinities in U.S. Presidential Campaigns"; on popular perceptions of candidates' masculinity as the driving force behind presidential contests in the United States, see Jackson Katz, *Leading Men: Presidential Campaigns and the Politics of Manhood* (Northampton, MA: Interlink Books, 2013).

[93] For excellent exceptions, see Riabova and Riabov, "Nastoiashchii muzhchina Rossiiskoi politiki?"; Elizabeth Wood, "Performing Memory: Vladimir Putin and the Celebration of WWII in Russia," *Soviet and Post-Soviet Review* 38 (2011): 172–200; Elizabeth Wood, "The New Facade of Autocracy"; Helena Goscilo, ed., *Putin as Celebrity and Cultural Icon* (London: Routledge, 2013).

the Russian case, addressing the question: Why have we seen the use of gender norms and sexualization in Russian politics in the Putin era? The chapter reviews the Kremlin's apparent strategy of accentuating Putin's machismo and considers multiple intersecting factors (political, cultural, economic, historical, and international), rooted in the 1990s, that contributed to the emphasis on gender norms and homophobia in twenty-first-century Russian politics.

The next two chapters analyze Russian political activists' use of femininity, masculinity, and homophobia (heteronormativity) as tools in their political organizing efforts. Chapter 3, *Who's Macho, Who's Gay? Pro- and Anti-Kremlin Activists Gendering Russia's Political Leadership*, is the first of three case-study chapters on the use of gender norms and sexualization as political tools in Russia. It shows how activists use gender norms in their efforts to demonstrate support for the political leaders whom they favor and to undermine the positions of their opponents. Examining the discourses and actions of several political youth groups shows how masculinity has been "materialized" in Putin's practices and portrayals, how it has been supported and reinforced by the political endorsement of women identified with traditional ("emphasized") femininity in the political arena, and how it has been symbolically challenged by Putin's political opposition. To provide political context, the chapter briefly describes the pro-regime political youth groups that operate under regime auspices and the extra-systemic liberal opposition groups. The second case study, Chapter 4, *Fight Club: Gendered Activism on Patriotism, Conscription, and Pro-Natalism*, analyzes the use of gender norms in political activism on patriotism and two policy issues typically linked to patriotism: military conscription and pro-natalism.

Arguing that gender norms are invoked as tools of authority-building to take advantage of widespread misogyny and homophobia, Chapter 5, *Everywhere and Nowhere: Sexism and Homophobia in Russian Politics*, explores the ways in which sexism and homophobia have been reflected in Russia's public sphere as well as within the political groups that engage young activists. Theorizing that a strong women's movement can serve as a brake on public misogyny, the chapter also examines the failure of the nascent women's movement in early post-Soviet Russia to mobilize significant popular support between its foundation in the late 1980s and the end of Putin's first decade in power.

Chapter 6, *When Pussy Riots: Feminist Activism in Russia*, as the third case-study chapter, investigates a new wave of Russian feminist activism that began in 2010 and the analysis of politics and political legitimacy that it offers. In the chapter, I show that some self-identified feminist groups, such as Pussy Riot, consciously make use of the same patriarchal paradigm used by the pro-regime and liberal activists earlier discussed (using gender norms in their discourse and actions as a means of legitimation and delegitimation), while other Russian feminist groups—outside the cultural spotlight—overtly critique the sexism and homophobia that they see displayed across the political arena. The chapter includes feminists' explanations for the prevalence of gender norms and sexualization in Russian politics. I also use the Pussy Riot trial and other examples to highlight the regime's antagonism to feminist ideology and the threat that it presents to the legitimation strategy that political actors have been exploiting in Russia.

The Conclusion, *"The First Time, Do It for Love": Sexism, Power, and Politics under Putin*, examines the ways in which gender norms and sexualization have been used in political advertising as a means of bolstering Russia's increasingly nondemocratic political regime. Gender norms can influence public understandings of politics, just as politics is shaped by cultural ideas about sex and gender. As an ideology founded on equality and inclusion, feminism reveals and critiques the patriarchal hierarchy that values masculinity over femininity, and decries the use of machismo and misogyny in political competition. Feminism also valorizes the individual right to choose and is thus at odds with regime efforts and societal notions that reinforce the conformist strictures of gender norms. Gender norms can be used in politics to undermine the authority of undemocratic regimes, for instance, by labeling political leaders as unmanly. However, in the long run, making use of sexualization and gender norms in political legitimation reinforces traditional notions of gender and the subordination of women to men, restricting people's personal and political freedom and undercutting democracy more broadly.

2

Putin the Sex Back in Politics: Gender Norms, Sexualization, and Political Legitimation in Russia

Fostering a macho image has been one of the central features of Russian president Vladimir Putin's political legitimation strategy. Since masculinity does not inhere in the male body, macho image-reinforcing stunts have to occur in series to advertise and maintain the impression that a politician wants to make. Following his first election to the presidency in March 2000, Putin's numerous masculinity-displaying feats have included his "saving" a crew of journalists from a Siberian tiger (by shooting it with a tranquilizing dart),[1] zooming around a track in a Formula-One racecar,[2] braving rough seas to garner a skin sample collected with a crossbow from a gray whale,[3] and showing off his martial arts skills.[4]

Historian Elizabeth Wood has referred to this as Putin's special brand of "political spectacle," where his image is that of the solo ruler who commands the realm, a "masculine posturing" that coexists with real failures of governance and an increasingly nondemocratic political system.[5] Wood traces the emphasis on Putin's machismo to his first stint in office as Russia's prime minister—that is, to the last few months before then-President Yeltsin resigned at

[1] "Putin Saves TV Crew from Siberian Tiger."
[2] "Vladimir Putin: F1 Driver," *The Telegraph*, November 8, 2010, http://www.telegraph.co.uk/news/worldnews/europe/russia/8116882/Vladimir-Putin-F1-driver.html.
[3] Andrew Osborn, "Vladimir Putin Tracks Whales with Crossbow," *The Telegraph*, August 25, 2010, http://www.telegraph.co.uk/news/worldnews/europe/russia/7963982/Vladimir-Putin-tracks-whales-with-crossbow.html.
[4] Michael Schwirtz, "Putin in Martial Arts Video," *New York Times*, October 8, 2008, http://www.nytimes.com/2008/10/08/world/europe/08iht-putin.1.16776325.html.
[5] Elizabeth Wood, "Russia's Anti-Putin Protests Are More Than Just a Generational Temper Tantrum," *Boston Globe*, January 18, 2012, http://www.boston.com/bostonglobe/editorial_opinion/blogs/the_angle/2012/01/putins_failures.html.

the close of 1999, leaving Putin as the acting president and soon-to-be incumbent.[6] The public relations (PR) campaign accenting his macho status—associated closely at first with militarism, itself tightly linked to masculinity—kicked off with Putin's flight in a fighter jet in October 1999 while visiting a military base in southern Russia and only accelerated thereafter.[7]

A significant element of Putin's machismo, Wood writes, rests on his assertion of power over other men—from state officials and economic powerhouses to journalists and foreign diplomats.[8] This process of "topping" makes challengers appear relatively less masculine and, thus, less powerful. Putin's insults were bold-faced in this regard. At a joint press conference held with European Union leaders in 2002, Putin berated a male foreign journalist who asked him about civilian deaths in Chechnya, suggesting that the journalist—apparently so empathetic to the Chechens—might consider converting to Islam and undergoing circumcision. "We have specialists in this area," Putin emphatically stated, adding, "I will recommend that they do the operation on you in such a way that nothing will grow back."[9] A profound silence followed this remark.

As Putin's prime minister, Dmitrii Medvedev, prepared to become president for the 2008–2012 term (as something of a placeholder for Putin who, according to the Russian Constitution, was not allowed to serve three presidential terms in a row), the Kremlin seemed careful to continue the message that Putin remained in charge. While the language Putin directed at Medvedev was not insulting, Wood notes that Medvedev was "feminized" during the faux campaign as a means to highlight Putin's macho image. In February 2008, for example, Medvedev was sent to meet with a gathering of mothers in Novosibirsk, while Putin was charged with attending a massive press conference in Moscow. Medvedev also visited sheep farms and maternity hospitals, emphasizing his connection to animal husbandry and family issues over high politics.[10] And when the regime's political vehicle, the United Russia party, formulaically nominated Medvedev as its presidential candidate in December 2007, one of the delegates to the United Russia convention—a well-known singer in the Soviet era and a member of the Russian parliament's lower house—told a journalist that he was happy with the party's choice, as he had "always dreamed that a woman would become president."[11] Although Putin would be relegated

---

[6] Wood, "The New Façade of Autocracy," 4.

[7] Ibid.

[8] Ibid., 4.

[9] Cited in Ibid., 14. For a video of the quote, see "Putin gotov obrezat'" [video], August 25, 2008, http://www.youtube.com/watch?feature=player_embedded&v=owAXfnSI5zA.

[10] Wood, "The New Façade of Autocracy," 5, 24–25.

[11] Ibid., 26.

to the prime ministerial position for the next four years, his masculinity—in comparison to that of his tandem-mate, Medvedev—was intact.

Masculinity on the Campaign Trail

Russia in the 2000s has been labeled a "managed democracy," an "illiberal democracy" and a "competitive authoritarian regime," all of these monikers indicating a less than fully democratic political system.[12] Between Putin's first election in 2000 and his reelection to a third presidential term in 2012, by many indicators Russia became an increasingly authoritarian state. Press freedom declined, investigative journalists perished, television stations returned to state control, restrictions on nongovernmental organizations increased, and elections suffered from fraud. Reflecting these trends, in 2005, Freedom House changed Russia's democracy rating from "partly free" to "not free," and in 2012 Russia was classified as a "consolidated authoritarian regime."[13] Timothy Colton's study of democratic competition in Russian presidential elections between 1996 and 2004 also found that contestation had declined over time. If the 1996 election had been truly competitive, with Yeltsin winning only 38 percent of the vote and having to endure a second round of elections to take office, and the 2000 election was moderately competitive, with Putin winning 53 percent of the vote, by 2004 the election was minimally competitive, with Putin easily gaining election with an official 71 percent of the vote, a trend that would continue.[14] In 2008, Medvedev, Putin's handpicked successor, drew 70 percent of the vote, and in 2012 Putin reportedly emerged victorious with the support of nearly 64 percent of the electorate (his nearest rival, the Communist Party candidate, was far behind at 17 percent).[15]

All political regimes need and use legitimation strategies. Even the most violent totalitarian regimes—like Cambodia under the Khmer Rouge or the USSR under Stalin—use propaganda in an effort to achieve political hegemony and try to secure their position. Because the balance between coercion and consent leans toward the former in dictatorships and tips toward the latter in democracies, political actors in democratic polities make more

[12] Steven Levitsky and Lucan A. Way, *Competitive Authoritarianism: Hybrid Regimes After the Cold War*, 1st ed. (Cambridge: Cambridge University Press, 2010).

[13] "Nations in Transit: Russia 2012," http://www.freedomhouse.org/report/nations-transit/2012/russia.

[14] Timothy Colton, "'Putin and the Attenuation of Russian Democracy,'" in *Putin's Russia*, ed. Dale Herspring, 3rd ed. (Lanham, MD: Rowman and Littlefield, 2007), 37–52.

[15] Central Electoral Commission of the Russian Federation, "Svedeniia o provodiashchikhsia vyborakh i referendumakh," March 4, 2012, http://bit.ly/1md7IDz.

of an effort to acquire legitimacy in the eyes of their potential constituents (rather than simply beating, jailing, or liquidating opponents as dictators feel more free to do). Under democratic rules of the game, politics may take on the air of a contest over perceived legitimacy. Although political campaigns in post-Soviet Russia have yet to entail the full-fledged political competition one can witness in long-standing democracies, in the wake of the Soviet collapse Russia's political leaders became the subject of far closer scrutiny in the official and unofficial media both while in office and while "running" for office. Despite the decreasingly free political environment in Russia as Putin's reign wore on, political actors both pro- and anti-Putin made efforts to build their political legitimacy and undermine that of their opponents.

Evidence of masculinity was one component of Russian politicians' new-found interest in having a legitimation strategy. In this, Russian political actors and image-makers were not alone. In an article on the construction of US presidential candidates' masculinity, Karin Wahl-Jorgensen elaborates on four arenas traditionally highlighted in campaigns where candidates' masculinity is on view: military prowess, sports and athletic ability, male bonding with a vice-presidential running mate, and family.[16] In his legitimation strategy (whether as a candidate or as an incumbent), Putin drew on some but not all of these, given the vast differences between the Russian and American political systems and the two countries' dramatically distinct legacies of political leadership.

While Putin never served in the Soviet military, he did (in the Russian context) one better by joining the Soviet Committee on State Security (KGB) directly after graduating from college in 1975. In addition to its fearsome and well-deserved reputation for brutality, during the Soviet era the KGB was said to have attracted "the most honest, incorruptible people," a belief that did not decay after the Soviet collapse, according to the deputy director of a major Russian public opinion polling firm.[17] As a former KGB operative in East Germany and later as head of the KGB's successor (the Russian Federal Security Service; FSB) for a year before being appointed prime minister by Yeltsin, Putin's "militarized" credentials were impeccable. These, predictably, were highlighted as Putin's rise to power began in earnest. The start of the second round of the Chechen war in fall 1999 began on Prime Minister Putin's watch. When several residential apartment buildings in Moscow and two other Russian cities blew up in September 1999, Putin's promise to corner and kill the

---

[16] Wahl-Jorgensen, "Constructing Masculinities in U.S. Presidential Campaigns."

[17] Maksim Ivanov, "Grazhdane veriat v tserkov', armiiu i spetssluzhby," November 2, 2012, http://www.kommersant.ru/doc/2058340?isSearch=True.

terrorists wherever they might be found reassured (or warned) the population that the new prime minister would not hesitate to apply violence and exact revenge.[18] And to augment his militarized credentials, in March 2000, just before the presidential election that began Putin's long term in Russia's top political office, Putin flew into Chechnya's capital, Grozny, in a Sukhoi-27 fighter jet (though he was not the pilot).[19] Maya Eichler's study of militarism and masculinity in Russia notes that the initiation of the second phase of the Chechen war smoothed Putin's path into the presidency, as the regime used Putin's prosecution of the war to successfully draw on and foster a "militarized patriotism."[20] This emphasis on militarism was not unique to Putin's political ascent. Tatiana Riabova's analysis of Russian news sources in Russia's 2004 and 2008 presidential campaigns suggests a picture similar to that in US politics, with frequent mention made of the "military competence" of candidates, whether by referring to a candidate's skills with weapons or simply showing the contender in camouflage or holding a machine gun.[21]

Sports constituted another element visible in Putin's legitimation strategy. Like US presidential candidates, the incumbent Putin (even without the motivating benefit of a serious political challenger in any of his political races) was shown playing team sports (hockey), individual sports (martial arts), and outdoor sports (shirtless fishing).[22] Many news outlets commented on his athleticism and physique.

Male bonding between presidential and vice-presidential running mates—a key part of US campaign strategies—was largely absent from the Russian political scene until the mid-Putin era. This is chiefly due to the fact that before the 1990s there *were* no public campaigns for the Russian presidency (or for the top positions in the Soviet Communist Party leadership). Moreover, the Russian political system does not include a vice-presidency (this having been eliminated by Yeltsin in the late-1993 draft of the constitution after his own vice president, Alexander Rutskoi, betrayed him and joined with angry communists in rebellion against the president, and after Gorbachev's vice president, Gennady Yanaev, joined the group of

[18] "Putin on 'Wasting Terrorists in the Outhouse': Wrong Rhetoric, Right Idea," July 15, 2011, http://rt.com/politics/putin-honesty-president-magnitogorsk/.

[19] Jim Heintz, "Birds, Bears, Bikers All Play into Putin's Stunts," September 6, 2012, http://bigstory.ap.org/article/birds-bears-bikers-all-play-putins-stunts.

[20] Maya Eichler, *Militarizing Men: Gender, Conscription, and War in Post-Soviet Russia* (Stanford, CA: Stanford University Press, 2012), 47–48.

[21] Tat'iana Riabova, *Pol vlasti: Gendernye stereotypy v sovremennoi rossiiskoi politike* (Ivanovo, Russia: Ivanovo State University, 2008).

[22] Wahl-Jorgensen, "Constructing Masculinities in U.S. Presidential Campaigns," 59; Alexey Druszinin, "Vladimir Putin's Passion for Sports," http://en.ria.ru/photolents/20121007/176420 498.htm, accessed April 16, 2013.

coup-plotters who attempted to unseat Gorbachev in August 1991). Campaign footage picturing the male running mates playing sports together, talking, laughing, and otherwise bonding, as is common in U S campaign coverage[23] arose only indirectly in Russia with images of the "tandem" of President Putin and Prime Minister Medvedev (and later, President Medvedev and Prime Minister Putin) playing badminton, biking, and trying to look cool together in their sunglasses.[24] One can speculate that media images showing Putin engaged in sports and of Putin and Medvedev bonding as a "tandem" may have come about as a result of the spread of US campaign techniques—whether brought by Western consulting companies or by political osmosis. While Medvedev was not Putin's "running mate," the two were clearly understood as something of a political team in which Medvedev (regardless of his official title) was the junior partner and not unlike a vice president in that regard. These male-bonding opportunities cement the image of political leadership as a man's job—though they also leave open implications of homoeroticism.[25]

The only part of the paradigm of masculine candidate image-making that finds no parallel in the Putin era is the "family values" element.[26] There are two aspects to the "family" realm where masculinity is on display. The first comprises the notion of safety and protection. Traditional masculinity entails the idea that the "man of the house" (or political leader) is responsible for protecting "his" family (or "his" nation). Putin has certainly adopted this rhetoric while in office, stressing the need to assert Russia's sovereignty against Western interference and to protect Russia from the threat of terrorism and political challengers. The second element, however, revolves around the candidate's family relationships, particularly, the spousal relationship.[27]

Whereas American families are accustomed to seeing the First Lady in a very public light, Soviet citizens—and even post-Soviet Russians—have no tradition of highly visible political wives, not to mention extensive media probes into the personal lives of their political rulers. Although Raisa Gorbacheva, Naina Yeltsin, and Liudmila Putina were more visible in public than Leonid Brezhnev's wife, Victoria, or Nina Khrushcheva (who did accompany

---

[23] Wahl-Jorgensen, "Constructing Masculinities in U.S. Presidential Campaigns," 60–63.

[24] Wil Longbottom, "Fancy a Bike Ride in the Park? How an 'Informal' Meeting in Moscow Could Decide Who Runs Russia Next Year," The Daily Mail, June 11, 2011, http://www.dailymail.co.uk/news/article-2002504/Fancy-bike-ride-park-How-informal-meeting-Moscow-decide-runs-Russia-year.html.

[25] Wahl-Jorgensen, "Constructing Masculinities in U.S. Presidential Campaigns," 61–63.

[26] Ibid., 67.

[27] Ibid.

her partner[28] on trips abroad and socialized with the wives of other heads of state, which was not typical for previous Soviet leaders), the Russian public in the 1990s and 2000s was not treated to intimate family scenes or romantic displays by male political leaders and their spouses.[29] Indeed, Putin's family has been "conspicuously absent from the public domain."[30] This method of demonstrating heterosexuality—and thus, masculinity—has therefore been less available to Russia's political leadership. Although the Putins would announce their impending divorce in 2013,[31] Liudmila Putina, interviewed in the first year of her husband's presidency, described herself and her husband in terms that did not challenge his masculinity or paint anything other than a happy family portrait. Putina noted that she was "not a feminist" herself but that she wanted women to "occupy a worthy place in the world." In answer to the question, "Does [Putin] look at women?" she reassured readers that "beautiful women draw his attention," and when asked whether this troubled her, she was quick to emphasize Putin's masculine credentials: "What kind of man [would he be] if he wasn't attracted to beautiful women?" Putina also confirmed that her husband was "indifferent" to alcohol but added that he was not opposed to it, having "loved to drink beer" during their years in Germany and that drinking "a little vodka or cognac" was also in his repertoire.[32] Putin's relative sobriety—compared to his predecessors, Yeltsin in particular—made him something of an aberration from the "regular guy" image that the Kremlin sought to cultivate. Such pronouncements thus made it clear that Putin was not above having a mug of quality beer from time to time or drinking other alcoholic beverages "in moderation."[33]

---

[28] Nina Kukharchuk did not officially marry Nikita Khrushchev until 1965, after his political career ended. See "Khrushcheva, Nina Petrovna," *Vikipediia*, http://bit.ly/18D8VNP, accessed November 9, 2012.

[29] Geraldine Baum, "The Reluctant First Lady: Profile: Naina Yeltsin Is No Raisa Gorbachev: But She Is Giving the Russian people What They Expect—A Political Wife Who Is Traditional, Anonymous and Colorless," *Los Angeles Times*, June 15, 1992, http://articles.latimes.com/1992-06-15/news/vw-405_1_raisa-gorbachev; Anna Nemtsova, "Vladimir Putin's Wife, Lyudmila, Has All But Vanished, and Russians Don't Seem to Care," *The Daily Beast*, January 13, 2013, http://www.thedailybeast.com/articles/2013/01/13/vladimir-putin-s-wife-lyudmila-has-all-but-vanished-and-russians-don-t-seem-to-care.html.

[30] Fiona Hill and Clifford G. Gaddy, *Mr. Putin: Operative in the Kremlin* (Washington, DC: Brookings Institution Press, 2012), 3.

[31] Ellen Barry and David M. Herszenhorn, "Putins Finally Appear Together, to Announce Split," *New York Times*, June 6, 2013, http://www.nytimes.com/2013/06/07/world/europe/putins-finally-appear-together-to-announce-split.html.

[32] Nataliia Gevorkian, Natal'ia Timakova, and Andrei Kolesnikov, *Ot pervogo litsa: Razgovorys Vladimirom Putinym* (Moscow: Vagrius, 2000), 140–141.

[33] Riabova and Riabov, "Nastoiashchii muzhchina Rossiiskoi politiki?," 55.

A "Real Man" (Muzhik)

The Russian notion of muzhik is also an important factor when considering masculinity and political legitimation. In Russian, "muzhik" means "man," but its connotations differ somewhat from muzhchina, the standard word for man. In the early Soviet era, according to historian Esther-Kingston Mann, a muzhik was a male peasant—backward, ignorant, and potentially counterrevolutionary (as opposed to the celebrated "worker"). His counterpart was the baba, a similarly derogatory term for a peasant woman—a politically retrograde female of limited intellectual scope and concerns.[34] In the post-Soviet period, however, "muzhik" gained a positive valence and came to connote the "norm of modern Russian masculinity," finding its way into advertisements, movies, pop songs, and elegies as a signifier of "real" manhood.[35] "Baba," however, underwent no such renovation and continues to be an insulting or denigrating term.[36] Attainment of "real male" (muzhik) status requires that a man prove that he is "not a woman, not a child, and not a homosexual."[37] Drawing on Olga Shaburova's analysis, Russian social scientists Oleg Riabov and Tatiana Riabova explain that "muzhik" came to signify the Russian national masculine identity by being defined "in opposition to representations of western masculinity," blending liberal and Soviet types of masculinity instead:

> This type [of masculinity] is founded on self-sufficiency, economic independence, [and] respect for private property (in that sense, a "muzhik" is anti-communist). It is also far from 100-percent support for liberalism—values that are interpreted as a cult of individualism and egoism—while comradeship (tovarishchestvo) and male

---

[34] Elizabeth A. Wood, *The Baba and the Comrade: Gender and Politics in Revolutionary Russia* (Bloomington: Indiana University Press, 1997), 1; Esther Kingston-Mann, personal communication by email, March 20, 2013; Valentina Zaitseva, "National, Cultural, and Gender Identity in the Russian Language," in *Gender and National Identity in Twentieth-Century Russian Culture*, eds. Helena Goscilo and Andrea Lanoux (DeKalb: Northern Illinois University Press, 2006), 34.

[35] Riabova and Riabov, "Nastoiashchii muzhchina Rossiiskoi politiki?," 53.

[36] Words describing privileged groups are not typically construed as insults, while those describing oppressed groups are, such as "yid," or "fag." See Anna Brius, "Baby, pedy, zhidy," *Net—znachit net* 3 (March 2011): 22–25; Emil A. Draitser, *Making War Not Love: Gender and Sexuality in Russian Humor* (New York: St. Martin's Press, 1999), 35.

[37] Riabova and Riabov, "Nastoiashchii muzhchina Rossiiskoi politiki?," 53–54, citing O. Shaburova, "Muzhik' kak konstrukt russkoi muzhestvennosti i ego reprezentatsiia v rossiiskoi massovoi kul'ture," in *Vater Rhein under Mutter Wolga: Diskurse um Nation und Gender in Deutschland und Russland*, eds. Elisabeth Cheaure, Regine Nohejl and Antonia Napp (Würzburg, Germany: Ergon, 2005); O. Shaburova, "Muzhik ne suetitsia, ili pivo s kharakterom," in S. Ushakin, ed., *O muzhe(N)stvennosti* (Moscow: NLO, 2002), 534.

brotherhood are crucial components of the image of a "muzhik." A "muzhik" does not agree with the liberal values of political correctness; sexism and homophobia are not considered faults in the [post-Soviet] environment. Unlike the imagined man in the contemporary West, a "muzhik" is hardy, strong, and powerful; he doesn't say much, but always stands by his word. Finally, he is a patriot—he prefers the values of his own national culture, and expresses his readiness to defend the Motherland.[38]

Backing this notion, a Russian survey firm reporting on Russians' homophobic attitudes toward gay pride events titled its press release, "We're not in America, you know" (My zhe ne v Amerike), emphasizing the idea that homosexuality is regarded as normal in the United States, and that—almost as a point of pride—the same was not true in Russia.[39]

The term "muzhik" and its content have become part of the Putin regime's legitimation strategy. Not only is this type of masculinity "exploited" by Russia's leadership, the regime takes an "active role in reproducing it and promoting it ... as American elites during the cold war [made use of] the masculinity in the image of John Wayne."[40] Putin's image was brought into line with the muzhik mold, as his presidency coincided with the rise of the muzhik as a masculine type. While initially—by contrast to Yeltsin's brash and sometimes outlandish behavior—Putin's persona reflected a Western-style masculinity featuring the qualities of a "rational, practical, cool-headed manager," soon the Russian electorate was offered a different image. This Putin was painted as a "tsar-father" figure who would protect the country from the wily Westerners aiming to weaken Russia from without and from the corrupt bureaucrats within.[41]

Putin's image and discourse also increasingly matched that of the muzhik. His tough language against Chechens accused of terrorist acts (he promised to "waste the terrorists in their outhouses") signaled the speech of a Russian-style "macho man."[42] Putin's use of colorfully foul language and criminal underworld slang is an element of the current Russian construction of political masculinity largely unfamiliar in public American political discourse. Indeed, Wood points out that Putin's language was even more vulgar than usually translated and that he frequently referred to bodily excretions when making

[38] Riabova and Riabov, "Nastoiashchii muzhchina Rossiiskoi politiki?," 54.

[39] Fond Obshchestvennogo Mneniia, "My zhe ne v Amerike," June 9, 2011, http://fom.ru/obshchestvo/123.

[40] Riabova and Riabov, "Nastoiashchii muzhchina Rossiiskoi politiki?," 54.

[41] Ibid., 55.

[42] Ibid., citing Kolonnitskii 2004. http://www.idelo.ru/312/14.html.

pointed remarks.[43] In trying to put to rest rumors of his own hidden wealth, for instance, in 2008 Putin told a journalist that this was simply "nonsense—excavated from someone's nose and then smeared on bits of paper."[44] Putin's choice turns of phrase reinforced his manly and occasionally rough persona.[45]

The images of Putin fishing with bared chest, shooting wild animals, throwing his martial arts opponents, and generally showing off his physique are part of the muzhik aura as well. Riabov and Riabova note that even Western commentators like Michael Gove, a Conservative British member of parliament, regarded the exhibition of Putin's body as a means to show his political counterparts (outside of Russia) that he was the "physical embodiment of his nation's strength and energy" and that his "bare-chested peacockery [was] in line with the cult of Putin as his nation's silverback—the leader of the band."[46] Masculine domination was a political legitimation strategy both at home and abroad. Occasional jabs at the masculinity of Western democratic political institutions that issued threats to Russian sovereignty constitute part of this strategy as well. In February 2008, for example, frustrated by the negative evaluations of Russian electoral processes by the Organization for Security and Co-operation in Europe (OSCE), Putin remarked at a major press conference that OSCE "election monitors should teach their wives 'how to make cabbage soup' rather than teach Russia about democracy."[47] In addition to the idea that the monitors' time would be better spent in the kitchen than impugning Russia's elections, Putin's comment contained the unmistakable implication that OSCE monitors were so unmanly that they would be able to perform a classically female cooking feat better than their own wives.

While the "real man" (muzhik) may constitute the current image of hegemonic masculinity in Russia, there are disagreements about what the "right" way to be masculine might be. Some Russian public figures regarded the new muzhik image in a negative light. Artemii Troitskii, a music critic and former editor of Russian *Playboy* magazine, stated in a 2009 interview that he wished

[43] Wood, "The New Façade of Autocracy," 7, 10.

[44] Quoted in ibid., 15.

[45] For analysis of Putin's linguistic style, see Michael S. Gorham, "Putin's Language," in *Putin as Celebrity and Cultural Icon*, ed. Helena Goscilo (London: Routledge, 2013), 82–103; Lara Ryazanova-Clarke, "The Discourse of a Spectacle at the End of the Presidential Term," in *Putin as Celebrity and Cultural Icon*, ed. Helena Goscilo (London: Routledge, 2013), 104–132.

[46] Michael Gove, "Putin's Bare Chest Is a Display of Power Best Kept Secret," August 31, 2007, http://grumpymanflashfictioncontest.blogspot.com/2007/08/putins-bare-chest-is-display-of-power.html (citation from Riabov and Riabova, "Nastoiashchii muzhchina Rossiiskoi politiki?," 56).

[47] "International Election Observers Highlight US Voting Problems," RIA Novosti, November 8, 2012, http://en.rian.ru/world/20121108/177284443.html.

the "real Russian muzhik" would become extinct and be replaced by modern men who were "clean, neat, smart, romantic and respectful to women." By contrast, Troitskii regarded the standard image of a Russian "muzhik"—or the "Russian myth" of one—as a "fat, vile creature from a . . . beer commercial . . . who likes to fight, and regards women with a mixture of suspicion and fear." Troitskii voiced concern that "the archetypal [woman] in the universe of a 'real muzhik' [was] a wife, who should put up the soup . . . and provide the comforts of home; a piece of meat who should spread her legs and then get lost; and a hateful mother-in-law who should be despised."[48] While images of ideal masculinity are obviously varied, Troitskii's effort to counter the misogynistic muzhik image suggests that he believed it to be common.

A Sexy Man

Testimonials by attractive women constitute another aspect of heteronormative masculinity. Likely aware of this, image-makers in the Kremlin were attentive to Putin's—and the regime's—depiction in popular culture and, in particular, on the Internet, where young people were most likely to get their information. The popular culture manifestations of support for Putin not only as a politician but as a man began with a 2002 song resulting from a collaboration between a Soviet-era rocker, Alexander Yelin, and his friend, Nikolai Gastello. Gastello, a government employee running the press division of Russia's national courts, also had a sideline business in the music industry. Yelin reportedly wrote the song in a successful bid to win a bet; he claimed that he could produce a hit song in Russia for $300. "A Man Like Putin" (Takogo kak Putin) was the result.[49] Performed by a female duo who endorsed Putin as a politician and as an "ideal man," the song rose to the top of Russia's pop charts and became a "propaganda song" often heard at state-sponsored pro-Putin rallies.[50] Its lyrics decry the bad behavior of a boyfriend who gets into fights and takes drugs, provoking the female narrator to break up with him and set her sights higher. Now, she explains, "I want someone like Putin, full of strength / Someone like Putin, who doesn't drink / Someone like Putin, who

---

[48] Nataliia Rostova, "'Ia schitaiu, chto "nastoiashchii russkii muzhik" dolzhen vymeret'," January 15, 2010, http://slon.ru/russia/ya_schitayu_chto_nastoyashhiy_russkiy_muzhik_dolz-238959.xhtml; see also Riabov and Riabova, "Nastoiashchii muzhchina Rossiiskoi politiki?," 56.

[49] "Takogo kak Putin/One Like Putin, English Subs" [video], YouTube.com, December 6, 2008, http://www.youtube.com/watch?v=zk_VszbZa_s&feature=related.

[50] Alexis Bloom, "A Man Like Putin" [video], accessed March 27, 2013, http://www.pbs.org/soundtracks/stories/putin/, accessed March 27, 2013.

won't treat me badly / Someone like Putin, who won't up and leave me."[51] In his song, Yelin tapped into the sentiments of the "average Russian woman," for whom finding a man like Putin—athletic, strong, and sober—would be "her lifelong dream."[52]

In mid-2011, several music videos similar in theme to their popular predecessor circulated on the Internet, posted by a group called "DevochkiZa" (Girls For). The catchiest of these was called "I Want to Be Your Konni" (Konni, or "Connie," is the name of Putin's dog). The video showed several attractive young women pining for a chance to get with Putin (primping, plotting, getting drunk, and finally smashing a watermelon with a baseball bat in apparent frustration). Projecting an almost campy level of driven sexual desire, the women sing, "I want to be your Konni / On the table and on the balcony/ You'll be mine in any case!"[53] A second clip called "Fistfight for Putin" (Draka za Putina) brings together seven young women in an apartment where they initially greet each other with smiles, kisses, and bottles of wine. They complain about their treatment at their boyfriends' hands, and then one points to the television where the news is showing Putin and proclaims: "There's my hero!" Hearing this, the women begin to cast suspicious glances at each other, recognizing one another as potential competitors. The doorbell rings and their friendly gathering deteriorates into a knock-down drag-out bar fight, as they compete to be the first to open the door to their guest—presumably, Putin.[54] Rather than voicing their desire simply for a man "like" Putin, the rather histrionic young women of DevochkiZa now appeared to want the man himself and acted as if they were ready to fight for him.

Some observers could not decide whether such clips were pro- or anti-Putin.[55] The Konni video's description stated simply, "A group of young women (devushek) recorded a song for Putin, 'I want to be your Konni.' Vladimir Putin is the ideal man," and offered like-minded viewers a social networking site to join if they were so inclined.[56] The site proclaimed itself to be apolitical and uncensored, a "group for the most beautiful girls in the country." The site's introductory paragraph inquires: "Do you think HE's sweet [and] sexy, or do

[51] The lyrics can be found in Helena Goscilo, "The Ultimate Celebrity: VVP as VIP Objet d'Art," in *Celebrity and Glamour in Contemporary Russia: Shocking Chic*, ed. Helena Goscilo and Vlad Strukov (London: Routledge, 2011), 38, 51.

[52] Bloom, "A Man Like Putin."

[53] "Devochki za Putina" [video], July 5, 2011, http://www.youtube.com/watch?v=7TC_N9qQLJ8.

[54] DevochkiZa, "draka za Putina" [video], September 29, 2011, https://www.youtube.com/watch?v=vPvVgSOi1yg.

[55] Feodorff, "Seks-klip o Putine: Ia khochu byt' tvoei Koni. . . . , " July 7, 2011, http://newsland.com/news/detail/id/733701/.

[56] "devochki za Putina."

you want to have his children? Then you're with us. Get closer to the sex-symbol and the most envied man in the country."[57] Such talk implies either considerable irony or actual support. However, DevochkiZa's YouTube user channel linked to and "liked" a video posted by a pro-Kremlin youth group, "Stal'" (the video records Stal' activists banging on drums in front of the Tver city administration building, demanding that hot water be turned back on in the city), which suggests a pro-Kremlin stance and renders practically impossible an anti-Kremlin one.[58]

Putin's positive image as an appealing heterosexual man was projected not only in such pop culture manifestations as these songs (if they were not, in fact, underwritten by the Kremlin) but was also reflected in the way that the main pro-Kremlin youth movement, Nashi, expended its funds. An email-hacking incident in early 2012 broke open a minor scandal when several nominally "grassroots" pro-Putin groups were exposed as Nashi-funded projects.[59] These groups included "Putin's Army" (famous for the "Rip it for Putin" contest) and another group that held a bikini car wash in Putin's honor. Both groups' activities served to advertise Putin's desirability in the eyes of attractive young women.

Putin "undoubtedly" represents an example of hegemonic masculinity in twenty-first century Russia.[60] This image, with its emphasis on physical masculinity, was not created accidentally. Journalist Steve LeVine asserts that Putin's political makeover was the brainchild of Kremlin ideologist Vladislav Surkov, who was in charge of "the transformation of the president's visage into a savior-of-Russia icon, gargantuan and granite-faced, gazing from billboards, television screens, and newspapers throughout Moscow."[61] As an example of the PR campaign promoting Putin's body, in 2007 the national newspaper *Komsomolskaia Pravda* published a series of photos of Putin on his fishing trip with the prince of Monaco, followed by an article titled "Become Like Putin," containing advice for civil servants and elected officials on how to exercise to achieve a Putinesque physique. Eliot Borenstein similarly attributes the

---

[57] "Devochki za Putina," http://vk.com/club28392848, accessed April 17, 2013.

[58] "Kanal pol'zovatelia DevochkiZa" [video], https://www.youtube.com/user/DevochkiZa?feature=watch, accessed April 17, 2013; MadeOfSteelChannel, "'Im po fig!'/'Stal'' v Tveri/Boi—4" [video], September 26, 2011, https://www.youtube.com/watch?v=rfXnhZyVG2Y.

[59] Miriam Elder, "Polishing Putin: Hacked Emails Suggest Dirty Tricks by Russian Youth Group," *The Guardian*, February 7, 2012, http://www.guardian.co.uk/world/2012/feb/07/putin-hacked-emails-russian-nashi?newsfeed=true; Kremlingate, "Proplachennoe v gazetakh pravil'noe osveshchenie Seligera," February 3, 2012, http://lj.rossia.org/users/kremlingate/345.html.

[60] Riabova and Riabov, "Nastoiashchii muzhchina Rossiiskoi politiki?," 50.

[61] Goscilo, "The Ultimate Celebrity," 32, citing Steve LeVine, *Putin's Labyrinth: Spies, Murder, and the Dark Heart of the New Russia* (New York: Random House), 2008, 34.

success of Putin's "brand" to the "political handlers . . . [who] created the image of a tough no-nonsense 'man's man' who was sober, athletic and decisive," in contrast to his predecessor.[62] The top–down plan, labeled "Project Putin" by Putin's deputy campaign manager, which aimed to reconsolidate power in the Kremlin "starting with the election of an unknown secret police chief" into Russia's presidency, had machismo as a centerpiece.[63] As Helena Goscilo points out, photographers perpetually trailed Putin as he went about the travels obligatory to his official position as well as on "vacations in Siberia, where a bare-chested Putin fishing, riding, and climbing trees became immortalized as a sexual commodity when snapshots of his leisurely self flooded the Internet."[64] These pictures—along with women's fawning expressions of love and desire for Putin as reported in the media—reinforced the "sexualization" of Putin's image. By the end of his second presidential term, Putin was regarded as the "post-Soviet exemplar of seductive, reassuring virility."[65]

It is widely accepted that Putin's image is controlled by Kremlin image-makers. Their task is to ensure that Putin's PR efforts target specific groups within his domestic audience, portraying him "as the ultimate Russian action man, capable of dealing with every eventuality."[66] As Fiona Hill and Clifford Gaddy note, each of these stunts or "performances" is "based on feedback from opinion polls suggesting the Kremlin needs to reach out and create a direct connection to a particular group among the Russian population," even as the Russian intelligentsia and opposition ridicule his efforts.[67]

As a legitimation strategy, machismo is risky, as it leaves the user open to persistent demands to prove his masculinity as well as to suggestions that his masculinity has been exaggerated. After a 2012 incident in which Putin apparently injured his back during a hang gliding flight alongside some Siberian cranes, opposition activists likened him to the geriatric Brezhnev for staying in power past his expiration date. Nearly two dozen opposition activists, including

---

[62] Eliot Borenstein, *Overkill: Sex and Violence in Contemporary Russian Popular Culture* (Ithaca, NY: Cornell University Press, 2007), 226–227.

[63] Peter Baker and Susan Glasser, *Kremlin Rising* (New York: Scribner, 2005), 6.

[64] Goscilo, "The Ultimate Celebrity," 40.

[65] Ibid., 40; On Putin's hypermasculine image and status as an erotic icon—and even as an object of female worship—see Helena Goscilo, "Putin's Performance of Masculinity: The Action Hero and Macho Sex-Object," in *Putin as Celebrity and Cultural Icon*, ed. Helena Goscilo (London: Routledge, 2013), 180–207.

[66] Hill and Gaddy, *Mr. Putin*, 5.

[67] Ibid., 4; Elements of satire and the presence of both official and unofficial "Putiniana" distinguish the Putin "craze" from the personality "cults" that surrounded Soviet leaders. See Julie A. Cassiday and Emily D. Johnson, "A Personality Cult for the Modern Age: Reading Vladimir Putin's Public Persona," in *Putin as Celebrity and Cultural Icon*, ed. Helena Goscilo (London: Routledge, 2013), 48–49.

Roman Dobrokhotov of the liberal political youth group "My" (We), took the occasion of Putin's sixtieth birthday later that fall to hold a "Let's Send Grandpa into Retirement" protest and were arrested for their trouble. Dobrokhotov had purchased a rake that he bedecked with a white ribbon (the symbolic color of Russia's political opposition) as an ostensible gift for Putin to use in his retirement at a penal colony. Dobrokhotov was not able to deliver his gift on the day of the action; it fell from the activist's grasp as he was dragged off the sidewalk into a waiting police bus.[68]

Fears that the aging Putin (only 60 in 2012) was losing his virile, manly edge apparently provoked the Kremlin's fixers to consider replacing Putin's macho image with that of the "wise patriarch of Russian politics," able to properly manipulate the conflicts and contests between his underlings, irrespective of his age. This plan to alter Putin's public profile was revealed in a report ordered by one of Russia's governors for his own use.[69] One danger of the regime relying on an ideology of political celebrity and glamour, selling the "Putin brand" as a partial basis for its political legitimation and power,[70] is that the popularity of brands—and the fads based on them—shifts and fades with age. By early 2013, however, Putin had apparently rejected the "wise patriarch" plan, as a "full slate of his traditional macho stunts" was planned for the ensuing months.[71]

At Putin's late-2012 press conference (a four-hour affair in a large auditorium), the connection between the Russian leader's masculine image and his political legitimacy was still in force. Putin's response to a question from a female reporter from Magadan, a city in Russia's far East, highlighted this explicitly:

Q. Antonina Lukina, Magadan, "Magadanskaia Pravda": Dear Vladimir Vladimirovich! When I was leaving for the press conference, I was preparing to ask you a regional question. But now, literally a little while ago, I was looking on the Internet and again I saw some fairly specific information about the health of the President.

v. PUTIN: You shouldn't be [on the Internet] so much; it'll teach you bad things.

[68] Oliver Englehart, "Roman v Kremlin," *Al Jazeera*, November 20, 2012, http://www.aljazeera.com/programmes/activate/2012/10/20121014132816101445.html.

[69] Aleksei Gorbachev, "Spokoinyi mudrets vmesto macho—Vladimiru Putinu prognoziruiut kardinal'nuiu smenu imidzha," *Nezavisimaia Gazeta*, December 4, 2012, http://www.ng.ru/politics/2012-12-04/1_wiseman.html.

[70] Goscilo, "The Ultimate Celebrity," 48.

[71] Fred Weir, "Putin Eyes Trip to Antarctica, Shuns Elder Image," *Christian Science Monitor*, January 29, 2013, http://www.csmonitor.com/World/Global-News/2013/0129/Putin-eyes-trip-to-Antarctica-shuns-elder-image.

A. LUKINA: Sometimes one has to. And now I'm looking at the screen (you're far away from me), and on the screen you're such an energetic, handsome man. My colleague from Primor'e—she's always saying how she loves you, and it seems today there's reason to do that.

V. PUTIN: Thank you.

A. LUKINA: So this is my question: Tell me, please, where does that information come from, and who benefits from it? Thank you.

V. PUTIN: It benefits the political opponents who are trying to call into question the legitimacy and the capacity of the authorities. I can answer the question about my health in the traditional fashion: Don't hold your breath! (ne dozhdetes'). [Laughter.][72]

Whether Putin's ongoing macho image-creation was largely planned or coincidental, conscious or unconscious, his variant of masculinity (including strength, sobriety, decisiveness, and attractiveness to women) was met with popular approval, reinforcing his position of power and authority. As we have seen, this support was expressed in cultural productions highlighting Putin's machismo—especially feminine endorsements of Putin's masculinity. It was also reflected in a variety of public opinion polls.

"I'm Sexy and I Know It!" The Machismo Legitimation Strategy Works

According to public opinion polls before and after the presidential elections of 2004, Putin was more popular among women than men. Women reportedly found him reliable, responsible, sober (literally), and strong.[73] In December 2011, as protesters objecting to widespread fraud in Russia's recent parliamentary elections filled the streets, and the proportion of the vote projected to be in Putin's favor in the upcoming March 2012 elections declined, women's support for Putin remained consistent.[74] Perhaps echoing the strains of the pop song, "A Man Like Putin," in a 2012 poll 20 percent of the female population said they would like to marry Putin.[75] Russian news media

[72] "Press-konferentsiia Vladimira Putina," kremlin.ru, December 20, 2012, http://kremlin.ru/transcripts/17173; translation is mine.

[73] Riabova and Riabov, "Nastoiashchii muzhchina Rossiiskoi politiki?," 52.

[74] "Putin's Rating Down but over 50 % of Voters May Support Him in Election," Interfax-Ukraine, December 29, 2011, http://bit.ly/1m0j2AV.

[75] "20 percent rossiianok khoteli by vyiti zamuzh za Vladimira Putina," Levada-Tsentr, October 5, 2012, http://www.levada.ru/05-10-2012/20-rossiyanok-khoteli-vyiti-zamuzh-za-vladimira-putina.

"repeatedly reported stories about women who had had erotic dreams about Putin," reinforcing the sexualization of his image,[76] and a survey conducted during Putin's first year in office ostensibly found that 3,500 out of 5,000 Russian women found Putin to be "the sexiest man in Russia" (samyi seksual'nyi muzhchina v Rossii).[77] Women have "publically profess[ed] 'mad' love" for their president, and one reportedly created an embroidered version of Putin's torso, based on his well-known, bare-chested fishing trip photos. A candy company, tapping into the potential for sublimated desire, created a chocolate Putin portrait in 2003.[78] As Riabova and Riabov point out,

> The eroticization of the political leader occurs against the backdrop of the eroticization of political discourse in general, which is manifested in the use of sexual images and metaphors, including metaphors of marriage, potency and impotence, prostitution, and so on. Being applied in order to signify the relationship between power and subordination, such active use of that kind of language makes the sexual sphere relevant to politics in the voters' eyes.[79]

How well has this legitimation strategy worked outside of the lovestruck subset of the Russian population? There is no question that Putin has been a remarkably popular president. In 2007, as expected, Putin was number one on the newspaper *Kommersant*'s listing of Russia's "elite," as he had been for the previous six years, earning 82 percent of the ballots.[80] When he took office as Russia's acting president in January 2000, Putin's approval rating was 84 percent. In March 2004, when he was elected to a second term, it was 81 percent. In December 2007, as the country voted in Russia's parliamentary elections, Putin's approval rating was 87 percent. His popularity maintained these levels, reaching 88 percent in September 2008 (in the aftermath of Russia's war with Georgia and near the end of Putin's second term as president). In January 2005, his rating slipped to 55 percent (a policy that replaced social benefits, such as free public transportation for the elderly, with

---

[76] V. Timchenko, *Putin i novaia Rossiia* (Rostov-na-donu, Russia: Feniks, 2005), 134, cited by Riabova and Riabov, "Nastoiashchii muzhchina Rossiiskoi politiki?," 53.

[77] "Rossiiskie zhenshchiny schitaiut glavu gosudarstva ideal'nym liubovnikom," December 18, 2000, http://www.businesspress.ru/newspaper/article_mId_33_aId_46,130.html, cited by Riabova and Riabov, "Nastoiashchii muzhchina Rossiiskoi politiki?," 53.

[78] Goscilo, "The Ultimate Celebrity," 30–31. For more evidence of the "Putin cult" see Stephen White and Ian McAllister, "The Putin Phenomenon," *Journal of Communist Studies and Transition Politics* 24, no.4 (2008): 604–628.

[79] Riabova and Riabov, "Nastoiashchii muzhchina Rossiiskoi politiki?," 53.

[80] Goscilo "The Ultimate Celebrity," 29, citing A. Alekseev, "VIP-parad 2007," *Kommersant*, December 28, 2007.

monetary benefits, had generated a wave of discontent), but by January 2006, it was back up to 71 percent.[81]

Russia's young electorate was particularly enamored of Putin. In November 2009, 87 percent of Russians aged 18–24 thought Putin was doing a good job in office as prime minister (compared to 78 percent across the population). In March 2011, 78 percent of Russian youth surveyed nationally approved of Putin's actions in power (the average approval rating across the entire population was 69 percent).[82] Putin was regarded as responsible for solving Russia's economic troubles (though, in reality, those troubles were at least temporarily solved by the rise in oil prices—making Russia's main export considerably more profitable) and resuscitating the country's national image after the dismal 1990s.[83]

Putin's popularity declined somewhat over the course of 2010–2011, with his approval ratings dipping into the sixties,[84] and slipped "irreversibly" after the post-election protests began in December 2011 (this latter finding was based on questions about Putin's qualities as a leader, as opposed to his overall approval ratings, which bottomed out at 63 percent in December 2011).[85] Still, his regime continued—sensibly—to rely on the presidency, the Russian Orthodox Church, and the Russian army as sources of political legitimation, since these were Russia's three most trusted institutions. Trust in Putin as president in June 2012 was voiced by 49 percent (down from 66 percent in November 2009); trust in the Church and other religious groupings registered at 49 percent, and the Russian army earned third place, with the trust of 41 percent of the population.[86] It is worth nothing that strong gender stereotypes pervade and are associated with each of these institutions, lending them additional credibility with the traditional-conservative sector of Russia's population from which Putin's regime is hoping to draw support: the macho presidency; the masculinized army, which relies upon its recruits' toughness and their protection of "weaker" citizens, including women (to whom soldiers are contrasted); and the Russian Orthodox Church, which excludes women from its hierarchy and embraces conservative and mutually exclusive notions of masculinity and femininity and ties them to a sex-based biological determinism.

[81] Levada Center, "Indeksy odobreniia deiatel'nosti Vladimira Putina i Dmitriia Medvedeva," 2012, http://www.levada.ru/indeksy.

[82] Levada Center, *Material No. 3 'Ustanovki rossiiskogo obshchestva na peremeny: tri pokoleniia (Po materialam kolichestvennykh sotsiologicheskikh issledovanii)* (Moscow; Levada Center, April 2011), 7, 16.

[83] Goscilo, "The Ultimate Celebrity," 29.

[84] Levada Center, *Indeksy odobreniia deiatel'nosti Vladimira Putina i Dmitriia Medvedeva.*

[85] Ibid.; "Pollster: Putin's Attractiveness Sagging 'Irreversibly,'" *Moscow Times*, May 18, 2012, http://www.themoscowtimes.com/news/article/pollster-putins-attractiveness-sagging-irreversibly/458718.html.

[86] "Russians Increasingly Trust President, Church—Poll," Interfax, June 26, 2012, http://www.interfax-religion.com/?act=news&div=9459.

By fall 2012, Putin's popularity had recovered somewhat: his approval rating had risen to 67 percent in October, the same as it had been the previous fall.[87] Although this represented a significant decline from the height of Putin's popularity, he was still in an enviable position with two-thirds of Russians surveyed stating that they approved of him. For comparison, on the eve of US President Barack Obama's reelection in November 2012 his approval rating hovered around 50 percent.[88]

It is impossible to disaggregate the impact of Putin's masculine aura on his generally high political approval rating from that of rising oil prices and their positive effect on Russia's economy and standards of living during his first two terms. Yet, citizens certainly take seriously the overall image of their political leaders, and it is not purely economics that determine regime legitimacy. Widespread attention to Putin's masculinity did not inoculate his regime from criticism, as the protests that developed after the fraud-plagued elections of December 2011 proved. However, the fact that Putin, his supporters, and the anti-regime protesters played upon gender norms during the protests (as we shall see in Chapter 3) suggests that actors on both sides of Russia's political fence took masculinity and femininity quite seriously as a factor in regime legitimation and in political authority-building in general.

That actors across the Russian political spectrum have made liberal use of femininity, masculinity, homophobia, and sexualization in their public acts and pronouncements during the Putin era is not in doubt. The previous chapter's discussion of ways in which gender norms are used as legitimation tools suggests that these concepts are wielded publicly in a variety of places and political systems. What is it about Putin's Russia that allowed these tactics to flourish so dramatically there? The next section addresses this question.

Explaining the Rise of Gender Norms and Sexualization as Tools of Political Legitimation in Putin's Russia: A Multiple Opportunity Structure Model

Designed to describe social movements' political, economic, cultural, historical, and international opportunities and obstacles to success, a "multiple opportunity structure" model can also be fruitfully employed to reveal the reasons

---

[87] Levada Center, *Indeksy odobreniia deiatel'nosti Vladimira Putina i Dmitriia Medvedeva.*

[88] Brett LoGiurato, "Obama Approval Rating Jumps before Election Day," November 4, 2012, http://www.businessinsider.com/obama-approval-rating-polls-rasmussen-50-percent-gallup-2012-11.

why gender-based discourses and practices appear as an element of political legitimation in any given country.[89] That a social movement studies model would
apply to political contests makes sense. Political actors who desire a particular
outcome (be it ongoing incumbency, renovation of the political system, or
social change) will face a set of opportunities and barriers and will make tactical
decisions based on what they encounter. Just as social change movements do,
political activists and politicians try to frame their ideas in culturally resonant
ways, take advantage of the resources available to them, and strengthen their
positions through networks of supporters.

While patriarchy and sexism are fairly ubiquitous societal conditions, the
relative balance of opportunities and obstacles to the use of gender norms and
sexualization as tools of legitimation in politics varies across states and historical periods. In the contemporary Russian case, the model reveals a "perfect
storm" of opportunities and few obstacles. The Kremlin deployed a strategy of
stressing Putin's masculinity and encountered a similarly gender-norm-laced
response from forces opposed to the Putin-centered regime. The ensuing political contest has included homophobic discourse along with competing
claims to femininity and masculinity both by regime supporters and
detractors.

The first component of the model to consider is the *political opportunity
structure*, which refers to changes in the Russian political system that created
space enabling a legitimation strategy featuring gender normative rhetoric to
flourish or that, alternatively, could have obstructed it. An essential feature of
the political opportunity structure is the presence or absence of a women's
movement able to draw critical attention to public sexism. It is likely that, in
any given country, the strength and cultural acceptance of a feminist movement has an inverse correlation with the use of overt misogyny in politics.[90]
The weakness of the Russian women's movement—having thrived briefly in
the 1990s and then declined in the first decade of Putin's rule before a new
wave of feminist organizing began in 2010—probably enabled some of this
sexist and homophobic political legitimation to pass unnoticed or (largely)
without drawing major criticism. The relative "invisibility" of women's

[89] Valerie Sperling, *Organizing Women in Contemporary Russia: Engendering Transition* (Cambridge: Cambridge University Press, 1999); Conor O'Dwyer, "Does the EU Help or Hinder Gay-
Rights Movements in Post-Communist Europe? The Case of Poland," *East European Politics* 28,
no. 4 (December 2012): 6.

[90] Multicountry studies have already demonstrated the significance of feminist movement
strength in achieving women-friendly policies (such as those combating violence against
women). See Mala Htun S. and Laurel Weldon, "The Civic Origins of Progressive Policy Change:
Combating Violence against Women in Global Perspective, 1975–2005," *American Political Science Review* 106, no. 3 (August 2012): 548–569.

movement organizations and women's movement issues in the public eye in the first decade of Putin's rule left the field open for uncontested sexist stereotyping in political, economic, and cultural spaces.[91]

Women's organizing, however, is far from being a preventative measure against the expression of sexism in the political realm. It is enough to recall that—despite the relative historical strength of the women's movement in the United States—Justice Clarence Thomas was confirmed to the US Supreme Court after his alleged sexual harassment of Anita Hill was revealed in 1991, and that in 2012 Republican member of the US House of Representatives Todd Akin was able to win more than a million votes (39 percent of the ballots) in his run for a Senate position even after claiming that "legitimate rape" would not result in pregnancy.[92] Republican Richard Mourdock, the state treasurer of Indiana, likewise earned 44 percent of the vote in Indiana's Senate race after claiming that pregnancies resulting from rape reflected "something that God intended to happen."[93] The fact that both men lost their races, however, suggests that within the United States feminist ideas had been assimilated to the point that such pronouncements were seen as unacceptable. Previous to these misogynist comments, the Akin and Mourdock races had been close calls.[94]

Feminism's reputation as an ideology is also important as an aspect of the political opportunity structure for public misogyny in any given country. In the Russian case, feminism has long been assigned a low status, which itself can suppress the strength of the women's movement. During its seven decades in power, the Soviet Communist Party demonized feminism. It was painted as a "bourgeois" movement, accused of splitting the working class by highlighting women's interests, and outlawed.[95] Decades of negative representation made it that much harder to spread the very notion that feminism or a women's movement questioning gender norms would be beneficial on post-Soviet territory.

---

[91] Elena Kovalenko, "Sovremennoe Rossiiskoe zhenskoe dvizhenie: Problema 'nevidimosti,'" in *Zhenskoe dvizhenie v Rossii: Vchera, segodnia, zavtra: Materialy konferentsii*, ed. Galina Mikhaleva (Moscow: RODP "Yabloko" and KMK Publishers, 2010), 89–93.

[92] Lori Moore, "Rep. Todd Akin: 'Legitimate Rape' Statement and Reaction," *New York Times*, August 20, 2012, http://www.nytimes.com/2012/08/21/us/politics/rep-todd-akin-legitimate-rape-statement-and-reaction.html; "Missouri Senate Race—2012 Election Center," November 8, 2012, http://www.cnn.com/election/2012/results/state/MO/senate.

[93] "Indiana Senate Race—2012 Election Center," December 10, 2012, http://www.cnn.com/election/2012/results/state/IN/senate; Lucy Madison, "Richard Mourdock: Even Pregnancy from Rape Something 'God Intended,'" October 23, 2012, http://www.cbsnews.com/8301-250_162-57538757/richard-mourdock-even-pregnancy-from-rape-something-god-intended/.

[94] "All 2012 Senate Polls," http://www.electoral-vote.com/evp2012/Senate/Graphs/all.html, accessed April 16, 2013.

[95] Sperling, *Organizing Women in Contemporary Russia*, 64–66.

Not only did the Soviet regime ban feminist organizing, it also established cultural norms about women's and men's proper roles in the labor force and family. The Soviet state used its extensive propaganda machine to impart the tenets of Soviet-style socialism, among which were the importance of individuals' hard work for the benefit of the collective, the Party, and the state. In this schema, women were expected to labor extensively in the family as well as outside of it, an arrangement that came to be known as the "double burden."[96] Strongly entrenched gender roles persisted through the Soviet era and afterward, tying women (but not men) to household labor. In a joint interview, two members of the Moscow Feminist Group, Elizaveta Morozova and Nadia Plungian, explained that across the culture women's double burden "was the absolute norm." While women were expected to work in the paid labor force, full responsibility for household chores and care also fell to them. Women were therefore not expected to climb the career ladder; the ominous notion that "a successful career woman would of necessity be single and alone" had been foisted on the population through Soviet films and other propaganda. As Morozova explained, "The scenario for my mother's generation was very clear: if a woman has a career it means she doesn't have a family, because you really have to slave away (vkalyvat') in the family. . . . And when the Soviet Union ceased to exist," she concluded, "those arrangements remained."[97] Feminism, with its endorsement of alternative family structures and advocacy for an equitable division of household responsibilities, clashes with long-held Soviet and post-Soviet notions about gender norms in the family.

National surveys suggest that feminism's reputation suffered under Soviet rule and recuperated only slightly thereafter. In 2001, only 19 percent of Russians knew the word "feminism," though 28 percent had heard it, while for 41 percent the survey was their first exposure to the term.[98] By 2012, the term was more familiar; 31 percent now knew the word, 23 percent had heard it, and 38 percent were hearing it for the first time. But of those who knew or had heard the term, only 13 percent had a positive opinion of it in 2001, declining to only 8 percent in 2012.[99] The remaining respondents in 2012 saw "feminism" as negative (12 percent) or were indifferent to it (29 percent).[100]

---

[96] Gail Warshofsky Lapidus, *Women in Soviet Society: Equality, Development, and Social Change* (Berkeley: University of California Press, 1978), 5–6.

[97] Nadia Plungian and Elizaveta Morozova, Moskovskaia Feministskaia Gruppa, interview by author, Moscow, June 20, 2012.

[98] Fond Obshchestvennogo Mneniia, "'Zhenshchina—tozhe chelovek': Predstavleniia rossiian o feminizme," September 2, 2012, http://fom.ru/obshchestvo/10611.

[99] Ibid.

[100] Ibid.

The negative connotations of feminism were so strong in the post-Soviet period that even among self-identified Russian women's movement activists in the 1990s many were hesitant to adopt the term to describe themselves or their organizations.[101] The aversion to feminism was associated loosely with age, however. In the mid-1990s, those activists with more positive views on feminism tended to be about ten years younger than those who regarded it with less enthusiasm (average age 42 as versus 52).[102] Nearly all of the young women activists I interviewed in 2012 had adopted the feminist label; only three said they didn't entirely identify as feminists. One 27-year old member of an art collective, asked whether she considered herself a feminist, answered "more yes than no," but added that she chose not to "call herself that," as feminism was a "red flag" in the Russian context.[103] Two activists in their mid-20s who volunteered with a small organization focusing on educating college-aged students about domestic violence voiced similar reluctance to adopt the term:

Q. You said the project was not feminist as such. Do you consider yourselves feminists, or not really?
A. (IRINA): It depends. Well, not a strict feminism (takoi nezhestkii feminizm). . . . Let's say, more yes than no (skoree da chem net). (MASHA, agreeing): Yes.[104]

Feminism and its adherents continued to suffer from their Soviet-era status as the 2000s passed under Putin's rule. Women activists' impressions in 2012 coincided with the statistical data finding that feminism was either unknown or unloved among Russia's citizenry:

Q. How do people regard feminism in Russia in general?
A. Nobody knows what feminism is. Typically, people think that it's an outdated movement . . . for the civic rights of women. And inasmuch as all those rights have been received, what more do you want? People generally think in stereotypes about feminists. They're completely unacquainted with the real, contemporary feminist agenda. Of course that's related to the fact that the feminist movement is very small, fragmented, and barely noticeable. And it must be said that in the media those very prejudices get

---

[101] Sperling, *Organizing Women in Contemporary Russia*, 59–73.
[102] Ibid., 64. The average age of the feminist activists I interviewed was considerably lower in the 2012 sample than in the mid-1990s sample.
[103] Polina Zaslavskaia, Verkhotura, interview by author, St. Petersburg, June 14, 2012.
[104] Irina Fetkulova and Mariia Tronova, Molodezhnoe Dvizhenie "Ostanovim Nasilie," interview by author, Moscow, June 18, 2012.

voiced because journalists, like the majority of the population, think feminism is something marginal and not of interest to anyone except in tabloids and on March 8 [International Women's Day].[105]

A. I can tell you precisely: badly (otnosiatsia plokho). And the most surprising thing is that even well-educated people, and even people who come into contact with that issue through their work . . . like psychologists, or substance abuse experts, specialists in the area of mental health in general, psychiatrists—their sexism is just through the roof.[106]

A. Well, here it was made into a dirty word (rugatel'noe slovo). People still don't understand what it's about.[107]

Galina Mikhaleva, the 55-year old leader of the Gender Caucus (gendernaia fraktsiia) of the liberal Yabloko Party, likewise bemoaned the difficult task of educating people, even the liberals within her party, about feminism and gender-based discrimination:

The women who come to us, particularly from the provinces, for them, feminism is a very frightening (strashnoe) word. You probably know that in our country a "feminist" is some kind of a bluestocking (sinnii chulok), a man-hater, and so on. Therefore, when they come to us, at the beginning, they say, "No! I'm not a feminist! God forbid!" Right? And then we need to gradually, step by step, explain it. Earlier, by the way, our title didn't include the word "gender." We're advancing. At the start, we were the "women's" [caucus], then the "women's" and in parentheses, "gender" [caucus]. And now we're called the "gender" [caucus]. It's this kind of a long-term operation. I've been working on this within our party since 1998; can you imagine? And when I started working on it, everybody laughed at me, made fun of me; at our [party] Congress they stomped their feet and clapped [to drown me out]. But now, it's no problem; all our men have learned the word "gender," although maybe in their hearts they're, you know, like many elderly Germans who remained anti-Semites in their hearts but don't admit it to anyone [Laughs].[108]

[105] Vera Akulova, Moskovskaia Feministskaia Gruppa, interview by author, Moscow, June 6, 2012.

[106] Tat'iana Grigor'eva, Initsiativnaia Gruppa Za Feminizm, interview by author, Moscow, June 18, 2012.

[107] Mariia Mokhova, Sestry, interview by author, Moscow, June 9, 2012.

[108] Galina Mikhaleva, Chair, Gendernaia Fraktsiia Partii Yabloko, interview by author, Moscow, June 8, 2012.

Other activists agreed that feminists bore a negative, unfeminine image in Russian society and that feminism continued to be associated with lesbianism (which itself carried a negative charge):

> In Russia, there's a very widespread opinion that feminists are ugly (strashnye) women, very masculine, very tough (zhestkie), who hate men, are unattractive, and aggressive. And I've talked a lot with men about this topic, too, and men—their faces change when you try to talk to them about feminism. It's very complicated to change your views [about this] because from the start, you have a picture [in your mind] and it's hard to move [someone] away from that position.[109]

> [If you identify as a feminist] you will immediately be seen as a butch ball-buster (muzhlanka), like a *muzhik* in the worst sense of the word. [There's the idea that feminists are] angry (zlye), aggressive, and of course, none of them get enough sex. There's the term "nedotrakhannaia" [i.e. needs a good fucking].[110]

> Why are there still negative attitudes toward feminists? Because a lot of people think that if someone's a feminist, it means she's a lesbian (esli feministka, znachit lesbianka). And the attitude toward people of nontraditional [sexual] orientation is very often negative (plokhoe).[111]

One member of the Moscow Radical Feminists illustrated the off-putting power of feminism by telling the story of a friend who had used her feminist identity to ward off unwanted advances:

> She and I talked not long ago, and [she told me] that some guy had been hitting on her. She told him right away that she was a feminist and the guy immediately lost interest (otkleilsia). . . . Feminists aren't liked; they're seen as scary. It's like that everywhere, I think, that kind of attitude. Here, of course, it's amplified. There's more of it, of the idea that a feminist is marked, that you've been branded (kleimo na tebe). An unattractive woman, an unsuccessful woman who didn't luck out in some way or another, and so on.[112]

---

[109] Zaslavskaia, interview by author.

[110] Zhenia Otto, Komitet za Rabochii Internatsional, Kampaniia protiv ekspluatatsii i diskriminatsii zhenshchin, interview by author, Moscow, June 18, 2012.

[111] Fetkulova, interview by author.

[112] Elena Maksimova, Moskovskie Radikal'nye Feministki, interview by author, Moscow, June 22, 2012.

Natalia Bitten, coordinator of the Initiative Group "Pro-Feminism" (za feminizm), noted that not only was feminism's reputation negative but that Russians had been subjected to a veritable "anti-feminist hysteria" whipped up in the media in connection with Pussy Riot's infamous performance and the court case that followed it:

> People have no idea what feminism is; by and large, it has this negative image. But the anti-feminist *campaign* began after Pussy Riot's action. If before that, people regarded feminism in a dismissive or aggressive way, then; now there's a hysteria that's begun in the mass media, since February [2012].[113]

Seventeen years earlier, feminist activists in Moscow had made strikingly similar statements about how feminism was popularly perceived. Ongoing aversion to feminism was one of a number of factors limiting women's movement growth and popularity in Russia, both in the politically turbulent 1990s and the more tightly controlled 2000s.

The Russian regime under Putin had concrete reasons to endorse a negative view of feminism. First, feminism, like any ideology that argues for a change in the distribution of privilege (such as antiracism), threatens to disrupt the existing hierarchy of power. As Polina Zaslavskaia, an activist in St. Petersburg, put it: "The authorities and the whole way of life in our country are organized on a vertical basis," and efforts to shake up the structure are therefore met with resistance. "If we're talking about the male point of view, it all makes sense—total fear [of losing their place in the hierarchy]."[114] Russian socialist feminist Zhenia Otto likewise argued that feminism was frowned upon by Russia's political-economic elite because increasing women's labor rights would make women workers more expensive, and an organized push by women to increase social welfare support for families would be costly if successful. That, she believed, was the real reason that the contemporary Russian state had embraced the notion that women's "mission" was to "stay home with the children," lionized the image of women raising multiple children, and made feminism (with its ideology of personal choice and equality) anathema.[115] Otto maintained that the government's desire to increase the birthrate—while not making an effort to increase living standards—was also motivated by the desire to maintain a "cheap" labor force.[116]

---

[113] Natal'ia Bitten, Initsiativnaia Gruppa "Za Feminizm," interview by author, Moscow, June 4, 2012.

[114] Zaslavskaia, interview by author.

[115] Otto, interview by author.

[116] Zhenia Otto, "Diskussiia s Frau-derrida: O neoplachivaemom trude," *Net—znachit net* 1 (May 2010): 12.

Feminism, with its insistence on reproductive rights, could derail this plan. Finally, as we shall see in Chapter 6, during Putin's reign the Russian Orthodox Church has fixated on feminism as a serious threat to the family and even to the entire country. With its increasing reliance on the Church as a pillar of support, the regime thus has an interest in keeping feminist organizing to a minimum.

Another critical piece of the Russian political opportunity structure, which enabled the emergence and albeit limited growth of the Russian women's movement as well as the increased use of gender norms in political tactics, was the relatively new political system introduced in the Soviet Union in 1990. This system eliminated media censorship and established competitive voting for public officeholders. The Soviet state collapsed at the close of 1991. In the new Russian regime that followed, politicians, including presidential candidates, would need to attract the voting public. Whereas Putin's election to his first presidential term was more an appointment than a competitive race, by the time of his second election in 2004, even as political freedoms of assembly and speech were contracting, the leaders of Russia's "hybrid" regime sought to appeal to the population for political support.[117]

The Kremlin under Putin employed PR, something the Soviet leaders had not considered. Through the late-Soviet era, inertia and coercive pressures had sufficed to get the population to at least feign support for the regime by attending holiday parades and turning out to vote for the sole party on the ballot. The Russian regime had clumsily begun to utilize PR under Yeltsin, particularly in the lead-up to his 1996 presidential election, hiring Western consultants to that end.[118] But as the twenty-first century broke, PR took on a new prominence. Putin was portrayed as a paragon of masculinity, and pro-Kremlin youth groups such as Nashi embraced physical fitness in emulation of their leader. This trend continued over the course of Putin's rule; in October 2012, to celebrate Putin's birthday, a gathering of young men from pro-Putin organizations did public pull-ups in front of a portrait of the president.[119] Putin's political advocates were not alone in their admiration for him. Russian

---

[117] For an astute explanation for why elections constitute a critical juncture, even for semi-authoritarian regimes like Russia's, see Andrew Little, "Noncompetitve Elections and Information: A Theoretical Perspective on the 2011 Russian Elections," December 9, 2011, http://themonkeycage. org/blog/2011/12/09/noncompetitve-elections-and-information-a-theoretical-perspective-on-the-2011-russian-elections/.

[118] Irina Hakamada, "Flights with Siberian White Cranes and Other PR Events of Vladimir Putin," October 11, 2012, http://valdaiclub.com/politics/49961.html; David W. Guth, "The Emergence of Public Relations in the Russian Federation," *Public Relations Review* 26, no. 2 (2000): 196.

[119] See photo #7 in Alissa de Carbonnel, "Plaudits Vie with Pensioner Jibes as Russia's Putin Turns 60," Reuters, October 7, 2012, http://www.reuters.com/article/2012/10/07/us-russia-putin-birthday-idUSBRE8940ZW20121007.

adolescents surveyed in the mid-2000s articulated "overwhelming support" for the president, admiring his sobriety, his physical fitness, his directness, and his efforts to improve Russia's living standards and international status, and 74 percent of them voiced trust in Putin in 2005.[120] Putin's masculinity became a political resource in a semi-authoritarian but still competitive regime. So too did the visually pleasing bodies of Putin's female supporters (as seen in the 2010 birthday calendar and other similar productions), given that they indirectly testified to his masculinity.

The increase in authoritarianism during Putin's reign—witnessed in the cessation of elections for governors in 2004, regular arrests of nonviolent protesters, and raids on nongovernmental organizations in 2013—constricted the opportunities for civic organizing across the board, marginalizing many voices but not eliminating the regime's efforts to advertise itself, often by advertising Putin. While keeping the media spotlight on an incumbent dictator may be a defining characteristic of "competitive authoritarian" regimes (along with limited freedoms of press and assembly, an executive branch that uses its power to limit political pluralism while still holding regular elections, and opposition groups that try to compete for power despite the grossly unequal playing field),[121] a focus on gender norms as a means of political regime legitimation is not unique to that type of political system. Although Russia shifted from a nascent democratic system in the 1990s to an authoritarian one in the 2000s, it was not the change in political regime type that solely drove the increased use of gender norms in politics under Putin. Indeed, in the Russian case, it might be more accurate to paint this shift in the use of gender norms as a "textbook case"—the result of a set of conditions creating an overdetermined situation. The renewal of authoritarianism in the early 2000s did nothing to stop it and may have facilitated it further, but that is not the single cause, as the other elements of the opportunity structure elaborated below make clear.

The second element to consider is the *economic opportunity structure* that facilitated the popularization of images of femininity, masculinity, and sexuality in the political realm. As commercial capitalism was introduced to Russia in the 1990s, the state's new and somewhat deficient system of political competition evolved alongside a new and somewhat deficient system of economic competition. Although the market in Russia's major assets (factories, buildings, natural resources) was in many ways monopolized by a privileged stratum of well-connected Soviet tycoons and former

[120] Olena Nikolayenko, *Citizens in the Making in Post-Soviet States* (London: Routledge, 2011), 41–42, 36.

[121] Levitsky and Way, *Competitive Authoritarianism*, 3, 11.

Communist Party bureaucrats, in the day-to-day economy consumers were now subject to a barrage of product advertising. Advertising had been nearly absent from the Soviet economy, where all production and sales had been owned by the state. In Russia, as elsewhere, commercial capitalism commodified and objectified women's bodies in particular. Print and television advertisements began regularly to feature skimpily dressed women, while classified ads for secretarial positions began demanding that applicants submit photos of themselves along with their applications and encouraged only "uninhibited" women to apply.[122] By the end of the decade, women's bodies were a regular feature of public advertising and remained so into the Putin era.

Women's bodies have long been used in advertising to symbolize—and sexualize—products. Ads for women's bicycles in the 1890s constituted one of the first examples in the United States, for example, where some companies' advertisements showed women biking in "daringly short skirts." Other advertisers, eager to prove that women could ride bicycles without deviating from their gender role expectations and becoming "mannish," showed women in unrealistically long skirts that covered their feet even as they pedaled.[123] Railroad companies, too, used the female body as a vehicle to market their wares; a nineteenth-century advertisement for the Pennsylvania Railroad Company showed a railroad map superimposed over the stylized bust and shoulder area of a woman in a puffy-sleeved dress.[124] Later, car advertisements frequently sought to link automobiles to women's bodies, implying that male car owners would likewise be able to attract (or "own") female sexual partners. A 2011 BMW ad for pre-owned vehicles exemplifies the sexualized process of purchasing a car. Picturing only a close-up of an apparently unclothed woman looking alluringly at the camera, the ad was captioned, "You know you're not the first. But do you really care?"[125] Air transportation, too, continued to associate modes of travel with the objectification of the female figure. Joining an international trend toward sexy airline advertisements, in 2010 the Russian trademark national carrier Aeroflot created a calendar (for internal use) featuring naked female flight attendants posing with aircraft, while a cheap Russian airline (Avianova) published a two-minute pornographic advertisement

[122] Sperling, *Organizing Women in Contemporary Russia*, 74–75.

[123] Ellen Gruber Garvey, "Reframing the Bicycle: Advertising-Supported Magazines and Scorching Women," *Armerican Quarterly* 47, no. 1 (1995): 70.

[124] Amy G. Richter, *Home on the Rails: Women, the Railroad, and the Rise of Public Domesticity* (Chapel Hill: University of North Carolina Press, 2005), 2.

[125] Mimi Seldner, "Still Using the Old Model for Sexist Car Advertisements," *Ms. Magazine*, August 29, 2011, http://msmagazine.com/blog/blog/2011/08/29/still-using-the-old-model-for-sexist-car-advertisements/.

on the Internet showing planes being soaped up by stewardesses in bikinis while a squad of firemen looked on.[126]

Along with openness to Western products and advertisement styles, Russia's economic opening brought an avalanche of Western images highlighting the importance of Hollywood glamour and new models of feminine and masculine attractiveness.[127] The stars of Soviet feature films had been—if better than average looking—more often built along the healthy, robust peasant-or-worker archetype, rather than supremely pretty, slender-yet-busty women and cleft-chinned handsome men of chiseled physique, whose abs could be displayed as exemplary in an anatomy class.[128] Depictions of women in Soviet art had played up the sexless worker angle; a 2013 exhibit on female beauty in Soviet painting and sculpture compared the iconic American woman worker, "Rosie the Riveter," with her "feminine sexuality," "makeup," and "cheeky glint," to her Soviet counterpart, who "almost disappeared into her boiler suit."[129]

Glossy magazines (mainly Russian versions of Western publications) popped up in kiosks in large numbers in the mid-1990s, instructing men and women on how to achieve the glamour previously unachievable under socialism.[130] Like their equivalents on the impulse-buy shelves in Western supermarkets, women's glossy magazines in Russia "teemed with ads and advice about makeup, clothes, plastic surgery, and modes of maintaining an enticing figure."[131] They also introduced new topics earlier untouched by relatively stodgy Soviet women's journals. The May 1995 issue of Russian *Cosmopolitan* magazine, for instance, in addition to beauty and fashion tips, featured articles on sex ("Results of Our Sex Survey"), sexual positions ("The CAT Position: A Sexual Revolution?"), relationships ("Do You Love Your Lovers?"), and advice on how to start your own business ("Arm Yourself with an Original Idea, and

[126] Lidia Okorokova, "Raunchy Avianova Ad Sparks Sexism Row," *Moscow News*, July 12, 2010, http://themoscownews.com/news/20100712/187926015.html; "Avianova Airlines Banned Commercial" [video], July 3, 2010, https://www.youtube.com/watch?v=owL9OqQ00og.

[127] On the importance of glamour in post-Soviet Russia, see Helena Goscilo and Vlad Strukov, eds., *Celebrity and Glamour in Contemporary Russia: Shocking Chic* (London: Routledge, 2011).

[128] I thank Al Evans for this insight about the incursion of Hollywood beauty standards into Russian popular and political culture. Alfred B. Evans Jr., Personal communication via email, March 8, 2012.

[129] Aliide Naylor, "The Changing Face of Russian Beauty," *Moscow Times*, January 28, 2013, http://www.themoscowtimes.com/arts_n_ideas/article/the-changing-face-of-russian-beauty/474647.html.

[130] Helena Goscilo and Vlad Strukov, "Introduction," in *Celebrity and Glamour in Contemporary Russia: Shocking Chic*, eds. Helena Goscilo and Vlad Strukov (London: Routledge, 2011), 3.

[131] Ibid., 13.

Then Analyze the Market for It"). In April 1995, *Cosmo* informed its Russian readers how to do self-breast exams. Also, buried at the back of the magazine, were two letters-to-the-editor from women who had experienced attraction to—or had sex with—other women (they did not use the term "lesbian"). These fleeting acknowledgments of lesbianism, however, were drowned in a sea of sex and fashion advice aimed at heterosexual women. Such magazines reinforced the sexualization of the everyday body, particularly for women. They also brought a new level of attention to personal appearance, underscoring the propriety of modifying one's appearance if it did not meet the beauty standard propagated by both the magazines and the beauty product companies whose ads littered their pages.

Femininity in 1990s Russia became economically accessible in a way that it had not been during the Soviet era, when consumer goods (including those that traditionally facilitated the display of femininity, such as hair dye, makeup, and fashionable clothes) had been in short supply. By the start of the twenty-first century, Russian women with sufficient cash could indulge in unlimited opportunities for makeovers and plastic surgery. The market for women's clothing was also transformed from a somewhat puritanical Soviet model to a more risqué and revealing standard.[132] On the positive side, for some women these new conditions may have represented an opportunity for sexual assertiveness and freedom of choice.[133] The editor of Russian *Playboy*, Artemii Troitskii, looking back on the advent of glossy magazines, felt that the Russian edition of *Cosmopolitan* had been a tool of women's empowerment, encouraging women to stand up for themselves and throw off the notion that women—in the Russian cultural paradigm—were second-class creatures.[134] These magazines may have preached women's empowerment, but it was an empowerment surrounded by messages designed to provoke feelings of inadequacy and to spur women to buy merchandise to address those feelings. From the market perspective, women's bodies and the norms of femininity were fundamentally and primarily for sale. Soon, they would be for sale in the political marketplace as well.

Masculinity was also subject to the vagaries of economic shifts. As Katherine Verdery notes, by the close of the Soviet period people were complaining that the practice of Soviet-style communism had perverted traditional gender relations, infantilizing men by depriving them of the opportunity for private ownership, responsibility, and independence. Along with the political

---

[132] Gregory Feifer, "Sex Booms, but Traditional Views Prevail in Russia," November 25, 2008, http://www.npr.org/templates/story/story.php?storyId=96,175,017&ft=1&f=1001.

[133] Lis Tarlow, personal communication, Cambridge, Massachusetts, September 22, 2012.

[134] Rostova, "'Ia schitaiu, chto "nastoiashchii russkii muzhik" dolzhen vymeret'."

and economic order, Soviet masculinity was in need of some perestroika, and the "muzhik" model fit the bill—for the leadership and the public alike.[135] However, the advent of a market economy and the initial impoverishment that came along with it had more of a "demasculinizing" effect, as many men could not meet the new market-derived standards for masculine achievement.[136] Russian cultural studies scholars Helena Goscilo and Vlad Strukov refer to the 1990s as a time of "crisis in gender identities, and particularly masculinity."[137] Male success in the new market derived from financial success—something emphasized in the glossy magazines directed at men—and was embodied in a tough masculinity summarized by the adjective "krutoi" (derived from prison lingo and indicating a "macho, authoritative demeanor").[138] This masculine image of the "traditional Slavic macho" in the 1990s carried over into the Putin era (with the political leader as its most conspicuous representation), while its rough "risibly crude" edges were softened.[139]

In short, the sexualization of economic products starting in Russia in the 1990s helped lay the groundwork for the sexualization of political products, such as candidates and their supporters. During the Putin era, the gender norms relied upon for advertising and image-making in the economic sphere crossed into the political realm. This is not to say, however, that gendered appeals were unknown in Russian politics earlier. Under Yeltsin's administration in the 1990s, for example, there were instances where feminization (or demasculinization) was used to undermine male political opponents' reputations. Liberal politician Grigorii Yavlinsky was said to dye his hair (a feminizing trait); it was also alleged that he and Communist Party leader Gennadii Ziuganov had gotten plastic surgery to improve their appearance (a behavior characteristic more of women than of masculine men).[140] Likewise, economist Yegor Gaidar and his team, which had implemented the first round of Russia's

---

[135] Riabova and Riabov, "Nastoiashchii muzhchina Rossiiskoi politiki?," 57, citing Katherine Verdery, "From Parent-State to Family Patriarchs: Gender and Nation in Contemporary Eastern Europe," *East European Politics and Societies* 8, no. 2 (Spring 1994).

[136] Ibid.

[137] Goscilo and Strukov, "Introduction," 11; On this issue see also Rebecca Kay, *Men in Contemporary Russia: The Fallen Heroes of Post-Soviet Change?* (Burlington, VT: Ashgate, 2006); Elena Zdravomyslova and Anna Temkina, "The Crisis of Masculinity in Late Soviet Discourse," *Russian Studies in History* 51, no. 2 (Fall 2012): 13–34.

[138] Goscilo and Strukov, "Introduction," 12, 24.

[139] Ibid., 13–14.

[140] Boris Barkanov, personal communication, September 22, 2012; T. B. Riabova and O. V. Riabov, "U nas seksa net: Gender, Identity, and Anticommunist Discourse in Russia," in *State, Politics, and Society: Issues and Problems within Post-Soviet Development*, ed. Aleksandr Markarov (Iowa City: University of Iowa, 2002), 29–38.

unpopular market reforms in the early 1990s, were mockingly referred to by their detractors as "little boys in pink pants, red shirts, and yellow shoes."[141]

In this context, one can fathom why the image-makers working with Putin as the new president following Yeltsin's surprise resignation in December 1999 might have seized on a model of attractive, physical masculinity as a way to set Russia's current leadership apart from its gut-boasting, boorish, boozy predecessor, not to mention from the gerontological Soviet leadership of the late Brezhnev era. As with Soviet and Russian leaders before him, Putin's PR image has drawn on the "father of the nation" trope.[142] The sexualized emphasis on his masculinity, however, is new in the context of the Russian and Soviet leadership. This concentration on Putin's physique continued throughout his terms as president (2000–2008), prime minister (2008–2012), and president again. The week that Putin turned 60, in October 2012, a state-owned television station aired a documentary focusing on Putin "as known by those closest to him." The camera crew spent a week shadowing President Putin, documenting the arenas from which cameras are usually forbidden but into which they were strategically permitted in this case. At the forefront of the documentary were questions including: What does the president's swimming pool look like, and how much time does he devote daily to staying in shape? The advertisement for the documentary showed Putin in the pool and using universal gym equipment, emphasizing his physical strength in the face of aging.[143] The leader's physical fitness and capacity to lead the state were thus tactically conflated; by remaining in shape—in the public eye—Putin was demonstrating (indirectly) his leadership superiority as an "eternally young, sporty man" compared both to his predecessors (such as Yeltsin) and his would-be rivals.[144]

The notion of glamour, relatively novel in the 1990s, ultimately crossed the boundary between economics and politics, becoming influential in both realms. Glamour played well in the new capitalist economy, though it would rise to the fore in politics only after Yeltsin's exodus, when Putin evolved into

---

[141] Boris Barkanov, "Mercantilist Development in Russia: The Legitimacy of State Power, State Identity, and the Energy Charter Regime (1990–2010)" (PhD diss., University of California, 2011), 232.

[142] See Tatiana Mikhailova, "Putin as the Father of the Nation: His Family and Other Animals," in *Putin as Celebrity and Cultural Icon*, ed. Helena Goscilo (London: Routledge, 2013), 65–81.

[143] "Putin the Unknown: TV Host Walks & Talks with Russian President," October 7, 2012, http://rt.com/news/putin-birthday-documentary-life-864/; "Tsentral'noe televidenie: Vypusk ot 7 oktiabria 2012 goda" [video], October 7, 2012, http://www.ntv.ru/peredacha/CT/m23400/o113999/comments/.

[144] Yevgeny Minchenko, "Putin's Public Actions: A Unique Style Is a Competitive Advantage," October 11, 2012, http://valdaiclub.com/politics/49960.html; Hakamada, "Flights with Sibrian White Cranes and Other PR Events of Vladimir Putin."

something of a glamour object. Putin became "a major—indeed, perhaps the ultimate—sex symbol" of a new political regime resting on a new economic order.[145] Glamour was now a selling point, and political leaders as well as economic goods could be desired and consumed.[146] The ascendancy of glamour continued into the 2000s; in 2007, the word "glamour" won Russia's "Word of the Year" contest, suggesting that the importance of appearance—and highly gender-normed appearance, at that—had not lost its grip on the country.[147] Goscilo and Strukov note that the wealthy middle class—a potential pillar of support for the Putin regime that oversaw that stratum's growth during the oil boom of the 2000s—had to be ideologically constructed (as the Bolsheviks had earlier constructed the working class). Glamour constituted a significant part of this ideology, and glossy magazines, directed at men as well as women, "served as the early primers" in glamour-and-consumer literacy.[148] The "Happy Birthday, Mr. Putin" calendar and other similar political advertisements featuring women in lingerie and high heels looked not unlike the advertisements in glossy magazines, where women illustrated and performed these new expectations.

To teach the ideology of glamour properly, however, the lessons would have to be clearly delineated for men and women. Glamour magazines were not unisex—quite the opposite. Indeed, part of a person's ability to exhibit the new standards of consumption and style was the ability to discern the correct gender norms of dress, appearance, and behavior—in short, to assimilate what was appropriate for men and women. Goscilo and Strukov refer to the post-Soviet project coinciding with the Putin regime's ascension as replacing "homo sovieticus" with "homo glamuricus."[149] In fact, however, homo glamuricus was not one being but two. The glossy instruction manuals were aimed at men and women separately, creating not "*homo* glamuricus" but "*hetero* glamuricus"— men and women who understood that gender norms were even more clearly delineated than they might have earlier believed.

The examples presented here highlight the obvious fact that these "opportunity" categories overlap. In post-Soviet Russia, political and economic opportunity structures converged to turn femininity and masculinity into both economic and political goods for sale in their respective marketplaces. Against the backdrop of commercial capitalism and Hollywood images, Putin's body,

---

[145] Goscilo and Strukov, "Introduction," 14.
[146] Goscilo, "The Ultimate Celebrity."
[147] Goscilo and Strukov, "Introduction," 3.
[148] Ibid., 4; Helena Goscilo, "Style and S(t)imulation: Popular Magazines and the Aestheticization of Postsoviet Russia," ed. Helena Goscilo, *Russian Culture of the 1990s*: Studies in 20th Century Literature 24, no. 1 (Winter 2000): 15–50.
[149] Goscilo and Strukov, "Introduction," 4.

along with the female bodies of his loyalists, became political commodities, facilitating political legitimation strategies based on contestation over masculinity and femininity. To some extent, the sexualization of the political realm (whether in Putin's macho virility or in the display of female beauty by his ostensible supporters) is explained by the confluence of commodification and political rule.

As gender sociologist Anna Temkina explained, sexualization in politics was not only a matter of commodification and capitalism but also took on an anti-Soviet flavor:

> Any product sells better if it's sexualized, especially after Soviet times. Everything has become more sexualized, more hedonistic. Since the state and capitalism have become one and the same thing, the government needs to be seductive—to not be like the Soviets; there was no profit there. Commodification and sexualization—this is also an anti-Soviet phenomenon. Putin is anti-Soviet, even if today's political structures are centralized and similar to [those of the Soviet era]. The Russian Orthodox Church, sexualization, capitalism—they're all in place now because they illustrate Putin's "anti-Soviet" perspective.[150]

The sexualization of politics, not only an aspect of Putin's macho PR strategy, was thus also a means of legitimating Putin as a political leader who distanced himself from certain Soviet precepts.[151] If Soviet rule had been anticapitalist, the Putin era lauded private property and trade (albeit in a rather kleptocratic, crony-capitalist way); if the Russian Orthodox Church had been suppressed under Soviet rule, under Putin's rule it was restored to its rightful place; if there had been "no sex in the Soviet Union," as a female participant in a 1985 "space bridge" program had asserted, the Putin era resolved to "bring the sex back in."[152] The

---

[150] Anna Temkina, interview by author, St. Petersburg, June 14, 2012.

[151] Putin's anti-Sovietism is tactical, not universal. Witness the Putin-era continuity with the national-patriotic trappings of Soviet rule, such as Putin's discursive emphasis on national pride, focusing on the Great Patriotic War, and on his pursuit of Russian influence in the now-independent states of the former Soviet Union. See Gorham, "Putin's Language," 92–94; Lara Ryazanova-Clarke, "The Discourse of a Spectacle at the End of the Presidential Term," in *Putin as Celebrity and Cultural Icon*, ed. Helena Goscilo (London: Routledge, 2013), 109–115.

[152] The space bridge event was a town hall meeting of sorts between Americans and Soviets. Reportedly, the woman from Leningrad who made the famous remark had been saying that there was no sex shown on television in the USSR, but that part of her answer went unheard due to audience "laughter and applause." See Olga Pigareva, "Prominent Russians: Vladimir Pozner," http://russiapedia.rt.com/prominent-russians/politics-and-society/vladimir-posner/, accessed March 20, 2013

very dearth of sexuality in Soviet public discourse lent it considerable power in the public sphere once the Soviet period had come to an end.[153]

Soviet legacies in the economic, political, and cultural arenas clearly created opportunities for the use of gender norms and homophobia as tools (or weapons) of political legitimation. *Political history* constitutes a third component of the multiple opportunity structure, describing how legacies of the previous political ideology condition the present one. The "Russia needs a strong leader" myth has never dissolved. Following Stalin's death in 1953, Soviet leaders on the Politburo—hoping in a self-serving way henceforth to avoid the dangers inherent in one-man dictatorship—embraced the idea of a nominally collective but still highly autocratic model where several top leaders would share power. Despite his colleagues' intentions to the contrary, this deteriorated into personalized rule by Nikita Khrushchev several years later. Subsequent general secretaries of the Soviet Communist Party also rhetorically espoused collective rule but tended to amass personal power instead.

No matter how individually power hungry the Soviet Union's leaders may have been, however, there was common agreement within the party hierarchy that collective behavior—at least for the Soviet population—was preferable to the greed-driven, Western capitalist ideal that lauded individual success. Soviet propaganda lionized the "socialist" collective and condemned the "capitalistic" individual. The "cowboy" model of fighting one's way out of a contest or the "bootstrap" model of achieving success on one's own not only represented an ideological contradiction to the Soviet model but a concrete danger to it. This perspective applied to the political realm as much as to the economy; after all, it was against Soviet Communist Party leaders' interests for individual citizens to assert their rights (political or economic) against the state; those who did so were punished as political dissidents or economic speculators.[154] While the top Soviet leadership, which was exclusively male, could share in the machismo that came from running one of the world's two nuclear superpowers, the idea of a Party leader attracting public attention and support as an individual via masculine assertiveness and dominance was frowned upon. For all his authoritarian tendencies, Putin's rule thus reflected a rhetorical political shift from the late-Soviet collective and from power purportedly shared among individual members of the Politburo, to power overtly hoarded by only one. However, the legacy of concentrating power around a single person at the top

---

[153] I thank Helena Goscilo for this insight. On the uneasy intrusion of sexuality into Russian popular discourse in the 1990s, see Eliot Borenstein, "*About That*: Deploying and Deploring Sex in Postsoviet Russia," ed. Helena Goscilo, *Russian Culture of the 1990s: Studies in 20th Century Literature* 24, no. 1 (Winter 2000): 51–83.

[154] Frau Derrida, Moskovskaia Feministskaia Gruppa, interview by author, Moscow, June 7, 2012.

of the political hierarchy had persisted from the Soviet era as had a discomfort with citizens asserting their rights as individuals against the regime.

Another aspect of political history and the ideological shift that occurred at the close of the Soviet Union was that more attention began to be directed toward sexuality and sexual issues in Russia's economy and polity. Communist Party leader Mikhail Gorbachev loosened the strictures of censorship in the late 1980s, and within a few years there was an enormous influx of pornography being sold above board. The political, economic, and social reorientations of the 1990s came along with increased attention to sexual issues and materials. Following the Soviet state's dissolution, previously taboo topics like homosexuality entered the realm of popular discussion and political-legal rethinking. By the mid-1990s, the widespread availability of pornographic magazines at newsstands even provoked Moscow residents to refer to the "perekhody"— the city's underground street crossings lined with newsstands and other small stores—as "pornokhody."[155] Following its political and economic departure with Soviet communism, in 1990s Russia the public role of sex blossomed—in advertising, in the economy, and as a political commodity.

In the 1990s, Vladimir Zhirinovskii, the bombastic and clownish head of Russia's inaptly named Liberal Democratic Party (LDPR), better described as a nationalist-fascist entity, facilitated this shift by bringing his own sexual obsessions into the public sphere. Several years after his party's initial and stunning showing in the 1993 parliamentary elections (the LDPR gained over 20 percent of the party-list vote—more than any other party), Zhirinovskii released a book titled *The ABCs of Sex* (Azbuka seksa). This peculiar volume, in somewhat schizophrenic fashion, alternated between being a detailed although not illustrated sex manual and a set of policy prescriptions aiming to facilitate sexual satisfaction and improve Russia's economic standing simultaneously. Specifically, Zhirinovskii and his neglected co-author, Vladimir Iurovitskii, proposed that Russia should model itself on Thailand and place sex at the center of its economy, by marketing the sexual potency of Russia's young men and selling the sadly domestically undervalued virginity of its young women for a far higher price on the world market. By penning this publication, large swathes of which read like a paean to sperm and the hymen, Zhirinovskii brought sex further into the public sphere, albeit in an absurd and misogynist way.[156]

---

[155] In this way, the first post-Soviet decade had much in common with the decade following Russia's 1905 revolution. In her examination of sexuality and its regulation in Russia, historian Laura Engelstein found that after 1905, sexual life (from health issues, to behavior then considered deviant such as prostitution and homosexuality) was far more widely discussed than it had been before. See Engelstein, *The Keys to Happiness*, 216, 267.

[156] Vladimir Zhirinovskii and Vladimir Iurovitskii, *Azbuka seksa: Ocherki seksual'noi kul'tury v rynochnom mire* (Moscow, Russia: Politbiuro, 1998), 169–177.

Zhirinovskii prided himself on being the first Russian politician to take sex out of the private sphere and pose it as an issue deserving public discussion.[157] He therefore did not hesitate to make freewheeling use of sexual language part of his political profile. Running as a candidate in Russia's 1996 presidential election, for instance, Zhirinovskii described his party as a desirable "virgin" and stated with certainty that "forty million men" would "desert" all the other parties (these he labeled as political prostitutes) and "rush after the virgin LDPR."[158] He also offered sexual characterizations of the eras of Soviet political history. "Masturbation" described the Khrushchev period and "impotence" the Brezhnev reign, while Gorbachev's perestroika and the early post-Soviet period under Yeltsin were "a time of orgies and sexual confusion."[159] Zhirinovskii's relative electoral success showed that sexualizing politics in these gratuitous ways found a potential constituency within the Russian public and paved the way for the future use of such rhetorical devices in political contests. With Putin's ascension to the presidency, the sexualization of politics was no longer primarily associated with the anomalous and outlandish Zhirinovskii but instead was harnessed to the agenda of a respected and comparatively staid incumbent.

Sex scandals also made an appearance in the 1990s as a political tool. These were virtually unknown in ruling circles in the Soviet era, when ostensible communist asceticism dictated that party leaders prioritize their commitment to building communism and put their sexual desires and personal lives on the back burner.[160] "Good communists" were portrayed in state-approved literary works and films as subordinating their individualistic romantic longings to the loftier collective goal of serving the party-state; to do the reverse was condemned as bourgeois. Sex and sexuality thus could not be foregrounded in politics under Soviet-communist rule for ideological reasons, and the Communist Party's highest functionaries were never caught with their pants down in public.[161]

---

[157] Ibid., 222.

[158] Eliot Borenstein, "About That," 64–65.

[159] Helena Goscilo, "Post-ing the Soviet Body as Tabula Phrasa and Spectacle," in *Lotman and Cultural Studies: Encounters and Extensions,* ed. Andreas Schonle (Madison: University of Wisconsin Press, 2006), 271.

[160] Moreover, without a free media, there would have been no outlet in which to disclose any indiscretions by top Soviet leaders should such have been discovered.

[161] Lavrentii Beria, the last head of the secret police (NKVD) under Stalin, is something of an exception. Beria was reportedly a serial rapist who used his powerful position to force women into his bed. Beria's sexual exploits were raised (among Communist Party leaders, not in the press) after his own arrest following Stalin's death in 1953. See Amy Knight, *Beria: Stalin's First Lieutenant* (Princeton, NJ: Princeton University Press, 1995), 97.

But on the verge of Putin's assumption of the presidential office, Yeltsin's regime used a sex scandal as a means to defang a significant opponent, Russian Attorney General Yurii Skuratov. Skuratov, who had been investigating corruption in Yeltsin's closest circles, was brought down in 1999 by the public release of a compromising video (parts of which were shown on television) in which a man who bore a close resemblance to Skuratov was seen in bed with two women said to be "call girls." The video had initially come into the possession of the Federal Security Service (FSB); Putin, as the agency's head at that time, likely played a key part in compromising Skuratov with the aid of this device.[162] Similar principles were at work later in the Putin era, when a handful of men counting themselves among the regime's opponents were set up in sexual situations and then filmed without their knowledge—the videos finding their way to the Internet soon after.[163] By the advent of Putin's regime, the political-historical opportunity structure had moved away from the ideology of communist ascetics to a potentially more sex-infused ideological setting.

The opportunity structure for any legitimation strategy's success also includes a *cultural* component.[164] We must therefore explore the cultural ground in which a legitimation strategy based on gender norms could grow. Numerous studies have documented sex-based discrimination and misogyny in various Russian, Soviet, and post-Soviet Russian settings, from the family to the workplace and from politics to popular culture, suggesting that ideas rooted in "natural" gender differences and female inferiority have been widespread there

---

[162] Iurii Fel'shtinskii and Vladimir Pribylovskii, "Rossiia i KGB vo vremena prezidenta Putina. Glava 4: Direktor FSB spas tron El'tsina," January 21, 2010, http://www.kasparov.ru/material. php?id=4B5811FDB4E78; Stcukov, "Namedni—99. Skuratov" [video], October 13, 2009, http://www.youtube.com/watch?v=4icOg44nRWQ&feature=related; Brian D. Taylor, *State Building in Putin's Russia: Policing and Coercion after Communism* (Cambridge: Cambridge University Press, 2011), 103–104.

[163] The use of sex scandal to tarnish a government official's image is obviously not found only in Russia. But whereas there have been a number of sex scandals raised in the US media, for instance (from the infamous Bill Clinton–Monica Lewinsky tryst to the discomfiting disclosure of South Carolina Governor Mark Sanford's Argentine connection), these are typically actual affairs that are discovered, rather than set-ups orchestrated by political opponents. One exception to this in the United States was a move directed against then-Senator Edward Kennedy by Republican Party-based supporters of President Richard Nixon. In 1972, in an effort to avert the chance of a Democratic victory in the upcoming presidential election, Nixon's operatives reportedly created campaign advertisements featuring Kennedy with a "buxom blonde sitting on his lap" who had been "spliced" into the footage. If Kennedy had ended up as the Democratic presidential nominee, the Republican party was prepared to use the ads as fuel, painting Kennedy as a womanizer with inappropriate or excessive sexual desires and as a cheater—given that the woman in question was not his wife. See Bob Woodward and Carl Bernstein, *All the President's Men*, 2nd ed. (New York: Simon & Schuster, 1994), 254.

[164] This is not to suggest that cultures are static; indeed, they contain elements of continuity and change (stemming from resistance). See Yuval-Davis, *Gender and Nation*, 41.

or, at the very least, uncontested publicly for a range of reasons.[165] Public celebration of women's inferiority was on display in the Putin era, for instance, in a popular television show called "Insanely Beautiful" (BezUmno krasyvie) that premiered in October 2011. The show featured attractive young women (aged 18–27) trying and often failing to answer questions posed by the host (such as "What was the Holocaust?," a question that a pair of twins answered awkwardly by saying, "We think that the Holocaust is wallpaper paste"), while young men attempted to guess how the women would answer (a task complicated by the "beautiful young women's attempts at logical reasoning"). The first word in the show's title constitutes a pun in Russian, translating literally as "Without Brains," perhaps making "Brainless Beauties" a better English translation. Unsurprisingly, the show proceeded to win a Russian feminist group's annual prize for "Sexism in the Media."[166]

A decade after the collapse of the Soviet Union, the cultural context enabling the political use of gender norms, sexism, and homophobia in Russia was firmly in place. Despite its egalitarian ideology, the Soviet government had presided over a grossly sex-segregated labor market, unequal pay for men and women, high rates of domestic violence (albeit rarely discussed in public policy circles), and a division of domestic labor that left women responsible for household labor and childrearing, often on top of full-time paid jobs. These conditions of gender-based discrimination did not evaporate with the collapse of the Soviet state. In the 1990s, women's unemployment initially exceeded men's, and women were pressured to return to the home. Gorbachev had endorsed this idea in 1987 when, in his book on perestroika, he called for establishing conditions to facilitate returning Soviet women to their "purely

---

[165] Discussion of these issues can be found in Hilary Pilkington, ed., *Gender, Generation and Identity in Contemporary Russia* (London: Routledge, 1996), esp. 9–10; Lynne Atwood, "Young People, Sex, and Sexual Identity," in *Gender, Generation and Identity in Contemporary Russia,* ed. Hilary Pilkington (London: Routledge, 1996), 95–120 (on naturalized/essentialized gender differences and homophobia); Sue Bridger, Rebecca Kay, and Kathryn Pinnick, *No More Heroines: Russia, Women and the Market* (London: Routledge, 1996) (on the labor market); Anastasia Posadskaya, ed., *Women in Russia: A New Era in Russian Feminism* (London: Verso, 1994); Laurie Essig, *Queer in Russia: A Story of Sex, Self, and the Other* (Durham, NC: Duke University Press, 1999) (on homophobia); Sperling, *Organizing Women in Contemporary Russia,* 54–97 (on the cultural obstacles to feminist organizing); Draitser, *Making War Not Love* (this work documents a wide range of misogynist Russian and Soviet jokes objectifying and belittling women at the level of popular culture).

[166] "Shou: Bezumno krasivye," http://www.vokrug.tv/product/show/Bezumno_krasivye/, accessed January 17, 2013; Mumin Shakirov and Aleksandr Kulygin, "Game Show Shocker Raises Questions about Holocaust Education," May 2, 2012, http://www.rferl.org/content/game_show_shocker_raises_questions_holocaust_education_russia/24531474.html; Wander Woman, "Seksist goda-2011: Itogi," March 6, 2012, http://www.zafeminizm.ru/2012/03/06/seksist-goda-2011-itogi.html.

womanly mission"—the private sphere of household and family.[167] A 1999 survey reflected stereotypical ideas about gender roles: 56 percent of 2000 respondents polled across the state agreed that "men should have priority" if there were not enough paid jobs to go around; 71 percent agreed that a woman "needs to bear children" in order to be fulfilled in life; and 47 percent thought that "sometimes when a woman says she doesn't want to have sex, she doesn't really mean it."[168]

While women's organizing in the 1990s brought these issues far more public attention than they had earlier received, sex stereotyping and a firm belief in sexist gender norms persisted through Putin's first three terms. As of 2011, surveys showed that the lion's share of housework remained on women's shoulders: the wife was responsible for ironing in 74 percent of families, did the dishes in 57 percent of families, prepared the food in 65 percent of families, and did the laundry in 74 percent of families.[169] In 2009, 52 percent of Russians thought there were not enough women in positions of power (up from 46 percent in 2005), though men were more likely to think that there were "as many women in power as needed to be" (40 percent of men and 24 percent of women).[170] In 2006, a survey asking how women's status in various areas had changed over the past fifteen years found that 68 percent of women thought it was harder to protect themselves from violence than in the past; 46 percent of Russians surveyed thought that men had a real chance of getting a worthy salary and finding work in their chosen professions, while only 3 percent of Russians believed that women had similar chances.[171]

Over the course of fifteen years (to 2006), the percentage of people who believed that women were discriminated against in salaries grew from 46 percent

---

[167] Mikhail Gorbachev, *Perestroika: New Thinking for Our Country and the World* (New York: Harper and Row, 1987), 116–117.

[168] Rossiiskoe Obshchestvennoe Mnenie i Issledovanie Rynka (ROMIR), "Zhenshchiny Rossii," September 1999, http://web.archive.org/web/20040529075740/http://www.romir.ru/socpolit/socio/october/women.htm.

[169] VTsIOM: Vserossiiskii Tsentr Izucheniia Obshchestvennogo Mneniia, "Domashnie khlopoty: Kto i chto delaet v Rossiiskoi sem'e," May 23, 2011, http://wciom.ru/index.php?id=459&uid=111631. Russian public opinion data should be treated with caution. That said, while VTsIOM is a state-owned agency, the portrait its data paints here is not particularly rosy. On the politics of Russian public opinion polling, see Anna Arutunyan, "Foreign Agents and Pollsters: Research Held Hostage?," *Moscow News*, May 27, 2013, http://themoscownews.com/news/20130527/191548967-print/Research-held-hostage.html.

[170] VTsIOM: Vserossiiskii Tsentr Izucheniia Obshchestvennogo Mneniia, "Zhenshchiny i vlast': Kak garantirovat' ravenstvo polov v politike?," March 6, 2009, http://wciom.ru/index.php?id=459&uid=11527.

[171] VTsIOM: Vserossiiskii Tsentr Izucheniia Obshchestvennogo Mneniia, "Muzhchiny i zhenshchiny ravny, no kto iz nikh 'ravnee'?," June 3, 2007, http://wciom.ru/index.php?id=459&uid=4120.

to 57 percent.[172] Public opinion polls also found a perceived gap in men's and women's chances in the labor market over time. In 2012, Russians surveyed were convinced that men had better opportunities to be promoted at work than women: 48 percent thought so, and only 32 percent thought women's chances were equally good; in 2001, 59 percent thought men's chances were better versus 30 percent who believed that opportunities were equal.[173] Sex-based role stereotypes persisted as well. Although in 2007 the majority of citizens surveyed thought that men and women could be equally good parents, workers, and managers, among the other respondents 34 percent thought that women were likely to be good parents, and only 5 percent saw men's potential to succeed in that area.[174] In 2012, perhaps reflecting economic realities for women, a national survey found that Russians increasingly believed that the future for their teenage daughters (hypothetical or real) was more likely to be linked to a "successful marriage" than to having a "good job" (21 percent thought so in 2007, and 37 percent in 2012; in 1995, during a period of disproportionate female unemployment, a full 46 percent thought this was the case).[175]

The Putin era was also accompanied by an increasingly sexist and biologically driven view of men's and women's roles, associated in part with the rising influence of the Russian Orthodox Church. In the words of a gender sociologist in St. Petersburg,

> The ideological trend toward a biodeterministic understanding of women's reproductive destiny is obvious as a clear sign of the ascendancy of neopatriarchal tendencies in state social policy. It has been grafted to the religious propaganda of stereotypical social roles for men and women (right up to the introduction of these precepts in the educational process in schools, instead of educating teachers about the necessity of undermining these stereotypes and developing gender tolerance in their students). Journalists' incompetence and ignorance about stereotyped discourse, and the media's frequent use of discriminatory images based on social stereotypes in entertainment programs and in ads, only strengthens [those stereotypes].[176]

---

[172] Ibid.

[173] Fond Obshchestvennogo Mneniia, "'Zhenshchina—tozhe chelovek.'"

[174] Vtsiom: Vserossiiskii Tsentr Izucheniia Obshchestvennogo Mneniia, "Muzhchiny i zhenshchiny ravny, no kto iz nikh 'ravnee'?."

[175] Fond Obshchestvennogo Mneniia, "'Zhenshchina—tozhe chelovek.'"

[176] Tat'iana Barandova, "Sovremennyi etap zhenskogo dvizheniia Sankt-Peterburga: Strukturnye ogranicheniia, okna vozmozhnostei, vektory razvitiia i tochki rosta," in Zhenskoe dvizhenie v Rossii: Vchera, segodnia, zavtra: Materialy konferentsii, ed. Galina Mikhaleva (Moscow: RODP "Yabloko" and KMK Publishers, 2010), 74–75.

Suppressed during the Soviet era, the Orthodox Church was resuscitated in the 1990s (regaining church buildings previously commandeered by the Soviet Communist Party, increasing the ranks of priests, and attracting more people to services) and came to occupy an increasingly prominent place on the socio-political scene under Putin. Russian Orthodoxy, having been shielded from liberalizing pressures in part by its dissident status under communist rule, remained a highly male-dominated religion, excluding women from the priesthood. According to historian Nadieszda Kizenko, in the contemporary period "many Orthodox Christians reject both Soviet and Western languages of equality as being hostile to Orthodox Christian values and damaging to Russia" and largely embrace "the traditional gender roles increasingly rejected by their coreligionists outside postcommunist spaces."[177] Putin's alliance with the Russian Orthodox Church hierarchy has given Church activists greater access to the public sphere, creating a louder and more prevalent voice for the endorsement of sharply defined sex roles and the defamation of feminism.

Russia also ranks fairly high on the sexism scale in a comparative cultural context, where sexism is measured by examining attitudes toward women's presence in "stereotypically male domains."[178] A 2011 study comparing levels of sexism across fifty-seven countries—based on World Values Survey data in the mid-2000s—ranked Russia's mean level of sexism at 2.7 on a 4-point scale, where 1 indicates strong disagreement with the statements, "On the whole, men make better political leaders than women do" and "On the whole, men make better business executives than women do," and 4 indicates strong agreement with those statements. Average across the multistate sample was 2.42 (the midpoint between "least sexist" and "most sexist" is 2.5). As was common across the board, male Russian citizens' level of sexism (2.95) was higher than women's (2.49). Russia ranked forty-sixth of the fifty-seven states, tied with Morocco; Iran, number fifty-two, scored 2.96, and Iraq finished last (or worst), at 3.57. For comparison, the United States scored 2.03 and was ranked number eighteen, while Norway, Sweden, and France took the top three "least sexist" slots, scoring 1.59, 1.65, and 1.7 respectively.[179] The study also reported the United Nations' Gender Empowerment Measure (GEM), which takes into account men's and women's shares of elected political positions, earnings, and managerial-level and professional positions. Russia's GEM at that time was

[177] Nadieszda Kizenko, "Feminized Patriarchy? Orthodoxy and Gender in Post-Soviet Russia," *Signs* 38, no. 3 (2013): 595. Also see Kizenko's article for a discussion of women's influence within the contemporary Russian Orthodox Church.

[178] Mark J. Brandt, "Sexism and Gender Inequality across 57 Societies," *Psychological Science* 22, no. 11 (November 2011): 1414.

[179] Ibid., 1414–1415.

0.482 (where a score of zero indicates complete gender inequality, and 1 indicates complete gender equality). Morocco scored 0.325, Iran scored 0.316; the United States scored 0.808, and Norway, at the top, scored 0.901.[180] Even Valentina Matvienko, a strong Putin ally who has served as the governor of St. Petersburg and speaker of the Russian parliament's upper house, acknowledged in a 2012 television interview that societal views prescribe women a secondary role, stating (in a rather geographically stereotypical formulation): "We are a European country and also an Asian country, and the public mentality holds that a woman should occupy a certain place."[181]

Putin's Russia was fertile ground for homophobia as well. Its roots can be traced to the Soviet era and even earlier.[182] Considered taboo as a topic for public discussion under Communist Party dictatorship, homosexuality had been kept under wraps.[183] Moreover, homosexuality had been criminalized in the Soviet period for men; Article 121 of the Criminal Code made male–male sex punishable by prison terms of up to five years. While Soviet law was silent on lesbianism, some lesbians (upon others' discovery of their orientation) were committed to psychiatric hospitals, forcibly treated with medication, and registered as mentally ill, requiring regular psychiatric visits.[184] The Soviet Union's gay community had no "Stonewall" and was not able to organize openly until the 1990s. Sex education courses, briefly introduced in the 1990s, met with resistance from religious and other groups, while the general resurgence of the Russian Orthodox Church following the end of Communist Party rule was accompanied by an openly "homophobic ideology."[185]

Gay sex was legalized in 1993, and by the end of Putin's first presidential term, general attitudes toward homosexuals had improved significantly over those in the early 1990s. Nearly half of citizens polled in 1990 thought that homosexuals should be "isolated from society," whereas by 2005, the proportion

[180] Ibid.

[181] Alexander Bratersky, "Female Leaders Manage Mentalities," *Moscow Times*, March 7, 2013, http://www.themoscowtimes.com/news/article/female-leaders-manage-mentalities/476634.html.

[182] On homosexuality and heteronormativity in sixteenth to eighteenth century Russia, see Marianna Muravyeva, "Personalizing Homosexuality and Masculinity in Early Modern Russia," in *Gender in Late Medieval and Early Modern Europe*, eds. Marianna Muravyeva and Raisa Maria Toivo (London: Routledge, 2012), 205–224.

[183] Elena Iarskaia-Smirnova, "Vezde kul'tiviruetsia obraz samtsa," June 15, 2011, http://fom.ru/obshchestvo/136.

[184] Masha Gessen, *The Rights of Lesbians and Gay Men in the Russian Federation: An International Gay and Lesbian Human Rights Commission Report* (San Francisco: IGLHRC, 1994), 7, 9, 17–18.

[185] Iarskaia-Smirnova, "Vezde kul'tiviruetsia obraz samtsa."

who felt this way fell to 31 percent, and 49 percent thought gays should be left to their own devices (predostavit' samim sebe).[186]

Still, popular attitudes toward homosexuality failed to catch up with the newly tolerant legal regime. As of mid-2011, 69 percent of Muscovites (and 60 percent of the general population) believed that the government acted correctly by banning gay pride parades (11 percent disagreed), with young men (aged 18–24) feeling most strongly in that regard (71 percent thought it was right to ban such events). Women aged 25–34 were the age group most likely to oppose the bans; still, only 17 percent of this cohort supported gay citizens' right to free speech and assembly.[187] In 2012, public opinion polls showed that respondents regarded gays and lesbians with even stronger distaste than they did people of nationalities or religions different from their own; 45 percent of people surveyed across Russia reportedly "experienced negative emotions when interacting with homosexuals" (whereas such interactions with people of different ethnic background were displeasing to only 10 percent of those surveyed). The majority of Russians (61 percent) also believed that homosexuality was acquired rather than inherent (25 percent), and 47 percent believed that homosexuality resulted from exposure to the mass media and other sources propagandizing it.[188] A poll by the Levada Center (which is not state-affiliated) likewise found that three-fourths of Russians thought homosexuality was the result of "an illness or loose morals."[189] In December 2012, the biggest fan club supporting St. Petersburg's most famous soccer team, Zenit (owned by the Russian state-run gas company, Gazprom), posted a public letter calling for the team to hire only heterosexual and light-skinned players.[190]

Nor did the state discard its distaste for citizens with a "non-traditional orientation." In March 2012, a homophobic law banning promotion of homosexuality to minors was passed in St. Petersburg; this joined previous laws passed in multiple Russian cities, in effect outlawing gay rights rallies and the distribution of literature about homosexuality.[191] In January 2013 a nationwide ban

[186] VTsIOM: Vserossiiskii Tsentr Izucheniia Obshchestvennogo Mneniia, "Odnopolaia Liubov'—Normal'no, braki—Rano," February 15, 2005, http://wciom.ru/index.php?id=459& uid=1084.

[187] Fond Obshchestvennogo Mneniia, "My zhe ne v Amerike."

[188] VTsIOM: Vserossiiskii Tsentr Izucheniia Obshchestvennogo Mneniia, "Gomoseksualistami ne rozhdaiutsia?," May 17, 2012, http://wciom.ru/index.php?id=459&uid=112769.

[189] Marc Bennetts, "Vitaly Milonov: Laying Down God's Law in Russia," RIA Novosti, August 30, 2012, http://en.rian.ru/analysis/20120830/175525037.html.

[190] Rob Hughes, "An Ugly Reminder in Russia That Bigotry Lingers," *New York Times*, December 18, 2012, http://www.nytimes.com/2012/12/19/sports/soccer/19iht-soccer19.html.

[191] The first of these was Riazan in 2006. See Leonid Bershidsky, "'Curing' Homosexuality in Russia and Ukraine," Bloomberg, October 10, 2012, http://www.bloomberg.com/news/2012-10-10/-curing-homosexuality-in-russia-and-ukraine.html.

on homosexual "propaganda" was passed by the Russian parliament (on the first of three readings) by a whopping 388 to 1. Any false hopes engendered by the one parliamentary ally were dashed when he explained after the fact that he had intended to support the law and had simply hit the wrong button.[192] In June of that year, the bill was passed in its final incarnation by a vote of 436 to zero, with one abstention, before Putin signed it into law. It outlawed the distribution or expression of information that portrayed "nontraditional" sexual relationships in a positive light or that equated them in value with heterosexual relationships and that did so in such a way that minors could be exposed to this information.[193] Duma Deputy Elena Mizulina, one of the law's main sponsors, explained that Russian lawmakers had avoided the word "homosexual" in the text of the law because, as she put it, using the term would "involuntarily propagandize it—this homosexuality."[194]

The Russian Orthodox Church, newly empowered to take public positions after having been largely silenced and coopted by Soviet rulers, did not hesitate to embrace patriarchal and homophobic positions, endorsing amendments to Russian legislation that would dramatically restrict abortion access, while some Russian Orthodox Church personnel lauded hate crimes perpetrated against gays.[195] When a masked mob beat up a group of patrons at a gay-friendly Moscow club in October 2012, Father (Igumen) Sergii Rybko, a Russian Orthodox priest in Moscow, sympathized with the attackers and justified their actions: "I understand the Russian people's indignation. The Holy Scriptures command [us] to stone all of these people with a nontraditional [sexual] orientation. Until that trash has been cleared off the Russian land, I will fully share the views of those who are trying to cleanse our Motherland of it. If the state doesn't do it, the people will." Rybko added regretfully that as a priest he "could not take part in such actions."[196] Church and state came together on this issue

---

[192] BBC World Service (WBUR), February 25, 2013; David M. Herszenhorn, "'Propaganda' by Gays Faces Russian Curbs Amid Unrest," *New York Times*, January 25, 2013, http://www.nytimes.com/2013/01/26/world/europe/propaganda-by-gays-faces-russian-curbs-amid-unrest.html.

[193] Alec Luhn, "Gay Pride Versus 'Gay Propaganda,'" *The Nation*, June 28, 2013, http://www.thenation.com/article/175035/gay-pride-versus-gay-propaganda.

[194] Andrew E. Kramer, "Russia Passes Bill Targeting Some Discussions of Homosexuality," *New York Times*, June 11, 2013, http://www.nytimes.com/2013/06/12/world/europe/russia-passes-bill-targeting-some-discussions-of-homosexuality.html.

[195] Dar'ia Zagvozdnina, "Delo Pussy Riot—V interv'iu 'Gazete.Ru' Ekaterina Samutsevich rasskazala o patriarkhe, feminizme i zhizni v tiur'me," October 17, 2012, http://www.gazeta.ru/social/2012/10/17/4815193.shtml.

[196] Sergii Rybko, "Igumen Sergii (Rybko) o razgone gei-kluba," October 12, 2012, http://www.pravmir.ru/igumen-sergij-rybko-o-razgone-gej-kluba-sozhaleyu-chto-kak-svyashhennik-ne-mogu-prinyat-uchastie-v-akcii/.

in Moscow in 2006, when Russian Patriarch Alexei II supported then-Mayor Yuri Luzhkov's ban on public gay pride events; in justifying the ban, Luzhkov had called such events "satanic."[197] Despite a small but increasingly visible movement for LGBT rights, Russia's cultural soil was fertile for political legitimation strategies based on homophobia.

The *international* arena presents the last piece of the multiple opportunity structure for the use of gender norms in political legitimation. Tying into the political-historical and cultural opportunity structures, Russia's international context at the close of the Cold War created an opening for masculine contestation in foreign affairs. The new Russian state inherited the Soviet Union's nuclear materials but not its superpower status. Russia's size and population had declined from their Soviet heights, and the country was plagued by economic disruptions as the state-owned economy was painfully transformed into a market-capitalist one. The early 1990s brought waves of Western consultants, advisors, and the inevitable conclusion that Russia had been reduced from the status of a world leader equal to the United States to that of a troubled and recalcitrant pupil in need of outside assistance. By the end of the decade Russians' feelings of patriotism and national pride had considerably deteriorated. Economic chaos, a devastating war in Chechnya (Russia's rebellious southern province), the loss of communism as an official state ideology that had at least proclaimed that the country was in the vanguard of a worldwide communist movement toward paradise on earth—these woes and others plagued Russia's government and population in the first post-Soviet decade. A nationwide public opinion poll in 2002, asking what "in the modern life of our country" gave rise to feelings of pride, allowed respondents to provide an open-ended answer: half the respondents provided answers deemed "not pertinent" or simply left it blank, and an additional 20 percent stated frankly that there was "nothing to be proud of," making that the most popular answer.[198] Contests to develop a "national idea" were held to no avail, and the new lyrics finally adopted in 2000 for Russia's national anthem were vague and unmemorable.[199]

When Yeltsin resigned at the end of 1999, leaving then-prime-minister Putin as the acting president and putting him in an advantageous position to win the

---

[197] "Moscow Bans 'Satanic' Gay Parade," January 29, 2007, http://news.bbc.co.uk/2/hi/europe/6310883.stm.

[198] "Russia: Pride and Shame," Fond Obshchestvennogo Mneniia Report/Population Poll, February 14, 2002, cited in Valerie Sperling, "Making the Public Patriotic: Militarism and Anti-Militarism in Russia," in *Russian Nationalism and the National Reassertion of Russia*, ed. Marlene Laruelle (London: Routledge, 2009), 218.

[199] "State Symbols of the Russian Federation," http://www.montreal.mid.ru/inf_symb_e.html, accessed October 19, 2012.

presidential contest in March 2000, the population eagerly awaited new leadership. Appealing as Yeltsin had been in 1991 as a democrat standing against his former communist colleagues, he had become something of an embarrassment at the international level—drunkenly attempting to conduct the Berlin Police Orchestra while visiting Germany in 1994, for instance—and was increasingly seen as a figurehead at home (where powers behind the throne were running the political and economic show).[200] Putin, as the head of the FSB, came to power as a relative unknown, though the agency he had headed exuded an aura of strength, and—as discussed earlier—Putin's sober persona made him a welcome contrast to his predecessor. While Putin was hard at work asserting his power at home, having initiated a second wave of war in Chechnya in late 1999 with the promise to rub out the Chechen rebels, he faced a simultaneous challenge internationally.[201] According to women's studies scholar Kimberly Williams, the image of Russia abroad had become feminized, particularly in US popular and elite-political culture. Russia was seen as a backward woman in need of guidance from the West. Even magazine advertisements picked up on this gendered imagery. Williams describes a 2005 Diesel Jeans ad in the American men's periodical, GQ, in which a cowboy has apparently dropped off to sleep after enjoying fellatio provided by a set of open-mouthed Russian nesting dolls (matrioshki)—thus putting Russia in the "penetrated," feminized sexual role described by Chauncey in the previous chapter.[202]

The Kremlin's desire to resuscitate the country's pride and international image—what Goscilo and Strukov refer to as "re-branding the nation—and particularly its leadership"[203]—was linked to the resuscitation of state masculinity. In a 2010 study examining Putin and masculinity in Russian politics, Riabov and Riabova argue that Putin's macho image accompanied a broader strategy to "remasculinize" the country domestically and internationally.[204] As they put it, "The renewal of national dignity was Putin's unique business card."[205] Putin made it clear that Russia had to embody—or be perceived as

---

[200] Gabriel Schoenfeld, "Boris Yeltsin's Ambiguous Legacy," *Commentary*, April 24, 2007, http://www.commentarymagazine.com/2007/04/24/boris-yeltsins-ambiguous-legacy/.

[201] Anna Politkovskaya, *A Dirty War* (London: Harvill Press, 1999), 91.

[202] Kimberly A. Williams, *Imagining Russia: Making Feminist Sense of American Nationalism in U.S.–Russian Relations* (Albany: State University of New York Press, 2012), 1–3; Pamela Jordan, "Review of Kimberly A. Williams, Imagining Russia: Making Feminist Sense of American Nationalism in U.S.–Russian Relations. Albany: State University of New York Press, 2012.," *H-Diplo, H-Net Reviews*, July 2012, https://www.h-net.org/reviews/showrev.php?id=36221; Chauncey, *Gay New York*, 66.

[203] Goscilo and Strukov, "Introduction," 1.

[204] Riabova and Riabov, "Nastoiashchii muzhchina Rossiiskoi politiki?," 56–57. Wood makes a similar point in "The New Façade of Autocracy," 26.

[205] Riabova and Riabov, "Nastoiashchii muzhchina Rossiiskoi politiki?,", 57.

embodying—a set of traditionally masculine characteristics like independence and strength. In that way, the Kremlin's PR strategy of emphasizing Putin's outward physical signs of masculinity echoed Putin's own declarations in 1999 about Russia's need to "get off its knees" and demonstrate its power.[206]

Putin's early encounters with US President George W. Bush presented a symbolic challenge in this regard. Williams claims that the "informal manly activities such as clearing brush on Bush's Texas ranch or saltwater fishing at the Bush family resort in Maine" that permeated the leaders' summit meetings served as a vehicle to highlight Bush's "virule [sic], rugged masculinity" and assert the masculine power of the United States itself.[207] Putin, meanwhile, was caught short in Crawford with footwear that suggested "urban and urbane effeteness" by comparison to Bush's ranch get-up and cowboy boots.[208] By 2007, however, Putin's PR team had caught on, releasing bare-chested photos of Putin on a Siberian fishing trip—apparently responding to or echoing the "rugged outdoorsman" image used by Bush.[209] In a more jocular instance of symbolic "topping," during a visit by Bush to Putin's residence at Novo-Oga-revo, Putin bragged that his black Labrador retriever, Konni, was "bigger, stronger [and] faster" than Bush's Scottish terrier, the diminutive Barney.[210] National pride required meeting or exceeding the masculine image of the Western rival and his country.

National masculinity, like individual masculinity, is thus a relative or relational condition. State leaders can endeavor to enhance their own masculinity by demeaning their foreign rivals' manliness. In this regard, the concepts of "in-groups" and "out-groups" are useful in explaining how images of "one's own people" and "Others" (or outsiders) come to be polarized in a gendered way. Riabov and Riabova suggest that these concepts from social identity theory apply internationally as well as locally and that people are inclined to identify "Others" metaphorically as feminine, while holding up one's own people as masculine (and thus superior).[211] A gendered power relationship is thereby rhetorically established and can play a part in domestic political struggles as well as international ones.

---

[206] Ibid., 58.

[207] Williams, *Imagining Russia*, 186.

[208] Ibid., 186; David E. Sanger, "Putin Is Target of the Pecan Pie Tactic," *New York Times*, November 15, 2001, http://www.nytimes.com/2001/11/15/international/15RANC.html.

[209] Williams, *Imagining Russia*, 186–188.

[210] "Putin to Bush: My Dog Bigger Than Yours," November 4, 2010, http://www.reuters.com/article/2010/11/03/us-bush-book-putin-idUSTRE6A275X20101103.

[211] Riabova and Riabov, "Nastoiashchii muzhchina Rossiiskoi politiki?," 59; For an extended discussion of how the "ours versus others" discourse has been gendered in Russia, see Riabov, "*Rossiia matushka.*"

Under Putin, for example, as prices for oil (one of Russia's main exports) rose, Russia's international clout followed suit, and Russia reasserted itself in the "near abroad"—the region of the former Soviet states. Countries in Russia's post-Soviet orbit that underwent attempts at democratizing revolutions (which were presumed to decrease Russia's influence and enhance America's power in the region) found themselves rhetorically demasculinized. Putin made clear that his regime would hold firm against the threat of a "color revolution," such as Ukraine's "Orange" Revolution, which nonviolently ousted the incumbent president after fraudulent elections in 2004, and the "Rose" Revolution in Russia's southern neighbor, Georgia, the previous year. Following the Orange Revolution, when Russia raised the price of gas exported to Ukraine, on Russian television Ukraine was painted as America's female mistress, a "greedy, kept woman," and Russian protesters' posters outside the US embassy in Moscow instructed the United States to pay Ukraine's subsequent debts to Russia: "A Gentleman Always Pays for His Girlfriend."[212] Putin used homophobic terms to similarly dismiss the Rose Revolution, casting it as gay. Reacting to a reporter's question following the Georgian events, Putin stated, "A rose revolution—next they'll come up with a light blue one" (To rozovaia revoliutsiia, to golubuiu eshche pridumaiut). In Russian, "light blue" is slang for "gay male." Putin's ally in that conflict, the president of South Ossetia, likewise remarked of Georgia's president, "Saakashvili is far from having democratic values—not to speak of male ones—he doesn't have any of those at all."[213]

In this context, Putin's self-assertion as a tough, strong, masculine, and, above all, patriotic leader protecting Russia from the chaotic demands for "mob rule" and the nefarious plans of Western states to weaken Russia and take advantage of her copious natural resources, was both personally pragmatic and eagerly welcomed by the citizenry. By 2007, Putin was winning the hypothetical "real-man" competition; in one mid-sized Russian city 44.8 percent of Russians surveyed named Putin when asked to name a "real man" in Russian politics.[214] A larger, national-level survey in 2009 also put Putin in first place with a plurality of 14 percent naming him as a "real man in Russia," with the next closest contestant, the revered Soviet performer Vladimir Vysotskii, named by only 7 percent.[215] National pride, too, had rebounded by the end of Putin's first decade in power. A countrywide survey in 2010 found that only 2 percent of respondents claimed that there was "nothing" for which to be proud

---

[212] Riabova and Riabov, "Nastoiashchii muzhchina Rossiiskoi politiki?," 59–60.

[213] Ibid., 60.

[214] The survey was conducted in Ivanovo, among four hundred people. Putin was chosen for various reasons including his decisiveness, the firmness of his convictions, his manliness (*muzhestvennost'*) and male strength of character, and his power (*sila*). See ibid., 51.

[215] Ibid., 48.

of Russia, and only 9 percent could not or did not provide a response.[216] Russia's formerly shaky position in the international realm, combined with the other elements of the opportunity structure described here, enabled a conflation of Putin's masculinity and Russia's international status. The emphasis on Putin's patriotic machismo gained him popularity while also enhancing the Russian public's perception of their country's strength and influence abroad.

* * *

The constellation of circumstances described above provides the setting in which a regime legitimation strategy using gender norms and homophobia could take root and flourish in the Russian case. Because all states' politics operate against a backdrop of patriarchy and misogyny to some degree, the multiple opportunity structure for the political use of gender norms reveals how conducive the circumstances are for such tactics in a given polity. Taken together, analogous studies of other states should reveal more general principles regarding the reasons why gender norms appear as a means of political legitimation and why they encounter greater or lesser degrees of public opposition.

---

[216] *Gordost' i styd za Rossiiu* (Dominanty no. 35, Fond Obshchestvennoe Mnenie, September 9, 2010), http://bd.fom.ru/pdf/d35gis10.pdf; "BBC News: Russia Country Profile," March 6, 2012, http://news.bbc.co.uk/2/hi/europe/country_profiles/1102275.stm.

3

Who's Macho, Who's Gay? Pro- and Anti-Kremlin Activists Gendering Russia's Political Leadership

On the occasion of Vladimir Putin's fifty-eighth birthday in 2010, a group of young women students from Moscow State University's journalism department produced the aforementioned erotic calendar. At that time, having served two serial terms as Russia's president (from 2000–2008), Putin had found an appropriately subservient man to take the presidency for a term— Dmitrii Medvedev—while he sat out the requisite period in the prime minister's chair and prepared to reoccupy the presidential office following the March 2012 elections, sure to be decided in his favor. With a series of double-entendre captions, the scantily clad would-be journalists offered Putin their personal and political affections. "If not you, then who?" wondered a sensuously smiling Miss August, suggesting that Putin was the only reasonable choice—for president, presumably. "As the years pass, you only get better," agreed Miss September, wearing a green and black demi-push-up bra and ruffled panty. "Everyone would [like to] have such a man," Miss January frankly stated, while Miss February, in leopard print lingerie, asked, "Vladimir Vladimirovich, how about a third time?" "You're my premier," pouted Miss October, while Miss May went with the straightforward message, "Vladimir Vladimirovich, I love you!"[1] A few days later, a response calendar appeared, this time portraying a different group of Moscow State University journalism department students. Six young women in black suits and dresses, with yellow tape pasted in an "X" over their mouths, posed uncomfortable political questions to the prime minister, inquiring, for instance,

---

[1] Kristina Potupchik, "Devushki zhurfaka MGU razdelis' dlia Putina," October 6, 2010, http://krispotupchik.livejournal.com/92592.html.

when jailed oligarch Mikhail Khodorkovsky would be released from prison and whether freedom of assembly would be guaranteed.[2]

While technically no concrete organizations claimed responsibility for either of these pieces of political propaganda, the first was clearly produced by young people partial to the prime minister and his politics and the latter by budding journalists more inclined to criticize the incumbent regime. When asked about their views on the calendars, activists with pro- and anti-Kremlin youth organizations responded with some predictability according to their political convictions. "It's the embodiment of political prostitution," noted one anti-Kremlin activist, referring to the first calendar.[3] Others on the anti-Kremlin side labeled the birthday calendar "offensive"[4] and "degrading,"[5] and regarded it as an attempt to undermine the profession of journalism more generally.[6] Anti-Kremlin activists asked about the response calendar respected the young women's bravery for speaking up.[7]

Pro-Kremlin activists, while not necessarily enthusiastic about the birthday calendar, held more positive opinions about it. "Sure, they were being a little naughty," remarked a pro-Kremlin activist, expressing some appreciation for the first calendar and for the young women who had taken the initiative to embody their birthday greetings in this fashion by "adding some glamour."[8] Another liked the "creative" one-liners voiced in the first calendar, which she contrasted to the "sillier" response calendar, which had, in her view, merely parroted the kinds of questions that represent "good tone" in liberal circles and therefore had made less of a splash.[9] But political youth activists on both sides of the Kremlin generally agreed that making a calendar featuring semi-naked young men would have been nontraditional for Russia and would no doubt have implied that its models and consumers alike were gay. "I wouldn't look at

[2] Sasha Utkin, "Kalendar,'" October 7, 2010, http://sasha-utkin.livejournal.com/147833.html; Goscilo, "Putin's Performance of Masculinity: The action hero and macho sex-object," 196. The response calendar could only be printed from the web, whereas the original calendar was for sale in stores.

[3] Tivur Shaginurov, Oborona, interview by author, Moscow, June 11, 2011.

[4] Olga Vlasova, Molodezhnoe Yabloko, interview by author, Moscow, June 14, 2011; Vera Kichanova, Libertarianskaia partiia, interview by author, June 16, 2011.

[5] Igor' Iakovlev, Molodezhnoe Yabloko, interview by author, Moscow, June 14, 2011.

[6] Oleg Kozlovskii, Oborona, interview by author, Moscow, June 8, 2011.

[7] Kirill Goncharov, Molodezhnoe Yabloko, interview by author, Moscow, June 10, 2011; Roman Dobrokhotov, My, interview by author, Moscow, June 9, 2011.

[8] Alena Arshinova, Molodaia Gvardiia, interview by author, Moscow, June 14, 2011. She considered the second calendar to be "fairly clever" as well.

[9] Irina Pleshcheva, Nashi, interview by author, Moscow, June 16, 2011. A second pro-Kremlin activist labeled the second calendar's questions as foolish or silly; Anton Smirnov, Stal'/Nashi, interview by author, Moscow, June 17, 2011.

men [on a calendar]," laughed the male head of a pro-Kremlin youth organization.[10] "Let me put it this way," said one male anti-Kremlin activist, "many
women might look at both women and men, but men definitely wouldn't look
at men."[11]

This chapter explores some of the gendered ways in which political youth organizations and other political actors have voiced their criticism of and support
for the Putin-centered regime that began ruling Russia at the turn of the twenty-
first century.[12] How have political youth groups on both sides of the Kremlin
used gender as an organizing principle for exhibiting or withholding support for
state leaders and opposition leaders? And how have pro- and anti-Kremlin political activists used masculinity, femininity, and heteronormativity to bolster
their own political authority and try to undermine that of their opponents?

Political Youth Organizing in Russia: Pro-Kremlin Groups and Liberal Anti-Kremlin Groups

Government-sponsored youth organizations designed to propagate state ideas
and implement state goals have a long history in Russia. Like the present-day
pro-Kremlin youth organizations, the Soviet-era Communist Youth League
(Komsomol) was both a "transmission belt" enabling the Communist Party to
spread its ideology within the population as well as a vehicle for the social mo-
bility of its members.[13] Such groups, then and now, were designed to foster the
dual illusion of mass support for the regime and popular participation in the
polity. The collapse of the Soviet Union and its single-party rule in 1991, however, brought an end to the Komsomol and enabled a broad array of political
organizing during the chaotic but relatively free 1990s. Vladimir Putin's ascension, first to Russia's prime ministership in 1999 and then to the presidency
in March 2000, signaled a sea change in Russia's political direction. As the
decade wore on, the incumbent regime's intention to remain in power was
manifested in several anti-democratic changes to the political system. These

---

[10] Nikita Borovikov, Nashi, interview by author, Moscow, June 9, 2011.

[11] Kozlovskii, interview by author.

[12] Given that a growing percentage of the protestors across Russia's somewhat restive political
field are aged 34 and under, political youth activists' tactics and views are particularly relevant. As
of June 2012, 65 percent of demonstrators attending rallies fell in that age group. See Natal'ia
Korchenkova, "Protest smenil vozrast i liderov," *Kommersant*, June 28, 2012, http://www.
kommersant.ru/doc/1968592?isSearch=True.

[13] Jim Riordan, "The Komsomol," in *Soviet Youth Culture*, ed. Jim Riordan (Indiana University
Press, 1989), 16–44; Ralph Talcott Fisher Jr., *Pattern for Soviet Youth: A Study of the Congresses of
the Komsomol, 1918–1954* (New York: Columbia University Press, 1959).

included eliminating elections for the governorships of Russia's eighty-three federal subregions, increasing state control over television, and the growing marginalization of opposition parties and politicians from political institutions and public life.[14]

By the mid-2000s, Russia's set of vocal political youth organizations included both pro- and anti-Kremlin groups actively staking out their political terrain. In this chapter and the next, I discuss the views and actions of participants in three pro-Kremlin groups: Nashi (Ours; understood as meaning, "Those on Our Side"), Stal' (Steel), and Molodaia Gvardiia Edinoi Rossii (the Young Guard of United Russia, the youth wing of the dominant political bloc, United Russia); and three liberally oriented, anti-Kremlin groups: Oborona (Defense), My (We), and Molodezhnoe Yabloko (Youth Yabloko, the youth wing of the liberal democratic Yabloko Party).

The 2004 Orange Revolution in Russia's neighboring country, Ukraine, served as a catalyst for the formation of youth organizations on both sides of Russia's political spectrum. Following the November 2004 announcement of presidential runoff election results that were widely perceived to be fraudulent, hundreds of thousands of Ukrainian citizens—many of them youth—had forced a political turnover by occupying the capital's main square in protest.[15] An activist with Oborona explained,

> [The Orange Revolution] had a strong influence on how people evaluated what was going on here. Because up until that time, the people in [liberal] youth organizations believed in something—we were doing something—but nobody believed that we could realistically . . . win [and] change something. What we'd been doing was keeping our consciences clean; I knew I was doing all I could. . . . But after the Orange Revolution, we saw that . . . it was possible to get results, that it was realistically possible to change the whole political situation in the country.[16]

While motivating liberal activists to strive for democratic change, the prospect of a "color revolution" in Russia spurred the Kremlin's creation of Nashi, a youth organization designed to defend and enthusiastically support the regime in power. Nashi's leader, Nikita Borovikov, was motivated to participate in the organization at its founding, for that reason:

[14] Joel M. Ostrow, Georgiy A. Satarov, and Irina M. Khakamada, *The Consolidation of Dictatorship in Russia* (Westport, CT: Praeger Security International, 2007), 105–118.
[15] The wave of civic activism resulted in a second runoff and the victory of the opposition candidate (rather than the victory of incumbent Prime Minister Viktor Yanukovich, the Kremlin's preferred candidate).
[16] Kozlovskii, interview by author.

As it happens, I had in fact just come back from the presidential elections in Ukraine—I'm a lawyer, by education—and I was one of the election observers there. And therefore, I was watching the news, and, having been in the Ukraine, had a good idea of what had gone on there, and a clear understanding that I didn't want that happening here.

Q. What put you off?

A. What put me off was, first, as a lawyer, the fact that this was an illegal means of [solving] political problems, a political crisis. . . . We had, and continue to have, the sense that this [the Orange Revolution] constituted a serious threat to the Russian Federation at that moment. And I'll say again that our task was not to allow such a thing [to take place here].[17]

As the brainchild of then-Kremlin ideologist Vladislav Surkov, Nashi was intended to help preserve the political status quo and prevent the onset of a revolution aimed at unseating the ruling regime and holding the incumbent Russian government to a more democratic set of political standards.[18]

By contrast, Russia's politically liberal youth organizations sought to democratize a regime that they had seen become narrow and politically restrictive and to do so precisely by the means used in Ukraine. A co-coordinator of Oborona in 2011 explained that the organization's main goal was "to achieve democracy in Russia. Not to overthrow Putin's regime, because if you overthrew Putin and did it only half way, whoever took his place could be even worse. But [what we want is] precisely the establishment of democracy in Russia, by means of a nonviolent revolution."[19] Another activist from the same organization elaborated:

The basic goal is democracy in Russia. All the [aspects of democracy]: freedom of choice, freedom of speech, freedom of association, freedom of assembly, multipartyism, the rule of law, the division of powers. . . . And in addition to that, you have to add the struggle against corruption . . . and some kind of justice for people who have suffered at the hands of the authorities.[20]

---

[17] Borovikov, interview by author.

[18] Ellen Barry, "Surkov, Architect of Putin's Political System, Is Reassigned," *New York Times*, December 27, 2011, http://www.nytimes.com/2011/12/28/world/europe/putin-takes-another-swipe-at-russian-protesters.html?_r=1.

[19] Mariia Savel'eva, Oborona, interview by author, Moscow, June 8, 2011.

[20] Kozlovskii, interview by author.

Ukraine's Orange Revolution constituted a turning point for Russian politics. However, political youth organizations existed in Russia prior to that time at both ends of the spectrum. Molodezhnoe Yabloko, for example, as the youth wing of "grown-up Yabloko" (as some activists referred to their parent political party), had been founded in 1995 in Moscow and St. Petersburg, with a Russia-wide organization chartered in 2005.[21] One memorable Molodzhnoe Yabloko action took place in July 2004, when a group of activists wearing t-shirts with Putin's face, a stop sign, and the slogan, "Down with big brother!," approached the building housing secret police headquarters in Moscow, unfurled a poster reading, "Down with police autocracy!," and splashed red paint on a plaque attached to the building's exterior. The plaque commemorated the career of Yuri Andropov, a former head of the secret police (from 1967 to 1982) famous for persecuting Soviet dissidents.[22] In 2011, there were roughly fifty Molodezhnoe Yabloko activists continuing the group's activities in Moscow; most of them were students, aged 18–25.[23] On the pro-Kremlin side, Nashi's predecessor, a patriotic pro-Putin youth group called Idushchie Vmeste (Walking Together) was created in 2000 and held its first mass action in May 2001. There, several thousand young people, most sporting Putin t-shirts and the slogan, "Everything is on track" (vse putem—a pun in Russian, as "on track" sounds similar to "Putin"), came together in Moscow to celebrate Putin's first year as Russia's president.[24]

More groups formed as political tensions heightened under Putin's rule. In March 2005, Oborona was founded by three activists, two of whom were adherents of the youth wings of liberal political parties (Yabloko and the Union of Right Forces [Soiuz Pravykh Sil, or SPS]); the third was an activist with the Institute of Collective Action, a left-inclined organization. The activists, wanting not to be subject to the dictates of their parent parties, decided to create an amalgamation "of people, not of organizations," and brought about fifty individuals together for the founding conference.[25] Using "direct action," Oborona carried out unauthorized protests to draw attention to state authoritarianism. In February 2007, for instance, activists gathered at the state television broadcasting station in Moscow (Ostankino), where they blocked the entrance

---

[21] Il'ia Iashin, *Ulichnyi protest* (Moscow, Russia: Galleia-Print, 2005), http://stevanivan.igp.ru/Solidarnost/2009-10-18_Solidarnost/Ilya.html; "Molodezhnoe Iabloko—O nas," http://youthyabloko.ru/ru/about.html, accessed March 24, 2013.

[22] "V godovschinu kazni dekabristov iablochniki obideli Andropova," July 29, 2004, http://novayagazeta.ru/data/2004/54/06.html.

[23] Goncharov, interview by author.

[24] Jussi Lassila, *The Quest for an Ideal Youth in Putin's Russia II: The Search for Distinctive Conformism in the Political Communication of Nashi, 2005–2009* (Stuttgart: *ibidem*-Verlag, 2012), 43.

[25] Kozlovskii, interview by author.

to the facility, hung a poster that read "Enough Lying!" (khvatit vrat'), hand-cuffed themselves to the fence, and distributed leaflets until the police arrived. The activists demanded the privatization of all but one television station and the termination of the "blacklists" that kept opposition figures off the air-waves.[26] In 2011, one of Oborona's coordinators reported that the group had thirty people in Moscow and about as many in St. Petersburg, plus several other regional branches. If at its start Oborona's members had been college students, by 2011 their average age was closer to 27, and a handful of activists had paired up as married couples.[27]

We, another group on the anti-Kremlin front, formed in 2005 as well, and, like Oborona, held creative actions to make political points. One playful action parodied a peculiar situation in 2006, when a venerable Russian dissident in her late 70s, Liudmila Alekseeva, was accused of having put listening devices into rocks and then handing them over to MI-6, the British intelligence agency.[28] As the leader of We explained, the group decided to do its "civic duty" and help the state in its quest to extinguish this threat to national security:

> We announced that we were going to help the FSB [Federal Security Service], and that we were going to go around Moscow and find suspi-cious rocks and bring them to the FSB to be checked out. And because the TV program [in which Alekseeva had been accused] had started with the words, "Look at this rock—on the surface it looks like a typi-cal rock," we also said we would gather rocks that appeared to be typ-ical on the surface, because they could also turn out to be "spy rocks." So we bagged up these huge rocks and brought them to the Lubianka [the FSB headquarters]. And of course, OMON [the riot police] im-mediately pounced on us, arrested us. And at that time it was rare to arrest people for no apparent reason. . . . So people saw the arrest as being fairly absurd, that is, they were saying, "People brought rocks across the street and they were arrested, for who knows what reason; they were saying they were helping out, after all." So it was pretty funny, and it got into all the media.[29]

---

[26] "Oborona (molodezhnoe dvizhenie)," http://bit.ly/1173JZM, accessed March 24, 2013; Ko-zlovskii, interview by author.

[27] Savel'eva, interview by author.

[28] In a bizarre twist, the British government admitted six years later that it had indeed used a fake rock as a listening device. Janet Stobart, "British Admit Using 'Embarrassing' Fake Rock to Spy on Russians," *Los Angeles Times*, January 20, 2012, http://articles.latimes.com/2012/jan/20/world/la-fg-britain-spy-rock-20120120.

[29] "Dvizhenie 'My' poneset na Lubianku shpionskie kamni," February 2, 2006, http://y.tagora.grani.ru/Politics/Russia/activism/m.101439.html; Dobrokhotov, interview by author.

As with Oborona, We activists' average age when the group was chartered was 22 or 23 but had increased over time; its leader was 27 in 2011, and he estimated that there were approximately 120 members based in Moscow.[30]

The scale of youth activism on the other end of the political spectrum was larger. Founded in 2004, the pro-Kremlin group Nashi consisted mostly of college-aged students and became the face of pro-regime youth organizing.[31] The "favorite son" of the Kremlin family, this politicized youth organization was the beneficiary of the many resources at the regime's disposal. Having ballooned to one hundred thousand reported members by 2011, Nashi towered over the liberal anti-Kremlin youth groups.[32] Nashi's original purpose was to support Putin, promote Russia's modernization, and bolster patriotism, particularly among youth.[33] The group's manifesto, penned in 2005, painted the task of Russia's young generation as understanding their country's crucial location in the globalized twenty-first century world as a bridge "uniting the economy and culture of our planet into a unified whole." To accomplish this, Russia would need to be strong, as weakness would "turn the country into a victim of its stronger competitors." But if Russia took advantage of its strengths, it would achieve a position of "global leadership—the task of our generation."[34]

Nashi's manifesto also clearly identified the two threats to Russia's success: the United States and international terrorism, both of which sought "to control Eurasia and the entire world." For Russia's youth, then, the task was to defend their state's "sovereignty," as their grandfathers had done against the Nazis in the Second World War. Not only did Nashi's program statement imply parallels between Nazi fascists and the US government, the manifesto also derided Russia's liberal leaders in the decade after the Soviet collapse, who "look[ed] to the West" for examples to follow and who took Western "orders." To assure Russia's modernization, Nashi argued, Russia needed a new, active generation that would focus on economic development under the watchful eye of a strong government. Rather than calling for a new regime, Nashi's

---

[30] Demokraticheskoe dvizhenie MY, "Ustav," May 14, 2005, http://web.archive.org/web/20121010140926/http://www.wefree.ru/?id=8; Dobrokhotov, interview by author.

[31] Molodezhnoe demokraticheskoe antifashistskoe dvizhenie NAShI, "Proekty," http://nashi.su/projects, accessed August 3, 2011; Borovikov, interview by author.

[32] James Jones, "Putin's Youth Movement Provides a Sinister Backdrop to Russia's Protests," *The Guardian*, December 8, 2011, http://www.guardian.co.uk/commentisfree/2011/dec/08/putin-russia-elections.

[33] On Nashi's predecessor (Idushchie vmeste), Nashi's origins, its efforts to communicate to its young target audience and its uneven relationship with the Kremlin, see Lassila, *The Quest for an Ideal Youth in Putin's Russia II*.

[34] "Manifest molodezhnogo dvizheniia 'NAShI,'" October 25, 2005, http://web.archive.org/web/20051025115524/http://www.nashi.su/pravda/83974709.

manifesto claimed that political stability was the linchpin of Russia's economic progress. The group's task, then, was to endorse the political status quo under Putin and prevent the return of those political forces who preferred to have Russia run from outside, "as was the case in the 1990s." Those political forces, identified by Nashi as an "unnatural union of liberals and fascists, of western-izers and ultranationalists, of international foundations and international ter-rorists," wanted only one thing: "to undermine the first positive changes in Russia, and to permanently return the country to the era of ineffective, weak government and collapsing society."[35]

What Russia's fascists and liberals had in common, Nashi's manifesto ex-plained, was their hatred for Putin. Nashi, on the other hand, assured its devotees that Putin, "having strengthened the state," was the right person to take Russia forward to its "claim to leadership in the world of the 21st cen-tury." This forward movement, however, was threatened by Putin's adversar-ies. Nashi, therefore, was committed to supporting Russia's leader: "This will not be support for Putin as an individual, but for his political course of action, directed to preserving the sovereignty of the state, carrying out its economic and political modernization, and securing its stable nonviolent development, and achieving its future global leadership." Stressing the value of action rather than liberal "verbiage," Nashi's leaders encouraged youth to join in making Russia great again[36] and, at the national level, engaged its supporters in mass rallies and other manifestations of patriotic-political obeisance.[37]

Stal' (Steel), whose name shares a linguistic root with "Stalin"—the alias adopted by the Soviet Union's most deadly leader—began as a Nashi project.[38] With approximately two thousand members across Russia and roughly ten ac-tivists who could be relied on to carry out actions in Moscow, Stal' became an independent entity in 2009–2010 and prided itself on being willing to operate at the boundary between legality and illegality. As Anton Smirnov, a Stal' leader, described, his group's goals were consonant, with Nashi's but the meth-ods Stal' used ran more toward the unofficial. For example, he explained,

---

[35] Ibid.

[36] Ibid.

[37] These reportedly included physical attacks on oppositionists. See "Masked Men Attack NBP Activists," *The Moscow Times*, August 31, 2005, http://www.themoscowtimes.com/news/arti-cle/masked-men-attack-nbp-activists/210256.html.

[38] "Molodezhnoe Patrioticheskoe Dvizhenie STAL,'" http://madeofsteel.ru/, accessed January 11, 2011. In the lower right corner of their homepage, Stal' features a trilogy of hyper-tough movie figures: the Terminator's mechanical skeleton, the Predator, and Darth Vader. Beneath their images lies the phrase "They were not made of steel." I thank Michael Metelits for identify-ing these characters.

It could take a long time to go through the court system to shut down places where illegal drugs are sold. You can draw public attention to it. Or shut it down immediately by [stirring up some trouble], at a moment's notice. If we're not prepared to wait half a year for a judge's decision, we can shut things down more quickly.[39]

Unlike Nashi and Stal', which are not officially affiliated with any political parties, Molodaia Gvardiia was the youth wing of the United Russia Party, the vehicle that had brought Putin into power and helped keep him there. Molodaia Gvardiia was founded in 2005, replacing its predecessor, Molodezhnoe Edinstvo (Youth Unity), the youth wing of United Russia's forerunner, the Unity Party.[40] As of 2011, Molodaia Gvardiia had branches across the Russian Federation, totaling up to 160,000 participants, ranging in age from 15 to their early 30s.[41] With populist themes, such as a demand against Russia's major oil companies (such as Lukoil) to lower the price of gas at the pump, Molodaia Gvardiia carried out a countrywide campaign at gas stations, calling on oil magnates to develop a conscience and "stop living off the people."[42] The group also held mass rallies supporting Putin, and (as we shall see) engaged in unfriendly propaganda against regime detractors.[43]

Some of the groups' names suggest their ideological perspective. "Molodaia Gvardiia" emphasized the group's patriotic alliance with the state; the organization shared its name with a group of young Soviet citizens who were venerated for their resistance activities in Nazi-occupied Ukrainian territory and were made famous in Soviet postwar propaganda.[44] Nashi's title set up a baldly and simply stated dichotomy between those loyal to Putin's regime—"Ours"—and those who were not (implicitly suggesting that everyone who was not "Ours" was "Theirs"—presumably taking orders from liberal forces outside the Russian state). On the opposite side of the political spectrum, the anti-regime group We took its politically significant title from Russian author Evgenii Zamiatin's remarkably prescient novel of the same name.[45] Zamiatin's futuristic dystopian tale describes a totalitarian regime intent on observing and

[39] Smirnov, interview by author.

[40] "Molodaia gvardiia Edinoi Rossii," http://bit.ly/sLDXMA, accessed November 8, 2010.

[41] Arshinova, interview by author.

[42] Molodaia Gvardiia, "Ia—za chestnoe toplivo!," February 13, 2011, http://mger2020.ru/nextday/2011/02/13/25831; Molodaia Gvardiia, "Dollarovaia ataka na 'Lukoil,'" April 28, 2011, http://www.molgvardia.ru/nextday/2011/04/28/29369.

[43] Bendzhamin Bidder, "Krasivaia molodaia gvardiia Putina," October 5, 2011, http://newsland.com/news/detail/id/795740/.

[44] Juliane Furst, *Stalin's Last Generation: Soviet Post-War Youth and the Emergence of Mature Socialism* (Oxford: Oxford University Press, 2010), especially chap. 4.

[45] Yevgeny Zamyatin, *We* (New York: Harper Voyager, 2001).

regulating its citizens' behavior full-time and keeping the notion of individual freedom at bay. The regime isolates itself from other communities behind a "Green Wall" and reduces dissidents to puddles of water in public execution ceremonies. Finally, to guarantee the collective good and its own perpetuity in power, the regime imposes an operation on the citizens that excises their imaginations. Zamiatin's novel in 1921—well before Stalin's takeover—imagistically had described the totalitarian regime that the Soviet Union would become. By adopting Zamiatin's title, the founders of We advertised their antagonism to dictatorship past and present.[46]

Although all the groups discussed here are technically political youth organizations, given the disparity in their size, support base (with some being supported by the regime and its ruling party and others being targeted by that regime), and autonomy from the state, it is fair to wonder whether the pro- and anti-regime groups should best be treated as analytically distinct types of political formations. In other words, by examining these groups together, might this study be artificially comparing tiny "grassroots" groups with massive Kremlin-synthesized "astroturf."[47] As Russian political scientist Dmitrii Kamnev points out, groups like Nashi and Molodaia Gvardiia were formed intentionally by state officials to put their members through a desirable process of "political socialization." He finds, however, that the national authorities were incapable of regarding their creations as "independent political subjects" and that conformism and the desire for personal gain were the dominant motives of the pro-Kremlin group participants.[48] For a select few, a prominent role in Nashi or Molodaia Gvardiia could serve as a launching point into a political career in the United Russia Party or into a comfortable government post. Particularly active membership in these groups could lead to useful networking connections for young people (particularly those from Russia's provinces) hoping to find employment in the capital. This made the pro-regime activists rather different from their liberal counterparts who, if anything, ran the risk of losing status due to their anti-regime organizing.

While the pro- and anti-regime groups constitute analytically distinct phenomena in that regard, they can still be fruitfully compared in this context. Although the "astroturf" groups were supported and funded by the state, some subset of their members—just like the activists in the small political

---

[46] Dobrokhotov, interview by author.

[47] The term originates with US Senator Lloyd Bentsen. See Rosemarie Ostler, *Slinging Mud: Rude Nicknames, Scurrilous Slogans, and Insulting Slang from Two Centuries of American Politics* (New York: Penguin Books, 2011).

[48] Dmitrii Grigor'evich Kamnev, "Molodezhnye politicheskie dvizheniia v sovremennoi Rossii: Avtoreferat dissertatsii na soiskanie uchenoi stepeni kandidata politicheskikh nauk" (Higher School of Economics, Moscow, 2009), 22, http://www.hse.ru/en/sci/diss/7791729.

opposition groups—were highly engaged politically and seemingly sincere in their beliefs. Anthropologist Julie Hemment, in an ethnographic study of Nashi members in Tver (a city about one hundred miles northwest of Moscow), conducted between 2006–2010, likewise found committed civic activists among Nashi members. These young people sought to apply their energies to what they saw as the betterment of Russian society, to promote political engagement, and to try to unseat corrupt officials.[49] However, the pro-Kremlin activists did this without appearing to question the leadership of the Putin administration. Hemment describes Nashi as an element of "state-initiated" civic organizing, a variant of what she labels "civil society" embraced by the Russian regime under Putin: "Based on the principle of sovereignty (gosu-darstvennost'), it advances a new vision of state/societal relations: civil society in the service of the nation or state."[50] While I define civil society differently, as an intermediary realm between citizens and the state, where citizens organize in their own interests and attempt to provide a check on the state's abuse of power—not as a terrain in which actors do the state's bidding—Hemment's perspective enables us to see the commonalities between some of the activists engaged in both types of organizations. Activists across the spectrum also populated the same relative age group and had been molded by the same set of political and economic events—though they reacted to them differently—and are to a large extent embedded in the same paradigm of gender norms.

In summer 2011, a decade into a renewed authoritarian trend in Russia, the pro-Kremlin groups enjoyed considerable budgetary and media dominance over the opposition groups. Groups on both sides largely used tactics that reflected their relative scale and political position. While the most visible pro-Kremlin group, Nashi, was capturing media attention with mass marches and politicized summer camps for activists, the considerably smaller liberal youth groups used creative direct actions to grab what media attention they could in an environment with shrinking press freedoms and publicized their efforts on the Web, largely on blogs and their organizations' websites.

Regardless of their origins and their political perspectives, groups on both sides were operating in the same political field. While some were the targets of regime repression and others the targets of taxpayer dollars redistributed by the regime, the organizations carried out their actions and attempted to gain popular attention and trust by framing their messages using culturally familiar concepts. Among these concepts were masculinity, femininity, and homophobia. As we shall see in

---

[49] Julie Hemment, "Nashi, Youth Voluntarism, and Potemkin NGOs: Making Sense of Civil Society in Post-Soviet Russia," *Slavic Review* 71, no. 2 (Summer 2012): 234–260.
[50] Ibid., 244–245.

the remainder of this chapter and in the one that follows, groups on both sides of the political continuum made use of gender norms as tools to build their own political legitimacy and undermine the perceived legitimacy of their opponents.

Loving the Leadership?: Political Youth Organizing for and against the Russian Regime

Pro- and anti-Kremlin groups clearly disagreed about the nature of the country's incumbent political leadership, centered on Vladimir Putin. While the pro-Kremlin organizations predictably exhibited appreciation for and support of Putin's leadership (both as president and as prime minister), youth organizations in the liberal opposition viewed Putin instead as the head of a corrupt, criminal, and anti-democratic regime. A brief survey of public actions by youth organizations readily reveals this distinction.

Mass gatherings in support of Putin's leadership, such as the early rally by Nashi's precursor, Walking Together, were a marker of the regime from the outset. Pro-Kremlin youth organizations continued to make their positive opinions of Putin resoundingly clear.[51] Witness the throngs of enthusiastic youth who greeted Putin at the Nashi-sponsored annual summer event, Camp Seliger[52] or the thousands of young people (including children) who marched with Molodaia Gvardiia in St. Petersburg, bearing flags with Putin's visage on May 1, 2011 under the banner "Youth for United Russia" (molodezh za Edinuiu Rossiiu!)[53] or the tens of thousands of Nashi, Stal' and other pro-Kremlin group participants who marched down Moscow's Sakharov Prospect in April 2011 for a state-sanctioned protest against corruption.[54] Activists supporting these organizations attribute Russia's recovery in the first decade of the twenty-first century to Putin, lauding the state's supposed reassertion of control over the oligarchs (widely perceived as having "stolen the state" in the 1990s), improvement in the population's economic standing, and the reinstatement of Russia's status as a global political and economic power to be reckoned

---

[51] Yashin, "Putin i politicheskaia pedofiliia" [video], May 3, 2011, http://yashin.livejournal.com/1027773.html. While the marchers may vote with their feet for Putin's regime, a number of children as well as adults questioned at these events (and captured on video) were unable to articulate the reasons why they supported Putin.

[52] Ilya Varlamov, "Fotoputeshestviia i eshche—Seliger," August 2, 2011, http://zyalt.livejournal.com/432712.html#cutid1.

[53] Yashin, "Putin i politicheskaia pedofiliia."

[54] "'Belye fartuki' na prospekte Sakharova," Echo Moskvy, April 16, 2011, http://www.echo.msk.ru/blog/echomsk/766717-echo/; Ilya Epishkin, "Belye fartuki," On Life, April 16, 2011, http://bit.ly/TrIohX.

with.[55] In 2008, a national public opinion poll found that a whopping 92 percent of 18 to 24 year olds supported Putin and his policies.[56]

Meanwhile, anti-Kremlin youth activists had not mobilized large numbers of Putin opponents, relying instead on small, provocative actions that illustrated their perspective. In November 2009, for instance, Oborona activists handed out leaflets with an unflattering portrait of Putin (eyes crossed, apparently examining a fly on the tip of his nose) and the headline, "A fish rots from the head!" The flyers called on Putin—as the chief of a corrupt political regime—to resign. Passersby regarded a sculpture on display at the event, embodying the protesters' message: on a table rested the body of a fish with a clay head designed to look like Putin, being fed upon by yellow clay worms.[57] Rather than praising Putin's stewardship of the economy and political system, opposition youth activists accused him of fostering the "disintegration of democracy" in Russia.[58] Instead of encouraging Putin to continue in power, anti-Kremlin activists voiced their preference for his retirement.

Other actions highlighted opposition activists' belief that a prison cell would be a more fitting location for Prime Minister Putin than the "White House," the seat of Russia's government. In December 2010, proclaiming, "Freedom to Khodorkovsky—Bread and Water for Putin!" (Khodorkovskomu—svobodu! Putina—na khleb i vodu), a group of Oborona activists in Moscow protested against the second sentencing of the already imprisoned businessman Mikhail Khodorkovsky and proposed that Putin should be jailed in his stead. With the Russian government building as a backdrop, the activists quickly created a "jail cell" using construction fencing and "imprisoned" one of their own—a female activist, wearing a rather convincing Putin mask—inside it. When federal security forces approached, the activists took off, prompting a most unlikely chase scene, as the police, brandishing weapons, yelled for "Putin" to stop his flight.[59] One participant in the action described

[55] Armine Ishkanian, "Nashi: Russia's Youth Counter-Movement," August 3, 2007, http://www.opendemocracy.net/article/democracy_power/politics_protest/russia_nashi.

[56] Christa Case Bryant, "Nashi and the Young Guard: Two Paths toward Building Support for Putin," February 26, 2008, http://www.csmonitor.com/World/Europe/2008/0226/p13s01-woeu.html.

[57] Eva Brauning, "Chudo-iudo ryba-Putin sgnila s golovy," Ekaterinburg NEWS, November 28, 2009, http://www.eburgnews.ru/photoreport/1607.html; International Center on Nonviolent Conflict, "On the Ground Interview with Oleg Kozlovsky" [video], January 7, 2011, http://www.youtube.com/watch?feature=player_embedded&v=ef2Oue76xGQ#at=310. The rotting fish protest can be seen on the interview video at 5:08.

[58] International Center on Nonviolent Conflict, "On the Ground Interview with Oleg Kozlovsky."

[59] Polosatiy_ez, "Pod gorbatym mostom poimali Putina s khvostom," December 27, 2010, http://polosatiy-ez.livejournal.com/19875.html.

its conclusion: "They're yelling, 'Stop!' (Stoiat'!) And it was really funny for me to see Putin running at full speed, away from the White House, while they're yelling, 'Stop! Freeze! Or we'll shoot!' That was one of my favorite actions."[60] Likewise, in February 2011, a handful of protesters with We hung a large banner from a Moscow bridge next to Red Square, displaying a photograph of Putin on the right and Mikhail Khodorkovsky on the left, proclaiming, simply, "It's time to switch!" (pora meniat'sia).[61]

Which Leaders Are Macho and Which Leaders Are Gay? Constructing Political Masculinity and Femininity

One way to shed analytical light on political groups' support or disparagement of political leaders is to examine the ways in which those groups use masculinity, femininity, and homophobia in their proclamations and propaganda. This section considers how political actors in Russia have used gender norms to try to affirm and undermine regime leaders' and opposition leaders' perceived legitimacy.

The calendars mentioned at the outset of this chapter are among a series of blatantly gendered moves within Russia's political arena in recent years. However, political organizations in Russia have been using sexualized images of women as political currency for some time. As early as the 1990s, the National Bolshevik Party (NBP)—a politically peculiar animal combining far left and far right elements—posted photographs of male activists' purported "girlfriends" in NBP leader Eduard Limonov's newspaper, *Limonka*.[62] Labeled "Nashi Boevye Podrugi" (also NBP) or "Our Battle-Ready Girlfriends," they later appeared on the NBP's website in a range of poses and stages of undress. The images ranged stylistically from the more or less traditional feminine portrayal of a young woman surrounded by flowers (albeit with a leather studded wrist cuff) to soft-porn depictions (one woman, clad in a velvet dress, is shown revealing one breast, complete with nipple, and a grenade [the NBP party symbol] tattooed on her shoulder). Other photos portrayed pairs of young women, stripped to the waist, in the lesbian duo so

---

[60] Shaginurov, interview by author, 2011.

[61] Andy Potts, "Putin Invited to Swap Places with Khodorkovsky," *The Moscow News*, February 21, 2011, http://themoscownews.com/politics/20110221/188435044.html?referfrommn.

[62] I thank Mischa Gabowitsch for bringing to my attention this early manifestation of the NBP's sexualized recruitment imagery, as well as its later incarnation on the web. Mischa Gabowitsch, personal communication, July 20, 2011.

familiar in heterosexual male pornography, as well as fully clothed young women attending NBP rallies.[63]

While displays of women's bodies in this way could serve as an organizational recruitment tool (for men and women alike), they also send messages about the masculinity of the male political leaders with whom the women are ostensibly affiliated. Viewed in this way, the "Happy Birthday, Mr. Putin!" calendar featuring Moscow State University journalism students served not only to publicly assert Putin's support from a group of young women but also to highlight Putin's machismo. Whether his machismo in the calendar case was being accentuated specifically by a particular organization, however, is unclear, as the provenance of the calendar has been disputed. Although Nashi technically denied responsibility for producing the calendar, Ksenia Basilashvili, the talk show host of an independent radio station program, said the calendar project was "initiated" by Nashi.[64] Vladimir Tabak, himself a graduate of Moscow State University's journalism department, ran the publishing house that printed the calendar and was also said to be an employee of the Russian government's Federal Youth Affairs Agency (Rosmolodezh), headed by Nashi's former leader, Vasilii Iakemenko.[65] Whether Nashi was involved or not, their spokeswoman (the organization's press secretary, Kristina Potupchik, who was also a spokesperson for Rosmolodezh),[66] announced and embraced the calendar's publication on her blog. The caption accompanying her photo of the calendar (shown for sale in a bin among other calendars) stated, "Having heard the hullabaloo, I went over to Ashan [a retail chain superstore in Moscow] and bought multiple copies, just in case."[67]

Whether Putin took the gift as a collective outpouring of support from Nashi or as the pleasant caprice of a dozen female fans, he responded to it favorably. In an interview with supermodel Naomi Campbell, Putin asserted, "I like the girls a lot, they are beautiful," adding that "they were courageous and they weren't scared."[68] What the students had to be scared of is not entirely clear; the

[63] "NBP-Info, "Nashi boevye podrugi," http://bit.ly/1paAdR4, accessed April 2, 2009.

[64] "Kseniia Basilashvili Interview of Maksim Shevchenko," October 7, 2010.

[65] Oleg Kozlovsky, "Controversial Sexy Gift for Putin and the Future of Russian Journalism," *Huffington Post*, October 7, 2010, http://www.huffingtonpost.com/oleg-kozlovsky/controversial-sexy-gift-f_b_753952.html; Julia Ioffe, "Happy Birthday, Mr. President (NSFW)," https://themoscowdiaries.wordpress.com/2010/10/06/happy-birthday-mr-president/, accessed July 27, 2011.

[66] Mikhail Zubov, "Lift Iakemenko," *Moskovskii Komsomolets*, December 1, 2010, http://www.mk.ru/politics/article/2010/11/30/548359-lift-yakemenko.html.

[67] Potupchik, "Devushki zhurfaka MGU razdelis' dlia Putina."

[68] Alina Lobzina, "When Naomi Met Vladimir—Supermodel Interviews Putin," *The Moscow News*, February 1, 2011, http://themoscownews.com/politics/20110201/188382669.html.

dean of the Journalism Department, Elena Vartanova, while decrying the calendar's use of the department's name, stated that the young women would not
be punished for their actions.[69] By contrast, after the regime-criticizing response calendar appeared on the Internet, Federal Security Service (FSB) personnel reportedly visited the department to read professors' email, because, as
one journalism department student had heard, "they were sure that one of the
professors had come up with the idea, and had put the students up to it."[70]

As discussed in Chapter 2, a key element of Putin's legitimation strategy has
been the cultivation of a macho image. His various public relations stunts sub-
duing wild animals, playing rough sports, displaying his muscular torso, serving as an honorary firefighter to help save Moscow from a spate of threatening
wildfires, and the like drew on widely familiar ideas about masculinity. The
purpose was to portray Putin as a strong, decisive leader who could be counted
upon to solve challenging problems with a convincing mixture of cool level-
headedness and the credible threat to use force as needed.

But while hegemonic masculinity is earned—or conferred—through such
displays, it is also conferred or, in something of a cyclical fashion, reinforced
and enhanced by the attention of traditionally feminine, attractive young
women. Putin's birthday calendar was only one element in a larger propagandistic campaign with machismo at its center. One opposition activist with
Oborona explained the calendar in this context:

> It's an attempt to show how macho the political leader is. It's about
> *him*. There was even a [pop] song about wanting a man like Putin. It's
> an attempt to put out a "brand": "What kind of political leader do you
> want? You don't know much about politics, but you're supporting a
> cool dude (klevogo parnia), a cool guy (klevogo muzhika), a real
> tough guy (muzhik). He flies planes, sails submarines, and the ladies
> love him (tetki ego liubiat). So, you see [what a great guy he is]?" He's
> like the hero in American films. It's basically the same thing as when
> they put Arnold Schwarzenegger forward to be the governor of Cali-
> fornia: "Here's your brand."[71]

In short, clues like the calendar, with its desirable women offering themselves
to Putin (voting with their bodies), help instruct the average voter in understanding political masculinity. The right leader is the most macho leader. In

[69] "The Heads of the Moscow State University Didn't Appreciate Putin's Saucy Congratulation,"
NewsBCM, October 17, 2010, http://bit.ly/1j69yjb.

[70] Kichanova, interview by author.

[71] Shaginurov, interview by author, 2011.

that sense, Putin's actions, as well as women's endorsement, constitute evidence of Putin's normative, hegemonic masculinity.

Further evidence of this political masculinity and femininity emerged in the wake of the calendars and as the parliamentary and presidential elections of 2011 and 2012 approached. In July 2011, a video clip called "Putin's Army" (Armiia Putina) went viral on the Web.[72] A cleavage-boasting, stiletto-heeled young woman named Diana strides through the clip, regaling viewers with her appreciation for Putin as she fondles her iPhone. "In addition to being a worthy politician, he's a classy man" (shikarnyi muzhchina), she declares. Millions of people are crazy about him, she assures us, except a handful of people who want to smear him with dirt—perhaps out of jealousy that they will never "be in his position." Ultimately, Diana meets up with two of her friends and explains that they are among the "young, smart, and beautiful" women of Putin's Army, who are starting a competition called "I'll Rip [it] for Putin" (porvu za Putina). The film ends with Diana tearing her white tank top in two, while asking viewers, "What are you prepared to do for your president?"—a question made only slightly more peculiar in that context by the fact that Russia's president was, at the time the clip was made, Dmitrii Medvedev.[73]

Rip it for Putin contestants proceeded to post their own videos on the Web. The first contender was a martial artist who filmed herself initially wearing a low cut black dress and heels and then outfitted in a martial arts uniform and using a sword, fighting an imaginary opponent. As she fought, she ruminated aloud about Putin, noting that he was an "ideal man" and concluding, "[probably] I'm just in love with him." The video emphasized her femininity with a close-up of her cleavage intercut with a fighting sequence and visually reassured viewers that the contestant appreciated "typical" female symbols by showing her stopping to smell some flowers as she walked down the street. "What I am prepared to do for him?" the contestant asks, followed by a cut to her performing a succession of boxing moves, which end with her grinning and saying, "I'll rip for Putin." The implication was that she could be relied upon to

---

[72] It seems likely that Putin's Army was inspired by the comedy videos "Crush on Obama" and "Super Obama Girl!" produced in the United States in the run-up to the 2008 presidential election. Obama Girl—like the star of the Putin's Army video—tears off her suit jacket to reveal a white midriff-bearing t-shirt with Obama's portrait emblazoned on it. See Barelypolitical, "Crush On Obama" [video] June 13, 2007, http://www.youtube.com/watch?v=wKsoXHYICqU, and Barelypolitical, "Super Obama Girl!" [video], January 31, 2008, http://www.youtube.com/watch?NR=1&v=AIiMa2Fe-ZQ&feature=pinned.

[73] "Porvu za Putina!" [video], July 13, 2011, http://www.youtube.com/watch?v=1Easr8WTwxs; Julia Ioffe, "Taking It Off for Putin," *The New Yorker*, July 21, 2011, http://www.newyorker.com/online/blogs/newsdesk/2011/07/putins-army.html; Goscilo, "Putin's Performance of Masculinity," 196, 198.

rip up some*one*—rather than some*thing*—if need be.[74] The second entrant was a skinny woman in a black dress, shown entering a building, taking an elevator, and then walking up to the roof, where she removed a handful of dollars from a money-packed metal briefcase, tore them in half, and released them like confetti into the street below.[75] In October 2011, Putin's Army continued its activity by filming a video for Putin's fifty-ninth birthday. Promising that their birthday gift would be "the sweetest," a handful of women from the group were shown baking their idol a chocolate birthday cake (decorated with a heart) while wearing white button-down shirts and underpants and squirting whipped cream into their mouths.[76]

Putin's outwardly confirmed masculinity was further bolstered by a July 2011 "car wash for Putin event," where bikini-clad young women from a pro-Putin group titled "I Really Do Like Putin," promised to wash Russian-made cars (for which Putin had voiced his support) for free at the scenic location of Moscow's Sparrow Hills.[77] The promotional ad for the event showed Putin sitting behind the wheel of a car while a young woman in a bikini top and daisy dukes sponged his windshield. Masculinity, reinforced by the adoring and highly sexualized femininity projected by Putin's Army, the Moscow State University birthday calendar women, and the bikini-boasting car washers was Putin's political trademark.

Putin's Army and "I Really Do Like Putin," both with presences on social networking sites in addition to their occasional "live" actions, were at the time assumed to have government sponsorship, though the Kremlin denied having a direct connection to the organizations.[78] As mentioned in the previous chapter,

---

[74] ArmiaPutina, "Armiia Putina—Konkursantka No. 1" [video], July 22, 2011, https://www.youtube.com/watch?v=1DoEjxMKMdk&feature=relmfu.

[75] ArmiaPutina, "Armiia Putina—Konkursantka No. 2" [video], July 24, 2011, https://www.youtube.com/watch?v=PtmOVMQMffs&feature=relmfu.

[76] ArmiaPutina, "Tortik dlia Putina! Chocolate cake!" [video], October 6, 2011, https://www.youtube.com/watch?v=rVCiwYqX180; Anna Arutunyan, "Birthday Craze Sweeps Moscow," *The Moscow News*, October 10, 2011, http://themoscownews.com/politics/20111010/189110902.html.

[77] Gruppa "Mne real'no nravitsia Putin," "Otkrytie "aVVtomoiki,'" July 21, 2011, http://forsmi.ru/announce/38308/; "Scantily-Clad Girls in Putin's 'Army' Wash Russian-Made Cars" [video], July 21, 2011, http://www.youtube.com/watch?v=aOe4JRry5j8&feature=player_embedded. Although the Russia Today broadcast states that the car wash was a Putin's Army event, it was in fact sponsored by a group on the Russian social networking site, VKontakte, which has held other events including a nonspontaneous "flash-mob" where a group of young people (male and female) publicly sang "Blueberry Hill" (a song that Putin had sung for a Hollywood fundraiser in 2010). See "Singing PM: 'Fats' Putin over the Top of 'Blueberry Hill' with Piano Solo" [video], December 11, 2010, http://www.youtube.com/watch?v=IV4IjHz2yIo.

[78] Arutunyan, "Birthday Craze Sweeps Moscow."

when the email accounts of several people connected with the pro-Kremlin group Nashi were hacked the following year, the exposed emails—sent among Nashi leader Nikita Borovikov, Kristina Potupchik (Nashi's outspoken press secretary), and Vasilii Iakemenko, who had originally headed Nashi and was, at the time, running the Federal Agency for Youth Affairs – provided evidence that Putin's Army and the "I Really Do Like Putin" group were both Nashi ventures.[79] Nashi had also disbursed large sums of taxpayer money to Internet "trolls"—people paid to post positive comments about the Putin regime and its allies, such as Nashi itself, and negative comments about representatives of the opposition. It had also spent over ten million rubles (about $300,000) on positive media coverage of the state-sponsored political-patriotic education camp, Seliger.[80] Moreover, the emails revealed Internet tactics consistent with using female sexualization as a means to promote Putin's popularity. In one email, Potupchik instructed Nashi-friendly bloggers to grow their readership by posting humorous content along with pictures of buxom women "willing to pose in underwear."[81]

A few weeks after Diana exhibited her eagerness to ruin a tank top for Putin, a low-budget clip echoing the "I'll Rip It for Putin" campaign emerged in support of Russia's President, Dmitrii Medvedev.[82] This, too, turned out to be a Nashi-sponsored endeavor.[83] In the video, two young women in low-cut tank tops and short-shorts with stiletto heels explained that they, having heard of Putin's Army, "decided to create our own women's brigade" (zhenskii otriad) to support the president. "You can call us "Medvedev Gerlz," explains one, using the English word, "girls." The Medvedev Girls proceeded to declare their readiness "to do anything for Dmitrii Anatol'evich," including supporting his recent signature on a Russian law categorizing beer as an alcoholic drink and outlawing public beer consumption starting in 2013.[84] But 2013 could not

[79] Elder, "Polishing Putin"; Kremlingate, "Razmeshchenie prokremlevskogo kontenta v internete," February 3, 2012, http://lj.rossia.org/users/kremlingate/1166.html.

[80] Victor Davidoff, "Kremlin's Youth Agency Resembles Cosa Nostra," *The Moscow Times*, February 12, 2012, http://www.themoscowtimes.com/opinion/article/kremlins-youth-agency-resembles-cosa-nostra/452893.html; Kremlingate, "Proplachennoe v gazetakh pravil'noe osveshchenie Seligera."

[81] Rolf Fredheim, "Quantifying Memory: Putin's Bot Army—Part Two: Nashi's Online Campaign (and Undesirable Bots)," June 2013, http://quantifyingmemory.blogspot.com/2013/06/putins-bot-army-part-two.html.

[82] solar2000, "Medvedev Girls" [video], August 3, 2011, http://www.youtube.com/watch?v=mLdoJb4mOXM.

[83] Fredheim, "Quantifying Memory."

[84] The law took effect on January 1, 2013. Jim Heintz, "Russia Rings in New Year with Ban on Kiosk Beer Sales," *The Globe and Mail*, January 1, 2013, http://russialist.org/newslink-russia-rings-in-new-year-with-ban-on-kiosk-beer-sales/.

come soon enough for the Medvedev Girls, who decided to teach people not to drink in public, starting immediately. "The time has come for you to make a choice," smiled the shorter of the two. "Beer or us!" continued the other, lifting up her shirt to the bustline and exposing her midriff, on which was superimposed the announcement of an event on August 4, in Moscow's Novopushkinskii Square, where participants would be able "to see the continuation" of the action. The promised continuation turned out to be a strip tease, where three Medvedev Girls removed articles of clothing down to their bikinis, in exchange for men pouring out their beers into a bucket and thus renouncing—temporarily—their public drinking habits.[85] Asserting that they were not getting undressed *for* Medvedev but rather to distract public beer drinkers from their typical pastime, the participants in the event thus claimed to distinguish themselves somewhat from the young women who had evinced their support for Putin more explicitly.[86] However, the Medvedev Girls had earlier carried out an event (without acquiring police permission), where women in Gorky Park were invited to freshen their lipstick and kiss a cardboard cutout of Medvedev, suggesting that he, too, was a plausible object of female attention.[87] These sexualized expressions of fondness should not be construed as an attempt by Medvedev (or his fans) to "out-macho" Putin and thus to portray the former as a competitor for the role of top political leader in Russia. Indeed, according to its description, the Web-based social networking group "Medvedev Is Our President" (which spawned the Medvedev Girls) posed "no goals at all" and thus should not be construed as an enterprise supporting Medvedev for president over Putin, for example.[88]

In a further indication that none of these events was symbolic of some kind of actual political competition between Putin and Medvedev, on August 8, 2011, eight supporters of the groups, "Medvedev Is Our President" and "I

---

[85] Alina Lobzina, "Stripping for Beer and Medvedev," *The Moscow News*, August 4, 2011, http://themoscownews.com/politics/20110804/188898817.html; "Medvedev's Female Fans Strip for Anti-Booze Law," August 4, 2011, http://rt.com/news/girls-medvedev-striptease-beer/.

[86] Lobzina, "Stripping for Beer and Medvedev."

[87] Tom Washington, "Puckering Up for Russia's President," *The Moscow News*, July 7, 2011, http://themoscownews.com/politics/20110707/188818857.html.

[88] MedvedevGroup, "Medvedev—nash Prezident!," http://vkontakte.ru/medvedev_group, accessed August 3, 2011. For Medvedev's birthday in September 2011, a group of five Medvedev Girls, dressed in cheerleading outfits and against the backdrop of Red Square, sang Marilyn Monroe's version of "Happy Birthday, Mr. President" in his honor. One young woman declared Medvedev the "best president ever elected," coming closer to an overt endorsement of Medvedev over Putin for president in 2012. See "Cheerleaders Wish Medvedev Happy Birthday," *Herald Sun*, September 14, 2011, http://www.heraldsun.com.au/news/breaking-news/cheerleaders-wish-medvedev-happy-birthday/story-e6frf7jx-1226137424712.

Really Do Like Putin" climbed onto four tandem bicycles and rode from the Kremlin to the Russian White House (young men sat in front, and young women behind). Further wrapping up the loose ends of the noncompetition, this physical embodiment of support for the Putin–Medvedev "tandem" leadership package was apparently sponsored by the creators of the "Happy Birthday, Mr. Putin" calendar, who paid to rent the tandem bikes for the event.[89]

Adding to the trend of video clips sexualizing young women's political support, in early August 2011 members of Eduard Limonov's aforementioned NBP responded to the emergence of Putin's Army with a somewhat sinister clip reminiscent of the US television show *Charlie's Angels*. The video was not an official NBP project: it was initiated by the wife of an NBP activist, but the women featured were actual members of the party.[90] Posted on YouTube, the video shows three slender young women in black, sleeveless minidresses, heels, and dark glasses, who enter a building, pull out handguns, and shoot little wooden bear-shaped effigies labeled "The Party of Crooks and Thieves" (the moniker that the political opposition has adopted for the ruling party, United Russia), while explaining that Putin has discredited himself as a politician and should leave power. Instead of calling Charlie afterward, however, the three young women rip the necklines of their dresses to reveal white tank tops inscribed not with Diana's lipsticked slogans and kisses but with a sketched hand grenade—the symbol of Limonov's party.[91] The clip, with this clear allusion to its Putin's Army predecessor, retains the traditionally feminine and sexualized elements of the previous clips (the minidresses, the suggestive fleshy revelations) but also shows the women firing handguns, an activity more traditionally coded masculine. In that sense, the clip was an effort to defy Putin and his monopolistic claim to political power. The fact that this challenge was offered by young women bearing firearms also suggests an indirect challenge to Putin's theoretical monopoly on masculine toughness.

The effective use of femininity to enhance regime leaders' perceived masculinity hinges on a concurrent depreciation of any femininity deployed by the opposition. To that end, a blog post by Nashi's press secretary, Kristina Potupchik, commenting on the Moscow State University birthday calendar, included an unfavorable comparison between the Moscow State University journalism

[89] "Poklonniki i poklonnitsy Dmitriia Medvedeva i Vladimira Putina na velosipedakh-tandemakh prokatilis' ot Kremlia k Belomu Domu," August 8, 2011, http://www.echo.msk.ru/news/800631-echo.html; "Molodye storonniki rossiiskogo duumvirata reshili segodnia udarit' veloprobegom za prezidenta Medvedeva i prem'era Putina," August 8, 2011, http://www.echo.msk.ru/news/800580-echo.html.

[90] Aleksandra Kachko, Drugaia Rossiia, interview by author, St. Petersburg, June 15, 2012.

[91] Fltvstudio, "Razgrom armii Putina" [video], August 4, 2011, http://www.youtube.com/watch?feature=player_embedded&v=VviBzQ9VVhc.

department "beauties" (krasavitsy) and the "flat chested" women of Femen—a women's group in Ukraine that has protested topless against the sex industry and also against Putin and Russian influence in Ukraine.[92] For instance, in an October 2010 outdoor protest during a visit by Putin to Kiev, six Femen members revealed posters (and their breasts) on an inclement fall day in a Kiev public square featuring a statue of Lenin, while chanting, "Fuck Alina, Not Ukraine!"[93]

Likewise, Internet commentary on the attractiveness of the women photographed for the two calendars emerging from the Moscow State University journalism department included critiques of their appearance and occasionally branded the "Happy Birthday" calendar women as prostitutes or sluts (identifying them as embodying a "pariah femininity" rather than the traditional variant).[94] Commentary on one blog post where photographs of the "alternative" calendar could be found included a lively dialogue about whether the women on the "birthday" calendar or the response calendar were better looking. In general, commenters there sought to contradict critical evaluations of the response calendar women's appearance (probably because most of the blogger's readers were inclined toward liberal political positions). Witness the following exchange:

> October 7, 2010, 16:36 the pretty ones are for putin; the ugly ones are against [him] (krasivye za putina, strashnen'kie—protiv)

> October 8, 2010, 14:50 [responding to: "the pretty ones are for putin; the ugly ones are against"] Maybe first you should learn the difference between BEAUTY and PORN? (Mozhet s nachala vy nauchites' razlichat' krasotu ot porno?)

> October 7, 2010, 19:05 [responding to: "the pretty ones are for putin"] What lowbrow taste you have.... (Kakoi u vas nepritiazatel'nyi vkus....)[95]

The credibility of the birthday calendar women as journalists was also put into question. Russian satirist Viktor Shenderovich, interviewed on the independent

[92] Kristina Potupchik, "Devushki zhurfaka MGU razdelis' dlia Putina," October 6, 2010, http://krispotupchik.livejournal.com/92592.html.

[93] Femen, "Ucraina: In topless contro Putin" [video], October 27, 2010, http://www.youtube.com/watch?v=jsh0jGk2PnU, accessed November 10, 2010. The Alina in question was a Russian rhythmic gymnast rumored to be romantically involved with Putin.

[94] See, for example, the comments on these sites: Elizabeth Menschikova, "O zhurnalistakh, kotorye s zhurfaka MGU," October 7, 2010, http://liz-anderson.livejournal.com/76145.html; Sasha Utkin, "Kalendar,'" October 7, 2010, http://sasha-utkin.livejournal.com/. On "pariah femininities" see Schipper, "Recovering the Feminine Other."

[95] Il'ya Varlamov, "'Kogda sleduiushchii terakt?'—Kalendar' dlia prem'era/Kommentarii," October 7, 2010, http://www.echo.msk.ru/blog/varlamov_i/716443-echo/.

radio station, Ekho Moskvy, the day after the first calendar's release, summed it up in a memorable phrase: "As for these students, of course it's more about fucking than it is about journalism" (eto, konechno, ne stol'ko ZHUR, skol'ko FAK).[96] And finally, the female voiceover for the Limonov NBP video began by referring to Putin's Army as being a collection of "cheap chicks" (deshevye kurochki) and to themselves, by contrast, as "young, successful women (devushki) [who] have already drawn our conclusions," namely, that eleven years of rule by Putin, Medvedev, and the oligarchs whom they shelter had led to levels of corruption that were going to result in Russia disappearing from the world stage.[97] Insulting a male politician's female fans—particularly by devaluing their femininity and proper womanhood ("sluts," "prostitutes")—is an attempt to lower that male politician's own status and legitimacy.

Similarly, after the "I'll Rip It for Putin" video emerged, pro-Kremlin Molodaia Gvardiia activist-turned-Moscow-City-council-member, Kirill Shchitov, mused on his blog about why attractive young women (such as those in the video) weren't showing their support in similar ways for opposition leaders. "How come we've never seen successful, attractive young women, joining together in the opposition's ranks? Apparently, they bypass [the opposition]. It'd be interesting to know: why is that? Is it [the opposition's] ideas, slogans, or leaders that fail to entice them?"[98] Shchitov's rumination implied that men in the opposition lacked the support of successful, attractive women because they themselves were insufficiently masculine to attract such supporters, while also suggesting that opposition women were simply not as attractive as those on the pro-Kremlin side.[99] Meanwhile, opposition activists asserted their own perspective on Putin's Army. Veronika Belozerskikh, a member of Molodezhnoe Yabloko's Moscow-based regional council, penned a response (accompanied by an attractive photograph of herself) explaining—in part—why "young and educated young women (devushki) should be ashamed to be filmed" for the "devushki for Putin" genre.[100] For her, Putin stood not as an admirable manly man but as a symbol of the administration's "patriarchal policies," its "sex-based

---

[96] "Kseniia Basilashvili Interview with Viktor Shenderovich," October 7, 2010, http://www.echo.msk.ru/programs/personalno/716199-echo/. The phrase is less clunky and more clever in Russian than in English, since "Journalism Department" is abbreviated "zhurfak" (fakul'tet zhurnalistiki) allowing Shenderovich to combine the Russian abbreviation for "journalism" along with the English word "fuck."

[97] f1tvstudio, "Razgrom armii Putina."

[98] Kirill Shchitov, "Devushki porvut za Putina," July 17, 2011, http://kirillschitov.livejournal.com/211912.html.

[99] Ibid.

[100] Veronika Belozerskikh, "Ia protiv armii putina," *Molodezhnoe Iabloko*, July 18, 2011, http://www.yabloko.ru/blog/2011/07/18_1.

discrimination," and its propagation of women's economic dependence on men. Belozerskikh also noted that one of the women in the "I'll Rip It for Putin" film had been identified as the 16-year-old sister of a Nashi activist, subtly accusing the pro-Kremlin youth group's filmmakers of inappropriately sexually exploiting the femininity of a minor for political purposes.

Like femininity, homophobia can also be wielded as a political tool aimed at male political leaders' masculinity but with the intent to undermine rather than enhance the target's legitimacy.[101] Homophobia as a political instrument relies on the involuntary rescinding of someone's masculinity, thereby "feminizing" the man and reducing his societal authority. It has been used by Russian youth organizations and other political actors, both liberal and pro-Kremlin.

Pro-Kremlin organizations have painted male political opposition leaders as unmasculine and sexually "deviant" in a variety of ways. In explaining this tactic, it is useful to recall that one element of national identity consists of the images of masculinity and femininity seen as typical in one's own national group ("Us") and in national groups beyond those community borders ("Them"). In a national comparison or conflict, one's own side's "gender order, as a rule, is represented as the norm, while the gender order of the Others is represented as being deviant (Our men are the most manly; Our women are the most feminine)." This is true not only of political comparisons or competition across ethnic or national lines but also of those across political lines *internal* to a country.[102]

In addition to painting one's political opponents as gay and therefore deviant from the heterosexual norm, deviance is implied by metaphors of prostitution.[103] A march in April 2007 by the strange-bedfellows opposition coalition, "The Other Russia"—which includes self-declared "National Bolsheviks" such as Eduard Limonov as well as mainstream opposition liberals like former chess champion Garry Kasparov—was met by pro-Kremlin youth activists carrying signs accusing the marchers of being funded and coopted by Russia's enemies in the West: "Greetings to the March of Political Prostitutes Bought with Western Currency!" (politicheskikh valiutnykh prostitutok).[104] In similar fashion, at the state-sponsored camp organized for pro-Kremlin youth that

---

[101] Homophobia can also be used against female political leaders (the imputation of lesbianism), but since the candidates for Russia's top political positions (both those in power and in the opposition) are men, I focus here on the use of anti-gay homophobic messaging.

[102] Riabova and Riabov, "Nastoiashchii muzhchina Rossiiskoi politiki?," 53.

[103] Ibid., 60.

[104] Ibid. "Valiutnaia prostitutka" is the term used to describe Soviet/Russian prostitutes who were paid in Western currency, when rubles were not yet convertible currency on the world market.

summer, a large poster exhibit of three male opposition leaders (Mikhail Kasy-anov, Garry Kasparov, and Eduard Limonov) portrayed their faces photo-shopped onto apparently female bodies clad in bustiers and thigh-high stock-ings. Labeled the "Red Light District," the installation's purpose was to renounce the opposition visually as a bunch of prostitutes who had "sold out" Russia to the West and to make the male opposition leadership out to look like low-status drag queens.[105] The theme of Russian prostitutes plying their wares specifically to foreigners became a motif in late-Soviet films and novels, serv-ing as a precursor to the image of "political prostitution" on display at Camp Seliger.[106]

The portrayal of male opposition figures as transvestite prostitutes can be usefully contrasted to the images of the women photographed for the first Moscow State University calendar, who showed off their bodies in the same kinds of outfits. Those in power used images of allied women that highlighted the sexuality and femininity of the latter, thus enhancing the masculinity of the political ruling group to which these women were committed. Likewise, the male opposition was attacked as transvestites to show that the opposition was insufficiently or inappropriately masculine (i.e., was feminized). In short, the pro-Kremlin organizations that created such pictorial political propaganda were using sexism and homophobia to tarnish the opposition's masculinity while highlighting Putin's masculinity and the desirability and femininity of the women who supported him.

One joke (posted in the comment section of a liberal radio station's website) about the Russian political scene neatly sums up the pro-Kremlin condemna-tion of liberal oppositionists in deviant sexual and homophobic terms (in this case, by hypersexualizing liberal women and labeling liberal men as gay):

> A teacher walks into class. "My name is Oleg Petrovich, and I'm a lib-eral. Children, please take turns introducing yourselves the way I did."
>
> "My name is Masha, and I'm a liberal."

---

[105] Maksim Stribnyi, "Ulitsa krasnykh fonarei na Seligere," August 17, 2007, http://mc-masters.livejournal.com/394646.html; Alexander Osipovich, "Lectures, Red-Light District at Nashi Camp," *St. Petersburg Times*, July 24, 2007, http://www.sptimes.ru/index.php?action_ id=2&story_id=22425. Portraying one's political opponents as transvestites is not unique to Russia; one human rights activist in South Korea sends propagandistic DVDs over the border to North Korea, which include cartoons of the North Korean leader Kim Jong-Il "as a stiletto-heeled transvestite, spilling out of a bustier." See Mark McDonald, "Balloon-Borne Messages to North Korea Have Detractors on Both Sides of Border," *New York Times*, April 26, 2011, http://www.nytimes.com/2011/04/27/world/asia/27iht-korea.html.

[106] Helena Goscilo, *Dehexing Sex: Russian Womanhood during and after Glasnost* (Ann Arbor: University of Michigan Press, 1996), 42–44.

"My name is Stepa, and I'm a liberal."

"My name is Vovochka, and I'm a Stalinist." [Note that Vovochka is a diminutive for Putin's first name, Vladimir.]

"Vovochka!" cries the teacher. "Why are you a Stalinist?"

"My mom is a Stalinist, my dad is a Stalinist, my friends are Stalinists, and I'm a Stalinist, too," he responds.

"Vovochka, what if your mom were a prostitute, your dad were a drug addict, your sister were a slut, and your friends were gays—then what would you be?" the teacher asks.

"Then I would be a liberal."[107]

Regime supporters have been eager to wield homophobia against the liberal opposition. After the violent dispersal of an attempted gay pride event in Moscow on May 28, 2011, when activists in the anti-regime group, Oborona, were prompted to discuss LGBT discrimination on their website in an effort to reach a position on the topic, regime-supporters at opposition demonstrations just a few days later began to attack them with homophobic comments:

> Literally, there were just a couple of posts [about LGBT discrimination] on our site. But just after that, it was the 31st [of the month] and there were [opposition] actions all over the country.[108] We went out [to protest] in Moscow, and we were detained and put in a police vehicle (avtozak). And they put a provocateur in there with us. He seemed to be a provocateur; he kept saying, "Oborona is all faggots (pidery) and gay activists, and I know that 50 percent of your activists are gay." We didn't know whether he was a provocateur or not, but later we found out that some [of our] folks (rebiata) were in Kirov, and they also had gone to an action, and someone came up to them, too, and said, "You're gay activists, you're homosexuals." That is, it was obvious that people had been constantly looking at our site; these questionable individuals [meaning provocateurs] had made an appearance

[107] "Skandal v efire: Dobrokhotov vs Kurginian" [video], December 17, 2008, http://www.youtube.com/watch?v=-tw_yd9srGQ.

[108] Starting in 2009, the opposition coalition, Strategy 31, has held protest actions on the 31st day of each month that has 31 days, to demand that Article 31 of the Russian Constitution (freedom of assembly) be honored.

in two cities already. And it was very strange to us; he [the provoca-
teur] had this constant verbal diarrhea (slovesnii ponos postoiannyi).
Judging by everything that happened, he was provoking us so that
we'd beat him up, so that they could bring a criminal action against
us. And the cops themselves started saying, "Shut him up!" And we
were saying [sarcastically]: "In front of the cameras, in front of you,
yes, let's go beat him up." That is, they were trying to provoke us to
beat him up, right there in the vehicle. So the topic of homosexuality
is a dangerous one here. You get these kinds of frame-ups.[109]

Other opponents of Putin's regime have also fallen victim to homophobic
campaigns. After his election in 2011, Artem Samsonov, a 38-year old Communist Party deputy in the legislature of one of Russia's far East regions, felt it
necessary to go to court to defend his honor and reputation when various
photos appeared on the Web purporting to show him wearing a "woman's
dress," kissing a man, and with his underwear pulled down. He sued for 5.5
million rubles and argued that his political opponents (i.e., regime supporters)
were behind the defaming materials posted on the Web. Samsonov wrote on
his Twitter feed:

I share the opinion that "United Russia" is the party of crooks and
thieves, and that Putin is leading the country toward collapse and
civil war, but I have a normal sexual orientation, I'm not an exhibition-
ist, not a transvestite, I've never taken off my clothes for the public,
and never put photos of myself naked or in women's dresses on the
Internet.[110]

Impugning a politician's masculinity by questioning his heterosexual orientation had become a tool of political legitimation and delegitimation in Russia.

In a tactically similar—if more convoluted—case, Evgenii Urlashov, who
had been elected mayor of Yaroslavl in April 2012 by trouncing his Kremlin-
favored opponent, soon found himself in open conflict with Putin's United
Russia party. As part of the local campaign to discredit the mayor, Putin-
supporters pretending to be LGBT-rights activists held demonstrations in
June 2013 ostensibly backing Urlashov, raising rainbow placards and signs
declaiming "Urlashov Is Our Favorite Mayor." This attempt to affiliate

---

[109] Savel'eva, interview by author.
[110] Tat'iana Dvoinova, "Kommunist pleiboem byt' ne mozhet—Primorskii parlamentarii dokazyvaet svoiu normal'nuiu orientatsiiu," *Nezavisimaia Gazeta*, December 5, 2012, http://www.
ng.ru/regions/2012-12-05/1_playboy.html.

Urlashov with the LGBT community was an unambiguous effort to decrease his popular support.[111]

Also along these lines, in a perhaps unique propaganda campaign launched in early January 2011, activists with the pro-Kremlin youth organization Stal' attempted to unman (or feminize) opposition leader Boris Nemtsov by suggesting that he had been sexually violated while in prison (Nemtsov had been arrested on December 31, 2010, following participation in an anti-Kremlin rally). An article on the Stal' website promised that their organization would bring a copy of the book, "Free Yourself: How to Overcome Violence and Its Effects" to the "petty hooligan" Nemtsov and voiced their ostensible sympathy for him.[112] Meanwhile, a group of four young female activists (two wearing blue jackets with "Stal'" printed on the back) collected signatures on a petition in Moscow asking the attorney general to investigate whether Nemtsov had indeed been sexually abused while serving out his fifteen-day sentence.[113] With this rather unsubtle example of political sleight of hand, Stal,' relying on innuendo rather than evidence, in effect accused Nemtsov of being the victim of sexual abuse and thus of being insufficiently masculine (or perhaps even being a willing participant in gay male sex). Nemtsov, brandishing a similarly homophobic political-rhetorical device, countered by publicly stating that all the pro-Kremlin youth group activists (from Nashi to Stal' to Molodaia Gvardiia) were "Putin's roosters" (petukhi), that is, homosexual "bottoms."[114]

The homophobic imputation of homosexuality, sexual deviance, and a general lack of masculine allure has also been deployed by anti-Kremlin political youth organizations to undermine the attractiveness of the leaders of the Putin regime. The anti-Kremlin youth organization We, for instance, carried out a Valentine's Day action in Moscow in 2009 designed to make Putinism (and, by association, Putin) appear less attractive. The action was called "We Don't Sleep with Putinists" (s putinistami ne spim) and echoed the ancient Greek

---

[111] Urlashov was arrested on corruption charges a few weeks later. David M. Herszenhorn, "Russian Mayor, an Opposition Figure, Is Arrested," *New York Times*, July 3, 2013, http://www.nytimes.com/2013/07/04/world/europe/russian-mayor-an-opposition-figure-is-arrested.html; Aleksei Gorbachev, "Iaroslavskii mer poshel na otkrytyi konflikt s 'Edinoi Rossiei,'" *Nezavisimaia Gazeta*, June 18, 2013, http://www.ng.ru/politics/2013-06-18/3_yaroslavl.html.

[112] Molodezhnoe Patrioticheskoe Dvizhenie STAL', "'Stal'' pomozhet Nemtsovu preodolet' posledstviia nasiliia," January 7, 2011, http://bit.ly/1oSiFeZ.

[113] The women were captured on film conducting their petition drive. See "Stal' 'nasiluet' Nemtsova" [video], January 9, 2011, http://www.youtube.com/watch?v=5iEMZ7bHJfg. As of August 2011, the video had been removed by the user from YouTube.

[114] "Russia's pro-Kremlin youth group launches smear campaign against jailed opposition leader," RIA Novosti, January 10, 2011, http://en.rian.ru/russia/20110110/162092486.html; Dan Healey, "Active, Passive, and Russian: The National Idea in Gay Men's Pornography," *The Russian Review* 69 (April 2010): 210–230, 215.

play, *Lysistrata*. Eight activists handed out badges (znachki) to female pass-ersby, reading "We don't sleep with Putinists!" and "We don't date Puti-nists!"[115] The group's leader explained it this way:

> The point of the action was that we were calling on all young women not to sleep with [men] who were supporting Putin and United Russia, because then the Putinists would become extinct; it would no longer be fashionable to be a Putinist. . . . And, in fact, although the action was mostly humorous, it also had a rational purpose, because it's true that the first thing to do is to make loyalty to the authorities really unfashionable. And in many ways, that's very much the task of any young women who have an adverse reaction to [Putin loyalists], and who would [turn them down and] say, "No, you're behind the times!" That would be much more effective than any kind of propa-ganda work (agitatsiia). That is, what's fashionable (moda) is a very important thing. Let's say in 1968, in Paris, or in America, the propor-tion of smart and stupid young people was the same as it is today. But to be on the side of the authorities (byt' storonnikom vlastei) was [at that time] simply impossible for a decent person.[116]

Predictably enough, given the gendered analysis that I have suggested here, the We action was interrupted by a group of male and female pro-Kremlin ac-tivists who clambered out of a nearby subway station with sparklers, balloons, and a large cardboard photo-portrait of Putin, showing traces of lipstick (pre-sumably from kisses), chanting, "Our men are the best!"[117]

Activists on both sides likewise have hurled the epithet "faggot" (pidoras) at their opponents, reinforcing homophobia in general while undermining the target's perceived masculinity in particular.[118] One activist with the anti-Kremlin group Oborona called this mutual accusation a "political trend":

> I have an acquaintance who went out with the slogan, "Putin is a faggot" (pidoras). And then Nashi came out with the same slogan against [opposition leader Boris] Nemtsov, and he got very offended and almost brought a court case against them [Laughs]. So within this

[115] "V Moskve proshla aktsiia 'S putinistami ne spim!,'" February 14, 2009, http://www.grani. ru/Politics/Russia/activism/m.147569.html.

[116] Dobrokhotov, interview by author.

[117] "V Moskve proshla aktsiia 'S putinistami ne spim!'." Somewhat ironically, the pro-Kremlin youth had failed to get a permit for their action, and were detained by police.

[118] The term "pidoras" or "pider," like its English equivalent, does not always have a sexual under-tone when used as an insult. It can also be found spelled "pidaras" and "pideras."

context of insulting each other with this word, in politics—it's a very strong word. Let's say LGBT activists come to a Strategy 31 [opposition] rally. You can often hear—on the side—Nashi and others saying, "Yeah, they're all faggots" (pidorasy). About us. Or [Eduard] Limonov, who organized the Strategy 31 rallies with us. In one of his books, "It's me, Eddy" (Eto ia—Edichka), there's a description of homosexual experience (gomoseksual'nogo opyta).[119] And they'll say, "Yeah, you're all that way" (Da vy vse takie).[120]

Even within the left, homophobia was a tool of delegitimation. One young activist with the socialist group, Committee for a Workers' International (KRI), explained that KRI was somewhat unusual among Russian socialist groups due to its cooperation with LGBT activists and its endorsement of gay rights. As she put it, "When other organizations get into arguments with [us] over political issues, they use homophobia against us. Like, 'Oh, KRI, they're all faggots'" (Oh, KRI-shniki, eto vse pidorasy).[121]

While use of the term is widespread, there can be serious consequences for those who use it against the regime. In late 2010, a criminal case was initiated against a journalist in Russia's Komi region who had called Putin a "pidaras" on his blog. The case was dismissed when the public prosecutor's office decided that although the term constituted a criticism, its use was not a punishable act; however, the incident was not the last of its kind. In spring 2011, when Georgii Sarkisian, an opposition activist in the Orlov region, posted a photo on his blog that featured a banner reading "Putin is a faggot" (Putin—pidaras), the FSB threatened to bring a criminal case against him for insulting the prime minister.[122]

Addressing the regime's hypothetical distress over such appellations, a song was posted on YouTube in October 2011 titled "Putin is a Fag and a Nit" (Putin pidoras i gnida). The timing of the video may have been provoked by Putin and Medvedev's joint announcement in September that Putin would be seeking another term as president the following March and that Medvedev would then serve as Putin's prime minister. Many Russians found this "castling" move insulting, since it highlighted the prearranged, noncompetitive nature of high politics. Over a montage of comical and pointed photos showing Putin in

[119] Eduard Limonov, "Eto ia—Edichka," http://lib.ru/PROZA/LIMONOV/edichka.txt, accessed August 12, 2011.

[120] Shaginurov, interview by author, 2011.

[121] Zhenia Otto, Komitet za Rabochii Internatsional, Kampaniia protiv ekspluatatsii i diskriminatsii zhenshchin, interview by author, Moscow, June 18, 2012.

[122] "Delo o rastiazhke 'Putin—pidaras.'"

many guises (including as a Russian tsar and as a Nazi), a catchy punk track tells the story of how Russia's parliamentary deputies had come together for an emergency session to determine who had said "Putin is a fag!" and how that person should be punished:[123]

> Though nobody's died,
> there's an emergency in the State Duma.
> For over two hours, the Deputies have been searching.
> They still can't imagine—but want to find out—
> who said, "Putin is a fag"?
>
> Chorus:
> Putin is a fag
> Putin is a fag
> Putin is a, Putin is a, Putin is a fag
> Putin is a fag, Putin is a fag,
> Putin is a fag and a nit
>
> Whoever said that Putin was a bad guy
> Is going to get it from us in the eye!
> In fact, he's very, very good.
> They're outright lying that Putin is a fag!
>
> His kimono [Putin's martial arts uniform] sparkles
> and he's always well kempt.
> We can picture him like that right now.
> They must hang, those fucking scum,
> who were shouting, "Putin is a fag!"

While its lyrics express a mock sense of being appalled, the song manages to repeat at least thirty times its message that "Putin is a fag."[124]

Although reportedly some oppositionists cracked jokes among themselves about what kind of relationship Putin and Medvedev might have, lending a "blatantly homophobic subtext" to the Putin–Medvedev tandem,[125] on balance

---

[123] "Putin Pidoras i Gnida" [video], http://www.youtube.com/watch?v=ExFyv5qBvTk, accessed May 18, 2012. I thank Nataliya Kun for help with the translation.

[124] A similar song, "Vova Putin Is a Fag," was posted to YouTube in February 2011, featuring a series of portraits of Putin reimagined as a woman. "Vova Putin pidoras" [video], February 16, 2011, https://www.youtube.com/watch?v=3JvVeFjm0jo.

[125] Vera Akulova, Moskovskaia Feministskaia Gruppa, interview by author, Moscow, June 6, 2012; Otto, interview by author.

there have been few concrete attempts to portray Russia's current top leadership as sexually deviant, gay, or effeminate. In a semi-authoritarian context, the regime in power controls, to some extent, the range of the gendered debate. When a department store advertisement (unauthorized by the regime) appeared on a Moscow billboard in May 2011 portraying Putin and Medvedev "in shorts with their hands almost touching," the ads, with their "slightly effete image," were quickly removed after the Kremlin's negative reaction.[126] In short, the regime established parameters about the permissible. In 2009, an artist in Voronezh who attempted to publicly portray Putin as a woman wearing a black spaghetti-strap top, with long hair and hoop earrings, was arrested, interrogated, beaten, and fined for his effort to project the painting onto the mayor's office building (his alleged crime was to use "obscene language in public").[127] In his composition, Putin's face was superimposed over a woman's torso, and flirty words to match the woman's pose appeared in the upper left corner of the painting, reading: "Oh, I just don't know ... A third presidential [term]? That'd be a bit much. Though god does love a Trinity (troitsa)!"[128] To the regime, the artistic wielding of homophobia against its leadership (not to mention concrete accusations of sexual deviance) was no joke. Alexander Litvinenko, the former Russian spy who died in a London hospital in November 2006 as a result of radioactive polonium poisoning, alleged several months before his death that Putin was a pedophile. This allegation, which may have sealed Litvinenko's fate, was made shortly after an incident in summer 2006, where Putin spontaneously chatted with some tourists in Moscow and then unexpectedly knelt, lifted the shirt of one young boy, and kissed his tummy.[129]

Even satirical portrayals of Putin in masculinized sexual terms are not fondly received by the regime. Following a speech in which then-president Putin drew attention to Russia's declining birthrate and proposed incentives to reverse it, Vladimir Rakhmankov, the editor of an independent Russian news

---

[126] Tom Washington, "Shorts Stunt Gives Putin a Sharp Shock," *Moscow News*, May 31, 2011.

[127] "V Voronezhe arestovan khudozhnik, napisavshii portret Putina v zhenskom plat'e," June 16, 2009, http://www.newsru.com/russia/16jun2009/shurik.html.

[128] Will Stewart, "The Portrait of Vladimir Putin as a Woman Which Got Artist Arrested by Secret Service," June 17, 2009, http://www.dailymail.co.uk/news/article-1193430/Artist-arrested-secret-service-portraying-Vladimir-Putin-woman.html; Goscilo, "Putin's Performance of Masculinity," 199; Helena Goscilo, "Russia's Ultimate Celebrity: VVP as VIP Objet d'Art," in *Putin as Celebrity and Cultural Icon* (London: Routledge, 2013), 25, 27.

[129] Litvinenko had worked for Russia's FSB. In 1998, he publicly accused FSB leaders of corruption and other misdeeds. He was soon fired from his position and was later granted assylum in the United Kingdom. Alexander Litvinenko, "The Kremlin Pedophile," July 5, 2006, http://www.informationliberation.com/?id=18244. I thank Mark Kramer for bringing Litvinenko's allegation to my attention. For a different interpretation of the tummy kiss incident, see Mikhailova, "Putin as the Father of the Nation," 76.

website, published a satirical article calling Putin "Russia's phallic symbol" and proposing the production of souvenirs portraying "the president's head as the head of a penis." He was subsequently charged under Article 319 of the Russian Criminal Code ("insulting a government official"), tried in September 2006, and sentenced to pay a 20,000 ruble fine (roughly $750) the following month.[130]

Media coverage highlighting Putin as a masculine supermodel (photographed shirtless, bearing weapons, conquering nature, etc.) allowed for little competition, even from pro-Kremlin activists.[131] The bodies of young female Putin-supporters enhanced Putin's political masculinity, as they enhanced (by association) the perceived masculinity of all pro-Kremlin male activists. The latter, meanwhile, were made in the image of Putin but not in competition with him. They were encouraged to be traditionally masculine, to join the army (as we will see in the next chapter), and protect the state from enemies foreign and domestic. They shared Putin's masculinity but did not threaten it.

Gender Norms, Homophobia, and Political Legitimation in the Protests of 2011–2012

The aftermath of the December 4, 2011 elections to Russia's parliament, the Duma, dramatically altered Russia's political dynamics. Volunteer election monitors documented electoral fraud in many locations and uploaded their findings to the Web, where their videos went viral. Protests began on the evening of December 5, with several thousand people gathering near a central Moscow subway station to express their anger at this apparent case of election theft.[132] In a bid to cut the protests off early, police detained protesters, including Ilia Iashin, a long-standing opposition youth activist and leader of the anti-regime political movement Solidarity, and the increasingly well-known anti-corruption blogger, Aleksei Navalny; they each received fifteen-day prison sentences. When Navalny emerged from jail on December 21, he noted that he had entered prison in one country and had exited it into quite another.[133]

---

[130] Committee to Protect Journalists, "Russia: Journalist Goes on Trial for Satirizing Putin," September 21, 2006, http://www.cpj.org/news/2006/europe/russia21sept06na.html; Reporters Without Borders, "In 'Grotesque' Sentence Court Fines Website Editor for Insulting Putin," October 27, 2006, http://en.rsf.org/article.php3?id_article=19473.

[131] Alan Taylor, "Vladimir Putin, Action Man," *The Atlantic*, September 13, 2011, http://www.theatlantic.com/infocus/2011/09/vladimir-putin-action-man/100147/.

[132] Michael Schwirtz and David Herszenhorn, "Voters Watch Polls in Russia, and Fraud Is What They See," *New York Times*, December 5, 2011, http://nyti.ms/Tuo0wJ.

[133] Michael Birnbaum, "Russian Blogger Alexei Navalny Released from Jail," *Washington Post*, December 21, 2011, http://www.washingtonpost.com/world/russian-blogger-alexei-navalny-released-from-jail/2011/12/21/gIQAiFK18O_story.html.

The tide of protest had shifted. Although on December 6, the pro-Kremlin group Stal' reportedly sent twelve hundred activists into Moscow's Manezhnaia Square for a drumming "flash-mob" in support of United Russia's victory at the polls[134] and, on the first two nights of protesting, pro-Kremlin youth were said to have outnumbered the demonstrators decrying election fraud,[135] a forty-minute pro-Kremlin protest held on December 12 next to Red Square turned up relatively small numbers of participants, some of whom proved unable to articulate the reasons for their presence.[136] Meanwhile, at least forty thousand citizens, many of them first-time protesters, flooded Moscow's Bolotnaia Square on December 10 and roughly one hundred thousand showed up on Sakharov Prospect on December 24 to voice their dissatisfaction with the regime and the election that it had allegedly stolen.[137] No longer was the pro-Kremlin movement mobilizing impressively large demonstrations on Moscow's thoroughfares; crowds were now pouring onto the streets to critique the Putin regime instead.

The anti-Kremlin political youth activists who had felt utterly marginalized up until that point were simultaneously elated and stunned by these developments. One activist with Molodezhnoe Yabloko responded to my inquiries about her reaction to the protests, saying, "Of course [it makes me] insanely happy that citizens' consciousness has changed. . . . It's no longer shameful to stand on a picket line or go to a rally, but rather, it's fashionable."[138] The leader of the same organization cheerfully noted, "The opposition no longer looks marginal; now we are the majority."[139] In the words of an Oborona activist,

> All that's going on here is a big surprise for us. Sitting on the tip of the iceberg we, in many ways, didn't imagine this mass that was moving under [the surface of] the water. . . . Even before the elections, we

[134] Dvizhenie Stal', "V Moskve proshel 'Marsh barabanshchikov,'" December 6, 2011, http://madeofsteel.ru/news/cat/Drugie_36/nov_V_Moskve_proshel_Marsh_barabansh-chikov__998.

[135] Jones, "Putin's Youth Movement Provides a Sinister Backdrop to Russia's Protests."

[136] Daisy Sindelar, "How Many Demonstrated for the Kremlin? And How Willing Were They?," December 13, 2011, http://www.rferl.org/content/how_many_and_how_willing/24420674.html. While official government estimates put the number of attendees at twenty-five thousand, people at the scene put the number in the "low thousands."

[137] William Mauldin, "Russian Paper Counts 102,486 Protesters, Several Times Police Tally," *Wall Street Journal*, December 23, 2011, http://blogs.wsj.com/emergingeurope/2011/12/26/russian-paper-counts-102486-protesters-several-times-police-tally/.

[138] Olga Vlasova, Molodezhnoe Yabloko, personal communication via email, January 5, 2012.

[139] Kirill Goncharov, Molodezhnoe Yabloko, personal communication via email, January 3, 2012.

activists talked a lot about the fact that, say, we are alone and aban-
doned, the masses at best sympathize with us, but they won't go out
into the streets. . . . And suddenly, on December 5—there it was!
People came out! . . . Activists were surprised to see a lot of new faces in
the crowd. For once, citizens were willing to stand up for themselves.[140]

Another echoed his sentiment, noting that the scale of the protests had "come
as a surprise to most of us, although we had been preparing for something like
this for the last seven years."[141] One activist stated frankly that he had not expected such protests, adding:

You ask how I feel about it? If we set aside political assessments, and I
describe what I feel, then it's probably better to compare my reaction to
the reaction of a person who for long years argued the obvious, but no
one believed him, no one paid attention to him, but at a certain moment
everyone saw the light and said, "Damn, he was right all along!":)[142]

Yet while opposition activists were enjoying this unanticipated level of societal support, the public discourse continued to reflect the gender-related
legitimation and delegitimation strategies documented before December
2011. These included efforts to undermine the normative masculinity or femininity of opponents. On December 6, the second night of election protests,
anti-Kremlin demonstrators clashed with youth activists from Nashi, Stal',
Molodaia Gvardiia, and other pro-Kremlin organizations in Moscow's
Triumfal'naia Square. Against the background of the pro-Kremlin activists'
drums, the anti-regime protesters hurled epithets at the young Putin supporters.[143] "All the 'Nashists' are prostitutes!" (Vse "nashisty"—prostitutki)
shouted the anti-Kremlin activists, thereby maligning the traditional masculinity and femininity of Nashi members, independent of their sex.[144] Likewise, as the police cornered the opposition demonstrators, roughed them up,
and arrested them, the pro-Kremlin youth expressed their support for these

[140] Tivur Shaginurov, Oborona, personal communication via email, January 3, 2012.
[141] Oleg Kozlovskii, Oborona, personal communication via email, January 3, 2012.
[142] Igor' Iakovlev, Molodezhnoe Yabloko, personal communication via email, January 3, 2012.
[143] Alexander Bratersky, Nikolaus von Twickel, and Rina Soloveitchik, "250 Held in 2nd Night of
Vote Protests," *The Moscow Times*, December 6, 2011, http://www.themoscowtimes.com/news/
article/250-held-in-2nd-night-of-vote-protests/449405.html.
[144] Il'ya Varlamov, "Nashi protiv NAShIkh," December 7, 2011, http://echo.msk.ru/blog/
varlamov_i/836960-echo/. Some opposition activists refer to Nashi members as "Nashisti"—a
play on the Russian word for "fascists" (fashisti).

uniformed representatives of the authorities, shouting, "The riot police are handsome!" (OMON—krasavchiki).[145]

The use of homophobia was particularly visible among the continuing pro- and anti-Kremlin authority claims. For example, following the initial post-election protests, on the night of December 6, President Medvedev retweeted a crude message from a 32-year old United Russia politician, Konstantin Rykov, stating, "Today it became obvious that a person who uses the phrase 'party of swindlers and thieves' on his blog is a stupid, cocksucking sheep :)."[146] The reference was to Aleksei Navalny—the originator of the catchy phrase demeaning the United Russia party and, by extension, to Navalny's supporters. During Putin's annual call-in show on December 15, the prime minister had declared that he thought the protesters' white ribbons—standing for clean elections—looked like condoms and that perhaps the vast crowd of protesters who gathered at Bolotnaia Square on December 10 were actually AIDS activists (a not-too-subtle code for "homosexuals"): "I decided that it was an anti-AIDS campaign ... that they pinned on contraceptives—I beg your pardon—only folding them in a strange way."[147] Then, a week into the new year, in an ongoing attempt to discredit Navalny and the protesters, a newspaper distributed in Ekaterinburg (fictively claiming to be part of the *Argumenty i fakty* chain of newspapers) printed a concocted photograph portraying Navalny alongside the widely disliked oligarch, Boris Berezovsky (who was living in exile), while the accompanying article asserted that the rank and file protesters who came by the thousands to Sakharov Prospect were all gay.[148]

Navalny was also feminized in an animated cartoon posted on the Web in mid-December 2011, apparently created by a Nashi activist and supported by Vasilii Iakemenko (the former Nashi leader and head of the Russian Federal Youth Affairs Agency). Portrayed primarily as a fascist compulsively giving the Nazis' "Sieg Heil" salute, in one scene of the video Navalny is shown holding up one end of a laundry line with his saluting arm while a woman, presumably his wife, hangs out clothes to dry and sharply instructs him to hold the line up higher.[149] Navalny

---

[145] Ibid.

[146] "Medvedev opublikoval v Twitter netsenzurnuiu zapis' o 'partii zhulikov i vorov,'" December 7, 2011, http://newsru.com/russia/07dec2011/ryktwitter.html.

[147] Tom Balmforth, "Putin Affirms Duma Vote in Annual Call-In Show," December 15, 2011, http://www.rferl.org/content/putin_annual_callin_tv_show/24422335.html.

[148] Boris Bakir, "Naval'nogo mochat chernukhoi: 'on nikogda ne skryval....'" January 8, 2012, http://www.weekjournal.ru/politics/2282.htm.

[149] Navalny4, "Pervyi kanal pokazal mul'tfil'm o Naval'nom" [video], December 15, 2011, http://www.youtube.com/watch?v=fLKOm-PIaHI&feature=player_embedded#%21; Miriam Elder, "Emails Give Insight into Kremlin Youth Group's Priorities, Means and Concerns," *The Guardian*, February 7, 2012, http://www.guardian.co.uk/world/2012/feb/07/nashi-emails-insight-kremlin-groups-priorities?newsfeed=true.

is also shown cooking eggs that, in the frying pan, take on the shape of a swastika. Being subordinated to a woman and engaged in clearly female-identified tasks was symbolically demasculinizing.

The homophobia-inflected attacks on political opponents in 2011 were not an entirely new feature of Putin-era elections. In 2007, the Russian musical group Leningrad had posted a short song called "Vybory" (election) on YouTube to mark the occasion of the parliamentary election occurring that December. Singer Sergei Shnurov growls a set of lyrics about the upcoming election, concluding with his own voting process: he's given a ballot and promptly ticks off the box for "against all." The song ends with a simple summary of Shnurov's disgusted disappointment: "Elections, elections. . . . The candidates are fags!" (Vybory, vybory, kandidaty pidory!)[150]

Other homophobic actions were aimed more concretely at undermining the legitimacy of the opposition forces. During the 2007 parliamentary election campaign, for instance, the SPS—a liberal party among whose founders was opposition politician Boris Nemtsov—was impugned in leaflets as having hired AIDS-infected canvassers. Some campaign literature handed out, ostensibly from SPS, included condoms and promised an opportunity for SPS supporters to travel to Amsterdam for a gay pride event. And in the run-up to the elections, SPS party headquarters "was ransacked and spray-painted with profanities and graffiti that proclaimed it the 'Party of Gays.'"[151]

But if in 2007 opposition parties had little recourse to counter such claims by the dominant party, in December 2011 the situation had changed. In the post-election fray, regime critics threw Putin's own sexuality and manliness into question. During Putin's mid-December call-in show, Roman Dobrokhotov, the leader of We, sent out tweets referring to Putin as #botox, thus pointing to the rumor that Putin had undergone botox treatments on his face and, simultaneously, feminizing him (given that facial plastic surgery is more strongly associated with women than men).[152] As Putin faced reelection as Russia's president in March 2012, former Soviet leader Nikita Khrushchev's great-granddaughter, Nina Khrushcheva (a professor of international affairs in the United States) pointed to Putin's "botox moment" (when people began to muse on the Internet about Putin's oddly taut and shiny skin) as symbolizing the loss of his status as a strong, tough, Russian "muzhik" and that, as such,

---

[150] "Vybory! Vybory! Kandidaty—pidory!" [video], October 11, 2007, http://www.youtube.com/watch?v=1CLBANCVHTw. I thank Nataliya Kun for the citation.

[151] Ian McAllister and Stephen White, "'It's the Economy, Comrade!' Parties and Voters in the 2007 Russian Duma Election," *Europe-Asia Studies* 60, no. 6 (2008): 931–957, pp. 943–944.

[152] Luke Harding, "Vladimir Putin Question and Answer Session in Russia."

people had ceased to fear him.[153] Undermining Putin's masculine legitimacy created a potential opening for the belief that political change was possible.

Putin's reference to the protesters at Bolotnaia Square in December 2011 as condom-toting AIDS activists also provoked a critical reaction. Several demonstrators attending the December 24 mass rally brought signs identifying Putin as a condom and suggesting he depart from political office. One protestor carried a handmade poster featuring a line drawing of a condom and the words "You're one yourself." Another showed Putin's face plastered on the side of a condom-shaped rocket, blasting off with Soviet astronaut Yurii Gagarin's famous words, "Off we go!" (Poekhali!) beneath, and Putin's arm waving goodbye.[154] "Not for re-use," proclaimed another poster portraying Putin along with a condom.[155] No longer an icon of virility, Putin had become its mere receptacle.

The portrayal of Putin as a condom was joined by implications of his homosexuality. Russian journalist and music critic Artemii Troitskii took the stage at the December 24 protest dressed as a condom, suggested that Putin's private life was too private and hinted that all was not well in the prime minister's bedroom. The would-be president of Russia, Troitskii said, must be "transparent and honest," adding, "Popular wisdom has it that if the president isn't doing it with his wife, he's doing it with his country."[156] Wearing a baggy white jumpsuit and a red bow tie, Troitskii explained that he wore the costume to allude to Putin's earlier remarks about the protesters and to express his concern "that the authorities were contagious."[157] It is possible that Troitskii was suggesting Putin was impotent, rather than a closeted homosexual, though the charge of being insufficiently masculine is central to both insinuations.[158] A joke circulating on

---

[153] James Kimer, "The Botox Czar: An Interview With Nina Khrushcheva—OpEd," *Eurasia Review*, March 5, 2012, http://www.eurasiareview.com/05032012-the-botox-czar-an-interview-with-nina-khrushcheva-oped/.

[154] Anton Burkov, "Fotoreportazh s prospekta Sakharova 24 dekabria 2011 goda" [video], December 24, 2011, http://sutyajnik.ru/news/2011/12/1902.html.

[155] Lynn Berry, "Putin Sends New Year's Greetings, with a Wink," December 31, 2011, http://news.yahoo.com/putin-sends-years-greetings-wink-125847229.html.

[156] Lucian Kim, "A Russian Fairy Tale for Christmas," December 25, 2011, http://lucianinmoscow.blogspot.com/2011/12/russian-fairy-tale-for-christmas.html; "Miting na prospekte Sakharova: Khronika," December 24, 2011, http://grani.ru/Politics/Russia/activism/m.194408.html#child-201713.

[157] Kseniia Vershinina, "Artemii Troitskii: Mitingi dolzhny privesti k perenosu prezidentskikh vyborov i smene TsIK," December 26, 2011, http://www.1tvnet.ru/content/show/artemii-trocikii-mitingi-doljni-privesti-k-perenosu-prezidentskih-viborov-i-smene-cik_07202.html.

[158] Following Ukraine's Orange Revolution, a survey of adolescents in Ukraine documented one pro-Russian (male) teenager's critique of the new incumbent president based on virility: "Yushchenko is an impotent, Yanukovich is the president." See Nikolayenko, *Citizens in the Making in Post-Soviet States*, 29.

the Internet in 2012 also played upon the condom/homosexuality theme: Putin and Medvedev walk into a drugstore, and say to the druggist, "Two condoms (gondona)." "I know," says the druggist, "Now what can I get for you?"[159]

As the protests wore on, homophobic attempts to undermine Putin continued. At the second "March of Millions" opposition rally, held on June 12, 2012 in Moscow, some protesters (though not from the LGBT or feminist contingents) chanted a rhyming couplet as they marched from Pushkin Square toward Sakharov Prospect: "One, two, three: Putin get out! Three, two, one: Putin is a fag!" (Raz, dva, tri: Putin ukhodi! Tri, dva, raz: Putin—pidoras!).[160]

In November 2012, opposition figure Kseniia Sobchak, on her Internet-TV program "State Department" (so named after the regime's accusation that the opposition was all on the US State Department's payroll), similarly implied that Putin could be gay, given his failure to parade his opposite-sex spouse in public. In the context of a discussion about whether gay marriage should be legalized, when one of her guests was endorsing the "restriction of certain freedoms" for gays, Sobchak commented about Putin's "hypocritical" tendency to appear at public events without his wife. Sobchak "likened this behaviour to that of 'parents who forbid their children to smoke while secretly puffing in the kitchen.'"[161]

Even Gleb Pavlovskii, a former Putin ally and adviser to the Kremlin until April 2011,[162] noted several days after the December 4 elections that Putin's upcoming presidential run would no longer be the kind of no-contest race that he had won in the past, in part because the "popular multitude who used to pant erotically for Putin [had] vanished."[163] As if to illustrate Pavlovskii's remark, at a large Moscow demonstration in February 2012 protesters' signs included one that read: "We know you want a third time, but we have a headache."[164]

---

[159] "Dva gondona!!!," http://pikabu.ru/story/dva_gondona_639316, accessed April 16, 2013.

[160] Author's fieldnotes. Similar chants could be heard at other marches. Footage of a nationalist "Russian March" posted to YouTube in November 2011 featured a call-and-response chant by the marchers: "Putin—Is a Fag." See "Putin pidoras! Russkii marsh!" [video], November 11, 2011, https://www.youtube.com/watch?v=aCscB25cjxY.

[161] "Russian TV Show Discusses Public Attitudes to Homosexuality: Dozhd Online," BBC Monitoring, November 11, 2012, http://conta.cc/1nq9ChC.

[162] Brian Whitmore, "The Pavlovsky Affair," April 29, 2011, http://www.rferl.org/content/the_pavlovsky_affair/16798268.html.

[163] Viktor Savenkov, "Interview with Effective Policy Foundation President Gleb Pavlovskiy," *Svobodnaya Pressa*, December 6, 2011.

[164] Gregory White, "Russia after Putin," *Wall Street Journal*, February 25, 2012, http://online.wsj.com/article/SB10001424052970203960804577241392587109400.html?mod=WSJ_hpp_RIGHTTopCarousel_1; Potupchik, "Devushki zhurfaka MGU razdelis' dlia Putina."

The opposition also used sexualized imagery to characterize the regime's political vehicle, the United Russia party, as illegitimate and powerless. One poster at a mass rally on February 4, 2012 used this technique to play on the notion of "topping," putting the regime in a subordinate, nondominant position. The poster, held by a young woman, showed a poodle mounting a stylized bear—the symbol of the United Russia party. The caption read, "Today we'll bark, tomorrow we'll bite, or even. . . . " The "unspeakable" and deviant image of the poodle and bear that accompanied the words "or even," where the bear (representing the regime) had lost its traditional power and was submitting to a mere poodle (standing in for the opposition), was a means of using gender norms to change the terms of the debate. While the United Russia party had resources and power (including police power) at its disposal as well as owning the "strong" image of the bear, the party's opponents could attack the regime on the basis of that very strength, using the implication of violence (rape) or just plain deviance from the sexual norm (a poodle topping a bear), to mark United Russia as no longer reliably dominant—in short, as vulnerable.[165]

Protesters also continued to use variations on "pidoras" to impugn Putin's political reputation. However, homophobic slurs directed at Putin could not reliably be counted upon to go unpunished. On May 6, 2013, an activist in Saratov attended a local demonstration to support a group of protesters who had been arrested and jailed following a major demonstration held in Moscow on the eve of Putin's presidential inauguration a year earlier. The activist carried a sign that bore a linguistic provocation: "Putin, count your remaining days of freedom." On his poster, the activist had used the Ukrainian imperative form of the verb "to count" (pidrakhui), which lexically resembles a combination of the Russian words for "fag" (pidor) and "dick" (khui)—producing a hard-to-translate slogan: "Putin, you fag-dick, count your remaining days of freedom" (the implication being that, sooner or later, Putin would find himself in prison for crimes committed while in office). This homophobically insulting wordplay was enhanced by a photo pasted in the corner of the poster, portraying Medvedev and his wife (her hair covered by a white shawl) standing next to Putin and Moscow's Mayor Sergei Sobyanin (whose head, thanks to photoshop, appeared to be similarly wrapped in a shawl). The original picture, taken during an Easter Service at the Cathedral of Christ the Savior a few days earlier, created the visual image of a double wedding ceremony: Medvedev and his wife, plus

---

[165] Lucian Kim, "A Hot Winter's Day in Moscow," February 5, 2012, http://lucianinmoscow. blogspot.com/2012/02/hot-winters-day-in-moscow.html. The poster is image 14 of 18 in Kim's slideshow.

Putin and his male "bride," standing four abreast on a church dais and all holding tall, red, lit candles.[166]

The poster-wielding activist, Mikhail Shapovalov, was the former coordinator of the Saratov Voters' League. Police on the scene at the Saratov rally reportedly deemed the term pidrakhui "inappropriate" and arrested him. After spending the night at a police station, Shapovalov appeared before a judge who convicted him of "petty hooliganism," sentenced him to a one-day prison term, and released him with time served. The next day, activists in Moscow announced a plan to hold "the first political flash mob" of the summer season and called upon participants to bring "creative posters" featuring the words "Putin pidrakhui" to Gorky Park for their unauthorized protest.[167] The twenty protesters who showed up there on May 8 were arrested; police found the "Putin pidrakhui" inscription on protesters' posters (and one t-shirt) "offensive" and "insulting" when addressed to Russia's president.[168] Likewise, a few months later, an art exhibit in St. Petersburg was closed down by the authorities because several of the paintings implied that Putin, Medvedev, and other political leaders who had outspokenly supported the national ban on homosexual "propaganda" were themselves gay. One painting, for instance, portrayed Putin and Medvedev as romantic partners; in the painting, Putin is wearing a pink negligee and stands behind Medvedev, running his fingers through Medvedev's hair. A voluptuous Medvedev, meanwhile, is shown wearing a matching demi-bra and panties with a flowery print. The paintings were carted off by police to be examined as evidence of "extremism."[169]

The regime, meanwhile, continued to delegitimate the protesters in the same vein. In his 2011 New Year's eve greeting to Russia's citizens, Putin used a sexual implication when referring to the protesters, sending his good wishes

---

[166] "Putin, pidrakhui* ostavshiesia svobody dni," May 8, 2013, http://www.compromat.ru/page_33340.htm; "Vladimir Putin pozdravil sograzhdan s Voskreseniem Khristovym," May 5, 2013, http://www.pravoslavie.ru/news/61349.htm.

[167] The term "pidrakhui," which means "count" or "calculate" in Ukrainian, had cropped up years earlier on many posters at Ukraine's Orange Revolution protests, directed at the head of the Ukraine's Central Electoral Commission who was blamed for helping steal the 2004 presidential election there. "8 maia v Moskve proidet aktsiia 'Putin pidrakhui….,'" May 8, 2013, http://www.kasparov.ru/material.php?id=518A30FA49413; "Putin, pidrakhui* ostavshiesia svobody dni"; "Pravozashchitnik popal v tiur'mu za plakat 'Putin, pidrakhui ostavshiesia svobody dni,'" May 8, 2013, http://newsru.co.il/world/08may2013/shapovalov456.html.

[168] "Moskovskaia politsiia razognala nesanktsionirovannyi 'lager' oppozitsii', vdokhnovlennyi plakatom 'Putin pidrakhui,'" May 8, 2013, http://m.newsru.com/arch/russia/08may2013/okkupay.html; "Aktivisty skandirovali: 'Doloi vlast' chekistov!'," May 8, 2013, http://www.kommersant.ru/doc/2185825.

[169] EchoMSK, "Politsiia iz"iala kartiny khudozhnika Konstantina Altunina," August 27, 2013, http://www.echo.msk.ru/blog/echomsk/1144458-echo/.

"to all our citizens regardless of their political persuasion, including those who sympathize with leftist forces and those who are located on the right, above, below, however you like."[170] Exhibitions of female support for the Putin regime—featuring displays of sexualized femininity—continued as well. In February 2012, an auto race event was held in support of Putin's candidacy in the Russian presidential elections slated for March 2012. The race featured Putin supporters driving their creatively decorated cars along Moscow's "ring road." Among those who sought to express their support for the president were several cars full of women who, despite the chilly winter weather, showed up for the race wearing only their bras and panties. From behind her steering wheel, one explained, "I came here because I wanted to, and I'm going to go vote—100 percent—only for him." Another woman stood in a bright green convertible waving a flag, while a group around her car belted out a rendition of the laudatory pop song "A Man Like Putin." [171]

Nor did the pro-Kremlin groups let Putin's next birthday pass without a new proclamation of young women's love for the president in his third term. In early October 2012, United Russia's youth wing, Molodaia Gvardiia, produced a four-minute video greeting for Putin's sixtieth birthday.[172] The clip begins with a blonde woman sitting in a wheat field with her iPhone, looking at a text message from "The Very One" (tot samyi) that reads, "I'm on my way!" (Vyezzhaiu!). She smiles broadly, and we hear a male voice singing "Blueberry Hill" (echoing Putin's performance of that song two years earlier at a celebrity fundraiser). She then walks through the field, coming to rest on a blanket with two other attractive young women in sundresses. The blonde lets grains trickle out of her fist onto the blanket, spelling out "Happy Birthday." The music shifts, and we see a woman riding on horseback through the field, carrying a banner that reads "You can't beat Putin in a race!" (Putina ne obskakat'). We then observe a series of events where the women are pictured miming a variety of Putin's manly exploits (flying a fighter jet, playing ice hockey in a Putin jersey, and scuba diving for pottery). In each setting, the women's femininity is exaggerated, and most of the women pictured are shown receiving a text message from Putin ("The Very One") or being reminded of him in some other fashion while carrying out their tasks. The fighter pilot, for example, who has long wavy red-brown hair and wears a skin-tight flight suit, strolls down the tarmac under the

---

[170] Berry, "Putin Sends New Year's Greetings, with a Wink"; "Putin pozhelal blagopoluchiia i protsvetaniia kazhdoi rossiiskoi sem'e," December 31, 2011, http://www.rosbalt.ru/main/2011/12/31/930649.html.

[171] "Avtoprobeg 'Za Putina!'" [video], February 19, 2012, http://www.gazeta.ru/video/politics/my_prosto_hotim_sdelat__emu_priatno.shtml. I thank Rob Boatright for the citation.

[172] Molodaia Gvardiia, "Molodaia Gvardiia—Videopozdravlenie Prezidentu Vladimiru Putinu ot molodogvardeitsev," October 7, 2012, http://mger2020.ru/nextday/2012/10/07/39219.

camera's gaze. She sits down in the cockpit of a fighter jet, puts on her helmet, and turns to contemplate a framed portrait by the dashboard of Putin in his flight suit and helmet. She smiles at it, lowers her visor, and flies off. The final scene, against the music of "Blueberry Hill," shows all the women standing together on a city street, smiling and talking while they wait in great anticipation. One holds a cake with candles. A small yellow car approaches, and the women gesticulate and clap, looking extremely excited. The car pulls up next to them. Its door opens and a presumably male foot emerges in a shiny black shoe. The final frame reads "Happy Birthday!" as we hear the "Blueberry Hill" lyric ostensibly ringing in each woman's mind: "My dreams came true."

In the video, each of the women appears to be able to do anything Putin can do—hypothetically challenging the gender norms that would keep traditionally "masculine" jobs like fighter-pilot and ice hockey player in male hands. Yet in the end, it is patently clear that the women are not honing in on Putin's territory; they yearn only to be in Putin's fan club, leaving the serious activities to him. The video thus playfully spoofs Putin's stunts but also upholds his image as a highly desirable man from the standpoint of the young and attractive women who thrill over his text messages and grow giddy at the prospect of seeing him drive up in person. As far as the United Russia videomakers were concerned, Putin remained a sex symbol, the center of attention for attractive young women—or at least they were committed to portraying him that way.

In short, as Putin entered his third term as president in 2012, even while his machismo was under attack in a more publicly accessible way than had been possible before the critical juncture of the Duma elections in December 2011, the political legitimation and delegitimation strategies earlier in evidence, rooted in patriarchal gender norms, clearly remained in place.

* * *

The masculinity upheld by the Putin regime and its enthusiasts relied for its power on femininity. Incumbents' perceived masculinity, propped up by the sexualization of their female supporters, helped legitimate their rule. Once politicized in this way, masculinity and femininity can serve as beacons to attract young men and young women into activism on their respective sides of the political spectrum. By the same token, painting a political perspective and portraying especially its male supporters as being sexually deviant or as feminized (often by using homophobia) undermines the authority of that perspective and its supporters. Pro-Kremlin activists aimed to portray themselves as correctly or traditionally masculine and feminine, while exposing the opposition as being atypically gendered. Opposition activists followed a similar set of tactics in that regard, though with more limited resources and fewer opportunities, given their relatively limited power in the Putin era's political context.

Viewed in this light, gender norms constituted a significant part of the scaffolding of political power in Putin's Russia. Political legitimacy was measured in part by whether (male) political leaders could attract young women to their cause, as evidenced by those women's willingness to physically "reveal" their politics, to wear their politics on their sleeves—or, rather, to dispense with the sleeves altogether. As anti-Kremlin organizer Oleg Kozlovsky mused with regard to the Moscow State University journalism department's dueling calendars contest and the true purpose of journalism: "is it about getting naked before public officials or is it about discovering and making public naked truth?"[173] The same could be asked of the political arena and the forms of political legitimation and contestation in Russia during the Putin era.

[173] Oleg Kozlovsky, "Controversial Sexy Gift for Putin and the Future of Russian Journalism."

4

Fight Club:
Gendered Activism on Patriotism,
Conscription, and Pro-Natalism

With Putin's ascension to the presidency in 2000, Russia's state bureaucracy placed a greater emphasis on building up popular patriotism, which had declined precipitously during the chaotic 1990s. During the Yeltsin era, Russia's citizens watched as their former country, the Soviet Union, dissolved and, in short order, lost its superpower status. Communism, as an alternative economic model to capitalism, had become a laughingstock, and the once-powerful Soviet Communist Party was revealed as little more than (at worst) an apparatus of repression and (at best) a tool for careerists. National pride plummeted along with the economy as the 1990s wore on.

Putin's advent brought a renewed national self-assertion. Russia's statesmen voiced anti-Western (and particularly, anti-American) sentiments, charging the United States with malign intent to undermine Russia's economy and asserting Russia's right to rule itself after its own fashion. This was embodied in Kremlin ideologist Vladislav Surkov's notion of "sovereign democracy"—a "hands-off" warning to Western democratic states that Russia's internal affairs were its own business. For the domestic audience, the Putin administration established a multifaceted patriotic education program aimed at bolstering national identity and providing some counterbalance to Western liberal appeals, especially among Russia's youth.[1]

As we have seen, political organizations in Russia contest each other's legitimacy by asserting the normative masculinity and femininity of their own

---

[1] Douglas W. Blum, *National Identity and Globalization: Youth, State, and Society in Post-Soviet Eurasia* (Cambridge: Cambridge University Press, 2007), 121. On Russia's patriotic education programs, see Valerie Sperling, "Making the Public Patriotic: Militarism and Anti-Militarism in Russia," in *Russian Nationalism and the National Reassertion of Russia*, ed. Marlene Laruelle (London: Routledge, 2009), 218–271.

members and the political leaders whom they support, and trying to undermine that of their opponents. Political actors also make use of gender norms when trying to carve out authority on matters of policy. Focusing on patriotism and two related policy areas—military conscription and pro-natalism—this chapter continues the exploration of how gender norms have been used by Putin-era political actors, both pro- and anti-Kremlin, as tools of political legitimation.

The pro- and anti-regime groups discussed in Chapter 3, with their widely divergent sentiments toward Putin's rule, largely adopted opposing positions on patriotism and related policies. As Putin's first decade in power wore on and as his second took off, the young pro-Kremlin supporters who populated groups such as Nashi, Stal,' and Molodaia Gvardiia and those opponents who joined Oborona, My (We), and Molodezhnoe Yabloko organized a variety of actions to demonstrate their patriotism and display their views on the state's conscription and pro-natalist policies.

Individual politicians and their political parties draw on a plethora of strategies, ideologies, and norms to legitimate and sustain their rule. One of the most frequently encountered strategies is to emphasize patriotism and nationalism, as the Putin regime chose to do. Nationalism and patriotism, in turn, are closely tied up with gender norms—perceptions about what constitutes "correct" sex roles and about masculinity and femininity within a given national population. Nira Yuval-Davis's examination of gender and nationalism, for instance, finds gender norms crucial to the construction of nationhood as a concept. Her book, *Gender and Nation*, examines various "national" projects, such as reproducing the population (and the concept of its own national culture) and mobilizing the citizenry for war, and shows that women and gender construction are central to these endeavors.[2]

Fostering patriotism, following a desirable demographic policy (whether to reduce or increase the population), and being prepared for military conflict are projects that state leaders pursue—at least in part because they believe success in these areas will reinforce their own political legitimacy. The Putin-centered regime and the pro-Kremlin youth groups that supported it tried to foster state-desired patriotic behavior among Russia's citizenry by speaking out in favor of the Kremlin's military conscription and pro-natalist policies. In so doing, these groups wielded gender norms as an inducement to compliance, arguing that "real men want to serve in the military," that "good patriots produce multi-child families," and so on. Anti-regime groups, meanwhile, made use of gender norms in their efforts to undermine military conscription policy and assert women's right to choose in reproductive matters. In this

---

[2] Yuval-Davis, *Gender and Nation*.

chapter, I show how gender norms were interwoven with and served to legitimate political actors' positions on patriotism, military conscription policy, and pro-natalism.

Patriotism, Policy, and Political Youth Organizing

Political actors perceive patriotism variously depending on their ideological standpoint. While the pro- and anti-Kremlin activists I interviewed in June 2011 largely defined patriotism as "love for one's motherland," several anti-Kremlin activists further specified that patriotism did not necessitate agreement with state policies and pointed out that it also represented the desire to change things for the better in the country, often by contravening existing policy.[3]

One area where patriotic opinions differ is on state policy regarding military conscription. Although the Russian army includes contract soldiers, it is staffed mainly by conscripts who serve one-year terms. Pro-Kremlin activists promoted conscription and actively encouraged military service, whereas anti-Kremlin activists favored a professional (volunteer) army and preferred to regard military service as an individual choice rather than an obligation. One Nashi activist provided an unqualified endorsement of army service:

Q. What position does Nashi have regarding service in the army?
A. The position is very simple. If you're supposed to serve, you should.[4]

Similarly, when asked how Molodaia Gvardiia (the youth wing of the United Russia political party that has dominated the Duma in the Putin era) viewed conscription, an activist on the organization's coordinating council described an action promoting conscription both inside and outside of the group: "Oh, we held an Army Call-Up. That is, we put out propaganda within Molodaia Gvardiia that young people, as well as our leaders [in the organization] absolutely should serve in the army. And we spread the word on this topic among the youth [in general]. That is, we want the guys (rebiata) to serve in the army."[5]

---

[3] In defining patriotism as love for one's country, the activists echoed Russian public opinion polls on the subject, where 27 percent provided that same response in 2006 ("hard to say" was the most popular answer, with 32 percent). See Fond Obshchestvennogo Mneniia, "Patriotizm: kriterii i proiavleniia," December 7, 2006, http://bd.fom.ru/report/cat/socium/dd064825.

[4] Nikita Borovikov, Nashi, interview by author, Moscow, June 9, 2011.

[5] Alena Arshinova, Molodaia Gvardiia, interview by author, Moscow, June 14, 2011.

To a significant extent, in the popular imagination, patriotism was associated with military service. In a 2006 survey, 69 percent of Russians believed that someone who tried to avoid army service could not be considered a patriot.[6] The pro-Kremlin groups' position on the obligation of military service echoes this view. Yet the vast majority of Russians also believe that few young people are eager to serve in the army; in 2012, 73 percent were confident that today's youth did not want to serve, and only 17 percent imagined that they wanted to do so.[7] Perhaps reflecting this reality, activists with pro-Kremlin organizations endorsed conscription, while in some cases acknowledging the potential benefits of a professional army:

Q. How does Nashi feel about conscription?

A. Well, we have the kind of country where the length of our borders is such that a professional army at this moment [couldn't ensure border security]. Therefore conscription [is still necessary].[8]

A. We can't allow ourselves a professional army. There are too many people living on our territory, and the border is too big. We understand that the border always has to be guarded. Moreover, the border regions we have—the Near East is right next door, and the problems in Afghanistan haven't been solved yet, there's drug trafficking—and China is right nearby, too. . . . We've evaluated the situation, and we're prepared for a threat from any country, because the riches of our country are enormous and, in fact, inexhaustible. And naturally, that all needs to be guarded.[9]

Q. What is Molodaia Gvardiia's position on conscription, as opposed to having a contract army?

A. I have a dual opinion on this—that it's possible that everyone should serve in the army, but on the other hand, I understand that professionalism also plays a large role. At this point, you could put together a professional army that would be responsible for responding to modern threats and so on. But, on the other hand, if you had a general mobilization, there would be more people who were constantly acquiring some skills. That is, this issue needs to be worked on; I can't really say that I have a precise position on it.[10]

---

[6] Fond Obshchestvennogo Mneniia, "Patriotizm: kriterii i proiavleniia."

[7] Fond Obshchestvennogo Mneniia, "Vesennii prizyv," April 16, 2012, http://fom.ru/obshchestvo/10405.

[8] Borovikov, interview by author.

[9] Anton Smirnov, Stal'/Nashi, interview by author, Moscow, June 17, 2011.

[10] Arshinova, interview by author.

These statements echoed the Russian government's position—retaining a conscripted army while rhetorically endorsing the eventual shift to a professional force.

By contrast, youth activists on the anti-Kremlin side were uniformly opposed to the draft. A 19-year old activist with Molodezhnoe Yabloko consigned the notion of conscripted armies to the previous century and argued that the draft should be eliminated in favor of the more rational system of professional armies used in Europe:

> We think that there should be a professional army, where soldiers receive a fitting salary, instead of having these 19-year-olds trying to avoid the draft board for several years, and then being forcibly inducted into the army, where who knows what they do. Instead of learning about military affairs, and learning military trades, they're doing construction projects for generals, cleaning their boots, and so on—that is, things that have nothing to do with the army.... He could be an excellent manager, or an excellent artist, or a singer, or actor— but instead, he's wasting a year carrying out unnecessary orders, building somebody's summer house (dacha). And no good comes of this—neither for the country, nor for him personally. So we need to get rid of that system.[11]

An activist with the opposition group, My (We) likewise rejected the draft, arguing that conscripted soldiers were "sitting in the army instead of doing something productive in their profession" and enhancing Russia's economy. He echoed the argument that a modern military required paid professionals capable of handling high technology and that soldiers' pay could be increased if the number of servicemen was cut significantly, as it would be if conscription ended. Moreover, the issue of individual rights was at stake: "The main reason is that the very idea of conscription violates freedom of choice. A person should choose for himself what profession he wants to pursue."[12] A member of the anti-Kremlin group Oborona asserted that his group, too, opposed the draft and favored a professional army and had been "quite active in campaigns on that issue."[13]

In the eyes of the Kremlin, army service and submission to military conscription are both direct forms of supporting the state. The state-sponsored

---

[11] Kirill Goncharov, Molodezhnoe Yabloko interview by author, Moscow, June 10, 2011. Recruits often end up laboring for their superior officers.

[12] Roman Dobrokhotov, My, interview by author, Moscow, June 9, 2011.

[13] Oleg Kozlovskii, Oborona, interview by author, Moscow, June 8, 2011.

patriotic education programs initiated in 2001 were designed in part to counter significant draft evasion and to improve the faltering image of the Russian
army. These programs centered to a large extent on World War II, in part with
the aim of boosting popular pride in Russia's history, while also encouraging
Russian (male) youth to serve their terms in the army rather than attempt to
evade the draft, an ongoing and significant problem from the perspective of
Russia's Ministry of Defense.[14]

One of the most widely publicized reasons for draft evasion is the practice
of violent hazing (*dedovshchina*) characteristic of the Russian army.[15] In part to
combat the hazing process, army service policy was changed as of 2008, reducing draftees' term of service to one year instead of two. The idea was that a
single-year term of service would eliminate the bifurcated hierarchy whereby
second-year soldiers felt free to abuse new draftees. However, dedovshchina
did not decrease as expected with the introduction of one-year terms. In 2009,
three thousand Russian soldiers reported being physically attacked in hazing
cases, and in the first five months of 2010, 1,167 Russian army soldiers were
subjected to such incidents (including four killings).[16] Reported hazing events
increased in 2010 by more than a third over 2009.[17] According to Russia's chief
military prosecutor, however, the form of hazing was changing, as increased
numbers of incidents were reported in which money or valuables (such as cell
phones) were "extorted" from new recruits.[18] Draft evasion did, however, decline, pointing perhaps to decreased fear due to the shorter term of army service or to effective propaganda under the rubric of the state patriotic education
programs.[19]

To a significant extent, the program of the pro-Kremlin youth organization
Nashi supported the state's patriotic educational goals, particularly those re-
lated to what Russians refer to as the Great Patriotic War (World War II).[20]
World War II and its commemoration have been central to the legitimation

[14] Sperling, "Making the Public Patriotic."

[15] Françoise Daucé and Elisabeth Sieca-Kozlowski, eds., *Dedovshchina in the Post-Soviet Military:
Hazing of Russian Army Conscripts in a Comparative Perspective* (Stuttgart: *ibidem*-Verlag, 2006).

[16] "Editorial: Renaming the Army," *Vedomosti*, November 1, 2010.

[17] Ethnic-based hazing is also prevalent within Russian army units, provoking the creation of
separate Chechen units and the possibility of creating ethnically distinct units for Slavs and
ethnic groups from the North Caucasus. Valery Dzutsev, "Ethnic Rivalries Appear to Be Tearing
Russia's Army and Society Apart," *North Caucasus Weekly* (Jamestown Foundation), December
17, 2010).

[18] "Hazing in Russian Military Still Rampant—Chief Prosecutor," Interfax/AVN, January 11,
2011.

[19] Ibid.

[20] Sperling, "Making the Public Patriotic," 249–252.

strategy of the Russian government under Putin and Medvedev and of the pro-Kremlin groups who offer support for it.[21] One Stal' activist who also served on Nashi's coordinating council noted that Nashi members were creating a video archive containing interviews with veterans. These interviews were designed to capture veterans' recollections on film, in part to counter the "falsification of history" (i.e., the failure to properly credit the importance of the Soviet Union's role in the war).[22] In June 2011, Stal' likewise initiated a series of events commemorating the seventieth anniversary of the start of the Great Patriotic War in Russia; the first was an exhibit of unique archival photographs from the war years, held at the All-Russian Exhibit Center in Moscow. There, Stal' activists, dressed in 1940s military uniforms, served as guides and invited young men to join the project. This entailed going to a local home for veterans to record veterans' recollections on the topic, "Where were you when the war began?" and "How did you end up at the front?"[23] Other Nashi activities also focused on making a connection between contemporary youth and war veterans, focusing on the commitment of the former to protect the current regime and the service and sacrifices of the latter during the war.

Several Nashi activists counted among their favorite programs those that focused on the commemoration of World War II and veterans. These included Nashi's first large-scale event, called "Our Victory" (Nasha Pobeda)—variously referred to by interviewees as "Civic Oath" (grazhdanskaia prisiaga) and the "Generational Relay" (estafet pokoleniia).[24] Here, Nashi gathered sixty thousand participants on Moscow's Leninskii Prospect for a symbolic occasion at which World War II veterans passed the "baton" (representing the defense of Russia's independence) to the younger generation. One activist described the action as having forged "a connection between the older and younger generations," reinforced by an exchange between the two: "Young people swore an oath to the veterans that they wouldn't ever hand over the country, and that they'd carry on and preserve the history of the country. The symbol was a shell casing (gil'za) from the time of the Second World War.

---

[21] On war memorialization as a contested act of state legitimation, see Maria Bucur, *Heroes and Victims: Remembering War in Twentieth-Century Romania* (Bloomington: Indiana University Press, 2009). On the Kremlin's ongoing efforts to enhance Putin's image by linking him with World War II, see Wood, "Performing Memory."

[22] Smirnov, interview by author. For more on this particular Stal' project, see Molodezhnoe Patrioticheskoe Dvizhenie STAL,' "Proekt: Bor'ba s fal'sifikatsiei istorii," http://www.made ofsteel.ru/projects/Borba_s_falsifikatsiey_istorii_4, accessed August 3, 2011.

[23] Molodezhnoe demokraticheskoe antifashistskoe dvizhenie NAShI, "Vystavka fotografii voennykh let otkrylas' na VVTs," June 9, 2011, http://nashi.su/news/36449.

[24] Molodezhnoe demokraticheskoe antifashistskoe dvizhenie NAShI, "Proekty." Nashi's major events are described here.

Veterans presented the shell casings to the participants."[25] Each shell casing was inscribed with a directive: "Remember the war, protect the Motherland."[26] This intergenerational message, while important to the Russian government for its value in burnishing the image of the army, was also meaningful to the pro-regime activists:

> I'm talking about this because that generation of veterans, our grand-parents, defended the country during the Great Patriotic War. And now we're taking up the baton. There's no war, but there are various threats to the country, and we're ready to respond to those threats. But that was not the only action we did with veterans, because it brings [one] joy to see that even though today's youth can be apolitical and might not know its history very well, they feel sincerely grateful toward veterans.[27]

The same message was echoed in a major Nashi action in 2006, called "Return the Holiday to the Veterans" who had been deprived of a New Year's celebra-tion sixty-five years earlier, when fighting off Hitler's troops just outside Moscow. Tens of thousands of Nashi activists, dressed as Father Frost (Ded Moroz, the Russian/Soviet equivalent of Santa Claus) and his companion, Snow Maiden (Snegurochka), arrived in downtown Moscow for an enormous parade, followed by activists bringing gifts to veterans and visiting their homes. One Nashi activist recalled the immense amount of work involved in bringing two trains full of activists from her region into the city as well as the experience of interacting with the veterans. Reflecting on the event, she explained that the knowledge that she gained by going to a veteran's house and talking about the war had "enriched" her experience: "Because unfortunately, when I was born, before I had any real awareness, my grandfather died, so he couldn't tell me about [the war]. And for me . . . maybe that was the most memorable action by the movement."[28]

The overwhelming majority of Russians, Muscovites in particular, have positive regard for symbolic means of commemorating World War II. In 2012, Russians were surveyed about a relatively new tradition—tying the familiar black and orange "St. George's Ribbon" (georgievskaia lentochka), used in Im-perial Russian and Soviet military medals of honor, to their car antennae or

[25] Smirnov, interview by author.
[26] "Esli rodilsia Grazhdaninom—bud' im!—Pomni o voine, beregi Rodinu!," http://mostachev.livejournal.com/187081.html, accessed August 3, 2011.
[27] Borovikov, interview by author.
[28] Irina Pleshcheva, Nashi, interview by author, Moscow, June 16, 2011.

pinning the ribbon to their clothes in advance of Victory Day. Seventy percent approved of the practice, with most regarding the ribbon as a commemoration of the war and those who perished and as a mark of respect and gratitude for veterans.[29]

It is therefore not surprising that opposition youth organizations, too, carry out actions commemorating the war and showing concern for veterans' well-being. In June 2011, for instance, the St. Petersburg branch of Molodezhnoe Yabloko lit candles at the spot where the residents of Leningrad had drawn water during the nine hundred-day siege of their city by the Nazis.[30] Meanwhile, Moscow's branch of the organization protested against a situation where veterans of the Great Patriotic War were being illegally evicted from their apartments.[31] One activist remarked on the notable case of Anton Karavanets, an 83-year old World War II veteran living in St. Petersburg, who wrote to US President Barack Obama asking if the United States might grant him housing; the authorities in St. Petersburg had failed to offer Karavanets the free apartment that Russian President Dmitrii Medvedev had promised to all surviving war veterans back in 2008.[32] "This is a very shameful case for Russia, when people who fought— who are, in fact, heroes in our country—end up in such a lowly position," said the leader of Molodezhnoe Yabloko, "In my view that's a very big problem for Russia and a very shameful one."[33]

By contrast to the pro-Kremlin organizations' mass marches commemorating the war and their explicit endorsement of conscription, the anti-Kremlin youth organizations campaigned against the draft. In April 2011, for instance, the Moscow branch of Molodezhnoe Yabloko hung a banner proclaiming, "Down with conscription slavery" from a third-floor walkway in GUM, the high-end mall on Red Square. Three of the activists (including two interviewees for this project, Kirill Goncharov and Igor Iakovlev) were detained by the police, and the banner—which also illustrated abuse within the army, showing a photograph of one soldier striking another with a chair—was confiscated. [34] A month later, the same group organized an anti-draft protest "performance,"

---

[29] Fond Obshchestvennogo Mneniia, "Georgievskaia lentochka."

[30] Liubov' Bakunin and Oleg Chizhova, "Veteranov vne elektorata ne predlagat'," June 22, 2011, http://www.svobodanews.ru/content/article/24243126.html.

[31] Goncharov, interview by author.

[32] "Russian Asks Obama for New Home," May 6, 2011, http://www.bbc.co.uk/news/world-europe-13312713.

[33] Goncharov, interview by author.

[34] "Aktivisty 'Molodezhnogo Iabloka' vyvesili v GUMe antiprizyvnoi banner," April 6, 2011, http://www.grani.ru/Society/m.187592.html.

creating a stylized military encampment in Moscow's Novopushkinskii Square.[35] Oborona, too, has marched in favor of a professional army to replace the practice of "forced conscription."[36]

Pro-Kremlin and anti-regime groups differed fundamentally in their threat perception; the former regard foreign countries—"the West" in particular—as threats to Russia, both militarily and ideologically. Over the course of Putin's regime, among all foreign countries the United States served as the most prominent perceived threat to Russia. The perception of that threat grew over time. If in 2000, when Putin's first presidential term began, 21 percent of Russia's population surveyed believed that the United States presented the greatest threat, that perception had escalated slightly to include 26 percent of the population in 2011.[37] To some extent, then, pro-Kremlin groups' embrace of mandatory army service was linked to the notion of Russian patriotism and Russian national sovereignty. Protecting against threats stemming from the West was a categorical imperative, whether the threats emerged in domestic Russian politics (the liberal opposition, for instance, was said to be in the pocket of Western countries) or as foreign menaces (such as the 2004 Orange Revolution in Ukraine, ostensibly sponsored by the West).[38] To the anti-regime groups, Western liberalism was not so much a threat as a desired end-goal for Russia's own political system.

For the pro-Kremlin youth groups, therefore, patriotism extended beyond support for army service and shaded over into protecting the domestic political status quo. From that view, the United Russia Party's (or Putin's) power in office should be sustained and violence applied to that end, if necessary. In November 2010, Russian journalist Oleg Kashin was brutally beaten in a life-threatening attack that he later blamed on former Nashi leader, Vasilii Iakemenko.[39] Previous to the attack (in which Kashin's jaws, fingers, and leg were broken, and his skull fractured), Molodaia Gvardiia, the youth wing of United

---

[35] Moskovskoe Iabloko, "Molodezhnoe Iabloko' provelo antiprizyvnoi festival' v tsentre Moskvy," May 13, 2011, http://www.mosyabloko.ru/archives/9082.

[36] Oleg Kozlovsky, "Oborona Marches for a Volunteer Army," April 2, 2008, http://olegkozlovsky. wordpress.com/2008/04/02/oborona-marches-for-a-volunteer-army/.

[37] Fond Obshchestvennogo Mneniia, "Staryi vrag luchshe novykh dvukh," July 14, 2011, http:// fom.ru/globe/10096.

[38] Nashi's retributive actions against Estonia (when its government relocated a World War II monument to Soviet soldiers from a central location in Tallinn to a military cemetery) are indicative of the link between patriotism and political action. See Jussi Lassila, "Making Sense of Nashi's Political Style: The Bronze Soldier and the Counter-Orange Community," *Demokratizatsiya* 19, no. 3 (2011): 253–276.

[39] Alexander Bratersky, "Yakemenko's Departure Signals End of Era for Youth Politics," *The Moscow Times*, June 14, 2012, http://www.themoscowtimes.com/news/article/yakemenkos-departure-signals-end-of-era-for-youth-politics/460310.html#ixzz1xk4Eo3xN.

Russia, had posted on their website the names of journalists who covered the activities of Russia's domestic political opposition, labeling those journalists as traitors and enemies of the people, and posting images of journalists (including Kashin) with a caption stamped in purple: "Will be punished."[40] In the aftermath of Kashin's beating, Molodaia Gvardiia was accused of extremism; the group responded to these criticisms by removing the offending articles from their website and condemning the attack.[41] Shortly thereafter, however, Molodaia Gvardiia's website threatened opposition activist Aleksei Navalny, posting a photo of him with a bloodied face under the heading, "They promise to kick Navalny's ass" (Naval'nomu obeshchaiut navaliat').[42] Nor was Nashi silent on the issue of opposition journalists and their deserved fates. When Kashin's beating was discussed at the Public Chamber, Nashi activist Irina Pleshcheva baldly stated that it would be easy as pie to prevent attacks on journalists. Reporters would simply have to stop "giving people reasons to murder them."[43]

This was not the first or last instance where violence against political opponents was implicitly endorsed or embraced by pro-Kremlin groups. In October 2007, as youth activists mobilized to promote United Russia during the parliamentary elections in December that year, Nashi ran twenty-five "political shooting ranges" where images of opposition politicians served as targets for young activists' darts and paintball guns. In a similarly motivated paintball action, one hundred Molodaia Gvardiia activists in Vladivostok engaged in a "symbolic execution" of the Russian state's "enemies."[44]

Ideologues promoting violent reprisals against their political opponents can also be found outside of Russia. In the United States, for example, in March 2001 right-wing television personality Glenn Beck mentioned Congressman Charles Rangel as one of the people "we'd like to beat to death with a shovel," and "joked"

---

[40] Aleksandr Chernykh, "The Young Guard's Word Is Being Put to the Test: Human Rights Activists Suspect the Organization of Extremism," *Kommersant*, January 14, 2011.

[41] Alexander Marquardt, "Caught On Tape: Reporter Beaten into Coma," November 9, 2010, http://abcnews.go.com/Blotter/russian-reporter-oleg-kashin-beaten-coma/story?id=12101001; Julia Ioffe, "Oleg Kashin's Horrible Truth," *Foreign Policy*, November 6, 2010, http://www.foreignpolicy.com/articles/2010/11/06/the_horrible_truth_about_oleg_kashin?page=0,1.

[42] Zubov, "Lift Iakemenko."

[43] Aleksandra Samarina, "Prosto 'ne davat' povod dlia ubiistva'—Prostota argumentatsii rukovoditel'nitsy Tsentra razvitiia molodezhnykh SMI shokirovala," *Nezavisimaia Gazeta*, November 10, 2010, http://www.ng.ru/politics/2010-11-10/1_kashin.html.

[44] CanWest News Service, "Youths Take Aim at Russian Foes," *Calgary Herald*, October 25, 2007, quoted in Thomas Ambrosio, *Authoritarian Backlash: Russian resistance to democratization in the former Soviet Union* (Burlington, VT: Ashgate, 2009),196.

about poisoning House Speaker Nancy Pelosi.[45] Likewise, Sarah Palin posted a US map on her Facebook page, with gun sights superimposed over the districts of twenty House Democrats, listed by name and location below the map.[46] This tasteless move was preceded by several incidents and threats of violence against Democrats who had voted for passage of the health-care reform bill.[47] The ad was taken down from the Internet only after Arizona Representative Gabrielle Giffords—one of the twenty Democrats listed on the map—was shot in the head at a meeting with constituents in January 2011.[48]

Preparation for war and for the political defense of the regime overlapped under the rubric of patriotism for Russia's pro-Kremlin groups. Patriotism also guided the anti-Kremlin groups' desire to democratize the regime and spread the notion of individual choice—including on military service. As discussed in the next section, pro- and anti-regime actors also made use of gender norms in their patriotic activism as they contested each other's positions on conscription.

What Kind of Army Is More Masculine?: Gendering the Debate over Conscription

In their actions both for and against the draft, pro- and anti-Kremlin youth groups employed concepts of masculinity and femininity in ways designed (whether consciously or not) to reinforce the image of their male participants as "real men" and of their organizations as befitting the membership of real men.[49]

In addition to fostering an ongoing connection between the Soviet army and the contemporary Russian army, Nashi created programs to reinforce its

[45] "Glenn Beck 2001: Rep. Rangel and Other People 'We'd Like to Beat to Death with a Shovel'" [video], September 1, 2009, http://mediamatters.org/blog/2009/09/01/glenn-beck-2001-rep-rangel-and-other-people-wed/154105; "It's Patriotic Duty to Stop Glenn Beck, according to Beck," August 10, 2009, http://foxnewsboycott.com/glenn-beck/its-patriotic-duty-to-stop-glenn-beck-according-to-beck/.

[46] Jillian Rayfield, "Palin Uses Crosshairs to Identify Dems Who Voted for Health Care Reform," March 24, 2010, http://talkingpointsmemo.com/news/palin-uses-crosshairs-to-identify-dems-who-voted-for-health-care-reform.

[47] Justin Elliott, "MAP: A Guide to Recent Vandal Attacks on Democrats," March 24, 2010, http://tpmmuckraker.talkingpointsmemo.com/2010/03/map_a_guide_to_recent_vandal_attacks_on_democrats.php.

[48] John T. Burke, Jr., "A Loner Named Loughner," January 10, 2011, http://www.thecenterlane.com/?tag=sarah-palin-crosshairs.

[49] For analysis of the linkages between masculinity and military service in Russia—and challenges to militarism—see Eichler, *Militarizing Men*.

support for military service and enhance the reputation of Russia's conscript army. The "Nasha Armiia" (Our Army) program, initiated in 2006, involved Nashi members signing up for military service together (so that they would serve in the same unit and attenuate the problem of dedovshchina), and was intended to "reinforce the prestige of military service among youth and in society on the whole."[50] In reaching out to potential members, one description of the program on Nashi's website highlighted the promise of participants becoming "a real example of courage for those who hadn't yet made up their mind to head over to the military enlistment office (voenkomat)." It also emphasized that program participants would be taught how to handle crisis situations (such as hostage-takings) and modern weaponry: "An enormous number of weapons of all calibers and models won't leave you feeling indifferent. Now don't you want to serve?"[51] As Finnish scholar Jussi Lassila points out, the text reveals Nashi's "assumption of a natural connection between masculinity and a positive attitude towards weapons."[52] The Nasha Armiia program appealed not only to male youth by proffering masculinity (join the program, master the weapons, become an exemplar of courage) but also, by pointing to the masculinity of the men in the program, attempted to enhance Nashi's authority.[53]

The website of the pro-Kremlin organization, Stal', itself a former Nashi project, echoed the connection made on the Our Army section of Nashi's website between masculinity and military service. In December 2010, for instance, a news item from Stal' in the city of Nizhnii Novgorod appeared on the group's website, lauding a young man's "masculine deed" (muzhskoi postupok). Anton Kudriavtsev, an activist who reportedly never shied away from participating in movement events and who made many friends and comrades at the civil service academy where he was studying, went off to do his army service without complaint: "I'm off to the army on November 25th. Here's my number, if you want to tell me anything—call or write. And make Russia better while I'm not around! Bye for now!" The authors of the item reported that they were proud of him: "Today, when many young men's knees begin to shake when they hear the word 'army,' [Anton] calmly and without unnecessary fuss went off to serve.

---

[50] Jussi Lassila, "Anticipating Ideal Youth in Putin's Russia: Symbolic Capital and Communicative Demands of the Youth Movements 'Nashi' and 'Idushchie Vmeste'" (PhD diss., University of Jyvaskyla, Finland, 2011), 125.

[51] Ibid., 125. Lassila presents the Russian text (which is no longer available on Nashi's website).

[52] Ibid., 127.

[53] The Nasha Armiia program evaporated in 2008 when the activists working on that issue "decided they wanted to work on something else" as well as due to a lack of interest on the part of the Ministry of Defense (Borovikov, interview by author).

Without a doubt, that is the act of a real man and a patriot. Well done, Anton!"[54] Viewers of this story can see a close up of Anton as well as a photo of him standing with a young woman who could plausibly (given their proximity and body positions) be a girlfriend.

The gendered aspect of protection is closely entwined with military service and with war in general. A central dimension of patriarchy is the idea that women require protection and that men can and should assert their masculinity by exercising that protective function, whether in war or personally as the protector of individual women from other men's violence.[55] Completing a term of military service is an easily identifiable step establishing masculinity and conferring the achievement of "manhood."[56]

This protector/protected dichotomy persisted through the Soviet era and afterward, though it was disrupted somewhat by Soviet women's large-scale participation as combatants in World War II.[57] As Helena Goscilo documents, however, Soviet wartime propaganda downplayed women's military contributions and engaged the male soldier/female victim trope in dramatic fashion. Despite more than eight hundred thousand female enlistees, women were only rarely portrayed as armed soldiers on propaganda posters.[58] Typically, female images were visually or lexically identified with the Soviet homeland under threat and showcased female vulnerability. On these posters, female prisoners of war and women grieving their wounded or dead children implored their implicitly male brethren at the front to save them from their Nazi tormentors and avenge their violent victimization by mercilessly crushing the enemy forces.[59]

Contemporary programs that endorse military service are masculinized in that one of their underlying goals is largely addressed to young men: to

---

[54] Molodezhnoe Patrioticheskoe Dvizhenie STAL', "Nizhnii Novgorod: muzhskoi postupok," December 7, 2010, http://madeofsteel.ru/news/cat/Drugie_36/nov_Nizhniy_Novgorod:_muzhskoy_postupok_71. The article can also be found on Nashi's website: http://nashi.su/news/33620.

[55] In both cases, the women being protected are often referred to as belonging to their male protectors (e.g., "our women"). For a brief discussion of and citations to further literature on the "'protector/protected' dichotomy" and war, see K. R. Carter, "Should International Relations Consider Rape a Weapon of War?," *Politics & Gender*, no. 6 (2010): 352.

[56] Healey, "Active, Passive, and Russian," 226, citing Rebecca Kay, *Men in Contemporary Russia: The Fallen Heroes of Post-Soviet Change?* (Aldershot, UK, 2006), 60–63.

[57] Anna Krylova, *Soviet Women in Combat: A History of Violence on the Eastern Front* (New York: Cambridge University Press, 2010).

[58] Helena Goscilo, "Graphic Womanhood under Fire," in *Embracing Arms: Cultural Representation of Slavic and Balkan Women in War*, ed. Helena Goscilo and Yana Hashamova (Budapest: Central European University Press, 2012), 156.

[59] Ibid., 158–161. Examples of these posters can be found following page 177 of "Graphic Womanhood under Fire."

decrease draft evasion and promote higher rates of service in Russian military forces. The implication of Nashi's anti-Orange Revolution goal was also that defense of the Putin regime might have to take a military form and thus might imply mostly male participation. But despite its orientation toward promoting military service and its construction of protective force as masculine and manly, the youth movement that served as the backbone of support for the Kremlin's patriotic education programs and military recruitment efforts was far from being a men-only movement. Women comprised roughly 50 percent of both Nashi's and Molodaia Gvardiia's members and were counted among the ranks of Stal' as well, although there were fewer women than men in the top leadership of all three organizations (Mariia Kislitsina became a leader of Nashi in 2010; the top three leaders of Molodaia Gvardiia in 2011 included one woman—Alena Arshinova—and none of the six top leaders of Stal' were women).[60] As of September 2011, of the Nashi members identified and pictured on the main page of their website under "Contacts," forty were male and eleven were female.[61] Women were designated as the contacts for nine of the twenty-one regional divisions of Stal',[62] and of the twenty-one people listed on Molodaia Gvardiia's coordinating council, three were women.[63]

As Cynthia Enloe has argued, masculinized military (and militarized) forces could not function without women playing a variety of roles.[64] At the most basic level, militaries (and youth organizations that reinforce the value of military service) sell men the notion that their masculinity will be enhanced when they act in ways that either dominate or protect women. Women's messages to political youth organization members should be consistent with this social construction of gender roles and practices if the recruitment process is to play effectively on ideas about masculinity.

Alongside masculinized militarism, femininity is also militarized in the name of patriotism. However, the relationship of men and women to weapons of war is not identical. At a Nashi-sponsored pro-conscription rally in 2007, 19-year old Nashi member Valeriia Chernobrovkina distributed leaflets featuring

[60] Borovikov, interview by author; Arshinova, interview by author; Smirnov, interview by author.
[61] "Molodezhnoe demokraticheskoe antifashistskoe dvizhenie NAShI / Koordinaty," http://nashi.su/coords/, accessed September 19, 2011.
[62] "Molodezhnoe Patrioticheskoe Dvizhenie STAL'," http://www.madeofsteel.ru/regions/, accessed September 19, 2011,
[63] "Molodaia Gvardiia—Koordinatsionnyi sovet," http://www.molgvardia.ru/persons/koordinatsionnyi-sovet, accessed September 19, 2011.
[64] See, for example, Cynthia Enloe, *Bananas, Beaches, and Bases: Making Feminist Sense of International Politics* (Berkeley: University of California Press, 1990); Cynthia Enloe, *Globalization and Militarism: Feminists Make the Link* (Lanham MD: Rowman & Littlefield, 2007).

"female Nashi recruits posing provocatively with Kalashnikovs."[65] While weapons are typically associated with masculinity and men, when women wield them in a sexualized way they show that their femininity is intact despite their contact with weaponry (and that men's masculinity, too, is not under threat). At the rally, deputy Nashi leader Katia Mikhailova, wearing military-style clothes and holding a Kalashnikov, also emphasized the importance of beefing up Russia's declining population, urging the crowd to help "make Russia great again," a goal to which she and her Nashi-member boyfriend were hoping to contribute by producing "two or three babies."[66] Pro-regime activists made use of ideas about femininity and masculinity when exhibiting patriotic commitment to the state, whether through army service or reproduction.

Women in Nashi have also rhetorically supported the association between military service and desirable masculinity. For instance, at the aforementioned Nashi rally, a young woman on the stage harangued the crowd about the side benefits of army service. As presumed Nashi members looked on, she declaimed, "A man who hasn't learned to protect his Motherland, who hasn't served in the army, won't be able to protect his girlfriend. So until you've completed your military service, I won't be marrying you!"[67] The same message—that men will not be rewarded with attractive female companionship unless their own behavior exhibits patriotic support for the state—showed up in 2011 on a Russian calendar featuring young women in revealing undergarments (a clear successor to the "Happy Birthday, Mr. Putin" calendar published the previous year). The calendar, produced by Nashi activists as part of their "White Aprons" (belye fartuki) program, was designed to help counter the corruption that plagued Russia's male-dominated bureaucracies, businesses, and police force.[68] The calendar was titled, "Sex against Corruption: Love against Evil," and its jacket featured women covering themselves (barely) with white aprons. The woman on the January page, brandishing a frying pan and rolling pin, threatens, "I'll re-educate a bribe-taker!" The woman featured for May, sporting a bridal veil and white corset, gives viewers the finger (albeit a nicely polished finger) and announces, "I won't marry a corrupt official!" (ne vyidu zamuzh za korruptsionera).[69] In a neat historical parallel, Soviet propaganda

---

[65] Oliver Harvey, "Babes 'n arms," *The Sun* (United Kingdom), October 8, 2007.

[66] Ibid.

[67] Journeyman Pictures, "Nashi: Putin's Enthusiasts" [video], November 30, 2007, http://www.youtube.com/watch?v=CeA6y2vFXgU.

[68] "Kremlin Activists Pose for Lingerie Calendar," *The Telegraph*, April 7, 2011, http://www.telegraph.co.uk/news/worldnews/europe/russia/8435668/Kremlin-activists-pose-for-lingerie-calendar.html.

[69] "Nashi Anti Corruption Calendar 2011," http://www.metro.co.uk/news/pictures/photos-10865/nashi-anti-corruption-calendar-2011/1?ITO=HPPIX, accessed April 9, 2011.

following the 1917 Bolshevik revolution had similarly encouraged women to be on the lookout for counterrevolutionary misbehavior. They were to use their "sharp eyes" to shame men into compliance with the new economic order and to catch deserters who were shirking their military duties.[70] These various "performances"—from the calendar to the brave recruits enlisting together— constitute examples of how gender norms are used in the service of patriotism and thus in support of the regime.

Youth groups oriented against the Putin regime similarly played on notions of masculinity in their anti-draft and other activism. However, opposition activism in Russia conferred on its male participants a "protest masculinity" somewhat distinct from that cultivated by the regime.[71] Oppositionists' perceived masculinity was enhanced by going against the mainstream, taking risks against the police and special forces (OMON) during small protests and demonstrations, and generally exhibiting the kind of bravery that accompanies public resistance to a semi-authoritarian regime. As Kirill Goncharov, the 19-year old leader of Molodezhnoe Yabloko put it, when asked what his participation in the movement said about him as a man:

> Oh—[Laughs]—Well, you know, it always seemed to me that young women (devushki) like the bad boys! Maybe it's true. In the organization, we have more than a few young women who joined the organization after seeing us at some kind of action, after which they understood that these are brave people who don't want to make peace with [the situation]. Well, speaking of "as a man," I think that any man, as a matter of honor, fights for the freedom of various institutions in our country.[72]

A belief that any political activism bolsters the perception of a young man's masculinity can be witnessed in the response of the former leader of Nashi to the same question:

Q. What does your participation in this movement say about you as a man?
A. I said a little about this before—about having the opportunity to accomplish [some kind of] a feat, right? Well, of course that's an exaggeration. But it's also true in a way. Because now, thankfully, there's no war going

[70] Wood, *The Baba and the Comrade*, 60–61.

[71] The term "protest masculinity" typically refers to masculinity as it is perceived and enacted by men in ethnically (or otherwise) marginalized communities or groups. For discussion, see Connell and Messerschmidt, "Hegemonic Masculinity," 847–848. I use the phrase differently here.

[72] Goncharov, interview by author.

on. And our country's not participating in any hot conflicts, only [in certain places] as peacekeepers, perhaps. And, I'll say it again, that's good—but given that, the opportunity for a man to show he's a man remains only at the everyday level, where you can open a door when a young woman comes along, or beat up a hooligan [Laughs]. But again, that's at the everyday level. But here [in the movement], there's the sense that you're doing an important, and sometimes rather dangerous, thing. And therefore, probably, lots of boys join.[73]

Military service is closely identified with the notion of "being (or becoming) a man"—witness the common notion that "the army will make a man out of you."[74] Resistance to military service, whether by draft evasion or disagreement with the policy of mandatory service therefore carries connotations of anti-patriotism and insufficient manliness. As Karin Wahl-Jorgensen writes: "The commitment to military service means a willingness to die for the country. This type of patriotism, of course, is reserved for men. Thus, military service becomes a marker of masculinist patriotism."[75] However, "protest masculinity"—such as that expressed by Goncharov above—enables activists and the public to construe draft evasion or opposition to conscription as both masculine and patriotic. This was the case to some degree when in 1992, US presidential candidate Bill Clinton's reputed draft avoidance was framed in some media outlets as "an alternative, and more peaceful, act of patriotism" than the "aggressive militarism" of his opponent, George H. W. Bush.[76]

By contrast to the principle of men's required military service willingly embraced by some of the pro-Putin activists, a professional army system enables wider-ranging choices that include the decision not to volunteer for military service. While such a position may not be interpreted as patriotic, taking that position could itself be construed as evidence of masculinity, gained by standing up to a seemingly unified societal insistence that manliness and military service are linked. In the Vietnam war era, for example, men in the United States who refused military service were seen—at least on the left—as exercising a masculinity similar to that embraced by liberal youth activists who risked arrest at present-day Russian anti-regime protests. As pro-feminist activist John Stoltenberg argues, during the era of demonstrations against the Vietnam war,

[73] Borovikov, interview by author.
[74] Helen Michalowski, "The Army Will Make a 'Man' Out of You," in *Reweaving the Web of Life: Feminism and Nonviolence*, ed. Pam McAllister (Philadelphia: New Society Publishers, 1982), 326–335.
[75] Wahl-Jorgensen, "Constructing Masculinities in U.S. Presidential Campaigns," 64.
[76] Ibid., 65.

for young males, resistance to military service came to be viewed culturally as being consistent with conventional masculinity: If a young man refused to fight, his power and prerogative in the culture over women was completely intact—in the eyes of himself and in the eyes of enormous numbers of others ("Girls say yes to men who say no" and "Make love not war" were two popular slogans of the time).[77]

Protesting against the war, in Stoltenberg's view, "became a new and acceptable option for being a real man, instead of an occasion for examining the fundamental relationship between militarism and male supremacy."[78]

Russian anti-draft activism, in fact, made use of some of the same markers of traditional masculinity that were at work in the Nasha Armiia program and in pro-Kremlin activists' encouragement of military service. At the May 2011 anti-draft "performance" mentioned earlier, Molodezhnoe Yabloko activists created a festival-like atmosphere in one of Moscow's public squares, attracting roughly five hundred people who watched and participated in the events that included break-dancing, graffiti, opportunities to shoot guns at targets, ways to test one's strength against other participants, and the chance to eat military rations, while learning about the benefits of a professional army over a conscripted one.[79] As part of the performance, participants acting out the role of soldiers in the current (conscripted) army were also commanded to march around pointlessly and then to scrub the paving stones on the Square using toothbrushes, making an unsubtle commentary on the utility of military conscript labor.

The Moscow-based Yabloko Party described the event and its components in starkly gendered terms on its website. "All the men who came to Novopushkinskii Square on Friday evening were able to try out the role of a contract soldier, and measure their strength against each other," including the strength-measuring sledgehammer test common at carnivals (this test was reportedly the most popular among the "strong guys" [krepkie parni] in attendance, the strongest of whose hammer blows would register as a "King-Kong") and an "ancient" form of wrestling involving a seated, sole-to-sole struggle to pull a pole away from one's opponent. Young women's attention was said to have been drawn to a group of professional break-dancers. All comers could duck into a military-style tent and receive instruction about how to take apart and

---

[77] Stoltenberg, *Refusing to Be a Man*, 83.

[78] Ibid.

[79] Kirill Goncharov, "Sobytie vcherashnego dnia," May 14, 2011, http://goncharov-kiril.livejournal.com/43750.html; Moskovskoe Iabloko, "Molodezhnoe Iabloko' provelo antiprizyvnoi festival' v tsentre Moskvy."

reassemble Kalashnikovs and Makarov pistols. While women and men alike attended the action, photographs on the website showed an apparent division of labor echoing what was described in Yabloko's text. Women were shown painting children's faces and adding to the large graffiti billboard announcing opposition to the draft, while in the rest of the photos men lifted weights, competed in strength contests, handled and aimed weapons, showed off their musculature, tried consuming the field rations, and break-danced, while onlookers (women and men) observed.[80]

Another attraction at the event was a photographic centerpiece: a large stand showing a poster for the film "Mr. and Mrs. Smith" (2005), with the faces of Angelina Jolie and Brad Pitt cut out, so that protest participants could be photographed in their stead.[81] The name of the film was substituted by the slogan, "We [fuck] the draft (prizyv); We [love] the contract," where the word "fuck" was replaced by a graphic representation of the middle finger, and "love" was replaced by a red heart.[82] In a gender-bending moment, several pairs of men had themselves photographed at the stand, producing humorous images of scruffy male faces floating over the body of Angelina Jolie in a slinky, high-cut black evening dress, with a small, ladylike pistol tucked into the top of "her" thigh-high stocking, standing alongside "Brad Pitt" in a suit and with gun in hand.[83]

The leader of the Molodezhnoe Yabloko organization disputed (somewhat) the impression created by the photographs posted on the Yabloko party's website:

Q. Based on the photos, I thought that only young men took part in the strength-measuring contests and target shooting—is it true that young women didn't take part, or did it just seem that way to me from the photos?

A. No, young women did take part in that. . . . Of course young women couldn't measure their strength against the guys; physically, we wouldn't consider that the right thing to do. But we had young women artists. . . .

---

[80] For photos of the event, see Moskovskoe Iabloko, "Molodezhnoe Iabloko' provelo antiprizyvnoi festival' v tsentre Moskvy."

[81] Doug Liman, dir., *Mr. & Mrs. Smith* [DVD]. Los Angeles: Twentieth Century Fox, 2005; for more information, see http://www.imdb.com/title/tt0356910/.

[82] The organizers chose to use Latin letters to spell out the slogan, which gave rise to some Internet discussion about the event and its flyer, as did the use of the rude "fuck" gesture and the use of camouflage on the announcement poster. See the comment section of Kirill Goncharov, "I Fuck Prizyv/I Love Contract," May 5, 2011, http://goncharov-kiril.livejournal.com/43499.html.

[83] Moskovskoe Iabloko, "Tantamareska I fuck prizyv!/I love contract!," http://www.mosyabloko.ru/tantamareski, accessed August 3, 2011.

Q. Yes, I saw that; they were doing some of the graffiti, and children's face painting.

A. Yes, yes. That is to say, what the young women could do, they did with pleasure (to mogli delat' devushki, oni delali s udovolstviem).

Q. Did they do the target shooting, or didn't they try it?

A. No, whoever wanted to tried it, of course. There were some young women like that (byli takie devushki). Moreover, there were young women who hit the [column] with the hammer and measured their strength, and didn't do at all badly! Some of them even won. Anyone who wanted to participate [in those strength measuring contests] did—we didn't prevent anyone from doing anything along those lines.[84]

Making weapon assembly and disassembly and target-shooting available for an anti-draft protest (as well as the strength contests and their implied element of military training) echoed the underlying connection that the Nasha Armiia program had made between masculinity and the opportunity that the program offered to handle weapons. The crude language and imagery of the flyer advertising the anti-draft event ("Fuck the draft, love the contract!" printed against a camouflage background) also signifies a certain youthful masculine bravado.[85] While opposing the draft and army service under conscription, male participants in the event could simultaneously enjoy the conferment of masculinity by "trying on" a military persona, complete with target shooting and the consumption of field rations. The apparent—even if not strictly gendered—division of labor (women engaging in art and largely serving to observe men's participation in strength contests and weapons training) also reinforced the connection between military activity and masculinity.

Just as women play a role in reinforcing military masculinity when it comes to recruitment and the draft so too do women activists participate in the social construction of gender roles in anti-draft protests. One event illustrating this connection was a less grandiose and smaller-scale anti-draft protest that took place about a week after the one held by Molodezhnoe Yabloko, titled "Girls against the Draft" (devochki protiv prizyva).[86] The protest on Moscow's Chistoprudnyi Boulevard was organized by Vera Kichanova, a young journalism student at Moscow State University, press secretary of Russia's Libertarian Party, and an activist with a human rights organization called Society and the Army (Obshchestvo i armiia), focused on campaigning against the draft. As

[84] Goncharov, interview by author.

[85] Goncharov, "I Fuck Prizyv/I Love Contract."

[86] "Devochki protiv prizyva (Grani-TV)" [video], May 11, 2011, http://www.youtube.com/watch?v=g39U7a2zjYk.

Kichanova explained, "For boys (mal'chiki) protesting against the draft, it's dangerous to take part in street actions because they can be caught and taken into the army. So it's up to young women to speak up for them."[87]

Goncharov considered conscription as a young women's issue for a different reason. Noting that it was young women in Molodezhnoe Yabloko who had helped organize the big anti-draft event and had even pushed for the idea, he explained that young women were also victimized by the military draft:

> In fact, young women turn out to be one of the targets of the draft, in that the draft deprives them of their young men, who get sent off to the army, and for a year they [the young women] basically don't see them, they're alone, and in general, that's a big problem. It's also a problem for mothers, for grandmothers—women also undergo discrimination when young men are taken into the army.[88]

This reasoning was also reflected in the "Girls against the Draft" protest. In the presence of about fifteen onlookers, including perhaps as many journalists,[89] a handful of young women held hand-lettered cardboard signs voicing opposition to the draft: "Girls against the Draft!" (Devochki protiv prizyva), "People shouldn't go into the army by conscription, but according to their calling" (V armiiu ne po prizyvu, a po prizvaniiu), "Enough conscription! Only by contract!" (Khvatit prizyva! Tol'ko kontrakt), "Let's serve together under contract" (Po kontraktu poidem sluzhit' vmeste), and "That kind of army won't make you a man!" (Takaia armiia ne sdelaet iz tebia muzhchinu).[90] The latter slogan in particular invoked the commonly made link between masculinity and military service but did so in a way that endorsed a professional army over a conscripted one.

Like Molodezhnoe Yabloko's anti-draft action a week earlier, "Girls against the Draft" called upon masculinity and femininity to emphasize the rightness of anti-draft activism. One subtheme was women's influence over men's military choices. A video of the event showed a passing wedding party that joined the protest; the bride proudly hoisted a sign decorated with a heart in the corner, reading, "I won't let [him go] into that kind of an army!" (V takuiu

[87] Vera Kichanova, Libertarianskaia partiia, interview by author, June 16, 2011.
[88] Goncharov, interview by author. While not part of the same organization, as activists, Goncharov and Kichanova supported each other's protests and posted about them on their websites.
[89] Kichanova, interview by author.
[90] "Devochki protiv prizyva" [video], May 21, 2011, http://www.youtube.com/watch?v=MDSHV-7L24k&feature=related. Passersby were also offered a new version of army food—canned dog food (sobachie konservy), dished out by a young man at a folding table; one participant was shown tasting it and then turning away to spit it out politely into his hand.

armiiu ia ne otpushchu!) and then kissed the groom. Not unlike the woman at Nashi's rally for conscription (but endorsing the opposite policy position), the young women protesters also voiced an implicit threat to men choosing whether to register with the army: "Either me, either me, or the army-y!" (Ili ia, ili ia, ili ar-mi-ia!)[91] In another phase of the protest, three young women in khaki and camouflage jackets and skirts marched in place, chanting (in the call-and-response style characteristic of the army), "I want to be protected/By a professional!" (Ia khochu chtob za-shchi-shal/menia pro-fes-si-o-nal), reinforcing the protection of women as a characteristic component of masculinity.

Gender norms and practices are complex, and political actions can both resist patriarchy and comply with it at the same time. The "Girls against the Draft" protest complied with patriarchal assumptions about women—both in using the rhetoric of women's need for male protection and by reinforcing the notion that adult women are, in essence, "girls" ("devochki" generally refers in Russian to girl children, though, as in English, adult women may call each other "girls"). Asked why they chose "devochki" rather than the term "devushki" (which is more typically used to refer to young women like those at the protest), Kichanova explained: "In fact, I don't know. It sounded more lively—less formal. . . . Though we were also told that it was a little strange-sounding; some others didn't like the title, either. They said it sounded childish (detskii sad)."[92] Yet the protest itself, enacted in public by young women who mimicked male military behavior and voiced clear political opinions, also resisted traditional femininity (what Connell calls "emphasized" femininity) that complies with patriarchal norms and that thus would dictate against the public expression of dissent by women—on a "men's" issue in particular.

Just as there exists a "protest masculinity" embraced by oppositionists, so too exists "protest femininity." This "opposition" femininity can take a semitraditional form—as in the "girls'" anti-draft protest—and also shares techniques with opposition masculinity (taking physical and legal risks to express one's opposition to the regime). While female Nashi activists at pro-conscription rallies had also crossed traditional gender lines by speaking out on a military issue in public, they had done so in ways consonant with regime goals and thus ran no risk of arrest or sanction. At a women's movement conference in 2010, a speaker seeking to explain the paucity of women holding positions of political power in Russia noted that women "have the

[91] Ibid.
[92] Kichanova, interview by author.

desire to please men" and are also pressured by their families and by society more broadly to remain outside of politics.[93] The same could be said of young women who supported opposition positions but hesitated to engage in political street actions. There were also physical reasons to avoid unsanctioned protests. Women (and men) in anti-regime youth groups explained that opposition tactics frequently dictated against women's participation because of the danger and risk involved, but for some female activists this was precisely the appeal of taking part in such actions.[94]

Anticipating a standard critique from Kremlin supporters, the "Girls against the Draft" event's organizer explained the point of the protest: "We're not protesting against the army or for the collapse of the country and its takeover by other states. We're in favor of a strong army, and a strong army can only be one that's professional, whose soldiers have professional preparation."[95] An army composed of conscript "slaves" would, in essence, be insufficiently masculine to do the challenging job of military defense in the modern era.

Just as the debate over patriotism, conscription, and military service took on gendered tones—consciously or unconsciously—and thereby helped recruit supporters by appealing to their sense of appropriate masculinity and femininity, so too did the Russian political debate over patriotism and population growth. The next section addresses this policy issue, fraught with gendered overtones and implications.

Patriotism and Pro-Natalism: Gendering the Debate over Demographic Policy

Under Putin, along with patriotic education programs came a highly publicized demographic policy overtly intended to increase the country's population. Russia's declining birthrate was framed as an issue of national health, of international status, of labor force needs, and of military consequence. In keeping with the government's patriotic-nationalist agenda, pro-Putin youth activists backed the Kremlin's goals by supporting the regime's policies on pro-natalism as well as on conscription.

---

[93] Tat'iana Chertoritskaia, "U istokov zhenskoi konsolidatsii na novom etape (2007–2010)," in *Zhenskoe dvizhenie v Rossii: Vchera, segodnia, zavtra: Materialy konferentsii*, ed. Galina Mikhaleva (Moscow, Russia: RODP "Yabloko" and KMK Publishers, 2010), 57–58.

[94] Mariia Savel'eva, Oborona, interview by author, Moscow, June 8, 2011.

[95] "Devochki protiv prizyva (Grani-TV)."

PRO-NATALIST POLICY

Ethnic nationalists typically seek to regulate marriage, reproduction, and sexual behavior in an effort to define "who counts" as members of a given nation, and to encourage that national group's increase.[96] In the Russian case, while at times there have been elements of Slavic nationalism in the state's program to raise the birthrate, pro-regime groups like Nashi at least rhetorically embraced an anti-fascist agenda that would dictate against an understanding of Russia as a community made up exclusively of ethnic Russians. Against the backdrop of a nominally multi-ethnic perspective, the drive to encourage population growth can be understood as part of the Putin regime's patriotic nationalist agenda. That agenda included repressing homosexuality, since it contravenes the traditional idea of heterosexual partnership and reproduction. The regulation or restriction of abortion is an area in which the gendered effects of pro-natalist agendas can be seen even more clearly, as women's reproductive rights are set aside in favor of a national goal, suggesting that women's bodies are regarded "as state property."[97]

Throughout the 1990s in Russia, as Michele Rivkin-Fish shows, pro-natalist nationalist voices were increasingly audible, and Russian Orthodox Church activists agitated to radically reduce abortion access. Following Putin's election, however, pro-natalism was more overtly endorsed at the state level. Access to second-trimester abortion was restricted in 2003, and exhortations to grow the population (at the expense of women's reproductive choice) gained ground.[98] In addition to anti-abortion rulings and rhetoric, the Russian government's pro-natalist policy under Putin entailed various reproductive incentives aimed at women and general encouragement of heterosexual partnership and childbearing (coupled with disparagement of homosexuality).

Support for military service and support for pro-natalism are both aspects of a particular expression of patriotism. That expression of patriotism is also gendered: if it is the ideal patriotic male citizen's duty to protect Russia's internal and external sovereignty (i.e., to protect the Putin regime from left-wing or liberal ideological opponents at home and to protect Russia from external threats), it is the ideal patriotic female citizen's duty to encourage military

---

[96] Yuval-Davis, *Gender and Nation*, 22. On the gendered nature of pro-natalist political discourse in Soviet and post-Soviet Russia, see Michele Rivkin-Fish, "From 'Demographic Crisis' to 'Dying Nation': The Politics of Language and Reproduction in Russia," in *Gender and National Identity in Twentieth-Century Russian Culture*, ed. Helena Goscilo and Andrea Lanoux (DeKalb: Northern Illinois University Press, 2006), 151–173.

[97] See Roza Tsagarousianou, "'God, Patria and Home': 'Reproductive Politics' and Nationalist (Re)Definitions of Women in East/Central Eruope," *Social Identities*, 1, no. 2 (1995): 283–313, cited in Yuval-Davis, *Gender and Nation*, 37.

[98] Rivkin-Fish, "From 'Demographic Crisis' to 'Dying Nation,'" 164, 167.

service among men (by linking women's admiration and sexual availability to men's military service) and to do her part to reproduce—and increase—the Russian state's population and, by association, its might.

The regime's policy on military conscription and its pro-natalism were also related to the broader notion of Russia's state strength. Putin himself has linked (albeit indirectly) the issue of fertility rates and population decline in Russia with the need for a more robust male population of conscript age in the future. In his annual address to Russia's Federal Assembly in May 2006, Putin stressed the demographic issues facing Russia, promoting a plan to increase birthrates by offering various incentives. The tie to military service was highlighted when Putin introduced the topic of fertility. "And now for the most important matter," Putin stated. "What is most important for our country?" A male voice from the audience interrupted him, calling out, "Love (liubov')!" It was Sergei Ivanov, then Russia's defense minister. "Correct (pravil'no)!" answered Putin. "The Defense Ministry knows what is most important. Indeed, what I want to talk about is love, women, children. I want to talk about the family, about the most acute problem facing our country today—the demographic problem."[99] Responding to these remarks, Andrei Illarionov, a former aid to the president, believed Putin's distress over demographic trends was motivated by his desire for a larger draft pool. "It seems that the Defense Ministry is the only institution that understands why it is necessary to solve the demographic problem in Russia," Illarionov stated after the address.[100]

State concern over Russian demographic decline continued over the course of Putin's first two terms as president and into his third. In November 2012, Dmitrii Medvedev—then in the position of prime minister—announced that the Russian government's "top priority" was population growth.[101] Along these lines, in June 2012, while attending a Kremlin ceremony to hand out "Order of Parental Glory" awards, President Putin declared that state support for "motherhood" and multi-child families was an "unconditional national priority."[102] These statements were preceded by the introduction of a "maternity capital" program in 2007, which made state funds available to women and families, rewarding them for giving birth to (or adopting) more than one

---

[99] Vladimir Putin, "Annual Address to the Federal Assembly [video/transcript]," May 10, 2006; C. J. Chivers, "Putin Urges Plan to Reverse Slide in the Birth Rate," *New York Times*, May 11, 2006, http://www.nytimes.com/2006/05/11/world/europe/11russia.html.

[100] "Putin's Address Heralds Return to Soviet Times—Illarionov," May 12, 2006, http://www. fulfilledprophecy.com/bb/viewtopic.php?f=7&t=7754.

[101] "Russia Government Sets Population Growth as Top Priority," ITAR-TASS, November 29, 2012, http://en.itar-tass.com/archive/686148.

[102] "Putin Says Support for Big Families, Mothers, Children priority of Govt," ITAR-TASS, June 2, 2012, http://en.itar-tass.com/archive/676588.

child.[103] Amounting to about $13,000 in 2012, the maternity capital (received in voucher form) could be used toward the acquisition of housing (or to pay off a mortgage), for children's education, or as an addition to the mother's future pension.[104]

Discussions of the problem of Russia's demographic decline echoed widely across the population. In May 2011, a "flash mob" was organized in the Moscow subway by hundreds of elderly people (largely women) wearing ponchos reading, "Is something the matter? Have babies!" (Chto-to ne tak? Rozhaite detei!"). The goal of the action—organized by a group called the Older Generation—was to attract young Muscovites' attention to the low birthrate and to call upon them to correct the problem. The takeover apparently provoked irritated passengers to exit the trains after being subjected to lectures about the importance of childbearing as well as to songs spontaneously voiced by the mob of retirees.[105]

Pro-Kremlin youth activists, too, have upheld state-approved patriotic policy, embracing gender norms in tandem with support for military conscription and pro-natalism. The gendering of pro-Kremlin youth activism on these issues was evident at the state-sponsored summer camp, Seliger, where marriage and reproduction among "patriotic youth" were fostered alongside the complicated reinforcement of gender norms.

SEX, SELIGER, AND THE STATE

Camp Seliger, a massive annual event focused on patriotism, political education, and physical fitness, was organized by the pro-Kremlin group Nashi, starting in 2005. In that year, five thousand campers were brought to the shores of Lake Seliger as part of the Kremlin's initiative to resist developments like the Orange Revolution, which had occurred in Ukraine the previous year.[106] By 2011, Seliger was bringing in approximately fifteen thousand youth to sleep in tents, cook over campfires, and participate in nine thematic "shifts," such as "Innovations and Technical Creativity," "Entrepreneurship," "Politics," and "Run after Me" (which focused on health and fitness).[107]

---

[103] A similar program to encourage births exists in Japan. See Yuval-Davis, *Gender and Nation*, 29.

[104] Michele Rivkin-Fish, "Pronatalism, Gender Politics, and the Renewal of Family Support in Russia: Toward a Feminist Anthropology of 'Maternity Capital,'" *Slavic Review* 69, no. 3 (Fall 2010): 701–724; Pension Fund of Russian Federation, "Maternity (Family) Capital," 2012, http://www.pfrf.ru/ot_en/mother/.

[105] Ilya Varlamov, "Fotoputeshestviia i eshche—Chto-to ne tak? Rozhaite!," May 18, 2011, http://zyalt.livejournal.com/399790.html.

[106] "Putin Promises to Lose 1/2 kg of Weight in 6 Months," ITAR-TASS, August 1, 2011.

[107] Ibid.

Particularly in its first few years, the Seliger encampment supported the regime's demographic policy in multiple ways. Most dramatically, to encourage marriages between patriotic citizens Seliger held a mass wedding for more than two dozen couples among the campers in 2007, after which they directed the newlyweds to a group of red "dormitory tents arranged in a heart shape" to start the reproductive process (no condoms were on sale).[108] As part of the marriage ceremony agenda, couples were exhorted verbally to help grow the Russian population by having at least three children, and some were sent off to red tents on floating barges to consummate their patriotic unions.[109] That year, camp organizers also offered young women the chance to "hand in thongs and other skimpy underwear"—because these could supposedly render women infertile—in exchange for "more wholesome and substantial undergarments."[110] Along the same pro-natalist lines, in 2008 Nashi had created a "mock graveyard" in Moscow as a means of protesting the high abortion rate in Russia.[111]

Marriages continued to be a regular feature of the Seliger gathering. In 2011, Nashi's leader, Nikita Borovikov, noted that each year more than ten couples generally went through the marriage ceremony at Seliger, though the red tents had been discontinued. "I don't even remember what the deal was with the red tents," Borovikov said. "A lot of things that catch the attention of journalists just go past us, unnoticed." Linking the encouragement of marriage and reproduction to Russian national interests, as well as to pragmatic, logistical issues associated with traditional weddings, he explained:

> To go back to the question of national interests, it's obvious that getting married and having children is good. And therefore, we are stimulating

[108] A reporter at the camp three years later noted that condoms were on hand at Seliger, though it is not clear whether they were made available by the camp organizers or brought by campers themselves. See Edward Lucas, "Sex for the Motherland: Russian Youths Encouraged to Procreate at Camp," *Daily Mail*, July 29, 2007, http://www.dailymail.co.uk/news/article-471324/Sex-motherland-Russian-youths-encouraged-procreate-camp.html; Julia Ioffe, "Russia's Nationalist Summer Camp," *The New Yorker*, August 16, 2010, http://www.newyorker.com/online/blogs/newsdesk/2010/08/seliger.html.

[109] Oliver Harvey, "Babes 'n arms"; Journeyman Pictures, "Nashi."

[110] Aleksei Iaushev, "Medal' za komissarskoe telo," August 26, 2010, http://www.vkrizis.ru/news.php?news=2318&type=rus&rub=soc; Lucas, "Sex for the Motherland."

[111] Andrew Osborn, "Kremlin Youth Group Does Its Bit to Reverse the Depopulation crisis," *The Telegraph*, April 21, 2011, http://www.telegraph.co.uk/news/worldnews/europe/russia/8464040/Kremlin-youth-group-does-its-bit-to-reverse-the-depopulation-crisis.html. The high abortion rate is likely an ongoing legacy of the deficit of contraceptives in the Soviet era and of inadequate sex education, which continues to the present day. See Chloe Arnold, "Abortion Remains Top Birth-Control Option in Russia," June 28, 2008, http://www.rferl.org/content/Abortion_Remains_Top_Birth_Control_Option_Russia/1145849.html.

this in every possible way. I know some guys who are planning to go to Seliger and who want to get married there. And they don't want to do the traditional wedding, going to ZAGS [the registry office], and having a whole bunch of drunken relatives [whom you don't even know].... They'll happily get married among their friends.[112]

Anton Smirnov, a 28-year old leader of Stal' who had come to Seliger initially as a participant as well as having been in charge of a 2000 person delegation (including campers from his own organization) was not sure that he would want to get married at Seliger but noted that marriage at Seliger had its advantages: "Why not have five thousand guests at your wedding!"[113]

Irina Pleshcheva, a 24-year old Nashi activist, further explained why marriage and reproduction were encouraged at Seliger:

In 2007, there was a book called "Putin's Plan." And one of the chapters in that plan addressed demographic issues. It's no secret that Russia is experiencing demographic degradation, right? That [the birthrate] is falling.... And, accordingly, the ideology on that issue is, "If you love each other, then why are you giving each other the runaround (*golovu morochit*')?" That is, if you've said, "I love you," then why should you go on living just like that, when you could get married and do it legally? You're allowed to live in a "civil marriage" (*grazhdanskii brak*)—that's what it's called if you live together, but you haven't gotten married [officially]. But typically, it's rare for those couples to have children. What we're saying is, "If you love each other, get married, and have children." ... Here, we have these ideas, probably from the village [way of life], along the lines of, "You're not married, but here you are having a baby, what kind of dim-witted (*bestolkovyi*) [person are you]?" That's why people don't have children in civil marriages. And if someone gets [unexpectedly] pregnant [in a civil marriage], then they register their marriage officially. But given that there are a lot of young women (*devushki*) and guys at Seliger, couples who have a lot of friends who have gotten married at Seliger, or not at Seliger, but who are in the movement—well, if you love each other, then get married. Have children.[114]

---

[112] Borovikov, interview by author.

[113] Smirnov, interview by author.

[114] Pleshcheva, interview by author. Neither she nor the two male activists from pro-Kremlin groups interviewed for the project were married or had children. And although Irina had a "candidate" in mind for marriage (not a Nashi member), she had no plans to get married at Seliger, citing her "traditional" family.

Borovikov also cited a connection between improving Russia's birthrate and opposing homosexuality. "It's evident that the birthrate is in the national interest of any country," he noted, "and it's obvious that we have a relatively difficult demographic situation here. And in that sense, of course, it's obvious that [homosexuality] lies beyond the bounds of national interests." In support of his position, Borovikov made reference to a speech he had heard by a prominent Rabbi with an "iron-clad argument: God . . . said, 'Be fruitful and multiply.' And [homosexuality] is a direct violation of the will of God. And that's not good. And it's hard to argue with that," he added, chuckling.[115]

Opposition activists, meanwhile, generated their own messages about Russia's demographic situation. Most famously, in February 2008, several years before the now-famed punk-feminist group, Pussy Riot, was created, one of its participants, college student Nadezhda Tolokonnikova, and her husband, Petr Verzilov—along with several other pairs of activists from the art-group War (art-gruppa Voina)—organized a "protest orgy" in Moscow's State Biological Museum. At the time, Tolokonnikova had been just a few days short of giving birth to her daughter. Afterward, a video of the event circulated on the Web and was shown on a Russian television station (Ren-TV). Titled "Fuck for the Heir Teddy-Bear!" (Ebis' za naslednika Medvezhonka) and widely critiqued for its exhibitionism, the action was reportedly "explained as a satire of then-presidential candidate Dmitry Medvedev's call to increase the birth rate in Russia."[116]

In a different kind of assertion of reproductive rights, in 2011 a Russian feminist organization, the Initiative Group "Pro-Feminism," awarded one of their "Sexist of the Year" prizes to State Duma Deputy Elena Mizulina after she called for legal changes that would limit access to abortion and made statements that, in essence, blamed women for Russia's low birthrate.[117] And at a demonstration held on International Women's Day 2011 (March 8), the Committee for a Workers' International (a Russian socialist group with a campaign to eradicate gender-based discrimination) lampooned a governmental advertisement in circulation at the time intended to encourage women to have more children and break their birthrate "records." The regime's pro-natalist poster—plastered throughout Moscow—bore the image of a woman and three children, with the slogan "The country needs your records!" The group's rejoinder was a poster that read, "The authorities need [a high] birthrate;

[115] Borovikov, interview by author.

[116] "Voina ebetsia za naslednika Medvezhonka (ren-tv)" [video], April 18, 2008, https://www.youtube.com/watch?v=BstpfQuQzuw; Robert Bridge, "Pussy Riot: Hell's Angels behind the Headlines," November 27, 2012, http://rt.com/politics/pussy-riot-russia-law-putin-medvedev-696/.

[117] Wander Woman, "Seksist Goda-2011."

mothers need child welfare benefits and childcare centers," making the point that the demographic situation could not be improved without addressing women's poverty as well.[118]

Over time, Seliger's mission shifted toward entrepreneurship and away from reproduction but retained a patriotic focus, as the camp received yearly visits from top political leaders. At its outset, Seliger had been a project of Nashi, then headed by Vasilii Iakemenko.[119] As such, the camp had embraced the internally and externally directed patriotism for which Nashi was known, supporting the regime and attacking its domestic opposition—often, by linking opposition figures to the West and labeling them as traitors and fascists. This trend reached its height at an "installation" at Seliger in 2010, when mockups of the heads of domestic and international political actors deemed to have anti-Russian interests were planted on stakes under a banner proclaiming, "You are not welcome here." Renowned Russian human rights activist and Kremlin critic Liudmila Alekseeva, former US Secretary of State Condoleeza Rice, Georgian president Mikheil Saakashvili, and ten others were pictured in this way, wearing Nazi Wehrmacht caps complete with swastikas.[120] A set of posters caricaturing the individuals provided the details of their "betrayals." The exhibit was organized by Stal'—the pro-Kremlin youth project whose leadership overlapped with Nashi's—and its insignia was visible on the posters.[121]

The exhibits at Seliger not only tied Russia's domestic opposition forces to the West but also entailed a display of normative feminine images that highlighted the "correct" femininity and sexuality of the regime's allies. This was compared to the inadequate femininity of the ostensibly traitorous women affiliated with Russia's political opposition forces. On one poster with the Stal' logo, the airbrushed face of Anna Chapman, the pretty, young, undercover Russian spy made famous in 2010 (when she was arrested and deported from the United States), with a Russian flag in the corner, was counterpoised to a close-up of Valeriia Novodvorskaia, a jowly, 60-year-old Soviet and Russian dissident political figure, with an American flag. The poster's caption read: "Their secret agents are cool (*byvaiut krutymi*) only in the movies."[122] The feminine attractiveness of the assumed-to-be pro-regime women at Seliger

---

[118] Zhenia Otto, "8 Marta: Vernut' utrachennyi smysl," *Net—znachit net* 3 (March 2011): 7.

[119] Bratersky, "Yakemenko's Departure Signals End of Era for Youth Politics."

[120] Sergey Borisov, "Youth at Seliger Camp Use Nazi Symbols to Portray Ideological Enemies," July 29, 2010, http://rt.com/politics/roar-seliger-installation-scandal/.

[121] "seliKhER. mnogo foto," July 28, 2010, http://tapirr.livejournal.com/2516191.html. In 2010, for the first time, young people from outside Russia attended Seliger, but their shift ended before the Nazi-heads-on-pikes exhibit went up. See Ioffe, "Russia's Nationalist Summer Camp."

[122] "seliKhER. mnogo foto," July 28, 2010, http://tapirr.livejournal.com/2516191.html.

was also revealed by photos of the 2010 session posted on the Web. One photo revealed four shapely young women in bikini bottoms, bared from the waist up, with red Xs made of what appeared to be tape covering their nipples, standing in front of a Nashi banner.[123] Also in 2010, young bikini-clad women at Seliger engaged in mud wrestling (posing afterward, grinning, in the embrace of a man, lending a heterosexual accent to the event), and the camp exhibits included a display of a large, fake ten-ruble note with a long-haired young woman in a silver bikini pictured in its center.[124]

Starting in 2009, Seliger ceased to be officially sponsored by Nashi, as control of the camp passed to the Federal Agency for Youth Affairs—though that agency was headed by Vasilii Iakemenko, Nashi's former leader, suggesting that the project was still closely tied to Nashi.[125] While that year the camp was no longer restricted to Nashi members, anti-Kremlin participants were not invited to attend,[126] and the camp retained a pro-regime tone, with likenesses of Putin and Medvedev prominent at the site.[127] At the camp's evening "disco," for instance, the backdrop for the stage was a huge portrait of Putin and Medvedev.[128]

In 2011, although Nashi's press secretary, Kristina Potupchik (also Iakemenko's press-secretary at the Federal Agency for Youth Affairs) stated that Nashi was involved only in Seliger's "political" shift, unambiguously pro-regime elements remained. In 2011, for instance, one of the planned topics of the political program was "What [is it], if not treason? Faces of the opposition in Russia," suggesting that an echo of the 2010 exhibit was in store.[129] That summer, great banners of Putin's and Medvedev's faces framed the stage before which campers conducted their morning exercises, and posters of Putin could be found alongside the boardwalk that ran through the camp.[130] In his speech

[123] Iaushev, "Medal' za komissarskoe telo."

[124] "seliKhER. mnogo foto."

[125] Alexander Bratersky, "Camp's Challenge Is also the Kremlin's," *The Moscow Times*, June 9, 2011, http://www.themoscowtimes.com/news/article/camps-challenge-is-also-the-kremlins/438538.html; "Putin Promises to Lose 1/2 kg of Weight in 6 Months."

[126] Andrey Kozenko, "Youth Being Prepared for Camps: Seliger-2009 to Be Main Event of 'Year of the Youth,'" *Kommersant*, March 9, 2009.

[127] Vadim Volkov, interview by author, Boston, November 14, 2009.

[128] "Seliger 2009: Putin-Medvedev Disco" [video], August 4, 2009, http://www.youtube.com/watch?v=6Ii8cJdRqO4&feature=related.

[129] Bratersky, "Camp's Challenge Is also the Kremlin's"; Iuliia Balashova, "Bezdonnyi Seliger, ili 'Ne vse doma,'" *Novaia Gazeta*, April 26, 2011, http://novayagazeta.ru/data/2011/045/22.html.

[130] Varlamov, "Fotoputeshestviia i eshche—Seliger"; Sergei Loiko, "Kremlin Youth Camp at Russia's Lake Seliger: Framework," *Los Angeles Times*, August 10, 2011, http://framework.latimes.com/2011/08/10/kremlin-youth-camp/#/0.

to the campers in August 2011, Putin himself pointed out that it was a pleasure to be among "likeminded people" and that the forum was supported by his party, United Russia, and by youth movements.[131] Seliger was also well funded—in large part by Russia's taxpayers. In 2012, 280 million rubles (over $8 million) came out of the federal budget to finance the camp, up from 178 million rubles (roughly $5.6 million) in 2011 and 100 million rubles ($3 million) in 2010.[132]

Gendered activities reinforcing notions of femininity and masculinity were in evidence at Seliger. Irina Pleshcheva, who had attended Seliger every summer (starting in the camp's second year in 2006), asserted that Seliger's events were open to everyone, regardless of their sex, but that campers did organize "optional" events that had a more traditionally gendered cast:

> Some of the girls (devchonki) held a beauty contest for themselves, "Miss Seliger"—that was more for their interests, to be acknowledged as "the beauties of Seliger," right? But the organizers didn't split anybody up [on that basis]. . . . The boys (mal'chishki) created a fight club (boitsovskii klub) for themselves, fighting in a boxing ring—that's more in their area of interest.
>
> Q. I heard that devushki also took part in the boxing club.
> A. Yes. The boys organized it, and girls (devchonki) came along and said, "We can do it, too."
> Q. So the [fight club] wasn't organized by the leadership [of Seliger]?
> A. No, it was optional; it's a civil society. The guys came [to the camp] and came up with something to do in the evenings, "Let's organize this"—and that's all there was to it.[133]

Russian sociologist Vadim Volkov, who lectured at Seliger in 2009, also witnessed the boxing club, which was titled "The Vladimir Putin Fight Club."[134]

---

[131] Tiffany Gabbay, "Why Is Vladimir Putin Arm Wrestling and Trying to Bend a Frying Pan?," August 3, 2011, http://www.theblaze.com/stories/why-is-vladimir-putin-arm-wrestling-and-trying-to-bend-a-frying-pan/.

[132] Ol'ga Kuz'menkova, "Uchastniki 'Seligera-2012' pytaiutsia oboitis' bez politiki," July 2, 2012, http://www.gazeta.ru/politics/2012/07/02_a_4660937.shtml; Alina Garbuzniak, "Oppozitsiia smenit 'Nashikh' na 'Seligere,'" *Moskovskie Novosti*, June 30, 2012, http://mn.ru/society_civil/20120630/321788235.html; "Kremlin Youth Camp Spending to Double Despite Reluctant Sponsors," *The Moscow Times*, April 10, 2012, http://www.themoscowtimes.com/news/article/kremlin-youth-camp-spending-to-double-despite-reluctant-sponsors/456474.html; Bratersky, "Camp's Challenge Is also the Kremlin's."

[133] Pleshcheva, interview by author.

[134] The Fight Club remained in 2011, when campers received martial arts instruction before being allowed to join the club. See Loiko, "Kremlin Youth Camp at Russia's Lake Seliger."

According to Volkov, the club was organized into male and female divisions and also by regions, such that men fought men and women fought women, while regions fought against each other. The audience (both male and female) reportedly supported the fighters, cheering for their regions regardless of the boxers' sex. The campers' living quarters were also divided according to region but not by sex. In general, Volkov noticed no gender bias, other than that the "internal police" for the camp were all male and that it was not clear who was doing the cooking. There were male and female fitness instructors, and an apparent mix of the sexes at all the events that he witnessed at the camp. Alcohol was forbidden, and there was a stress on fitness, economic innovation, and entrepreneurship.[135]

Nikita Borovikov, who had been present at Seliger since its first year, lauded the opportunities for contact and conversation that the camp enabled by bringing people together from across the country and echoed Pleshcheva's impression that Seliger events did not discriminate on a gendered basis. Even the military-related "eternal flame" marking respect for Russia's World War II dead, lighted at the start of the camp and extinguished at the end, was guarded by male and female campers alike.[136] A journalist at Nashi's Seliger gathering in 2007 likewise reported that male and female attendees "practiced shooting, wrestling and how to strip down guns."[137] Borovikov's description of the exercise regime, however, was enlightening from a gendered perspective, reflecting societal understandings of normative feminine and masculine behavior:

Q. At Seliger, were there any events that were just for men and just for women?

A. Yes. Every morning, there were exercises (zariadka). And it's obvious that it's hard to have a bunch of people doing exercises all in one place, and if it's several thousand, it's also complicated. And on the one hand, for these technical reasons, and on the other hand, so that, let's say, the men wouldn't forget that they are men, we decided that the boys (mal'chiki) would go running and that the girls (devushki) would do aerobics. So that's probably the most striking difference (if there are any) that we have. And nobody stopped the girls from going running; if you want—go ahead and run. But they like aerobics better. And in that sense, there's discrimination against men.

Q. They weren't allowed to do aerobics?

---

[135] Volkov, interview by author.
[136] For footage of two young women standing guard, see "Seliger 2009: Honour Watch" [video], August 4, 2009, http://www.youtube.com/watch?v=rNcXqRYWX_4.
[137] Harvey, "Babes 'n Arms."

A. Well, it's that an atmosphere is created where it'd be shameful (stydno) to stay behind at the girls' exercises. [Laughs][138]

Modeling the desirable features of strength and masculinity, Prime Minister Putin arm-wrestled several male campers during his visit in 2011 and made an effort to bend a frying pan.[139] Not all efforts to secure a masculine image succeeded; Putin failed in this particular enterprise, looking on afterward in awe as a bulky male Seliger attendee managed to roll up not one but two stacked frying pans.[140] Still, that year young female campers were pictured on the Web asking for Putin's autograph and had reportedly shouted, "We love you!" to the prime minister during his visit. This public declaration of female desire reinforced Putin's masculinity, while the overall association between physical strength and masculinity was affirmed as a fitting characteristic for male supporters of the regime.[141]

Despite participants' belief that Seliger presented a reasonably nondiscriminatory atmosphere, some of those outside of it gained a different impression. Twenty-five-year-old socialist-feminist activist Zhenia Otto believed Nashi relied on Seliger simply as a recruiting tool, based on the attractiveness of the women in attendance:

The way they use Nashi is understood—if you look at their booklets, in general the subtext is, "Look what cool babes come to us at Seliger" (Posmotrite kakie u nas klevye telki priezhaiut k nam v Seliger). Well, the photos they take of them, it's obvious what they're targeting, and it's clearly not [done] with the subtext that these are women activists (activistki), but simply that it's an ad for Seliger—that "we have pretty girls (krasivye devchonki)" and nothing else (i bol'she nichego).[142]

In an effort to attract English-speaking foreigners to Seliger in 2011, the forum's organizers put out a recruitment video in March of that year, whose music echoed Otto's viewpoint. The Guns and Roses soundtrack of "Paradise

---

[138] Borovikov, interview by author. A male camper at Seliger confirmed that "we have to jog in the morning—all the boys have to." See Anna Sulimina, "Occupy Seliger," *The Moscow News,* July 19, 2012, http://themoscownews.com/politics/20120719/189979244.html.

[139] Sergei Loiko, "Russia Youths Seek 'Social Lift' at Kremlin Political Camp," *Los Angeles Times,* August 11, 2011, http://articles.latimes.com/2011/aug/11/world/la-fg-russia-youth-camp-20110811.

[140] See "Putin Supporter Bends Frying Pans—Video," Reuters, August 3, 2011, http://www.reuters.com/video/2011/08/04/putin-supporter-bends-frying-pans?videoId=217853042.

[141] For photos of Seliger 2011, see Varlamov, "Fotoputeshestviia i eshche."

[142] Zhenia Otto, Komitet za Rabochii Internatsional, Kampaniia protiv ekspluatatsii i diskriminatsii zhenshchin, interview by author, Moscow, June 18, 2012.

City" played over footage of Seliger's various activities: "Take me down to Paradise City/Where the grass is green/And the girls are pretty."[143]

Indeed, opposition activists saw nothing peculiar about Nashi's efforts to attract young people to their organization by drawing attention to the sexual attractiveness of the women ostensibly linked to it. Commenting on Nashi's anti-corruption calendar, with its sexily dressed young women, an opposition activist with Oborona explained that the pro-Kremlin groups were in the habit of using the promise of pleasure to attract new followers:

> At first, [Nashi] was an organization called "Walking Together" (Idushie Vmeste), which from the start made itself known for giving its activists things like movie tickets and gym passes, and played not so much on people's convictions, but on their desire for pleasure. It was a way of getting people to participate—not by using ideology, but by using pleasure. That is to say, "Our ideology is better, because we've got more sex."[144]

In another activist's opinion, Nashi's motivation to play up the sexual angle stemmed from the group's reputation as a Soviet-esque official youth group, akin to the Komsomol, and bound to do the authorities' bidding. This perhaps explained the organization's occasional choice of tactics: "As we know, sex sells. And they understood that perfectly, too. They clearly are trying to be very unofficial, very informal, because they still can't rid themselves of that Komsomol overtone [shleif], and they're afraid that's going to ruin them completely. So they always want to be on the edge, or beyond the edge [of propriety]."[145]

The group's edginess, however, did not extend to "nontraditional" sexuality. Like other political actions associated with pro-regime youth groups, Seliger reinforced the "correctness" of its participants' sexual orientation. Vasili Iakemenko, speaking in 2011 to the young men and women gathered at Seliger, called the participants "true heroes" and contrasted them to Nashi's targets in Russian society—"drug-dealers, pedophiles, and bandits supporting illegal casinos."[146] Iakemenko's reference to "pedophiles" here was likely a stand-in for "homosexuals." Although homosexuality and pedophilia are unrelated, in

---

[143] "Seliger 2011" [video], March 20, 2011, http://www.youtube.com/watch?v=97yQVX RgdMo.

[144] Tivur Shaginurov, Oborona, interview by author, Moscow, June 11, 2011.

[145] Kozlovskii, interview by author.

[146] "Party Prospects for Seliger Youth forum," July 27, 2011, http://rt.com/politics/seliger-youth-forum-party/.

Russia they are linked in the public and political imagination. For instance, a law passed in St. Petersburg in 2012 banned the "propaganda of homosexuality and pedophilia among minors," and the bill's supporters typically echoed its sponsor, Vitalii Milonov, in arguing that the bill was "simply defending children," implying that children required protection from homosexuals and homosexuality.[147] Indeed, few gay Nashi members felt comfortable coming out to their fellow campers. One former Nashi organizer, Ruslan Savolainen, recalled being the only noncloseted gay person at Seliger, out of "tens of thousands" of youth from across the country, and noted that people would even "come over to look at him"—and occasionally try to convince the teenager that his orientation was wrong (though his friends would "chase them off"). Savolainen recalled Iakemenko's position as one of personal indifference mixed with pronatalist concern: "I'm not against it, but it's bad for the demographic [situation]." In Savolainen's final year at Seliger, he knew one gay male couple who openly lived together, and a "small community of lesbians."[148] Even as a handful of campers carved out some gay-friendly space, Nashi's public orientation was "traditional," and the messages about sex at Seliger clearly encouraged and supported the state's pro-natalist agenda.

Public disclosures about sex, however, occasionally endangered the organization's reputation. Iakemenko himself was caught in something of a scandal when opposition activist Roman Dobrokhotov (the leader of We), revealed that Iakemenko had had a sexual liaison at Seliger with a camper in her mid-teens.[149] Dobrokhotov had uncovered a photograph posted on a blog written by Nashi member Anastasiia Korchevskaia, in which she was standing next to Iakemenko; the caption read: "Seliger-2008. Iakemenko still thinks that I'm madly in love with him." Iakemenko's commentary on the blog followed, seeming to confirm their liason: "Korchevskaia, if you came to my tent twice for the night, i.e., once a year, and we had something, that doesn't mean that I think you're in love with me. Got it?"[150] While this alleged encounter was not an illegal act, given that 16 is the age of consent in Russia, Dobrokotov's public revelation of it was intended to undermine Iakemenko's reputation as a man.[151]

---

[147] "St. Petersburg 'Gay Propaganda' Law Author Defiant after Milan Snub," RIA Novosti, November 28, 2012, http://en.rian.ru/russia/20121128/177798647.html; "Gay Propaganda Bill Challenged in Court," RIA Novosti, April 2, 2012, http://en.rian.ru/society/20120402/172562401.html.

[148] Alla Mel'nikova and Kristina Markhotskaia, "'Ia mogu vstat' i skazat': Tak bol'she ne budet': 27 istorii iz zhizni rossiiskikh geev," *Afisha*, February 22, 2013, http://www.afisha.ru/article/gay-issue/. Savolainen does not say what year this was at Seliger.

[149] Samofalova, "Samye gromkie seks-skandaly 2010 goda."

[150] For a screen shot, see Gera_DOT, "Khroniki mirovoi blogosfery," August 26, 2010, http://f5.ru/geradot/post/290395.

[151] Samofalova, "Samye gromkie seks-skandaly 2010 goda."

Whereas a man could get "masculinity credit" for having a female lover or as many female lovers as possible—and Iakemenko was married at the time—a man in his late 30s taking up with a 16-year-old appeared potentially deviant. As one blogger responding to the information wrote,

> You can ask Vasia Iakemenko on his blog what he's teaching young people; is he recommending that they cheat (in particular when they have a legal wife and son), is he recommending sex with under-age schoolgirls, and what would the attitude of his brother—the leader of an Orthodox [religious] sect—be toward his betrayal and sex with a minor?[152]

In making this information public, Dobrokhotov was exacting revenge on the regime. Unknown players, presumed to be acting on state orders, had provoked a reputation-scarring scandal earlier that year (2010) by setting up several regime opponents (including Russian satirist Viktor Shenderovich and the leader of the National Bolshevik party, Eduard Limonov) to engage in sex with young women, filming them, and releasing the videos on the Web in an effort to erode the oppositionists' reputations. Several men had been approached by two young women—one of them was a model, Katia Gerasimova, with the nickname Mu-Mu—who invited them to an apartment and offered them sex and cocaine.[153] The editor of Russian *Newsweek*, Mikhail Fishman, for example, was shown in a video clip—released on the Molodaia Gvardiia site, titled "Fishman Is an Addict"—snorting a white powder while sitting next to a partially dressed young woman on a couch (earlier in the video Fishman was also shown naked in the same apartment).[154] When the video of Fishman appeared, Ilia Iashin, a 25-year old liberal activist and former member of Oborona, recognized the apartment, and revealed that he, too, had been contacted by Mu-Mu. After Iashin slept with her in 2008, Mu-Mu invited him to come over for a "surprise," which turned out to be an invitation to a threesome with herself and a young woman named Nastia Chukova. Iashin did not decline. However, when the young women took out a variety of sex toys, Iashin asked whether they were being filmed on a hidden camera. The women denied it but then offered him drugs—after which "everything became clear as day," and he left, despite their attempts to get him to remain.[155] Dobrokhotov himself was

---

[152] Quoted in Gera_DOT, "Khroniki mirovoi blogosfery."

[153] Samofalova, "Samye gromkie seks-skandaly 2010 goda."

[154] "'Mishka Fishman narkoman': V Set' vylozhen ocherednoi 'kompromat' na glavreda 'Russkogo Newsweek,'" March 25, 2010, http://www.nakanune.ru/news/2010/3/23/22190466.

[155] Yashin, "Ulybaites'. Vas snimaet skrytaia kamera," March 23, 2010, http://yashin.livejournal.com/894296.html.

approached by the same woman (Katia) in 2009 but apparently got wise to the situation and did not fall for the "porno-provocation."[156]

While having multiple female lovers can reinforce a man's perceived hetero-masculinity, being set up could erode it, as that might suggest he was not clever enough to avoid being caught, that he had fallen for a trap set by a woman, and so on. The "Mu-Mu" technique—using a woman to entrap a man into drug use—was reminiscent of that used by the FBI and Washington, DC, police to arrest then-Mayor Marion Barry in 1990 for smoking crack cocaine. The woman involved in the Barry case—like Mu-Mu, a model—had been an FBI informant.[157] Dobrokhotov and Iashin likewise concluded that the perpetra-tors were acting on behalf of Russia's Federal Security Services (the FSB, suc-cessor to the Soviet KGB).[158] It was also rumored—perhaps because the Fish-man video appeared on the website of United Russia's youth wing, Molodaia Gvardiia—that people affiliated with that organization or with Nashi were behind the reputation-smearing acts.[159]

CHANGES AFOOT—NASHI IN TROUBLE

The reinvigoration of mass protest in Russia following the December 4, 2011 parliamentary elections shifted the perceived balance of power between pro-regime and opposition forces more generally, carrying the latter into public view with a vengeance. Fraud uncovered in the voting process had brought thousands of Russians into the streets criticizing their government and de-manding honest elections. Within a year of the first protests a notable change had taken place, particularly in Nashi's fortunes. It was as if the large-scale, authentic, grassroots-generated protest movement had acted on Nashi like daylight on a vampire, sending the pro-Kremlin group scurrying off into something of a political graveyard. The very timing of Nashi's waning—after a brief spurt of activity initially countering the December 2011 protests—points to an element of its artificiality as an organization. This is not to say that Nashi, as a state-sponsored group, had no authentic existence or counted no committed political activists among its ranks. But it does suggest that there was something inauthentic about the size of this pro-Kremlin collective;

[156] Samofalova, "Samye gromkie seks-skandaly 2010 goda."

[157] Sharon LaFraniere, "Barry Arrested on Cocaine Charges in Undercover FBI, Police Opera-tion," *Washington Post*, January 19, 1990, http://www.washingtonpost.com/wp-srv/local/long-term/tours/scandal/barry.htm.

[158] Yashin, "Ulybaites'"; Dobrokhotov, "Kokainovaia provokatsiia. Lichnyi opyt," March 23, 2010, http://dobrokhotov.livejournal.com/447278.html.

[159] "Mumugeit (MuMugate)," April 2010, http://traditio-ru.org/wiki/%CC%F3%EC%F3%E3%E5%E9%F2.

surely an organization of one hundred thousand loyal activists could not unravel in the midst of a threat—the first real threat, after all—to the regime to which they were supposedly so strongly committed.

In June 2012, Vasilii Iakemenko lost his position at the Federal Agency for Youth Affairs, symbolically suggesting that the Kremlin's youth policy had shifted.[160] But the agency's ties to Nashi had not fully evaporated. Its new press secretary, Anna Biriukova, had previously worked for Nashi's press office,[161] and another of the Camp Seliger organizers, Mariia Abdulaeva, was a former Nashi member. Meanwhile, Nashi's own fate was growing insecure. During Seliger 2012, in an interview to a Russian journalist, Abdulaeva proclaimed that the Nashi movement had died; for transmitting this information to the public the journalist was ejected from Seliger.[162]

Less than a year later, further reports of Nashi's demise surfaced. In March 2013 Kremlin sources announced that by the end of the year Nashi would be disbanded and "rebooted" as a new youth organization—as yet nameless. The leaders of that organization would be tasked with managing the movement's projects, though how that would differ from the current leaders' tasks remained unclear. The new purpose of the movement was said to be to foster young people's "social adaptation" (itself a vague concept), though political projects "could arise from below." Existing Nashi projects such as a consumer-rights initiative called Piggies Opposed (Khriushi protiv), an effort to stop drivers from parking on the sidewalk (a considerable problem in Moscow) called Stop [Being] Rude (Stop Kham), and the physical-fitness centered program, Run after Me, would be reconstructed as nongovernmental organizations. Nashi's Web-based projects were to be united under the Foundation for Open New Democracy, run by Nashi's former press secretary, Kristina Potupchik, intended to help nonpolitical Internet-based projects find funding. The Russian Federal Agency for Youth Affairs would cease to be the sponsor of the movement and instead would run eight different summer camps for youth (one camp for each of Russia's seven federal districts—including Seliger, as the "central federal district" camp plus one "Federal" camp whose status would rotate). As political scientist Aleksei Makarin concluded, following the December 2011 mass election protests, it "became clear that Nashi was ineffective in fighting regime opponents" and that therefore the Kremlin would now put its energies into "less ambitious, local, but perhaps more effective projects."[163]

---

[160] Bratersky, "Yakemenko's Departure Signals End of Era for Youth Politics."

[161] "Den' pamiati," Interfax, August 8, 2010, http://www.interfax.ru/society/txt.asp?id=148529.

[162] Alina Garbuzniak, "'Nashi' zakryli 'Seliger' dlia 'MN,'" Moskovskie Novosti, July 2, 2012, http://mn.ru/politics/20120702/321981004.html.

[163] Maksim Glikin and Liliia Biriukova, "Kreml' otkazhetsia ot 'Nashikh,'" March 5, 2013, http://www.vedomosti.ru/politics/news/9743881/bolshe_ne_nashi.

As a harbinger of this impending change, in summer 2012, for the first time since Seliger's inception, there were no posters and banners of Putin and Medvedev festooning the stage and walkways of Seliger, and the camp's doors were opened even to liberal and nationalist oppositionists.[164] The logo for the "Politics" shift was now British graffiti-artist Banksy's familiar image of a man preparing to hurl a bouquet of flowers.[165] Still, the camp retained signs of its state connection, with Putin making a visit to the site. This time, however, he expressed his respect for government critics, including "those who wear white ribbons."[166] Respect for such critics was not universal at Seliger that year. Roman Dobrokhotov, for instance, presented a lecture that summer on state corruption. Following his talk, some members of the audience gave him a "gift" as per the Seliger tradition—aiming paper airplanes at him and suggesting that he fly to the United States—while others flocked around him asking how they could contact him to find out more about corruption in contemporary Russia.[167]

Still, the anti-Western images and pro-regime slogans that had been arrayed in the forest for public consumption in the past were absent that year; the trees at Seliger 2012 were bare of agitational banners.[168] However, the eternal flame persisted, as did the Putin Fight Club,[169] and a Russian newspaper reporter who arrived at the start of Seliger was told by its new director that portraits of Putin might appear closer to the end of the session, when the "Politics" shift began—now under the new name, "Politics and Civil Society."[170] Despite the shift in political tone, campers were still encouraged by Seliger organizers to marry each other. During morning exercises attendees were asked whether anyone had paired up overnight. "Raise your hands!," they were told, and those who did received applause and an explanation of how to apply for a marriage license at the camp. "Find each other, love each other, and 'Seliger' will help you with that!," called a young woman from the stage.[171] While

---

[164] Alexander Roslyakov and Laura Mills, "Kremlin Youth Camp Seeks Image Change," August 2, 2012, http://bigstory.ap.org/article/kremlin-youth-camp-seeks-image-change.

[165] The logo can be seen on Seliger-2012's main page: "Vserossiiskii molodezhnyi forum Seliger 2012," http://www.forumseliger.ru/, accessed December 4, 2012.

[166] Margarita Bogatova, "Putin Visits Youth Camp on Lake Seliger," July 31, 2012, http://english.ruvr.ru/2012_07_31/Putin-visits-youth-camp-on-Lake-Seliger/.

[167] Roman Dobrokhotov, "Pochemu ia edu na Seliger," July 25, 2012, http://slon.ru/russia/pochemu_ya_edu_na_seliger-813688.xhtml; Englehart, "Roman v Kremlin."

[168] Dmitrii Ternovskii, "Seliger 2012. Reportazh s otkrytiia," July 3, 2012, http://www.ridus.ru/news/38565/.

[169] Egor Zhokhov, "Pro Seliger, nashistov i Putina," Feburary 11, 2013, http://yagrazhdanin.ru/post1230.

[170] "Rosmolodezh' obeshchaet na 'Seligere' dat' slovo vsem," RIA Novosti, July 26, 2012, http://ria.ru/politics/20120726/709775594.html.

[171] Garbuzniak, "'Nashi' zakryli 'Seliger' dlia 'MN.'"

campers' "sterility inducing" sexy underwear was no longer being policed, the regime's pro-natalist policies had retained a voice at Seliger.

Patriotic Underwear

Underwear—and, more broadly, fashion—played a role in the regime's patriotic policies supporting military service and pro-natalism as well as in pro-regime youth organizations' support of those policies. In 2008, a Nashi activist named Antonina Shapovalova brought together her interest in fashion and pro-regime political activism. The eponymously named "Shapovalova" clothing line, which included t-shirts and undergarments featuring politicized graphics and slogans, was the result.[172] Finnish scholar Jussi Lassila described the patriotic and demographic emphases in Shapovalova's early collections, no longer visible on the Web.[173] An early Shapovalova creation—reportedly purchased by future president Dmitrii Medvedev—featured a pro-natalist policy-endorsing slogan: "It's pleasant and useful to multiply!" (raznmozhat'sia priatno i polezno).[174] Medvedev was not the only bigwig among Shapovalova fans; her website noted that Putin, Vladislav Surkov (the Kremlin's chief ideologist), Sergei Ivanov (the defense minister), and governors of various Russian regions also "had her clothes in their closets."[175] Other Shapovalova-brand tops, such as one declaring, "I want three!," with the word "children" on the back (khochu troikh . . . detei), used double entendre to express the regime's message about raising the birthrate.

Shapovalova's patriotic undergarments likewise upheld the regime's assertion of internal and external sovereignty. Underwear intended for women used the same medium to express both political support and desire for Putin, with a mini-bikini reading, "Vova, I'm with you!" (Vova, ia s toboi!).[176] Men's briefs expressed a patriotic message about Russia's political independence: "Russia must not be under the Entente!" (Rossiia ne byt' pod Antantoi). This was likely a reference to the French–British–Russian alliance leading up to World War I (and joined by the United States a few years later) and thus constituted a warning against Russia's loss of independence to contemporary Western powers.[177]

---

[172] "Shapovalova," http://www.shapovalova.ru/, accessed November 21, 2012.

[173] Lassila, "Anticipating Ideal Youth in Putin's Russia," 216–220, 338–341.

[174] "Shapovalova."

[175] Lassila, "Anticipating Ideal Youth in Putin's Russia," 217.

[176] Ibid., 218. The "Happy Birthday, Mr. Putin" calendar two years later would again feature skimpy underwear worn with the purpose of supporting Putin's masculinity, but the Putin-enamored messages that time were not printed on the underwear itself.

[177] Ibid., 217.

General patriotic—and gendered—themes were also expressed in Shapovalova's clothing lines. Her "Matreshki" (nesting dolls) collection from 2008–2009 showed male and female models wearing t-shirts that pictured a busty blonde woman in a red bikini emerging out of the lower half of a Russian nesting doll, with "Love things Russian" (liubi russkoe) written across it in script.[178] Shapovalova's later collections continued to feature patriotic themes, from designs based on Russian folk tales, to the military-themed "Victory No. 22" line in 2010, commemorating Russia's victory in the Great Patriotic War.[179]

Not all underwear generated by Russia's young activists endorsed the regime's patriotic goals. An experimental fashion exhibit called "Unusual Underwear" (neobyknovennye trusy) opened in St. Petersburg on March 8, 2012—International Women's Day. It provided an interesting contrast to the pro-regime groups' use of underwear as a means to reinforce patriotism and Russian sovereignty. While the exhibit's participants did not label their work "feminist," the idea for the exhibit grew out of a small-group discussion of the purpose of underwear and emerged as "Women's views on women's underwear." As explained by Polina Zaslavskaia, one of the participants in the exhibit,

> The basic thesis was that, to a large degree, underwear is worn not for oneself but for someone else, usually for men. And in general, underwear is typically exploited in advertising, especially women's underwear. Though you can also see men in underwear now, in ads. [The exhibit] was an experiment in the opinions and views of specific young women on the question, "What does femininity mean to you?"[180]

Among the underwear on display was a series that Polina designed, called "Hairstyles" (pricheski), which constituted a commentary on cultural expectations regarding shaving the pubic area.[181] Another, designed from a woman-friendly functionalist perspective by Ada Chereshnia, was labeled "Always Ready" (an echo of the Soviet youth organization's slogan) and could be removed at any moment using zippers and without having to take off one's other garments.[182] The exhibit was linked to a roundtable held a few days later at a St. Petersburg bookstore, where participants discussed the topic "What Is Feminism the Russian Way?: Prospects for the Development of a Mass

---

[178] "Shapovalova"; Lassila, "Anticipating Ideal Youth in Putin's Russia," 338.
[179] "Shapovalova."
[180] Polina Zaslavskaia, Verkhotura, interview by author, St. Petersburg, June 14, 2012.
[181] Ibid.
[182] "Na Pushkinskoi, 10 pokazali 'Neobyknovennye trusy,'" March 9, 2012, http://www.tv100.ru/news/na-pushkinskoy-10-pokazali-neobyknovennye-trusy-53298/.

Feminist Movement in Russia in the Coming Years."[183] Rather than adopting wholesale the notions that women's bodies could and should be subject to the state's plans and that fashion could similarly be harnessed to the state's demographic program, the Unusual Underwear exhibit used fashion statements to express an ideology interrogating common cultural assumptions.

*   *   *

While disagreeing with the government and with pro-Kremlin youth organizations about the proper way of constituting Russia's armed forces, neither the Molodezhnoe Yabloko anti-draft extravaganza nor the "Girls against the Draft" protest had contradicted the state's assumed "need" for a military. Nor did they undermine militarism, as the protesters had worn camouflage, marched, and chanted in army rhythm. Meanwhile, youth activism on both sides of the conscription policy debate relied heavily on traditional ideas about masculinity, femininity, and desirability. Whether it was a female activist with Nashi instructing young men about their worth as potential husbands or a female activist in the political opposition suggesting that a young man would not truly acquire masculinity from joining the wrong kind of army—a conscripted army—but would, by implication, become a man if he served under contract in a professional army, what counts or what is evaluated as masculine depended in part on enlisting young women's endorsement. The debate over conscription, as one example of contested regime policy, was thus inextricably bound up with gender norms. Pro-natalist policy, too, came out in youth political activism in ways that featured patriotism and patriarchy. While the patriotic male citizen's duty was to protect Russia—and to protect women—the patriotic female citizen's duty was to support men in that endeavor and to bear a new and larger generation of patriotic citizens.

This chapter's exploration of liberal and pro-Kremlin political youth activism in Russia on the topics of patriotism, military conscription, and pronatalism illustrated how political activists in Russia have used femininity and masculinity in efforts both to boost their own authority and damage that of their opponents. Yet most of the activists, regardless of their pro- or anti-regime political positions, did not regard these uses of gender norms as problematic, in part because sex stereotyping was so ubiquitous in the society surrounding them. The next chapter explores sexism in Russia—the foundation on which political legitimation strategies resting on femininity, masculinity, and homophobia are built.

---

[183] For links to the seven-part video of the roundtable (in Russian), see sergeyyugov, "feminizm po-russki?," [video], March 11, 2012, http://www.youtube.com/playlist?list=PLAB65D4BD49 285A0A.

5

Everywhere and Nowhere: Sexism and Homophobia in Russian Politics

Like racism and other types of institutionalized discrimination, sexism and homophobia have the peculiar quality of being visible to some people while remaining invisible to others. Once they become aware of sexism, for instance, whether through conversations with friends, reading books, taking courses, or experiencing discrimination themselves, people find that they can no longer stop seeing evidence of it practically everywhere that they look. For those who have not yet found their "gender lenses," evidence of sexism remains obscure or difficult to believe. This chapter illustrates the normalization of sexism and homophobia that renders them unremarkable or invisible to many political activists in Russia—both regime supporters and liberal opponents.

Political legitimation strategies that rely on gender norms include "topping," or asserting masculine dominance over other men, enhancing political authority by claiming the sexual allegiance of attractive, feminine women, and undermining opponents' positions by attacking their masculinity or femininity as deviant. These techniques only work effectively in a cultural-political context where sexism and homophobia are widely accepted or at least little questioned in public. While small feminist and LGBT movements in Russia tirelessly work to raise public consciousness about sexism and homophobia, popular beliefs about strictly delineated gender norms remain powerful and block many people's perception of sex- and gender-based discrimination.

This chapter begins with the perceptions of young male and female political activists, both pro- and anti-Kremlin, about sex-based discrimination in contemporary Russia. If such discrimination remained largely invisible to them, it had not remained so to Russia's feminist activists, who saw it as pervasive in the spheres of political, economic, social, and personal life. I also present selected data about sex-based discrimination in Russia and examine public sentiments and public policies on homosexuality that indicate pervasive homophobia in Russian society and politics. Whereas a powerful women's movement might be able to constrain sexism in the public sphere, Russia's women's movement has faced a variety of obstacles—from its failure to become a popular movement in the decade immediately following the Soviet collapse to the increased authoritarianism of the Putin era. The chapter concludes with a discussion of the rise and fall of the women's movement that developed in Russia in the 1990s and the generational rift between it and the new feminist movement that has come into being over the past several years.

Sex Discrimination in Russia: Pro- and Anti-Kremlin Activists' Views

About half of the young political activists I interviewed in 2011—who were not explicitly involved in feminist or women's movement activity—acknowledged the presence of sex discrimination in Russian politics, society, and private life. While on the whole pro-regime activists were more likely than anti-regime activists to believe that gender discrimination was not a problem in Russia, neither political ideology nor sex was predictive. Three (two men and one woman) of the four pro-regime activists believed that sex discrimination was not a relevant issue in Russia, whereas only three (two men and one woman) of nine anti-regime activists held this opinion. However, two more male anti-regime activists thought that Russia evinced only mild discrimination, taking the form of role stereotypes and manifesting in lower levels of women's representation in government, and one female anti-regime activist identified sex discrimination as existing mainly within the private sphere of family life (thus six of nine anti-regime activists did not believe sex-based discrimination was widespread). Since the number of interviewees was small, these data cannot be construed as representative, but the interviewees' beliefs show that similar impressions about discrimination (or its absence) could be found on both sides of the political fence.[1]

Two male activists with the pro-Kremlin group Nashi, both in their late 20s, believed that there was little evidence of gender-based discrimination. Nashi's leader, Nikita Borovikov, noted, "Here, as opposed to in the USA and in Western Europe, that issue, the gender issue, isn't on the

---

[1] Whatever degree of sex-based discrimination pro-regime activists and their anti-regime liberal contemporaries acknowledged in Russian political, economic, or private life, they saw next to none of it in the youth organizations where they had found their respective political homes. Feminist activists, however, who had collaborated with left-wing political youth groups, were often alienated by the sexism that they encountered there. Interviews by author, 2011 and 2012.

agenda."[2] As evidence, he pointed to Russia's experience with communism, which generated gender-neutral terms like "comrade" and had upheld women's electoral rights:

> And therefore, I'd say in principle that on that issue we don't have any serious problems. And we had the first woman astronaut [Laughs].
> Q. So would you say that discrimination on the basis of sex doesn't exist in Russia?
> A. I wouldn't be prepared to make such serious pronouncements because that's for the sociologists to do. But in general, I don't see any such problems. Probably, if we look at the roster of the state Duma, it'll turn out that there are more men. But maybe women just don't want [to be in the Duma]. Maybe this has to do with their internal aspirations— so, then, why should they [be in it]?[3]

Anton Smirnov, a Nashi member and the leader of the pro-Kremlin group Stal', doubted that any such discrimination existed, noting that he had not "come across any," and drew a contrast to the situation in other states:

> That problem [discrimination on basis of sex] isn't an issue in Russia. . . . No, nobody poses this as an issue for discussion here. I know that in Western countries there's a powerful feminist movement, right? And so on. But we don't have that. People are respectful to women here, and women respect men, too. It's not the East. And it's not the West. I think we're in an excellent position.[4]

Roman Dobrokhotov, a 27-year-old liberal activist and leader of the group My (We), agreed:

> I think that for Russia, now, the gender issue—I don't know why—is just completely irrelevant (*sovershenno neaktualen*). In general, it seems to me that the gender issue can only be relevant when there's some kind of obvious, severe gender inequality, like in, let's say, Iran, or in other Muslim countries. Or when it's the other way around, when society is already so highly developed and prosperous that there's nothing left to complain about other than gender equality. . . .

[2] Nikita Borovikov, Nashi, interview by author, Moscow, June 9, 2011.
[3] Ibid. Voting rights under dictatorial Soviet rule enabled women—and men—to vote only in sham elections.
[4] Anton Smirnov, Stal'/Nashi, interview by author, Moscow, June 17, 2011.

In Russia, it's a topic that's not under discussion because there are far more severe problems, both with nationalism—that is, with discrimination on the basis of nationality, and with discrimination on the basis of sexual orientation. And those bigoted things are manifested in very obvious ways. But attitudes toward women are fairly normal, I think. That is, in fact, maybe somewhere in the provinces there are some gender stereotypes, but personally, in Moscow, I've never noticed gender based discrimination going on whether at work, or in politics, not to mention in any youth movement.

Q. So women's issues aren't very relevant here because there are more severe forms of discrimination?

A. Well, there *are* harsher types of discrimination, but secondly, I honestly don't see even mild forms of discrimination against women. That is, of course, you can't say women are particularly well respected, but here men aren't particularly well respected either. That is, here, we disrespect both men and women equally, and in that sense, we adhere to equality.[5]

This view was not only held by male activists. A 20-year-old journalism student and Libertarian Party activist, Vera Kichanova, echoed the notion that discrimination ceased at Moscow's borders:

Q. I'd be interested to know whether you think there's any discrimination on the basis of sex.

A. Where?

Q. In Russia.

A. In Russia? I don't know—it's hard for me to say anything about that; I have read, for example, some reports by human rights organizations about discrimination on the basis of sex, sexual orientation, and so on. But in Moscow, in this fairly educated environment, it'd be hard to spot something like that. Where I live and work, people are quite liberal, progressive, and I haven't seen [any discrimination].[6]

Noting that she had a feminist acquaintance who, as it turned out, would be arrested and jailed the following year for her alleged participation in Pussy Riot's "punk prayer" in Moscow, Kichanova explained that her own knowledge of feminism was limited but that she was curious about it:

[5] Roman Dobrokhotov, My, interview by author, Moscow, June 9, 2011.
[6] Vera Kichanova, Libertarianskaia partiia, interview by author, Moscow, June 16, 2011.

People say it's women's struggle for equal rights (ravnopravie). So I think that it'd definitely be needed in places where women don't have equal rights, like in the Arab countries. But I don't know what feminists *here* are doing. I don't know. As I said, I live in a certain progressive liberal circle, and within that circle, it's OK. People with a nontraditional sexual orientation, that's OK. [But] even on the outskirts of Moscow, two boys walking arm in arm, they can be beaten up for that.

The situation was the same for racist bigotry, Kichanova asserted, "It depends on whom you interact with."[7]

Some women activists had felt the burden of gender stereotypes personally, as political activists. Alena Arshinova, a 26-year-old coordinator of the ruling United Russia party's youth wing, Molodaia Gvardiia, had not "noticed" any discrimination against women but pointed to gender stereotypes that she felt were far more evident in Moscow (where she had spent the past four years) than in her home region of Transdniestria:

There are just stereotypes. That in the grand scheme of things, that politics, or some serious job, isn't for women—there is that. A little. But in Transdniestria, there's none of that. . . . Here, I've felt it, that people can look at a young woman (devushka) and there's a little—but not everywhere, I'll say that, too. Not everywhere. A little—something like [slowly, as if imitating someone who is thinking aloud], "She's young, she's pretty, she thinks . . . That's strange. Strange." [Laughs]. That's what it's like.[8]

Gender stereotypes, Arshinova believed, also led people to regard young women superficially and to fail to take women seriously as being accomplished in their own right:

People look, say, even at me, and see a young, pretty devushka (molodaia krasivaia devushka), like a type (obraz). But on the other hand, I also have a certain vision, I have ideas, I have ways to carry out various projects that could turn out better than everyone else's, for instance! But there's this prejudice: "She's a *devushka*, and that's all there is to it." That kind of thing exists. It does. Or, they look [at me], and they think, "Oh, she's probably somebody's lover, or somebody's girlfriend, or daughter" and so on. That is, [people think], "For her to have gotten

---

[7] Kichanova, interview by author.
[8] Alena Arshinova, Molodaia Gvardiia, interview by author, Moscow, June 14, 2011.

there [to that position] on her own—that's hard to believe." That kind of thing still exists in Russia. And therefore it's a little harder. That's my position, I wouldn't hide it, and of course I'd like it if something changed. It'd be nice if there were more respect—if [people could see] that devushki and women are often also professionals! [Laughs][9]

Asked what she thought her activism said about her as a young woman, Arshinova added that people might regard her as having departed from the traditional gender norm:

You know, people could say different things. Someone might say that I must have nothing better to do [Laughs]. Someone might say that I'm a strange person and that a young lady (molodaia devchonka) should find herself a guy and marry him. But. . . I've been involved in socio-political activity since I was 18 or 19. That is, even though I think I'm pretty young, that's a long time—for me.

Optimistically, Arshinova added, taking into account her years of activist experience, someone observing her could also conclude, "That's the kind of woman I want—who has enough energy and strength to do it all. That is, [she has] enough for politics, for [her] family, for [her] parents, enough for all of it."[10]

A 25-year-old anti-regime Yabloko activist, Olga Vlasova, similarly noted that her political activity appeared somehow suspect in the eyes of (male) society: "People fear it (boiatsia). That is, it's as if men's attitude [toward me] is strange and strained (strannoe, napriazhennoe). That is, it's not typical at my age to [be involved in politics, to be an activist]; it's more typical to work, to make money."[11]

Some activists, both pro- and anti-regime, spoke readily and in detail about sex-based discrimination. Irina Pleshcheva, a 24-year-old Nashi activist whom Putin had personally selected as a member of a political advisory body, the Public Chamber, after meeting her at Camp Seliger in 2007,[12] linked some of her own experiences to more widespread societal discrimination:

Q. Do you think any discrimination on the basis of sex exists in Russia today?
A. I think you'd have to be the last chauvinist not to admit that [there is]. I think there is, absolutely. I think our country won't be ready for a woman

[9] Arshinova, interview by author.
[10] Arshinova, interview by author.
[11] Ol'ga Vlasova, Molodezhnoe Yabloko, interview by author, Moscow, June 14, 2011.
[12] "Vladimir Putin promenial Iuliu na Iru (foto)," 2007, http://www.mosstroy.su/news-word/various/Vladimir-Putin10/.

president for a long time yet. We have a patriarchy here, after all (u nas vse-taki patriarkhat).... Unfortunately, in the state leadership, we [only] have three women ministers. Maybe, in principle, that's okay, but it seems to me there are other positions that women could hold. But there's also a lot of competition. And when, at every step, there are women who are discredit-ing the image of a professional woman, it's very hard to prove that you're worthy. Even in the Public Chamber, where I've been for four years— when I arrived, I was seen as being just some chick (menia vosprinimali kak devchonku).[13]

Pleshcheva went on to clarify that women themselves contributed to this prob-lem by dressing inappropriately in professional settings, feeding preexisting stereotypes that attribute women's success only to their looks. "I'm a profes-sional person (delovoi chelovek)," she explained. "If we want them to take us seriously, then we shouldn't be wearing short skirts and showing cleavage—we should be leading with our brains. In Russia, there's an enormous stereotype that a woman can only make a career thanks to her appearance, to her curves (vypuklosti), her smile, whatever. And for people who really work hard, that's really insulting (obidno)."[14]

Pleshcheva herself had been on the receiving end of this kind of discrimina-tion. As part of her work with Nashi and as a Public Chamber deputy, Plesh-cheva on occasion met with male politicians, only later to find photos of the event on the Internet, accompanied by offensive sexist statements implying that her job in the movement was to provide sexual services:

When you start reading the kinds of things that were written about me on the Internet, it's as if there's a platoon of men who, as honorable people, should be obligated to marry me. But I've encountered some of them maybe once or twice in my life, roughly speaking, and only in professional situations. For instance, take the Commission on Regional Development of the Public Chamber of Karachaevo-Cherkessia. We were meeting with the president of Karachaevo-Cherkessia. Getting out of the plane, he shook my hand—so there's a photograph of me with the president of Karachaevo-Cherkessia—and [people say], "Look— you see? The girl (devitsa) is hanging around with him, too!" Or take the time when Mikhail Prokhorov came to Seliger. He's a famous oli-garch, he's leading [the political party] Right Cause (Pravoe Delo). Vasilii Iakemenko [the former leader of Nashi] called me and said, "I've

[13] Irina Pleshcheva, Nashi, interview by author, Moscow, June 16, 2011.
[14] Pleshcheva, interview by author.

got a big favor to ask you. Could you make it to the plane [to meet Prokhorov], and [then] I'll come over?" He didn't call me because he needed some chick (devchonka) with a beautiful appearance—because frankly, I'm not much of a match for Prokhorov, who is a fairly tall person—I only come up to about his waist!—but because when I meet him, I can explain to him what's been going on at the [Seliger] Forum in an articulate way (vniatno). I can talk with him about Russia's development strategy, I know what I'm talking about to some extent—I don't just have to sit there and smile, I'm also perfectly capable of having a normal conversation with him. There's a photograph of me with Mikhail Dmitrievich Prokhorov at Seliger, where I'm telling him about the donors program, and the photo shows up on the Internet, with the comment, "She's sleeping with Prokhorov, too!" Well, you understand, right? In general, a woman, to prove that she's a professional and so on, always has to do two times more and better than a man. Otherwise, it's as though it's hard to prove that.[15]

Given her association with Nashi—and that organization's links to the "Happy Birthday, Mr. Putin" calendar—I wondered whether Pleshcheva would critically regard the journalism students who had disrobed for Russia's leader the previous year, given that they had posed in clothing far less professional than short skirts and revealing blouses. Pleshcheva considered that the wardrobe choices for both the birthday calendar and the response to it had been appropriate to the tasks at hand:

But, in the first calendar, they weren't putting their emphasis on professionalism. From the very start their emphasis was on sexuality (seksual'nost). [Quoting the calendar:] "The fires are out, but I'm still burning." If they'd said that while posing with high collars in black suits—that is, they weren't trying to, in any way—and if they [in the response calendar]—excuse me—were showing cleavage with a low necked garment, asking, "When will Khodorkovsky be released?," it would have been sarcastic, right? . . . I don't want to come off as a prude; I have shirts that show cleavage too. But everything has its place. If you're going to a professional meeting, like a conference, then why would you wear something revealing? If you're going with your fiancé to a restaurant, then go ahead and [wear something that] shows your cleavage. To a ball, to a disco, to the beach—not long ago, somebody took some photos from my webpage and republished them

<hr />

[15] Ibid.

[elsewhere on the Web]. It was a pair of photos of me in Barcelona, at the sea, and, accordingly, I was in a bathing suit. But I'm not sitting at a session of the Public Chamber in a bathing suit! [It's as if they're saying to me], "How dare you say that a woman should dress accordingly—and yet here you are in a bathing suit!" And I answer, "And you probably wear a burqa to go swimming!" Everything has its time and its place.[16]

Several activists pointed to the widespread sexualization and objectification of women's bodies, albeit without using those terms (and with varying degrees of approbation for the practice). Responding to my query about why the birthday calendar had featured women, rather than men, Pleshcheva noted that images of partially dressed women had become ubiquitous in Russian advertising:

> You know, I went home to Voronezh recently, and while on the way, I was very surprised by the large billboards advertising, for instance, forged metal doors, with a young woman (devushka) in a bathing suit. It's an ad for doors, and there's a devushka in a bathing suit. Onward. Elite European Furniture, and there's a devushka. Not in a bathing suit this time—in a dress. But again, a devushka. I don't know to what extent in Europe advertising has moved away from that, but in Russia, unfortunately, all advertisements feature some kind of nudity and, accordingly, [they feature] a woman.[17]

Pleshcheva's colleague from Nashi, Nikita Borovikov, responded to the same question by pointing to the use of women's bodies in advertisements:

> There's this expression that I like: Young women (devushki) with beautiful wrists can advertise watches; devushki with beautiful necks can advertise jewelry; devushki with beautiful breasts can advertise underwear, real estate, tourism. . . . [Laughs]. There it is. Well, I'm saying this because devushki always attract more attention. I don't know why. Apparently it's because it's understood that men will pay attention to devushki for obvious reasons, yes? And women [will pay attention] out of jealousy.[18]

Liberal activists recognized this trend as well. Igor Iakovlev, a 24-year-old Molodezhnoe Yabloko member (who, like Vlasova, also worked for the party

[16] Ibid.
[17] Ibid.
[18] Borovikov, interview by author.

itself), noted that while it was atypical for young men to be photographed in that fashion, by contrast, "images of half-dressed devushki are all over the place—in newspapers, in magazines; everybody understands it. It's an image that's clear to everyone."[19]

Male and female activists with the Yabloko Party's youth wing readily identified other aspects of sex discrimination as being among the outstanding issues on Russia's political agenda. This is probably not coincidental, given that their "parent" party was the only one boasting a Gender Caucus (fraktsiia). Iakovlev summed up the situation:

Q. Do you think any sex-based discrimination exists in Russia?
A. Without a doubt. Our country continues to be quite patriarchal to this day, and women run into serious problems when it comes to everyday life (byt), and domestic violence, and labor discrimination; it's much harder for women to find jobs, and women's salaries are far lower than men's, and the leadership positions in business, in the civil service, and so on are mostly filled by men. That is, without a doubt there's discrimination.[20]

The 19-year-old leader of Molodezhnoe Yabloko, Kirill Goncharov, pointed to women's "second-class status" in Russia, based primarily on role stereotypes:

A woman, today, is basically a second-class person in Russia. It's as if a man is supposed to drive the car, he's the one who's supposed to work, bring home the money, but his wife is [supposed to be] in the kitchen, with a child, and only concern herself with family matters. That's probably the biggest form discrimination takes. . . . There's that stereotype that women absolutely must have children. By the age of 30 they have to have children and take care of them [for her whole youth], and only later, when she's got the child standing on his own two feet, can she then do her own thing. But everybody knows it's late to begin your career at 40 or 50 . . . and unfortunately, that's also a type of discrimination, that people would have fewer opportunities than they would have had twenty years earlier. That's why I think it should be each person's choice—when to have children, what to do when they're young, if and when to get married—it's not necessary to insist that people [follow a certain pattern] and propagandize them about it.[21]

---

[19] Igor' Iakovlev, Molodezhnoe Yabloko, interview by author, Moscow, June 14, 2011.
[20] Iakovlev, interview by author.
[21] Kirill Goncharov, Molodezhnoe Yabloko, interview by author, Moscow, June 10, 2011.

Olga Vlasova seconded the notion that stereotypes about family roles played a strong role in Russia, noting that it was "hard to imagine, for instance, a man who would stay home with a child [on leave from work]—and a woman would hardly agree to that, anyway [laughing]—that's where the problem lies." While she had not experienced or observed "any particular discrimination or strong types of discrimination" at her university, Vlasova mused about sex discrimination within the Yabloko Party: "It's not that there's glaring discrimination; it's just that it so happens that all the people in leadership roles are men. And among the women [in Yabloko] at present; there probably isn't one who could be competitive with [the men in the leadership]. That's a question, too: is it discrimination, or is it just a natural competition?"[22]

Two other liberal activists, both formerly involved with the anti-regime group Oborona, believed that role-stereotypes created discrimination, particularly in politics. Oleg Kozlovskii, a 27-year-old student writing his PhD thesis on nonviolent activism, contrasted the "formal" absence of discrimination with "reality":

> I think there exists, so to speak, a kind of notion that people have, that there are certain social roles for women that they're not supposed to go beyond. To the extent that I can judge this, I think these ideas act very strongly on women. For instance, if a woman is running for office, especially a young woman—women themselves don't vote for other women. But men will vote [for a woman] if she's pretty (*simpatichna*). And in that sense, especially in elected posts, it exists.[23]

Human rights activist Nikolai Zboroshenko similarly thought that "traditional ideas" about gender roles were "not uncommon" and that discrimination played its largest role in the political arena. Arguing that one could find female bosses at private companies but that it was a relative rarity to find a woman manager within a government institution, he noted, "In the private sector, there's a more appropriate approach. And in NGOs [nongovernmental organizations], too. To some extent it depends on concrete people at particular organizations, but in principle I think there's more discrimination within government institutions; unfortunately, government institutions are more traditional."[24]

---

[22] Vlasova, interview by author.

[23] Oleg Kozlovskii, Oborona, interview by author, Moscow, June 8, 2011.

[24] Nikolai Zboroshenko, Oborona, interview by author, Moscow, June 6, 2011.

Sex Discrimination in Russia

How do these activists' views and experiences regarding sex discrimination comport with broader empirical analyses of the subject? Women's movement activists and scholars wielding a wide expanse of statistical information assert that Russia, like the rest of the world, has not escaped sex-based discrimination. Sexism at the social-cultural level, discussed in Chapter 2, is echoed in the political and economic spheres as well.

POLITICAL DISCRIMINATION

Women are only weakly represented in Russian politics, particularly in positions of political power. In 2008, the United Nations ranked Russia in seventy-first place, based on the number of women in positions of executive power and in eighty-fourth place for women's representation in the legislative branch.[25] In the communist era, a quota system had given Soviet women one-third of the seats in the state legislature. This was a powerless entity compared to the small body of decision-makers in the Soviet Politburo, which, in reality, led the state. Over the course of its 72-year lifespan, the Politburo had only two full-fledged female members: Soviet Minister of Culture, Ekaterina Furtseva (1957-1961), and journalist Galina Semenova, who diversified that body for its final year (1990-1991).[26]

No such political assurances were in place in what became the independent Russian Federation after 1991. In post-Soviet Russia's first elections, in 1993, a women's political bloc aptly titled Women of Russia won 8 percent of the party list vote in the parliamentary elections (helping earn women a total of 13 percent of the seats in the parliament's lower house, the Duma) but failed to assert itself on issues of gender discrimination or to make common cause with the burgeoning women's movement at that time.[27] Women of Russia failed to clear the 5 percent threshold in the next two parliamentary elections and then evaporated from the political scene.[28] Women constituted just less than 10 percent of the Duma in 2003 and made up 14

---

[25] Galina Mikhaleva, "Est' li politicheskii potentsial u zhenskogo dvizheniia v Rossii?," in *Zhenskoe dvizhenie v Rossii: Vchera, segodnia, zavtra: Materialy konferentsii*, ed. Galina Mikhaleva (Moscow, Russia: RODP "Yabloko" and KMK Publishers, 2010), 63.

[26] "Semenova, Galina Vladimirovna," *Vikipediia*, http://bit.ly/1kCVSlQ, accessed March 24, 2014; "Furtseva, Ekaterina Alekseevna," *Vikipediia*, http://bit.ly/1mSrweF, accessed May 20, 2014.

[27] Mikhaleva, "Est' li politicheskii potentsial u zhenskogo dvizheniia v Rossii?," 67.

[28] Sperling, *Organizing Women in Contemporary Russia*, 116–118.

percent of the Duma elected in 2007. The parliamentary elections of December 2011 generated a similar result, with women winning 13.5 percent of the seats.[29] As of 2010, none of Russia's active, registered political parties had a woman among its leaders, and few women were present in those parties' leadership bodies. Even within Russia's "unregistered" political movements, women played largely "secondary roles."[30] Women in the state administration were also few and far between, holding only three ministerial portfolios (health care, agriculture, and economic development) of seventeen at the national level.[31] In 2014, women held the governorships of only two of Russia's eighty-three regions; Natalia Komarova served as the head of the Khanty-Mansiisk autonomous district, itself a subregion of the larger oil-rich Tiumen' province, and Marina Kovtun ran the region of Murmansk, in the Russian Artic.[32]

Women's representation in Russia's "extra-systemic" political sphere, composed of Russia's nonregistered political movements and parties, was little better. In October 2012, Russia's political opposition forces, tired of hearing that the elected government had "no one to talk to" in the opposition, thus making dialogue impossible, held an online election to a forty-five-member Coordinating Council designed to bring together the liberal, leftist, and nationalist sectors of Russia's opposition movement. Thirty council members were elected from a general list, while leftist, nationalist, and liberal forces were entitled to five additional seats each. The results were not encouraging for women: only five of the thirty general mandates went to women. To their five additional seats, the liberals and leftists elected one woman apiece. The nationalists' five additional mandates were all won by men (they had put forth thirteen candidates; none of them female). In short, at 15.5 percent female, the most representative body of opposition political leaders only slightly outdid the Duma.[33]

---

[29] Inter-Parliamentary Union, "IPU Parline database: Russian Federation, election archives," http://www.ipu.org/parline-e/reports/2263_arc.htm, accessed March 18, 2013.

[30] Mikhaleva, "Est' li politicheskii potentsial u zhenskogo dvizheniia v Rossii?," 64.

[31] Ibid., 63.

[32] Trude Pettersen, "Marina Kovtun appointed Governor of Murmansk Oblast," *Barents Observer*, April 16, 2012,http://barentsobserver.com/en/politics/marina-kovtun-appointed-governor-murmansk-oblast.

[33] "Rezul'taty vyborov v Koordinatsionnyi Sovet Oppozitsii," October 22, 2012, http://www.echo.msk.ru/blog/echomsk/943408-echo/; Tsentral'nyi vybornyi komitet, "Spisok kandidatov," October 2, 2012, http://compass.cvk2012.org/candidates/; Anna Arutunyan, "Politics—from Scratch," *The Moscow News*, October 1, 2012, http://www.themoscownews.com/politics/20121001/190300786.html.

VIOLENCE AGAINST WOMEN

While violence against women has long been regarded as an interpersonal rather than a political problem per se, the state ostensibly plays a role in maintaining public order and protecting individuals against assaults on their person and property. In that regard, domestic violence and the state's response to it can be a telling measure of discrimination. Domestic violence, rape, and domestic murder are directed disproportionately against women and are discriminatory for that reason. The way that these crimes are treated by law enforcement bodies can also constitute gender-based discrimination.

According to the Russian Ministry of Internal Affairs in 2008, approximately fourteen thousand women perish each year as a result of domestic violence in Russia.[34] This oft-cited statistic, first publicized in the mid-1990s, is most assuredly incorrect, despite its official source. According to a UN Global Study on Homicide, a total of 15, 954 homicides were registered in Russia in 2009.[35] World Health Organization data in 2008 found that women made up 25.7 percent of Russia's homicide victims, suggesting that something closer to 3,700 women are killed annually in Russia.[36] Another World Health Organization report in 2013 found that 40 percent of the women killed across the globe died at the hands of a partner.[37] If that statistic bears out for Russia, then approximately fifteen hundred women's deaths could be attributed annually to domestic violence in that state. The number of nonfatal domestic violence cases is far higher. As of 2003, 184,000 such cases were officially registered with Russian police.[38] To date, the most reliable data on this subject has come from a multiregion survey in Russia in 2003, which

---

[34] ANNA National Centre for the Prevention of Violence, "Violence against Women in the Russian Federation: Alternative Report to the United Nations Committee on the Elimination of Discrimination Against Women, 46th session, July 2010, Examination of the 6th and 7th reports submitted by the Russian Federation" (henceforth, ANNA Alternative Report), July 2010, 6, citing Police Lieutenant General M. Artamoshkin.

[35] Evgeniya Chaykovskaya, "UN Report Puts RUSSIA among Leaders in Homicide Rates," *The Moscow News*, October 24, 2011, http://themoscownews.com/russia/20111024/189146825.html.

[36] United Nations Office on Drugs and Crime, *2011 Global Study on Homicide* (Vienna, Austria: UNODC, 2011), 124.

[37] "One-Third of Women Assaulted by a Partner, Global Report Says," *New York Times*, June 20, 2013, http://www.nytimes.com/2013/06/21/world/one-third-of-women-assaulted-by-a-partner-global-report-says.html?_r=0.

[38] These represent only a fraction of actual cases because domestic violence reporting rates are low. Network Women's Program, Violence against Women Monitoring Program, *Violence against Women: Does the Government Care in Russia?* (New York: Open Society Institute, 2007), 50, http://www.stopvaw.org/sites/3f6d15f4-c12d-4515-8544-26b7a3a5a41e/uploads/Russia_2.pdf.

found that half of married women had undergone at least one instance of physical violence at the hands of their husbands.[39]

Meanwhile, across Russia there are no more than twenty crisis centers offering counseling and, in a very few cases, a place to stay.[40] Nonfatal domestic violence cases, after changes to the Russian Penal Code in 2003, are generally prosecuted as "private prosecutions" where the individual survivor must initiate the proceedings, collect the evidence and present it, and pursue the case—generally, while living with the person who battered her (since restraining orders—which mandate a certain distance be maintained between the abuser and the victim—have not been established in Russia). The lion's share of private prosecutions ends without a verdict, because the complainant is insufficiently versed in the legal requirements of the process, is too frightened to proceed, or (in 90 percent of cases) because the parties reportedly reconciled.[41]

Exacerbating this problem is the fact that police often respond to domestic violence and rape complaints by blaming the victim or accusing her of fabricating the charges.[42] Maria Mokhova, director of the "Sisters" Center in Moscow, contended that no more than 50 percent of rape complaints brought to law enforcement were acted upon by officers investigating the claims, initiating proceedings in a timely fashion, and so on.[43] According to a psychotherapist and member of the Russian youth movement "Stop Violence," a common response by police to women seeking law enforcement intervention in the face of domestic battering is, "Come see us after he's killed you."[44] Russia has no law specifically concerning domestic violence, despite many attempts to introduce such legislation since the mid-1990s. In 2012, hearings were held by the Public Chamber about introducing a simplified process to prosecute domestic violence cases, including a restraining order system that would be initiated by a phone call from the victim to the police and would result in fifteen days' administrative arrest of the perpetrator in the event of a reoccurrence and a criminal

---

[39] I. D. Gorshkova and I. I. Shurygina, "Nasilie nad zhenami v sovremennykh rossiiskikh sem'iakh: Materialy obshcherossiiskogo issledovaniia, predstavlennye na konferentsii 16–16 maia 2003 v MGU im. M. V. Lomonosova i Gorbachev-Fonde" (Moscow, 2003), 38, http://www. owl.ru/rights/no_violence/.

[40] "Brutal Murder Highlights Russia's Domestic Violence Problem," RIA Novosti, January 16, 2013, http://en.rian.ru/crime/20130116/178800003.html.

[41] ANNA Alternative Report, 11.

[42] ANNA Alternative Report, 29.

[43] ANNA Alternative Report, 26–27.

[44] Irina Fetkulova, Molodezhnoe Dvizhenie "Ostanovim Nasilie," interview by author, Moscow, June 18, 2012.

case after a third incident.[45] Two years later, however, no such law had been passed by the Duma.

ECONOMIC DISCRIMINATION

According to studies conducted by several labor rights organizations, there is widespread and multifaceted labor discrimination in Russia, including sex discrimination in job advertising, hiring, and wages. In 2009, 27 percent of want ads specified the sex of the desired applicant. On job applications and in interviews, women—but not men—are routinely asked whether they have children and the ages of the children.[46] Women with young children or who are planning to have children in the future encounter major difficulties landing a position. It is also practically impossible for a pregnant woman to get hired into a new job, although Russian law makes it illegal to refuse to hire a woman for that reason. Women's salaries on average are one-third lower than men's, in part because women choose different professions and because men and women tend to dominate different branches of the economy (and those where men predominate offer higher pay). However, the salary gap persists, even for equal work. As of 2007, office managers (91 percent of whom are women) have different salaries based on sex; men's are 1.5 times higher than women's. Sex is the third most popular reason for labor discrimination complaints (age and trying to assert one's labor rights are the first two), and women make up 78 percent of employees bringing sex-based discrimination cases.[47]

Women's rate of promotion on the job is also slower than men's, in part because of the perception that, for women, the most important sphere of life is the family as well as the reality that women have less time to spend on raising their professional qualifications because they spend more time on childcare and housework than do their male counterparts. Employers frequently fail to pay pregnant women their benefits while they are on leave to take care of children. Employers also fire pregnant women and use threats, blackmail, and other means to rid themselves of pregnant employees—or women employees with young children—despite the fact that doing so is illegal.[48] Because of the

---

[45] Vladislav Kulikov, "Ne vse doma: Ezhegodno bolee 10 tysych zhenshchin pogibaiut ot ruk muzhej ili drugikh blizkikh,"/Each Year, More Than 10,000 Women Die at the Hands of Their Husbands or Other family Members, *Rossiiskaia Gazeta*, March 7, 2012, http://www.rg.ru/2012/07/03/nasilie.html.

[46] Elena Gerasimova, "Zhenshchiny v trudovykh otnosheniiakh v Rossii," in *Zhenskoe dvizhenie v Rossii: Vchera, segodnia, zavtra: Materialy konferentsii,* ed. Galina Mikhaleva (Moscow: RODP "Yabloko" and KMK Publishers, 2010), 15.

[47] Ibid., 16.

[48] Ibid., 18.

"extra" benefits that employers are obligated to provide for women—which are specified in Russia's Labor Code under Article 41, titled "Regulations specific to regulation of women's labor, and that of people with family obligations," but are largely regarded as applying only to women—employers believe that "women cost more" and are likely to pay women less or to avoid hiring them for that reason.[49] Finally, women are restricted from more than 450 jobs in heavy industry and underground labor on the ostensible grounds that such occupations endanger women's reproductive health. Women are allowed, however, to perform lower-paid jobs that entail similar conditions. Women are forbidden to work as subway train drivers but may work freely as janitors in underground subway stations, for example.[50]

Sexual harassment in Russia offers another example of sex-based workplace discrimination, as it grossly disproportionately affects women. While Russia's Labor Code does not include sexual harassment, Russia's Criminal Code could be used in such cases, as its Article 133 outlaws "coercion to perform acts of a sexual nature by exploiting the material or other dependence of the victim." However, Russian law makes a distinction between coercion and "seduction to commit sexual acts, one variation of which is a promise of privileges and benefits (for example, a promise of ... promotion in office....)." Such cases of sexual interaction, being deemed consensual and based on personal choice, are not considered coercive and are not covered by the Criminal Code.[51] Sexual harassment is widespread in Russia. One Russian academic paper analyzing "power and sex in the workplace" found that 80 percent of women reported that any promotion at work had been tied to a proposal to sleep with their boss. Meanwhile, across the country, only ten cases of harassment per year were brought under Article 133.[52]

That it did not occur to liberal and pro-regime activists in Moscow—whose groups were not explicitly concerned with feminist issues—to discuss these problems when asked about discrimination is perhaps unsurprising. Lacking consistent media coverage, the women's movement and its efforts to spread the word about sex discrimination in Russia have been highly constrained since the mid-1990s.

---

[49] Irina Kozina, "Rabotaiushchie materi: Usloviia zaniatosti i sotsial'naia podderzhka," in *Zhenskoe dvizhenie v Rossii: Vchera, segodnia, zavtra: Materialy konferentsii*, ed. Galina Mikhaleva (Moscow: RODP "Yabloko" and KMK Publishers, 2010), 23.

[50] "Jobs Women Can't Do in Russia," June 12, 2009, http://www.pri.org/stories/world/jobs-women-can_t-do-russia1427.html.

[51] United Nations, Committee on the Elimination of Discrimination against Women, "Responses to the List of Issues and Questions with Regard to the Consideration of the Combined Sixth and Seventh Periodic Report: Russian Federation" (CEDAW/C/USR/Q/7/Add.1), May 22, 2010, 36.

[52] R. T. Iuldashev and I. G. Kornilova, "Vlast' i seks na rabochem meste," n.d., 2, http://www.miir.ru/e107_plugins/library/books/bib0012.pdf, accessed May 22, 2014.

Sex Discrimination in Russia: Feminists' Views

Feminist activists, interviewed in 2012, talked readily about the sex-based discrimination that they perceived in politics and economics and that, in some cases, they had experienced personally. First, like their political activist counterparts whose groups were not explicitly focused on sex-based discrimination, feminist activists pointed to the striking absence of women in politics. As one anti-violence activist, Irina Fetkulova, put it: "Nobody wants to—well, not *nobody*—people don't really want to see a woman in power."[53] Feminists also fluently referred to the widespread labor discrimination described above. One 23-year-old feminist activist in Moscow summed the situation up as follows:

> In Russia, even according to official statistics, they acknowledge that there's a 35 percent gap in pay for equal work on average. The state statistics on rape are very strongly reduced. But they don't even consider it necessary to hide labor discrimination, it doesn't even occur to anyone to hide it. Therefore, the statistics about differences in salary are collected and are openly available. Women also encounter an enormous amount of discrimination in hiring. That is, if a young woman has children, she can be refused work because she has children. If she doesn't have children, they'll tell her that they won't hire her because she could become pregnant. And therefore, young women are the first to be fired when there are staff cuts.... Another big problem concerns mothers who go on maternity leave (dekretnyi otpusk), because an enormous number of employers don't pay the maternity benefits; they use the law to try to avoid paying the benefits.... And there's another big problem—the list of jobs forbidden [to women].[54]

Several young feminists shared stories from their own lives, highlighting discriminatory societal expectations for young women in the working world. Oksana Zamoiskaia, an aspiring cinematographer in St. Petersburg, related the peculiar experience of being harangued on this subject by her (female) professor at the University of Film and Television:

> Here it's absolutely bizarre. Even at the university, there was a class where the teacher told the young women (devushki)—this was because the young women camera-operators (devushki-operatora) who

[53] Fetkulova, interview by author.

[54] Vera Akulova, Moskovskaia Feministskaia Gruppa, interview by author, Moscow, June 6, 2012.

were shooting were all wearing—they looked like they were heading off to go fishing. With lots of pockets. Without heels. And she started teaching us about how to dress properly, to wear heels to class. In front of the boys. She said, "You're in school now. But in two years you'll be done. And you'll have to find a husband by then. And then you'll work for a couple of years, and then have a baby. You'll have to stay with the children, and take care of (obsluzhivat') your husband." . . . Again, it's that bourgeois model, that is, to find yourself a good husband and everything will be fine. He'll solve your problems. But nobody says at what cost.[55]

Natalia Bitten, who had graduated from an art institute and sought work as a designer, heard similar words from her employers:

I brought my documents to the client, showing what it would cost, what the expenses would be. And he sat there, smoking, and said, "Girl (devochka), what do you need money for?" So I said, "What, are you some kind of idiot?" I had done accounting work, and this old fool (staryi chulan) says these things to me! . . . People were always saying things to me like, "What do you need to work for? You need to get married. Why do you need an apartment? Why do you need money?" "Why do you need money for an apartment?" said the chief editor [at a newspaper where she had been employed]. "Just get married and live off your husband." And I said to him, "You want me to take up social prostitution? No, I don't want to get married in order to get an apartment. Because I can work myself."[56]

Even in these professional-educational and workplace settings, people in positions of authority did not hesitate to propagate the notion that marriage founded on financial dependency constituted young women's economic destiny.

Patterns of sex discrimination—whether manifested in the economy, in Russia's political institutions, or in the harsh array of violent crimes against women—were evident to feminists, as well as to some of the political activists whose groups devoted little to no energy to addressing such issues. The gender stereotypes that they had encountered also closely echoed those mentioned by several of the pro- and anti-regime activists. While those activists, however,

[55] Oksana Zamoiskaia, Rossiiskoe Sotsialisticheskoe Dvizhenie, Interview by author, St. Petersburg, June 16, 2012.
[56] Natal'ia Bitten, Initsiativnaia Gruppa "Za Feminizm," interview by author, Moscow, June 4, 2012.

largely perceived their own organizations as being immune to the gender stereotyping and discrimination present in broader Russian society, feminist activists cast a critical eye across the political spectrum, finding that sexism per-
vaded the Russian political realm and was characteristic of pronouncements
by regime politicians, liberal opposition leaders, and even the marginalized
socialist groupings for whom little space was available in the public sphere.

Sexism across the Russian Political Spectrum

Feminist activists readily provided concrete examples of sexism in Russian
politics—by regime actors as well as oppositionists. When asked to do so,
however, several interviewees initially felt stymied by the overwhelming
number of options. Said one 25-year-old socialist feminist:

> It's constant. Every time a women's issue comes up, a wave of sexism
> immediately rises along with it. Really, every time Putin or anyone
> [talking about social policy] pronounces the word "woman," it's fol-
> lowed by a torrent of sexism. It's hard for me to give you an example;
> the radical feminists have their Sexist of the Year competition—and
> it's not like they don't have enough material.[57]

A radical feminist activist concurred:

> It might be better to try to recall some kind of statement that *wasn't*
> sexist! [Laughs] That would be much easier. But in fact it's hard to give
> a concrete example because, first of all, it's better not to listen to our
> politicians if you [value your nerves]. Second, they use sexism as a
> platform so often that you don't even notice it anymore. You don't pay
> attention—oh, look what he said. If they say something progressive,
> you're more likely to pay attention to that.[58]

Nevertheless, feminists pointed to plenty of sexist statements made by
public figures representing a range of political positions. To illustrate Putin's
sexism, for example, Moscow-based feminist activists pointed to a little-no-
ticed incident in 2006. After Israel's president, Moshe Katsav, was accused of

[57] Zhenia Otto, Komitet za Rabochii Internatsional, Kampaniia protiv ekspluatatsii i diskriminatsii zhenshchin, interview by author, Moscow, June 18, 2012.
[58] Elizaveta Morozova, Moskovskaia Feministskaia Gruppa, interview by author, Moscow, June
20, 2012.

raping two women on his staff, Putin (while at a meeting in the Kremlin) asked the Israeli prime minister to send the president his regards. Believing he was off-mic, Putin then commented that President Katsav turned out to be a "mighty man," adding, "He raped 10 women—I would never have expected this from him. He surprised us all—we all envy him!" Putin's press secretary dismissed this as a joke, and it was reported that the (male) members of both delegations laughed out loud at it.[59] Katsav was later convicted of rape.[60] As Vera Akulova, a young feminist organizer in Moscow, put it, "Nobody sees the difference between rape and sex, right up to the head of the government."[61]

Several activists brought the same point home in reference to remarks made by a well-known Putin critic, Artemii Troitskii, at an opposition rally at the close of 2011. As noted earlier, Troitskii, the former editor of Russian *Playboy* magazine, had appeared on stage dressed as a condom, and in a "vivid incident that shocked all the feminists at the demonstration on Sakharov Prospect . . . said this: 'Putin is doing with the country what he ought to do with his wife. (Putin delaet so stranoi to, chto dolzhen delat' s zhenoi.)'"[62] Troitskii's antipathy toward Putin's politics made clear that he thought what Putin was "doing with the country" was neither a consensual nor enjoyable act. One feminist activist spelled out the ramifications: "He thinks Putin should be raping his wife."[63] Another activist elaborated on Troitskii's meaning: "That is, [Putin is] wielding hierarchical violence against the country because he's not able to do it with his own wife. But if he *were* to do that with his wife, then it would be completely fine and right (normal'no i pravil'no). He would be a *muzhik*. And if he can't, then tee-hee-hee, we would laugh at him."[64] This popular liberal oppositionist and his political opponent, Putin, though on different sides politically, had found a small plot of common ground in making rape jokes.

Feminist analysis of the incident pointed to sexism as a legitimation strategy in two ways. By criticizing Putin's political rule in this fashion, Troitskii had attacked Putin's masculinity and endorsed marital rape at the same time.

[59] "Putin's 'Rape Joke' Played Down," October 20, 2006, http://news.bbc.co.uk/2/hi/6069136.stm; Natal'ia Melikova, "Putin voskhitilsia liubovnymi podvigami Katsava," *Nezavisimaia Gazeta*, October 19, 2006, http://www.ng.ru/politics/2006-10-19/4_putin.html.

[60] Isabel Kershner, "Israeli Ex-President, Katsav, Is Convicted of Rape," *New York Times*, December 30, 2010, http://www.nytimes.com/2010/12/31/world/middleeast/31israel.html.

[61] Akulova, interview by author.

[62] Ibid. Troitskii had actually said, "If the president isn't doing it with his wife, he's doing it with his country" (esli prezident ne delaet eto so svoei zhenoi, to on delaet eto so svoei stranoi). "Miting na prospekte Sakharova: Khronika."

[63] Bitten, interview by author.

[64] Frau Derrida, Moskovskaia Feministskaia Gruppa, interview by author, Moscow, June 7, 2012.

The paucity of politically active women in the public sphere, one activist argued, helped enable this kind of discourse:

> You can find plenty of that; they're not shy about it at all. They don't filter themselves at all, and nobody slaps their hands for it, because there are very few women in the Duma [parliament], and the ones who are there—it's understandable—they're afraid to lose their power. Therefore, of course they have to stay absolutely within the bounds (v ramkakh), and say what they're told to and no more. There are just very few women who speak out in public.[65]

Another noted that the women who had made it into the Duma were there in a decorative capacity, not as serious politicians or to put forth feminist positions:

> There was a photograph going around the Internet where one female [Duma] deputy was bending over to kiss another deputy, and [a third] deputy had his hand on her rear end. It seems to me that's what [the women deputies] are there for. And our sportswomen end up in the Duma, too, like Alina Kabaeva, and [Svetlana] Khorkina; there's also someone's 22-year old daughter—I can't remember her name. That is, they're there [in the Duma] to provide decoration and entertainment, and in no way to do work.[66]

Moreover, she added, Putin reinforced this gender norm of traditional femininity in his yearly address to Russia's women on International Women's Day: "If Putin is wishing women a happy holiday on March 8, and recommends that they continue to beautify men's lives, or people's lives, as it was said, then what more can you even say? And it's at all levels among the authorities, everywhere, it's ubiquitous, every day."[67]

Putin and other politicians were similarly faulted for reducing women to their reproductive capacity:

> One example, when Putin was prime minister, he was meeting with a group of entrepreneurs, and a woman spoke up there—I forget her last name, but she's a successful entrepreneur. And when Putin spoke, he said, "Yes, yes, yes, that's all very good, but I don't want women to

[65] Elena Maksimova, Moskovskie Radikal'nye Feministki, interview by author, Moscow, June 22, 2012.
[66] Tat'iana Grigor'eva, Initsiativnaia Gruppa Za Feminizm, interview by author, Moscow, June 18, 2012.
[67] Ibid.

forget about their civic duty of bearing children." He said that publicly to her. It was all broadcast by the mass media. And everybody [just] giggled about it.[68]

Putin made a similar remark when speaking with journalists at the state-sponsored television channel, RT (Russia Today) in 2013. When a Serbian journalist seeking Russian citizenship expressed her frustration at Russia's immigration rules, Putin acknowledged that, for people like her, the process should be adjusted: "We have to welcome people like you. You are a young and beautiful woman. I am sorry, but it is true that you are a woman of childbearing age."[69]

This biological functionalism was evident among liberal male oppositionists as well. Zhenia Otto, leader of a socialist group's campaign to eliminate discrimination against women, explained:

> On that subject, regarding liberals, Ania, one of our [Committee for a Workers' International] participants, wrote an article that I really liked about a well-known journalist from *Novaia Gazeta*, [Dmitrii] Bykov. He had written another in his series of political poems on Russia. For the most part, he wrote about Russian politics, but his literary approach was to compare Russia to a woman—that in all her actions, she conforms not to reason and common sense but to her menstrual cycle, and so on. It was a completely sexist text. I bring this up to show the extent to which even liberals, who claim to have some intellectual superiority or critical thinking, are just—it's commonplace. If something has to be demonstrated (dokazat') then the main way they'd all go about it is by using sexism, *all* of them.[70]

Whether inside or outside of the political system, opinion-makers apparently had few qualms about resorting to gender norms in their pronouncements.

Women also often found themselves rhetorically absent from the opposition. After a December 2010 rally memorializing a Russian soccer fan (killed in a fight with a young man from Russia's north Caucasus region) turned into a Russian-nationalist pogrom, with multiple attacks on people of non-Slavic appearance, a counterdemonstration was announced.[71] In an increasingly

---

[68] Bitten, interview by author.

[69] "Visit to Russia Today Television Channel," June 11, 2013, http://eng.kremlin.ru/news/5571.

[70] Otto, interview by author.

[71] Julia Ioffe, "Race Riots in Russia," *The New Yorker*, December 16, 2010, http://www.newyorker.com/online/blogs/newsdesk/2010/12/russia-race-riots.html; Ilya Varlamov, "Besporiadki v Moskve," December 11, 2010, http://zyalt.livejournal.com/330396.html.

familiar trope, the press release covering the event reduced women to the status of everyday male property:

> [After the riots on Manezh Square], the liberals organized an action, "Russia for Everyone" (Rossiia dlia vsekh). And in the press release, it said, "We are all used to having a regular way of life, to our cup of coffee, [our] books, [our] women"—separated by commas—"but now let's go into the streets and say we're opposed to fascism!" So they weren't calling for women to come to the protest; women are something like the books and cups of coffee. And that's what's considered the elite of the nation [Laughs]: We're so intelligent, we liberals, we're so high-brow—and everyone else is cattle (bydlo).[72]

Vera Akulova referred similarly to an opposition poet, Emelin, who had published a book of poems dedicated to the protest movement. Here, too, the protestor-protagonist's image was consistently male: "There's an image there, of the man who says goodbye to his wife and goes off to a protest. And that's particularly strange because in reality an enormous number of women are going to these demonstrations—it's unprecedented. I've never seen so many women at street actions." Akulova considered that this image of a default-male protestor stemmed in part from the composition of opposition organizations, where, even in liberal groups, "there are few women, and they never hold leadership positions."[73]

If women protesters seemed—despite their presence—to be invisible, women with high visibility in the political realm fared just as badly. Female political figures who crossed the regime, such as long-time dissenter Valeriia Novodvorskaia, could find themselves labeled "ugly, unattractive, and hysterical" or, like Ksenia Sobchak, an attractive young reality-TV show star turned oppositionist, characterized as easy sex objects. As a feminist in Moscow explained, "We have very few women in politics—almost none. Like [Ksenia] Sobchak, who started speaking out lately. Of course [she gets called things like] soska." Stemming from the verb, "to suck," soska has the derogatory connotation of a "blow-job giver," providing men with pleasure at their request and receiving nothing in return.[74]

As one of the only recognizable women among the opposition, Sobchak had been singled out for derision in this and other ways. The young and famously pretty daughter of one of the most renowned democrats of the perestroika era,

[72] Otto, interview by author.
[73] Akulova, interview by author.
[74] Frau Derrida, interview by author. I thank Mariia Zolotukhina for the detailed explanation of the term.

Leningrad mayor Anatolii Sobchak (himself Putin's sometime mentor), started her political career as a television celebrity and "it girl," making a splash with photographs in *Playboy* and the Russian version of the men's magazine *Maxim*.[75] But after the December 2011 elections, Sobchak turned her energies to the opposition, despite being Putin's goddaughter. Painted as a socialite who was now trying her hand at a new means of attention-getting, Sobchak was criticized by oppositionists for being uncommitted and too middle of the road. She and one of the prominent young liberal opposition figures, Ilia Iashin, became romantically involved, and in June 2012 Sobchak's apartment was ransacked by Federal Security Service (FSB) agents who found around two million dollars, a fact that was widely advertised in an attempt to smear her reputation on the right and left alike.[76] Sobchak responded by filming an ad (for a bank) that satirized the FSB's invasion of her home and seizure of her cash.[77]

But Sobchak had been the subject of derision before she turned to the opposition. Internet blogs had mocked her by emphasizing what Vlad Strukov identifies as the "artificiality of her identity" and blending her image in ways that "transgress Sobchak's essentialist claims to beauty, elegance, and intelligence"—portraying her face on the body of a horse, for example.[78] These images constituted an attack on Sobchak's trademark femininity, the gender-normative basis of her popular success. Attacks on her sexual and feminine propriety continued after her conversion to the opposition. In 2011, for instance, Nashi activist and Federal Youth Affairs Agency press secretary Kristina Potupchik labeled Sobchak a "cheap whore" after Sobchak posted a video of then-Putin ally Vasilii Iakemenko (the former Nashi leader and Potupchik's boss at the Agency) eating out at an expensive restaurant.[79]

In April 2013, Sobchak's traditional femininity was attacked anew when a recording of an angry phone conversation between Sobchak and the manager of her apartment building was publicized in the press. A television broadcast aiming to further discredit Sobchak as an oppositionist honed in on the parts

[75] Goscilo and Strukov, "Introduction," 10–11.

[76] Alexander Kolesnichenko, "Dilettante, Polymath, Traitor," February 18, 2013, http://www.tol.org/client/article/23606-dilettante-polymath-traitor.html.

[77] In the ad, when the masked FSB men saw open her safe and find only an envelope with credit cards, Sobchak tells viewers that it's better not to keep your money in cash at home. See Tcsbank, "Obysk-2 u Ksenii Sobchak" [video], July 11, 2012, http://www.youtube.com/watch?v=wqdSLXCyCwA.

[78] Vlad Strukov, "Russian Internet Stars: Gizmos, Geeks, and Glory," in *Celebrity and Glamour in Contemporary Russia: Shocking Chic*, ed. Helena Goscilo and Vlad Strukov (London: Routledge, 2011), 152.

[79] Natalia Antonova, "2011: Russia's Year in Quotes," *The Moscow News*, December 26, 2011, http://themoscownews.com/politics/20111226/189326055.html.

of the conversation where Sobchak reportedly stated that she had no interest in bearing children. A medical sex expert on the television program high-lighted Sobchak's abnormality in this regard, arguing, "When a woman con-sciously does not want to have children, it means that she has a certain inner pathology and lacks a mother's instinct." On the basis of this opinion, the pro-gram drew the inevitable conclusion that knowledge of Sobchak's "strong hatred of children" and reported rejection of women's reproductive mission had rendered her even less popular in the public eye.[80] Sobchak, while not a figure in Russian feminism, has defended women's right to abortion and has remarked on the fact of labor discrimination (i.e., that men prefer to hire men), arguing that women have to overcome the widespread societal mentality ac-cording to which "women themselves think their greatest value is their ability to cook cabbage soup." Women, Sobchak argued in her book ironically titled *Marry a Millionaire* (Zamuzh za millionera), needed to change their conscious-ness. And marrying a millionaire, she explained in an interview, "is in no way a necessity."[81]

Aware of the stereotypes associated with feminism, some Russian female opposition figures took pains to distinguish themselves from feminists, assert-ing their own gender normativity and heterosexuality. Evgeniia Chirikova, Russia's best-known environmental activist (who won a seat on the opposi-tion's Coordinating Council in 2012) asserted that her activism stemmed pre-cisely from her position as a mother and a "homemaker." When asked, in an interview with the liberal newspaper *Nezavisimaia Gazeta*, whether she was more of a leftist or a liberal, Chirikova highlighted her traditionally feminine position. As she explained,

> I'm not a specialist in that area. People should have traditional values. I think the main value is the family and children. . . . I think, for ex-ample, that homosexual marriage is vulgar (poshlo). It can't be a norm. And at the same time, I don't understand the idea of feminism, either. A happy woman cannot be a feminist. The guarantee of a stable, normal society is a strong family.[82]

---

[80] "Russian Media Personality Turned Opposition Activist 'Hates Children'—TV," BBC Moni-toring, April 7, 2013.

[81] Aleksei Gorbachev, "Kseniia Sobchak: 'Putin nashchupal iz"ian u rossiiskoi oppozitsii i ochen' gramotno im vospol'zovalsia,'" *Nezavisimaia Gazeta*, April 3, 2012, http://www.ng.ru/ng_ politics/2012-04-03/9_sobchak.html; Oksana Robski and Kseniia Sobchak, *Zamuzh za millio-nera, ili Brak vyshego sorta* (Moscow: Astrel' ACT, 2009).

[82] Aleksei Gorbachev, "Evgeniia Chirikova: 'Ia vovse ne oppozitsioner, ia domokhoziaika!,'" *Ne-zavisimaia Gazeta*, April 3, 2012, http://www.ng.ru/ng_politics/2012-04-03/9_chirikova. html.

One Moscow-based organization (with international members), the Initiative Group "Pro-Feminism" (IGZF), held a regular "Sexist of the Year" award contest, where prizes were conferred for the most sexist statements made by public figures. One 2011 award went to Russian Orthodox archpriest Vsevolod Chaplin, who had spoken out after the above-mentioned ethnic riots in December 2010 with a peculiar proposition. Chaplin, as head of the Church's Department for Church-Society Relations, was described by feminist activist Natalia Bitten as Russia's "chief misogynist." He earned his prize by arguing for the legal imposition of a Russian Orthodox "dress-code" for women as a means of stopping rape (which he believed was provoked by women wearing mini-skirts) and preventing subsequent interethnic violence.[83] "It is obvious," Chaplin reportedly stated, "that a woman who is conducting herself carelessly, dressed like a prostitute, and, moreover, drunk and coming on to men, is not worthy of any respect and is not right in any case, regardless of whether she was raped or not."[84] Following Chaplin's initial statement about women in mini-skirts provoking rape, the IGZF penned an Internet petition objecting to Chaplin's assertion. They collected over two thousand signatures on line and earned their first media attention. Invited by journalists to appear on a television program, the feminist activists agreed, only to be asked by the program's editor if they could come to the studio wearing miniskirts. Bitten, the coordinator of the IGZF, recalled: "They were calling us 'defenders of the miniskirt.' That's also a gimmick (triuk), that kind of devaluing—as if we're not standing for women's rights or fighting for women's right not to be called prostitutes and not to be blamed for interethnic conflicts."[85]

Russian Orthodox Church figures were implicated in other misogynist statements reducing women to men's auxiliaries. As Elizaveta Morozova, a founder of the Moscow Feminist Group, explained:

> The Russian Orthodox Church is playing a larger and larger role in Russian politics. Its leaders have practically become political figures, they are constantly making political proclamations, and they are very patriarchal. For example, one of the leaders of the ROC [Russian Orthodox Church], a priest, [Dmitrii] Smirnov, on the eve of the [2011 parliamentary] elections, said, "Why do women have the right to vote? The right to vote should be taken away from them." He said, "Imagine if the husband votes one way, and the wife votes the other

---

[83] Bitten, interview by author.

[84] "RPTs predlozhila vvesti obshcherossiiskii dress-kod," January 18, 2011, http://lenta.ru/news/2011/01/18/dresscode/; Wander Woman, "SEKSIST GODA-2011: ITOGI."

[85] Bitten, interview by author.

way—that's unacceptable! She's basically not supporting what her husband is supporting!" You can allow women to vote if they're not married, and if they've achieved a lot in life—then you can let them vote. But married women voting separately from their husbands? That's bad, that can't be allowed [Laughs].[86]

Russia's politicians reportedly met such remarks with silence, offering no reaction at all.[87]

Finding that even liberal oppositionists tended at best to disregard and at worst to embrace traditional gender norms and sexism, feminist activists held out little hope for a more progressive politics even in the event that the liberal opposition successfully replace Putin's regime. The chances of electoral success for the Yabloko Party—the one liberal party whose registration was still intact, enabling its candidates to stand for election—were minimal for the foreseeable future as the party regularly failed to gain sufficient votes to earn parliamentary seats. Of all the registered parties, however, Yabloko was the most "feminist friendly." Feminist activists had attended events at Yabloko Party headquarters, such as lectures at a School of Feminism (shkola feminizma) hosted by Galina Mikhaleva, chair of the party's Gender Caucus. But in general, feminists expressed despair about the potential for Russia's extant political parties to raise feminist issues, as there was no apparent constituency for that. As one activist in Moscow put it,

[Most politicized people] consider feminism to be nonsense—entertainment for homemakers who have nothing else to do. Or they say that equality has already been achieved, so calm down. That's not our task: our job is to chase Putin out of power, or something else along those lines. There are very few people who share [positive] views [on feminism] and almost nobody supports it or spends time on it. There's no support from any of [the political organizations]. The only exception is Yabloko, which has a small section, and those people pay at least a little attention to [feminism], they organize meetings. I don't know of any other party that's taken up the issue of feminism.[88]

[86] For Smirnov's contention that only educated, successful, accomplished property owners should be able to vote, see Oksana Golovko, "Protoierei Dimitrii Smirnov: Ia protiv vseobshchego izbiratel'nogo prava!," November 29, 2011, http://www.pravmir.ru/protoierej-dimitrij-smirnov-ya-protiv-vseobshhego-izbiratelnogo-prava/.

[87] Morozova, interview by author.

[88] Grigor'eva, interview by author.

Things looked little better among the extra-systemic political opposition. So-cialist activist Zhenia Otto found that the protest movement was no stranger to sexist terms and imagery:

> For instance, there was an action about the sharp rise in gas prices, and there was a sticker with a drawing of a busty young woman (gru-dastaia devushka) with a little shirt that's falling open, and the cap-tion said, "We won't hand ourselves over to be fucked (Ne dadim sebia poimet')." It was a totally sexist symbol, and it was hard to ex-plain it.[89]

Russia's young feminist activists in Moscow and St. Petersburg believed that sexism had permeated the political sphere writ large. This included the left (which had no official representation in politics, aside from the Russian Com-munist Party, which was widely regarded as more a nationalist than a socialist entity) as well as those with more conservative views:

> The attitude toward feminism isn't dictated by any political move-ment, but by the culture on the whole. And those cultural founda-tions can be found among leftists, and rightists—they are all identi-cal. If you take a left activist, or a right activist, or a libertarian, or someone else, as far as gender is concerned, it'll all be the same. Maybe one would talk about [Russian] Orthodoxy, and how it's im-perative to have a good, monogamous family with ten children, and another would say that you have to make contraception and abor-tion completely available because a man should be able to have one hundred [female] lovers. But the difference would be in what the *man* wants; whether it's one orientation or another. And what *women* want, regardless of their political preferences, there's no con-sciousness of that, there's none of that. That is, the differences in political positions concerning family arrangements, daily life (byt), and the like, all depend entirely on the preferences of the men who are in those movements.[90]

Sexism and the notion of male privilege on which it rested could be found across the board.

In bringing their feminist analysis to bear, Nadia Plungian and Elizaveta Morozova (two members of the Moscow Feminist Group, interviewed

---

[89] Otto, interview by author.
[90] Morozova, interview by author.

together in 2012) found the politics of liberal anti-Putin protesters indistin-
guishable in its essence from that of the ruling regime:

> NADIA: If the liberals come to power, they'll mistreat all of the
> oppressed groups in just the same way. . . .
> ELIZAVETA: . . . It's the very same people. It's just that some of them are
> in power, and the others aren't."

Men, they argued, benefitted from the advantages granted them under patriarchy whether or not they were politically empowered. As such, men in Russia's liberal opposition had a common interest in sustaining the prevailing
patriarchal system, not in embracing an anti-sexist ideology; they were far
more interested in expanding their own power than in redistributing it. In
that light, Plungian described the goals of a male former classmate of hers,
now a "liberal" within Russia's Occupy movement (an anti-Putin movement
that arose in May 2012):

> NADIA: He simply wants to create an in-crowd (tusovka) of young
> white men who have money, who have cars, who have apartments in
> the center [of Moscow], so that they can go out and have drinks at
> cafes and say to each other, "Guys (rebiata), we're so totally cool!"
> (my zhe krutye).
> ELIZAVETA: "The only thing missing [for us] is political power."
> NADIA: Yes. [Speaking in a lower register, simulating a conversation
> between two men]: "I've got two kids, by the way, and what have you
> got?" "I've got two more." "And I go to prostitutes, do you?" "Oh, yes,
> I go—I always go." "I go to [the ones] over here, where do you go?" "I
> go over there." "Great! Let's go together!" I'm not joking, that's really
> how it is. That's exactly how it happens. . . .
> ELIZAVETA: It's logical, in fact. These are people with a high level of
> education, with a high level of income, but despite that, they have no
> access to political power within the current political system. It's in-
> teresting from the political point of view, because these are people
> who are privileged, and who have—I don't know how to say this in
> Russian—"entitlement." That is, they think that people like them
> should have it all. This is why the elections became a prod for the
> development of the opposition. They don't have any opportunities to

go into politics, because there everything is decided behind closed doors by Putin's inner circle. That's what provoked that upsurge of opposition.[91]

Plungian and Morozova regarded the liberal intelligentsia as thoroughly elitist and disinterested in (or, more accurately, deeply committed to suppressing the views of) anyone who did not fit the elite mold.[92] As the Russian Orthodox archpriest, Dmitrii Smirnov, rejected the idea of suffrage for married women and the lower class,[93] so too did liberals reject voices of the socio-economically disadvantaged. In this view, Russia's liberal intelligentsia was similarly dependent on the extant male-dominated, elite-based system of power that marginalized everyone else: the poor, women, feminists, sexual minorities, people with disabilities. Liberals displacing Putin in power would therefore likely reproduce the same sexist, homophobic political regime that was already in place.

Like sexism, homophobia was pervasive in Russia's political field, and, as I argued in Chapter 3, gender norms and homophobia alike have been used in efforts to assert and to undermine political actors' legitimacy. The next section briefly examines the perspectives on LGBT rights and homophobia held by young political activists and their organizations.

Homophobia and LGBT Rights in Russia: Political Activists' Views

In June 2011 the gay rights issue was fresh on people's minds, since (for the sixth year in a row) Moscow's city administration had just banned the annual Gay Pride event scheduled for the end of May. A year later, a Moscow court—in a burst of homophobic efficiency—banned gay pride events in the city for the next one hundred years.[94] Despite the 2011 ban, LGBT activists had gathered in central Moscow, where a group of Russian Orthodox extremists physically attacked them, bringing the gathering to a hasty end with arrests on both

[91] Nadia Plungian and Elizaveta Morozova, Moskovskaia Feministskaia Gruppa, interview by author, Moscow, June 20, 2012.

[92] Plungian develops this critique of the Russian liberal intelligentsia in her review of Masha Gessen's biography of mathematician Grigorii Perelman. See Nadia Plungian, "Istoriia odnoi diskreditatsii," *Neprikosnovennyi zapas* 81, no. 1 (2012), http://www.nlobooks.ru/node/1535.

[93] Golovko, "Protoierei Dimitrii Smirnov."

[94] Steve Clemons, "Not the Onion: Moscow Bans Gay Pride for Next 100 years," *The Atlantic*, June 8, 2012, http://www.theatlantic.com/international/archive/2012/06/not-the-onion-moscow-bans-gay-pride-for-next-100-years/258296/.

sides.[95] One young woman who, on the eve of attending the event, had posted a moving blog entry about her own lesbian relationship and against Russia's rampant homophobia, reportedly received a concussion in the melee, giving rise to discussion and outrage within progressive circles on the Web.[96] Not surprisingly, then, in answering interview questions about their groups' positions on discrimination regarding sex, ethnicity, and sexual orientation, a number of the pro- and anti-regime activists I talked with referred to the "gay parade"/gay pride event (gei parad).[97]

While activists across the board unhesitatingly stated that their groups stood against xenophobia and ethnic discrimination (a significant issue in Russia, given the state's multinational character and widespread popular bigotry, particularly toward people from Chechnya and other regions of the Caucasus), their groups' positions on discrimination against "sexual minorities" were largely unofficial, if they existed at all. The activists' own sentiments ran the gamut from support for gay rights and tolerance to relative intolerance and opposition.

None of the pro-Kremlin groups (Nashi, Stal', and Molodaia Gvardiia) had endorsed gay rights, although activists from those organizations voiced a range of individual views on the subject. After linking homosexuality to the matter of "national interests" and birthrates, Nashi's leader elaborated further:

> I think it's an example, a negative example, of the devaluation of the concept of freedom. I remember one history professor said that the people who thought that up, the philosophers, who talked about freedom a few hundred years ago, would be turning in their graves if they could see what had become of their brainchild. Our position is that nobody should violate anybody's personal rights, and if you have that kind of need (potrebnost'), then clearly you're going to have to do it somehow. But, first of all, you shouldn't attract any children to it, especially in a coercive way, and, second, propaganda about those kinds of relations is unacceptable, because, well, propaganda has to do with societal attitudes, and that it would be harmful to society's interests is obvious. And on that score, I won't lie—many of us are very intolerant. I don't know whether any of my friends would have gone down

[95] Mitra Mobasherat, "Dozens Arrested in Moscow Gay Rights Parade Clashes," May 28, 2011, http://www.cnn.com/2011/WORLD/europe/05/28/russia.gay.rights.parade.clashes/index.html.
[96] Veronika Khokhlova, "Russia: Moscow Pride 2011," May 29, 2011, http://globalvoicesonline.org/2011/05/29/russia-moscow-pride-2011/.
[97] Some Russians refer to "gay pride" and "gay parade" interchangeably, as the Russified version of the English word "pride" sounds similar to "parade" (gei praid; gei parad).

there—recently, there [to the pride event], yes?—and beaten [people up], but they [view it] most negatively (rezko otritsatel'no)—and I also view it most negatively. I think it's a deviation from the norm—that is, it's an abnormal attitude.[98]

Anton Smirnov, a Nashi member and leader of Stal', responded in a similar vein to my queries about his organizations' positions, alluding to popular intolerance:

Regarding the gay parade (gei parad), if I understand your question: personally, I'm against it. No—I just don't want it. It doesn't mean that if I see a person who has a different [i.e., gay] orientation that I'm going to go beat him up (polezu s kulakami na nego). Let him live in peace. And I'll live in peace. You understand, average people, including foreigners, we all project our way of life onto others, and ask why they don't do things like we do. Things are OK here [in that regard]. Nobody is oppressing gays here (pritesniaiut). But you know, our historical development and our culture don't approve of it. At the end of the day, this isn't Sparta. It's Russia. It's just not accepted. If someone has a gay orientation, it's just not accepted to discuss it. But there's no discrimination on that basis.

He concluded by noting, "To be honest, I don't even have any [gay] acquaintances," reflecting, perhaps, the relative rarity of disclosing homosexual orientation, given societal bias on the subject.[99]

Alena Arshinova, a co-coordinator of Molodaia Gvardiia, also endorsed the ban:

Q. About two weeks ago, when people were going to have a gay pride event (gei parad) in Moscow, and [Mayor] Sobianin decided to forbid it—.
A. He did the right thing.
Q. He did the right thing? Is that Molodaia Gvardiia's position?
A. It's more like my position than like Molodaia Gvardiia's; neither I nor Molodaia Gvardiia has anything against sexual minorities. But, on the other hand, I'll tell you that, in principle, in Russia, [people] aren't very accepting of it, and I even understand why that is. It's the mindset, it's the country's history. It's not ancient Greece [laughing], where that was the norm! And therefore, Sobianin took the right (and understandable) step, because he couldn't guarantee the safety of the people who were going out

---

[98] Borovikov, interview by author.
[99] Smirnov, interview by author.

into the square. It's just too *soon*. That is, he *saved* them [laughing], that's what I'd say. So . . . my position is that if I gave birth to a son, I'd want him to have a traditional [sexual] orientation. I have nothing against it, but I would want my children, and my friends' children, say, to have a traditional orientation. For him to marry a young woman (devushka), so that they'd have a child who's really theirs, and so on. It's a very particular kind of issue (Eto osobyi takoi vopros).[100]

By contrast, Roman Dobrokhotov, the leader of the liberal opposition group My (We), stressed the mutual support between his group and the gay community:

We participated in various actions against homophobia, and when I was running for a seat in the Moscow City Duma (though the authorities wouldn't register me), I found that the gay community—though I hadn't ever tried to contact them—on their own had started calling me and writing to me. And some financing was necessary in order to organize the collection of signatures [to get on the ballot], half of which was done by volunteers. But since it was a difficult task and a lot of people just wouldn't open their doors to us, we needed people to help with financing, and several people from that community came forward, independently of each other, to help in that way. It was really unexpected for us. And it turned out that way because I was one of only a few people willing to speak out publicly, and very sharply, against homophobes and in support of equality in that area.[101]

Given the prevalence of homophobic attitudes, the gay community's endorsement would hardly have endeared Dobrokhotov to the broader pool of voters, even if the authorities had agreed to register him as a candidate in the race.

Reflecting societal anxieties over the public assertion of gay rights, in several cases liberal, anti-regime activists noted that this was a controversial issue for their organizations. Molodezhnoe Yabloko's program, in the words of the group's leader, opposed "all forms of discrimination—on the basis of gender identity and sexual orientation, on the basis of nationality, because all people are created equal, and we don't see the point in dividing them up."[102] A Molodezhnoe Yabloko activist who worked for the "grown-up" Yabloko political party, however, believed that the issue for both groups was more complex:

[100] Arshinova, interview by author.
[101] Dobrokhotov, interview by author.
[102] Goncharov, interview by author.

As concerns sexual minorities, there's nothing in the party program about it, and we're having tumultuous debates about it. But up to this point, the party has had no position on it.

Q. Does Molodezhnoe Yabloko take a position on it?

A. It doesn't have one either, because a federal-level congress of Molodezhnoe Yabloko hasn't been held yet, and opinions on this issue differ very strongly. There's also a tactical issue, which is that this is an election year, and people have very negative attitudes about sexual minorities. So, we'll probably just be silent on this issue, as a tactical matter. It's understood that, as a liberal party, at some point down the line we should probably adopt something on that issue. But this is not the time or place.[103]

Mariia Savel'eva, a co-coordinator of the anti-regime group Oborona, noted that activists held diverse opinions within her organization on the subject and that her own view was more liberal. However, the violence that had taken place at the banned gay pride event had led the organization and some of its members to define or reconsider their positions:

In the past month we had a relevant topic come up about sexual minorities, because of the gay pride event (gei parad). There was a dramatic story because one young woman (devushka) was hit in the head, a lesbian, and there were a lot of postings about it, and Oborona posted about this too.... And some activists spoke out on our website [on this topic]; that is, we tried to come to some kind of position. And even those guys, like [she names an Oborona activist] for instance, who was always saying, "No, I'm opposed to gay parades. . . . That is, I'm not opposed to homosexuals, but why should they make a show of it? They aren't being deprived of their political rights." But when that devushka was hit in the head, he wrote, "I'm against gay parades, but I'm also against them being broken up."

Once violence had been used against the protesters to break up their action, gay rights was redefined as a "political matter," leading the organization to "stand up for them," Savel'eva explained.[104]

Overall, opposition-oriented activist groups were friendlier to gay rights than were their regime-supporting counterparts. While LGBT contingents

---

[103] Vlasova, interview by author.

[104] Mariia Savel'eva, Oborona, interview by author, Moscow, June 8, 2011.

were present and visible at large-scale protests against the Russian regime in 2011 and 2012, none of the mass actions sponsored by regime-supporting youth organizations like Nashi or Molodaia Gvardiia had ever featured even a glimmer of support by or for gay citizens. Pro-regime groups, in fact, spoke out against public manifestations celebrating gay rights. Molodaia Gvardiia activists, for instance, had protested against gay pride events, organizing a picket outside the Council of Europe building in Moscow in October 2010, after the European Court of Human Rights declared that the repeated bans on gay pride parades in the city constituted a violation of Russia's international obligations.[105] It is worth noting, in that context, that when the opposition-friendly Internet-TV station Rain (Dozhd') ran a show in 2012, titled "Legalization of Single-Sex Marriages: For and Against," the tally of viewer voting at the close of the program showed 57 percent of viewers supporting legalization and 38 percent against.[106] One of the representatives of the "against" position who had spoken on the program was newly elected United Russia deputy Alena Arshinova, the former co-coordinator of Molodaia Gvardiia (United Russia's youth wing); she had endorsed the ban on gay pride events when interviewed in 2011.[107] United Russia had repeatedly acted to restrict freedom of speech for the LGBT community. In the eight Russian regions where laws had been passed making it illegal to "propagandize" homosexuality in front of minors, United Russia deputies had sponsored them.[108]

Feminist activists interviewed in 2012 uniformly supported LGBT rights and typically protested jointly with LGBT groups when opportunities arose (see Chapter 6 for examples). In this, they differed from most of their politicized counterparts outside of the feminist movement, who were more likely than not to share in the majority's homophobic viewpoints about political activism on that subject. As two activists with the youth movement "Stop Violence" put it in a joint interview in June 2012, Russian popular culture in the twenty-first century had become marginally more friendly to gay entertainers while society remained virulently homophobic:

[105] Vladimir Laktanov, "Gei-parada v Moskve ne budet!," October 29, 2010, http://web.archive.org/web/20101104042115/http://www.molgvardia.ru/mg/2010/10/29/20465.
[106] "Russian TV Show Discusses Public Attitudes to Homosexuality: Dozhd Online," BBC Monitoring, November 11, 2012; "GOSDEP-3: Legalizatsiia odnopolykh brakov: Za i protiv," November 10, 2012, http://tvrain.ru/articles/gosdep_3_legalizatsija_odnopolyh_brakov_za_i_protiv-332762/?autoplay=false.
[107] "Russian TV Show Discusses Public Attitudes to Homosexuality"; "GOSDEP-3: Legalizatsiia odnopolykh brakov: Za i protiv," November 10, 2012, http://tvrain.ru/articles/gosdep_3_legal-izatsija_odnopolyh_brakov_za_i_protiv-332762/?autoplay=false.
[108] "Russian TV Show Discusses Public Attitudes to Homosexuality."

IRINA: In the modern world somehow it's become fashionable, here, at least, to be on stage as a gay or lesbian, it's seen as cool (kruto). . . . People eat it up, they like it. But they don't like it in politics. . . . And they try in various ways to suppress it, not to see it, not to look at it, not to pay attention to it. Recently, here, they forbade—.

MARIIA: That law on [outlawing homosexual] propaganda [in St. Petersburg]. . . . When that law passed, I even heard people say, first-hand, at work, "Yes, it's good that they forbade it, they shouldn't be allowed to do those things." Well, they didn't forbid the fact of [LGBT] existence. But that's exactly how people view it.[109]

Some opponents of the regime embraced homophobia while protesting against Putin's rule. On May Day 2011, the annual left-wing protest organized by the Russian Communist Party and various other left-wing groups for the first time had included a "gender" contingent. This was the initiative of the Committee for a Workers' International (KRI), a socialist group mainly staffed by young people, who the previous year had created a campaign against discrimination and women's exploitation.[110] As Vera Akulova recalled:

There were feminists and LGBT there, with different flags. And people from other left organizations attacked us several times [during the march]. At the beginning, when the contingent was gathering, a young man ran up to us from the Left Front contingent, Udal'tsov's group, and tried to tear a poster out of a gay activist's hands. I was standing next to him at that moment. After that, during the march, people from the Left Front contingent ran over and yelled insults and threats [at us], like "Send [all the] Fags to Auschwitz!" (Piderasy v Osvientsim). And then a man ran up to us, one of the KPRF [Russian Communist Party] organizers, and tried to tear up the rainbow flag. And the LGBT activists got the flag away from him and handed him over to the police who were walking with the protest. The situation was completely distorted in the media coverage. In fact, it was presented the other way around. They wrote mockingly about how gays tried to join in with the KPRF contingent, and—they just got it all mixed up. They said LGBT activists were handed over to the police, when in fact it was the other way around.[111]

---

[109] Irina Fetkulova and Mariia Tronova, Molodezhnoe Dvizhenie "Ostanovim Nasilie," interview by author, Moscow, June 18, 2012.

[110] Otto, interview by author.

[111] Akulova, interview by author.

Despite this display, Akulova believed that homophobia was becoming less popular within the political opposition. This change had occurred, somewhat ironically, as a result of the homophobic law passed in St. Petersburg in 2012 banning homosexual "propaganda":

> I think something is shifting a little, that gradually it's becoming un-seemly (neprilichno) to be a homophobe openly. At least, within the extra-systemic opposition. Although Udal'tsov [leader of the Left Front] continues to say that.... For instance, he was being interviewed on television, and they asked him a question about LGBT, and he an-swered, "I don't support faggots (piderasov)." That is, he said it openly. But I believe that the majority in the opposition, at least among the leftists, will just try not to say anything on that issue.[112]

The law's passage had motivated more public organizing by LGBT activists and their allies (in the feminist movement in particular), which in turn had spurred more discussions of gay rights and had made an impact on the opposition.

Tivur Shaginurov, an activist formerly with Oborona, reinterviewed in June 2012, similarly pointed out that the LGBT movement had earned a lot of respect among anti-Putin activists during the post-parliamentary election pro-tests in December 2011. "LGBT people are getting much more recognition and support. People on the left and in the opposition see that the LGBT activ-ists and Pussy Riot are real fighters (nastoiashchie boitsy)," he explained.[113] As evidence of this change, Shaginurov cited a widely viewed opposition parody of a Mastercard ad that circulated on YouTube in summer 2012.[114] In an echo of the Mastercard "priceless" campaign, the video enumerated a series of new fines that could be levied against protesters (a law to that effect had come into force in June 2012 as the regime attempted to decrease popular enthusiasm for bringing discontent into the streets). Its footage concluded with a still photo of people at a protest holding a rainbow flag and a poster with the words, "We won't allow Putin a third time," accompanied by a voiceover that intoned, "Not being afraid to say what you think: priceless."

Sexism and homophobia have a common core. But in addition to the mi-sogyny on which both concepts rest (i.e., the idea that being "like a woman" is demeaning for a man), homophobia additionally thrives on the notion that a "real man" is a heterosexual alpha-male.[115] Sociologist Elena Iarskaia-Smirnova

[112] Ibid.

[113] Tivur Shaginurov, Moscow, interview by author, June 20, 2012.

[114] Good Moments Box, "Novyi zakon o mitingakh i Masrecard [sic]" [video], June 10, 2012, http://www.youtube.com/watch?v=GTP8ZaN9rJc.

[115] Homophobia directed against lesbians (lesbophobia) attacks women for defying the patriar-chal order that mandates women's sexual and other dependence on men.

notes that the Russian political realm is practically female free and that media events like the Moscow State University birthday calendar for Putin only emphasize the widespread understanding that Russia's political leadership is male and heterosexual.[116] Manifestations of politicized sexism and homophobia thus serve to reinforce each other and ongoing male domination in the political realm.

Resistance to Sexism and Homophobia in Politics: Constraints on Women's Movement Mobilization (1989–2010)

As discussed in Chapter 2, women's movements can restrict the degree to which political actors feel free to rely on misogyny as a legitimation tool or as a source of ideological support. Russia is at something of a disadvantage in this respect. For most of the twentieth century, Russia lacked a well-institutionalized women's movement, although Russian women had organized actively and influentially before the Bolshevik revolution in 1917.[117] Once in power, the Communist Party's assertion of authoritarian rule made it impossible for women to organize separately in support of their own interests, since this was seen as detracting from the class struggle against capitalism and imperialism. With the exception of some efforts by female Soviet dissidents in the late 1970s (whose issues went unrecognized by the male dissident community),[118] women in the Soviet Union had no space for organized activism.[119] Russia's "second wave" of feminism broke only as the Soviet regime itself was nearing its end, emerging in the late 1980s and growing through the mid-1990s.

The women's movement of the late-Soviet "perestroika" era and the first post-Soviet Russian decade grew and diversified rapidly. Advocacy and

---

[116] Iarskaia-Smirnova, "Vezde kul'tiviruetsia obraz samtsa."

[117] On the roots of women's organizing in the Russian empire and in the early twentieth century, see Natal'ia Pushkareva, "Nachalo zhenskogo dvizheniia v Rossii," in *Zhenskoe dvizhenie v Rossii: Vchera, segodnia, zavtra: Materialy konferentsii*, ed. Galina Mikhaleva (Moscow: RODP "Yabloko" and KMK Publishers, 2010), 29–34; Rochelle Goldberg Ruthchild, *Equality and Revolution: Women's Rights in the Russian Empire, 1905–1917* (Pittsburgh: University of Pittsburgh Press, 2010); Richard Stites, *The Women's Liberation Movement in Russia: Feminism, Nihilism, and Bolshevism, 1860–1930* (Princeton, NJ: Princeton University Press, 1978).

[118] Nadezhda Azhgikhina, "Proshloe i budushchee zhenskogo dvizheniia v Rossii," in *Zhenskoe dvizhenie v Rossii: Vchera, segodnia, zavtra: Materialy konferentsii*, ed. Galina Mikhaleva (Moscow: RODP "Yabloko" and KMK Publishers, 2010), 111.

[119] For a detailed description of the production of the first Soviet feminist samizdat publications, see Anna Nataliia Malakhovskaia, "20 let tomu nazad v Leningrade zarodilos- zhenskoe dvizhenie," in *Propushchennyi siuzhet* (Moscow: ROO: Tsentr Obshchestvennoi informatsii, 2008), 54–69.

lobbying groups (some explicitly feminist and others not) raised women's issues with Russia's legislators and held innumerable seminars and conferences to discuss and strategize about varied aspects of sex-based discrimination, from the labor market to violence in the family. For all its successes in bringing taboo topics into common parlance, creating women's studies programs at universities around the country and placing issues like women's unemployment and domestic violence on the political agenda, the women's movement in the 1990s failed to become a mobilizational movement.[120]

The absence of mobilizational organizations from the Putin-era political scene was not peculiar to the women's movement, but fairly typical of Russian civic organizing overall.[121] As the twentieth century drew to a close, something of an historical parallel to the advent of Bolshevik rule occurred for the Russian women's movement. Like its pre-revolutionary predecessor, the movement encountered an atmosphere of increased authoritarianism, this time under Putin's reign. The ruling regime suppressed independent civic activism once again (though nowhere near as thoroughly as the Communist Party had done in its time), adding another constraint on popular mobilization for social change in a feminist direction.[122]

---

[120] For analyses of Russian civil society, examining issues of gender, foreign funding, and organizations' interaction with their potential constituents and with the state in the first two post-Soviet decades, see, for example, Julie Hemment, *Empowering Women in Russia: Activism, Aid, and NGOs* (Bloomington: Indiana University Press, 2007); Sarah L. Henderson, *Building Democracy in Contemporary Russia: Western Support for Grassroots Organizations* (Ithaca, NY: Cornell University Press, 2003); Suvi Salmenniemi, *Democratization and Gender in Contemporary Russia* (London: Routledge, 2008); Sperling, *Organizing Women in Contemporary Russia*; Lisa McIntosh Sundstrom, *Funding Civil Society: Foreign Assistance and NGO Development in Russia* (Stanford, CA: Stanford University Press, 2006); Lisa McIntosh Sundstrom, "Russian Women's Activism: Two Steps Forward, One Step Back," in *Women's Movements in the Global Era: The Power of Local Feminisms*, ed. Amrita Basu (Boulder, CO: Westview Press, 2010), 219–244; James Richter, "Evaluating Western Assistance to Russian Women's Organizations," in *The Power and Limits of NGOs*, ed. Sarah E. Mendelson and John K. Glenn (New York: Columbia University Press, 2002), 54–90.

[121] Sarah L. Henderson, "Civil Society in Russia: State–Society Relations in the Post-Yeltsin Era," *Problems of Post-Communism* 58, no. 3 (June 2011): 25.

[122] This is not to say that there was no social protest in Russia during the Putin period (i.e., before the cycle of larger-scale political protests that began in December 2011). Russia has experienced sporadic labor protests as well as a wave of protests in 2005 against the monetization of certain in-kind benefits (such as free transportation and utility subsidies) and occasional protests on concrete ecological and housing-related issues. See Alfred B. Evans Jr., "Protests and Civil Society in Russia: The Struggle for the Khimki Forest," *Communist and Post-Communist Studies* 45, nos. 3–4 (December 2012): 233–242; Alfred B. Evans Jr., "Civil Society and Protest," in *Return to Putin's Russia: Past Imperfect, Future Uncertain*, ed. Stephen K. Wegren (Lanham, MD: Rowman and Littlefield, 2012), 103–124; Elena Vinogradova, Irina Kozina, and Linda Cook, "Russian Labor: Quiescence and Conflict," *Communist and Post-Communist Studies* 45, nos. 3–4 (December 2012): 219–231.

Twenty years after the collapse of the Soviet dictatorship, no nationwide grassroots membership organizations for women had yet been created to pressure lawmakers on issues like abortion rights, violence against women, common violations of women's labor rights, or equal access to education.[123] As one long-term political player and women's activist put it, Russia contained a wealth of women's groups, including many academic feminist groups. However, as of 2010, "there [was] not a single active feminist group prepared to organize mass actions."[124]

Political parties, accordingly, showed little interest in reaching out to their potential female constituencies. In 2012, only one of the political parties regularly listed on Russian ballots—the liberal Yabloko Party—proffered a gender equality plank in its platform and had an intra-party gender caucus.[125] Even this was little consolation, however, given that Yabloko had failed to gain any seats in Russia's parliamentary elections via the party list system in 2003, 2007, and 2011.[126] At a women's movement conference in Moscow in early 2010, feminist journalist Nadezhda Azhgikhina pointed out a certain irony in the fact that the conference was hosted by Yabloko:

> I remember well how in the mid-1990s activists in the very young— and at that time, independent—women's movement were trying to make contact with Yabloko. We took part in meetings and tried to get women's issues on the agenda. Unfortunately, in those years, a strong alliance didn't develop. Now, Yabloko has no seats in the parliament, and the women's movement simply doesn't exist as a significant or even recognizable societal force.[127]

---

[123] One new high school in Kazan, for instance, specializing in information technology education, failed to accept any young women into its first entering class in 2012, although more than half of the applicants who had made it to the final selection round for admission were girls. In October, the local attorney general's office found the school in violation of federal education law and demanded that thirty young women who had scored higher than their male counterparts be accepted, but two months later, the young women had not been allowed to register. See "Prokuratura trebuet ustranit' polovuiu diskriminatsiiu v IT-litsee pri universitete," October 17, 2012, http://pravo.ru/news/view/78750/; Natasha Bitten, "Russia: Gender Segregation in IT (Information Technology) Education: for Boys Only," September 19, 2012, http://www.zafeminizm.ru/171-russia-gender-segregation-in-it-information-technology-education-for-boys-only.html.

[124] Mikhaleva, "Est' li politicheskii potentsial u zhenskogo dvizheniia v Rossii?," 66.

[125] Galina Mikhaleva, "Predislovie," in *Zhenskoe dvizhenie v Rossii: Vchera, segodnia, zavtra: Materialy konferentsii*, ed. Galina Mikhaleva (Moscow: RODP "Yabloko" and KMK Publishers, 2010), 5.

[126] Centre for the Study of Public Policy and the Levada Center, "Results of Previous Elections to the Russian State Duma," http://www.russiavotes.org/duma/duma_elections_93-03.php, accessed January 4, 2013. Four Yabloko members won independent mandate seats in the 2003 election.

[127] Azhgikhina, "Proshloe i budushchee zhenskogo dvizheniia v Rossii," 110.

The most natural ally of the women's movement (outside of the various left-wing socialist groups that, in some cases, rhetorically supported women's rights) had found itself largely excluded from mainstream politics.

After the September 11, 2001 attacks, US foreign aid priorities shifted, and Russian women's movement groups (particularly those with a feminist orientation) were challenged by the withdrawal of foreign funds that had supported their activity.[128] Nonforeign-funded grassroots women's groups existed, but neither they nor the formerly funded groups made the Russian national news.[129] While a number of the women's organizations founded in the 1990s continued to exist (such as the Consortium of Women's NGOs, a women's informational network called Women and Information, and a network of women's crisis centers) along with several strong gender-studies-oriented research centers, they lacked political clout and social recognition.[130] The political impetus in the 1990s to support women's rights (strengthened somewhat by the Fourth World Conference on Women, held in Beijing in 1995) had weakened, and the political gains achieved by the movement, such as the establishment of a presidential commission on women during Yeltsin's presidency, were reversed.[131] Efforts to pass legislation supporting a quota for women's representation on party lists failed.[132] Women's issues, aside from official calls for raising the birthrate, had fallen off the regime's agenda.[133] Media coverage of women's movement issues and organizations was slight and the public had "no clear idea about women's issues in contemporary Russia, while a multitude of sexist stereotypes and beliefs persisted."[134] As we have seen, a decade into Putin's administration, even politically engaged youth on the

---

[128] For a discussion of the foreign funding of Russian civil society, see Hemment, "Nashi, Youth Voluntarism, and Potemkin NGOs," 241–243.

[129] On the differences between funded and unfunded groups, see Sarah Henderson, "Importing Civil Society: Foreign Aid and the Women's Movement in Russia," *Demokratizatsiya* 8, no. 1 (2000): 65–82.

[130] On the key role played by gender studies scholars in the Russian women's movement, see Irina Iukina, "Rol' akademicheskogo soobshchestva v sovremennom zhenskom dvizhenii Rossii (na primere Sankt-Peterburga)," in *Zhenskoe dvizhenie v Rossii: Vchera, segodnia, zavtra: Materialy konferentsii,* ed. Galina Mikhaleva (Moscow: RODP "Yabloko" and KMK Publishers, 2010), 84–88.

[131] Mikhaleva, "Est' li politicheskii potentsial u zhenskogo dvizheniia v Rossii?," 67.

[132] Ibid.

[133] In St. Petersburg, the situation was somewhat different, as the city had a cooperative relationship with some women's groups, and city adminstrators were somewhat amenable to feminist perspectives on the resolution of gender inequality, largely due to the efforts of academics who taught gender-related courses to civil servants. Iukina, "Rol' akademicheskogo soobshchestva v sovremennom zhenskom dvizhenii Rossii (na primere Sankt-Peterburga)," 88; Barandova, "Sovremennyi etap zhenskogo dvizheniia Sankt-Peterburga."

[134] Kovalenko, "Sovremennoe Rossiiskoe zhenskoe dvizhenie," 91.

liberal side of the political spectrum found it difficult to believe that sexism was a serious issue in contemporary Russia.

The contraction of democracy during the Putin era combined with a variety of other factors to restrict women's movement activity. At the 2010 conference in Moscow, women activists who had experienced the movement's heyday in the mid-1990s made critical self-assessments of the contemporary movement, enumerating its weaknesses, while also pointing to the challenging political and social context faced by feminist activism in the Putin era. The movement itself, some argued, was weak, fragmented, lacked charismatic leadership, and bore an "elite character."[135] Activists distrusted attempts to coordinate activities between groups, fearing the loss of their independence; coalition activity, whether with other women's groups or with other political forces (such as parties or trade unions), was lacking.[136] The techniques of the 1990s movement persisted as well, focusing on expert analysis and closed-door seminars and conferences; one study analyzing one hundred women's NGO reports between 2000 and 2007 identified their main form of activity as organizing lectures, roundtables, and seminars. This rendered the movement publicly "invisible" to its potential constituents, partners, and opponents—and to the media.[137] As Elena Kovalenko, a Russian graduate student analyzing the movement, argued, the "potential that the Russian women's movement had in the 1990s had been nearly exhausted," and new, "alternative" forms of action would be required to alter that situation and raise the movement's visibility.[138] Specifically, she explained, the women's movement had avoided "direct action," preferring to rely on the "expert community" of gender studies scholars to do the work of connecting with decision-makers. This was a fraught approach: "Experts' efforts could be ineffective without the weight and influence that can only be gained by serious societal support in the form of vigorous activism on the part of women's NGOs. The nature of expert activity is such that the experts themselves are speaking not as representatives of a concrete social group seeking to solve a particular problem but are representing a scholarly position on a given issue. One gets the impression that the women whose interests are being supported by the experts are passive when it comes to expressing and defending those interests."[139]

---

[135] Nadezhda Shvedova, "Zhenskoe dvizhenie v Rossii: Problemy sovremennogo etapa," in *Zhenskoe dvizhenie v Rossii: Vchera, segodnia, zavtra: Materialy konferentsii*, ed. Galina Mikhaleva (Moscow: RODP "Yabloko" and KMK Publishers, 2010), 39.

[136] Ibid.

[137] Kovalenko, "Sovremennoe Rossiiskoe zhenskoe dvizhenie: Problema 'nevidimosti,'" 90.

[138] Ibid., 89.

[139] Ibid., 89–90.

The need for public outreach was evident in the virtual realm as well. As Russian society was becoming increasingly attuned to the Internet, the movement's public Web presence was limited. In particular, it lacked an arena in which strategies and interorganization plans could be discussed; groups remained largely uninformed about one another's activities.[140] Moreover, as of 2010, there was an ongoing gap between the women's movement and its "target groups" or potential constituencies: "Women know almost nothing about the activity of even the organizations for which demand is highest—women's crisis centers supporting women who have survived domestic violence and sexual violence."[141] No stable channels for communication were in place, and efforts to contact and educate a broad audience were few and far between.[142]

In the view of some of the conference-goers, the movement had gotten stuck in its ways. Tatiana Fediaeva, a woman journalist in attendance, pointed out that at the conference she saw people with whom she had been discussing the conference themes (such as the absence of women in political power, violence against women, and the need for public enlightenment about gender issues) for twenty years and that it would be "self-deceptive" to suggest that very much had changed over that period of time.[143] Her recipe for strengthening the movement was to take up issues with broad popular resonance, such as alcoholism, and thereby create a movement representing a significant force: "Everyone respects strength. But strength can only be demonstrated by achieving concrete results that everyone can understand. It can't be achieved by loudly yelling words like 'gender' that the majority of people don't understand, or by using scary words like 'feminism.'"[144]

The term "gender"—imported into Russian from English, with a hard "g"—started out, as it did in the United States, as an academic term unfamiliar to the average citizen. Although it had not achieved universal familiarity by 2010 in Russia—a government document prepared for the fifteenth anniversary of the adoption of the Beijing Declaration reportedly confused "gender" and the financial term "tender" (also an import)[145]—it had become a considerably more

[140] Nikolai Vinnik, "Zhenskoe dvizhenie i runet: Naiti drug druga," in *Zhenskoe dvizhenie v Rossii: Vchera, segodnia, zavtra: Materialy konferentsii,* ed. Galina Mikhaleva (Moscow: RODP "Yabloko" and KMK Publishers, 2010), 94.

[141] Ibid., 94–95.

[142] For a brief analysis of the reach of several main informational women's movement sites as of 2010, see ibid., 95–96.

[143] Tat'iana Fediaeva, "Skaz o parallel'nykh mirakh," in *Zhenskoe dvizhenie v Rossii: Vchera, segodnia, zavtra: Materialy konferentsii,* ed. Galina Mikhaleva (Moscow: RODP "Yabloko" and KMK Publishers, 2010), 107.

[144] Ibid., 108.

[145] Barandova, "Sovremennyi etap zhenskogo dvizheniia Sankt-Peterburga," 74.

common term than it was in the mid-1990s, when it was not universally known even among the leaders of Russia's women's organizations (particularly those outside of Moscow and St. Petersburg).[146] Young Moscow-based political activists—even those who were not concerned with feminist issues—freely used the term "gender" in interviews in 2011. As the leader of the pro-Kremlin group, Nashi, explained with a chuckle, "Yes, the word is common now—you can't say it's a Russian word, but it's like 'parliament.'"[147] As discussed in Chapter 2, however, the term "feminism" was a different story, retaining its negative reputation in the broader society.

Meanwhile, at the end of Putin's first decade in power, the political and cultural context for feminist organizing was unfriendly. "Widespread sexist convictions" and general opposition to the idea of gender equality made it difficult for the women's movement to flourish, though struggling against that very sexism was regarded by some scholar-activists as the main goal of the movement.[148] The topics of gender equality, women's rights, and democratic development had been "essentially crowded off the Russian societal agenda, despite the fact that those issues had not yet been resolved."[149] Just as problematic was the political system in which the movement operated. Under Putin, the women's movement—like the human rights movement and other civic initiatives—was subject to a new set of political constraints. As foreign grants declined, a domestic system of grants distributed by Russia's Public Chamber (an advisory body, one third of whose members are chosen by the Russian president) was established, largely supporting apolitical organizations or those that "directly supported the ruling group."[150] The Chamber reportedly funded neither gender-based nor feminist initiatives.[151] As one historian of the Russian women's movement remarked with regard to the movement in 2010 and its widely bemoaned weakness, like Russia's other civic movements "the women's movement is in no condition to be what it could be in a society where citizens accepted democratic freedoms as the norm in their lives, in a society with developed democratic institutions, freedom of the press, and [a well-formed sense of] respect for the individual as such."[152] What Janet Johnson and Aino Saarinen refer to as Russia's "neomasculinism" under Putin also limited the opportunities for feminist organizing and increased the

[146] Sperling, *Organizing Women in Contemporary Russia*, 246.

[147] Borovikov, interview by author.

[148] Shvedova, "Zhenskoe dvizhenie v Rossii," 40, 46.

[149] Kovalenko, "Sovremennoe Rossiiskoe zhenskoe dvizhenie,'" 89.

[150] Mikhaleva, "Est' li politicheskii potentsial u zhenskogo dvizheniia v Rossii?," 68.

[151] Barandova, "Sovremennyi etap zhenskogo dvizheniia Sankt-Peterburga," 75.

[152] Iukina, "Rol' akademicheskogo soobshchestva v sovremennom zhenskom dvizhenii Rossii (na primere Sankt-Peterburga)," 85.

"pressure on activists to frame their activism in ways that do not counter neo-traditional gender norms."[153]

Despite these obstacles and a "near total silence" about the women's movement within the Russian mass media, more than one thousand participants came together for a Second All-Russian Women's Congress in November 2008, marking the centennial anniversary of the first, pre-revolutionary Russian women's congress. Nadezhda Azhgikhina described the Congress as a peculiar event supported by Putin's regime and organized by little-known women entrepreneurs, where no mention was made of the previous twenty years of independent women's organizing in Russia. It soon became clear, wrote Azhgikhina, that these "spunky gals (devushki) were pursuing a clear and simple goal: to offer the authorities a movement with a century-old history as a commodity for further financing."[154] Others saw the event as having "demonstrated that women's non-governmental organizations were alive" and that women's organizing (in the form of conferences, seminars, and roundtables) was occurring in Russia's far-flung regions as well as in its metropolitan centers.[155]

Following the Congress, its organizing committee created the Council to Consolidate the Women's Movement, along with a website that the organizers hoped would, by mid-2010, "become a space bringing together participants in the women's movement, and allowing them to solve their problems with the support of the community and of experts, to plan to carry out joint actions, to get 'firsthand' news, conduct virtual Council sessions" and generally help to consolidate the otherwise scattered activities of women organizing on a wide range of issues.[156] Four years later, however, the Council's website (http://www.gensovet.com) had been taken over by a Russian industrial repair services company, and its Facebook page was essentially empty.[157] The movement

---

[153] For instance, Johnson and Saarinen document the tactical shift that Russia's crisis centers adopted in toning down feminist rhetoric in the 2000s. See Janet Elise Johnson and Aino Saarinen, "Twenty-First-Century Feminisms under Repression: Gender Regime Change and the Women's Crisis Center Movement in Russia," *Signs* 38, no. 3 (2013): 550, 553.

[154] Nadezhda Azhgikhina, ed., *Propushchennyi siuzhet: Istoriia novogo nezavisimogo zhenskogo dvizheniia Rossii s nachala 1990x do nashikh dnei v zerkale SMI* (Moscow: ROO: Tsentr Obshchestvennoi informatsii, 2008), 246.

[155] Shvedova, "Zhenskoe dvizhenie v Rossii," 41.

[156] Natal'ia Dmitrieva, "Zhenskoe dvizhenie Rossii: Sovremennoe sostoianie i potentsial rosta," in *Zhenskoe dvizhenie v Rossii: Vchera, segodnia, zavtra: Materialy konferentsii*, ed. Galina Mikhaleva (Moscow: RODP "Yabloko" and KMK Publishers, 2010), 52.

[157] "Sovet po konsolidatsii Zhenskogo Dvizheniia Rossii," http://on.fb.me/11Hpd5p, accessed January 4, 2013, but no longer available. The original website for the Council, http://www.gensovros.ru, was also not in operation, and another Council site had not been updated for several years: http://style-nes.com/assets/files/verstka/2010/sowet/article.html#.

whose political influence (albeit limited) had peaked in the mid-1990s had begun its descent shortly thereafter.[158]

GENERATIONAL RIFT

By the late-2000s, a new wave of feminist organizing had arisen in Russia (see Chapter 6). When the movement reemerged, it was largely populated by a younger generation, quite disconnected from the 1990s activists. Russia's new wave of feminism found expression on the Web as well as in small conscious-ness-raising groups and street protests. Its largest Web-based presence was on the three-thousand-member LiveJournal blog called Feministki (feminists), created with the aim of spreading the word about feminism (posting founda-tional texts of feminism in translation) and providing the Russian Internet with its most significant discussion platform on gender issues.[159] However, representatives of the established "women's movement" (the major groups of the 1990s that had continued to exist) reportedly "paid little attention" to the Feministki community.[160] Several of the new groups adopted the forms of direct action endorsed by Kovalenko at the February 2010 conference, believ-ing that, as she had argued, educational lectures and seminars were not "up to the task" of increasing movement visibility.[161] If in February 2010 "cultural ac-tions, as a means of fighting sexism and gender stereotypes (through exhibi-tions, performances, festivals, and so on)"[162] had not been in evidence, the small street protests conducted by women's groups starting in April of that year (not to mention the performances by Pussy Riot in late 2011 and early 2012) changed the tactical palette that the women's movement had used until that time.

Indicative of the generational gap, the Council to Consolidate the Women's Movement, which brought together the leaders (now in their 50s and 60s) of several Russian women's movement groups founded in the 1990s, did not count any of the new feminist groups among its membership.[163] Co-chaired by Galina Mikhaleva, the head of the Yabloko Party's Gender Caucus, the Council

---

[158] Mikhaleva, "Est' li politicheskii potentsial u zhenskogo dvizheniia v Rossii?," 67.

[159] Frau Derrida, interview by author. On the founding and later development of the Feministki blog, see Frau Derrida, Isya, and Myjj, "Pol'za ot razgovorov (Ob opyte odnogo prosvetitel'skogo proekta v blogosfere)," in *Zhenskoe dvizhenie v Rossii: Vchera, segodnia, zavtra: Materialy konferen-tsii*, ed. Galina Mikhaleva (Moscow: RODP "Yabloko" and KMK Publishers, 2010), 97–102.

[160] Vinnik, "Zhenskoe dvizhenie i runet: naiti drug druga," 96.

[161] Kovalenko, "Sovremennoe Rossiiskoe zhenskoe dvizhenie," 91.

[162] Ibid.

[163] Galina Mikhaleva, Chair, Gendernaia Fraktsiia Partii Yabloko, interview by author, Moscow, June 8, 2012; Bitten, interview by author.

proceeded to establish some connections with Russia's Public Chamber, where it made efforts to lobby for women's interests.[164] The new generation of feminist activists, however, was not to be found calling on lawmakers or on the citizens designated as advisors to Putin's regime who sat in the Public Chamber.

The tech-savvy young feminists who had begun to mobilize on the Web and engage in small street protests had not displaced the activists who had brought the movement into the public eye in the 1990s. But cooperation across that generational divide was largely absent, and the groups that got their start in different decades were mainly unaware of each other's existence. Reflecting this "generational isolation," one analyst in 2010 noted that the movement that had formed in the 1990s was "aging," as it had not actively recruited new supporters and had not become a "truly influential" societal force.[165]

Young feminist activists interviewed in summer 2012 agreed with this assessment. They had few ties with their feminist foremothers who had been active in the first post-Soviet Russian decade. The strongest connections across the generational divide were to women activists at several crisis centers established in the 1990s—one in St. Petersburg and two in Moscow—the "Sisters" (Sestry) center, which works with rape survivors, and ANNA, which focuses on domestic violence.[166] In St. Petersburg, young feminists were in touch with well-established gender studies scholars and activists from that city's Gender Center who participated together at events such as a 2012 roundtable discussion titled, "What Is Feminism in Russian? Prospects for the Development of a Mass Feminist Movement in Russia in the Coming Years."[167] But intergenerational connections in Moscow between women activists were rare. A young feminist working on a socialist organization's campaign to eliminate sex discrimination noted that her job was to do outreach and that she had no knowledge of the women's groups founded fifteen to twenty years earlier. Nor had anyone from such groups reached out to her.[168]

Efforts to establish cross-generational connections were sometimes frustrated. One of the moderators of the Feministki blog had made an attempt to visit what had been the scholarly hub of the Moscow women's movement in the mid-1990s, the Moscow Center for Gender Studies, but found the venture frustrating:

---

[164] Mikhaleva, interview by author.

[165] Vinnik, "Zhenskoe dvizhenie i runet," 94.

[166] Frau Derrida, interview by author; Maksimova, interview by author; Tat'iana E., FemInfoteka, interview by author, St. Petersburg, June 14, 2012.

[167] Sergeyyugov, "Feminizm po-russki?"; Tat'iana E., interview by author.

[168] Otto, interview by author.

With other organizations—for instance, the Moscow Center for Gender Studies—we don't have any contact with them. Some time ago, I wanted to get into their library, which is open something like one day a week for two hours. I found the address on the Internet, I went over there, but there was nothing there. I called, nobody answered—and that was that."[169]

Another activist, discussing the likelihood of coalition building among women's organizations, seemed pessimistic:

Of course, if we're talking about whom to build coalitions with, it would be with organizations from the 1990s, but based on my experience, building those coalitions with them is very complicated. It requires a great deal of energy; that is, it's harder to make a coalition with those organizations than it is to recruit an antifeminist into a feminist group. Because if a person comes to feminism from nothing, then they don't have any feminist convictions or identification and so on. But the people who worked in feminism in the 1990s very often—how to say this so as not to offend?—they might have, so to say, a "mentor" complex, a teacher complex (kompleks metrov). That is, very often—If you start to raise a subject for discussion, asking if you'd like to discuss this issue, or if you send an invitation to someone from that old generation—and when I say "old" I don't mean age. They could be my age. I mean that they'd been working in those organizations of the 1990s. And when you send them an invitation to a meeting, the classic reaction is that you get an answer like, "Yes, of course, my organization and I have been studying this issue since such-and-such a year, when we carried out a such-and-such program. . . ." In other words, they always have to say that they've been working on it for so long, and you constantly have to prove to them that you're not at some lower level.[170]

Given these obstacles, from the perspective of Russia's new wave of feminist organizers, the probability of succeeding at intergenerational outreach appeared slim.

---

[169] Frau Derrida, interview by author. The Moscow Center for Gender Studies, formed in 1990, was soon accused by other Russian feminists of hoarding their Western contacts and funding sources. On this and other conflicts within the Russian women's movement in the 1990s, see Sperling, *Organizing Women in Contemporary Russia*, 182–205, 232–246.

[170] Morozova, interview by author.

It was not that the feminist activists who found themselves organizing to improve women's status in the late-Soviet and early post-Soviet period had nothing in common with their Putin-era counterparts. Activists in both generations of the movement pointed to similar struggles: intra-movement splits and conflicts, fragmentation, and the relative invisibility of the movement in the socio-political field. Activists in both eras had undergone similar processes of discovering feminism (the first generation had typically found it in English-language texts kept under lock and key in their academic institutes' libraries; the second had typically found it in English-language texts—or Russian translations of them—on the Web). Both movements had seen the value in creating informal consciousness-raising groups, and both were populated by highly intellectual, well-read women in social and political settings utterly unfriendly to feminism. But the two generations had few chances to connect. When they did intersect, the connection was uneasy. A Moscow-based gender sociologist acquainted with activists in both generations had organized a round table on gender research in Moscow in 2011, bringing together some of the academic feminist luminaries of the 1990s with the new feminist activists, but working relationships had not developed. Her collaborator, a young feminist activist, mused afterward about the failure to bridge the divide, attributing it in part to the 1990s researchers' tendency to "dominate the discussion, which seems strange to us."[171] It was a classic "generational rift," as one gender sociologist in St. Petersburg explained in 2012.[172]

Some cross-generational connections had occurred between activists at the individual, interpersonal level. In interviews in 2012, several young feminists mentioned having encountered women who got their start in women's movement activism in the 1990s. The controversial writer, television personality, and feminist Mariia Arbatova, for example, attended International Women's Day rallies where "new generation" feminists were present,[173] and Arbatova's mid-1990s TV show, "Ia sama" [I Myself], had brought the word "feminism" to the attention of several young feminists who had been teenagers at the time when they'd watched it.[174] Galina Mikhaleva invited several young feminist activists to the conference at Yabloko headquarters in 2010, enabling other

---

[171] Akulova, interview by author.

[172] Anna Temkina, interview by author, St. Petersburg, June 14, 2012.

[173] Grigor'eva, interview by author.

[174] Morozova, interview by author; Zamoiskaia, interview by author. On "Ia sama," see Azhgikhina, *Propushchennyi siuzhet*, 173–176. In the mid-1990s, Ol'ga Lipovskaia, the head of the St. Petersburg Center for Gender Issues publicly critiqued Arbatova as Russia's only "paid telefeminist." Arbatova, in turn, accused Lipovskaia and other Russian feminist activists who had received grants from Western sources of being more interested in money than in bringing feminist ideas to the general Russian population. See Sperling, *Organizing Women in Contemporary Russia*, 3–4.

connections. Two of the next-generation activists in Moscow were acquainted with feminist journalist Nadezhda Azhgikhina, and one activist had met Valentina Konstantinova, earlier a researcher at the Moscow Center for Gender Studies, at a civic forum in Fall 2011.[175] But these ties were sporadic and individual rather than between organizations.

A social movement can be strengthened by continuity, and intergenerational connection is "one of the relevant issues for the preservation and further development of the [women's] movement."[176] Twenty years after the Soviet dictatorship collapsed, Russia's women's movement lacked that intergenerational continuity. Young feminists empathized with the struggles faced by feminists in the 1990s, who, they imagined, might have been even more isolated in their activities and beliefs than the current group and who had had to fight for recognition while "constantly defending themselves" and their support of feminist principles.[177] The limited pluralism of Russia's political system, meanwhile, likely acted as a brake on the establishment of intergroup connections, leaving the women's movement—like all of Russia's other social movements—at an organizing disadvantage.

A decade into the twenty-first century, Russia lacked a popular women's movement that might otherwise have held in check some of the sexualization of politics and other patriarchal political phenomena in evidence under Putin. At the Yabloko-hosted women's conference in 2010, Galina Mikhaleva identified a range of problems troubling Russia from a feminist perspective. These included "the male face of Russian politics," which had made rude speech and insults against political opponents characteristic of the political field; the feminization of poverty and the minimalist nature of children's welfare benefits; women's disadvantaged position in the labor market; the pressures on women—caught between "harsh market conditions and patriarchal stereotypes"—to choose between motherhood and professional development; the ongoing and insufficiently critical societal attitude toward domestic violence against women and sexual harassment at work; legislative attempts to limit access to abortion (in the context of what Mikhaleva vividly called the "[Russian] 'Orthodox fashion show'"); and the tendency to regard women in "glamour culture" as "objects for purchase and sale."[178] "In large part," Mikhaleva noted, "this is the consequence of the absence of a strong and influential women's movement in society."[179] For reasons including the generation gap and the fact that the 1990s women's movement in Russia had

---

[175] Bitten, interview by author; Morozova, interview by author; Akulova, interview by author.
[176] Barandova, "Sovremennyi etap zhenskogo dvizheniia Sankt-Peterburga," 81.
[177] Morozova, interview by author.
[178] Mikhaleva, "Est' li politicheskii potentsial u zhenskogo dvizheniia v Rossii?," 66.
[179] Ibid.

not mobilized a domestic constituency, the women's movement had remained small and marginal. It had little opportunity to effectively counter the many-faceted embodiments of sexism. As gender sociologist Tatiana Barandova put it, summing up the somewhat disheartening situation for the Russian women's movement in 2010: "For a series of institutional and material reasons, the educational efforts by segments of the nonprofit sector, which includes crisis centers and feminist organizations, and also the small numbers of [progressively inclined academics] in a variety of regions, cannot counter the scale of the neo-patriarchy's attack."[180] In short, when sexism and homophobia entered into Russia's political debate, whether concretely and overtly or in the form of rhetorical discrimination based on gender-normative stereotypes, those who embraced it were not subject to political costs from an organized and powerful constituency of women.

* * *

At the close of the aforementioned women's movement conference in 2010, attendees affirmed a set of resolutions. These asserted the ongoing importance of women's issues and the necessity of struggling both against gender-based discrimination and for women's rights and opportunities. The resolutions avowed a need to unite the forces of disparate women's groups and expressed concern about the lack of governmental support for gender equality in the context of "growing patriarchal tendencies in Russia."[181] They identified the priorities of the movement as including lobbying to pass a law establishing a "national mechanism" to monitor the implementation of gender equality across the state and bringing together women's movement group actions for a range of purposes:

> To struggle against manifestations of patriarchy, discrimination, and violence against women; to protect women's political, social, and labor rights; to propose civic initiatives and state policies to guarantee equal rights and opportunities for men and women; to guarantee the balanced participation of men and women in the development and adoption of decisions at all levels of power, and to actively nominate women for positions in power; to increase social and financial support for mothers; to develop partner-like family relationships, increasing the role of fathers and protecting their rights; and to promote gender education.[182]

[180] Barandova, "Sovremennyi etap zhenskogo dvizheniia Sankt-Peterburga," 76.
[181] Galina Mikhaleva, ed., "Rezoliutsiia konferentsii: 'Zhenskoe dvizhenie v Rossii: Vchera, segodnia, zavtra,' Moskva, 26 fevralia 2010 goda," in *Zhenskoe dvizhenie v Rossii: Vchera, segodnia, zavtra: Materialy konferentsii* (Moscow: RODP "Yabloko" and KMK Publishers, 2010), 112.
[182] Ibid.

This was a tall order. The next chapter examines the various forms of feminist activism that developed over the course of the three years that followed. During that period, young feminists in Russia attempted to make their voices heard. They worked in the virtual world as well as in the real one. They gathered in small groups and planned creative actions to draw citizens' attention in public spaces. They did so under conditions that held out few promises of feminists' winning popular approval and that ran the risk of subjecting them to political repression. By the end of 2012, contrary to expectations, feminism had nonetheless entered Russia's public discussion. It did so in the context of the best-known political-musical event of the twenty-first century—the self-identified feminist punk band Pussy Riot's abbreviated "punk prayer service" in Moscow's Cathedral of Christ the Savior. Suddenly, "feminism" had become the word of the day in Russia—and, to many, it stood more for blasphemy than for gender justice. Pussy Riot's representation of feminism, however, was not the only one. And amidst the clamor over Pussy Riot's dramatic entry onto the political stage (and their equally dramatic exit into prison), other Russian feminists continued to organize. Russia's battle over gender norms and political legitimacy was heating up.

6

When Pussy Riots:
Feminist Activism in Russia

Patriarchy is powerful and persistent. Despite centuries of feminist organizing in some countries and decades in others, rampant discrimination on the basis of sex continues around the globe. Whether one points to the paucity of female representation in government, the global feminization of poverty, or the reports of rapes, domestic murders and honor killings that flicker across the news (not to mention those that do not make the news), it is clear that feminists' and pro-feminist allies' work is far from over.

Like their colleagues elsewhere, Russian feminist groups have publicized instances and patterns of sex discrimination and objected to the limits imposed on human freedom by strict gender norms. Against the backdrop of sexism observed in Russian politics, feminist activists in Russia have also exposed the use of patriarchy and misogyny as tools of political authority-building by both the regime and its opponents. In so doing, they have helped to undermine one of the ideological legitimation strategies of the Putin regime.

Yet not all feminist groups exempt themselves from the gender-normative paradigm in which so much political competition takes place. I start this chapter with a discussion of Pussy Riot, a self-identified feminist group that reacted to Putin's macho image with song lyrics portraying him as a weak, unmanly leader—echoing the gender-normative discourse used by regime-supporters against their adversaries and by Putin opponents against the regime. Another women's group—based in Ukraine but active in Russia—called Femen, similarly appeared to comply with some of patriarchy's precepts by protesting topless and invoking normative feminine attractiveness as the medium for their feminist messages. The bulk of this chapter, though, focuses on feminist groups in contemporary Russia that have eschewed patriarchal stereotypes in their actions, explicitly critiquing gender norms and homophobia without making use of them.

As an ideology, feminism reveals and seeks to disassemble the patriarchal hierarchy that values masculinity over femininity and relies on homophobia as an instrument of power. In recent years in Russia, feminists have been punished for their efforts—both by political actors outside the regime, such as Russian Orthodox Church activists, and by law enforcement institutions, such as the court that condemned Pussy Riot in 2012. The evidence presented in this chapter on feminist activism and anti-feminist retribution suggests that feminism presents a considerable threat to the gender-norm-infused legitimation strategies that both the regime and the opposition have been using in Putin's Russia.

Feminist Groups and Gender Norms: Pussy Riot

Pussy Riot achieved worldwide fame in March 2012 when three of their members were arrested after performing an anti-Putin "punk prayer" in Moscow's renowned Cathedral of Christ the Savior.[1] After months in pretrial detention, in mid-August 2012 three Pussy Riot members—Nadezhda Tolokonnikova, Ekaterina Samutsevich, and Mariia Alekhina—were sentenced for "hooliganism motivated by religious hatred" and handed two-year jail terms in a Russian penal colony.[2] While the court—widely viewed as a mouthpiece for the regime—alleged that the women's action in the church was a "hate crime," rather than politically motivated (and protected) speech, the band's earlier performances, like this one, had clearly been political acts, blatantly critical of the Putin regime.[3] By focusing on the religious angle, the court's job, in sociologist Vadim Volkov's view, was to conduct the trial as a means to mobilize

---

[1] For details on the process by which the three women were detained and incarcerated and on their interactions with the courts and penal system, see Masha Gessen, *Words Will Break Cement: The Passion of Pussy Riot* (New York: Riverhead Books, 2014).

[2] Natalya Krainova, "What Awaits Pussy Riot Musicians in Prison," *The Moscow Times*, August 30, 2012, http://www.themoscowtimes.com/news/article/what-awaits-pussy-riot-musicians-in-prison/467342.html. On October 10, 2012, after replacing her legal team, Samutsevich was freed on probation; on October 20, Tolokonnikova and Alekhina were taken from their Moscow detention center to labor colonies in Mordovia and the Perm region, respectively. Both were released as part of an amnesty in December 2013, two months ahead of schedule. Long-jailed oligarch Mikhail Khodorkovsky was also released, prompting speculation that Putin's government sought to minimize the potential sources for protests during the Sochi Olympics in February 2014. See Maria Vasilyeva and Nikolai Isayev, "Amnestied Russian Punk Band Pair Criticize Putin after Release," *Chicago Tribune*, December 23, 2013, http://www.chicagotribune.com/news/sns-rt-us-russia-pussyriot-release-20131222,0,5817915.story.

[3] Human Rights Watch, "Russia: Free Pussy Riot Members," March 1, 2013, http://www.hrw.org/news/2013/02/28/russia-free-pussy-riot-members.

societal conservatives in support of the Putin regime.[4] As the women in Pussy Riot had hoped, however, the trial, like the incident itself, directed public attention to the close ties between the Church and Putin's regime, one of a number of political issues important to their group.

While the "punk prayer" and its aftermath constituted something of a turning point for Russia politically, it was neither the first nor last of Pussy Riot's endeavors. The group's songs, performed in symbolic locations around Moscow and then uploaded as video clips on the Web starting in November 2011, had raised a range of topics. Among other things, their lyrics endorsed mass protest against the Putin regime, criticized state-sponsored homophobia, and praised feminism as a possible curative for Russia's many ills. In setting forth their ideas, however, Pussy Riot's lyricists made use of traditional gender norms and homophobia, wielding these against their opponents in the regime and thereby reinforcing them in ways that other self-identified Russian feminists found problematic at best.

PUSSY RIOT, HOMOPHOBIA, AND GENDER NORMS: COMPLIANCE OR CRITIQUE?

Pussy Riot explicitly positioned themselves and their musical productions as feminist. While not the only group of young women publicly identifying themselves as feminist in Russia in 2012, Pussy Riot could fairly be characterized as the only group of self-proclaimed Russian feminists who generated widespread media attention. One thing that was largely taken for granted in both the Russian and the Western media, however, was that the group members were, in fact, "feminists" (although this term was ill-defined or not defined at all by the press). In June 2012, when the three women arrested for the performance in the Cathedral had already been in jail for three months, I interviewed seventeen feminist activists in Moscow and St. Petersburg about a variety of subjects, including their views on Pussy Riot. Although all of the activists I talked with were supportive of Pussy Riot now that the latter had become literally "political prisoners," a significant subset was adamant that Pussy Riot itself was not a feminist endeavor. Several pointed out that Pussy Riot's singers had earlier participated in the performance art group Voina (War) and that a number of Voina's previous actions were violent and sexist. Likewise, they characterized Pussy Riot's lyrics as embracing violence rather than promoting a specifically nonviolent feminist agenda. Others regarded Pussy Riot with admiration and found feminist elements in their work. In this section, I review

[4] Sergey Chernov, "Why Do Russian Judges Act That Way?," February 6, 2013, http://www.tol. org/client/article/23588-russia-judges.html.

Pussy Riot's songs from 2011 and 2012, highlighting the areas where gender norms and apparent misogyny, sexism, and homophobia appeared.

Pussy Riot's first release, on the anniversary of the 1917 Russian Revolution (November 7) and also Tolokonnikova's birthday, was the song "Osvobodi Bruschatku." Translated literally as "Free the cobblestones" or, more liberally, as "Free the area," the title evoked the paving bricks of Red Square.[5] Contrasting the refreshing air of Egypt's revolution to the "putrefying" voting booths in the stuffy schoolrooms into which voters would soon be "herded" on Russia's election day, the song called upon listeners to "Create Tahrir on Red Square" and disrupt the "stability" that the regime was expecting the upcoming elections to reinforce.[6] Calling for Tahrir implied the desired overthrow of the existing Russian government, as Mubarak had been overthrown in the 2011 Arab Spring.

Tolokonnikova had long been discontented with Putin's reign. As a high school student in 2004, she and a friend had responded to Putin's election for a second presidential term by protesting next to their school with handmade signs proclaiming, "Down with tsarism! Long live revolution!"[7] Lending fuel to their call for an uprising, Pussy Riot's first song included a verse on the regime's suppression of protest: "The Khimki forest has been cleared / They won't allow Chirikova [an environmental activist who tried to protect the forest from a state plan to build a road through it] access / The feminists were sent on maternity leave," and ends with a prescription: "Russia could use a feminist whipping!" [literally, "A feminist whip is useful for Russia"] (feminist-skii khlyst polezen Rossii).[8]

Several feminist activists outside of Pussy Riot saw sexist language and violent discourse in the lyrics to "Osvobodi bruschatku," drawing particular attention to a verse that played on the bondage-and-domination theme: "It's never too late to become a dominatrix (gospozha) / The cattle prods have been charged; the cries are getting louder / Stretch the muscles of your arms and legs / The policeman [politseiskii (male)] licks you between the legs."[9] Natalia Bitten, a journalist and feminist activist in Moscow, regarded these lyrics as embracing the idea of sexual objectification—in this case, of the police officer—and the (assumed female) narrator's exertion of power over

---

[5] Vera Kichanova, *Pussi Raiot: Podlinnaia istoriia* (Moscow: Hocus-Pocus, 2012), 6. I am grateful to Nataliya Kun and Christopher Lemelin for their help translating and interpreting Pussy Riot's song lyrics.

[6] PussRiot, "Devchonki iz PUSSY RIOT zakhvatyvaiut transport" [video], November 6, 2011, http://www.youtube.com/watch?v=qEiB1RYuYXw&feature=related.

[7] Kichanova, *Pussi Raiot: Podlinnaia istoriia*, 6.

[8] PussRiot, "Devchonki iz PUSSY RIOT zakhvatyvaiut transport."

[9] Ibid.

him. As she explained it, "What does it mean, 'The policeman licked [you] between the legs'? That you want to be just the same [as him], that you want to have power over someone else—and that's not feminism." In the context of the song, the female narrator, with the aid of the cattle prod normally in police hands, was engaged in "forcible action of a sexual character. . . . It's not that [the police officer] himself wants to do it." In short, Bitten argued, this was a violent act, an endorsement of the abuse of power. Typically, Bitten explained, the situation is reversed, such that "the police force *her* to do something—the police have power, and they abuse that power (proizvol). But in *that* moment, *she* has the power, and she can abuse it." With this language, Pussy Riot had failed to position themselves as feminists: "For me, it's inarguable; it's not feminist discourse."[10] Reflecting on this and on Pussy Riot's lyrics more generally, Zhenia Otto, a socialist feminist in Moscow, faulted Pussy Riot for their "sexist" lyrics, finding that they "expressed aggression through sex, that sex and violence were the same thing, in the sense of 'having' somebody—that is to say, 'fucking somebody'—there's a lot of that language in Pussy Riot's lyrics."[11] Pussy Riot's debut "album" title, "Kill the Sexist," also suggests something other than a nonviolent feminist response to misogyny.

Tolokonnikova posted an announcement of the release of "Osvobodi bruschatku" on the Live Journal blog Feministki (feminists), giving rise to discussion of the new Pussy Riot phenomenon within Russia's feminist community. The reception was fairly chilly. In the comment section on the posting, feminist activist and art historian Nadia Plungian critiqued the group's lyrics and misappropriation of the feminist concept: "Rhetoric like 'It's never too late to become a dominatrix' and 'Russia could use a feminist whipping' discredit and distort the very point of feminism, which fights against hierarchy and inequality, as well as against degradation and discrimination. 'Kill the sexist' is a direct call for violence."[12]

For their part, after releasing the song, Pussy Riot noted on their own Live Journal blog that dozens of people had queried whether feminism was truly "relevant" in Russia and that people—"unfortunately, even among the opposition"—regarded feminism and LGBT rights as matters of secondary importance, compared to Putin's impending return for a third term as president. Pussy Riot explained that they regarded the question differently. For people to see these issues as "secondary," they argued, "suits Putin," whereas focusing on

[10] Natal'ia Bitten, IGZF, interview by author, Moscow, June 4, 2012.

[11] Zhenia Otto, Komitet za Rabochii Internatsional, Kampaniia protiv ekspluatatsii i diskriminatsii zhenshchin, interview by author, Moscow, June 18, 2012.

[12] Nadia Tolokno, "Nelegal'nye feministskie kontserty v Moskve," November 7, 2011, http://feministki.livejournal.com/1857679.html.

"concrete issues of feminism, LGBT [rights] and the environment would make opposition protests more meaningful and more convincing" and would bring in more resources with which to oppose the existing regime. In that sense, Pussy Riot contended, a "feminist whip" would be beneficial in the Russian political context.[13]

A month later, on December 1, 2011, Pussy Riot's "Kropotkin Vodka" video appeared, featuring the band members in their traditional balaklavas, touring expensive clothing stores, spraying fire extinguishers outdoors, and playing atop a plexiglass-encased Jaguar on a ritzy boutique-jammed Moscow side street.[14] Released on the eve of the Russian parliamentary elections, the song itself described the varied effects of "Kropotkin" vodka (named after Russian revolutionary anarcho-communist Petr Kropotkin) on regime officials and oppositionists; while emboldening the latter, it poisoned the former, with fatal results.[15] The song's obscenity-laced refrain can be translated approximately as "Fuck the fucking Putinist sexists!" (pizdets seksistam ebanym putinistam).[16]

The first verse of "Kropotkin Vodka" alludes to an action carried out by women in the art-performance group Voina in early 2011, mentioned by several feminist activists who questioned Pussy Riot's feminist credentials. The song begins:

> Occupy the city with a kitchen pan
> Go out with a vacuum cleaner, get yourself an orgasm
> Seduce battalions of police-girls
> The naked cops are happy with this new reform.[17]

While the first couplet is somewhat opaque, the instruction to "seduce battalions of police-girls" (politseiskikh devits) was a direct reference to a video that circulated on the Internet in March 2011.[18] Earlier that year, several female members of Voina, including Tolokonnikova and Samutsevich, entered Moscow's subway

---

[13] Gruppa Pussy Riot, "Pochemu feministskii khlyst polezen Rossii?," November 7, 2011, http://grani.ru/blogs/free/entries/192925.html.

[14] Gessen, *Words Will Break Cement*, 73.

[15] Pussy_riot, "Vtoroi nelegal'nyi tur Gruppy Pussy Riot s podzhogami i okkupatsiei," December 1, 2011, http://pussy-riot.livejournal.com/5164.html.

[16] PussRiot, "Gruppa pussy riot zhzhet putinskii glamur" [video], November 30, 2011, http://www.youtube.com/watch?v=CZUhkWiiv7M.

[17] Pussy_riot, "Vtoroi nelegal'nyi tur gruppy pussy riot s podzhogami i okkupatsiei."

[18] For the video, see "Art-gruppa 'Voina' zatselovyvaet mentov 1 marta" [video] March 1, 2011, http://www.youtube.com/watch?v=Aa_ZUj4Vx88.

stations, where they accosted female police officers by attempting to kiss them on the lips and filmed this "performance."[19] Members of the Moscow Feminist Group (Moskovskaia Feministskaia Gruppa; MFG) characterized this action as having had "nothing in common with feminism," as it amounted to uninvited sexual assault. "It's completely clear in the video that the women find it unpleasant, that they don't know what to do," observed Nadia Plungian.[20] Indeed, the policewomen frown, turn away, appear confused and disgusted, and attempt to push off the unexpected advances of their undesired suitors (a musical soundtrack to the video replaced any audio recorded in the subway).

The logic behind this action, as explained by MFG activist Elizaveta Morozova, was that Voina was engaged in a symbolic effort to fight the regime but was doing so with "very typical patriarchal discourse." For the Voina activists, attacking female police officers was a means to attack the male-dominated Russian state. Forcibly kissing the policewomen was a stand-in for rape. Voina's action addressed the state, saying, "You take us down—so now we'll take down *your* women." That is, Morozova continued,

> The women who serve in the police in this particular case are fulfilling the role of "their" women [the women who belong to the state]. It's like, "We're raping your women because you, the police, it's as if you're raping us as a country." It's absolutely, openly, that kind of discourse.[21]

From this view, the metaphorical (and symbolically physical) rape of the state in Voina's subway action is of a piece with the "topping" behavior discussed in Chapter 3, where political activists on both sides of the Kremlin made efforts to assert their masculine predominance over their perceived antagonists. As rape—in the context of war—becomes a means to attack the opponent, the policewomen involuntarily involved in Voina's action were being attacked as a means to undermine the machismo of a state unable to protect "its" women.

Pussy Riot's partial overlap with Voina led feminists as well as regime supporters to link the band with Voina's previous actions. After forming in 2007, Voina had split in 2009, leaving one faction in St. Petersburg and another in Moscow (with which Tolokonnikova and, later, Samutsevich were affiliated).[22] As a self-styled radical art performance group, Voina had gained notoriety for several of its actions, including the February 2008 "protest orgy" in which

[19] Tom Washington, "Voina Come Back for Kisses," *The Moscow News*, March 1, 2011, http://www.themoscownews.com/local/20110301/188458300.html.

[20] Nadia Plungian, MFG, interview by author, Moscow, June 20, 2012.

[21] Elizaveta Morozova, MFG, interview by author, Moscow, June 20, 2012.

[22] Kichanova, *Pussi Raiot: Podlinnaia istoriia*, 9–11, 26–27.

Tolokonnikova and her husband participated.[23] Another Voina action that—like the assault on Moscow's subway police, borrowed from the opposition's "topping" toolbox—took place in June 2010, when members of the Voina faction in St. Petersburg painted a 210-foot penis on a drawbridge, visually "screwing" the Federal Security Service (FSB) building in front of which it stood.[24] In a peculiar turn of events, Voina's "Dick in Captivity at the FSB" won a Ministry of Culture-supported "Innovation" prize in April 2011.[25] A month later, in July 2010, the male leader of the St. Petersburg branch of Voina went with his wife into a supermarket in St. Petersburg, where they a recorded video of themselves inserting a raw chicken into her vagina and then left the store, posting the visual documentation of their action on the Web afterwards.[26] Nadia Plungian argued that such actions have naught to do with social activism and merely reproduce "patriarchal aggression." In this view, Voina's actions were rooted in sexism—the "affirmation of male superiority." The "chicken" action, "despite its incredible formal novelty," Plungian wrote, was merely a "decision by a group of men to use a woman's body as a container."[27]

These two actions preceded Pussy Riot's formation and had been carried out by the Petersburg branch group after Voina's split in 2009.[28] However, the direct link between members of Pussy Riot and Voina—even if it applied to some of Voina's actions and not others—drove feminist activists to question Pussy Riot's commitment to feminism. In their view, Voina's tactics—such as the assault on policewomen—could not be understood as feminist, and because some of Pussy Riot's members had participated in those tactics, they could not be considered serious about having a feminist agenda in their new incarnation.[29]

Others gave Pussy Riot less authorial credit and less responsibility. Like the Bolsheviks' belief that rebellious peasant women resisting the collectivization

[23] "Voina ebetsia za naslednika Medvezhonka (ren-tv)."
[24] "Liteinyi most vstal na FSB" [video], June 15, 2010, http://www.youtube.com/watch?v=KIFZ41P6kfw&feature=related; Plucer, "Novaia aktsiia Voiny 'Khui v PLENu u FSB!' i inauguratsiia Nashego Prezidenta Leni Ebnutogo," June 24, 2010, http://plucer.livejournal.com/265584.html.
[25] Tom Parfitt, "Voina, Art Group Backed by Banksy, Wins Russian Prize for Erection," *The Guardian*, April 8, 2011, http://www.guardian.co.uk/world/2011/apr/08/voina-banksy-penis-prize; Nick Sturdee, "Don't Raise the Bridge: Voina, Russia's Art Terrorists," *The Guardian*, April 12, 2011, http://www.guardian.co.uk/artanddesign/2011/apr/12/voina-art-terrorism.
[26] For photographs and video of the "chicken" action (though I don't recommend it), see Plucer, "Novaia skandal'naia aktsiia gruppy Voina 'Poshto pizdili Kuru?' ili 'Skaz o tom, kak Pizda Voinu kormila,' July 24, 2010, http://plucer.livejournal.com/281211.html.
[27] Nadia Plungian, "Gendernye zerkala sovremennogo iskusstva: Mezhdu soprotivleniem i dedovshchinoi," *Neprikosnovennyi zapas* 2, no. 76 (2011), http://magazines.russ.ru/nz/2011/2/pl5.html.
[28] Kichanova, *Pussi Raiot: Podlinnaia istoriia*, 11.
[29] Plungian, interview by author; Morozova, interview by author.

of agriculture in the late 1920s and early 1930s were merely the pawns of their counterrevolutionary husbands and other men,[30] some contemporary commentators regarded Pussy Riot's actions as the creations of men in Voina—merely implemented by the women. Pussy Riot members particularly resented the implication that their project had been masterminded by Tolokonnikova's husband, Petr Verlizov. They explained that it would be "contradictory to the ideas of feminism if they were fronting for some man," noting that Verlizov was present at rehearsals, but only "in the role of a silent photographer . . . on the sidelines." Pussy Riot member Ekaterina Samutsevich was similarly struck that, following the action where women in the Moscow branch of Voina had forcibly kissed women police officers, Aleksei Plutser-Sarno, one of the (male) founders of the group (who had sided with the St. Petersburg faction) claimed that the action had been Verzilov's idea. "It's stunning! No matter what you do, since you're a woman, society will always find some man-boss or man-ideologist who (as you unexpectedly discover!) did all the intellectual work for you," Samutsevich complained afterward.[31]

Others hypothesized that (given their fairly shapeless outfits and balaklavas) Pussy Riot was composed of men—or had at least one male participant. According to the band members, their effort to contradict the typical image of female performers helped produce this impression, as they explained in an early 2012 video interview (where they used nicknames and wore balaklavas):

Q. Why do you wear masks?
SHAIBA: It seems to me that the main reason is that we could be anybody.
GARADZHA: This kind of image is very unusual for women's groups, because especially for commercial women's bands, they're very feminine in a commercial way, with very feminine faces, make-up—it's all so emphasized. But we don't want any of that; [we want] people to see—instead of the typical, standard feminine image, to see masks.
TIURA: The way we move is completely unfeminine. We choose [our] gestures intentionally. We box, we lurch back and forth, we use these totally unfeminine moves. That is, it's a multifaceted attack on traditional femininity. Many people even say, "There's a guy (muzhik) among you." They say, "Look, your Garadzha is really a guy." [Tiura laughs.]
GARADZHA: I'm not a male (muzhik), I'm a female (baba). [All laugh.][32]

---

[30] Lynne Viola, *Peasant Rebels under Stalin: Collectivization and the Culture of Peasant Resistance* (New York: Oxford University Press, 1996), 181–204.

[31] Kichanova, *Pussi Raiot: Podlinnaia istoriia*, 18, 27.

[32] Garadzha Matveeva, "Pussy Riot o kontserte 'Putin zassal,' feminizme i protestakh" [video], February 1, 2012, http://www.youtube.com/watch?v=YPAaPWoJ-b8.

Pussy Riot's next public performance occurred in a radically different political atmosphere. The falsified results of the Duma elections in early December 2011 had provoked mass protests by Russians who poured out into the streets to express their outrage. Although the first mass protest occurred on December 10, gathering tens of thousands in Bolotnaia Square, arrests had followed smaller protests on the nights immediately following the election. On December 5, Tolokonnikova's husband was among those arrested during a spontaneous march toward the Kremlin. On December 14, Pussy Riot members gathered and shouted their song "Death to Prison, Freedom to Protest" while standing on a roof across from the jail where several demonstrators (including Verlizov and two well-known opposition activists, Aleksei Navalny and Ilia Iashin) were being held following the protests.[33] A lyrical entreaty favoring nonviolent occupation, freedom for political prisoners, and relieving the police of their guns, the song called for direct action and for members of the LGBT and feminist communities to protect the country. As Pussy Riot explained on their blog, the December 10 protest had shown that "people were ready to make their own decisions" and that the protest movement had no need for a "father-leader."[34]

On January 20, 2012, as the protest mood continued to pervade the Russian political arena, eight women in Pussy Riot took to the center of Russia's political space—Red Square. After climbing up onto the circular, stone platform (Lobnoe mesto) in the Kremlin's shadow, the band members sprayed canisters of colored smoke, waved a purple feminist flag and performed the song "Putin Pissed Himself" (Putin zassal).[35] For the first time, Pussy Riot's performers were detained following their musical excursion onto Red Square but were merely fined and soon released.[36] Interviewed by *The Guardian* after their performance, three Pussy Riot members explained that they had chosen to perform in Red Square in homage to Anatolii Osmolovskii and Aleksandr Brener, irreverent performance artists of the 1990s who had held actions there.[37] In a challenge to then-president Boris Yeltsin's masculinity, Brener had stood atop

[33] Kichanova, *Pussi Raiot*, 14.

[34] Pussy_riot, "Nelegal'nyi kontsert gruppy pussy riot na kryshe tiur'my," December 14, 2011, http://pussy-riot.livejournal.com/5763.html.

[35] The song title could more figuratively be translated as "Putin Got Scared." Elena Kostiuchenko, "Feministki-khuliganki dali kontsert na Lobnom meste," *Novaya Gazeta*, January 20, 2012, http://www.novayagazeta.ru/news/53456.html.

[36] Miriam Elder, "Feminist Punk Band Pussy Riot Take Revolt to the Kremlin," *The Guardian*, February 2, 2012, http://www.guardian.co.uk/world/2012/feb/02/pussy-riot-protest-russia.

[37] The performers also mentioned their respect for the Soviet dissidents who had illegally protested in Red Square in 1968 against the USSR's invasion of Czechoslovakia. Garadzha Matveeva, "Pussy Riot o kontserte 'Putin zassal,' feminizme i protestakh."

Lobnoe mesto in the snow in 1995, wearing boxing gloves and shorts, challenging Yeltsin to a boxing match.[38] In 1991, Osmolovskii's group, ETI (the Expropriation of Art's Territory) had arranged their bodies on Red Square to spell out the obscenity "khui" (dick), violating the (then-Soviet) law against using obscene language in public spaces.[39] Oleg Kulik, another performance artist, surprised the Russian public in the mid-1990s by removing all of his clothes and pretending in public to be a dog (leashed in some instances by Brener).[40]

The profanity and references to bodily functions that pervade the lyrics to "Putin Pissed Himself" thus joined a tradition of Russian performance art. The song begins by describing a "rebel column" moving in on the Kremlin, windows exploding in the secret police's office building and the "bitches pissing behind the red [Kremlin] walls" in fear. Further verses criticize Russia's "culture of male hysteria" and complain that excessive devotion to the leadership "consumes people's brains," while "conformity" is the medicine doled out to the citizens. The Russian Orthodox religion is described as a "hard penis" (zhestokogo penisa), while, by contrast, the woman at the center of Christianity is on the side of the protesters: "The Madonna, in all her glory, will teach us to fight / The feminist Magdalene went to a demonstration." The chorus proclaims:

Rebellion in Russia—the charisma of protest
Rebellion in Russia—Putin pissed himself
Rebellion in Russia—we exist
Rebellion in Russia—riot, riot! [41]

The song's conclusion refers to the "sexist regime" as a "flock of bitches" (staia suk) and imagines them begging forgiveness from the "feminist wedge," implying a relationship of domination reversed, similar to the imagery from "Free the Cobblestones." The language of the title and chorus was also unambiguous in its gender-normative critique of Putin. The male-dominated regime was characterized and derogated in a misogynist fashion as female ("bitches"), and Putin, despite his reputed masculine strength, was demasculinized and di-

[38] Aleksandr Brener, "Pervaia perchatka dokumentatsiia aktsii Moskva, Krasnaia ploshchad,'" *Muzei 21 Artkladovka*, 1995, http://artkladovka.ru/ru/artists/02/brener/works/01/.

[39] "1991: Khui na Krasnoi ploshchadi: Osmolovskii," *Zapreshchennoe iskusstvo*, April 18, 1991, http://bit.ly/1jMOFR7.

[40] "Podlinnaia istoriia Olega Kulika, kotoryi byl chelovek-sobaka strashnaia," June 17, 2011, http://adindex.ru/publication/gallery/2011/06/17/67740.phtml.

[41] pussy_riot, "Proryv i arest pussy riot na lobnom meste krasnoi ploshchadi s pesnei 'putin zassal,'" January 20, 2012, http://pussy-riot.livejournal.com/8459.html.

minished to the status of a child; a truly macho leader would hardly urinate in terror upon facing rebellious citizens.

If feminists found little to admire in Pussy Riot's initial burst of musical material, they held more mixed opinions about the song accompanying the band's famed escapade in the Cathedral of Christ the Savior. On February 21, 2012, five Pussy Riot members entered the Cathedral of Christ the Savior, approached a church employee to ask about the proper placement of votive candles, and then proceeded to the ambo (the area in front of the altar), where they quickly set up their equipment and managed to film less than two minutes worth of footage, during which they recited part of the song's refrain ("Shit, shit, holy shit!"), pumped the air with their fists, and kicked up their legs, before being promptly removed.[42] That night, interwoven with footage shot earlier in a different church, the video clip of the song was posted on the Web. By mid-March, three of the alleged performers had been arrested.

The lyrics to Pussy Riot's "punk prayer," also titled "Mother of God, Chase Putin Away" (Bogoroditsa, Putina progoni), contained a mixture of feminist critique of Putin's regime and the Russian Orthodox Church, along with homophobic disparagement of male leaders:

Mother of God, Virgin, exorcise Putin
Exorcise Putin, exorcise Putin

Black cassocks, gold epaulettes
The parishioners all crawl and bow
The ghost of freedom is in the Heavens
Gay Pride has been sent to Siberia in shackles

The head of the KGB, their principal saint
Leads the protesters to detention under escort
So as not to insult the Most Sainted One
Women must give birth and love.

Shit, shit, Holy shit
Shit, shit, Holy shit

---

[42] "Church Employee Says Pussy Riot Show Has Given Her 'Unceasing Pain,'" Interfax, July 31, 2012, http://www.interfax-religion.com/?act=news&div=9615; Nikolaus von Twickel, "Punk Band's Legal Team Reveals Full Performance," *The Moscow Times*, June 6, 2012, http://www. themoscowtimes.com/news/article/punk-bands-legal-team-reveals-full-performance/ 459967.html#ixzz1x2CNf5X4; Garadzha Matveeva, "Pank-moleben 'Bogoroditsa, Putina progoni' Pussy Riot v Khrame" [video], February 21, 2012, http://www.youtube.com/watch? feature=player_embedded&v=GCasuaAczKY.

Mother of God, Virgin, become a feminist
Become a feminist, become a feminist

The sacred blessing of rotten leaders
A Crucession (krestnii khod) of black limousines
The preacher is planning to come to your school
Go to your class — and bring him some money!

Patriarch Gundiai believes in Putin
It'd be better to believe in God, you bitch
The Belt of the Virgin won't displace the demonstrations
The Ever Virgin Mary is with us at the protests!

Mother of God, Virgin, exorcise Putin,
Exorcise Putin, exorcise Putin[43]

In addition to making repeated requests to the Virgin Mary to exorcise Putin (explained by Pussy Riot as something of a last resort, after the mass demonstrations that winter had failed to do the trick), as feminists the band members had chosen to perform their "prayer" in proximity to the altar precisely "because women are not allowed to be there. If the Mother of God were in the Cathedral, for instance, she would not be allowed to stand at the altar."[44] Indeed, women's "second class status" in Russian Orthodoxy begins shortly after birth. At baptism, male infants are "triumphantly borne aloft by the priest behind the iconostasis into the altar," whereas baby girls are "placed on the floor in front of the royal doors," because access to the altar space is off limits to their sex.[45] Women are allowed on the ambo, the raised area in front of the altar, only for weddings, and, even then, this is at the priest's discretion.[46] Pussy Riot's members thus occupied the central space on the ambo where baby girls were entitled to baptism but did not proceed all the way to the altar, behind the royal doors. In taking this position, Pussy Riot physically highlighted sex-based inequality within Church practices.

[43] For the Russian lyrics, see Matveeva, "Pank-moleben 'Bogoroditsa, Putina progoni' Pussy Riot v Khrame." A crucession (or "cross procession") entails the churchgoers circling around the church building; here, the lyrics refer to Russian politicians' limousines parked around the church while they're inside of it.

[44] Pussy_riot, "Pank-moleben 'bogoroditsa, putina progoni' v khrame khrista spasitelia," February 21, 2012, http://pussy-riot.livejournal.com/12442.html.

[45] Kizenko, "Feminized Patriarchy?," 601.

[46] The sides of the ambo are not off limits to laypeople, but the central part, in front of the altar, is intended only for clerical personnel—male, by definition. Nadieszda Kizenko, personal communication, March 7, 2013. "Church Employee Says Pussy Riot Show Has Given Her 'Unceasing Pain.'"

The song's lyrics also voiced a feminist critique of the Church's endorsement of traditional gender roles. Calling upon the Virgin Mary to "become a feminist" and asserting that she "is with us at the protests," the song promised that the reliquaries on display at the Cathedral (such as the ostensible "Virgin's belt" that people lined up to see on the parliamentary elections' eve in November 2011) would not distract the citizens—the female vocalists included—from protesting against the regime. Lines from the second verse connected the violation of feminine gender norms to the threat of state- and Church-endorsed punishment: "The KGB's head, their chief saint / Leads the protesters to detention centers under escort / So as not to insult the Most Sainted One (sviateishego) / Women must give birth and love."[47] The injunction to "give birth and love" harked back to a line from "Free the Cobblestones" where, to fulfill their proper duty, the feminists were "sent on maternity leave."

While the identity of the "most sainted one" was ambiguous (it could be either Putin, as the former head of the FSB/KGB, or Patriarch Kirill, the head of the Church), the song's message about the conjoined interests of the Church and regime was not. On issues of demography and protest, government and Church institutions supported each other, rhetorically relegating women to reproductive roles, punishing all citizens (regardless of their sex) for anti-regime protest. On their blog, Pussy Riot explained that Church figures opposed feminists, as feminism offered women a range of choices, including parenthood: "The [Russian Orthodox Church] doesn't like feminists. In the opinion of archpriest Dmitrii Smirnov, 'Feminism is a powerful spearhead against the family!' Pussy Riot is indeed opposed to the traditional patriarchal family, where women are given a secondary, submissive role."[48] Smirnov, a prominent spokesperson for the Orthodox Church, also believed (as noted earlier) that married women should not enjoy the right to vote.[49]

Pussy Riot's "punk prayer" also critiqued the Church for its homophobia. Verses described the fusion of Church and state: the Church "blesses the rotten leaders" whose "black limousines circle the church," and the two institutions jointly preside while "gay pride is sent to Siberia in chains." In their exegesis, Pussy Riot explained that the "gay pride" lyric referred to the Church-supported laws banning homosexual propaganda that had recently been passed in several Russian cities. This legislation "effectively prevents the LGBT community from organizing public events," forcing them back into the closet. The band also objected to the laws' juxtaposition of homosexuality and pedophilia, "which is homophobic and insulting in and of itself."[50]

[47] Matveeva, "Pank-moleben 'Bogoroditsa, Putina progoni' Pussy Riot v Khrame."
[48] Pussy_riot, "Pank-moleben 'bogoroditsa, putina progoni' v khrame khrista spasitelia."
[49] Golovko, "Protoierei Dimitrii Smirnov."
[50] Pussy_riot, "Pank-moleben 'bogoroditsa, putina progoni' v khrame khrista spasitelia."

Pussy Riot's own lyrics, however, made use of homophobic denigration, while targeting the apparent merger of the Church and the regime. Not only was Putin the Church's "chief saint," but, Pussy Riot argued, the very head of the Church was not a believer in the traditional sense: "Patriarch Gundiai believes in Putin / It'd be better to believe in God, [you] bitch" (luchshe by v Boga, suka, veril).[51] In calling him a "bitch" (rather than using an expletive not gendered female, such as scoundrel), Pussy Riot was undermining the Patriarch's authority by identifying him as a woman in a subservient position. Other oppositionists have leveled a similar homophobic misogyny at Patriarch Kirill. Following the resignation of Pope Benedict, Kremlin opponent Stanislav Belkovskii published an article criticizing the Russian Orthodox Church for kowtowing to the state and advised Patriarch Kirill to end his career by moving to a women's convent. "That's right where he belongs" (tam emu samoe pravil'noe mesto), Belkovskii concluded.[52]

Yet Pussy Riot's public acts can be read as decidedly pro-feminist. Nikolai Uskov, for instance, the former editor of GQ magazine in Russia and a trained historian specializing in medieval Western European church history, was certain that Pussy Riot's action had been a "feminist gesture" by which the young women had "demonstrated their independence from the patriarchal culture and political model in which they are forced to exist." In turn, the arrest of two of the band members literally on the day before the presidential election as well as the group's ensuing trial had enabled Putin to "consolidate" the support of voters "wary about the collapse of traditional values, including patriarchal values, and who regard a woman either as a vessel of sin or as a housewife."[53] Part of Pussy Riot's impetus to perform their songs in public, without authorization, was to violate such sex stereotypes and traditional conceptions about sex roles and norms. Speaking to *The Guardian*, a Pussy Riot member, Garadzha, explained that the group opposed sex discrimination:

> It's a strange notion to divide people according to their sex, and not only to divide them, but to arrange their lives and make certain demands of them based on their sex. Unfortunately, this really influences people, to the point that when a woman is growing up she's told, "You're a woman. You should get married, have children." But we want to show that a

[51] Gundiai is a short and insulting form of Patriarch Kirill's surname, Gundiaev; it means to speak in a nasal tone, and also to drone on, boring the listener. Matveeva, "Pank-moleben 'Bogoroditsa, Putina progoni' Pussy Riot v Khrame."

[52] Stanislav Belkovskii, "Papa ukazal put' patriarkhu," *Moskovskii Komsomolets*, February 15, 2013, http://www.mk.ru/specprojects/free-theme/article/2013/02/14/812869-papa-ukazal-put-patriarhu.html.

[53] Nikolai Uskov, "Pro menia," 2013, http://www.snob.ru/profile/24889; "Osoboe Mnenie: Aleksandr Pliushchev Interviews Nikolai Uskov," August 7, 2012, http://echo.msk.ru/programs/personalno/915946-echo/.

woman isn't just someone who fulfills that role well, but also [is someone who does] something unusual, who can go out and do political protests.[54]

While many thousands of Russian women, over the years, had participated in political protests, Pussy Riot's performances and arrest no doubt provoked others to join in.

Some of Russia's other self-identified feminist activists likewise saw Pussy Riot as feminist allies in important ways. Olga Lipovskaia (described by feminist journalist Nadezhda Azhgikhina as "the face of radical Russian feminism of the 1990s," and an ongoing force in the Russian feminist movement) was among them.[55] Lipovskaia argued in April 2012 that while Pussy Riot's songs "contained no ideological or conceptual feminist positions," their actions could certainly be considered feminist because they "truly break the traditional ideas about the female role. And in that sense, even without having a feminist message, they were still carrying out feminist action and making a feminist gesture." The young women in the group had not shied away from calling themselves feminists (a rarity in the Russian socio-political arena) and, Lipovskaia noted, were widely regarded or labeled as feminists both by their opponents and their supporters.[56] Tatiana Egorova, a young feminist activist in St. Petersburg, similarly believed that Pussy Riot's actions were important, given that there were so few active feminist groups in Russia and that the discussions those groups provoked were correspondingly small in scope. Even if Pussy Riot's "feminist position" was not particularly well developed, Egorova suggested, "thanks to them, feminist rhetoric had finally appeared in the mass media." The group's lyrics, she thought, did include "a bit about women's position" and introduced the question of women's status into the political conversation.[57]

Several feminists, however, found Pussy Riot's affiliation with feminism superficial. In an article critical of Pussy Riot (written after their performance in the Cathedral, but before their arrest), MFG activist Vera Akulova frankly noted that the fundamental difference distinguishing Pussy Riot from other feminist initiatives lay in their "crazy media success"—which is "unsurprising, given that their main audience is the media itself." The band members, she believed, therefore "play by the rules and prepare bait that no popular publication can resist." The bait was "the image of 'protest feminism,'" which worked on liberal and conservative publications alike. The liberal media was "charmed by [Pussy Riot's] daring incursions into the city's spaces," while conservative

[54] Garadzha Matveeva, "Pussy Riot o kontserte 'Putin zassal,' feminizme i protestakh."
[55] Azhgikhina, *Propushchennyi siuzhet*, 208.
[56] "Chego khoteli i chego dobilis' Pussy Riot," June 28, 2012, http://polit.ru/article/2012/04/16/discussion/.
[57] Ibid.

media wrote "with a mixture of delight and revulsion about 'shameless femi-nists.'" Meanwhile, since "sexism rules the Russian media," publications across the spectrum were happy to publish photos of the young women's "slender legs in colorful tights" and their "fragile shoulders, bare in the cold." Pussy Riot had put forth a commonplace liberal viewpoint—to get rid of Putin—in an attention-getting wrapper; the rest of their texts were "slogans, meaningless, empty appeals ('Free the Cobblestones,' 'Mother of God, become a feminist!') and endless intoxication with the energy of protest." This essential superficial-ity, Akulova wrote, enabled conservatives to "confirm their prejudice that femi-nists are psycho girls who have nothing better to do with their lives, while liberal opposition protesters could identify with the fearless, joyful activists without risking hearing anything too serious or radical." By contrast, she noted, activists who aimed to address society and to overturn stereotypes "fly under the radar" of the mainstream media. Despite this critique, Akulova declined to privilege one kind of feminism over another and also made the case that Pussy Riot's public performance feminism had been productive in its own ways, empower-ing the young women in the group and inspiring others to civic activism.[58]

Another feminist activist based in Moscow declared that, despite the fact that Pussy Riot called themselves feminists, they had not understood the con-tent of feminism or of the punk culture they had superficially adopted. Instead, they were in it for "adolescent shock value" and that while their group members had been jailed because they had crossed the line of acceptable behavior from the government's and the Church's perspective, their actions were "calculated and designed to appeal to men and to raise their credibility in [the] male domi-nated environment" of the Voina group.[59] Whatever their feelings about Pussy Riot's feminist credentials, however, all of the feminist activists I spoke with following the band members' arrest were unanimous in stating that it no longer mattered whether or not Pussy Riot's performers were feminist; the three young women were being unjustly held in prison by the Russian government, and the state had grossly overstepped its boundaries.

Pussy Riot's last song (as of this writing), "Putin Is Lighting the Bonfires of Revolution," was released just after the three jailed band members were sen-tenced. Its first verse drew a connection between sexism and political repres-sion and made use of gender norms to undermine Putin's authority, proclaim-ing that every arrest made by the regime was carried out "with love for the sexist / who botoxed his cheeks and pumped up his chest and abs." Drawing attention to Putin's attempts at masculine posturing, the lyrics noted Putin's bodybuilding, adding the reference to his reputedly botox-enhanced face to

[58] Vera Akulova, "Konformizm v protestnoi obertke?," February 27, 2012, http://os.colta.ru/art/events/details/34649/?expand=yes#expand.

[59] Elena Maksimova, MRF, interview by author, Moscow, June 22, 2012.

imply that (like a stereotypical woman) he had had plastic surgery and that his masculinity was both superficial and artificial. Putin was further painted in the song as having a sexualized stake in political repression. Having lit the "bonfires of revolution" out of boredom, Putin was aroused by controlling his political opponents: "Every long prison sentence is the subject of wet dreams." The song's last verse, in a homophobic moment, suggested that Putin go and marry Belarus's male dictator, Alexander Lukashenko.[60] (Lukashenko had made a strikingly homophobic remark to Germany's foreign minister earlier that year, when the latter recalled the German ambassador from Belarus and referred to the country as "the last dictatorship in Europe." An indignant Lukashenko had responded: "When I heard him—whoever he is, gay or lesbian— talking about dictatorship, I thought, 'It's better to be a dictator than gay.'"[61]) Pussy Riot's last word on their own political persecution thus critiqued Putin's machismo as a means of regime legitimation, while also playing on homophobic derogation. Despite the band's vocal endorsement of feminism and opposition to sexism, when it came to reproducing or undermining gender stereotypes, the message of Pussy Riot's songs was mixed.

"FEMENISM" AND GENDER NORMS: FEMEN

Another attention-grabbing women's group on the Russian political scene was Femen, a constellation of topless Ukrainian protesters founded in 2008.[62] Based in Ukraine, many of Femen's activists were Russian speakers, and the group held actions in Russia as well as in their home state.

Whether or not Femen should be characterized as a feminist group is an issue of some dispute. The group consciously chose to display their naked breasts and, occasionally, more; one Femen poster with a nationalist message portrayed a woman with a Ukrainian flag on a stem held upright between her naked buttocks, with the slogan, "Hold on tighter."[63] Yet Femen spoke out on a

---

[60] "Pussy Riot singl dlia prigovora—'Putin zazhigaet kostry'" [video], August 17, 2012, https://www.youtube.com/watch?v=e9u06LD-l3g.

[61] "'I'd Rather Be a Dictator than Gay': Lukashenko to German FM," March 4, 2012, http://rt.com/news/lukashenko-gay-german-minister-807/.

[62] An early precursor to Femen appeared in 1970s West Germany, where women activists protested bare-chested, simultaneously decrying the sexual objectification of female bodies in the media and drawing "attention to their words . . . by virtue of their bodies." Belinda Davis, "Political Participation, Civil Society, and Gender: Lessons from the Cold War?," in *Women and Gender in Postwar Europe: From Cold War to European Union*, ed. Bonnie G. Smith and Joanna Regulska (London: Routledge, 2012), 143.

[63] Maria Mayerchyk and Ol'ga Plakhotnik, "The Femen Phenomenon: Reflections on New Grassroots Feminisms in Ukraine" (Paper presented at the Gender, Socialism and Postsocialism Working Group, Davis Center for Russian and Eurasian Studies, Harvard University, Cambridge, MA, 2012).

range of issues not difficult to recognize as within the feminist orbit. Their first protest (which was not topless) was held in 2008 under the banner "Ukraine is not a bordello" and was intended to protest against sex tourism in Ukraine—an issue to which Femen repeatedly returned, particularly with reference to the 2012 UEFA soccer championships (held partially in Ukraine), which they believed would bring a flood of sex tourists to their country.[64] Femen also opposed restrictions on abortion in Ukraine.[65]

A number of Femen's actions challenged Putin's political legitimacy. In December 2011, following Russia's parliamentary elections, Femen staged a topless protest outside Moscow's Cathedral of Christ the Savior, with Orthodox crosses inked on their naked chests, holding aloft signs that read "Lord, chase away the tsar!" Their aim was to condemn Putin for his government's authoritarianism and to support Russia's political opposition forces, who planned a mass protest in Moscow the following day. This presaged Pussy Riot's anti-Putin protest inside the same Cathedral two months later.[66] In another protest against Putin's less-than-democratic regime, in March 2012 three Femen members appeared at the polling place where Putin had cast a ballot, presumably supporting his own presidential candidacy. The Femen activists removed their shirts, revealing slogans penned across their chests, such as "I'll steal it for Putin!" and "Kremlin rats!" and yelled, "Putin is a thief!" while attempting to steal the ballot box into which Putin had cast his vote. Police dragged the shouting activists away.[67] In August 2012, Femen protested in support of Pussy Riot by sawing down a wooden cross in central Kiev that memorialized the victims of Stalin's political repressions. In a parallel to Pussy Riot's experience in the Cathedral, this action seemed to have motivated the Ukrainian Attorney General's office to announce its plans to prosecute Femen, whose core group then decamped for Paris.[68]

As with Pussy Riot, observers saw Femen as putting forth a mixed message. Using naked women's bodies to draw attention to political issues—in the aforementioned cases, lending their bodies to the Russian political opposition's

[64] Ibid.; Hammer, "Femen: UEFA Is Attacking Our Gates," December 2, 2011, http://www.mizozo.com/world/12/2011/02/femen-uefa-is-attacking-our-gates-nsfw.html.

[65] Mayerchyk and Plakhotnik, "The Femen Phenomenon."

[66] Femen, "Bozhe, tsaria goni!," December 9, 2011, http://femen.livejournal.com/182346.html.

[67] For video of the event, see "Putin progolosoval na vyborakh vmeste s zhenoi. Topless-desant opozdal smutit' prem'era," March 4, 2012, http://www.newsru.com/russia/04mar2012/putingolos.html. This was a response to the "I'll rip [it] for Putin" action carried out by the pro-Kremlin group "Putin's Army" in 2011 (see chapter 3).

[68] Mayerchyk and Plakhotnik, "The Femen Phenomenon." According to Mariia Alekhina, Pussy Riot's jailed members did not appreciate this particular form of support. See Elena Masiuk, "Posle prigovora," *Novaya Gazeta*, August 21, 2012, http://www.novayagazeta.ru/politics/54073.html.

cause—reinforced the notion that women's bodies were the main thing that women were capable of offering in the political marketplace.[69] The group also employed homophobia in their actions, referring to the Ukrainian Cabinet of Ministers as a "homosexual cabinet," for instance, while asserting Femen's own heterosexuality. Group members repeated the fact that they "love men" and did not protest for LGBT rights in Ukraine, so as to avoid being identified or linked with lesbians.[70] Yet some observers argued that Femen combined traditional Ukrainian flower wreaths (symbolizing chastity) and nubile flesh in an effort to "parody the Berehynia-Barbie choices young women face" in contemporary Ukraine ("berehynia" is the Ukrainian term for a woman dedicated to caring for her family and home and stems originally from the name of an ancient female fertility deity worshipped in the region).[71] From this perspective, the group was making an ironic challenge to women's expected roles in the post-Soviet symbolic field.[72]

Feminist activists interviewed in Russia in 2012 offered diverse opinions and evaluations of Femen. While some found the group's protests "impressive" and "vivid,"[73] others were troubled by Femen activists' self-objectification of the female body and by their fairly uniform appearance. Though the group's actions occasionally included larger-sized or older women—one heavy-set woman played Belarusian dictator Lukashenko in a Femen protest in 2011, for example[74]—the lion's share of the actions were carried out by women in their 20s who looked like runway models, fitting traditional "beauty standards."[75] As with Pussy Riot, feminist activists questioned the content of Femen's

---

[69] For an anthropological analysis of the tensions between feminism and Femen's methods, see Jessica Zychowicz, "Two Bad Words: Femen and Feminism in Independent Ukraine," *Anthropology of East Europe Review* 29, no. 2 (Fall 2011): 215–227.

[70] Mayerchyk and Plakhotnik, "The Femen Phenomenon." Femen activists did later join a march supporting gay marriage while safely abroad in France in late 2012, but this was the first time Femen showed any inkling of public support for LGBT rights. See Sara C. Nelson, "Topless FEMEN Members in Nuns Habits Clash with Same Sex Marriage Protesters in France," *Huffington Post* (UK), November 19, 2012, http://www.huffingtonpost.co.uk/2012/11/19/topless-femen-nun-same-sex-marriage-protestors-france_n_2157536.html?ncid=GEP.

[71] Alexandra Hrycak, "FEMEN-ism: FEMEN and the Ukrainian Women's Movement," *Ukraine Analyst* 3, no. 4 (April 2011): 3; Mary B. Kelly, "The Ritual Fabrics of Russian Village Women," in *Russia—Women—Culture*, eds. Helena Goscilo and Beth Holmgren (Bloomington: Indiana University Press, 1996), 152–176.

[72] Mariia Maerchik and Ol'ga Plakhotnik, "Fenomenologiia 'Femen': Metodologicheskie Kontroversii," *Socioprostir*, no. 3 (2012): 27.

[73] Anastasiia Khodyreva, Crisis Center for Women, interview by author, St. Petersburg, June 15, 2012.

[74] Femen, "V zhopu KGBat'ku!," December 19, 2011, http://femen.livejournal.com/183324.html; Mayerchyk and Plakhotnik, "The Femen Phenomenon."

[75] Vera Akulova, MFG, interview by author, Moscow, June 6, 2012.

actions as well as their methods, finding little evidence of a "feminist agenda" therein. As a member of the MFG put it:

> In their "Ukraine is not a brothel" actions, is their message about being an object of sex tourism and sexual exploitation? No, the message is that "our women aren't sluts," something like that, with this unbelievable inflection of nationalism.
>
> Q. I thought their action against UEFA, where they were objecting to sex tourism, had a feminist theme.
>
> A. Well, yes, but the form they choose for their protest is openly anti-feminist, with the exception of one case. I remember one time when an old woman (starushka) spoke out with them, bare-chested, with some slogan. That was OK. But typically, it's the devushki who look like [fashion] models being served up as a sexual commodity. When they protest in that way against trafficking, I think it's pretty strange. . . . That is, they're reproducing the objectification of women. There might be a way to use the naked body without doing it in such a sexist way. That is, if it was normal, varied bodies, not models . . . not being presented as sexual commodities, but as the variety of human bodies. . . ."[76]

In other words, to some feminists, Femen's use of their bodies did not aim to "deconstruct patriarchal femininity, but to use it and peddle it."[77]

In their analysis of Femen, Ukrainian scholars Olga Plakhotnik and Maria Mayerchyk argue that the criticisms of Femen stemming from the right-wing and the left-wing have much in common. Whereas right-wing commentators condemn Femen for revealing their breasts and wearing wreaths symbolizing chastity, arguing that this is shameful to Ukraine, many feminists regard the group's methods as sexist and exploitative of young women's bodies (and thus a shameful misrepresentation of feminism) and as upholding a particular, traditional standard of beauty while denying the validity of other body types. Both critiques, then, focus on Femen's use of their bodies and the sexualization of that exposure.[78] Femen members, however, seem equally enthusiastic to deny any affiliation with the traditional feminist camp. They do not tend to refer to themselves as feminists, preferring to devise new terms to describe their methods, such as "sextremism."[79] Anna Gutsol, the group's leader, has

---

[76] Frau Derrida, MFG, interview by author, Moscow, June 7, 2012.

[77] Mariia Dmitrieva, "Radikal'nyi eksgibitsionizm," *Chastnyi Korrespondent*, January 6, 2011, http://www.chaskor.ru/article/radikalnyj_eksgibitsionizm_18186.

[78] Mayerchyk and Plakhotnik, "The Femen Phenomenon."

refuted any association with feminism, emphasizing femininity instead and contrasting her group to feminists "who want to emulate men . . . and become women-men."[80] In an interview with Finnish television for a 2011 documentary, one Femen activist adopted the feminist label but with a lesbophobic twist, explaining that she wanted people to see feminists as "beautiful, naked women, not as butch, bald, and tattooed women."[81]

Mayerchyk and Plakhotnik root Femen's aversion to feminism and predilection for the display of feminine beauty in the Soviet legacy. That is, the group's glamorization and objectification of women's bodies can be seen as a reaction against the Soviet economic model (characterized by deficits of consumer desirables like beauty products and fashionable clothes) and the "gender regime" according to which women had been employed in manual labor, had worked full time inside and outside of the home, and had enjoyed few opportunities to celebrate their sexuality and traditional femininity.[82] Mayerchyk and Plakhotnik also note that the "Philistine" or commonplace male response to Femen is the one most often witnessed on the Femen blog site. Such comments tended to ignore Femen's political messages and focused exclusively on sexualization, along the lines of: "Are these Femen chicks for rent?"[83] Labeling politicized action by women as "prostitution" is a means of devaluing the political content of the action and denigrating its participants' normative femininity, as discussed in Chapter 3.

It is apparent that Femen's topless (and often nearly bottomless) method gains far more publicity than when women protest clothed. In 2010 the group carried out its first topless action, protesting against the candidacy of Victor Yanukovich for Ukraine's presidency. There, prefiguring their 2012 action in Moscow, they entered the polling station where Yanukovich was planning to vote, removed their shirts, and voiced their opinion: "Ukraine has been raped enough!" The nationwide response following this event convinced the activists that topless protest was more effective than the more traditional type. "No one paid attention to us before we demonstrated topless," noted Gutsol.[84] Maria Dmitrieva, in an article weighing the ramifications of Femen's topless protests, pointed out that whether women are naked or not, when they enter

[79] "Femen," http://femen.org/about, accessed March 15, 2013.

[80] Dmitrieva, "Radikal'nyi eksgibitsionizm."

[81] Femen. "Topless Warriors" [video], 2011, http://www.youtube.com/watch?v=PKDJxOm2Rf Y&feature=youtube_gdata_player, accessed October 26, 2012.

[82] Mayerchyk and Plakhotnik, "The Femen Phenomenon."

[83] Maerchik and Plakhotnik, "Fenomenologiia 'Femen' Metodologicheskie Kontroversii," 26.

[84] Jeffrey Tayler, "Femen, Ukraine's Topless Warriors," *The Atlantic*, November 28, 2012, http://www.theatlantic.com/international/archive/2012/11/femen-ukraines-topless-warriors/265624/.

the public sphere they are judged on their sexual attractiveness, their "suitability for sexual consumption" in the market for sex objects. The political messages of those who trade on their looks are ignored, while those women who fail to play up their sexual attractiveness are accused of letting themselves go and not trying hard enough to appeal to men and are then summarily dismissed. Women in the political arena are thus caught in a double bind.[85]

According to Plakhotnik and Mayerchyk, the openly feminist-identified group, Feministichna Ofenziva (Feminist Attack/Offensive), which consists largely of university students in Ukraine, was invisible in the state's media, though they protested on some of the same issues as Femen (e.g., resisting the close ties between church and state, protesting against restrictions on abortion, and supporting Pussy Riot).[86] Distinguishing themselves from Femen, they have protested while keeping their shirts on, have carried signs for LGBT rights, and have pointedly criticized the sexism of Ukrainian president Yanukovich, who, at the World Economic Forum Davos in 2011, encouraged the attendees to visit Ukraine in the spring, "when it gets warmer and women in Ukraine start undressing."[87] Presumably, in so saying, Yanukovich did not have Femen's typical antics in mind. Feministichna Ofenziva openly opposed "all forms of patriarchal power, such as sexism, transphobia, homophobia, ageism, and racism" and strived to raise awareness about the ramifications of widely held gender norms on women's rights, well aware that calling themselves feminists left them open to the "hostile stigma" associated with the term.[88] Like Pussy Riot in Russia, Femen garnered extensive media attention in Ukraine but was not the only group raising women's issues in the political arena.

Feminist Activism in Russia: Countering Sexism and Homophobia

Like Ukraine, with its Feministichna Ofenziva and other small groups advocating for women's rights, Russia at the end of Putin's first decade in power boasted a handful of recently formed feminist groups. Beyond the borders of

[85] Dmitrieva, "Zhenskoe dvizhenie Rossii."

[86] Feminist Ofenzyva, "Feministichnii marsh vidbuvsia!," March 8, 2012, http://ofenzyva.word-press.com/2012/03/08/feministychny-marsh-vidbuvsia/; Mark Rachkevych, "New Feminist Offensive Aims to Lift Women," *Kyiv Post*, March 22, 2012, http://www.kyivpost.com/guide/about-kyiv/new-feminist-offensive-aims-to-lift-women-124777.html.

[87] Tamara Martsenyuk, "Ukraine's Other Half: International Women's Day Brings Disappointment and Hope for the Sex Largely Excluded from Power in Kyiv," *Stanford Post-Soviet Post*, March 27, 2012, http://postsovietpost.stanford.edu/analysis/.

[88] Rachkevych, "New Feminist Offensive Aims to Lift Women."

the media spotlight that had fallen on Femen and before Pussy Riot's eruption onto the scene, these groups had been explicitly critiquing sexism and gender roles across the board for several years. Pithily summing up this sentiment, socialist feminist Zhenia Otto explained on a liberal radio station broadcast in 2012 (tellingly titled "Feminism: Is It a [psychiatric] Diagnosis or a Form of Protest?") that feminism should not be about "altering" men's and women's existing roles—where men dominate the economy and society and women serve others' interests—but rather, about "getting rid of them altogether."[89] The next sections describe the origins and actions of several small groups of activists who have brought feminist analyses into Russia's public sphere during the Putin era.

ORIGINS

Various events, such as a series of proposed amendments to Russian law aimed at further restricting access to abortion, and the announcement of a prize awarded by a Moscow art gallery to a man who had been convicted of rape, helped crystallize feminist civic action at the end of Putin's first decade in power. The small-scale, creative protest actions and public lectures organized by feminists (like those of the young liberal Kremlin opponents discussed in earlier chapters) epitomized voluntarism; the activists did not collect dues or seek out funding for their activities. In the almost total absence of foreign funding, young feminist activists in contemporary Russia engaged in civic activism, typically with the aid of such social networking sites as Facebook and Live Journal. They participated in large-scale political events such as the mass post-election protests that started in late 2011 and continued through the June 12, 2012 March of Millions in Moscow, so that in addition to voicing demands for Putin's resignation these events would include expressions of protest against homophobia and sexism in Russian society. Recent feminist activism also featured smaller public protests targeting issues of particular importance to feminists, such as protecting women's right to reproductive choice and objecting to homophobic legislation. Through street demonstrations as well as a rich presence on the Web, these small groups were able to reach out to a broader range of citizens than was possible in the 1990s, when feminist activists largely confined their activities to conferences, seminars, and other advocacy activities aimed at state officials rather than at changing public attitudes.

---

[89] "Feminizm—diagnoz ili forma protesta?: Irina Khakamada, Natal'ia Osipova, Evgeniia Otto" (Kul'turnyi shok, Ekho Moskvy, Moscow, September 8, 2012), http://www.echo.msk.ru/programs/kulshok/927417-echo/.

The feminist groups that began to populate the Russian public arena in 2010 had their origins in the virtual world. In 2005, Elizaveta Morozova, then in her late 20s, was inspired to try to create an Internet community about feminism, rather than for feminists per se, in hopes that over time it would result in the creation of a nonvirtual feminist community: "I understood that there was no mob of feminists who would come [to the site], because they simply didn't exist."[90] At that time, while Russian gender scholars had published a great deal of research in both English and Russian, their work was directed toward an academic audience rather than to the broader public. Little was available on the Internet for people "interested in the ideas of feminism or who were simply concerned with gender issues of one kind or another." Morozova thus set out to "popularize" the notion of feminism and simultaneously undo some of the "demonization" of the term. She created the Feministki blog on Live Journal and began by posting Russian translations of feminist essays and other articles written for the general public.[91] Her first post, on February 5, 2005, linked to a Russian translation of Gloria Steinem's iconic 1978 essay, "If Men Could Menstruate."[92] Morozova offered readers a chance to familiarize themselves with the "sweet fantasy" of this "famous feminist theorist" who had posed the question, "How would our society regard menstruation if it was men, rather than women, who menstruated?"[93]

It took almost two weeks for anyone to respond. Then, over the course of two days in mid-February, fourteen comments on the post appeared. Most of these consisted of a discussion between two people arguing about the nature of feminism and feminists. One poster, a now-deleted-and-purged Live Journal user called "ex_ex_apazh," argued that a feminist was a "hysteric, 'fighting for her gender rights'" and that a "normal man could not hold out for more than ten minutes with such a person," never mind have sex with her: "Do you seriously think that it would be possible to fuck normally, if one had to constantly ask his female partner something like, 'comrade vagina-bearing Russian citizen, may I have permission to spank you on the buttocks?' And 'would you not be degraded by assuming a position on your knees and elbows?'" His interlocutor, pell_mell, who, several days earlier, on her own website had posted a question about the ways in which men's and women's interests differed, wondered with a virtual "shrug" whether ex_ex was trying to sketch a portrait of

---

[90] Morozova, interview by author.

[91] Frau Derrida, Isya, and Myjj, "Pol'za ot razgovorov (Ob opyte odnogo prosvetitel'skogo proekta v blogosfere)," 97–98. This article neatly summarizes the history of the Feministki blog (http://feministki.livejournal.com).

[92] Steinem, Gloria, "If Men Could Menstruate," *Ms. Magazine*, October 1978.

[93] Sadcrixivan, "Esli by u muzhchin byla menstruatsiia....," February 5, 2005, http://feministki. livejournal.com/373.html.

the average feminist. If so, pell_mell thought the basis for such a characterization was dubious. Another reader noted that his girlfriend had said that feminists were women "who didn't get any sex," and he wondered whether this was true. One poster, however, got the point of Steinem's essay: "Men would have granted themselves a legal day off—with no fuss about it."[94]

Soon it was clear that Morozova's efforts had paid off. Within a year, there were daily multiple postings to the site, and by 2009 Feministki's members numbered fifteen hundred people. As Morozova explained it, "At that time, in Russia, women were boiling over. And a lot of them who were ready to browse through [feminist material] simply didn't have any information about it or a platform on which to do it."[95] Feministki created that forum, and it served a number of simultaneous functions. It was a source of information about sexist, patriarchal phenomena around the world and about feminist terminology (such as "sexism" and "internalized misogyny"). The site also served as a virtual consciousness-raising group, friendship network, and source of moral support among the likeminded, and it helped its readers overcome the "internal stigma" of identifying as a feminist. Finally, it raised important themes generally excluded from mainstream media discussion, such as violence against women, the impact of homophobia, and the experiences of women with disabilities.[96]

By 2012, Feministki boasted over three thousand readers, had four moderators, and covered as many topics as its readers were interested in posting.[97] A selection of posts to the Feministki blog in mid-February 2013 included a query about how people respond when they see women referred to on the Internet in denigrating ways, such as the widespread use of "TP," the Russian language initials for the term, "dumb cunt;" a discussion of a BBC article about women's unrealistically high expectations of marriage; a post noting the presence of a woman in the Soviet delegation for the negotiation of the Brest-Litovsk treaty in 1917; a selection of sex-specific want ads (one sales manager position sought candidates from 21 to 60 years old, specifying "for young women (devushek)—preferably without children, or children under 14 years of age; no limit for men)"; an informational discussion of a wide range of

---

[94] Pell_mell's query was itself inspired by a recent post by a third Live Journal blogger, Pelageya, who had noted that the interests of women who seriously call themselves feminists amount exclusively to male interests. Pelageya, "I o feminizme," January 21, 2005, http://pelageya.livejournal.com/241488.html; Pell_mell, "Potok soznaniia," February 2, 2005, http://pell-mell.livejournal.com/2005/02/02/; Sadcrixivan, "Esli by u muzhchin byla menstruatsiia. . . . "

[95] Morozova, interview by author.

[96] Frau Derrida, Isya, and Myjj, "Pol'za ot razgovorov (Ob opyte odnogo prosvetitel'skogo proekta v blogosfere)."

[97] Frau Derrida, interview by author.

women's rights violated in India; and a post titled, "Glossy Magazines: The Heavy Artillery of Patriarchy," about the "enormous number of stereotypes about women and their roles and place in the world" that such publications reinforced.[98]

A few years into the Feministki community's development, Morozova approached one of its moderators, Frau Derrida, with the idea of creating a consciousness-raising group. Morozova was inspired by the experience of American feminist groups such as the Redstockings, who wrote about the importance of consciousness-raising as a means of overcoming isolation and recognizing common experiences of patriarchal oppression.[99] The two women gathered a handful of acquaintances and people they knew through the Feministki blogging community and began to meet, founding the MFG in 2008.[100] As its founders had hoped, the group provided a "safe space" where women could "concretely discuss the issues that were troubling them." It also, with the establishment of MFG's website, http://www.ravnopravka.ru, created an informational platform about feminism and about Russian feminism in particular.[101] By 2012, the group had approximately twenty members, the majority of whom were aged 25 to 35.

Members of MFG soon intersected with feminist-oriented women from left-wing circles. Elena Maksimova, a feminist frustrated by the reception of her ideas within Vpered (Forward), a socialist group, encountered MFG members Frau Derrida and Nadia Plungian at a conference, "The Women's Movement in Russia: Yesterday, Today, Tomorrow," held in February 2010 at the liberal Yabloko Party's offices in Moscow, and exchanged contact information.[102] Two weeks later, all three attended an International Women's Day event organized by socialist activists at a Moscow bookstore. This led, in short order, to collaboration on a new feminist-oriented journal published by the

---

[98] Olga_future, "Klichki i rugatel'stva," February 11, 2013, http://feministki.livejournal.com/2535051.html; Litrlife, "Ozhidaniia sovremennoi zhenshchiny ot braka zachastuiu kraine vysoki i daleki ot real'nosti," February 11, 2013, http://feministki.livejournal.com/2534717.html; Hey_jan_ghapama, "Sovetskaia delegatsiia i nemtsy: Brest-Litovsk. dekabr' 1917," February 10, 2013, http://feministki.livejournal.com/2532798.html; Olga_future, "Nam nuzhny rabotniki, no Vy nam ne podkhodite," February 10, 2013, http://feministki.livejournal.com/2532259.html; Moloko2012, "Uzhasy Indii," February 10, 2013, http://feministki.livejournal.com/2531915.html#comments, accessed February 12, 2013; Galinakuksa, "Gliantsevye Zhurnaly - Tiazhelaia Artilleriia Patriarkhata," livejournal.com, February 9, 2013, http://feministki.livejournal.com/2531262.html.

[99] Redstockings, Feminist Revolution (New York: Random House, 1979).

[100] Morozova, interview by author.

[101] "Moskovskaia feministskaia gruppa," http://ravnopravka.ru/?page_id=37, accessed April 2, 2012.

[102] Maksimova, interview by author.

Committee for a Workers' International (KRI), called *No Means No* (Net—znachit net), the first issue of which emerged in May of that year. The journal was the project of KRI's Campaign against Discrimination and Exploitation of Women, spearheaded by Zhenia Otto, then in her early 20s. Otto, by her own admission, "didn't really know anything about women's issues" at the time and found her ensuing work on the journal with the radical feminists enlightening, as she read the theoretical literature that they had "opened up" for her.[103] For some of the feminists who had been operating largely on the Web, working on the journal felt important. Frau Derrida put it this way: "Fairly soon, I started thinking about how these CR groups in the United States were made up of people who were doing political activism, while in their groups they were talking at a more personal level. But we [in MFG] were discussing things and not doing anything beyond the group's borders." Although she was not a member of KRI, Frau Derrida felt "positively inclined [to collaboration on the journal] because it was like an answer to my need for some external political activity. I was happy that someone was doing that sort of thing."[104]

Events in Moscow soon pushed young feminists to organize in the brick-and-mortar world. On April 30, 2010, a Russian poet, Nikolai Nikiforov, described a frightening scene on his blog. He had been visiting a friend—a young artist, Ilia Trushevskii—and heard him and another acquaintance raping a young woman, an 18-year-old student, in the next room. Nikiforov called the police, and the woman filed a complaint, which led first to Trushevskii's release on bail, and, ultimately, to a jail sentence for rape and sexual assault.[105] Maksimova read about it on Feministki, called Frau Derrida and said, "We have to *do* something." Having already "divorced" the socialist group to which she had earlier belonged and finding the Feministki community more interested in writing than in going into the streets, Maksimova turned to KRI and organized "the first of our actions."[106] On the evening of May 13, participants from the feministki community, MFG, KRI and Vpered held an unauthorized march on Moscow's Arbat Street, chanting, handing out leaflets, and carrying a banner reading, "A woman is not a thing and not a commodity!" Two days later, the activists held a city-authorized picket condemning oppression and violence against women, under the slogan, "Society allows it—Trushevskiis commit it," to emphasize the general tendency for "typical" citizens to ignore or dismiss the crime of rape.[107]

---

[103] Otto, interview by author.

[104] Frau Derrida, interview by author.

[105] "Action!," *Net—znachit net* 2 (November 2010): 3–5.

[106] Maksimova, interview by author.

[107] "Action!," November 2010.

Testifying to this point, in May a Trushevskii supporter published a piece on the Liberty blog (http://www.liberty.ru), noting that "a normal way to look at this is that there is nothing that stands out about sexual violence . . . if a boy 'raped' a girl, a normal person, not a leftist, would see it just the same way as if a boy got in a fistfight with another boy. . . to howl about rapes is so senseless!"[108]

On June 2, 2010, Moscow's chic contemporary art gallery, Vinzavod, awarded its yearly "Moral Support" prize to several artists, including Trushevskii, motivating Maksimova, Otto, and other activists to organize a picket of the gallery and offer a prize "For Amoral Support" to the Vinzavod gallery administration. KRI, meanwhile, announced a Vinzavod boycott, collecting signatures on the Web.[109] The feminists' actions had shifted the dynamics of the situation. "In the end," Maksimova said, "we forced them to justify their decision, at least, so they couldn't just say, 'Well, it's OK to rape a young woman (devushka).'"[110]

Maksimova was eager to continue feminist street actions and began to pull activists together to that end. In late August, a collection of papers presented at the aforementioned February 2010 conference on the women's movement was published, and an event was held to mark the occasion at Yabloko party headquarters. There, Maksimova met Natalia Bitten, a feminist journalist who had been excited to read about the demonstrations concerning Trushevskii on Feministki, because, as she put it, the women who organized the actions "finally had done what needed to be done."[111] Together with several other activists, they created a new organization, the Initiative Group "Pro-Feminism" (Initsiativnaia gruppa "Za Feminizm"; IGZF). Oriented toward street actions rather than small-group consciousness-raising, with fewer than a dozen members, the IGZF went to work, organizing at least six such actions in its first five months and inaugurating the "Sexist of the Year" competition in December 2010.[112]

Over the next two years, Moscow's feminist groups divided and reformed as activists sorted out their differences over social class background, political persuasion, and inclination to street protest, leaving a constellation of small feminist groups with overlapping membership. After six months of fairly

[108] Ibid.

[109] "'Vinzavodu' ob"iavili boikot za podderzhku khudozhnika Trushevskogo," June 7, 2010, http://lenta.ru/news/2010/06/07/vinzavod/; "Action!," November 2010.

[110] Maksimova, interview by author.

[111] Bitten, interview by author.

[112] Akulova, interview by author; Bitten interview by author; Frau Derrida, interview by author; Maksimova, interview by author. Accounts of the organization's formation and later dissolution differ slightly.

frenzied organizing activity, the IGZF split in March 2011; one set of activists, including Bitten, retained the organization's name and the Sexist of the Year competition, while the rest, including Maksimova, created the Moscow Radical Feminists (Moskovskie Radikal'nye Feministki; MRF), featuring a reading group where feminist texts were discussed, and continued to take part in street protests. Several months later, in summer 2010, the MRF split, with Maksimova and several others remaining in the organization, and the rest created a consciousness-raising group called the Tea Group (Chainaia Gruppa), so named because one of its members worked at a tea house that allowed the group to meet on its grounds.[113] Similarly, in late May 2011, the School of Feminism (Shkola Feminizma) formed, a nonhierarchically organized assemblage that gathered to educate themselves about and discuss various topics, from the different strands of feminist theory and practice (liberal, socialist, radical) to key texts and developments in feminist history and organizing, and topics like sexuality, violence against women, and images of women in the media.[114] The group met eight times over the course of the year but had split in two by January 2012, with one School of Feminism holding its meetings at the Yabloko Party's offices (under the auspices of that party's Gender Caucus), and the other meeting more informally. The MFG was not as dramatically transformed; while it continued to focus on consciousness raising, over time its members gradually engaged the public sphere, organizing lectures, occasionally speaking to the media on gender issues, and participating in street actions.

Russia's twenty-first century feminists had not avoided the fragmentation common to many social movements. But neither had it demobilized them. By contrast to the Russian women's movement of the late- and post-Soviet period, the Putin era feminists worked together and separately to make a small but sustained impact in the public eye. In February 2012, a coalition of feminist groups was formed, pulling together the MFG, the MRF, and the Chainaia Gruppa, as well as participants from KRI and other groups, under the title "Forum Feministskaia Initsiativa" (Feminist Initiative), and proceeded to organize several protest actions over the course of 2012 and into 2013.[115]

---

[113] Akulova, interview by author; Bitten, interview by author; Morozova, interview by author.

[114] "Shkola feminizma" [audio], February 5, 2012, http://www.feminismru.org/load/audio/shkola_feminizma/2-1-0-57. Recordings of the sessions can be found on this site. On radical feminist theories, see Carol Anne Douglas, *Love and Politics: Radical Feminist and Lesbian Theories* (San Francisco: Ism Press, 1990).

[115] Akulova, interview by author; Bitten, interview by author; Frau Derrida, interview by author; Maksimova, interview by author; Morozova, interview by author; Plungian, interview by author; Elena Maksimova, "Feministki-nevidimki," June 3, 2012, http://grani.ru/blogs/free/entries/198158.html.

OPPOSING SEXISM, HOMOPHOBIA, AND THE ENFORCEMENT OF GENDER NORMS

Russia's feminist groups emerged into an increasingly authoritarian political environment, where sexism and homophobia were rampant. It was sensible, therefore, to use multiple methods to struggle against the patriarchal hydra. In addition to consciousness-raising and hosting public lectures—techniques that flew under the regime's political radar screen—Russia's young feminist activists took to the streets with their demands and with their efforts to alter public consciousness about the variegated forms of patriarchy, including sexist discrimination, misogyny, and homophobia. Given the relatively hostile social backdrop for these actions and the near total absence of public feminist protest in the first decade of Russia's twenty-first century, the small numbers of activists who engaged in both state-authorized and unauthorized (and thus illegal) protests benefited from having a supportive virtual environment. In that regard, the Feministki community served as something of a hub for feminist organizing in the Putin era; activists posted announcements on Feministki as well as on their groups' websites, enabling people to join in, provide suggestions for protest slogans, and generally cheer one another on before and after the fact.

Between 2010 and early 2013, feminists organized dozens of actions, from petitions and art exhibits to street-art performances, graffiti campaigns, and public rallies.[116] The frequency of feminist protests intensified with the formation of the IGZF in 2010. The IGZF's first action was motivated by the beginning that summer of what one activist called "the anti-women campaign"—a renewed initiative to restrict abortion, endorsed by the government and the Russian Orthodox Church, and widely discussed in the mass media.[117]

Part and parcel of the national "remasculinizing" of Russia under Putin (discussed in Chapter 2 and evidenced by a rhetorically aggressive foreign policy, Russia's avowal of "sovereign" democracy, and Putin's own macho posturing) was a related effort to reassert Russia's national power by boosting fertility rates and reversing the country's demographic decline. The new Russia was thus to be tough, assertive, potent—and pregnant. This demonstration of national virility would clearly require women's cooperation, but that could not be counted upon, especially given economic uncertainties and a variety of newly available contraceptive methods in addition to abortion (which had

---

[116] I present here only a small selection of the protests; many others can be found on feminist groups' websites, such as http://www.ravnopravka.ru (MFG), http://www.radical-fem-msk. livejournal.com (MRF), http://www.zafeminizm.ru (IGZF), and http://www.rosovi-bint. livejournal.com (the blog of a feminist graffiti artist and activist in St. Petersburg).

[117] Bitten, interview by author.

been women's main method of controlling fertility in the Soviet era). Russian nationalists' approach to the fertility issue was to claim that contraception was a Western plot to emasculate the state; they "construed abortion and contraception as issues of national security practices linked to the country's weakened geopolitical power."[118] The nationalists' solution was to decry contraception and outlaw abortion or at least restrict it as much as possible, actions that necessarily impinged on women's reproductive freedoms and choices. While abortion was available and widely used during the Soviet era, during Putin's first two terms as president access to second-trimester abortions was curtailed. These restrictions were enacted by Russia's Ministry of Health rather than by the parliament, cutting any pretense of public input out of the picture.[119] Anticontraceptive and anti-abortion rhetoric was accompanied by more calls for women to exit the workforce and raise multiple children apiece. As anthropologist Michele Rivkin-Fish notes, the "maternity capital" program introduced in 2007 was designed to facilitate that process, while also "further entrenching a vision of women as mothers and linking them to the domestic sphere."[120] Such policies would enable women to fulfill their "duty" to the state, thereby proving en masse that their male compatriots were not impotent after all.

Responding to the accumulating constraints on women's reproductive rights, IGZF activist Elena Maksimova proposed holding an action on World Contraception Day, September 26, 2010. In a fortuitous turn of events, the group was granted permission to hold their rally within shouting distance of the Cathedral of Christ the Savior, the most lavish embodiment of Russian Orthodoxy in the capital.[121] The action's twenty participants were drawn from the IGZF, the left-wing KRI, and several other groups, including ANNA and Sestry (Sisters) (two groups founded in the 1990s to address issues of domestic and sexual violence). Bearing banners and posters with the slogans, "Contraception [works] against abortion!" (kontratseptsiia protiv abortov), "No condom—no love," "Don't forbid, don't judge, educate!" and "The alternative to abortion is sex education and accessible contraception!", activists attracted the attention of passersby and distributed leaflets with information about contraception and reproductive health and also about ways to combat violence against women.[122]

---

[118] Michele Rivkin-Fish, "Conceptualizing Feminist Strategies for Russian Reproductive Politics: Abortion, Surrogate Motherhood, and Family Support after Socialism," *Signs* 38, no. 3 (2013): 573.

[119] Ibid., 573–574.

[120] Ibid., 584.

[121] Bitten, interview by author.

[122] "Vsemirnyi den' kontratseptsii: Aktsiia v Moskve—28 Sentiabria 2010—Za feminizm," September 28, 2010, http://www.zafeminizm.ucoz.ru/news/vsemirnyj_den_kontracepcii_akcija_v_moskve/2010-09-28-1.

A month later, IGZF organized a protest against the onslaught of sexist advertising that had been ubiquitous in print and broadcast media since the advent of capitalism and consumerism in the mid-1990s. Saying "No to sexist advertising" and the objectification of women's bodies that it promoted, a handful of activists gathered for a "flash mob" on Moscow's Gogolevskii Boulevard with hand-lettered signs, including "Good merchandise doesn't need sexist ads," and "A woman is neither a doll nor a commodity!" Activists also drew topless female torsos and held them up for onlookers in mock advertisements for beer, construction materials, and tires. Their captions highlighted the sexism of ads that typically featured women's bodies even when they had no relevance to the product in question. "Your car will go far," one sign promised, "After all, my large breasts (pyshnaia grud') are advertising it!" The previous day, to mark the national day recognizing Employees in the Advertising Industry, the group had written to major advertising agencies encouraging them to stop running sexist advertisements.[123]

Barely a month later, on November 27, the intrepid IGZF activists protested violence against women as part of the annual international "16 Days against Gender Violence" campaign.[124] Dressed in black garbage bags covered with handwritten statements, with black swaths of fabric tied across their mouths and a sign reading "Territory of Silence," the activists illustrated victims' reluctance to speak about violence and society's deafness to it. Activists testified to the varied forms of violence against women—from domestic violence and rape to the trafficking of women into sexual slavery and the use of rape as a war weapon. Dramatic and educational, the protest aimed to break the usual silence on these subjects in Russian society.[125] Having been given a permit for Bolotnaia Square that Saturday, the protesters worried that they would be isolated in the large park. But upon arrival, as one activist recalled, "We understood what a happy coincidence it was, because on Saturdays there are weddings, and big processions with a lot of people come through there. And so we . . . gave out leaflets to the newlyweds—like preventative medicine!"[126]

[123] Lena Maksimova, "Action!," Net—znachit net 3 (March 2011): 3–5; "Aktsiia IG 'Za feminizm' protiv seksistskoi reklamy 23 oktiabria v Moskve," October 25, 2010, http://www.zafeminizm. ucoz.ru/news/akcija_ig_za_feminizm_protiv_seksistskoj_reklamy_23_oktjabrja_v_ moskve/2010-10-25-4.

[124] On violence against women in post-Soviet Russia, see Janet Elise Johnson, Gender Violence in Russia: The Politics of Feminist Intervention (Bloomington: Indiana University Press, 2009).

[125] "Piket v podderzhku Mezhdunarodnoi kampanii za likvidatsiiu nasiliia v otnoshenii zhenshchin," November 30, 2010, http://www.zafeminizm.ucoz.ru/news/2010-11-30; "Ne tol'ko vos'mogo marta," March 24, 2011, http://www.union-report.ru/news/2011-03-24/ne-tolko-vosmogo-marta.

[126] Bitten, interview by author.

International Women's Day, March 8, offered yearly opportunities for activists to protest on a public holiday whose original intent—to highlight women's struggle for equal rights—had long since been forgotten in many countries (the United States included) and replaced with mere pleasantries and bouquets in Russia and other former Soviet bloc states. In 2011, International Women's Day was marked by two rallies in Moscow. Under the slogan "For Men's and Women's Equality," the first rally focused on the need for a state law backing gender equality. While Russia's Constitution includes an article stating that Russian men and women enjoy equal rights and opportunities, none of the several efforts to pass legislation implementing that article had been successful. Rally speakers objected to the absence of women in power as well as to labor discrimination and miserly child welfare benefits. While the rally was regarded as liberal-feminist, a speaker from the socialist KRI's anti-discrimination campaign was also given the microphone to state that even if women gained political power in greater numbers, capitalism would still continue to support conditions that help maintain an available, inexpensive, degraded female working class. Sexist advertising, inadequate provision of domestic violence shelters, and low welfare payments all constituted additional means to continue profits for the capitalist-run government.[127] An hour later, a second rally for women's rights took place, titled "Return [the Holiday] Its Lost Meaning," which drew attention to a similar and overlapping set of issues: sexism, domestic violence, the need for more accessible childcare centers, higher child welfare benefits paid to mothers, and equal pay for equal work. At this left-wing organized rally, a Yabloko representative also spoke about the need for more women in office. KRI had also reached out to LGBT activists who joined in, bearing rainbow flags, and who spoke about the importance of openly discussing LGBT discrimination and resisting insults and repression.[128]

In June 2011, parliamentary deputies in the ruling political party, United Russia, gave feminists a new impetus to organize, by proposing legislation that would grossly restrict abortion rights. On the table were proposals that would require the signature of a married woman's husband approving her abortion; enable doctors to refuse to perform abortions according to their beliefs; restrict second trimester abortions to those for medical reasons and in cases of rape; establish mandatory fetal ultrasounds; and impose obligatory meetings with psychologists (whose task was to convince women that any material or financial concerns a woman might have about bearing a child were, in fact,

---

[127] Anna Brius, "8 Marta: Za ravnye prava i vozmozhnosti," *Net—znachit net* 3 (March 2011): 6.
[128] Otto, "8 Marta."

psychologically based) before allowing an abortion to occur.[129] The Russian Orthodox Church was seen to have a hand in the proposed bills, and feminists reacted with a flood of protest.[130]

In St. Petersburg, where feminist organizing was drawn from a network of likeminded people (many, if not all of whom, were members of the Live Journal Feministki community) rather than from organized groups per se, activists came largely from left-wing circles, and several were involved with the St. Petersburg Crisis Center for Women, which had been founded in the 1990s. On June 25, 2011, feminists in Russia's "northern capital" came together and organized a rally against the proposed abortion-restricting legislation. Aleksandra Kachko, a co-organizer of the rally, appeared with a mock pregnancy under her modest, gray dress and a sign promising to "Give it into good hands," while her friend Oksana Zamoiskaia bore a bright red slogan on her bare abdomen: "My body is my business." Another woman encased in a human-sized plastic bag posed as a condom, and a sign alluding to the Church's medieval views on the subject read, "Today—a ban on abortion; tomorrow, 'witches' on bonfires."[131] Feminist protesters at the event continued to explain their opposition to the proposed amendments limiting women's access to abortion at a similar rally on September 3.[132] In Moscow, feminists gathered a crowd of one hundred protesters for an abortion rights rally on September 5. At the end of the month, under the banner "Fight abortion, not women!," activists held a smaller protest against the threatened limitations to abortion access and in memory of the victims of illegal abortion, who

---

[129] In the end, a waiting period was established; acceptable reasons for second-trimester abortions were restricted to rape and medical issues; psychological consultations were introduced into clinics by decree (and in practice, women were not offered a choice about whether to meet with the psychologist). Husbands' signatures were not required. Akulova, interview by author. Also see Vera Akulova, "Bez abortov?: Ogranichenie prava na abort—eto ne demograficheskaia politika," Net—znachit net 4 (March 2012): 11–14.

[130] The feminist reproductive rights campaign website is ProtivAbortov2011, "Za svobodnoe materinstvo!," https://sites.google.com/site/protivabortov2011/, accessed February 19, 2013. The misogyny of Russian Orthodox Church doctrine on reproductive matters is striking. The Church condemns abortion, but, recognizing the frequency of its use in Russia, provides "special prayer rules for women who have had abortions and are seeking to expiate their guilt." According to historian Nadieszda Kizenko, a prayer designed for women who have miscarried a pregnancy "essentially blames them for their child's death and bars them from the Eucharist." See Kizenko, "Feminized Patriarchy?," 599.

[131] Rosovi_bint, "Piket protiv antiabortnogo zakonodatel'stva proshel khorosho," June 25, 2011, http://rosovi-bint.livejournal.com/79363.html; Sergey Chernov, "Can't Keep Silent," The St. Petersburg Times, December 7, 2011, http://www.sptimes.ru/index.php?action_id=2&story_id=34935.

[132] For photos of the rally, see Rosovi_bint, "Vse na miting za prava zhenshchin!," August 29, 2011, http://rosovi-bint.livejournal.com/88777.html.

were represented by orange and red balloons.[133] For Vera Akulova, a key organizer of the abortion rights campaign, the September 5 rally marked a turning point, as it was "the biggest rally with a purely feminist agenda in I don't know how many years." Bringing that number of people into the public arena months before the mass post-election protests was a considerable achievement that Akulova believed had later "helped women go out to the civic rallies" after the December elections and that had promoted the feminist movement's visibility.[134] While the regime and the Orthodox Church aimed to legitimate themselves by limiting women's access to abortion, the feminist activists insisted on asserting their right to reproductive choice and control over their bodies.

That fall, two St. Petersburg activists undertook a graffiti campaign called "Rozovyi krest'" (pink cross). Pink stencils appeared on selected city walls showing a simple drawing of a woman in a dress, affixed to a cross, with the words, "A crime was committed here." Posting these in places where women had been raped and murdered, the activists sought to draw attention to the problem of sexual violence. In a related action feminists drew attention to the nexus of the Orthodox Church, patriarchy, and violence against women by posting graffiti showing a young blond woman on a cross, naked from the waist up, and wearing a miniskirt, with the caption, "Patriarchy kills, and the Church approves."[135] Highlighting the problem of state accountability to women, in late November St. Petersburg activists organized an art-rally about the need to pass legislation on domestic violence. A cartoon graphic advertising the rally played on the Russian expression advising people not to air their dirty laundry in public. It showed laundry hung outdoors with the text, "Violence in the family is not someone's 'dirty laundry,' it's the whole society's problem."[136]

Back in Moscow, on an evening in late November 2011, feminists from Yabloko's Gender Caucus and several other groups performed a dramatic sketch in support of women's rights in Novopushkinskii Square, where the Medvedev Girls had stripped to support Medvedev's ban on the public

---

[133] "Za svobodnoe materinstvo," https://sites.google.com/site/protivabortov2011/, accessed February 19, 2013; "Miting pamiati pogibshikh ot kriminal'nykh abortov sostoialsia—Za svobodnoe materinstvo!," October 1, 2011, https://sites.google.com/site/protivabortov2011/novosti-kampanii/mitingpamatipogibsihotkriminalnyhabortovsostoalsa.

[134] Akulova, interview by author.

[135] Aleksandra Kachko, Drugaia Rossiia, interview by author, St. Petersburg, June 15, 2012; Rosovi_bint, "Rozovyi krest 1.0," October 27, 2011, http://rosovi-bint.livejournal.com/95233.html; Rosovi_bint, "Okolo Kniaz'-Vladimirskogo sobora raspiali zhenshchinu," November 7, 2011, http://rosovi-bint.livejournal.com/97155.html.

[136] Rosovi_bint, "Vynosim sor iz izby! Miting za priniatie zakona v zashchitu zhertv nasiliia," November 23, 2011, http://rosovi-bint.livejournal.com/98480.html.

consumption of alcohol some months earlier. The participants reenacted scenes illustrating the gender roles enacted in a "typical day" in the life of a Russian family:

> A woman has to take care of the house, serve her husband, look after the children, and work—without getting help from her husband, who in his free time watches television and drinks beer, and even allows himself to raise his hand against his wife, who's bringing him a plate [of food]. The salary she gets is one third less than her male colleagues' for the same position. "You're married; your husband should take care of you," was the explanation her employer gave for the size of her salary. The scene ended with a domestic dispute and divorce.[137]

The mass protests following Russia's parliamentary elections in December 2011 gave feminists new opportunities for political exposure. While none of Moscow's small feminist groups chose to attend the first mass rally "For Fair Elections" on December 10, Nadezhda Tolokonnikova of Pussy Riot spoke in defense of women's and LGBT rights at the Bolotonaia Square event to a reportedly unreceptive crowd.[138] The second "For Fair Elections" protest, on December 24, however, brought a "feminist contingent" several dozen strong onto Moscow's Sakharov Prospect, along with tens of thousands of other protesters. Feminist activists from MFG, IGZF, and other groups (including LGBT activists mobilized through an open call on the Feministki community) carried a feminist flag, banners, posters, and leaflets, making feminist symbols and the activists themselves visible for the first time in the context of a Putin-era mass rally.[139] MFG member Frau Derrida recalled brainstorming slogans related to the election theme, like "Feminism is a choice" and "Feminism is freedom of choice."[140]

As the election protest rallies continued, so too did the feminist presence. On February 4, 2012, activists from MRF and other groups took part in the third "For Fair Elections" mass march and rally at Bolotnaia Square. If at their own earlier protests, handfuls of feminist activists had rattled around in that

---

[137] "V Moskve proshla teatralizovannaia aktsiia 'Odin den' iz zhizni rossiianki,'" November 29, 2011, http://www.yabloko.ru/regnews/Moscow/2011/11/29.

[138] Alaverin, "Apochitaite Golysheva," August 22, 2012, http://alaverin.livejournal.com/397696.html.

[139] Akulova, interview by author; Bitten, interview by author; Frau Derrida, interview by author.

[140] Frau Derrida, interview by author.

large public space, now the square was crowded with thousands of people, with the largest yet "gender contingent" comprising more than sixty of them.[141] As they marched, activists carried a white banner with purple letters proclaiming, "Feminists for civic freedom," a feminist flag (a white "woman" symbol with a fist in the center, on a purple background), and signs announcing: "My country, my life, my freedom: Feminists for the right to choose" (za pravo na vybor), and "The struggle for LGBT rights is a struggle for human rights." Feminists also made explicit their critique of the regime's gender-norm-based legitimation strategy with a poster aimed at Putin's efforts to curry popular favor by belittling gays: "A crook and a thief cannot rescue his ratings with homophobia."[142]

The next six weeks temporarily transformed the Russian political landscape, as Pussy Riot's brief but momentous "performance" in the Cathedral of Christ the Savior was followed by the arrest of three of the alleged vocalists in March 2012. Suddenly, issues of critical importance to feminists (such as the influential role of the Orthodox Church on public policy) became a source of heated socio-political argument, and liberals were lining up to demand Pussy Riot's immediate release, even as they dismissed the significance of the band's action. Russia's leading anti-corruption blogger, Aleksei Navalny, for instance, demeaned the young women in Pussy Riot as "foolish girls" (dury) and "crazy chicks" (choknutye devitsy) who were merely seeking publicity.[143] Three young "feminists" were now the focus of legal, political, and cultural attention, standing in for any and all other Russian feminist voices (which remained largely unheard), while quite literally, in the eyes of some Orthodox believers, demonizing feminism anew.

Appalled by the state's disproportionate reaction, Russia's feminists uniformly declared that, whether or not they thought Pussy Riot was "feminist" in a way that they recognized, they sought a quick end to the band members' confinement. Even when approached by the mainstream media seeking a "feminist bites feminist" story, activists refused to take the bait. MFG member Nadia Plungian, for instance, was interviewed by the major TV channel, "Rossiia," where she was asked multiple times whether she believed that Pussy Riot could be considered "feminists." Plungian staunchly repeated her position: the question was irrelevant. This excerpt from the interview (the Russian transcript of which was published on the MFG's webpage) transmits the flavor of the conversation:

---

[141] "Action!," *Net—znachit net* 4 (March 2012): 3–4.
[142] "Na shestvii 'Za chestnye vybory' 4 fevralia 2012g," February 5, 2012, http://radical-fem-msk.livejournal.com/5806.html.
[143] Navalny, "Pro pussi raiots," March 7, 2012, http://navalny.livejournal.com/690551.html.

INTERVIEWER: But are they feminists—from a methodological perspective?

NP: What differences does it make? What difference does it make in this case?

INTERVIEWER: It's a matter of curiosity.

NP: I don't think this is the time to discuss it. Once they're out, then I'll be prepared to talk about that.

INTERVIEWER [LAUGHING]: Good lord, why did you agree to meet with us if you yourself say you're not prepared?

NP: I'm meeting with you in order to voice the position, on the air, that feminists—at least, the feminists I know and can represent, the Moscow Feminist Group, in this case—are opposed to any activists or artists being imprisoned for such things. That's all there is to it.

In the course of the conversation, Plungian also noted that feminists' task was to support human rights—primarily, women's rights—and that the rights of one of the imprisoned band members, Maria Alekhina, had been violated when the regime had threatened to deprive her of parental rights and send her child to an orphanage. "That is a feminist issue," argued Plungian, "if that interests you." The broadcast deleted both of these sections of the interview, suggesting that was not, in fact, what the reporter had hoped to hear.[144]

Other feminist voices in the public arena also showed support for the imprisoned women. At an authorized International Women's Day event on March 8, 2012, organized by Yabloko's Gender Caucus with participants from IGZF and other groups, Moscow police labeled the slogans supporting Pussy Riot as "extremist" and attempted to break up the rally.[145] In particular, police demanded that a rhyming poster reading: "[Putin's] third term, one-two-three—feminists under lock and key?" (Tram-pam-pam, tretii srok—feministok pod zamok) be removed as well as a rainbow flag representing the LGBT community.[146] Another poster cast doubt on the fairness of Russian Orthodox Church encroachments on public institutions, musing: "Priests in schools—that's spirituality (dukhovnost'), but feminists in a cathedral—that's a crime?" The head of Yabloko's Gender Caucus, Galina Mikhaleva, spoke in favor of the young women's release, as did Mariia Arbatova, the aforementioned co-host of the "Ia sama" talk show.[147]

---

[144] "MFG na kanale 'Rossiia,'" March 24, 2012, http://bit.ly/10NoZou.

[145] Galina Mikhaleva, Chair, Gendernaia Fraktsiia Partii Yabloko, interview by author, Moscow, June 8, 2012.

[146] "Politsiia zopodozrila uchastnikov mitinga 'Za ravnye prava i vozmozhnosti dlia zhenshchin' v ekstremizme," Znak Ravenstva, April 2012, 19–20.

[147] Wander Woman, "Fotoreportazh s mitinga 8 marta 2012 g. v Moskve," March 9, 2012, http://www.zafeminizm.ru/137-fotoreportazh-s-mitinga-8-marta-2012-g-v-moskve.html; On Arbatova's TV program, see Azhgikhina, Propushchennyi siuzhet, 173–176.

Despite the media circus surrounding Pussy Riot, feminist groups continued their efforts to educate the public about a different notion of
feminism—one that explicitly criticized efforts to limit women's choices
and opportunities. Taking advantage of the occasion provided by International Women's Day, activists from MFG and MRF held the "March 8: In-
foAttack" and marched down Moscow's snowy Tverskoi Boulevard and
Tverskaia Street with signs undermining the notion that March 8 was merely
a celebration of love, beauty, and femininity. As the organizers explained on
the MRF website, "March 8 has long since been turned from a day to struggle for women's equality into a holiday for sexism." Posters affixed to the
marchers' fronts and backs informed spectators of a wide range of sexist
manifestations. "In nearly all families, housework falls to women," read one
poster. Another read: "Since the year 2000, women have not had the right to
drive a city bus. There are 456 other jobs closed to women. Maybe you could
decide on your own where to work?" The posters posed questions about
sexist discrimination to passersby: "The Russian Orthodox Church disap-
proves of contraception and considers abortion murder; the state is trying
to outlaw abortion. Wouldn't you like to plan your family life yourself?" "According to Crisis Centers' data, 22% of women in Russia are raped. Are you
sure it won't happen to you?" "One out of every four women is sexually ha-
rassed at work. Maybe the boss should be punished?" "According to [state
statistics agency] Rosstat, women get 60% of men's salaries working at the
same job. Are you sure that's fair?" Encouraging women to join the struggle
against sexism, an artistic banner read: "If not me, and you, then who? Feminism is liberation!"[148]

A few months later, on June 2, 2012, the coalition Feminist Initiative held
what was, in essence, the first-ever authorized gay pride event in Putin-era
Moscow, with participants from LGBT groups, left-wing organizations, and
other human rights and civic associations. Called the "March of Burning
Hearts" (Marsh Goriashchikh Serdets), the event addressed a variety of
issues, including sexism, homophobia, and discrimination against ethnic
minorities and people with disabilities. Rainbow flags, feminist flags, and a
wide variety of posters created a festive, determined atmosphere. The Feminist Initiative's series of hand-drawn posters cleverly illuminated—and
questioned the wisdom of—the double binds that patriarchy creates for
women across various social fields. One sign showed a woman wearing a
pink bikini, counterposed to a woman in a long-sleeved top who was avidly
reading a book: "If she agrees to sex, she's a slut—and if she doesn't, she's a

---

[148] "8 marta—nash prazdnik," March 9, 2012, http://radical-fem-msk.livejournal.com/
8393.html.

bitch?" Another examined the gendered judgments to which both home-makers (presumed to live off their husbands) and women who pursue careers fall prey: "If she builds a career, she's a 'man in a skirt,' and if she's a housewife, she's a parasite?" A woman who invades the career world regarded as properly belonging to men, loses her femininity and becomes masculine, while a homemaker suffers the stigma of dependence. A third poster illustrated the double bind facing women on the question of childrearing: "If she has a child, she's a 'hen' [klusha], and if she didn't, she's an egotist?" No matter what any woman chooses, the posters reminded viewers, patriarchy will tell her that she's bad. Other posters asserted disabled people's rights ("No to discrimination against people with limited physical abilities!"), the right to sex education ("Instead of lectures about morality, [we need] sex education and crisis centers"), gay rights, and the freedom to make choices ("Homosexuality is not an illness; Having children is a choice, not a destiny!" "For your right to parent, and for our right to abortion: reproductive rights for all!").[149]

In acquiring their protest permit, activists employed a strategy of deception-by-omission. Feminist activist Vera Akulova explained: "In the paperwork filled out for the Mayor's office, it didn't say anything about sexual minorities—it was about sex discrimination." For their part, the authorities granted the permit for the Taras Shevchenko embankment, "the place the Mayor's office proposes when they want an action to go unnoticed. There's nobody there; nobody ever walks by there." Neo-Nazis got wind of the protest and prepared to "ambush" the activists, but as the protesters had a permit, the police "did their job well and detained [the neo-Nazis] before they could attack."[150] While the activists succeeded in disguising the gay rights part of the planned protest in the paperwork, the name for the event—the March of Burning Hearts—reportedly came about in response to a statement made by Russian journalist Dmitrii Kiselev, who proposed incinerating gays' hearts to prevent any unwitting (putatively heterosexual) beneficiaries of organ transplants from receiving them. In adopting the "burning hearts" phrase for their protest, the event's organizers noted, "Bigots (mrakobesy) burn with hatred and fear, but our hearts burn with anger and indignation. They burn with the thirst for justice and are capable of igniting the hearts of others."[151]

---

[149] "Marsh goriashchikh serdets," June 3, 2012, http://radical-fem-msk.livejournal.com/10511.html; Plungian, interview by author; Morozova, interview by author.

[150] Akulova, interview by author.

[151] "Marsh ravenstva," Vikipediia, December 17, 2012, http://bit.ly/16wc4iy. The March of Burning Hearts was the fourth in a series of Marches for Equality.

Feminist and LGBT solidarity was common to Russia's small feminist groups.[152] Ten days after the March of Burning Hearts, feminists, LGBT activists, and Pussy Riot supporters (with a gigantic pink balaklava sculpted from styrofoam) joined Russia's second "March of Millions" to present their agendas while undermining the ruling regime's authority. Tensions ran high before the protest, as the first "March of Millions" in Moscow (marking Putin's inauguration in early May) had ended in violent clashes with the police. But the police presence on June 12 was minimal and the march proceeded in an orderly and lively fashion. Rain greeted the activists as they gathered at Pushkin Square but soon cleared, and thousands of shouting activists proceeded down the tree-lined boulevard heading for Sakharov Prospect. The feminist and LGBT contingent walked near a column of left-wing activists from the gay-friendly socialist KRI group, chanting anti-discriminatory slogans ("Down with fascists, homophobes, and sexists!"; "No to discrimination, yes to emancipation!"; "Fight capitalism, down with homophobia!"; "No to discrimination on the basis of sexual orientation!") along with more traditional anti-regime refrains ("Putin, leave!"; "The main thief is in the Kremlin!"). A large, fringed fabric banner (styled to look like a Russian Orthodox Church banner) that had also appeared at the March of Burning Hearts featured a pink triangle ("homophobia") intersecting with a black triangle ("sexism") to form a Jewish star and read: "They oppress us differently, but exterminate us the same way."[153]

In 2008, the Russian government had established a midsummer state holiday embodying some of its gender-normative principles. Called the "Day of Family, Love, and Loyalty," the holiday aimed at raising the birthrate and celebrating the nuclear, heterosexual family. It also, unwittingly, gave feminists a second annual holiday on which to organize public outreach. In 2012, feminists in St. Petersburg approached city authorities for a permit to gather on July 8 but instead received one for July 7 and thus held their protest on the eve of the holiday. Under the slogan, "Gender equality will save the family," activists rallied to emphasize the need for a state law on domestic violence and for an end to homophobia within the traditional family. With only a handful of protesters, the activists relied on a dramatic, eye-catching central image: Oksana Zamoiskaia, a feminist activist, volunteer at the St. Petersburg Crisis Center for Women, and member of the left-wing Russian Socialist Movement, posed

---

[152] This was a relatively new development; the small handful of out lesbians who attended the first independent women's movement conference in the USSR in 1991 got a mixed reception from other activists, and in the mid-1990s, lesbian rights were absent from women's movement groups' agendas (aside from small lesbian support organizations, one of which in Moscow got occasional media coverage: the Moscow Organization of Lesbian Literature and Art [MOLLI]). See Azhgikhina, *Propushchennyi siuzhet*, 214; Sperling, *Organizing Women in Contemporary Russia*, 27, 85.

[153] Author's fieldnotes: March of Millions, Moscow, June 12, 2012.

in a square across the street from Kazan Cathedral dressed in a bridal gown, one eye blackened (as if from a premarital punch), with her arm in a sling. In this guise, Zamoiskaia approached passersby to collect signatures on a petition to pass a law against domestic violence. Two other activists held a red and yellow banner addressed to Russia's parliament, reading "Deputies! We demand a law against domestic violence." In addition to stressing the need for legislation, the Petersburg activists' protest undermined the notion of the ideal traditional family, arguing that marriages fitting into the traditional gender schema could and did cover up violence. This included violence against LGBT and transgendered children, a topic rarely discussed, but captured on a poster: "A 'correct' family is a patriarchal hell for LGBT children: beatings, humiliation, house arrest, attempted rape, blackmail, murder, isolation. Stop homophobia and transphobia." Another poster featured an image of Rosie the Riveter and her muscular bicep, with the words, "Enough praying: defend yourself!" Such situations were pithily summarized on a poster: "Sometimes the home is the most dangerous place."[154]

Moscow's Feminist Initiative celebrated the holiday with an unauthorized street-art performance about women's rights, focusing on gender norms and woman's choice of clothes. Told by city authorities that there simply were no available spaces in the city for a small demonstration on July 8, the activists nonetheless had no trouble finding a spot in Bolotnaia Square for their protest. Three women dressed in ways often targeted by societal judgment—one in a midriff-revealing outfit with a pink wig, another in more traditionally "masculine" garb (jeans, a long-sleeved blouse, and a tie), and a third fully covered, in hijab—enacted skits making an "ironic commentary on gender stereotypes" and raised posters declaring: "Don't teach us how to dress, teach them not to rape!," "All women are real women," and "They judge us differently but rape us the same way."[155] Every woman, the organizers explained, "has the right to her own personal choice—how to dress, what parts of her body to reveal, and what parts to hide." Women's sartorial selections, "whether a miniskirt or hijab," constitute neither an "invitation to insults" nor a justification for sexual violence. How a woman dresses is nothing more than "her own business!" Leaflets offered to people strolling in the park critiqued the ironic proclamation of "Family" Day, given that traditional patriarchal family propaganda had little in common with some of the real facts of Russian family life: 5.6 million women

---

[154] Rosovi_bint, "07 iiulia 2012. Piket protiv nasiliia v sem'e," July 10, 2012, http://rosovi-bint.livejournal.com/118002.html; MFG Admin, "Feministkie pikety v 'Den' sem'i, liubvi i vernosti' proshli 7 i 8 iiulia v Moskve i Sankt-Peterburge," July 9, 2012, http://bit.ly/10EzMVj.
[155] "Moskovskie feministki otprazdnovali Den' Sem'i, Liubvi i Vernosti," July 9, 2012, http://radical-fem-msk.livejournal.com/11310.html; MFG admin, "Feministkie pikety v 'Den' sem'i, liubvi i vernosti' proshli 7 i 8 iiulia v Moskve i Sankt-Peterburge."

headed single-parent households; "loyalty" had failed to prevent men from infecting their wives with HIV; and the state refused to allow same-sex couples and unmarried couples to adopt any of the 650,000 orphans registered in 2012. Rather than blaming the demographic crisis on "western propaganda and the imposition of liberal values," the feminists suggested, the state and Church should stop ignoring the real obstacles to childbearing created by state- and Church-endorsed gender norms: the financial need for women to work outside the home plus the exhausting expectation that women will also perform the lion's share of household labor; miserly child welfare benefits; no protection for women from domestic abuse; the refusal to validate "alternative" family models, and so on.[156]

As societal attention to "feminism" waned in the wake of Pussy Riot's trial and sentencing in mid-August 2012, Russia's small groups of feminists persisted in their protests for abortion rights, against violence targeting women, and against proposed national legislation banning homosexual "propaganda." Continuing their opposition to the regime's pro-natalist agenda (backed wholeheartedly by Russian Orthodox Church spokesmen), on September 26, 2012 the MRF marked World Contraception Day by stenciling graffiti on sidewalks declaring, "Abortion is our right!" Pedestrians also encountered sarcastic reproductive-rights themed entreaties such as, "Give birth—the Church needs slaves" (a variation read: "Give birth—the state needs slaves!"), and a prophylactic suggestion: "Introduce your guy to a condom."[157] In early December, in an echo of the pink-cross graffiti action carried out in St. Petersburg in October 2011, the Silent Territory protest in November 2010, and the initial protest motivated by Trushevskii's publicized act of rape in April 2010, MRF organized an "Action in Memory of Raped Women," placing signs and lighted candles in various locations in Moscow where rape had been committed: park benches, cars, and stairwells. Rape, the activists argued, should not be excused, and its victims should not be silenced. Instead, it should be acknowledged as a serious, violent crime "for which the perpetrators, not the victims, are found guilty."[158]

The new year promised ongoing reasons to protest. After Russia's State Duma passed an initial version of a national law banning "homosexual propaganda" in January 2013, the Feminist Initiative organized a graffiti campaign in Moscow, responding with their own "propaganda" in favor of individual

---

[156] "Moskovskie feministki otprazdnovali Den' Sem'i, Liubvi i Vernosti."

[157] "Noch'. Ulitsa. Vsemirnyi den' kontratseptsii," September 30, 2012, http://radical-fem-msk.livejournal.com/12154.html.

[158] "Aktsiia Pamiati iznasilovannykh zhenshchin," December 3, 2012, http://radical-fem-msk.livejournal.com/13865.html.

freedom, rather than the imposition of conformity justified by traditional gender norms. Stenciled depictions of a young female couple appeared on buildings' outer walls, captioned: "If your guy is an asshole (mudak), live with a girlfriend! There's nothing bad about propaganda." In the drawing, the women appear happy and romantically close; one is affectionately kissing the other on the cheek. The Feminist Initiative's campaign criticized the devaluation of relationships between women (compared to the usual treatment of "normative heterosexual relationships") and objected to the default propaganda for heterosexuality that was taught in schools, advertisements, books, movies, and the media. These default messages endorsed "a single image" of heterosexual, patriarchal family structures and practices that inevitably entailed "love between a man and a woman, marriage, and children."

Drawing a link between normative heterosexuality and sexism, the Feminist Initiative explained:

> And of course, the woman in such a union is subordinate to the man. We are told that only this can be considered happiness and social success. Any departures from this standard are silenced, or, when they're not silenced, they're devalued, laughed at, and scorned. You're not romantically involved?—That's bad! You want a divorce?—Awful! You're in love with someone of your own gender?—A perversion! You don't want to have children?—Madness![159]

Rather than trying to fit the mold of heterosexual family norms as LGBT activists had traditionally done (in campaigns for gay marriage rights, for instance), the Feminist Initiative supported multiple ways of life and the pursuit of happiness and "will continue to propagandize our values: freedom, respect, and humanity." Making another link between the state's endorsement of gender norms and the regime's disdain for democracy, the activists declared that the state's "real goal" in banning public evidence of homosexuality was to "control citizens' sexuality—a true sign of totalitarianism. Because it is the deprivation of the most fundamental freedom—the right to one's own personality and body."[160]

The idea of free choice underlay many of these feminist protests: the choice to leave a violent relationship, to make one's own reproductive choices, and to choose one's sex partners, clothes, behaviors, gendered "performance" and identity. While the political aspect of some of these choices had to do with the

---

[159] MFG admin, "Soprotivlenie gomofobnomu zakonu: radikal'nyi analiz," January 27, 2013, http://ravnopravka.ru/2013/01/1785/.
[160] Ibid.

right to privacy (though it was phrased as autonomy—"her own business!"—rather than "privacy," a word missing from the Russian language), it also concerned democratic decision-making. In a variety of ways, these small feminist protests expressed the notion that individuals should have the power to make the decisions that affect them. Moreover, that decision-making power, to be made real, must occur in the presence of information about multiple options, enabling the freest possible choice. In essence, feminist protest on these issues was a demand for radical democracy. In that light, the state's role should be to create space for and protect these choices, not to punish or limit them with homophobic legislation, abortion restrictions, and an absence of the most fundamental protections for women living with domestic violence.

At the core of these protests also lay Russian feminists' effort to point out that society and the state were punishing people for violating gender norms, such as wanting the right to abortion and reproductive choice (or to live in intentionally child-free relationships), rather than fulfilling the religious and state expectation to be fruitful and multiply; wanting the right to leave an abusive relationship rather than to be subservient; or wanting to express any gender identity irrespective of its conformity with biological sex or a range of identities. As one of the post-election rally slogans had it in 2011, "Feminism is freedom of choice." Gender norms, as feminists explained, were socially constructed, not biologically determined, and should not serve to limit the fulfillment of men's or women's individual desires and life paths.

As Putin wrapped up his first decade in office and embarked upon a second one, feminists in Russia were busy. Sexism was ubiquitous, the enforcement of gender norms was rampant, the sexualization of Russian politics (itself also relying on the strict delineation of masculinity and femininity) was striking. While they could and did protest against these trends, Russia's feminists also analyzed them. The next section presents some explanations for why these phenomena took on importance in Russia in the Putin era.

Feminist Explanations for Sexism, the Enforcement of Gender Norms, and the Sexualization of Politics in Russia: Regime Legitimation

From the "Happy Birthday, Mr. Putin" calendar, on the one hand, to the sexist, homophobic, gender-norm-embracing statements on the part of the state, Church, and various political figures, on the other, Russia's feminists saw the widespread endorsement of gender norms and stereotypes as a means of reinforcing patriarchy and political power.

Asked to share their impressions of politicized efforts like the calendars and the Medvedev Girls' striptease, feminist activists generally began by labeling them as concrete embodiments of sexism, patriarchy, and gender norms. Regarding the 2011 "Rip it for Putin" campaign, the coordinator of the IGZF, Natalia Bitten, responded: "I can laugh about that as a person, but as a feminist, I know how dangerous those kinds of actions are; they are using women to do propaganda among women, propaganda for sexism and patriarchal values. It forces us to discriminate against ourselves."[161] Vera Akulova likewise regarded the "Happy Birthday, Mr. Putin" calendar as a conscious attempt to draw young people to the pro-Kremlin side by means of women's sexual objectification:

> I don't know whose idea it was to do the [birthday] calendar; I suspect that it was the Kremlin's political technologists [i.e., public relations people]. But I think that, consciously or unconsciously, the people who formulate the official policy of the Russian government make the assumption that the majority of the population, of course, has traditional values. But for the youth who want something more lively, relatively speaking—they get the sexual objectification of women.[162]

Feminists saw these productions as inherently political and, specifically, as designed to enhance the perception of Putin's masculinity:

> I remember that photo of Putin, fishing, with a naked torso, it was put out as an official photograph. And to me that was a little alarming, because, when it's all said and done, we need a "head" (golovo), not a [male] "member" (chlen)! I think so, anyway, if we're talking about the head of the government. In other situations, maybe you'd want it the other way! [Laughs][163]

> [Putin], as a man, as a soldier—he has to prove his importance, to shake his weapons in front of everyone [Chuckles]. It reminds me of the preparation for the [military] parade this year; they usually do a rehearsal, where they parade the equipment around the streets of Moscow. . . . I was struck that this year they did four or five rehearsals – a lot more than usual. That is, they had to show everyone in the whole world that we have a big, healthy—I don't know—missile (raketa).[164]

---

161 Bitten, interview by author.
162 Akulova, interview by author.
163 Bitten, interview by author.
164 Maksimova, interview by author.

From feminists' perspectives, these PR strategies emphasized the regime's use of machismo as a regrettable legitimation strategy for its highest leadership.

Machismo, in short, was a means to justify Putin's power. Asked to describe Putin's image in the mass media, Zhenia Otto explained that his macho aura was used to excuse the government's incompetence, on the one hand, and to vindicate Putin's repressive behavior, on the other:

> [He's a] bull (samets) [Laughs]. It's the only way to lend a romantic air to his rule, because the power apparatus, the repression, the [government's] inability to get any work done other than by [Putin's] hands-on management. . . . Here, one person does everything. He puts out fires for us, and test-drives cars—he does it all. And pulls amphoras out of the sea. And to justify that kind of behavior, which is clearly aggressive toward the majority of Russia's population, the only way to make this look good is to create an image for him as the alpha-male (al'fa samets), so that it's ostensibly good that he oppresses us, that he's incapable of organizing [the government's] work, and so on.[165]

The use of machismo as a political legitimation tool relied on a fairly strict division of gender norms, from heterosexuality to traditional ideas about men (associated with strength, protection, and breadwinning) and women (associated with sexual availability). Natalia Bitten saw the government's legitimation strategy as an intentional positioning of Putin, relying on women's willingness to see him as an ideal lover and, therefore, leader:

> Stalin was positioned as the "father of the peoples." He was like a universal father (vseobshchii otets). They're trying to position Putin, in my opinion, as a kind of "stud of the peoples" (ebar' narodov). In Russian, that [ebar'] is a very rude thing to say; it's the person who's having sex (zanimaetsia seksom), the man. And there are associations with it—inasmuch as in Russia, women have this tenacious dream about men—this idea is idealized. . . . The dream of that male shoulder [to lean on]. . . . And therefore, Putin is positioning himself not as the father, but as the lover, the Prince, the one you have erotic fantasies about. The Man of your Dreams.[166]

The leadership also relied on citizens' willingness to comply with the norms that helped keep the hierarchy of power in place—both gender norms and

---

[165] Otto, interview by author.
[166] Bitten, interview by author.

political norms, such as obeisance and offerings to the political leader. Tatiana E. in St. Petersburg saw Putin's birthday calendar in that light: "It's just the reproduction of the existing image of women, the traditional image, that's useful to the existing regime. . . . It doesn't change power relations; it doesn't reveal them; it just strengthens them and supports them."[167] In Moscow, Vera Akulova had a similar reaction to the calendar:

> I think it was a very natural thing, in fact. In a way, it's an indivisible aspect of the general official policy toward women. That is, the calendar and the action "Rip it for Putin" are based on the sexual objectification of women and on the notion (predstavlenie) of women as being devoted to a man who has power. I'd say it's just what one would expect.[168]

Irina Fetkulova, a psychotherapist and activist working against domestic violence, likewise saw the birthday calendar as problematic for its social implications for women in general. The willingness of a set of women to undress sent a society-wide message: "Unfortunately now, if a young woman (devushka) does it, or a group of young women, then it gets transposed onto everybody, that is, 'They're all like that.' And that's what's bad." She and another activist whom she had recruited into the organization, Mariia Tronova, agreed that the implications of women's public nudity in print were different from those for men:

> MARIIA: Consider how people react—if you see a calendar with naked male torsos, you look at them as sportsmen.
> IRINA: Yes.
> MARIIA: You perceive it differently. But when it's a naked woman, most people would think, "They're easy."[169]

In fact, a group of men from the St. Petersburg University journalism department had made a somewhat analogous calendar for the then-governor of St. Petersburg, Valentina Matvienko, a strong Putin ally. Created for April Fool's Day 2011 (shortly before Matvienko's birthday), the calendar featured a dozen young men, but lacked the degree of sexual objectification seen in its Putin-oriented predecessor. Two of the men were naked to the waist but were

[167] Tat'iana E., interview by author, St. Petersburg, June 14, 2012.

[168] Akulova, interview by author.

[169] Irina Fetkulova and Mariia Tronova, Molodezhnoe Dvizhenie "Ostanovim Nasilie," interview by author, Moscow, June 18, 2012.

not as straightforwardly offering themselves sexually to the Governor as the Putin calendar women had been. The most suggestive caption was that accompanying the photo of "Mr. March," a muscular third-year student: "Valentina Ivanovna, in the struggle against icicles, I can offer my laser."[170]

Irina Kosterina, a Moscow-based feminist sociologist, remarked that the Putin calendar had a dual motivation. While some of the enterprising young journalism students regarded the calendar as a means to draw attention to themselves and to show that they "liked Putin as a man," not as the prime minister per se, others were likely conscious participants in a public relations ploy ordered from above.[171] Several activists similarly doubted that the action reflected any sincere feelings for Putin and suspected that the calendar and other public outbursts of affection for Russia's male leaders had been purchased. As Irina Fetkulova put it: "If it's from the heart, then why advertise it like that? If a person wants to give flowers to the one he loves, he doesn't gather a bunch of people and present it to the person in Red Square, right? He just gives them."[172]

Aleksandra Kachko, a feminist graffiti artist (and ally of the National Bolshevik Party in St. Petersburg) believed that the Medvedev Girls, who had undressed to support public temperance in Moscow's Novopushkinskii Square in 2011, were paid, though she pointed out that the young women in question would have found the attention to their bodies flattering rather than humiliating or oppressive.[173] Frau Derrida, in Moscow, also believed that the public relations angle was central to such events, remarking, "Some people in the presidential administration, or whoever they hire, think that it's a normal political advertisement to hire young women (devushki) to go out with bare breasts and say how much they love Putin."[174] Political legitimation and feminine sexuality were intimately tied.

Normative conceptions of gender (masculinity and femininity) fostered by the state change over time. A member of the MFG and a moderator of the Live Journal Feministki community, Frau Derrida analyzed the interaction between political legitimation and gender norms as the Soviet and Russian political regimes themselves shifted and evolved:

---

[170] Icicles and ice dams that fall from the city's roofs, injuring and killing pedestrians, are an annual problem in St. Petersburg. Buzit, "STEP by STEB"; "Studenty SPbGU sdelali pervoaprel'skii kalendar' dlia Matvienko (foto)," April 1, 2011, http://www.rosbalt.ru/piter/2011/04/01/834965.html.

[171] Irina Kosterina, interview by author, Moscow, June 18, 2011.

[172] Fetkulova, interview by author.

[173] Kachko, interview by author.

[174] Frau Derrida, interview by author.

[Putin] needs the recognition of the electorate, so that people would
see him as the kind of person you can bring to power. And to that end,
I would say that, here, he would have to be masculine. A person who's
going to be making decisions, he should clearly look masculine.

Q. And why didn't they do that with Yeltsin, say, stressing his masculinity?

A. Probably there was some element of that. But in any case, Yeltsin
didn't have the problem of being insufficiently masculine. He was like
a heroic fighter, an oppositionist, which in and of itself provides for
that masculinity. . . . And then, times were also a little different. I
would say that back then, the Soviet Union was still close at hand,
with its notions about gender.[175]

Rather than emphasizing a strict division of gender norms, the Soviet government—rhetorically, if not in practice—had embraced the ideology of gender
equality, emphasizing, above all, the duty of all Soviet citizens to contribute to
the collective good:

In the Soviet Union, the gender [culture] was organized a little differently [from that in the West]. It wouldn't have been *comme il faut* on
the state level to accentuate the idea that women are essentially one
way, and men are essentially another way, such that a woman's job is
the home and the children, and nothing more. Of course, Soviet
women were supposed to be housewives (khoziaiki) and mothers, but
it was said that women should also work [outside the home] for the
good of society, and that's how women were supposed to fulfill themselves (samorealizuiutsia).[176]

Accordingly, under Soviet rule, less emphasis was placed on the leader's masculinity:

The way the Soviet leaders were painted, it doesn't seem to me that
they singled out that masculine element in particular. I think that the
Soviet state in and of itself was so strong that there was no need to add
some of that individual masculine strength. And also [take] into account that the *gensek* [General Secretary of the Communist Party]
didn't have to be advertised the way he would have to be in the West,
because he wasn't elected. Accordingly, there was no political technology [public relations] as such.[177]

[175] Frau Derrida, interview by author.
[176] Ibid.
[177] Ibid.

In the post-Soviet Putin era, gender norms, in Frau Derrida's conception, had become increasingly polarized along a Western model. As masculinity became a more overt legitimation tool for the regime, this required that masculinity be blatantly distinguished from femininity, enabling Putin to clearly enact his macho performance.

The polarization of gender norms had its advantages, from the state's perspective. Tatiana Grigor'eva, an activist with the IGZF, saw the strict division of gender norms as supporting several professed state policy goals:

> All our policies now that have to do with the birthrate and the rebirth of the Russian nation, the national idea—that fits in very well with the idea that women are there to raise children, while men go into the army and go into the workforce, as protectors, as breadwinners, and women maintain the domestic hearth. That's how [the authorities] are trying to solve the demographic problem and all the other problems, such as alcoholism and drug addiction. They want to kill all the flies with one blow, while not understanding the sources of these problems.[178]

THE PATRIARCHAL CHURCH-STATE NEXUS

For the Putin regime, another source of political legitimation was its increasingly strong connection with the Russian Orthodox Church, which itself rested on strictly segregated gender norms and heterosexuality. The Church and state under Putin have demonstrated a relationship of mutual reliance and apparent admiration. As Putin's presidential election in March 2012 approached, for example, Patriarch Kirill referred to Putin's previous twelve years at the apex of Russian politics as "God's miracle." For his part, while hosting a Kremlin celebration honoring the fourth anniversary of Kirill's reign as leader of the Russian Orthodox Church, Putin asserted that a "vulgar and primitive interpretation" of secularism was out of place in Russia and voiced his belief that the Church should enjoy greater influence over social welfare, education, and fostering patriotism within Russia's military forces.[179] That influence was visible in legislative policy relating to both reproductive rights and homosexuality. A self-identified "Christian politician," Vitalii Milonov, the

[178] Tat'iana Grigor'eva, IGZF, interview by author, Moscow, June 18, 2012.
[179] "Putin Opposes 'Primitive Interpretation' of Secularism," RIA Novosti, February 2, 2013, http://bit.ly/1ynH3aA; Thomas Grove, "Church Should Have More Control over Russian Life: Putin," Reuters, February 1, 2013, http://www.reuters.com/article/2013/02/01/us-russia-putin-church-idUSBRE91016F20130201.

St. Petersburg legislator from the United Russia party who had sponsored that city's homophobic law in 2012, also proposed legislation "granting full citizenship to embryos."[180] In a reversal of Soviet-era practice, under Putin the Russian state had become the Church's patron and ally, supporting laws favored by the Church and punishing perceived attacks by "neo-atheists" and artists (such as Pussy Riot) who sought to undermine Church authority.[181]

In the ideological netherworld between Soviet communism and "Western" liberalism, Russian Orthodoxy itself was increasingly seen as providing an ideological source of state legitimation.[182] A television station loyal to the Putin regime aired a film in January 2013 claiming that the Church–state nexus should not be cause for alarm, as Russian Orthodoxy was a "cornerstone of Russian statehood."[183] Whereas at a glance, it might seem as though Orthodoxy and the sexualization of politics run at cross purposes, in fact, both rely on the enforcement of gender-normative male and female behavior, including heterosexuality. In the Putin era, the state and the Church have shared an interest in promoting and sustaining clear gender norms of masculinity and femininity. The state's interest lay in promoting and sustaining gender norms to use Putin's machismo effectively as a legitimation tool, while the Church endorsed them as a means to help foster public disapproval of abortion, contraception, and homosexuality. To some extent, the agendas of the Church and state overlapped; the regime's interest in increasing the birthrate coincided rhetorically, if not empirically, with legislation restricting access to abortion, while both state budgets and religious practices found it desirable for women to perform unpaid labor in the home in exchange for minimal compensation for carrying out this "natural" feminine role. The Church appeared to want Putin's regime to remain in power, as it had been friendly to the Church (supporting anti-abortion and anti-gay initiatives), while the regime appeared to want to promote Church influence and respect, as the Church was seen as a pillar of regime support in an ideologically confused environment.

The convergence of state and Church interests was evident with regard to public opposition toward gay rights. In the absence of a recognizable "national idea," beyond overthrowing communism and resisting Western incursions on Russian state sovereignty, homosexuality has been posited as an ideological threat. Whereas in the 1990s, the Yeltsin regime largely failed to develop a

---

[180] Bennetts, "Vitaly Milonov."

[181] "NTV Sees Russian Church as Victim of Soviet-Era Style Attacks," BBC Monitoring, January 20, 2013.

[182] Charles Clover, "Putin and the Monk," *Financial Times*, January 25, 2013, http://www.ft.com/intl/cms/s/2/f2fcba3e-65be-11e2-a3db-00144feab49a.html#axzz2JNuBKxoc.

[183] "NTV Sees Russian Church as Victim of Soviet-Era Style Attacks."

"national idea" (beyond market capitalism and a militarized patriotism),[184] the Putin regime, confronted with popular displeasure over the loss of Russia's international status in the 1990s and the widespread impoverishment that accompanied capitalism, sought a new basis for ideological legitimacy. To some extent, this would be a "traditional" or conservative national ideology, relying in part on the gender-normative values embraced by Orthodoxy. In talking about the Moscow city authorities' firm opposition to gay pride events, Maria Mokhova, director of the "Sisters" rape crisis center, explained how the very notion of homosexuality threatened the state's tenuous grasp on the national ideology, rooted in traditional family values:

> There's a lot of talk about how Russia has lost its ideals. We believed that our goal was communism, that we were heading toward the bright future; we had a value system. There were children's organizations that grew up into youth organizations that turned into [Communist] Party organizations—and the goals were not contradictory. That was destroyed—and a new system hasn't been created. There are a lot of discussions about a "national idea." Where are we headed? Why? What is our country about? And one of the options is [family values]. At the political level, they say, "Let's inculcate family values. Let's talk about how we respect people and how people should unite as families, that they should have children, that they should think about the happiness of the next generation—these are good goals." But as soon as gays and lesbians appear, we encounter the fact that these family values don't work.
>
> Q. Why not? You can adopt children.
>
> A. Because they want to forbid that now. Those kinds of marriages aren't allowed here. The government doesn't accept that kind of family. That means [in the state's view] such a family can't have those values. That's one aspect. The second aspect is that only sound (polnotsennye) people can form a family. And gays and lesbians aren't sound; they are sick (bol'ny), they can't be part of society—that idea is imposed. And now it's being imposed very strongly.[185]

As the chair of the liberal Yabloko Party's Gender Caucus put it in 2010, the situation for Russia's gay-rights seekers is difficult due to the "strengthening of patriarchal, traditional attitudes supported by [the] government . . . , [which]

[184] Valerie Sperling, "The Last Refuge of a Scoundrel: Patriotism, Militarism, and the Russian National Idea," *Nations and Nationalism* 9, no. 2 (2003): 235–253.
[185] Mariia Mokhova, Sestry, interview by author, Moscow, June 9, 2012.

relies to a significant extent on Orthodoxy as a state religion, and openly demonstrates it."[186] With the passage of regional laws banning "homosexual propaganda" in 2012 and a national law passed in 2013, the joint Church–state campaign seems to have borne its desired fruit.

Several feminist activists remarked on the confluence between the interests of the Russian Orthodox Church and the Russian state leadership and their shared reliance on gender norms as a necessary basis for the achievement of their goals. One such point of common interest was demographic issues and reproductive rights, where the state sought to increase the population and, for religious reasons, the Church favored outlawing abortion and even contraception. Recalling Putin's verbal assault on the opposition protesters following the surge of tens of thousands of protesters on Moscow's streets following the December 2011 parliamentary elections, Natalia Bitten lent insight into Putin's choice of words, helping to explain why he called the protesters "condoms": "Inasmuch as they're fighting now to increase the birthrate, all those Orthodox are also against contraception, speaking out against contraception. [Putin] was alluding to that as well, speaking out against condoms. You get the feeling that, in reality, they don't need the demographics [birth rate]; they need an excuse to make the regime harsher, and they're starting with women."[187]

Others echoed Bitten's belief that the Church and regime had a common patriarchal interest in suppressing women's activism. As Elena Maksimova, of MRF, explained, this was particularly obvious in the treatment of Pussy Riot:

> I understand full well that they were jailed because they were women. I see it precisely in that light, because our ROC [Russian Orthodox Church] is thoroughly convinced that women should sit at home wearing long skirts, with their eyes downcast. And when a woman tries to shout something—and it doesn't matter at all what it is that she's going to shout about—she has to be clapped in prison (upech'), she has to be put away somewhere. So that she would be punished for having the audacity (naglost') to raise her head. This is the very confluence of the power of the Church and the power of the state; it's all merging, all that fascism from above, breaking out all over [us]. [Sighs][188]

---

[186] Galina Mikhaleva, "V Rossii eshche ochen' sil'ny ostatki tiuremnoi kul'tury, kak i ostatki stalinizma," *Znak Ravenstvo* 10 (September 2010): 12.

[187] Bitten, interview by author.

[188] Maksimova, interview by author.

The sexualized image of women (seen in the various pro-Putin actions earlier discussed) might appear to have little in common with the more conservative homemaker image endorsed by the Russian Orthodox Church. But the female sexualized image and the female reproductive image are not wholly disconnected. Anastasiia Khodyreva, a feminist activist in St. Petersburg, saw them as linked in affirming the norm of women's service:

> What's happening isn't anything out of the ordinary; it's the typical image of women being used to provide a service (obsluzhivaiushchie). ... That's clearly so simplistic—someone could phrase this better than I could. For me, on a subconscious level, I can simply see what's going on: It's the use of traditional feminine and masculine images, and the feminine image, as always, is about providing a service. Which gives you a very clear idea of what the role of women is in our traditional Orthodox Russian society. A woman now is something that should only serve (obsluzhivat') and reproduce, which is currently one of the main trends [here].[189]

Maksimova saw a related connection between the insistence on "traditional" family values, the prevalence of sexualization, and political authoritarianism:

> If before, the [Communist] Party was the basis for morality, then now, we have these *traditional* values. And traditional values and a traditional church means a traditional *family*, which means—I think that even they themselves couldn't explain what a traditional family is; they have some kind of a myth in their heads. That is, it's all of a piece. It's power, it's this standard, patriarchal power, it's violence; it can keep its hold only when it's got someone to dominate, and it carries out that domination via sex, via the family, by suppressing any freedoms of sexual self-expression and nontraditional families. That's the easiest way to rule the citizenry. That's on the one hand. And on the other hand, the more you strip down that image of women as accessible (podatlivyi), as someone who can be used by everyone, with a bunch of sexist advertising all around, saying that a woman should give it to absolutely everyone and that men should want absolutely all of it—again, it distracts people from politics, to the point of, "Well, I'll go look at some porn films," to jerk off or something, because everyone's got hormones coming out of their ears. ... It's easiest to rule the masses by ruling their sexuality. But for that, you need women to be of

[189] Khodyreva, interview by author.

a particular kind, so that they serve and cater to the males' sexual desires (seksual'nosti samtsov). It's like in fascist Germany; it's the same, except that they're not giving us cradles (liul'ki), and [they're not giving] the soldiers leave [to encourage the birth rate].[190]

Whether in the home as the mother to multiple children or pictured on an erotic calendar, women were supposed to be catering to men.

This notion of women's service fits with the Church's ideology, where women serve through reproduction and obedience, as well as with the state's legitimation model, where women also serve through reproduction and obedience and in addition make possible the female legitimation of regime masculinity. In this sense, pro-Kremlin activism by women was not problematic, as long as it continued to serve the regime's interests. Opposition women, however, from Oborona to Pussy Riot, refused to serve the state correctly (they were speaking out in public as regime critics), and feminist activists refused to "serve" in general (protesting for reproductive rights and asserting control over their own bodies, for example). Anti-regime Oborona activist Mariia Savel'eva, at 26, married to another activist and considering the prospect of trying to get pregnant, noted that her activism (which required her beloved protest activity of crawling on large buildings' roofs to hang banners, as well as the undesirable aftermath, which entailed risking arrests and beatings) was generally incompatible with pregnancy.[191] "Protest femininity" in that sense required violation of the feminine gender norm of service-provision.

For the regime, however, feminism – or what the regime saw as feminism – was the worst offender of all. Since both state and Church supported the notion of women's service (as reproductive or sexual objects), both required conformity with gender norms and thus attacked feminism, which critiqued the root of this legitimation strategy.

Feminism: Anathema to Church and State

The concurrent interests of the Russian Orthodox Church hierarchy and the Putin regime were nowhere more evident than in the prosecution of the Pussy Riot case. Within several weeks of the February 21, 2012 incident at the Cathedral of Christ the Savior, three of the alleged performers were arrested. The young women remained in jail until their trial began at the end of July, having

[190] Maksimova, interview by author.
[191] Mariia Savel'eva, Oborona, interview by author, Moscow, June 8, 2011.

been denied bail and told that their detention was for their own safety.[192] The trial concluded on August 17, when they were sentenced to two-year prison terms in women's "corrective labor" colonies, no easy regime.[193] According to a letter written from their detention cells, the singers claimed that their arrest had come as the result of a personal request from Patriarch Kirill to Putin:

> The problems began after the video of our punk-prayer was published, when the entire Orthodox world saw how heatedly one could ask the Mother of God to get rid of the earthly tsar who is hated by everyone. . . . After that, according to the story that was repeated in government circles, the Patriarch called Putin and the then-head of the Moscow police, General Kolokol'tsev, asking that those who had so loudly rebuked him, the Patriarch, for believing in Putin himself more than in God, and [who did so] in a space entrusted to him, be taught a proper lesson.[194]

The confluence of the Russian state and the Orthodox Church, having been foregrounded in Pussy Riot's "punk prayer," became weirdly obvious in the course of the band's prosecution. At several points during the trial, it was unclear whether the defendants were being tried under secular law or the strictures of Church canon. Initially, the prosecution sought to convict the performers under two articles of the seventh-century Quinisext Council, which forbade entry (except for ordained clergy) into the area of the Church where the young women had trespassed. Because Russia is governed by secular law, the judge could hardly find Pussy Riot guilty of violating the Quinisext Council's rules. Yet, in something of a compromise, the sentence did "cite as expert opinion the fourth-century Council of Laodicea," which ruled that the solea and ambo bore "special religious significance for believers," bolstering the case that Pussy Riot's action in the Cathedral had been motivated by religious hatred, as the prosecution claimed.[195] Making that connection more concrete was a piece of legislation proposed by Putin's United Russia party in 2012 that sought to impose jail terms of up to three years on those convicted of offending religious believers' feelings.[196]

---

[192] Victor Davidoff, "The Witch Hunt against Pussy Riot," *The Moscow Times*, June 25, 2012, http://www.themoscowtimes.com/opinion/article/the-witch-hunt-against-pussy-riot/460968.html.

[193] Galina Stolyarova, "Not a Pretty Picture," January 31, 2013, http://www.tol.org/client/article/23576-russia-prison-women.html.

[194] Kichanova, *Pussi Raiot*, 24. Translation is mine.

[195] Clover, "Putin and the Monk."

[196] Grove, "Church Should Have More Control over Russian Life."

Interviewed in June 2012, ten of eleven feminist activists (and two gender sociologists) who offered explanations for the state's strong adverse reaction to Pussy Riot following the group's "punk prayer" in the Cathedral, believed that the Russian Orthodox Church had played a role—directly or indirectly—in the government's choice to imprison the three young women who allegedly took part in the action.[197] Several interviewees thought that the main issue had been the women's outspoken criticism of Putin (even before their action in the Cathedral), both as members of Pussy Riot and as affiliates of the political art group Voina. In their view, the widely expressed outrage over the ostensible offense to Orthodox believers' feelings was largely an excuse for an arrest that served the government's interest.[198] Arresting the young women was a way to threaten the opposition without risking the kind of mass disturbances that could result from the imprisonment of better-known male opposition leaders such as the Left Front's Sergei Udal'tsov or the anti-corruption blogger, lawyer, and political activist, Aleksei Navalny.[199] In that sense, the young women were simply "convenient targets" of the regime's wrath; the three unknown and marginal Pussy Riot members were "on hand," and had insulted both the state's and the Church's leadership.[200] The state chose to make an example of them, hoping to win the allegiance of Church supporters in the process (74 percent of Russians polled in December 2012 identified as Russian Orthodox, though far fewer attended church on a regular basis).[201]

For seven interviewees, the connection between the Church and the government was key to the state's reaction. In their song lyrics, Pussy Riot had certainly highlighted the connection between the regime and the Church, referring to "their biggest saint" as the "head of the KGB" and, even more pointedly, declaiming the Patriarch's belief in Putin (rather than in God).[202] It would hardly have been possible to offend the two most powerful individuals in the country—the Patriarch and the president—more. As Vera Akulova put it: "[Pussy Riot's] sharp critique of the fusion of the government and the [Church] hit the sore spot. Because they said what everyone was thinking. And

---

[197] One interviewee saw a "hysterical aspect" to their harsh treatment, believing that if Putin were a more "balanced and calm person, he would have had the political will to let the young women (devushki) go free, to say 'enough already.'" Mokhova, interview by author.

[198] Nadia Plungian, interview by author; Morozova, interview by author.

[199] Bitten, interview by author.

[200] Mikhaleva, interview by author.

[201] Kristen Blyth, "Religious Radicalism in Russia: Hell, Heaven and the State," *The Moscow News*, February 4, 2013, http://www.themoscownews.com/russia/20130204/191202860/Religious-radicalism-in-Russia-hell-heaven-and-the-state.html.

[202] Matveeva, "Pank-moleben 'Bogoroditsa, Putina progoni' Pussy Riot v Khrame."

judging by the harshness of the repression [against them], you can see the degree to which that critique was painful."[203]

Anna Temkina, a gender sociologist at the European University of St. Petersburg, agreed. By highlighting the growing influence of the Church on the state, Pussy Riot had "revealed one of the sharpest contradictions." Despite the state's nominal secularism, the regime relied upon Church support, and Pussy Riot had called the question:

> They were punished because the government needs the [Russian Orthodox Church's] resources; it needs people, it needs an ideology. And the Church wants to—and does—affect gender policy, such as on the legislation restricting abortion. And that connection, and the influence of the Church, had not been so obvious until Pussy Riot did their action in the Cathedral. And after it, after their arrest, a lot of people started saying, "You have to let them out," and talking about the ties between the state and the Church, and the Church's influence on the state.[204]

By arresting, jailing, and sentencing the performers to two years in prison—arguing primarily that their action had been intended to offend Orthodox believers, rather than to take some kind of political position—the regime calculated that it would gain political support for Putin from the country's Orthodox (and sympathetic) community.

The Church, too, needed a reputational lift. A month after Pussy Riot's initial arrest, Patriarch Kirill had made headlines for apparently sporting a $30,000 Breguet wristwatch (later airbrushed out of a Church publicity photo—though the watch's reflection in the polished wood table remained, giving it away) and for having made a twenty million ruble fuss about dust penetrating his apartment following repairs in his neighbor's premises (the damages were awarded to the Patriarch in a Moscow court).[205] As feminist graffiti artist Aleksandra Kachko put it, the Russian Orthodox Church "lends its support to the state, and so [in exchange] the government helps the Church by arresting Pussy Riot."[206] Illustrating Patriarch Kirill's uncharitable perspective and far from ascetic way of life, Kachko created a cut-out-paper graffito of

---

[203] Akulova, interview by author.

[204] Anna Temkina, interview by author, St. Petersburg, June 14, 2012.

[205] "Former Minister Pays for 'Dusting' Patriarch's Flat," RIA Novosti, April 6, 2012, http://en.rian.ru/russia/20120406/172657429.html; Michael Schwirtz, "In Russia, a Watch Vanishes Up Kirill's Sleeve," *New York Times*, April 5, 2012, http://www.nytimes.com/2012/04/06/world/europe/in-russia-a-watch-vanishes-up-orthodox-leaders-sleeve.html?_r=0.

[206] Kachko, interview by author.

the Patriarch seated behind the wheel of a Porsche Boxster, being towed on a rope by Jesus as he carried a hefty cross on his other shoulder, and posted it on outdoor walls around St. Petersburg (and on her blog) in May 2012.[207]

In this symbiotic relationship, the Church provided an ideology and a constituency for Putin, and, in exchange for its support, the Church had gained access and influence in the policy sphere on such issues as abortion, gay rights, and religious education in schools. As Anastasiia Khodyreva at the St. Petersburg Crisis Center for Women put it, "Putin works on everything [in conjunction] with the Russian Orthodox Church; the Russian Orthodox Church works on everything with him."[208] An artistic young activist in St. Petersburg summed up the harsh treatment of Pussy Riot with regard to the mutual dependency between Church and state:

> The Russian government reacts to anything of that sort harshly because, it seems to me, they're afraid. They're afraid that they won't be able to control it. . . . With Pussy Riot, in addition to the government, there is also the Church, which is supposedly separate from the government. But in the last few years, [they've been] trying to unite the country on the grounds of Christianity. . . . In short, the Church is quite influential, including the Patriarch. And of course the Church was alarmed—and if the Church is alarmed, then the government is alarmed.[209]

The government was indeed alarmed, and its alarm had a gendered component. The young women of Pussy Riot—who had violated gender norms in a range of ways, from speaking out publicly against the regime and declaring Putin's machismo to be false, to standing on a space in the Church typically reserved for men—were forced to await their trial for five months behind bars. By contrast, an Orthodox activist, Roman Lisunov, who had punched a woman in the face at an attempted gay pride event in May 2011, was neither detained nor arrested, and the criminal case against him was closed.[210] In the regime's calculus, the "danger to society" posed by the young women of Pussy Riot apparently far outweighed that posed by Lisunov, who had upheld the regime's favored gender norms by attacking an apparent supporter of LGBT rights. A

---

[207] Rosovi_bint, "Iisus vs Gundiai," May 22, 2012, http://rosovi-bint.livejournal.com/2012/05/22/.

[208] Khodyreva, interview by author.

[209] Polina Zaslavskaia, Verkhotura, interview by author, St. Petersburg, June 14, 2012.

[210] Viktor Shenderovich, "Opasnost' dlia obshchestva," March 6, 2012, http://www.svobodanews.ru/content/article/24507039.html.

similar lack of reaction characterized the regime's response to attacks on pick-
eters protesting Pussy Riot's detention. At a picket in support of Pussy Riot in
March 2012, Aleksander Bosykh, the assistant to Vice Premier Dmitrii
Rogozin and a leader of the right-wing nationalist Congress of Russian Communities, punched a Pussy Riot supporter, videographer Taisiia Krugovykh,
in the head, while police at the scene stood by without acting to restrain him.[211]
As he later bragged (perhaps also trying to justify his violence), "A feminist
lesbian attacked me, and got it in the face."[212] In an interview following the
clash, Bosykh linked Pussy Riot's trespass into the Cathedral with efforts to
"Europeanize" Russia "in the negative sense of the word," affiliating such acts
with others like "homos' parades, the idiotic abolition of parental rights, epi-
demic feminism, and so on."[213] For her part, describing the incident, Krugovykh noted that pro-regime Nashi members on the scene (pretending to be
journalists) had also approached her and asked how she felt about "orgies" and
when the next one was scheduled.[214] This, as well as Bosykh's labeling of Krugovykh as a feminist and a lesbian, constituted efforts to undermine the authority of an anti-Kremlin activist by implying she was sexually deviant or had
violated gender norms by adopting feminism.

In a preamble to a blog post discussing feminism and the New Testament, a
blogger on the Feministki Live Journal community neatly summed up the
conflict between feminism and the Russian Orthodox Church:

> The entire 20th century in Russia and most of the world took place
> under the banner of the movement to liberate women from repres-
> sion, violence, and inequality, and for the freedom of reproductive
> choice. Currently in Russia we see the expansion of participation by
> the Church, by Orthodox clergy, and also representatives of Islam, in
> the trends in state family policy. In the press, on TV, and on the Inter-
> net, familiar faces from the Russian Orthodox Church are always
> popping up, such as Chaplin and Smirnov, and State Duma Deputy
> Milonov, who shocks the country with his pronouncements; in
> Muslim areas, situations where women are forced into a completely
> dependent way of life are becoming more and more common. All of
> them are adherents of a patriarchal, orthodox system honed under the

---

[211] Bosykh also smeared glue in Krugovykh's hair. She struck him and then received a "knock-
out" punch (and a concussion). Taisiia Krugovykh, "Kak oni b'iut," March 16, 2012, http://os.
colta.ru/art/events/details/35192/?attempt=1.

[212] Kichanova, *Pussi Raiot*, 28.

[213] "Za spravedlivost'!," March 27, 2012, http://kro-rodina.ru/all-news/207-za-spravedlivost.

[214] Krugovykh, "Kak oni b'iut."

rule of—and for the convenience of—the stronger half of human-kind, where women are assigned a secondary role, to serve the family and society. Talk is increasingly heard about women's main destiny being children and running the house, while a career, science, and any achievements not exclusively associated with the family come from evil. The church system, where only men make decisions, rejects feminism and its main goal—sex equality—as being inappropriate and not pleasing to God.[215]

For the state and the Orthodox Church, the very notion of "gender" had come to symbolize the danger of women or men asserting their individuality and refusing to abide by socially constructed sex roles and masculine and feminine norms. In 2012, in discussion of a proposed "gender equality" law, a prominent Church spokesman, archpriest Dmitrii Smirnov, equated use of the term "gender" with betraying the country's interests and (according to a summary of his remarks on a Russian feminist website) "affirmed that people's right to define their gender roles for themselves would lead to a 'blow to the birthrate' and the destruction of the institution of the family."[216]

In April 2013, in a speech to representatives of the Union of Orthodox Women of Ukraine (meeting, for some reason, in Moscow), Patriarch Kirill himself cautioned his listeners that feminism could lead to destruction of biblical proportions. A woman, the Patriarch warned, "must be focused inwards, where her children are, where her home is. . . . If this incredibly important function of women is destroyed then everything will be destroyed— the family, and, if you wish, the motherland."[217] Feminism, the Patriarch stated, "is a very dangerous phenomenon, because feminist organizations proclaim a pseudo-freedom for women, which primarily is supposed to stem from outside of marriage and the family. At the center of feminist ideology is not the family, not the raising of children, but a different women's role that often runs counter to family values." Hinting further that feminism led women to deviate from traditional gender norms, Kirill pointedly added, "It is probably no coincidence that the majority of the leaders of feminism are unmarried women." The Patriarch noted that women were perfectly capable

[215] Olga_future, "Novyi Zavet i feminizm," February 18, 2013, http://feministki.livejournal.com/2547661.html#comments.

[216] Wander Woman, "Predstavitel' RPTs v popytkakh diskreditirovat' idei gendernogo ravenstva," February 15, 2012, http://www.zafeminizm.ru/115-predstavitel-rpc-v-popytkah-diskreditirovat-idei-gendernogo-ravenstva.html.

[217] Miriam Elder, "Feminism Could Destroy Russia, Russian Orthodox Patriarch Claims," *The Guardian*, April 9, 2013, http://m.guardiannews.com/world/2013/apr/09/feminism-destroy-russia-patriarch-kirill.

of holding careers in areas like politics and business that are largely male dominated but explained that there was a right way and a wrong way for women to tread the professional path. "I must say that women have achieved great success in many professions. And that testifies to women's ability and capacity—under the right distribution of responsibility, and with the right system of priorities—to preserve her service as a wife and mother while simultaneously contributing to the community (prinosit' obshchestvennuiu pol'zu)."[218] The feminist path, with its prescription for a more equal division of labor in the home and outside of it, threatened to displace women's primary role as the "guardian of the domestic hearth, and the center of family life" and perhaps implied that men's roles and priorities were overdue for a change as well.[219]

Punishing Feminism: "The Women's Revolt Won't Be Allowed!"

If stereotypical gender norms prescribe and dictate women's subservience, on the one hand, and a clear distinction between men and women, masculinity and femininity, on the other, feminism takes the radical position that gender norms are flexible and utterly nondeterminative. From a feminist perspective, masculinity cannot be wielded as a legitimation tool politically, because it— and its counterpoint, femininity—are inherently fluid and inessential. In threatening the binary hierarchies on which patriarchy is built (strong/weak; rational/emotional; smart/dumb; decision-makers/subordinates; the public sphere/the home), where the more valued characteristics are affiliated with the masculine, feminism presents a threat not only to patriarchy but also to authoritarianism.

The relevance of feminism for the Putin regime was therefore dually striking. Feminist protests subverted both the regime's and the Church's messages about gender norms. If people failed to comply with and value these norms, then the legitimation strategy of both institutions could fail. If men and women were not clearly distinct categories, if heterosexuality was presented as one of multiple valid options, and if gender norms were questioned, then a legitimation strategy relying on machismo and feminine support (i.e., on clearly defined masculine/feminine qualities and behaviors) might break down.

---

[218] "Patriarkh Kirill schitaet feminizm ochen' opasnym iavleniem," April 9, 2013, http://www.vedomosti.ru/politics/news/2013/04/09/10955531.
[219] Ibid.

Setting aside the ambiguity of some of Pussy Riot's lyrics, the feminist demonstrations described in this chapter critiqued traditional, patriarchal gender norms and proclaimed that the alternative was as many individual different ways of being as can be imagined. Witness for instance the above-described graffiti protest by the Feminist Initiative in January 2013, which countered the typical argument for single-sex marriage (that gay couples were just like a patriarchal nuclear family, except for their sexual orientation) in favor of embracing an infinitely diverse set of arrangements. This notion of diversity was good for democracy, but bad for authoritarianism—particularly for an authoritarianism that rested in part on machismo, which required widespread acceptance of traditional gender norms and their boundaries.

The public disparagement of feminism was therefore an essential ingredient both for patriarchy and for political authority resting in part on gender norms or on a traditional gender order. Putin's machismo-laced legitimation strategy and the state's campaign to raise the birthrate were good examples of state reliance on traditional gender norms. Feminism reveals and critiques the very existence of gender norms, arguing instead that individuals must be free and unrestricted in their pursuit of self-realization, and thereby threatens the foundations of patriarchal systems. System supporters thus decried feminism thoroughly and publicly. The IGZF's annual competition for "Sexist of the Year" highlighted this fact. In February 2013, the group announced the nominees for its 2012 award, presenting a series of choice quotations and offering readers a chance to vote for the most offensive among them. First on the list came German Sterligov, a multimillionaire entrepreneur and patriotic monarchist who had initiated a media campaign against abortion in fall 2010. Interviewed on the Russia-RU television channel in December 2012, Sterligov spoke against the aforementioned proposal for a Russian law on gender equality. Along with arguing that equality in the socio-economic sphere would endanger women's health and lead to fewer births and more abortions, Sterligov voiced his belief that men were "genetically incapable" of raping modestly dressed women and that therefore female rape victims were to blame for failing to dress appropriately. In the course of the interview, Sterligov described feminists (who presumably endorsed gender equality) in strikingly unflattering terms:

> Any feminist is a wretched woman who had no luck with men. Men had no use for her; that's how it was. And that's why they [feminists] try to convince other women to be as unhappy as they are. And they try to put these foolish ideas into the heads of young, trusting girls (devchonkam), so that they won't have happiness in their lives, either. Because women are envious, especially those elderly, repulsive, filthy

feminists. [After pronouncing the word "feminists," Sterligov spits off to the side in disgust.] As many feminists as I've seen, they're all repulsive. I've never seen a single good-looking, charming feminist.[220]

Pussy Riot's trial and conviction illustrated the ruling regime's antipathy to feminism and served as a warning to those who would dare to protest in feminism's name. While the media blitz surrounding the trial focused on the growing schism between the secular and the sacred in Russian society, feminism lay silently at the center of the case. Feminists in Russia may have disagreed over whether Pussy Riot was "really" feminist, but from the regime's perspective, Pussy Riot's embrace of feminism—even if it was merely rhetorical—sat at the heart of their crime.

The prosecution attacked Pussy Riot for their feminism during the trial. On the first day of the proceedings, Liubov Sokologorskaia, the first witness for the prosecution, stated that the performers had taken to the ambo, jerked around in a "demonic" fashion and had caused her "enormous moral harm" in so doing. When, in turn, Sokologorskaia, whose job it was to mind the candleholders, icons, and blessed relics in the Cathedral, was asked by defendant Nadezhda Tolokonnikova whether "feminism" was a "dirty word" (brannoe slovo), she responded, "In the cathedral—yes."[221] Feminism was profane.

A week into the trial, Larisa Pavlova, the lawyer for the prosecution, provided another argument for regarding feminism adversely. Pavlova informed the court that feminism was "a mortal sin, like all unnatural manifestations associated with human life."[222] Pavlova also remarked on Tolokonnikova's participation in the performance-art group Voina's orgy-action in the Biological Museum: "Obscene copulation in front of everyone. This once again proves that [Tolokonnikova] had violated the law even before this." In this light, Pavlova added, the fact that a defendant's status as a parent is typically a mitigating circumstance should not be taken into account in this case. Tolokonnikova's transgression of gender norms, her engagement in sexual "deviance," and her feminism outweighed her traditional feminine status as the mother of a preschooler.[223]

Feminism was not only used as evidence against Pussy Riot at the trial but featured in the sentence itself. The band members' sentence clearly reflected the regime's antagonism to feminist ideology. Explaining that she could not

---

[220] Wander Woman, "Seksist goda-2012. Golosovanie," February 13, 2013, http://www.zafeminizm.ru/180-seksist-goda-2012-golosovanie.html.

[221] Denis Kriukov, "Pussy Riot—Sud po sushchestvu dela. Pervye tri dnia," August 6, 2012, http://echo.msk.ru/blog/kryukov/916560-echo/.

[222] Quoted in Kichanova, *Pussi Raiot*, 39.

[223] Ibid.

share the defense's supposition that the defendants simply bore no motive of enmity toward a social group (Orthodox believers), Judge Marina Syrova argued plainly that feminism lay at the root of Pussy Riot's "religious hatred." This, in turn, had motivated them to commit their criminal act of "hooliganism" in the Cathedral of Christ the Savior. The relevant portion of the sentencing document, which the judge read out loud at the end of the trial, began: "The judge sees the motive of religious hatred in the actions of the accused in the following: The accused position themselves as supporters of feminism, that is, of the movement for women's equal rights with men." After quoting the Russian Constitution's guarantee of equal rights and freedoms to all Russian citizens regardless of their sex, race, nationality, language, origin, and so forth, Syrova made the case against feminism in greater detail:

> At the present time, people who count themselves part of the feminist movement are fighting for the equality of the sexes in political, family, and sexual relationships. Affiliation with feminism in the Russian Federation is not a violation of the law or a crime. A series of religions, such as [Russian] orthodoxy, catholicism, and islam, have a religious-dogmatic basis that is incompatible with the ideas of feminism. And while feminism is not a religious teaching, its representatives are invading such spheres of social relations as ethics, norms of decorum, relations in the family, [and] sexual relations, including nontraditional [sexual relations], that were historically built on the basis of a religious worldview. In the modern world, relations between nations and peoples, between various [religious] confessions, should be built on principles of mutual respect and equality. The idea of the superiority of one [belief], and, accordingly, the inferiority and unacceptability (nepriemlemosti) of another ideology, social group, [or] religion, gives grounds for mutual animosity and hatred, for interpersonal conflictual relations.[224]

In essence, the judge suggested, when a belief (feminism, in this case) is posited as being superior to others, it creates grounds for "mutual animosity and hatred"—for which the performers were punished.

In the court's view, Pussy Riot had adopted feminism, which, by questioning and disagreeing with religious beliefs about power relations between the sexes, was, in fact, stirring up religious hatred and enmity. Feminism aimed to disrupt traditional relations in the family and gendered behavior ("norms of

---

[224] "Prigovor po delu Pussy Riot," August 21, 2012, http://www.vedomosti.ru/library/news/3115131/tekst_prigovora_po_delu_pussy_riot. The relevant passage is on page 32 of the sentencing document.

decorum"), while affirming "nontraditional sexual relations" (homosexuality) and questioning the precedence of heterosexuality. The three women arrested for the action in Moscow's Cathedral of Christ the Savior had been condemned for defying traditional gender-based power relations. Whether or not she understood it fully, in her sentence the judge made clear that feminism's danger lay precisely in its explicit questioning of gender norms and of a patriarchal hierarchy that valued masculinity over femininity.

Pussy Riot's sentence represented a complex juggling act that took into account the desires of the Church hierarchy, the presumed sentiments of Orthodox believers (some of whom averred that Pussy Riot should undergo no criminal penalty for their action), and the government's growing tendency to punish anti-Putin public statements with jail terms. Given the lack of independence of Russia's legal system from the executive branch, especially when it comes to politicized cases, it is not unreasonable to guess that, as Russian sociologist Vadim Volkov put it, "the judge understood her political role."[225] It is also plausible that the sentence had the approval of the top leadership; a few days before the sentence was announced, Putin stated that he did not think the sentence needed to be too harsh; the women then received two years out of a possible seven.[226]

Liberal oppositionists and feminist activists aside, Pussy Riot found little support for leniency among the Russian population. As the three arrested Pussy Riot members awaited trial in July 2012, 26 percent of Russians who had heard about the "punk prayer" (about 80 percent of the adult population) felt that the group's members deserved a prison sentence. Eleven percent thought that the time they had already served while awaiting trial should suffice, but 29 percent favored a sentence of forced labor. Still, much of the public appeared to have shared Pussy Riot's interpretation of the action. A total of 39 percent believed it had been directed against Putin (19 percent) or against the Church's "participation" in politics (20 percent), while 25 percent thought it had been directed against the Church and religious believers—something Pussy Riot firmly denied. Another 19 percent thought all three options were valid, with the final fifth finding it "hard to say."[227]

---

[225] Chernov, "Why Do Russian Judges Act That Way?"; M. Steven Fish, *Democracy Derailed in Russia: The Failure of Open Politics* (Cambridge: Cambridge University Press, 2005), 67; Anastasiia Kornia and Natal'ia Kostenko, "Rossiiskii sud pristrasten," *Vedomosti*, October 29, 2011, http://www.vedomosti.ru/newspaper/article/2009/10/29/217680; Ekaterina Mishina, "Prof. Ekaterina Mishina Reflects on 20th Anniversary of the Establishment of Judicial Reform in Russia: History Matters," Insitute of Modern Russia, October 24, 2011, http://bit.ly/11gtNWy.

[226] "Vladimir Putin Says Pussy Riot Should Not Be Treated Too Harshly," *The Telegraph*, August 2, 2012, http://www.telegraph.co.uk/news/worldnews/vladimir-putin/9448370/Vladimir-Putin-says-Pussy-Riot-should-not-be-treated-too-harshly.html.

[227] Levada-Tsentr, "Rossiiane o dele Pussy Riot," July 31, 2012, http://www.levada.ru/31-07-2012/rossiyane-o-dele-pussy-riot; Gessen, *Words Will Break Cement*, 159–160.

The gender normativity of the defendants continued to be contested outside the courthouse. On sentencing day, August 15, 2012, among crowds of supporters, detractors outside the court voiced their distaste for the defendants, who had failed to act in accordance with traditional femininity (setting aside the fact that two of the young women had already given birth to babies—one of the desiderata of the regime and Orthodox Church alike). While a clutch of Orthodox activists shouted, "All power comes from God," a group of Cossacks attempted to "light a bonfire 'for the witches.'"[228] A handful of violinists played classical compositions, accompanied by a sign reading "Pussy Riot—that's porn. But this is real music!" Making clear that Pussy Riot had overstepped the limits, specifically for *women's* political action, a group of young people shouted slogans: "The women's revolt won't be allowed!" and "Pussy should sit in a cell!" Approached by a police officer, one of the young men explained that he was a Molodaia Gvardiia member (the youth wing of the pro-Kremlin party, United Russia), after which they were left alone.[229]

Condemned as witches and sexual deviants who had penned pornographic songs, Pussy Riot's members were also incorrectly accused (by singer and United Russia Duma Deputy Iosif Kobzon) of having bared their breasts in the Cathedral.[230] In interviews Pussy Riot had distinguished themselves from the Ukrainian group, Femen, arguing that Femen had bought into the "normative femininity (feminnost') . . . that a young woman (devushka) should be feminine and beautiful, and should reveal her body, show everything and try to appeal to men." Although Pussy Riot, by contrast, avoided "this classic femininity" intentionally, the two groups were often compared and even mistaken for each other, as may have occurred in Kobzon's case. As one Pussy Riot member explained, "It's just that in the post-Soviet space there are so few [activist, political] radical groups who speak out, that the only thing left is to associate us with one another because we all have breasts and colorful skirts."[231] The conflation of Femen and Pussy Riot highlights a double standard about politics and gender norms. Revealing one's female body in a sexualized context in *support* of the regime—as the women in Moscow State University's journalism department did for Putin's birthday calendar or as the Medvedev Girls did with their striptease (see Chapter 3)—is treated as a display of normal (if somewhat frivolous) femininity, while doing so from an anti-regime perspective signifies deviance. Politics and gender norms interact to produce a range of outcomes. As Pussy Riot member Ekaterina Samutsevich suggested

[228] Kichanova, *Pussi Raiot*, 42.

[229] Ibid.

[230] Ibid., 28.

[231] Garadzha Matveeva, "Pussy Riot o kontserte 'Putin zassal,' feminizme i protestakh."

during the trial, "If we had sung 'Mother of God, preserve Putin!' we would not be sitting here right now."[232]

Whether naked or not, Pussy Riot's performance in the Cathedral was regarded by prominent Orthodox nationalists as a violation of the way in which women are supposed to behave. On their blog, Pussy Riot reported some of the negative—and sexualized—reactions, made in the name of Orthodoxy, to their "punk prayer." Pro-Kremlin journalist and self-described expert on religious policy issues Maksim Shevchenko[233] proposed a punishment for Pussy Riot: "I think that Orthodox women need to catch those bitches and whip them raw." Orthodox activist and journalist Egor Kholmogorov reportedly proposed that if he were in the place of the Cathedral's workers, he would have "undressed them down to their underwear, covered them in honey and tree fluff (pukh), shaved them bald, and put them out in the frost."[234] From this perspective, Pussy Riot's unfeminine behavior deserved responses that would echo the women's own gender deviance, mark them as unworthy of respect, and deprive them of the feminine attributes (such as hair and clothes) that they had symbolically renounced with their performance.

Pussy Riot's "punk prayer" took place in a religious and political context primed for scapegoat-seeking. In Russian religious-political discourse, the very concept of gender had been portrayed as synonymous with "otherness and the West, as a threat and a challenge," and this tone had crept into discussions of the amendments to the legislation on abortion and St. Petersburg's anti-gay propaganda law.[235] As Anna Temkina wrote, "The west-derived [notion of] gender and its Russian adherents [read: feminists] are blamed for declining birthrates, the high numbers of abortions, family instability, and the proclamation of minority rights."[236] As discussions about Pussy Riot's "punk prayer" mounted, the "gender" issue was thrown into high relief. Temkina described Pussy Riot's action as taking place in the context of a "conservative gender agenda," evidenced by the Duma's (repeated) refusal to consider legislation on gender equality, efforts to reduce access to abortion, and the passage of the St. Petersburg law banning homosexual propaganda. That agenda was also visible in "conservative policies supporting

[232] Kichanova, *Pussi Raiot*, 39.

[233] "Antioranzhevyi Komitet," 2012, http://anti-orange.ru/post/34.

[234] Pussy_riot, "Vyn' prezhde brevno iz tvoego glaza i togda uvidish,'" February 23, 2012, http://pussy-riot.livejournal.com/12658.html; Vladimir Abarinov, "Sviato mesto Pussy Riot," February 27, 2012, http://grani.ru/opinion/abarinov/m.195956.html; "Smeshenie Neba i preispodnei," *Vzgliad*, February 21, 2012, http://www.vz.ru/opinions/2012/2/21/563022.html.

[235] Anna Temkina, "Gendernyi vopros v sovremennoi Rossii," June 16, 2012, http://polit.ru/article/2012/06/16/gender/.

[236] Ibid.

neo-traditionalist gender relations that push mothers out of the paid labor sphere for long periods" and "increasingly stronger calls to return women to their traditional family roles."[237]

Feminism, which called upon people to see venerable sex roles as mere mutable "gender" constructions, threatened this conservative agenda. Following Pussy Riot's performance in the Church, an organization titled the Union of Orthodox Women published an announcement "against feminism" that labeled Pussy Riot's act blasphemous and the "punk prayer" an "extremist crime humiliating millions of women-believers." The Orthodox women demanded that society and the authorities react properly so as to prevent such acts from being repeated in the future.[238] According to the Union, feminism constituted a menace to "the very role and image of women," and to such characteristics of femininity as "tenderness . . . elegance . . . and self-sacrifice." Feminism also threatened "traditional family values" by promoting abortion, along with reproductive and LGBT rights. Finally, feminism was a threat to the practice of patriarchy, to "the gender stereotypes of male culture."[239] While they may well have misunderstood Pussy Riot, the Union of Orthodox Women had got feminism exactly right.

In the wake of the Pussy Riot trial, the regime took steps to link "feminism" and opposition in the popular imagination, joining them together in a devilish conspiracy to undermine the Russian Orthodox Church. In January 2013, the latest in a series of documentary films portraying opposition figures in an unflattering light was shown on a major state-run television channel and received a positive endorsement from Church spokesman Vsevolod Chaplin. The film purported to prove that a popular opposition blogger and several prominent television hosts, along with Pussy Riot and the Ukrainian group, Femen, were in cahoots in a campaign to "discredit" the Russian Orthodox Church. According to the film, Femen and Pussy Riot—neither of which got particularly ringing endorsements from Russia's young feminist activists sitting outside of the media spotlight but which were both repeatedly identified in the press as being "feminist"—were "among the most infamous manifestations of the campaign" aimed at ruining the Church's reputation. To further highlight the sexual deviance of this anti-Church cabal, the filmmakers repeated accusations of pedophilia directed at one of the oppositionists featured in the film, Rustam Adagamov.[240]

---

[237] "Chego khoteli i chego dobilis' Pussy Riot."

[238] Cited in ibid.

[239] Ibid.

[240] Jonathan Earle, "NTV Exposé Alleges Anti-Church Campaign," *The Moscow Times*, January 21, 2013, http://www.themoscowtimes.com/news/article/ntv-expos233-alleges-anti-church-campaign/474262.html.

Feminism critiqued the gender order on which the regime's legitimation strategy itself was based. This was a problem for liberals, right-wingers, and leftists as well as for pro-regime parties and the Russian Orthodox Church, which all relied to some extent on sexism and the gender hierarchy that accompanies it for their legitimation. All of these political forces, especially the regime in power, therefore had an interest in making feminism (and feminists) out to be something bad, disgraceful, dangerous, invalid, antipatriotic, abnormal, and so on. The more that feminism could be painted in that light, the harder it would be for women to recruit allies in the fight against sexism, and the harder it would be to overturn the political regime resting on the gender regime and to lay the groundwork for a more democratic society.

With Pussy Riot's adventure in the Cathedral, feminists (or what the regime tagged as feminists) had made the regime's Most Wanted List, where they joined homosexuals and opposition groups across the political spectrum from liberal to socialist to national-fascist. Pussy Riot had been punished in part for propagating an ideology that the regime identified as feminist, in part for their opposition to the regime and their lyrical threats to Putin's popular standing, and in part for the purpose of boosting Putin's reputation with conservatives. While Russia's other small feminist groups—despite their many public protests—had avoided Pussy Riot's fate, this would change in 2013, on International Women's Day, as the regime's antagonism to civic activism accelerated.

Conclusion

"The First Time, Do It for Love": Sexism, Power, and Politics under Putin

It is clear from the preceding chapters that sexism, homophobia, and stereo-typical ideas about masculinity and femininity are no strangers to the Russian political realm. Throughout the Putin era, despite their political polarization pro- and anti-regime political actors and activists, especially those in political youth organizations, have used normative ideas about femininity, masculinity, and heterosexuality as tools in their political organizing efforts to strengthen their own positions and undermine their opponents. In the foregoing, I have suggested that they do so primarily as a means of political legitimation and authority-building and that this is a particularly convenient means because of the accessibility and resonance of gender norms, given Russia's political, eco-nomic, cultural, ideological-historical, and international contexts.

The intersection of gender norms and politics is not peculiar to Russia. Gender norms—especially masculinity—have been wielded in a wide variety of countries and across historical periods as instruments of political legitima-tion. The sexualization of women's political support—a related phenomenon in the legitimation toolkit—also arises in varied types of states' political con-tests, particularly for incumbents. I have argued that while gender norms enter into political competition fairly universally where sexism and homophobia exist as spoken or unspoken cultural values, and while the presence of a strong women's movement can deter some degree of that public misogyny, a constel-lation of circumstances for the use of these tactics exists that may differ from state to state and over time. Using contemporary Russia as an in-depth case, I have sought to show that a close exploration of states where political legitima-tion strategies encompass the use of gender norms and sexualization enables us to understand more about how such norms are used as a means of reproduc-ing and contesting political power.

This chapter focuses on the broader ramifications of using gender norms to devalue opponents and recruit adherents in political contests. While it seems obvious that politics in any given country is shaped by mainstream ideas about gender, *the embodiment in politics of stereotypical gender norms and the patriarchal hierarchy on which they rest shapes citizens' perception of the public sphere and way in which political power should be distributed.* Where masculinity and femininity are strictly delineated in political discourse, where female support is sexualized, and where homosexuality and imputations of male weakness reflect a misogynist hierarchy that values the masculine over the feminine, the political arena can more easily be conceived as a place where certain types of men constitute the only legitimate rulers. Legitimate rule defined in this narrow way reinforces the idea of restricting political power to regime-supporting participants, enforcing political repression against opponents, and (naturally) limiting the peaks of the political realm to a certain stratum of men.

Because it exposes and criticizes the gender hierarchy in which masculinity is celebrated at the expense of equality and because it offers multiple ways to construe the meaning of gender identity, a feminist analytical lens helps citizens recognize (and possibly condemn) political discourses and practices rooted in gender norms and sexism. In valuing individual choices and differences over biological determinism, feminism runs counter to political legitimation strategies that rely on gender norms and the valorization of machismo in particular.[1] While a gender-norm-laden political strategy stressing the leader's machismo, for instance, can be undermined by challengers who successfully relabel the leader as unmanly, in the long run, tactics that buy into the patriarchal and heteronormative paradigm only reinforce freedom-limiting gender stereotypes, a gender hierarchy that privileges masculinity over femininity, and a limited conception of political pluralism.

In this final chapter, I consider instances of political sexualization and repression under Putin and argue that democratization has been hindered not only by concrete restrictions on political freedom but also by the infusion of gender norms into politics and the metaphorical sexualization of the electoral process. I then discuss feminist ideology as an instrument facilitating women's liberation and democratization in general and suggest that feminist activists, brandishing their critique of gender norms, are capable of curtailing authoritarian rule and inoculating the public against superficial and sexist strategies of political legitimation.

---

[1] On the dangers of biological determinism, see Andrea Dworkin, "Biological Superiority: The World's Most Dangerous and Deadly Idea," *Heresies No. 6 on Women and Violence* 2, no. 2 (Summer 1978), http://www.nostatusquo.com/ACLU/dworkin/WarZoneChaptIIID.html.

Sexualizing the Political Process: Advertising Political Monogamy

Under Putin's aegis, gender norms and sexualization have been employed in political advertising as a means of bolstering the regime in culturally familiar ways. In the lead-up to the December 2011 parliamentary elections, a public service announcement put out by the pro-Kremlin party United Russia showed a young man and woman hooking up at the polling station, entering a booth together, and then exiting in a tousled state to jointly place their ballots in the designated box. The tag line was, "Let's do it together."[2] The political acts of voting and of (heterosexual) sex were thus conflated; the voting process was sexualized.[3]

Likewise, Putin's presidential election campaign in February 2012 featured a series of advertisements put out by the pro-Kremlin youth group, Nashi, in which traditionally feminine, attractive young women were portrayed seeking medical, psychiatric, and psychic advice about how to go about "doing it for the first time." Each fresh-faced beauty expressed anxiety about the act itself, along with her desire to "do it for love," and was subsequently reassured by the relevant authority figure that she had made the right choice and would be "safe" with the man she loves and has chosen: Putin. Each woman then headed happily off to her local polling station to vote.[4] These advertisements tapped into a common heteronormative understanding of gender roles whereby women seek out male lovers to protect them (from harsh economic realities and from possible violence and sexual predation at the hands of other men).[5] Portrayed as the "toughest" public figure, Putin offered the best protection from dangers visible and invisible; women were thus "safest" affiliating themselves with him politically. As the director of the Moscow-based "Sisters"

---

[2] Bayanshik, "Davai sdelaem eto vmeste" [video], November 6, 2011, http://www.youtube.com/watch?feature=player_embedded&v=dK-nnASP7OY.

[3] As noted in chapter 2, there is precedent for describing elections in Russia in sexual terms. In 1996, promoting his own presidential candidacy, Vladimir Zhirinovskii publicly proclaimed, "Let's have group sex on June 16 [the day of the upcoming presidential election]." Quoted in Borenstein, *About That,* 64–65.

[4] Luke Allnutt, "How the Kremlin Is Using Sex to Sell Putin," February 22, 2012, http://www.rferl.org/content/how_the_kremlin_is_using_sex_to_sell_putin/24492979.html; Perviirazpolubvi, "Nevinnaia devushka khochet pervyi raz" [video], February 22, 2012, http://www.youtube.com/watch?v=VxU-WUtza9c&sns=em; Perviirazpolubvi, "Krasotka gadaet na pervyi raz" [video], February 20, 2012, http://www.youtube.com/watch?feature=player_embedded&v=Noo0lzJILaM; Perviirazpolubvi, "Otkroveniia devushki pro ee pervyi raz" [video], February 20, 2012, http://www.youtube.com/watch?feature=player_embedded&v=MbIzj21X0tU. The videos are subtitled in English.

[5] See K. R. Carter, "Should International Relations Consider Rape a Weapon of War?," 352.

Center explained, this understanding of gender roles was pervasive in Russia: "A great many women want a man to be a protector, a wall, that he'll take care of her, and so on."[6]

The Kremlin's political opponents questioned this image of Putin as Russia's only possible leader and citizens' only safe choice. Drawing on gender norms, Putin's opposition has used two means to undermine Putin's image as a desirably strong advocate for the Russian nation. The first method, discussed in Chapters 3 and 6, endeavored to deny Putin his masculine credibility by labeling him as weak and unmanly. But the opposition also attacked Putin as a masculine paragon by parodying his tough guy manner, making him out to be part of a criminal regime that operates by threats and punishments. In a video clip posted just a few days after the "Do it for love" ads that had wholeheartedly endorsed Putin as a leader and a lover, opposition activist and television personality Kseniia Sobchak played on Putin's masculine image and her own feminine vulnerability to convince viewers to draw the opposite conclusion. The clip begins with a close-up of the usually well-coiffed, pretty Sobchak looking disheveled and exhausted, with her white shirt pushed off one shoulder. She flatly notes in subdued and resigned tones that she has decided to vote for "this candidate" because the economy has improved significantly under his guidance and because, with the threat of an Orange-style revolution in Syria and Libya, this is not the time to rock the boat; everyone should unite around a single leader. As her unconvincing monologue draws to a close, the camera pans back to reveal that Sobchak has been tied to her chair with duct tape and forced to voice her support for Putin, the unnamed candidate. We watch the director approach her and announce that the take was successful. He then tapes her mouth shut, gives her a kiss on the head, and says, "Good job," over her muffled screams of protest. Two masked police officers pick up her chair and move her out of the room. In the clip, Sobchak is not voting for Putin because she wants to but because she has to.[7] He is not her imagined ideal lover, but instead, a vindictive opponent who has ordered her to be held captive, used, and then silenced completely. The clip not only parodied Putin's tough masculine image; it also intimated that he had gained and would maintain his political power through coercion, not legitimacy.

Eight months later, in October 2012, a political advertisement supporting Barack Obama's presidential campaign appeared on YouTube. Featuring Lena Dunham, the 26-year-old lead actress on the television show *Girls*, the clip clearly cribbed from the "first time" videos described above. With an earnest

[6] Mariia Mokhova, Sestry, interview by author, Moscow, June 9, 2012.

[7] "Ia golosuiu za!" [video], February 22, 2012, http://www.youtube.com/watch?feature=player_embedded&v=fxEWddT44BY.

sincerity, Dunham faces the camera and instructs viewers about how to handle their first time. "Your first time shouldn't be with just anybody. You want to do it with a great guy," Dunham says, "Someone who really cares about and understands women." Moments later, however, Dunham makes clear that the subject of her monologue is voting—and that women should select candidates who support gay marriage and women's access to birth control. The metaphor sexualizing the voting process continues, however, as she explains, "My first time voting was amazing. It was this line in the sand. Before, I was a girl, now I was a woman." With her first vote in a presidential election, Dunham lost her political virginity to Obama in 2008.[8]

These pro-Putin and pro-Obama ads exhibit a striking parallel: both rely on the same double-entendre to highlight the desirability of Putin and Obama as sexual partners and as political leaders, and both sexualized women's support for a male political leader. Yet in Dunham's version, the accent fell on making a choice between two viable candidates. A similarly choice-related message was expressed in a musical advertisement endorsing Obama's candidacy during the campaign. Lip synching Leslie Gore's 1964 hit song, "You Don't Own Me," a variety of women made the parallel between dating and voting, thereby sexualizing the latter. However, captions inserted throughout the video criticized the Republican Party for its efforts to decimate women's reproductive rights, and the song lyrics asserted the importance of individual choice ("Don't tell me what to say / Don't tell me what to do". . . "You don't own me / Don't say I can't go with other boys") rather than the Nashi-sponsored endorsement of a voting process resembling an arranged marriage.[9]

The use of sexual-cultural metaphors shapes the ways in which citizens understand politics and the rules of political engagement. From the pro-Putin perspective, the range of options in the 2012 election was limited by two threats to which Putin supporters frequently refer in their actions and rhetoric: the communicable "Orange Plague"—concerns about a Ukrainian style, democratically inclined revolution that would unseat the status quo—and the creeping danger that Russia would be "sold" to the West, as Yeltsin was widely said to have done in the 1990s. As the "Do it for love" advertisements suggested, for the pro-Kremlin forces there was really only one foreordained choice to keep Russia safe from these hazards: Putin. The joy of authoritarian political intercourse—a politics of limited choice—has been the Putin regime's ongoing message both metaphorically (with such ads) and in practice. In recent years the Russian parliament has passed a spate of laws

---

[8] BarackObamadotcom, "Lena Dunham: Your First Time" [video], October 25, 2012, http://www.youtube.com/watch?v=o6G3nwhPuR4.

[9] "'You Don't Own Me' PSA Official" [video], 2012, http://vimeo.com/51940856.

restricting political demonstrations, establishing outsized fines for participation in unauthorized protests, and forcing nongovernmental organizations that receive foreign funds to register as "foreign agents" if they engage in any political activity (including public opinion polling and organizing an LGBT film festival). The regime has also restricted citizens' choices by prosecuting political opponents on the basis of trumped up charges.[10]

State-supported homophobia has also contributed to a lack of choice and alternatives, not only in private life but also in public political life. The nationwide anti-gay propaganda law that passed on its first reading in the lower house of Russia's legislature in 2013 was endorsed by the Kremlin and by the Russian Orthodox Church authorities alike. Using unexpectedly well-informed vocabulary, the ban sought to outlaw the exposure of minors to the "propaganda of sodomy, lesbianism, bisexuality, and transgenderism," meaning that public events such as gay pride gatherings or other protests or even public displays of affection between same-sex couples could be criminalized.[11] Such legislation aimed not only to forcibly closet non-heteronormative behavior but also to squelch protest against the regime by opposition forces. As one gay activist in Moscow commented regarding the bill, the regime sought to suppress "minorities of any kind—political and religious as well as sexual."[12] The regime's message in politics as well as in gender norms (and sexual life) was uniformity, not pluralism. To reinforce that message, Russian officials openly conflated homosexuality with pedophilia. Indeed, when the Sochi Olympic games drew international attention to the propaganda law, Putin was quick to assert that gay athletes would be welcome at the Games, as long as they "stay away from the children" (ostav'te v pokoe detei).[13] Meanwhile, as the Olympics began, activists were prevented from holding an attention-garnering LGBT rights protest in the St. Petersburg subway. The plan had been to use helium balloons

---

[10] "Prokuratura: peterburgskii LGBT-kinofestival' 'Bok o bok' deistvuet kak 'inostrannyi agent,'" *Gazeta.ru*, May 8, 2013, http://www.gazeta.ru/social/news/2013/05/08/n_2898265.shtml; "Levada Pollster 'Told to Register' as Foreign Agent," *The Moscow Times*, May 7, 2013, http://www.themoscowtimes.com/news/article/levada-pollster-told-to-register-as-foreign-agent/479670.html; Lyudmila Alexandrova, "Arrests of Oppositionists, Suspected of Disorders at Rallies, Resumed," ITAR-TASS, February 21, 2013, http://www.itar-tass.com/en/c39/656986.html.

[11] Mansur Mirovalev, "Russia Moves to Enact Anti-Gay Law Nationwide," *Time*, January 21, 2013, http://world.time.com/2013/01/21/russia-moves-to-enact-anti-gay-law-nationwide/. The version signed into law in June 2013 used the general term "non-traditional sexual relations" rather than the specifics ones listed in the first version passed.

[12] Ibid.

[13] Elena Egorova, "Putin v Sochi prokommentiroval versiiu o 'gei-rastsvetke' olimpiiskoi formy," January 18, 2014, http://www.mk.ru/politics/article/2014/01/17/971861-putin-v-sochi-prokommentiroval-versiyu-o-geyrastsvetke-olimpiyskoy-formyi.html.

to hoist banners equating the Berlin 1936 Olympics to those being held in Sochi. Police got wind of the action and detained the would-be protesters outside the subway station, charging them with swearing and harassing passersby.[14] A few days earlier, it emerged that a ninth-grade girl in the Briansk region recently had been charged with propagandizing her own "nontraditional" sexuality by talking to her classmates openly about it and, in so doing, intending to "form a distorted picture of the social equivalence of traditional and non-traditional sexual relationships." While no criminal indictment was brought against her, the girl received a warning, and her name was recorded at the local Commission on Juvenile Affairs.[15] Patriarchy and political authoritarianism were in cahoots.

Feminism, with its critique of gender norms and of obligatory heteronormative behavior as well as its ideological embrace of the importance of choice could provide an antidote to the increasingly restrictive politics offered by the Putin regime but only if feminists could find the political space in which to do so. The state had already cracked down on Pussy Riot. Would the repression of other feminist groups be next?

Cracking Down on Feminism and Freedom of Speech

One young feminist in Moscow, Vera Akulova, saw antics such as the "Happy Birthday, Mr. Putin" calendar, governmental efforts to limit women's right to abortion, Putin's public reminder to a successful businesswoman not to forget her "demographic duty," and his infamous jest about rape (with regard to the Israeli president's indictment in 2007) as all of a piece. "To me, it all paints a singular picture in which the degree of women's freedom directly reflects the degree of freedom of the entire society," said Akulova, adding, "And however amusing it may be, Engels even talked about that."[16] If women's freedom was the measure of democracy, Russia under Putin was failing.

On March 8, 2013, International Women's Day, the degree of women's freedom and of the entire society was encapsulated in the outcome of an authorized protest held to mark the holiday. The Yabloko Party's Gender Caucus had obtained permission from the Moscow city authorities to hold an International

---

[14] Al'ians geteroseksualov za ravnopravie LGBT, "LGBT-aktivisty proveli 'Olimpiiskuiu' aktsiiu v Peterburge, nesmotria na protivodeistvie politsii," February 5, 2014, http://vk.com/straights_for_equality?w=wall-38905640_231797%2Fall.

[15] "Priekhali. Za gei-propagandu vpervye v Rossii nakazan rebenok (!). DOKUMENT," February 2, 2014, http://znak.com/urfo/news/2014-02-02/1017612.html.

[16] Vera Akulova, Moskovskaia Feministskaia Gruppa, interview by author, Moscow, June 6, 2012.

Women's Day rally at Novopushkinskii Square in central Moscow, whereas another group of feminist activists had been granted—and then denied—permission to conduct a march under the slogan, "Feminism Is Liberation."[17] The
organizers of the nonauthorized protest reached agreement with the Gender
Caucus to join their rally instead, and over one hundred people showed up at
Novopushkinskii Square representing a broad range of groups, from Yabloko
to LGBT organizations and left-wing groups such as Left Socialist Action and
the Committee for a Workers' International, as well as anarcho-feminists and
speakers on ecofeminism and transfeminism.[18] This might have been the largest International Women's Day protest in Moscow in the post-Soviet period.

But all did not go smoothly. Before the meeting's planned time was up,
police intervened, arresting seventeen activists and complaining that demonstrators had chanted slogans and brought signs "such as 'Feminism Is Liberation,' which had not been pre-approved."[19] Having authorized the Yabloko protest, law enforcement at the scene did not remove Yabloko's signs drawing
attention to sex discrimination; these included "Equal pay for the same job";
"Women—into power!"; "Divide the housework!"; and "The ability to give
birth isn't a reason to oppress!"[20] A purple feminist banner (featuring a "woman
symbol" ankh with a fist in the middle), however, was apparently not welcome;
police bundled it into the police bus along with the arrestees.[21] Police also forbade the distribution of any written materials, announcing that leaflets would
be confiscated as protesters entered the rally area; some activists thus chose to
distribute their "Feminism Is Liberation" leaflets outside of the square instead.[22] The first activist arrested, Vlad Tupikin, had attempted to hand out a
feminism-oriented issue of his magazine, *Volia* (Will), while the rest of the

---

[17] StreetFem, "Segodnia v Moskve proshel edinstvennyi feministkii miting," March 8, 2013,
http://radical-fem-msk.livejournal.com/15881.html.

[18] "Miting za zhenskie prava proshel, nesmotria na zaderzhaniia," March 8, 2013, http://www.
yabloko.ru/regnews/Moscow/2013/03/08; "Moscow Police Make Arrests after Feminist Protest," RIA Novosti, March 8, 2013, http://en.rian.ru/russia/20130308/179893843/Moscow-
Police-Make-Arrests-After-Feminist-Protest.html; Tat'iana Sukhareva and Olgerta Ostrov,
"Miting 8 marta—Feminizm eto osvobozhdenie," March 8, 2013, https://www.facebook.com/
events/218586968279328/.

[19] Kathy Lally, "Russian Women's Rights Rally Broken up," *The Washington Post*, March 8, 2013,
http://www.washingtonpost.com/world/europe/russian-womens-rights-rally-broken-
up/2013/03/08/eaa4cdbc-880b-11e2-9d71-f0feafdd1394_story.html.

[20] "Miting za zhenskie prava proshel, nesmotria na zaderzhaniia."

[21] "Massovye zaderzhaniia na feministskom mitinge v Moskve," http://avtonom.org/news/
massovye-zaderzhaniya-na-feministskom-mitinge, accessed March 8, 2013.

[22] StreetFem, "Segodnia v Moskve proshel edinstvennyi feministkii miting"; StreetFem, "Listovka k mitingu 8 marta," March 8, 2013, http://radical-fem-msk.livejournal.com/16382.html.

arrestees were reportedly detained for coming to his aid.[23] Another was seized for handing out issues of the feminist 'zine *Witches Hammer* (molot ved'm), as were activists bearing anarcho-feminist flags. "As we can see," wrote a blogger on the StreetFem site (formerly titled Moscow Radical Feminists), "state repression is increasing. It's increasing to the point that you're not even allowed to be at a rally with flags and to hand out leaflets." The writer concluded with a call to "Go into the streets and say 'NO' to state violence!"[24]

Adding insult to injury, Russian Orthodox activists in the crowd threw rotten eggs and aimed squirts from urine-filled syringes at the International Women's Day rally speakers, "arguing that feminism endangers the family."[25] A male Orthodox activist being videotaped by one of many camera operators in the square explained frankly that "Eve was the first feminist," adding that "the world fell because of Eve, because of a woman" and that the Orthodox believe men and women are equal but that "a wife should be completely subservient to her husband." A small mixed-sex group of Orthodox activists in the crowd disrupted the rally, yelling, "Yabloko is the party of satanists and perverts (izvrashchentsev)!"[26]

Following the arrests, one of the organizers of the nonauthorized meeting, Tatiana Sukhareva, posted an announcement to the event's Facebook page asking people to spread information about the arrests and expressing her outrage at the regime: "It's obvious that they won't let us even open our mouths, even to express our opinion. They don't let women raise their heads. For the authorities, the word 'feminism' is like a red flag for a bull. Shame on them!"[27] This was the first time that a public rally for feminism—a sanctioned rally, no less—had been broken up, ending in arrests. In fact, it was the first crackdown on an authorized rally since May 6, 2012, when hundreds of people had been arrested while protesting Putin's third inauguration as Russian president. Since that time, in the words of one of the feminist rally's organizers, the regime had "tolerated rallies supporting political prisoners, a march against Duma deputies, a social march, the anarchists' march, the Russian March, major rallies— but cracked down on the feminist rally. I think this is telling (pokazatel'no)."[28]

---

[23] "Massovye zaderzhaniia na feministskom mitinge v Moskve."

[24] StreetFem, "Segodnia v Moskve proshel edinstvennyi feministkii miting."

[25] Lally, "Russian Women's Rights Rally Broken Up"; Wander Woman, "The 100th Anniversary of International Women's Day in Russia: Details of the Forcibly Dispersed Feminist Meeting at Novopushkinsky Park on 8th March," March 9, 2013, http://www.zafeminizm.ru/186-the-100th-anniversary-of-international-womens-day-in-russia-details-of-the-forcibly-dispersed-feminist-meeting-at-novopushkinsky-park-on-8th-march.html.

[26] For video, see "Massovye zaderzhaniia na feministskom mitinge v Moskve."

[27] Sukhareva and Ostrov, "Miting 8 marta—Feminizm eto osvobozhdenie."

[28] For a detailed account of the rally, see Shagirt, "Feministskii miting ili kak ia provela 8 marta," March 10, 2013, http://feministki.livejournal.com/2592697.html#comments.

Writing on the eve of the crackdown, Galina Mikhaleva, the chair of the Yabloko Party's Gender Caucus, penned her yearly assessment of the struggle for women's rights in Russia. While she usually found that there was little to celebrate on this annual farce of a holiday, over the previous year, in her view, the situation for women's rights had become "catastrophically worse." The period since International Women's Day in 2012 had been characterized by a "massive offensive by the most reactionary circles within the Orthodox church, supported by the ruling powers." The insistence that everyone follow Orthodox teachings, that all women be made "to wear a kerchief and be forced to bear more children—to return to their 'original role' as mothers and wives" was coming across at an increasingly high volume. There was the "Inquisition-style" prosecution of Pussy Riot. The word "feminist" had become synonymous with a neologism: *koshchunnitsa* or "female blasphemer." There was the legislation attacking homosexual propaganda, the ongoing attack on reproductive rights, the absence of progress in getting laws passed on domestic violence and the implementation of equal rights. Meanwhile, images of women in the Russian media remained confined to "mother, wife, lover, commodity." On the bright side, Mikhaleva argued, street actions by feminist groups had made those groups "more noticeable." But rather than increasing feminist influence, she feared, their activism had "increased the number of our rabid opponents and enemies among radical Church activists, nationalists, and traditionalists. And [still] we remained invisible to the government, our demands unheard." In short, the state had ignored feminists' concerns all year.[29] The police response to the rally organized by Yabloko's Gender Caucus the following day, however, suggested that the state was no longer ignoring feminism and that, for their part, feminists were ignoring neither state nor society and were trying to raise public consciousness about regime-endorsed sexism and an increasingly restrictive political realm.

Gender Norms and Political Institutions: Is the Constitution a Beautiful Woman or a Stinking Corpse?

The suppression of free assembly is one of various formal institutions of democracy that have suffered a decline since Putin's first election in March 2000. This deterioration is sometimes described in gendered terms. In August 2011, former Soviet leader Mikhail Gorbachev, critiquing the decimation of Russian democracy under Putin, asserted, "The electoral system we had was nothing

---

[29] Galina Mikhaleva, "Prazdnik 8 marta: Pir vo vremia chumy," March 7, 2013, http://www.yabloko.ru/blog/2013/03/07.

remarkable but [Putin and his team] have literally castrated it."[30] After the December 2011 protests began, even when the regime reacted by making several reforms to the political system, these were not seen as providing for a robust, virile democracy. For instance, Dmitrii Gudkov, at that time a Duma Deputy from the vaguely oppositional party A Just Russia (Spravedlivaia Rossiia) described the new rules that reintroduced voting (rather than pure appointment) for Russia's regional governors by saying, "The very idea of elections has been emasculated."[31] Gudkov was reacting to the fact that gubernatorial candidates would now need to get signatures of support from 10 percent of the elected officials in their locales. This would be a near impossibility for opposition candidates, since legislatures are dominated by the ruling United Russia party, and front-party candidates loyal to the Kremlin are sent out early on by the local governor to acquire legislators' signatures preemptively.[32] In short, potentially robustly democratic political institutions had been, in Gudkov's view, unmanned.

At the hands of pro-Kremlin youth groups, even Russia's Constitution under Putin has been demeaned and devalued by association with frivolous, sexualized femininity. In 2008, the Russian Constitution played a supporting role in a Nashi-sponsored "Miss Constitution" contest, where young women competed for the title in Moscow.[33] Nikita Borovikov, Nashi's leader at the time, elaborated on the reasoning behind the contest:

> Every brand has its own face. Sportsmen, models, actors—simply successful people. You've seen it—you recognize it right away. But there's also a brand through which the government is reflected, as in a mirror. That's the Constitution, the government's brand. And today we want to select a young woman (devushka) who's worthy of being [the Constitution's] image. . . . We want this contest to become an annual, beautiful Russian tradition.[34]

As Finnish scholar Jussi Lassila points out, from Nashi's perspective, the Russian Constitution, lacking its own image to project, required an embodiment of

[30] "Putin 'Castrated' Democracy in Russia—Gorbachev," RIA Novosti, August 18, 2011, http://en.rian.ru/russia/20110818/165906628.html.

[31] Gregory L. White, "Having Vowed Reform, Kremlin Said to Dilute It," *Wall Street Journal*, April 18, 2012, http://online.wsj.com/article/SB1000142405270230351340457735174137036 0480.html?mod=googlenews_wsj.

[32] Simon Shuster, "The Managed Democracy: A How-to-Manual from Putin's Russia," *Time*, October 15, 2012, http://world.time.com/2012/10/15/the-managed-democracy-a-how-to-manual-from-putins-russia/.

[33] Lassila, "Anticipating Ideal Youth in Putin's Russia."

[34] Ibid., pp. 220–221.

feminine beauty to represent itself.[35] One of the contest's jury members, a lawyer, Pavel Astakhov, remarked: "The image of the Constitution should be as graceful, elegant, and rich in content (soderzhatel'nyi) as these young women. One must be on friendly terms with the law of the state, but when the Constitution is such a beautiful one, it's also very pleasant to be on friendly terms [with it]."[36] The Constitution, thus personified as a woman, becomes desirable, but it does not govern the state or hold the leaders of the state accountable as it is ostensibly supposed to do. Like the young women who posed for the "Happy Birthday, Mr. Putin" calendar, the Constitution, feminized and beautified, simply reflected the machismo of the Russian executive back upon itself.

By contrast, Russia's opposition positioned the Constitution as a corpse. In a joint action held in 2009 by Oborona, My (We), and the United Civil Front, a mock funeral was conducted for the Russian Constitution, pronounced dead after its key articles guaranteeing civic rights had ceased to function.[37] On this occasion, the regime in power was accused of sexual deviance when Roman Dobrokhotov, the leader of We, suggested that the Constitution had been the victim of "political incest" since Putin's first term as president began.[38] In the opposition's eyes, the rape of the Constitution (metaphorically, a body of unspecified sex) had ended in death. The sexually deviant and violent incumbent regime was thus made out to be unfit for rule. Using the metaphor of sexual violence, opposition forces suggested that the regime could not be trusted to safeguard democracy but rather could be counted upon to violate it.

Endangering Democracy: Gender Norms, Sexualization, and Political Legitimation

Svetlana Aivazova, a political scientist and the co-leader of a feminist discussion club in Moscow in the 1990s, remarked in 1997 that feminism had given rise to a

> new understanding of democracy as not just a system of political representation or state administration, but, primarily, as a way of life [that] starts with the relationship between men and women. And if that relationship is built on a hierarchical basis, then no matter what

[35] Ibid., p. 220.

[36] Cited in ibid., 336–337.

[37] "Constitution Day Marked with Mock Funerals, Arrests," December 13, 2009, http://www.theotherrussia.org/2009/12/13/constitution-day-marked-with-mock-funerals-arrests/.

[38] Ibid.

> democratic clothes you try to dress the regime up in, it will remain, in its essence, authoritarian. Only equal partnership relations between men and women provide for a stable and sustainable democratic society.[39]

Under Putin's leadership, Russia's political system discarded its flimsy democratic clothes, both metaphorically and literally. It found a new look in the wardrobe of Putin's masculinity, accessorized by the sexualization of women's political support. As the regime explored its new garb, it discovered that removing clothes (whether to bare Putin's chest or to reveal his female fans' lingerie) worked to boost political legitimacy for its incumbents. Indecent exposure produced decent approval ratings, even as it reinscribed an undemocratic gender hierarchy and helped direct attention away from a progressively less democratic field of political competition. Young women were being used to support and, in essence, prettify Putin's increasingly authoritarian regime with their bodies—simultaneously reinforcing political dictatorship and the repressive system of sexism.

The (hetero)sexualization of politics, which relies on a clear delineation of masculinity and femininity (and on the attendant notion that properly feminine, attractive women should love and support only properly masculine, macho men), is only one manifestation of how gender norms are used politically. Russia's increasingly nationalist and pro-natalist political establishment, together with the Russian Orthodox Church, has made use of a more conservative—but just as patriarchal—reading of gender norms that dictates women's subordination to men, and women's primary relationship to childbearing and childrearing. As we have seen, both of these intersecting interpretations of gender norms have been plied in Putin's Russia in the service of regime legitimation.

Legitimation strategies based on discrimination and hierarchy (whether grounded in racism and ethnocentrism, sexism and homophobia, classism, or any other demographic form of hierarchy) reinforce discrimination society-wide and, in something of a vicious circle, help to maintain a narrow representation of views and population groups in political power. While limited representation is characteristic of authoritarian regimes, democracies also continue to suffer the negative effects of sexism, racism, classism, and other systems of domination.

Studying the mechanisms by which power is reproduced and sustained is a critical part of dismantling any politically oppressive system. Regimes can and

[39] Azhgikhina, *Propushchennyi siuzhet*, 17; Sperling, *Organizing Women in Contemporary Russia*, 27, 127.

should be explored in their economic, political, cultural, historical, and international contexts with an eye toward analyzing the ways in which gender-normative and other stereotypes are used to justify the positions of political incumbents and their challengers. Comparing those analyses over time and space should help reveal those mechanisms and help citizens work together to understand how to undermine them without reinforcing them. As we have seen in the Russian case, using misogyny and homophobia as means of challenging an incumbent's legitimacy might temporarily seem to weaken a dictatorial regime. However, political actors using the same gender-authoritarian tools as the regime ultimately reinforce both sexism and the political repression that they seek to oppose. As Charles Blow writes, with regard to right-wingers' machismo-based attacks on Democratic Party candidates in the United States, "The problem with having your message powered by machismo is that it reveals what undergirds such a stance: misogyny and chauvinism."[40]

Much of this book has examined the way that gender norms and sexualization in the Putin era have been used to symbolically endorse or disparage political actors and policies. However, while incumbents and regime opponents may use sexualization, gender norms, and homophobia in instrumental ways to strengthen their own positions, the use of gender norms as tools of political legitimation has ramifications for the political system and polity more generally. Signifying metaphorically and concretely in the political realm that there is only one way to do things (heterosexually) and one way to behave (in line with the appropriate gender norms) likely has a deleterious effect on the way that people regard political pluralism and democracy. Emphasizing gender norms and reifying a gender hierarchy that values maleness over femaleness and values women most for their service (whether in reproduction or in their sexualized support) reinforces the idea that some should rule over others. Strict, power-driven hierarchy, however, is inimical to democracy. The gender-normative discourse that has proliferated in Russia's political realm under Putin thus bodes ill for democratic development in Russia—and in other states where the opportunity structure for misogyny is favorable and there is little to stop or restrain it ideologically.

Feminism Is Liberation: An Antidote to Authoritarian Rule

Despite the evidence brought to bear in this book, Russia is not hopelessly or permanently mired in anti-feminism and homophobia. Other states have

---

[40] Charles M. Blow, "The Masculine Mistake," *New York Times*, January 31, 2014, http://www.nytimes.com/2014/02/01/opinion/the-masculine-mistake.html?hp&rref=opinion&_r=1.

endorsed homophobia, for instance, only to renounce their previous decisions some years down the line. In 1986, the US Supreme Court case of *Bowers v. Hardwick* affirmed the criminality of oral sex between consenting homosexual adults, a decision that was reversed less than two decades later in the *Lawrence v. Texas* case (2003). In a rough parallel to the present-day homophobic laws outlawing "homosexual propaganda" in Russia, Great Britain passed a law (Section 28 of the Local Government Act of 1988) to prevent local governments from "promoting" homosexuality. This law, too, was overturned in 2003.[41]

States and societies change. However, movement away from homophobia and sexism should not be assumed to be teleological, any more than homophobia and sexism in a given society should be believed to be static or permanent. In being able to shift their governments' positions on these issues, social movements in Great Britain and the United States enjoyed certain advantages. The gay rights and feminist groups working for repeal of the homophobic law in Britain and the overturn of *Bowers v. Hardwick* in the United States were active and practiced enough to be able to increase—over almost two decades—support for gay rights in the face of state-sponsored discrimination.

Civic activists in longstanding democracies cumulatively share decades of experience mobilizing the public. The tradition of independent civic organizing in Russia, by contrast, is weak, and the gay rights groups and feminist groups that exist are tiny and lack a significant resource base. Conditions in Russia may thus be as slow—or slower—to change as they have been in longstanding democracies. As noted earlier in this book, in 2012 the city of Moscow outlawed gay pride events for the next century, while a small feminist coalition that same year held the first authorized gay rights demonstration in Moscow— a feat they accomplished by not using the word "gay" on their permit application. In short, the similarities between Russia and "consolidated democracies"[42] should not be overstated, whether we are talking about societal acceptance of feminism and the strength of homophobic sentiments or the likely duration of government policies and rhetoric that endorse strict gender norms and heteronormativity.

Perceiving sexism and homophobia in politics (and elsewhere) as problematic—and maybe just perceiving it at all—requires a particular set of analytical tools. Feminism can serve this purpose, shining a light on the

---

[41] Alex McBride, "Landmark Cases: Bowers v. Hardwick (1986)," December 2006, http://www. pbs.org/wnet/supremecourt/rights/landmark_bowers.html; "Section 28," http://en.wikipedia. org/w/index.php?title=Section_28&oldid=552693762, accessed May 3, 2013.

[42] Juan J. Linz and Alfred Stepan, *Problems of Democratic Transition and Consolidation: Southern Europe, South America, and Post-Communist Europe* (Baltimore: Johns Hopkins University Press, 1996).

ramifications of hierarchically arranged gender norms for democratic politics. For this reason, feminism and the anti-sexist notion of equal rights that it embraces constitute critical elements of democracy. This is why the presence or absence of a vocal women's movement is one of the key components of the political opportunity structure governing the degree of openly sexist politics in a given regime. As the insights of young feminist activists in Russia suggest, feminism gives citizens a lens through which to scrutinize political institutions and to recognize and resist the political authorities' oppression of societal groups— women, sexual minorities, migrants, or others who are marginalized. Continued and growing access to feminist viewpoints—conditions for which Russia's small but dedicated and active feminist groups strive—would support democratization and ultimately enable more citizens to take an interest in holding their political authorities publicly accountable for their behavior and their decisions. But feminist groups' freedom to protest in public, like that of other critics of authoritarian rule, is conditioned by the regime's decisions. Where power is hoarded, it will be difficult for feminists (or any groups that endorse an ideology inimical to the political incumbents) to raise their voices and gain influence. The use of masculinity as a vehicle for power and political legitimation can more easily, for this reason, pass unnoticed in a nondemocratic setting.

Feminists in any political context are neither fooled nor distracted when political leaders cloak themselves in the aura of traditional masculinity to justify the abuse of power. Nor do feminists accept the notion that women have no place in politics. In May 2013, a new Russian television station aimed at girls posted ads in Moscow's subway trains: a black cat with a human-hair wig and kerchief, wearing a white blouse, blue pinafore, and a red beaded necklace, states, "I'm a girl (devushka), and I don't want [to hear about] politics. I want a channel that's for me." Feminists posting about this on Live Journal's Feministki blog quickly mobilized to create stickers that could be downloaded, printed, and pasted to the offensive ads. In phrases that could serve as manifestos for the democratizing effects of feminist movements worldwide, they read:

> I'm a girl. I don't want to be interested only in dresses, makeup, and boys.
>
> I'm a girl. I can do anything.
>
> I'm a girl. I want to participate in decision-making and I'm interested in politics.
>
> I'm a girl. I will make my own choices about what I want.[43]

[43] Redvalkyria, "Telekanal 'dlia devushek,'" May 24, 2013, http://feministki.livejournal. com/2724173.html.

Appendix: Methodology

I began this project in 2009, using the Web to uncover stories of political youth activism in Russia as well as to find contact information for activists both on their organizations' websites and through their blogs and social networking pages. In June 2011, I traveled to Moscow and interviewed thirteen political youth activists (both pro- and anti-Kremlin) about their activism, their paths into politics, and the use of gender norms in their actions. Of the thirteen activists, four hailed from the pro-Putin camp (two women and two men), and nine opposed the regime (six men and three women). Activists came from three pro-Kremlin groups: *Nashi* (Ours), *Stal'* (Steel), and *Molodaia Gvardiia Edinoi Rossii* (Young Guard, the youth wing of the pro-Kremlin party United Russia), and from three liberal opposition groups: *Oborona* (Defense), *My* (We), and *Molodezhnoe Yabloko* (the youth wing of the liberal Yabloko Party).

One striking finding from my interviews in 2011 was that few activists, male or female, viewed the objectification of women (e.g., in the pro-Putin birthday calendar) as a political problem or as evidence of sexist discrimination. In part, this may have been because the Russian women's movement that reached its height in the mid-1990s had largely disintegrated since that time, meaning that there was little organized resistance to sexist assertions and behavior in the public realm.[1] Yet, in the past several years, a number of small feminist activist groups had emerged in Moscow, St. Petersburg, and elsewhere in Russia, as had a self-described feminist punk band called Pussy Riot (a handful of whose members stood up in front of the Kremlin and sang an anti-Putin anthem in January 2012, and gave an unsanctioned performance of a "punk prayer" at Moscow's most grandiose Orthodox church the next month, followed by the imprisonment of several group members).

---

[1] Sperling, *Organizing Women in Contemporary Russia*; Azhgikhina, "Proshloe i budushchee zhenskogo dvizheniia v Rossii," 110.

In June 2012, I returned to Russia to broaden my field of interviews, especially to include feminist activists. This second cohort included seventeen feminist activists (eleven in Moscow from eight different groups, plus the chair of the Gender Caucus of the liberal party, *Yabloko*, and five in St. Petersburg), and two gender studies sociologists (one in each city). The Moscow-based groups included: *Initsiativnaia Gruppa "Za Feminizm"* (Initiative Group "Pro-Feminism"), *Moskovskaia Feministskaia Gruppa* (Moscow Feminist Group), *Moskovskie Radikal'nye Feministki* (Moscow Radical Feminists), *Chainaia Gruppa* (the Tea Group), *Feministskaia Initsiativa* (Feminist Initiative), *Tsentr "Sestry"* (Sisters Center), *Kampaniia protiv ekspluatatsii i diskriminatsii zhenshchin – Komitet za Rabochii Internatsional* (Campaign against Discrimination and Exploitation of Women - Committee for a Workers' International), and *Molodezhnoe Dvizhenie "Ostanovim Nasilie"* (Youth Movement "Stop Violence"). In St. Petersburg, feminist activists largely networked with one another as individuals rather than being organized in specifically feminist groups; some of the women I interviewed worked (or volunteered) at the *Krizisnyi Tsentr dlia Zhenshchin* (Crisis Center for Women), and one was organizing a project called *FemInfoteka*, a feminist library and discussion platform; several were affiliated with other groups, including *Verkhotura* (an art collective), *Rossiiskoe Sotsialisticheskoe Dvizhenie* (Russian Socialist Movement, a fairly small left-wing organization), and the *Natsional-bol'shevistskaia partiia* (National Bolshevik Party).

Russia's young feminists were critical of the misogyny that they had encountered within left-wing political organizations (much as women in the second wave of the feminist movement in the United States had reacted to sexism in the civil rights and New Left movements)[2] and of what they saw as an almost universally sexist political environment, where homophobia and sexism were widespread in the actions and discourses of both the regime and its opposition. In these interviews, activists shared the ways they used gender analysis to make sense of their political context, as well as information about their groups and the paths they had traveled into feminist political awareness and activism.

While in Moscow, I attended the second "March of Millions" on June 12, 2012, marching largely with the LGBT (Lesbian, Gay, Bisexual, Transgendered) and Feminist contingents, and with the supporters of Pussy Riot (several of whose members were at the time in pre-trial detention; in August 2012

---

[2] See Robin Morgan, "Goodbye to All That," 1970, http://blog.fair-use.org/2007/09/29/goodbye-to-all-that-by-robin-morgan-1970/; Sara Evans, *Personal Politics: The Roots of Women's Liberation in the Civil Rights Movement & the New Left*, 1st ed. (New York: Vintage, 1980).

they would be handed two-year jail terms). In St. Petersburg I sat in on a meeting of young feminists to discuss sexism within left-wing groups. That summer I also reinterviewed three youth activists from the previous cohort (by that time two had left the anti-Kremlin group *Oborona*; another was transitioning from a leadership position in the pro-Kremlin group *Nashi* to become the head of a new political party).

The political youth activist cohort interviewed in 2011 was younger on average (a mean age of 25.5) than the feminist cohort (a mean age of 32), and their age range was smaller (19–30). Feminist activists' ages ranged from 23 to 55, but the majority (53 percent) were in their twenties, with 29 percent in their thirties, and only three activists over forty. One-quarter of the activists were married (three in the youth political activist cohort, and four in the feminist cohort), and several more in each group were in non-marital relationships with men or women. Few of the activists (14 percent overall) had children; one of the male activists in the political youth cohort had a toddler, and three of the feminist activists were raising children (ranging in age from six to twenty-two).

All of the interviews in 2011 and 2012 were conducted in Russian. In two cases, activists chose to be interviewed together (from the Youth Movement "Stop Violence"; and from the Moscow Feminist Group). The interviews ranged from thirty minutes to over two hours and were recorded. Most often, they took place in cafes, but several were conducted in people's apartments and at Yabloko Party headquarters; one took place in an interviewee's office at the Russian Public Chamber. Public parks in Moscow provided the setting for two interviews, and another transpired outdoors on a particularly sunny day in view of the Gulf of Finland in St. Petersburg. All of the interviewees were guaranteed anonymity unless they chose to opt out of it, which all of them readily did. The activists interviewed for the project thus granted permission for their words to be quoted in this book, though occasional exceptions were registered and observed.

Bibliography

"1991: Khui na Krasnoi ploshchadi: Osmolovskii." *Zapreshchennoe iskusstvo*, April 18, 1991. http://bit.ly/1jMOFR7.

"20% rossiianok khoteli by vyiti zamuzh za Vladimira Putina." October 5, 2012. http://www.levada.ru/05-10-2012/20-rossiyanok-khoteli-vyiti-zamuzh-za-vladimira-putina.

"8 maia v Moskve proidet aktsiia 'Putin pidrakhui.…'" May 8, 2013. http://www.kasparov.ru/material.php?id=518A30FA49413.

"8 marta—nash prazdnik." March 9, 2012. http://radical-fem-msk.livejournal.com/8393.html.

Abarinov, Vladimir. "Sviato mesto Pussy Riot." February 27, 2012. http://grani.ru/opinion/abarinov/m.195956.html.

Abduliaev, Nabi. "Bears and Mammoth Bones Keep Putin on TV." *The Moscow Times*, August 27, 2010. http://www.themoscowtimes.com/news/article/bears-and-mammoth-bones-keep-putin-on-tv/413788.html.

"Action!" *Net–znachit net* 2 (November 2010): 3–5.

"Action!" *Net–znachit net* 4 (March 2012): 3–4.

Addis, Michael, and Geoffrey Cohane. "Social Scientific Paradigms of Masculinity and Their Implications for Research and Practice in Men's Mental Health." *Journal of Clinical Psychology* 61, no. 6 (June 2005): 633–647.

"Aktivisty 'Molodezhnogo Iabloka' vyvesili v GUMe antiprizyvnoi banner." April 6, 2011. http://www.grani.ru/Society/m.187592.html.

"Aktivisty skandirovali: 'Doloi vlast' chekistov!'." May 8, 2013. http://www.kommersant.ru/doc/2185825.

"Aktsiia IG 'Za feminizm' protiv seksistskoi reklamy 23 oktiabria v Moskve." October 25, 2010. http://www.zafeminizm.ucoz.ru/news/akcija_ig_za_feminizm_protiv_seksistskoj_reklamy_23_oktjabrja_v_moskve/2010-10-25-4.

"Aktsiia Pamiati iznasilovannykh zhenshchin." December 3, 2012. http://radical-fem-msk.livejournal.com/13865.html.

Akulova, Vera. "Bez abortov?: Ogranichenie prava na abort—eto ne demograficheskaia politika." *Net–znachit net* 4 (March 2012): 11–14.

———. "Konformizm v protestnoi obertke?" February 27, 2012. http://os.colta.ru/art/events/details/34649/?expand=yes#expand .

Al'ians geteroseksualov za ravnopravie LGBT. "LGBT-aktivisty proveli 'Olimpiiskuiu' aktsiiu v Peterburge, nesmotria na protivodeistvie politsii." February 5, 2014. http://vk.com/straights_for_equality?w=wall-38905640_231797%2Fall.

Alaverin. "A pochitaite Golysheva." August 22, 2012. http://alaverin.livejournal.com/397696. html.

Alexander, Jeffrey. *Performance and Power*. Malden, MA: Polity, 2011.

Alexander Osipovich. "Lectures, Red-Light District at Nashi Camp." *St. Petersburg Times*, July 24, 2007. http://www.sptimes.ru/index.php?action_id=2&story_id=22425.

Alexandrova, Lyudmila. "Arrests of Oppositionists, Suspected of Disorders at Rallies, Resumed." ITAR-TASS, February 21, 2013. http://www.itar-tass.com/en/c39/656986. html.

All 2012 Senate Polls." http://www.electoral-vote.com/evp2012/Senate/Graphs/all.html, accessed April 16, 2013.

Allnutt, Luke. "How the Kremlin Is Using Sex to Sell Putin." February 22, 2012. http://www. rferl.org/content/how_the_kremlin_is_using_sex_to_sell_putin/24492979.html.

"Antioranzhevyi Komitet." 2012. http://anti-orange.ru/post/34.

Antonova, Natalia. "2011: Russia's Year in Quotes." *The MoscowNews*, December 26, 2011. http:// themoscownews.com/politics/20111226/189326055.html.ArmiaPutina. ArmiaPutina. "Armiia Putina—Konkursantka No. 1" [video], July 22, 2011. https://www.youtube.com/ watch?v=1DoEjxMKMdk&feature=relmfu.

———. "Armiia Putina: Konkursantka No. 2" [video], July 24, 2011. https://www.youtube. com/watch?v=PtmOVMQMffs&feature=relmfu.

———. "Tortik dlia Putina! Chocolate cake!" [video], October 6, 2011. https://www.youtube. com/watch?v=rVCiwYqX180.

Arnold, Chloe. "Abortion Remains Top Birth-Control Option In Russia." June 28, 2008. http://www.rferl.org/content/Abortion_Remains_Top_Birth_Control_Option_ Russia/1145849.html.

"Art-gruppa 'Voina' zatselovyvaet mentov 1 marta" [video], March 1, 2011. http://www.youtube. com/watch?v=Aa_ZUj4Vx88.

Arutunyan, Anna. "Birthday Craze Sweeps Moscow." *The Moscow News*, October 10, 2011. http://themoscownews.com/politics/20111010/189110902.html.

———. "Foreign Agents and Pollsters: Research Held Hostage?" *Moscow News*, May 27, 2013. http://themoscownews.com/news/20130527/191548967-print/Research-held-hostage.html.

———. "Politics—from Scratch." *Moscow News*, October 1, 2012. http://www.themoscownews. com/politics/20121001/190300786.html.

Atwood, Lynne. "Young People, Sex, and Sexual Identity." In *Gender, Generation and Identity in Contemporary Russia*, edited by Hilary Pilkington, 95–120. London: Routledge, 1996.

"Author's Fieldnotes: March of Millions, Moscow, June 12, 2012." June 12, 2012.

"Avianova Airlines Banned Commercial" [video], July 3, 2010. https://www.youtube.com/ watch?v=owL9OqQ00og.

"Avtoprobeg 'Za Putina!'" [video], February 19, 2012. http://www.gazeta.ru/video/politics/ my_prosto_hotim_sdelat__emu_priatno.shtml.

Azhgikhina, Nadezhda, ed. *Propushchennyi siuzhet: Istoriia novogo nezavisimogo zhenskogo dvizheniia Rossii s nachala 1990x do nashikh dnei v zerkale SMI*. Moscow: ROO: Tsentr Obshchestvennoi informatsii, 2008.

———. "Proshloe i budushchee zhenskogo dvizheniia v Rossii." In *Zhenskoe dvizhenie v Rossii: Vchera, segodnia, zavtra: Materialy konferentsii*, edited by Galina Mikhaleva, 110–111. Moscow: RODP "Yabloko" and KMK Publishers, 2010.

Baker, Peter, and Susan Glasser. *Kremlin Rising*. New York: Scribner, 2005.

Bakir, Boris. "Naval'nogo mochat chernukhoi: 'on nikogda ne skryval. . . .'" January 8, 2012. http://www.weekjournal.ru/politics/2282.htm.

Bakunin, Liubov', and Oleg Chizhova. "Veteranov vne elektorata ne predlagat'." June 22, 2011. http://www.svobodanews.ru/content/article/24243126.html.

Balashova, Iuliia. "Bezdonnyi Seliger, ili 'Ne vse doma.'" *Novaia Gazeta*, 26 2011. http:// novayagazeta.ru/data/2011/045/22.html.

Balmforth, Tom. "Putin Affirms Duma Vote in Annual Call-In Show." December 15, 2011. http://www.rferl.org/content/putin_annual_callin_tv_show/24422335.html.

BarackObamadotcom. "Lena Dunham: Your First Time" [video], October 25, 2012. http://www.youtube.com/watch?v=o6G3nwhPuR4.

Barandova, Tat'iana. "Sovremennyi etap zhenskogo dvizheniia Sankt-Peterburga: Strukturnye ogranicheniia, okna vozmozhnostei, vektory razvitiia i tochki rosta." In *Zhenskoe dvizhenie v Rossii: Vchera, segodnia, zavtra: Materialy konferentsii*, edited by Galina Mikhaleva, 73--83. Moscow, Russia: RODP "Yabloko" and KMK Publishers, 2010.

Barelypolitical. "Crush On Obama" [video], June 13, 2007. http://www.youtube.com/watch?v=wKsoXHYICqU.

———. "Super Obama Girl!" [video], January 31, 2008. http://www.youtube.com/watch?NR=1&v=AIiMa2Fe-ZQ&feature=pinned.

Barkanov, Boris. "Mercantilist Development in Russia: The Legitimacy of State Power, State Identity, and the Energy Charter Regime (1990–2010)" (PhD. diss., University of California, Berkeley, 2011).

Barry, Ellen. "Surkov, Architect of Putin's Political System, Is Reassigned." *New York Times*, December 27, 2011, http://www.nytimes.com/2011/12/28/world/europe/putin-takes-another-swipe-at-russian-protesters.html?_r=1.

Barry, Ellen, and David M. Herszenhorn. "Putins Finally Appear Together, to Announce Split." *New York Times*, June 6, 2013. http://www.nytimes.com/2013/06/07/world/europe/putins-finally-appear-together-to-announce-split.html.

Baum, Geraldine. "The Reluctant First Lady: Profile: Naina Yeltsin Is No Raisa Gorbachev, But She Is Giving the Russian People What They Expect—A Political Wife Who Is Traditional, Anonymous and Colorless." *Los Angeles Times*, June 15, 1992. http://articles.latimes.com/1992-1906-15/news/vw-405_1_raisa-gorbachev.

Bayanshik. "Davai sdelaem eto vmeste" [video], November 6, 2011. http://www.youtube.com/watch?feature=player_embedded&v=dK-nnASP7OY.

"BBC News: Russia Country Profile." March 6, 2012. http://news.bbc.co.uk/2/hi/europe/country_profiles/1102275.stm.

BBC World Service. WBUR-FM, February 25, 2013.

Belkovskii, Stanislav. "Papa ukazal put' patriarkhu." *Moskovskii Komsomolets*, February 15, 2013. http://www.mk.ru/specprojects/free-theme/article/2013/02/14/812869-papa-ukazal-put-patriarhu.html.

Belozerskikh, Veronika. "Ia protiv armii putina." *Molodezhnoe Iabloko*, July 18, 2011. http://www.yabloko.ru/blog/2011/07/18_1

"'Belye fartuki' na prospekte Sakharova." *Echo Moskvy*, April 16, 2011. http://www.echo.msk.ru/blog/echomsk/766717-echo/.

Bennetts, Marc. "Vitaly Milonov: Laying Down God's Law in Russia." RIA Novosti, August 30, 2012. http://en.rian.ru/analysis/20120830/175525037.html.

Berry, Lynn. "Putin Sends New Year's Greetings, with a Wink." December 31, 2011. http://news.yahoo.com/putin-sends-years-greetings-wink-125847229.html.

Bershidsky, Leonid. "'Curing' Homosexuality in Russia and Ukraine." Bloomberg, October 10, 2012. http://www.bloomberg.com/news/2012-10-10/-curing-homosexuality-in-russia-and-ukraine.html.

Bidder, Bendzhamin. "Krasivaia molodaia gvardiia Putina." October 5, 2011. http://newsland.com/news/detail/id/795740/.

Birnbaum, Michael. "Russian Blogger Alexei Navalny Released from Jail." *Washington Post*, December 21, 2011. http://www.washingtonpost.com/world/russian-blogger-alexei-navalny-released-from-jail/2011/12/21/gIQAiFK18O_story.html.

Bitten, Natasha. "Russia: Gender Segregation in It (Information Technology) Education: For Boys Only." September 19, 2012. http://www.zafeminizm.ru/171-russia-gender-segregation-in-it-information-technology-education-for-boys-only.html.

Blom, Ida. "Gender and Nation in International Comparison." In *Gendered Nations: Nationalisms and Gender Order in the Long Nineteenth Century*, edited by Ida Blom, Karen Hagemann, and Catherine Hall, 3–26. New York: Bloomsbury, 2000.

Bloom, Alexis. "A Man Like Putin." http://www.pbs.org/soundtracks/stories/putin/, accessed March 27, 2013.

Blow, Charles M. "The Masculine Mistake." *New York Times*, January 31, 2014. http://www.nytimes.com/2014/02/01/opinion/the-masculine-mistake.html?hp&rref=opinion&_r=1.

Blum, Douglas W. *National Identity and Globalization: Youth, State, and Society in Post-Soviet Eurasia*. Cambridge: Cambridge University Press, 2007.

Blyth, Kristen. "Religious Radicalism in Russia: Hell, Heaven and the State." *The Moscow News*, February 4, 2013. http://www.themoscownews.com/russia/20130204/191202860/Religious-radicalism-in-Russia-hell-heaven-and-the-state.html.

"The Body Politic: Women's Party Bares All on Election Poster." September 26, 2007. http://www.spiegel.de/international/europe/the-body-politic-women-s-party-bares-all-on-election-poster-a-508030.html.

Bogatova, Margarita. "Putin Visits Youth Camp on Lake Seliger." July 31, 2012. http://english.ruvr.ru/2012_07_31/Putin-visits-youth-camp-on-Lake-Seliger/.

Borenstein, Eliot. "*About That*: Deploying and Deploring Sex in Post-Soviet Russia." *Special Issue: Russian Culture of the 1990s*. Edited by Helena Goscilo. *Studies in 20th Century Literature*. 24, no. 1 (2000): 51–83.

———. *Overkill: Sex and Violence in Contemporary Russian Popular Culture*. Ithaca, NY: Cornell University Press, 2007.

Borisov, Sergey. "Youth at Seliger Camp Use Nazi Symbols to Portray Ideological Enemies." July 29, 2010. http://rt.com/politics/roar-seliger-installation-scandal/.

Brandt, Mark J. "Sexism and Gender Inequality across 57 Societies." *Psychological Science* 22, no. 11 (November 2011): 1413–1418.

Bratersky, Alexander. "Camp's Challenge Is also the Kremlin's." *The Moscow Times*, June 9, 2011. http://www.themoscowtimes.com/news/article/camps-challenge-is-also-the-kremlins/438538.html.

———. "Female Leaders Manage Mentalities." *The Moscow Times*, March 7, 2013. http://www.themoscowtimes.com/news/article/female-leaders-manage-mentalities/476634.html.

———. "Yakemenko's Departure Signals End of Era for Youth Politics." *The Moscow Times*, June 14, 2012. http://www.themoscowtimes.com/news/article/yakemenkos-departure-signals-end-of-era-for-youth-politics/460310.html#ixzz1xk4Eo3xN.

Bratersky, Alexander, Nikolaus von Twickel, and Rina Soloveitchik. "250 Held in 2nd Night of Vote Protests." *The Moscow Times*, December 6, 2011. http://www.themoscowtimes.com/news/article/250-held-in-2nd-night-of-vote-protests/449405.html.

Brauning, Eva. "Chudo-iudo ryba-Putin sgnila s golovy." Ekaterinburg News, November 28, 2009. http://www.eburgnews.ru/photoreport/1607.html.

Brener, Aleksandr. "Pervaia perchatka dokumentatsiia aktsii Moskva, Krasnaia ploshchad'." *Muzei 21 Artkladovka*, 1995. http://artkladovka.ru/ru/artists/02/brener/works/01/.

Bridge, Robert. "Pussy Riot: Hell's Angels behind the Headlines." November 27, 2012. http://rt.com/politics/pussy-riot-russia-law-putin-medvedev-696/.

Bridger, Sue, Rebecca Kay, and Kathryn Pinnick. *No More Heroines: Russia, Women and the Market*. London: Routledge, 1996.

Brius, Anna. "8 Marta: za ravnye prava i vozmozhnosti." *Net–znachit net* 3 (March 2011): 6.

———. "Baby, pedy, zhidy." *Net–znachit net* 3 (March 2011): 22–25.

"Brutal Murder Highlights Russia's Domestic Violence Problem." RIA Novosti, January 16, 2013. http://en.rian.ru/crime/20130116/178800003.html.

Bryant, Christa Case. "Nashi and the Young Guard: Two Paths toward Building Support for Putin." February 26, 2008. http://www.csmonitor.com/World/Europe/2008/0226/p13s01-woeu.html.

Bucur, Maria. *Heroes and Victims: Remembering War in Twentieth-Century Romania.* Bloomington: Indiana University Press, 2009.

Burke, Jr., John T. "A Loner Named Loughner." January 10, 2011. http://www.thecenterlane.com/?tag=sarah-palin-crosshairs.

Burkov, Anton. "Fotoreportazh s prospekta Sakharova 24 dekabria 2011 goda" [video], December 24, 2011. http://sutyajnik.ru/news/2011/12/1902.html.

Butler, Judith. *Gender Trouble: Feminism and the Subversion of Identity.* New York: Routledge, 2006.

Buzit. "STEP by STEB—Valentine Ivanovne s liubov'iu!" April 1, 2011. http://buzit.livejournal.com/55722.html.

Caiazza, Amy. *Mothers and Soldiers: Gender, Citizenship, and Civil Society in Contemporary Russia.* New York: Routledge, 2002.

Carter, K. R. "Should International Relations Consider Rape a Weapon of War?" *Politics & Gender,* no. 6 (2010): 343–371.

Cassiday, Julie A., and Emily D. Johnson. "A Personality Cult for the Modern Age: Reading Vladimir Putin's Public Persona." In *Putin as Celebrity and Cultural Icon,* edited by Helena Goscilo, 37–64. London: Routledge, 2013.

Caulfield, Philip. "Mexican Congressional Candidate Appears in Topless Billboard." *New York Daily News,* May 22, 2012. http://www.nydailynews.com/news/world/mexican-congressional-candidate-appears-topless-billboard-article-1.1082514.

Central Electoral Commission of the Russian Federation. "Svedeniia o provodiashchikhsia vyborakh i referendumakh." March 4, 2012. http://bit.ly/1md7IDz.

Center for the Study of Public Policy and the Levada Center. "Results of Previous Elections to the Russian State Duma." http://www.russiavotes.org/duma/duma_elections_93-03.php, accessed January 4, 2013.

Chauncey, George. *Gay New York: Gender, Urban Culture, and the Mak*ing of the Gay Male World, *1890–1940.* New York: Basic Books, 1994.

Chaykovskaya, Evgeniya. "UN Report Puts Russia among Leaders in Homicide Rates." *The Moscow News,* October 24, 2011. http://themoscownews.com/russia/20111024/189146825.html.

"Cheerleaders Wish Medvedev Happy Birthday." *Herald Sun,* September 14, 2011. http://www.heraldsun.com.au/news/breaking-news/cheerleaders-wish-medvedev-happy-birthday/story-e6frf7jx-1226137424712.

"Chego khoteli i chego dobilis' Pussy Riot." June 28, 2012. http://polit.ru/article/2012/04/16/discussion/.

Chernov, Sergey. "Can't Keep Silent." *St. Petersburg Times,* December 7, 2011. http://www.sptimes.ru/index.php?action_id=2&story_id=34935.

———. "Why Do Russian Judges Act That Way?" February 6, 2013. http://www.tol.org/client/article/23588-russia-judges.html.

Chernykh, Aleksandr. "The Young Guard's Word Is Being Put to the Test: Human Rights Activists Suspect the Organization of Extremism." *Kommersant,* January 14, 2011.

Chertoritskaia, Tat'iana. "U istokov zhenskoi konsolidatsii na novom etape (2007–2010)." In *Zhenskoe dvizhenie v Rossii: Vchera, segodnia, zavtra: Materialy konferentsii,* edited by Galina Mikhaleva, 56–60. Moscow: RODP "Yabloko" and KMK Publishers, 2010.

Chivers, C. J. "Putin Urges Plan to Reverse Slide in the Birth Rate." *New York Times,* May 11, 2006. http://www.nytimes.com/2006/05/11/world/europe/11russia.html.

"Church Employee Says Pussy Riot Show Has Given Her 'unceasing pain.'" Interfax, July 31, 2012. http://www.interfax-religion.com/?act=news&div=9615.

Clemons, Steve. "Not the Onion: Moscow Bans Gay Pride for Next 100 Years." *The Atlantic*, June 8, 2012. http://www.theatlantic.com/international/archive/2012/06/not-the-onion-moscow-bans-gay-pride-for-next-100-years/258296/.

Clover, Charles. "Putin and the Monk." *Financial Times*, January 25, 2013. http://www.ft.com/intl/cms/s/2/f2fcba3e-65be-11e2-a3db-00144feab49a.html#axzz2JNuBKxoc.

Cohn, Carol. "Wars, Wimps, and Women." In *Gendering War Talk*, edited by Miriam Cooke and Angela Woolacott, 227–246. Princeton, NJ: Princeton University Press, 1993.

Colton, Timothy. "Putin and the Attenuation of Russian Democracy." In *Putin's Russia*, edited by Dale Herspring, 37–52. 3rd ed. Lanham, MD: Rowman and Littlefield, 2007.

Conley Harris, William. *Queer Externalities: Hazardous Encounters in American Culture*. New York: SUNY Press, 2009.

Connell, R. W. *Masculinities*. 2nd ed. Cambridge: Polity Press, 2005.

Connell, R. W., and James W. Messerschmidt. "Hegemonic Masculinity: Rethinking the Concept." *Gender & Society* 19 (2005): 829–859.

"Constitution Day Marked with Mock Funerals, Arrests." December 13, 2009. http://www.theotherrussia.org/2009/12/13/constitution-day-marked-with-mock-funerals-arrests/.

Daucé, Françoise, and Elisabeth Sieca-Kozlowski, eds. *Dedovshchina in the Post-Soviet Military: Hazing of Russian Army Conscripts in a Comparative Perspective*. Stuttgart: *ibidem*-Verlag, 2006.

Davidoff, Victor. "Kremlin's Youth Agency Resembles Cosa Nostra." *The Moscow Times*, February 12, 2012. http://www.themoscowtimes.com/opinion/article/kremlins-youth-agency-resembles-cosa-nostra/452893.html.

———. "The Witch Hunt against Pussy Riot." *The Moscow Times*, June 25, 2012. http://www.themoscowtimes.com/opinion/article/the-witch-hunt-against-pussy-riot/460968.html.

Davis, Belinda. "Political Participation, Civil Society, and Gender: Lessons from the Cold War?" In *Women and Gender in Postwar Europe: From Cold War to European Union*, edited by Bonnie G. Smith and Joanna Regulska, 139–155. London: Routledge, 2012.

Day, Michael. "Former Italian Prime Minister Silvio Berlusconi Sentenced to a Year in Jail for Tax Fraud." *The Independent*, October 26, 2012. http://www.independent.co.uk/news/world/europe/former-italian-prime-minister-silvio-berlusconi-sentenced-to-a-year-in-jail-for-tax-fraud-8228441.html.

De Carbonnel, Alissa. "Plaudits Vie with Pensioner Jibes as Russia's Putin Turns 60." Reuters, October 7, 2012. http://www.reuters.com/article/2012/10/07/us-russia-putin-birthday-idUSBRE8940ZW20121007.

Deconde, Alexander. *Presidential Machismo: Executive Authority, Military Intervention, and Foreign Relations*. Boston: Northeastern University Press, 1999.

"Delo o rastiazhke 'Putin—pidaras': Avtor foto khochet predstat' pered sudom." April 13, 2011. http://grani.ru/Society/Media/Freepress/m.187737.html.

Demokraticheskoe dvizhenie MY. "Ustav." May 14, 2005. http://web.archive.org/web/20121010140926/http://www.wefree.ru/?id=8.

"Den' pamiati." Interfax, August 8, 2010. http://www.interfax.ru/society/txt.asp?id=148529.

"Devochki protiv prizyva" [video], May 21, 2011. http://www.youtube.com/watch?v=MDSHV-7L24k&feature=related.

"Devochki protiv prizyva (Grani-TV)" [video], May 11, 2011. http://www.youtube.com/watch?v=g39U7a2zjYk.

"Devochki za Putina" [video], July 5, 2011. http://www.youtube.com/watch?v=7TC_N9qQLJ8.

"Devochki za Putina." http://vk.com/club28392848, accessed April 17, 2013.

DevochkiZa. "Draka za Putina" [video], September 29, 2011. https://www.youtube.com/watch?v=vPvVgSOi1yg.

Dmitrieva, Mariia. "Radikal'nyi eksgibitsionizm." *Chastnyi Korrespondent*, January 6, 2011. http://www.chaskor.ru/article/radikalnyj_eksgibitsionizm_18186.

Dmitrieva, Natal'ia. "Zhenskoe dvizhenie Rossii: Sovremennoe sostoianie i potentsial rosta." In *Zhenskoe dvizhenie v Rossii: Vchera, segodnia, zavtra: Materialy konferentsii*, edited by Galina Mikhaleva, 49–52. Moscow: RODP "Yabloko" and KMK Publishers, 2010.

Dobrokhotov. "Kokainovaia provokatsiia. Lichnyi opyt." March 23, 2010. http://dobrokhotov.livejournal.com/447278.html.

Dobrokhotov, Roman. "Pochemu ia edu na Seliger." July 25, 2012. http://slon.ru/russia/pochemu_ya_edu_na_seliger-813688.xhtml.

Draitser, Emil A. *Making War Not Love: Gender and Sexuality in Russian Humor.* New York: St. Martin's Press, 1999.

Druszinin, Alexey. "Vladimir Putin's Passion for Sports." RIA Novosti. http://en.ria.ru/photolents/20121007/176420498.htm, accessed April 16, 2013.

"Dva gondona!!!" http://pikabu.ru/story/dva_gondona_639316, accessed April 16, 2013.

"Dvizhenie 'My' poneset na Lubianku shpionskie kamni." February 2, 2006. http://y.tagora.grani.ru/Politics/Russia/activism/m.101439.html.

Dvizhenie Stal.' "V Moskve proshel 'Marsh barabanshchikov,'" December 6, 2011. http://madeof-steel.ru/news/cat/Drugie_36/nov_V_Moskve_proshel_Marsh_barabanshchikov_998.

Dvoinova, Tat'iana. "Kommunist pleiboem byt' ne mozhet—Primorskii parlamentarii dokazyvaet svoiu normal'nuiu orientatsiiu." *Nezavisimaia Gazeta*, December 5, 2012. http://www.ng.ru/regions/2012-12-05/1_playboy.html.

Dworkin, Andrea. "Biological Superiority: The World's Most Dangerous and Deadly Idea." *Heresies No. 6 on Women and Violence* 2, no. 2 (Summer 1978). http://www.nostatusquo.com/ACLU/dworkin/WarZoneChaptIIID.html.

Dzutsev, Valery. "Ethnic Rivalries Appear to Be Tearing Russia's Army and Society Apart." *North Caucasus Weekly* (Jamestown Foundation), December 17, 2010.

Earle, Jonathan. "NTV Exposé Alleges Anti-Church Campaign." *The Moscow Times*, January 21, 2013. http://www.themoscowtimes.com/news/article/ntv-expos233-alleges-anti-church-campaign/474262.html.

EchoMSK. "Politsiia iz"iala kartiny khudozhnika Konstantina Altunina." August 27, 2013. http://www.echo.msk.ru/blog/echomsk/1144458-echo/.

"Editorial: Renaming the Army." *Vedomosti,* November 1, 2010.

Edwards, Janis L. "Visualizing Presidential Imperatives: Masculinity as an Interpretive Frame in Editorial Cartoons, 1988-2008." In *Gender and Political Communication in America: Rhetoric, Representation, and Display*, edited by Janis L. Edwards, 233–250. Lanham, MD: Lexington Books, 2009.

Egorova, Elena. "Putin v Sochi prokommentiroval versiiu o 'gei-rastsvetke' olimpiiskoi formy." January 18, 2014. http://www.mk.ru/politics/article/2014/01/17/971861-putin-v-sochi-prokommentiroval-versiyu-o-geyrastsvetke-olimpiyskoy-formyi.html.

Eichler, Maya. *Militarizing Men: Gender, Conscription, and War in Post-Soviet Russia.* Stanford, CA: Stanford University Press, 2012.

Elder, Miriam. "Emails Give Insight into Kremlin Youth Group's Priorities, Means and Concerns." *The Guardian*, February 7, 2012. http://www.guardian.co.uk/world/2012/feb/07/nashi-emails-insight-kremlin-groups-priorities?newsfeed=true.

———. "Feminism Could Destroy Russia, Russian Orthodox Patriarch Claims." *The Guardian*, April 9, 2013. http://m.guardiannews.com/world/2013/apr/09/feminism-destroy-russia-patriarch-kirill.

———. "Feminist Punk Band Pussy Riot Take Revolt to the Kremlin." *The Guardian*, February 2, 2012. http://www.guardian.co.uk/world/2012/feb/02/pussy-riot-protest-russia.

———. "Polishing Putin: Hacked Emails Suggest Dirty Tricks by Russian Youth Group." *The Guardian*, February 7, 2012. http://www.guardian.co.uk/world/2012/feb/07/putin-hacked-emails-russian-nashi?newsfeed=true.

"Election Resources on the Internet: Federal Elections in México." Election Resources, 2012. http://www.electionresources.org/mx/deputies.php?election=2012&state=14.

Elias, J. "Hegemonic Masculinities, the Multinational Corporation, and the Developmental State: Constructing Gender in 'Progressive' Firms." *Men and Masculinities* 10, no. 4 (2008): 405–421.

Elliott, Justin. "MAP: A Guide to Recent Vandal Attacks On Democrats." March 24, 2010. http://tpmmuckraker.talkingpointsmemo.com/2010/03/map_a_guide_to_recent_vandal_attacks_on_democrats.php.

Engelstein, Laura. *The Keys to Happiness: Sex and the Search for Modernity in Fin-de-Siecle Russia.* Ithaca, NY: Cornell University Press, 1994.

Englehart, Oliver. "Roman v Kremlin." Al Jazeera, November 20, 2012. http://www.aljazeera.com/programmes/activate/2012/10/20121014132816101445.html.

Enloe, Cynthia. *Bananas, Beaches, and Bases: Making Feminist Sense of International Politics.* Berkeley: University of California Press, 1990.

———. *Globalization and Militarism: Feminists Make the Link.* Lanham, MD: Rowman and Littlefield, 2007.

Epishkin, Ilya. "Belye fartuki." *On Life.* April 16, 2011. http://bit.ly/TrIohX.

"Esli rodilsia Grazhdaninom—bud' im!—Pomni o voine, beregi Rodinu!" http://mostachev.livejournal.com/187081.html, accessed August 3, 2011.

Essig, Laurie. *Queer in Russia: A Story of Sex, Self, and the Other.* Durham, NC: Duke University Press, 1999.

Evans, Jr., Alfred B. "Civil Society and Protest." In *Return to Putin's Russia: Past Imperfect, Future Uncertain,* edited by Stephen K. Wegren, 103–124. Lanhm, MD: Rowman and Littlefield, 2012.

———. "Protests and Civil Society in Russia: The Struggle for the Khimki Forest." *Communist and Post-Communist Studies* 45, nos. 3–4 (December 2012): 233–242.

Fltvstudio. "Razgrom armii Putina" [video], August 4, 2011. http://www.youtube.com/watch?feature=player_embedded&v=VviBzQ9VVhc.

Farrell, Maureen. "George W. Kowalski?: Bush's Macho Facade Goes Limp." September 23, 2003. http://www.buzzflash.com/farrell/03/09/23.html.

Fausto-Sterling, Anne. "The Five Sexes, Revisited." *Sciences* 40, no. 4 (August 2000): 18–23.

Fediaeva, Tat'iana. "Skaz o parallel'nykh mirakh." In *Zhenskoe dvizhenie v Rossii: vchera, segodnia, zavtra: Materialy konferentsii,* edited by Galina Mikhaleva, 107–109. Moscow: RODP "Yabloko" and KMK Publishers, 2010.

Feifer, Gregory. "Sex Booms, but Traditional Views Prevail in Russia." November 25, 2008. http://www.npr.org/templates/story/story.php?storyId=96175017&ft=1&f=1001.

Fel'shtinskii, Iurii, and Vladimir Pribylovskii. "Rossiia i KGB vo vremena prezidenta Putina. Glava 4: Direktor FSB spas tron El'tsina." January 21, 2010. http://www.kasparov.ru/material.php?id=4B5811FDB4E78.

Femen. "Bozhe, tsaria goni!" December 9, 2011. http://femen.livejournal.com/182346.html.

———. "V zhopu KGBat'ku!" December 19, 2011. http://femen.livejournal.com/183324.html.

Femen. "Ucraina: in topless contro Putin" [video], October 27, 2010. http://www.youtube.com/watch?v=jsh0jGk2PnU, accessed November 10, 2010.

"Femen." http://femen.org/about, accessed March 15, 2013.

Femen. "Topless Warriors" [video], 2011. http://www.youtube.com/watch?v=PKDJxOm2RfY&feature=youtube_gdata_player, accessed October 26, 2012.

Feminist Ofenzyva. "Feministichnii marsh vidbuvsia!" March 8, 2012. http://ofenzyva.wordpress.com/2012/03/08/feministychny-marsh-vidbuvsia/.

"Feminizm—diagnoz ili forma protesta?: Irina Khakamada, Natal'ia Osipova, Evgeniia Otto." Kul'turnyi shok, Ekho Moskvy, Moscow, September 8, 2012. http://www.echo.msk.ru/programs/kulshok/927417-echo/.

Feodorff. "Seks-klip o Putine: ia khochu byt' tvoei Koni. . . . " July 7, 2011. http://newsland.com/news/detail/id/733701/.

Ferree, Myra Marx and Wendy Christensen. "Cowboy of the World? Gendered Discourse in the Iraq War Debate." *Qualitative Sociology* 31, no. 3 (2008): 287-306.

Fish, M. Steven. *Democracy Derailed in Russia: The Failure of Open Politics.* Cambridge: Cambridge University Press, 2005.

Fisher, Ralph Talcott Jr. *Pattern for Soviet Youth: A Study of the Congresses of the Komsomol, 1918–1954.* New York: Columbia University Press, 1959.

Fond Obshchestvennogo Mneniia. "Georgievskaia lentochka." April 25, 2012. http://fom.ru/proshloe/10421.

———. "My zhe ne v Amerike." June 9, 2011. http://fom.ru/obshchestvo/123.

———. "Patriotizm: kriterii i proiavleniia." December 7, 2006. http://bd.fom.ru/report/cat/socium/dd064825.

———. "Staryi vrag luchhe novykh dvukh." July 14, 2011. http://fom.ru/globe/10096.

———. "Vesennii prizyv." April 16, 2012. http://fom.ru/obshchestvo/10405.

———. "'Zhenshchina—tozhe chelovek': predstavleniia rossiian o feminizme." September 2, 2012. http://fom.ru/obshchestvo/10611.

"Former Minister Pays For 'Dusting' Patriarch's Flat." RIA Novosti, April 6, 2012. http://en.rian.ru/russia/20120406/172657429.html.

Foucault, Michel. *The History of Sexuality.* Vol. 2, *The Use of Pleasure.* New York: Vintage, 1990.

Frau Derrida, Isya, and Myjj. "Pol'za ot razgovorov (Ob opyte odnogo prosvetitel'skogo proekta v blogosfere)." In *Zhenskoe dvizhenie v Rossii: Vchera, segodnia, zavtra: Materialy konferentsii,* edited by Galina Mikhaleva, 97–102. Moscow: RODP "Yabloko" and KMK Publishers, 2010.

Fredheim, Rolf. "Quantifying Memory: Putin's Bot Army—Part Two: Nashi's Online Campaign (and Undesirable Bots)." June 2013. http://quantifyingmemory.blogspot.com/2013/06/putins-bot-army-part-two.html.

Furst, Juliane. *Stalin's Last Generation: Soviet Post-War Youth and the Emergence of Mature Socialism.* Oxford: Oxford University Press, 2010.

"Furtseva, Ekaterina Alekseevna." *Vikipediia.* http://bit.ly/1mSrweF, accessed May 20. 2014.

Gabbay, Tiffany. "Why Is Vladimir Putin Arm Wrestling and Trying to Bend a Frying Pan?" August 3, 2011. http://www.theblaze.com/stories/why-is-vladimir-putin-arm-wrestling-and-trying-to-bend-a-frying-pan/.

Galinakuksa. "Gliantsevye Zhurnaly—Tiazhelaia Artilleriia Patriarkhata." February 9, 2013. http://feministki.livejournal.com/2531262.html.

Garadzha Matveeva. "Pussy Riot o kontserte 'Putin zassal,' feminizme i protestakh" [video], February 1, 2012. http://www.youtube.com/watch?v=YPAaPWoJ-b8.

Garbuzniak, Alina. "'Nashi' zakryli 'Seliger' dlia 'MN.'" *Moskovskie Novosti,* July 2, 2012. http://mn.ru/politics/20120702/321981004.html.

———. "Oppozitsiia smenit 'Nashikh' na 'Seligere.'" *Moskovskie Novosti,* June 30, 2012. http://mn.ru/society_civil/20120630/321788235.html.

"Gay Propaganda Bill Challenged in Court." RIA Novosti, April 2, 2012. http://en.rian.ru/society/20120402/172562401.html.

Gera_DOT. "Khroniki mirovoi blogosfery." August 26, 2010. http://f5.ru/geradot/post/290395.

Gerasimova, Elena. "Zhenshchiny v trudovykh otnosheniiakh v Rossii." In *Zhenskoe dvizhenie v Rossii: Vchera, segodnia, zavtra: Materialy konferentsii,* edited by Galina Mikhaleva, 15–18. Moscow: RODP "Yabloko" and KMK Publishers, 2010.

Gessen, Masha. *The Rights of Lesbians and Gay Men in the Russian Federation: An International Gay and Lesbian Human Rights Commission Report.* San Francisco: IGLHRC, 1994.

———. *Words Will Break Cement: The Passion of Pussy Riot.* New York: Riverhead Books, 2014.

Gevorkian, Nataliia, Natal'ia Timakova, and Andrei Kolesnikov. *Ot pervogo litsa: razgovory s Vladimirom Putinym.* Moscow: Vagrius, 2000.

Ghodsee, Kristen. "Electioneering on the Rocks." http://www.tol.org/client/article/20667-electioneering-on-the-rocks.html?print, accessed September 22, 2012.

Gitlin, Todd. *The Whole World Is Watching: Mass Media in the Making and Unmaking of the New Left*. Berkeley: University of California Press, 1981.

"Glenn Beck 2001: Rep. Rangel and Other People 'We'd Like to Beat to Death with a Shovel'" [video], September 1, 2009. http://mediamatters.org/blog/2009/09/01/glenn-beck-2001-rep-rangel-and-other-people-wed/154105.

Glikin, Maksim, and Liliia Biriukova. "Kreml' otkazhetsia ot 'Nashikh,'" March 5, 2013. http://www.vedomosti.ru/politics/news/9743881/bolshe_ne_nashi.

Goffman, Erving. *Frame Analysis: An Essay on the Organization of Experience*. New York: Harper Colophon Books, 1974.

Golovko, Oksana. "Protoierei Dimitrii Smirnov: Ia protiv vseobshchego izbiratel'nogo prava!" November 29, 2011. http://www.pravmir.ru/protoierej-dimitrij-smirnov-ya-protiv-vseobshhego-izbiratelnogo-prava/.

Goncharov, Kirill. "I Fuck Prizyv/I Love Contract." May 5, 2011. http://goncharov-kiril.livejournal.com/43499.html.

———. "Sobytie vcherashnego dnia." May 14, 2011. http://goncharov-kiril.livejournal.com/43750.html.

Good Moments Box. "Novyi zakon o mitingakh i Masrecard [sic]" [video], June 10, 2012. http://www.youtube.com/watch?v=GTP8ZaN9rJc.

Gorbachev, Aleksei. "Evgeniia Chirikova: 'Ia vovse ne oppozitsioner, ia domokhoziaika!'" *Nezavisimaia Gazeta*, April 3, 2012. http://www.ng.ru/ng_politics/2012-04-03/9_chirikova.html.

———. "Iaroslavskii mer poshel na otkrytyi konflikt s 'Edinoi Rossiei.'" *Nezavisimaia Gazeta*, June 18, 2013. http://www.ng.ru/politics/2013-06-18/3_yaroslavl.html.

———. "Kseniia Sobchak: 'Putin nashchupal iz"ian u rossiiskoi oppozitsii i ochen' gramotno im vospol'zovalsia.'" *Nezavisimaia Gazeta*, April 3, 2012. http://www.ng.ru/ng_politics/2012-2004-03/9_sobchak.html.

———. "Spokoinyi mudrets vmesto macho—Vladimiru Putinu prognoziruiut kardinal'nuiu smenu imidzha." *Nezavisimaia Gazeta*, December 4, 2012. http://www.ng.ru/politics/2012-2012-04/1_wiseman.html.

Gorbachev, Mikhail. *Perestroika: New Thinking for Our Country and the World*. New York: Harper and Row, 1987.

Gordost' i styd za Rossiiu. Dominanty No. 35. Fond Obshchestvennoe Mnenie, September 9, 2010. bd.fom.ru/pdf/d35gis10.pdf.

Gorham, Michael S. "Putin's Language." In *Putin as Celebrity and Cultural Icon*, edited by Helena Goscilo, 82–103. London: Routledge, 2013.

Gorshkova, I. D., and I. I. Shurygina. "Nasilie nad zhenami v sovremennykh rossiiskikh sem'iakh: Materialy obshcherossiiskogo issledovaniia, predstavlennye na konferentsii 15-16 maia 2003 v MGU im. M. V. Lomonosova i Gorbachev-Fonde." Moscow, 2003. http://www.owl.ru/rights/no_violence/.

Goscilo, Helena. *Dehexing Sex: Russian Womanhood During and After Glasnost*. Ann Arbor: University of Michigan Press, 1996.

———. "Graphic Womanhood under Fire." In *Embracing Arms: Cultural Representation of Slavic and Balkan Women in War*, edited by Helena Goscilo and Yana Hashamova, 153–177. Budapest: Central European University Press, 2012.

———. "Post-ing the Soviet Body as Tabula Phrasa and Spectacle." In *Lotman and Cultural Studies: Encounters and Extensions*, edited by Andreas Schonle, 248–296. Madison: University of Wisconsin Press, 2006.

———. ed. *Putin as Celebrity and Cultural Icon*. London: Routledge, 2013.

———. "Putin's Performance of Masculinity: The action Hero and Macho Sex-Object." In *Putin as Celebrity and Cultural Icon*, edited by Helena Goscilo, 180–207. London: Routledge, 2013.

———. "Russia's Ultimate Celebrity: VVP as VIP Objet d'Art." In *Putin as Celebrity and Cultural Icon*, 6–36. London: Routledge, 2013.

———. "Style and S(t)imulation: Popular Magazines and the Aestheticization of Postsoviet Russia." Edited by Helena Goscilo. *Russian Culture of the 1990s: Studies in 20th Century Literature* 24, no. 1 (Winter 2000): 15–50.

———. "The Ultimate Celebrity: VVP as VIP Objet d'Art." In *Celebrity and Glamour in Contemporary Russia: Shocking Chic*, edited by Helena Goscilo and Vlad Strukov, 29–55. London: Routledge, 2011.

Goscilo, Helena, and Andrea Lanoux, eds. *Gender and National Identity in Twentieth-Century Russian Culture.* DeKalb: Northern Illinois University Press, 2006.

Goscilo, Helena, and Vlad Strukov, eds. *Celebrity and Glamour in Contemporary Russia: Shocking Chic.* London: Routledge, 2011.

———. "Introduction." In *Celebrity and Glamour in Contemporary Russia: Shocking Chic*, 1–26. London: Routledge, 2011.

"GOSDEP-3: Legalizatsiia odnopolykh brakov: Za i protiv." November 10, 2012. http://tvrain.ru/articles/gosdep_3_legalizatsija_odnopolyh_brakov_za_i_protiv-332762/?autoplay=false.

Gove, Michael. "Putin's Bare Chest is a Display of Power Best Kept Secret." August 31, 2007. http://grumpymanflashfictioncontest.blogspot.com/2007/08/putins-bare-chest-is-display-of-power.html.

Grove, Thomas. "Church Should Have More Control over Russian Life: Putin." Reuters, February 1, 2013. http://www.reuters.com/article/2013/02/01/us-russia-putin-church-idUSBRE91016F20130201.

Gruber Garvey, Ellen. "Reframing the Bicycle: Advertising-Supported Magazines and Scorching Women." *American Quarterly* 47, no. 1 (1995): 66–101.

Gruppa "Mne real'no nravitsia Putin." "Otkrytie 'aVVtomoiki.'" July 21, 2011. http://forsmi.ru/announce/38308/.

Gruppa Pussy Riot. "Pochemu feministskii khlyst polezen Rossii?" November 7, 2011. http://grani.ru/blogs/free/entries/192925.html.

Guth, David W. "The Emergence of Public Relations in the Russian Federation." *Public Relations Review* 26, no. 2 (2000): 191–207.

Gutterman, Steve. "Putin Needs More Than Rhetoric to Win Over Weary Nation." Reuters, December 12, 2012. http://uk.reuters.com/article/2012/12/12/uk-russia-putin-id UKBRE8BB00L20121212.

Hakamada, Irina. "Flights with Siberian White Cranes and Other PR Events of Vladimir Putin." October 11, 2012. http://valdaiclub.com/politics/49961.html.

Hammer. "Femen: UEFA is Attacking Our Gates." December 2, 2011. http://www.mizozo.com/world/12/2011/02/femen-uefa-is-attacking-our-gates-nsfw.html.

Harding, Luke. "Vladimir Putin Question and Answer Session in Russia—Live Updates." *The Guardian*, December 15, 2011. http://www.guardian.co.uk/world/blog/2011/dec/15/vladimir-putin-question-and-answer-session-in-russia-live.

Harvey, Oliver. "Babes 'n arms." *The Sun* (UK), October 8, 2007.

"Hazing in Russian Military Still Rampant—Chief Prosecutor." Interfax/AVN, January 11, 2011.

"The Heads of the Moscow State University Didn't Appreciate Putin's Saucy Congratulation." NewsBCM, October 17, 2010. http://bit.ly/1j69yjb.

Healey, Dan. "Active, Passive, and Russian: The National Idea in Gay Men's Pornography." *The Russian Review* 69 (April 2010): 210–230.

Heintz, Jim. "Birds, Bears, Bikers All Play into Putin's Stunts." September 6, 2012. http://bigstory.ap.org/article/birds-bears-bikers-all-play-putins-stunts.

———. "Russia Rings in New Year with Ban on Kiosk Beer Sales." *The Globe and Mail*, January 1, 2013. http://russialist.org/newslink-russia-rings-in-new-year-with-ban-on-kiosk-beer-sales/

Hemment, Julie. *Empowering Women in Russia: Activism, Aid, and NGOs.* Bloomington: Indiana University Press, 2007.

———. "Nashi, Youth Voluntarism, and Potemkin NGOs: Making Sense of Civil Society in Post-Soviet Russia." *Slavic Review* 71, no. 2 (Summer 2012): 234–260.

Henderson, Sarah. "Importing Civil Society: Foreign Aid and the Women's Movement in Russia." *Demokratizatsiya* 8, no. 1 (2000): 65–82.

Henderson, Sarah L. *Building Democracy in Contemporary Russia: Western Support for Grassroots Organizations.* Ithaca, NY: Cornell University Press, 2003.

———. "Civil Society in Russia: State-Society Relations in the Post-Yeltsin Era." *Problems of Post-Communism* 58, no. 3 (June 2011): 11–27.

Herszenhorn, David M. "'Propaganda' By Gays Faces Russian Curbs Amid Unrest." *New York Times*, January 25, 2013. http://www.nytimes.com/2013/01/26/world/europe/propaganda-by-gays-faces-russian-curbs-amid-unrest.html.

———. "Russian Mayor, an Opposition Figure, Is Arrested." *New York Times*, July 3, 2013. http://www.nytimes.com/2013/07/04/world/europe/russian-mayor-an-opposition-figure-is-arrested.html.

Hey_jan_ghapama. "Sovetskaia delegatsiia i nemtsy. Brest-Litovsk. dekabr' 1917." February 10, 2013. http://feministki.livejournal.com/2532798.html.

Hill, Fiona, and Clifford G. Gaddy. *Mr. Putin: Operative in the Kremlin.* Washington, DC: Brookings Institution Press, 2012.

Hodal, Kate. "Anwar Ibrahim's moment of truth looms." *The Guardian*, July 10, 2012. http://www.guardian.co.uk/world/2012/jul/11/anwar-ibrahim-moment-truth-looms.

Hoganson, Kristin L. *Fighting for American Manhood: How Gender Politics Provoked the Spanish-American and Philippine-American Wars.* New Haven, CT: Yale University Press, 1998.

Hrycak, Alexandra. "FEMEN-ism: FEMEN and the Ukrainian Women's Movement." *Ukraine Analyst* 3, no. 4 (April 2011): 1–4.

Htun, Mala, and S. Laurel Weldon. "The Civic Origins of Progressive Policy Change: Combating Violence against Women in Global Perspective, 1975–2005." *American Political Science Review* 106, no. 3 (August 2012): 548–569.

Hudson, Roger. "The Great Helmsman Goes Swimming." *History Today* 62, no. 5 (2012). http://www.historytoday.com/roger-hudson/great-helmsman-goes-swimming.

Hughes, Rob. "An Ugly Reminder in Russia That Bigotry Lingers." *New York Times*, December 18, 2012. http://www.nytimes.com/2012/12/19/sports/soccer/19iht-soccer19.html.

Human Rights Watch. "Russia: Free Pussy Riot Members." March 1, 2013. http://www.hrw.org/news/2013/02/28/russia-free-pussy-riot-members.

"Ia golosuiu za!" [video], February 22, 2012. http://www.youtube.com/watch?feature=player_embedded&v=fxEWddT44BY.

Iarskaia-Smirnova, Elena. "Vezde kul'tiviruetsia obraz samtsa." June 15, 2011. http://fom.ru/obshchestvo/136.

Iashin, Il'ia. *Ulichnyi protest.* Moscow, Russia: Galleia-Print, 2005. http://stevanivan.igp.ru/Solidarnost/2009-2010-18_Solidarnost/Ilya.html.

Iaushev, Aleksei. "Medal' za komissarskoe telo." August 26, 2010. http://www.vkrizis.ru/news.php?news=2318&type=rus&rub=soc.

"'I'd Rather Be a Dictator than Gay': Lukashenko to German FM." March 4, 2012. http://rt.com/news/lukashenko-gay-german-minister-807/.

"Indiana Senate Race—2012 Election Center." December 10, 2012. http://www.cnn.com/election/2012/results/state/IN/senate.

Inter-Parliamentary Union. "Ipu Parline database: Russian Federation, Election Archives." http://www.ipu.org/parline-e/reports/2263_arc.htm, accessed March 18, 2013.

International Center on Nonviolent Conflict. "On the Ground Interview with Oleg Kozlovsky" [video], January 7, 2011. http://www.youtube.com/watch?feature=player_embedded&v=ef2Oue76xGQ#at=310.

"International Election Observers Highlight US Voting Problems." RIA Novosti, November 8, 2012. http://en.rian.ru/world/20121108/177284443.html.

Ioffe, Julia. "Happy Birthday, Mr. President (NSFW)." https://themoscowdiaries.wordpress. com/2010/10/06/happy-birthday-mr-president/, accessed accessed July 27, 2011.

———. "Oleg Kashin's Horrible Truth." *Foreign Policy*, November 6, 2010. http://www. foreignpolicy.com/articles/2010/11/06/the_horrible_truth_about_oleg_kashin? page=0,1.

———. "Race Riots in Russia." *The New Yorker*, December 16, 2010. http://www.newyorker. com/online/blogs/newsdesk/2010/12/russia-race-riots.html.

———. "Russia's Nationalist Summer Camp." *The New Yorker*, August 16, 2010. http://www. newyorker.com/online/blogs/newsdesk/2010/08/seliger.html.

———. "Taking It Off for Putin." *The New Yorker*, July 21, 2011. http://www.newyorker.com/ online/blogs/newsdesk/2011/07/putins-army.html.

Ishkanian, Armine. "Nashi: Russia's Youth Counter-Movement." August 3, 2007. http:// www.opendemocracy.net/article/democracy_power/politics_protest/russia_nashi.

"It's Patriotic Duty to Stop Glenn Beck, According to Beck." August 10, 2009. http://foxnews boycott.com/glenn-beck/its-patriotic-duty-to-stop-glenn-beck-according-to-beck/.

Iukina, Irina. "Rol' akademicheskogo soobshchestva v sovremennom zhenskom dvizhenii Rossii (na primere Sankt-Peterburga)." In *Zhenskoe dvizhenie v Rossii: Vchera, segodnia, zavtra: Materialy konferentsii*, edited by Galina Mikhaleva, 84–88. Moscow: RODP "Yabloko" and KMK Publishers, 2010.

Ivanov, Maksim. "Grazhdane veriat v tserkov', armiiu i spetssluzhby." November 2, 2012. http://www.kommersant.ru/doc/2058340?isSearch=True.

Jeffords, Susan. *The Remasculinization of America: Gender and the Vietnam War*. Bloomington: Indiana University Press, 1989.

"Jobs Women Can't Do in Russia." June 12, 2009. http://www.pri.org/stories/world/jobs-women-can_t-do-russia1427.html.

Johnson, Janet Elise. *Gender Violence in Russia: The Politics of Feminist Intervention*. Blooming-ton: Indiana University Press, 2009.

Johnson, Janet Elise, and Aino Saarinen. "Twenty-First-Century Feminisms under Repres-sion: Gender Regime Change and the Women's Crisis Center Movement in Russia." *Signs* 38, no. 3 (2013): 543–567.

Jones, James. "Putin's Youth Movement Provides a Sinister Backdrop to Russia's Protests." *The Guardian*, December 8, 2011. http://www.guardian.co.uk/commentisfree/2011/ dec/08/putin-russia-elections.

Jordan, Pamela. "Review of Kimberly A. Williams, Imagining Russia: Making Feminist Sense of American Nationalism in U.S.–Russian Relations. Albany: State University of New York Press, 2012." *H-Diplo, H-Net Reviews*, July 2012. https://www.h-net.org/reviews/ showrev.php?id=36221.

Journeyman Pictures. "Nashi: Putin's Enthusiasts" [video], November 30, 2007. http://www. youtube.com/watch?v=CeA6y2vFXgU.

Kamnev, Dmitrii Grigor'evich. "Molodezhnye politicheskie dvizheniia v sovremennoi Rossii: Avtoreferat dissertatsii na soiskanie uchenoi stepeni kandidata politicheskikh nauk." Higher School of Economics, Moscow, 2009. http://www.hse.ru/en/sci/diss/7791729.

"Kanal pol'zovatelia DevochkiZa" [video]. https://www.youtube.com/user/ DevochkiZa?feature=watch, accessed April 17, 2013.

Katz, Jackson. *Leading Men: Presidential Campaigns and the Politics of Manhood*. Northampton, MA: Interlink Books, 2013.

Kay, Rebecca. *Men in Contemporary Russia: The Fallen Heroes of Post-Soviet Change?* Burling-ton, VT: Ashgate, 2006.

Kelly, Mary B. "The Ritual Fabrics of Russian Village Women." In *Russia—Women—Culture*, edited by Helena Goscilo and Beth Holmgren, 152–176. Bloomington: Indiana Univer-sity Press, 1996.

Kershner, Isabel. "Israeli Ex-President, Katsav, Is Convicted of Rape." *New York Times*, Decem-ber 30, 2010, http://www.nytimes.com/2010/12/31/world/middleeast/31israel.html.

Khokhlova, Veronika. "Russia: Moscow Pride 2011." May 29, 2011. http://globalvoicesonline. org/2011/05/29/russia-moscow-pride-2011/.

"Khrushcheva, Nina Petrovna." http://bit.ly/18D8VNP, accessed November 9, 2012.

Kichanova, Vera. *Pussi Raiot: Podlinnaia istoriia*. Moscow, Russia: Hocus-Pocus, 2012.

Kim, Lucian. "A Hot Winter's Day in Moscow." February 5, 2012. http://lucianinmoscow.blogspot.com/2012/02/hot-winters-day-in-moscow.html.

Kim, Lucian. "A Russian Fairy Tale for Christmas." December 25, 2011. http://lucianinmoscow.blogspot.com/2011/12/russian-fairy-tale-for-christmas.html.

Kimer, James. "The Botox Czar: An Interview with Nina Khrushcheva—OpEd." *Eurasia Review*, March 5, 2012. http://www.eurasiareview.com/05032012-the-botox-czar-an-interview-with-nina-khrushcheva-oped/.

Kizenko, Nadieszda. "Feminized Patriarchy? Orthodoxy and Gender in Post-Soviet Russia." *Signs* 38, no. 3 (2013): 595–621.

Knight, Amy. *Beria: Stalin's First Lieutenant*. Princeton University Press, 1995.

Kolesnichenko, Alexander. "Dilettante, Polymath, Traitor." February 18, 2013. http://www.tol.org/client/article/23606-dilettante-polymath-traitor.html.

Kolonitskii, B. "Vladimir Putin. Velikii Macho, moguchii i mochashchii." *Delo*, February 9, 2004. http://www.idelo.ru/312/14.html.

Korchenkova, Natal'ia. "Protest smenil vozrast i liderov." *Kommersant*, June 28, 2012. http://www.kommersant.ru/doc/1968592?isSearch=True.

Kornia, Anastasiia, and Natal'ia Kostenko. "Rossiiskii sud pristrasten." *Vedomosti*, October 29, 2011. http://www.vedomosti.ru/newspaper/article/2009/10/29/217680.

Kosterina, I. V. "Konstrukty i praktiki maskulinnosti v provintsial'nom gorode: Gabitus 'normal'nykh patsanov.'" *Zhurnal sotsiologii i sotsial'noi antropologii* 4, no. 11 (2008): 122–140.

Kostiuchenko, Elena. "Feministki-khuliganki dali kontsert na Lobnom meste." *Novaya Gazeta*, January 20, 2012. http://www.novayagazeta.ru/news/53456.html.

Kovalenko, Elena. "Sovremennoe Rossiiskoe zhenskoe dvizhenie: problema 'nevidimosti.'" In *Zhenskoe dvizhenie v Rossii: Vchera, segodnia, zavtra: Materialy konferentsii*, edited by Galina Mikhaleva, 89–93. Moscow: RODP "Yabloko" and KMK Publishers, 2010.

Kozenko, Andrey. "Youth Being Prepared for Camps. Seliger-2009 to Be Main Event of 'Year of the Youth.'" *Kommersant*, March 9, 2009.

Kozina, Irina. "Rabotaiushchie materi: usloviia zaniatosti i sotsial'naia podderzhka." In *Zhenskoe dvizhenie v Rossii: Vchera, segodnia, zavtra: Materialy konferentsii*, edited by Galina Mikhaleva, 19–28. Moscow: RODP "Yabloko" and KMK Publishers, 2010.

Kozlovsky, Oleg. "Oborona Marches for a Volunteer Army." April 2, 2008. http://olegkozlovsky.wordpress.com/2008/04/02/oborona-marches-for-a-volunteer-army/.

Krainova, Natalya. "What Awaits Pussy Riot Musicians in Prison." *The Moscow Times*, August 30, 2012. http://www.themoscowtimes.com/news/article/what-awaits-pussy-riot-musicians-in-prison/467342.html.

Kramer, Andrew E. "Russia Passes Bill Targeting Some Discussions of Homosexuality." *New York Times*, June 11, 2013. http://www.nytimes.com/2013/06/12/world/europe/russia-passes-bill-targeting-some-discussions-of-homosexuality.html.

"Kremlin Activists Pose for Lingerie Calendar." *The Telegraph*, April 7, 2011. http://www.telegraph.co.uk/news/worldnews/europe/russia/8435668/Kremlin-activists-pose-for-lingerie-calendar.html.

"Kremlin Youth Camp Spending to Double Despite Reluctant Sponsors." *The Moscow Times*, April 10, 2012. http://www.themoscowtimes.com/news/article/kremlin-youth-camp-spending-to-double-despite-reluctant-sponsors/456474.html.

Kremlingate. "Proplachennoe v gazetakh pravil'noe osveshchenie Seligera." February 3, 2012. http://lj.rossia.org/users/kremlingate/345.html.

———. "Razmeshchenie prokremlevskogo kontenta v internete." February 3, 2012. http://lj.rossia.org/users/kremlingate/1166.html.

Kriukov, Denis. "Pussy Riot—Sud po sushchestvu dela. Pervye tri dnia." August 6, 2012. http://echo.msk.ru/blog/kryukov/916560-echo/.

Krugovykh, Taisiia. "Kak oni b'iut." March 16, 2012. http://os.colta.ru/art/events/details/35192/?attempt=1.

Krylova, Anna. *Soviet Women in Combat: A History of Violence on the Eastern Front.* New York: Cambridge University Press, 2010.

"Kseniia Basilashvili Interview of Maksim Shevchenko." Osoboe Mnenie (Ekho Moskvy), October 7, 2010.

"Kseniia Basilashvili Interview with Viktor Shenderovich." October 7, 2010. http://www.echo.msk.ru/programs/personalno/716199-echo/.

Kuz'menkova, Ol'ga. "Uchastniki 'Seligera-2012' pytaiutsia oboitis' bez politiki." July 2, 2012. http://www.gazeta.ru/politics/2012/07/02_a_4660937.shtml.

LaFraniere, Sharon. "Barry Arrested on Cocaine Charges in Undercover FBI, Police Operation." *Washington Post,* January 19, 1990. http://www.washingtonpost.com/wp-srv/local/longterm/tours/scandal/barry.htm.

Laktanov, Vladimir. "Gei-parada v Moskve ne budet!" October 29, 2010. http://web.archive.org/web/20101104042115/http://www.molgvardia.ru/mg/2010/10/29/20465.

Lally, Kathy. "Russian Women's Rights Rally Broken Up." *The Washington Post,* March 8, 2013. http://www.washingtonpost.com/world/europe/russian-womens-rights-rally-broken-up/2013/03/08/eaa4cdbc-880b-11e2-9d71-f0feafdd1394_story.html.

Lapidus, Gail Warshofsky. *Women in Soviet Society: Equality, Development, and Social Change.* Berkeley: University of California Press, 1978.

Lassila, Jussi. "Anticipating Ideal Youth in Putin's Russia: Symbolic Capital and Communicative Demands of the Youth Movements 'Nashi' and 'Idushchie Vmeste'" (PhD. diss., University of Jyvaskyla, 2011).

———. "Making Sense of Nashi's Political Style: The Bronze Soldier and the Counter-Orange Community." *Demokratizatsiya* 19, no. 3 (2011): 253–276.

———. *The Quest for an Ideal Youth in Putin's Russia II: The Search for Distinctive Conformism in the Political Communication of Nashi, 2005-2009.* Stuttgart: *ibidem*-Verlag, 2012.

Leonard, Andrew. "John Kerry: The Road Bike Warrior." September 3, 2008. http://www.salon.com/2008/09/03/john_kerry_road_rider/.

Levada Center. "Indeksy odobreniia deiatel'nosti Vladimira Putina i Dmitriia Medvedeva." 2012. http://www.levada.ru/indeksy.

Levada Center. "Material No.3 'Ustanovki rossiiskogo obshchestva na peremeny: tri pokoleniia' (Po materialam kolichestvennykh sotsiologicheskikh issledovanii)." Levada Center, Moscow, April 2011.

"Levada Pollster 'Told to Register' as Foreign Agent." *The Moscow Times,* May 7, 2013. http://www.themoscowtimes.com/news/article/levada-pollster-told-to-register-as-foreign-agent/479670.html.

Levada-Tsentr. "Rossiiane o dele Pussy Riot." July 31, 2012. http://www.levada.ru/31-07-2012/rossiyane-o-dele-pussy-riot.

Levitsky, Steven, and Lucan A. Way. *Competitive Authoritarianism: Hybrid Regimes After the Cold War.* 1st ed. Cambridge: Cambridge University Press, 2010.

Li, Zhisui. *The Private Life of Chairman Mao.* New York: Random House, 1996.

Liman, Doug, dir., *Mr. & Mrs. Smith* [DVD]. Los Angeles: Twentieth Century Fox, 2005.

Limonov, Eduard. "Eto ia—Edichka." http://lib.ru/PROZA/LIMONOV/edichka.txt, accessed August 12, 2011.

Linz, Juan J., and Alfred Stepan. *Problems of Democratic Transition and Consolidation: Southern Europe, South America, and Post-Communist Europe.* Baltimore: Johns Hopkins University Press, 1996.

"Liteinyi most vstal na FSB" [video], June 15, 2010. http://www.youtube.com/watch?v=KIFZ41P6kfw&feature=related.

Litrlife. "Ozhidaniia sovremennoi zhenshchiny ot braka zachastuiu kraine vysoki i daleki ot real'nosti." February 11, 2013. http://feministki.livejournal.com/2534717.html.

Little, Andrew. "Noncompetitve Elections and Information: A Theoretical Perspective on the 2011 Russian Elections." December 9, 2011. http://themonkeycage.org/blog/2011/12/09/noncompetitve-elections-and-information-a-theoretical-perspective-on-the-2011-russian-elections/.

Litvinenko, Alexander. "The Kremlin Pedophile." July 5, 2006. http://www.information liberation.com/?id=18244.

Lobzina, Alina. "Stripping for Beer and Medvedev." *The Moscow News*, August 4, 2011. http://themoscownews.com/politics/20110804/188898817.html.

———. "When Naomi Met Vladimir—Supermodel Interviews Putin." *The Moscow News*, February 1, 2011. http://themoscownews.com/politics/20110201/188382669.html.

LoGiurato, Brett. "Obama Approval Rating Jumps before Election Day." November 4, 2012. http://www.businessinsider.com/obama-approval-rating-polls-rasmussen-50-percent-gallup-2012-2011.

Loiko, Sergei. "Kremlin Youth Camp at Russia's Lake Seliger: Framework." *Los Angeles Times*, August 10, 2011. http://framework.latimes.com/2011/08/10/kremlin-youth-camp/#/0.

———. "Russia Youths Seek 'Social Lift' at Kremlin Political Camp." *Los Angeles Times*, August 11, 2011. http://articles.latimes.com/2011/aug/11/world/la-fg-russia-youth-camp-20110811.

Longbottom, Wil. "Fancy a Bike Ride in the Park?: How an 'Informal' Meeting in Moscow Could Decide Who Runs Russia Next Year." *The Daily Mail*, June 11, 2011. http://www.dailymail.co.uk/news/article-2002504/Fancy-bike-ride-park-How-informal-meeting-Moscow-decide-runs-Russia-year.html.

Lucas, Edward. "Sex for the Motherland: Russian Youths Encouraged to Procreate at Camp." *Daily Mail*, July 29, 2007. http://www.dailymail.co.uk/news/article-471324/Sex-motherland-Russian-youths-encouraged-procreate-camp.html.

Luhn, Alec. "Gay Pride Versus 'Gay Propaganda.'" *The Nation*, June 28, 2013. http://www.thenation.com/article/175035/gay-pride-versus-gay-propaganda.

MadeOfSteelChannel. "'Im po fig!'/'Stal'' v Tveri/Boi—4" [video], September 26, 2011. https://www.youtube.com/watch?v=rfXnhZyVG2Y.

Madison, Lucy. "Richard Mourdock: Even Pregnancy from Rape Something 'God Intended,'" October 23, 2012. http://www.cbsnews.com/8301-8250_162-57538757/richard-mourdock-even-pregnancy-from-rape-something-god-intended/.

Maerchik, Mariia, and Ol'ga Plakhotnik. "Fenomenologiia 'Femen': Metodologicheskie Kontroversii." *Socioprostir*, no. 3 (2012): 24–29.

Maksim Stribnyi. "Ulitsa krasnykh fonarei na Seligere." August 17, 2007. http://mc-masters.livejournal.com/394646.html.

Maksimova, Elena. "Feministki-nevidimki." June 3, 2012. http://grani.ru/blogs/free/entries/198158.html.

Maksimova, Lena. "Action!" *Net—znachit net*, no. 3 (March 2011): 3–5.

Malakhovskaia, Anna Nataliia. "20 let tomu nazad v Leningrade zarodilos- zhenskoe dvizhe-nie." In *Propushchennyi siuzhet: Istoriia novogo nezavisimogo zhenskogo dvizheniia Rossii s nachala 1990x do nashikh dnei v zerkale SMI*, edited by Nadezhda Azhgikhina, 54–69. Moscow: ROO: Tsentr Obshchestvennoi informatsii, 2008.

"Manifest molodezhnogo dvizheniia 'NAShI,'" October 25, 2005. http://web.archive.org/web/20051025115524/http://www.nashi.su/pravda/83974709.

Marquardt, Alexander. "Caught On Tape: Reporter Beaten into Coma." November 9, 2010. http://abcnews.go.com/Blotter/russian-reporter-oleg-kashin-beaten-coma/story?id=12101001.

"Marsh goriashchikh serdets." June 3, 2012. http://radical-fem-msk.livejournal.com/10511.html.

"Marsh ravenstva." Vikipediia, December 17, 2012. http://bit.ly/16wc4iy.

Martsenyuk, Tamara. "Ukraine's Other Half: International Women's Day Brings Disappointment and Hope for the Sex Largely Excluded from Power in Kyiv." *Stanford Post-Soviet Post*, March 27, 2012. http://postsovietpost.stanford.edu/analysis/.

Masiuk, Elena. "Posle prigovora." *Novaya Gazeta*, August 21, 2012. http://www.novayagazeta.ru/politics/54073.html.

"Masked Men Attack NBP Activists." *The Moscow TImes*, August 31, 2005. http://www.themoscowtimes.com/news/article/masked-men-attack-nbp-activists/210256.html.

"Massovye zaderzhaniia na feministskom mitinge v Moskve." http://avtonom.org/news/massovye-zaderzhaniya-na-feministskom-mitinge, accessed March 8, 2013.

Matveeva, Garadzha. "Pank-moleben 'Bogoroditsa, Putina progoni' Pussy Riot v Khrame" [video], February 21, 2012. http://www.youtube.com/watch?feature=player_embedded&v=GCasuaAczKY.

Mauldin, William. "Russian Paper Counts 102,486 Protesters, Several Times Police Tally." *Wall Street Journal*, December 23, 2011. http://blogs.wsj.com/emergingeurope/2011/12/26/russian-paper-counts-102486-protesters-several-times-police-tally/.

Mayerchyk, Maria, and Ol'ga Plakhotnik. "The Femen Phenomenon: Reflections on New Grassroots Feminisms in Ukraine." Davis Center for Russian and Eurasian Studies, Harvard University, Cambridge, MA, 2012.

McAllister, Ian, and Stephen White. "'It's the Economy, Comrade!' Parties and Voters in the 2007 Russian Duma Election." *Europe-Asia Studies* 60, no. 6 (2008): 931–957.

McBride, Alex. "Landmark Cases: Bowers v. Hardwick (1986)." December 2006. http://www.pbs.org/wnet/supremecourt/rights/landmark_bowers.html.

McDonald, Mark. "Balloon-Borne Messages to North Korea Have Detractors on Both Sides of Border." *New York Times*, April 26, 2011. http://www.nytimes.com/2011/04/27/world/asia/27iht-korea.html.

"Medvedev opublikoval v Twitter netsenzurnuiu zapis' o 'partii zhulikov i vorov.'" December 7, 2011. http://newsru.com/russia/07dec2011/ryktwitter.html.

"Medvedev's Female Fans Strip for Anti-Booze Law." August 4, 2011. http://rt.com/news/girls-medvedev-striptease-beer/.

MedvedevGroup. "Medvedev—nash Prezident!" http://vkontakte.ru/medvedev_group, accessed August 3, 2011.

Meier, Sam. "Gay Dad Defends AZ Principal Who Punished Male Students by Making Them Hold Hands." December 4, 2012. http://www.policymic.com/articles/20108/gay-dad-defends-az-principal-who-punished-male-students-by-making-them-hold-hands>.

Mel'nikova, Alla, and Kristina Markhotskaia. "'Ia mogu vstat' i skazat': Tak bol'she ne budet': 27 istorii iz zhizni rossiiskikh geev." *Afisha*, February 22, 2013. http://www.afisha.ru/article/gay-issue/.

Melikova, Natal'ia. "Putin voskhitilsia liubovnymi podvigami Katsava." *Nezavisimaia Gazeta*, October 19, 2006. http://www.ng.ru/politics/2006-10-19/4_putin.html.

Menschikova, Elizabeth. "O zhurnalistakh, kotorye s zhurfaka MGU." October 7, 2010. http://liz-anderson.livejournal.com/76145.html.

Messerschmidt, James. *Hegemonic Masculinities and Camouflaged Politics: Unmasking the Bush Dynasty and Its War against Iraq*. Boulder, CO: Paradigm Publishers, 2010.

MFG admin. "Feministkie pikety v 'Den' sem'i, liubvi i vernosti' proshli 7 i 8 iiulia v Moskve i Sankt-Peterburge." July 9, 2012. http://bit.ly/10EzMVj.

———. "Soprotivlenie gomofobnomu zakonu: Radikal'nyi analiz." January 27, 2013. http://ravnopravka.ru/2013/01/1785/.

"MFG na kanale 'Rossiia,'" March 24, 2012. http://bit.ly/10NoZou.

Michalowski, Helen. "The Army Will Make a 'Man' Out of You." In *Reweaving the Web of Life: Feminism and Nonviolence*, edited by Pam McAllister, 326–335. Philadelphia: New Society Publishers, 1982.

Mikhailova, Tatiana. "Putin as the Father of the Nation: His Family and Other Animals." In *Putin as Celebrity and Cultural Icon*, edited by Helena Goscilo, 65–81. London: Routledge, 2013.

Mikhaleva, Galina. "Est' li politicheskii potentsial u zhenskogo dvizheniia v Rossii?" In *Zhenskoe dvizhenie v Rossii: Vchera, segodnia, zavtra: Materialy konferentsii*, edited by Galina Mikhaleva, 61–72. Moscow: RODP "Yabloko" and KMK Publishers, 2010.

———. "Prazdnik 8 marta: Pir vo vremia chumy." March 7, 2013. http://www.yabloko.ru/blog/2013/03/07.

Mikhaleva, Galina. "Predislovie." In *Zhenskoe dvizhenie v Rossii: Vchera, segodnia, zavtra: Materialy konferentsii*, edited by Galina Mikhaleva. Moscow: RODP "Yabloko" and KMK Publishers, 2010.

———. "V Rossii eshche ochen' sil'ny ostatki tiuremnoi kul'tury, kak i ostatki stalinizma." *Znak Ravenstvo*, no. 10 (September 2010): 12–14.

———. ed. "Rezoliutsiia konferentsii: 'Zhenskoe dvizhenie v Rossii: vchera, segodnia, zavtra,' Moskva, 26 fevralia 2010 goda." In *Zhenskoe dvizhenie v Rossii: Vchera, segodnia, zavtra: Materialy konferentsii*, 112. Moscow: RODP "Yabloko" and KMK Publishers, 2010.

Minchenko, Yevgeny. "Putin's Public Actions: A Unique Style Is a Competitive Advantage." October 11, 2012. http://valdaiclub.com/politics/49960.html.

Mirovalev, Mansur. "Russia Moves to Enact Anti-Gay Law Nationwide." *Time*, January 21, 2013. http://world.time.com/2013/01/21/russia-moves-to-enact-anti-gay-law-nationwide/.

Mishina, Ekaterina. "Prof. Ekaterina Mishina Reflects on 20th Anniversary of the Establishment of Judicial Reform in Russia: History Matters." Insitute of Modern Russia, October 24, 2011. http://bit.ly/11gtNWy.

"'Mishka Fishman narkoman': V Set' vylozhen ocherednoi 'kompromat' na glavreda'Russkogo Newsweek.'" March 25, 2010. http://www.nakanune.ru/news/2010/3/23/22190466.

"Missouri Senate Race—2012 Election Center." November 8, 2012. http://www.cnn.com/election/2012/results/state/MO/senate.

"Miting na prospekte Sakharova: Khronika." December 24, 2011. http://grani.ru/Politics/Russia/activism/m.194408.html#child-201713.

"Miting pamiati pogibshikh ot kriminal'nykh abortov sostoialsia—Za svobodnoe materinstvo!" October 1, 2011. https://sites.google.com/site/protivabortov2011/novosti-kampanii/mitingpamatipogibsihotkriminalnyhabortovsostoalsa.

"Miting za zhenskie prava proshel, nesmotria na zaderzhaniia." March 8, 2013. http://www.yabloko.ru/regnews/Moscow/2013/03/08.

Mobasherat, Mitra. "Dozens Arrested in Moscow Gay Rights Parade Clashes." May 28, 2011. http://www.cnn.com/2011/WORLD/europe/05/28/russia.gay.rights.parade.clashes/index.html.

Molodaia Gvardiia. "Dollarovaia ataka na 'Lukoil.'" April 28, 2011. http://www.molgvardia.ru/nextday/2011/04/28/29369.

———. "Ia—za chestnoe toplivo!" February 13, 2011. http://mger2020.ru/nextday/2011/02/13/25831.

———. "Molodaia Gvardiia—Videopozdravlenie Prezidentu Vladimiru Putinu ot molodogvardeitsev." October 7, 2012. http://mger2020.ru/nextday/2012/10/07/39219.

"Molodaia gvardiia Edinoi Rossii." http://bit.ly/sLDXMA, accessed November 8, 2010.

"Molodaia Gvardiia—Koordinatsionnyi sovet." Accessed September 19, 2011. http://www.molgvardia.ru/persons/koordinatsionnyi-sovet.

Molodezhnoe demokraticheskoe antifashistskoe dvizhenie NAShI. "Proekty." http://nashi.su/projects, accessed August 3, 2011.

———. "Vystavka fotografii voennykh let otkrylas' na VVTs." June 9, 2011. http://nashi.su/news/36449.

"Molodezhnoe demokraticheskoe antifashistskoe dvizhenie NAShI / Koordinaty." http://nashi.su/coords/, accessed September 19, 2011.

"Molodezhnoe Iabloko – O nas." http://youthyabloko.ru/ru/about.html, accessed March 24, 2013.

Molodezhnoe Patrioticheskoe Dvizhenie STAL'. http://madeofsteel.ru/, accessed January 11, 2011.

———.http://www.madeofsteel.ru/regions/, accessed September 19, 2011.

———. "Nizhnii Novgorod: muzhskoi postupok." December 7, 2010. http://madeofsteel.ru/news/cat/Drugie_36/nov_Nizhniy_Novgorod:_muzhskoy_postupok_71.

———. "Proekt: Bor'ba s fal'sifikatsiei istorii." http://www.madeofsteel.ru/projects/Borba_s_falsifikatsiey_istorii_4, accessed August 3, 2011.

———. "'Stal'' pomozhet Nemtsovu preodolet' posledstviia nasiliia." January 7, 2011.http://bit.ly/1oSiFeZ.

"Molodye storonniki rossiiskogo duumvirata reshili segodnia udarit' veloprobegom za prezidenta Medvedeva i prem'era Putina." August 8, 2011. http://www.echo.msk.ru/news/800580-echo.html.

Moloko 2012. "Uzhasy Indii." February 10, 2013. http://feministki.livejournal.com/2531915.html#comments, accessed February 12, 2013.

Moore, Lori. "Rep. Todd Akin: 'Legitimate Rape' Statement and Reaction." *The New York Times*, August 20, 2012. http://www.nytimes.com/2012/08/21/us/politics/rep-todd-akin-legitimate-rape-statement-and-reaction.html.

"Moscow Bans 'Satanic' Gay Parade." January 29, 2007. http://news.bbc.co.uk/2/hi/europe/6310883.stm.

"Moscow Police Make Arrests after Feminist Protest." RIA Novosti, March 8, 2013. http://en.rian.ru/russia/20130308/179893843/Moscow-Police-Make-Arrests-After-Feminist-Protest.html.

"Moskovskaia feministskaia gruppa." http://ravnopravka.ru/?page_id=37, accessed April 2, 2012.

"Moskovskaia politsiia razognala nesanktsionirovannyi 'lager' oppozitsii', vdokhnovlennyi plakatom 'Putin pidrakhui.'" May 8, 2013. http://m.newsru.com/arch/russia/08may2013/okkupay.html.

"Moskovskie feministki otprazdnovali Den' Sem'i, Liubvi i Vernosti." July 9, 2012. http://radical-fem-msk.livejournal.com/11310.html.

Moskovskoe Iabloko. "Molodezhnoe Iabloko' provelo antiprizyvnoi festival' v tsentre Moskvy." May 13, 2011. http://www.mosyabloko.ru/archives/9082.

———. "Tantamareska I fuck prizyv!/I love contract!" http://www.mosyabloko.ru/tantamareski, accessed August 3, 2011.

"The Most Macho Leaders in History." October 7, 2012. http://msn.lockeroom.com.my/features/2012/10/the-most-macho-leaders-in-history#.UH7NaIXd7io.

"Mumugeit (MuMugate)." April 2010. http://traditio-ru.org/wiki/%CC%F3%EC%F3%E3%E5%E9%F2.

Muravyeva, Marianna. "Personalizing Homosexuality and Masculinity in Early Modern Russia." In *Gender in Late Medieval and Early Modern Europe*, edited by Marianna Muravyeva and Raisa Maria Toivo, 205–224. London: Routledge, 2012.

"Na Pushkinskoi, 10 pokazali 'Neobyknovennye trusy,'" March 9, 2012. http://www.tv100.ru/news/na-pushkinskoy-10-pokazali-neobyknovennye-trusy-53298/.

"Na shestvii 'Za chestnye vybory' 4 fevralia 2012g." February 5, 2012. http://radical-fem-msk.livejournal.com/5806.html.

"Nashi Anti Corruption Calendar 2011." http://www.metro.co.uk/news/pictures/photos-10865/nashi-anti-corruption-calendar-2011/1?ITO=HPPIX, acessed April 9, 2011.

"Nations in Transit: Russia 2012." http://www.freedomhouse.org/report/nations-transit/2012/russia.

Navalny. "Pro pussi raiots." March 7, 2012. http://navalny.livejournal.com/690551.html.

Navalny4. "Pervyi kanal pokazal mul'tfil'm o Naval'nom" [video], December 15, 2011. http://www.youtube.com/watch?v=fLKOm-PIaHI&feature=player_embedded#%21.

Naylor, Aliide. "The Changing Face of Russian Beauty." *The Moscow Times*, January 28, 2013. http://www.themoscowtimes.com/arts_n_ideas/article/the-changing-face-of-russian-beauty/474647.html.

NBP-Info. "Nashi Boevye Podrugi." http://www.nbp-http://bit.ly/1paAdR4, accessed April 2, 2009.

"Ne tol'ko vos'mogo marta." March 24, 2011. http://www.union-report.ru/news/2011-03-24/ne-tolko-vosmogo-marta.

Nelson, Sara C. "Topless FEMEN Members in Nuns Habits Clash with Same Sex Marriage Protesters in France." *Huffington Post* (UK), November 19, 2012. http://www.huffingtonpost.co.uk/2012/11/19/topless-femen-nun-same-sex-marriage-protestors-france_n_2157536.html?ncid=GEP.

Nemtsova, Anna. "Vladimir Putin's Wife, Lyudmila, Has All but Vanished, and Russians Don't Seem to Care." *The Daily Beast,* January 13, 2013. http://www.thedailybeast.com/articles/2013/01/13/vladimir-putin-s-wife-lyudmila-has-all-but-vanished-and-russians-don-t-seem-to-care.html.

Network Women's Program, Violence against Women Monitoring Program. *Violence against Women: Does the Government Care in Russia?* New York: Open Society Institute, 2007. http://www.stopvaw.org/sites/3f6d15f4-c12d-4515-8544-26b7a3a5a41e/uploads/Russia_2.pdf.

Nikolayenko, Olena. *Citizens in the Making in Post-Soviet States.*: Routledge, 2011.

"Noch.' Ulitsa. Vsemirnyi den' kontratseptsii." September 30, 2012. http://radical-fem-msk.livejournal.com/12154.html.

Nolan, Hamilton. "Bushmaster Firearms, Your Man Card Is Revoked." December 18, 2012. http://gawker.com/5969150/bushmaster-firearms-your-man-card-is-revoked.

"NTV Sees Russian Church as Victim of Soviet-Era Style Attacks." BBC Monitoring, January 20, 2013.

O'Dwyer, Conor. "Does the EU help or hinder gay-rights movements in post-communist Europe? The case of Poland." *East European Politics* 28, no. 4 (December 2012): 1–21.

"Obama vs Putin—Shirtless." December 24, 2008. http://rt.com/news/prime-time/obama-vs-putin-shirtless/.

"Oborona (molodezhnoe dvizhenie)." http://bit.ly/1173JZM, accessed March 24, 2013.

Okorokova, Lidia. "Raunchy Avianova Ad Sparks Sexism row." *The Moscow News,* July 12, 2010. http://themoscownews.com/news/20100712/187926015.html.

Oldfield, Sybil. "The Dubious Legacy of Bismarck and von Treitschke." In *Women against the Iron Fist: Alternatives to Militarism 1900-1989*, by Sybil Oldfield, 3–17. Cambridge, MA: Basil Blackwell, 1989.

Oleg Kozlovsky. "Controversial Sexy Gift for Putin and the Future of Russian Journalism." *Huffington Post,* October 7, 2010. http://www.huffingtonpost.com/oleg-kozlovsky/controversial-sexy-gift-f_b_753952.html.

Olga_future. "Klichki i rugatel'stva." February 11, 2013. http://feministki.livejournal.com/2535051.html.

———. "Nam nuzhny rabotniki, no Vy nam ne podkhodite." February 10, 2013. http://feministki.livejournal.com/2532259.html.

———. "Novyi Zavet i feminizm." February 18, 2013. http://feministki.livejournal.com/2547661.html#comments.

"One-Third of Women Assaulted by a Partner, Global Report Says." *New York Times,* June 20, 2013. http://www.nytimes.com/2013/06/21/world/one-third-of-women-assaulted-by-a-partner-global-report-says.html?_r=0.

Osborn, Andrew. "Kremlin Youth Group Does Its Bit to Reverse the depopulation Crisis." *The Telegraph,* April 21, 2011. http://www.telegraph.co.uk/news/worldnews/europe/russia/8464040/Kremlin-youth-group-does-its-bit-to-reverse-the-depopulation-crisis.html.

———. "Vladimir Putin Tracks Whales with Crossbow." *The Telegraph,* August 25, 2010. http://www.telegraph.co.uk/news/worldnews/europe/russia/7963982/Vladimir-Putin-tracks-whales-with-crossbow.html.

"Osoboe Mnenie: Aleksandr Pliushchev Interviews Nikolai Uskov." August 7, 2012. http://echo.msk.ru/programs/personalno/915946-echo/.

Ostler, Rosemarie. *Slinging Mud: Rude Nicknames, Scurrilous Slogans, and Insulting Slang from Two Centuries of American Politics*. New York: Penguin Books, 2011.

Ostrow, Joel M., Georgiy A. Satarov, and Irina M. Khakamada. *The Consolidation of Dictatorship in Russia*. Westport, CT: Praeger Security International, 2007.

Otto, Zhenia. "8 Marta: Vernut' utrachennyi smysl." *Net—znachit net* 3 (March 2011): 7.

———. "Diskussiia s Frau-derrida: O neoplachivaemom trude." *Net—znachit net* 1 (May 2010): 12.

Parfitt, Tom. "Voina, Art Group Backed by Banksy, Wins Russian Prize for Erection." *The Guardian*, April 8, 2011. http://www.guardian.co.uk/world/2011/apr/08/voina-banksy-penis-prize.

"Party Prospects for Seliger Youth Forum." July 27, 2011. http://rt.com/politics/seliger-youth-forum-party/.

Pascoe, C. J. *Dude, You're a Fag: Masculinity and Sexuality in High School*. Berkeley: University of California Press, 2007.

"Patriarkh Kirill schitaet feminizm ochen' opasnym iavleniem." April 9, 2013. http://www.vedomosti.ru/politics/news/2013/04/09/10955531.

Pelageya. "I o feminizme." January 21, 2005. http://pelageya.livejournal.com/241488.html.

Pell_mell. "Potok soznaniia." February 2, 2005. http://pell-mell.livejournal.com/2005/02/02/.

Pension Fund of Russian Federation. "Maternity (Family) Capital." 2012. http://www.pfrf.ru/ot_en/mother/.

Perviirazpolubvi. "Krasotka gadaet na pervyi raz" [video], February 20, 2012. http://www.youtube.com/watch?feature=player_embedded&v=Noo0lzJILaM.

———. "Nevinnaia devushka khochet pervyi raz" [video], February 22, 2012. http://www.youtube.com/watch?v=VxU-WUtza9c&sns=em.

———. "Otkroveniia devushki pro ee pervyi raz" [video], February 20, 2012. http://www.youtube.com/watch?feature=player_embedded&v=MbIzj21X0tU.

Pettersen, Trude. "Marina Kovtun Appointed Governor of Murmansk Oblast." *Barents Observer*, April 16, 2012. http://barentsobserver.com/en/politics/marina-kovtun-appointed-governor-murmansk-oblast.

Pigareva, Olga. "Prominent Russians: Vladimir Pozner." http://russiapedia.rt.com/prominent-russians/politics-and-society/vladimir-posner/, accessed March 20, 2013.

"Piket v podderzhku Mezhdunarodnoi kampanii za likvidatsiiu nasiliia v otnoshenii zhenshchin." November 30, 2010. http://www.zafeminizm.ucoz.ru/news/2010-11-30.

Pilkington, Hilary, ed. *Gender, Generation and Identity in Contemporary Russia*. London: Routledge, 1996.

Plucer. "Novaia aktsiia Voiny 'Khui v PLENu u FSB!' i inauguratsiia Nashego Prezidenta Leni Ebnutogo." June 24, 2010. http://plucer.livejournal.com/265584.html.

———. "Novaia skandal'naia aktsiia gruppy Voina 'Poshto pizdili Kuru?' ili 'Skaz o tom, kak Pizda Voinu kormila,'" July 24, 2010. http://plucer.livejournal.com/281211.html.

Plungian, Nadia. "Gendernye zerkala sovremennogo iskusstva: Mezhdu soprotivleniem i dedovshchinoi." *Neprikosnovennyi zapas* 2, no. 76 (2011). http://magazines.russ.ru/nz/2011/2/pl5.html.

———. "Istoriia odnoi diskreditatsii." *Neprikosnovennyi zapas* 81, no. 1 (2012). http://www.nlobooks.ru/node/1535.

"Podlinnaia istoriia Olega Kulika, kotoryi byl chelovek-sobaka strashnaia." June 17, 2011. http://adindex.ru/publication/gallery/2011/06/17/67740.phtml.

"Poklonniki i poklonnitsy Dmitriia Medvedeva i Vladimira Putina na velosipedakh-tandemakh prokatilis' ot Kremlia k Belomu Domu." August 8, 2011. http://www.echo.msk.ru/news/800631-echo.html.

Politkovskaya, Anna. *A Dirty War*. London: Harvill Press, 1999.

"Politsiia zopodozrila uchastnikov mitinga 'Za ravnye prava i vozmozhnosti dlia zhenshchin' v ekstremizme." *Znak Ravenstva*, April 2012, 19–20.

"Pollster: Putin's Attractiveness Sagging 'Irreversibly.'" *The Moscow Times*, May 18, 2012. http://www.themoscowtimes.com/news/article/pollster-putins-attractiveness-sagging-irreversibly/458718.html.

Polosatiy_ez. "Pod gorbatym mostom poimali Putina s khvostom." December 27, 2010. http://polosatiy-ez.livejournal.com/19875.html.

"Porvu za Putina!" [video], July 13, 2011. http://www.youtube.com/watch?v=1Easr8WTwxs.

Posadskaya, Anastasia, ed. *Women in Russia: A New Era in Russian Feminism*. London: Verso, 1994.

Potts, Andy. "Putin Invited to Swap Places with Khodorkovsky." *The Moscow News*, February 21, 2011. http://themoscownews.com/politics/20110221/188435044.html?referfrommn.

Potupchik, Kristina. "Devushki zhurfaka MGU razdelis' dlia Putina." October 6, 2010. http://krispotupchik.livejournal.com/92592.html.

"Pravozashchitnik popal v tiur'mu za plakat 'Putin, pidrakhui ostavshiesia svobody dni.'" May 8, 2013. http://newsru.co.il/world/08may2013/shapovalov456.html.

"Press-konferentsiia Vladimira Putina." December 20, 2012. http://kremlin.ru/transcripts/17173.

"Priekhali. Za gei-propagandu vpervye v Rossii nakazan rebenok (!). Dokument." February 2, 2014. http://znak.com/urfo/news/2014-2002-02/1017612.html.

"Prigovor po delu Pussy Riot." August 21, 2012. http://www.vedomosti.ru/library/news/3115131/tekst_prigovora_po_delu_pussy_riot.

"Prokuratura trebuet ustranit' polovuiu diskriminatsiiu v IT-litsee pri universitete." October 17, 2012. http://pravo.ru/news/view/78750/.

"Prokuratura: peterburgskii LGBT-kinofestival' 'Bok o bok' deistvuet kak 'inostrannyi agent.'" *Gazeta*, May 8, 2013. http://www.gazeta.ru/social/news/2013/05/08/n_2898265.html.

Pronina, Lyubov, and Henry Meyer. "Putin Says Berlusconi Sex Allegations 'Made Out of Envy.'" Bloomberg, September 16, 2011. http://www.bloomberg.com/news/2011-2009-16/putin-says-berlusconi-sex-allegations-made-out-of-envy-1-.html.

"Proof of Your Manhood: The Man Card from Bushmaster." May 7, 2010. http://www.ammoland.com/2010/05/bushmaster-man-card/#axzz2zjW6C3lv.

ProtivAbortov 2011. "Za svobodnoe materinstvo!" https://sites.google.com/site/protivabortov2011/, accessed February 19, 2013.

Pushkareva, Natal'ia. "Nachalo zhenskogo dvizheniia v Rossii." In *Zhenskoe dvizhenie v Rossii: Vchera, segodnia, zavtra: Materialy konferentsii*, edited by Galina Mikhaleva, 29–34. Moscow: RODP "Yabloko" and KMK Publishers, 2010.

PussRiot. "Devchonki iz PUSSY RIOT zakhvatyvaiut transport" [video], November 6, 2011. http://www.youtube.com/watch?v=qEiB1RYuYXw&feature=related.

———. "Gruppa Pussy Riot zhzhet putinskii glamur" [video], November 30, 2011. http://www.youtube.com/watch?v=CZUhkWiiv7M.

"Pussy Riot singl dlia prigovora—'Putin zazhigaet kostry'" [video], August 17, 2012. https://www.youtube.com/watch?v=e9u06LD-l3g.

Pussy_riot. "Nelegal'nyi kontsert gruppy pussy riot na kryshe tiur'my." December 14, 2011. http://pussy-riot.livejournal.com/5763.html.

———. "Pank-moleben 'bogoroditsa, putina progoni' v khrame khrista spasitelia." February 21, 2012. http://pussy-riot.livejournal.com/12442.html.

———. "Proryv i arest pussy riot na lobnom meste krasnoi ploshchadi s pesnei 'putin zassal,'" January 20, 2012. http://pussy-riot.livejournal.com/8459.html.

———. "Vtoroi nelegal'nyi tur gruppy pussy riot s podzhogami i okkupatsiei." December 1, 2011. http://pussy-riot.livejournal.com/5164.html.

———. "Vyn' prezhde brevno iz tvoego glaza i togda uvidish'." February 23, 2012. http://pussy-riot.livejournal.com/12658.html.

"Putin 'Castrated' Democracy in Russia—Gorbachev." RIA Novosti, August 18, 2011. http://en.rian.ru/russia/20110818/165906628.html.

"Putin gotov obrezat'" [video], August 25, 2008. http://www.youtube.com/watch? feature=player_embedded&v=owAXfnSI5zA.

"Putin on 'Wasting Terrorists in the Outhouse': Wrong Rhetoric, Right Idea." July 15, 2011. http://rt.com/politics/putin-honesty-president-magnitogorsk/.

"Putin Opposes 'Primitive Interpretation' of Secularism." RIA Novosti, February 2, 2013. http://bit.ly/1ynH3aA.

"Putin Pidoras i Gnida" [video]. http://www.youtube.com/watch?v=ExFyv5qBvTk, accessed May 18, 2012.

"Putin pidoras! Russkii marsh!" [video], November 11, 2011. https://www.youtube.com/ watch?v=aCscB25cjxY.

"Putin pozhelal blagopoluchiia i protsvetaniia kazhdoi rossiiskoi sem'e." December 31, 2011. http://www.rosbalt.ru/main/2011/12/31/930649.html.

"Putin progolosoval na vyborakh vmeste s zhenoi. Topless-desant opozdal smutit' prem'era." March 4, 2012. http://www.newsru.com/russia/04mar2012/putingolos.html.

"Putin Promises to Lose 1/2 kg of Weight in 6 Months." ITAR-TASS, August 1, 2011.

"Putin Saves TV crew from Siberian Tiger." Reuters, September 2, 2008. http://www.reuters.com/article/2008/09/02/us-putin-tiger-idUSLV19939720080902.

"Putin the Unknown: TV Host Walks & Talks with Russian President." October 7, 2012. http://rt.com/news/putin-birthday-documentary-life-864/.

"Putin Says Support for Big Families, Mothers, Children Priority of Govt." ITAR-TASS, June 2, 2012. http://en.itar-tass.com/archive/676588.

Putin, Vladimir. "Annual Address to the Federal Assembly" [video/transcript], May 10, 2006.

"Putin, pidrakhui* ostavshiesia svobody dni." May 8, 2013. http://www.compromat.ru/ page_33340.htm.

"Putin Supporter Bends Frying Pans" [video] Reuters, August 3, 2011. http://www.reuters.com/video/2011/08/04/putin-supporter-bends-frying-pans?videoId=217853042.

"Putin to Bush: My Dog Bigger Than Yours." Reuters, November 4, 2010. s.

"Putin's Address Heralds Return to Soviet Times—Illarionov." May 12, 2006. http://www.fulfilledprophecy.com/bb/viewtopic.php?f=7&t=7754.

"Putin's 'Rape Joke' Played Down." October 20, 2006, http://news.bbc.co.uk/2/hi/6069136.stm.

"Putin's Rating Down but over 50% of Voters May Support Him in Election—Public Opinion Foundation." Interfax-Ukraine, December 29, 2011. http://bit.ly/1m0j2AV.

Rachkevych, Mark. "New Feminist Offensive Aims to Lift Women." Kyiv Post, March 22, 2012. http://www.kyivpost.com/guide/about-kyiv/new-feminist-offensive-aims-to-lift-women-124777.html.

Rayfield, Jillian. "Palin Uses Crosshairs to Identify Dems Who Voted For Health Care Reform." March 24, 2010. http://talkingpointsmemo.com/news/palin-uses-crosshairs-to-identify-dems-who-voted-for-health-care-reform.

Redstockings. Feminist Revolution. New York: Random House, 1979.

Redvalkyria. "Telekanal 'dlia devushek,'" May 24, 2013. http://feministki.livejournal.com/2724173.html.

"Rezul'taty vyborov v Koordinatsionnyi Sovet Oppozitsii." October 22, 2012. http://www.echo.msk.ru/blog/echomsk/943408-echo/.

Riabov, Oleg. "Rossiia matushka": Natsionalizm, gender i voina v Rossii XX veka. Stuttgart: ibidem-Verlag, 2007.

Riabova, T. B., and O. V. Riabov. "Nastoiashchii muzhchina Rossiiskoi politiki? (K voprosu o gendernom diskurse kak resurse vlasti)." POLIS: Politicheskie Issledovaniia, no. 5 (2010): 48–63.

———. "U nas seksa net: Gender, Identity, and Anticommunist Discourse in Russia." In State, Politics, and Society: Issues and Problems within Post-Soviet Development, edited by Aleksandr Markarov, 29–38. Iowa City: University of Iowa, 2002.

Riabova, Tat'iana. *Pol vlasti: Gendernye stereotypy v sovremennoi rossiiskoi politike*. Ivanovo, Russia: Ivanovo State University, 2008.

Richter, Amy G. *Home on the Rails: Women, the Railroad, and the Rise of Public Domesticity*. Chapel Hill: University of North Carolina Press, 2005.

Richter, James. "Evaluating Western Assistance to Russian Women's Organizations." In *The Power and Limits of NGOs*, edited by Sarah E. Mendelson and John K. Glenn, 54–90. New York: Columbia University Press, 2002.

Riordan, Jim. "The Komsomol." In *Soviet Youth Culture*, edited by Jim Riordan, 16–44. Bloomington: Indiana University Press, 1989.

Rivkin-Fish, Michele. "Conceptualizing Feminist Strategies for Russian Reproductive Politics: Abortion, Surrogate Motherhood, and Family Support after Socialism." *Signs* 38, no. 3 (2013): 569–593.

———. "From 'Demographic Crisis' to 'Dying Nation': The Politics of Language and Reproduction in Russia." In *Gender and National Identity in Twentieth-Century Russian Culture*, edited by Helena Goscilo and Andrea Lanoux, 151–173. DeKalb: Northern Illinois University Press, 2006.

———. "Pronatalism, Gender Politics, and the Renewal of Family Support in Russia: Toward a Feminist Anthropology of 'Maternity Capital.'" *Slavic Review* 69, no. 3 (Fall 2010): 701–724.

Robski, Oksana, and Kseniia Sobchak. *Zamuzh za millionera, ili Brak vyshego sorta*. Moscow: Astrel' ACT, 2009.

Roslyakov, Alex and Laura Mills. "Kremlin Youth Camp Seeks Image Change." August 2, 2012. http://bigstory.ap.org/article/kremlin-youth-camp-seeks-image-change.

Rosovi_bint. "07 iiulia 2012. Piket protiv nasiliia v sem'e." July 10, 2012. http://rosovi-bint.livejournal.com/118002.html.

———. "Iisus vs Gundiai." May 22, 2012. http://rosovi-bint.livejournal.com/2012/05/22/.

———. "Okolo Kniaz'-Vladimirskogo sobora raspiali zhenshchinu." November 7, 2011. http://rosovi-bint.livejournal.com/97155.html.

———. "Piket protiv antiabortnogo zakonodatel'stva proshel khorosho." June 25, 2011. http://rosovi-bint.livejournal.com/79363.html.

———. "Rozovyi krest 1.0." October 27, 2011. http://rosovi-bint.livejournal.com/95233.html.

———. "Vse na miting za prava zhenshchin!" August 29, 2011. http://rosovi-bint.livejournal.com/88777.html.

———. "Vynosim sor iz izby! Miting za priniatie zakona v zashchitu zhertv nasiliia." November 23, 2011. http://rosovi-bint.livejournal.com/98480.html.

"Rosmolodezh' obeshchaet na 'Seligere' dat' slovo vsem." July 26, 2012. http://ria.ru/politics/20120726/709775594.html.

"Rossiiskie zhenshchiny schitaiut glavu gosudarstva ideal'nym liubovnikom." December 18, 2000. http://www.businesspress.ru/newspaper/article_mId_33_aId_46130.html.

Rossiiskoe Obshchestvennoe Mnenie i Issledovanie Rynka (ROMIR). "Zhenshchiny Rossii." September 1999. http://web.archive.org/web/20040529075740/http://www.romir.ru/socpolit/socio/october/women.htm.

Rostova, Nataliia. "'Ia schitaiu, chto "nastoiashchii russkii muzhik" dolzhen vymeret','" January 15, 2010. http://slon.ru/russia/ya_schitayu_chto_nastoyashhiy_russkiy_muzhik_dolz-238959.xhtml.

"RPTs predlozhila vvesti obshcherossiiskii dress-kod." January 18, 2011. http://lenta.ru/news/2011/01/18/dresscode/.

"Russia Government Sets Population Growth as Top Priority." ITAR-TASS, November 29, 2012. http://en.itar-tass.com/archive/686148.

"Russia's pro-Kremlin youth group launches smear campaign against jailed opposition leader." RIA Novosti, January 10, 2011. http://en.rian.ru/russia/20110110/162092486.html.

"Russian Asks Obama for New Home." May 6, 2011, http://www.bbc.co.uk/news/world-europe-13312713.

"Russians Increasingly Trust President, Church—Poll." Interfax, June 26, 2012. http://www.interfax-religion.com/?act=news&div=9459.

"Russian Media Personality Turned Opposition Activist 'Hates Children'—TV." BB Monitoring, April 7, 2013.

"Russian TV Show Discusses Public Attitudes to Homosexuality: Dozhd Online." BBC Monitoring, November 11, 2012.

Ruthchild, Rochelle Goldberg. *Equality and Revolution: Women's Rights in the Russian Empire, 1905–1917*. Pittsburgh: University of Pittsburgh Press, 2010.

Ryazanova-Clarke, Lara. "The Discourse of a Spectacle at the End of the Presidential Term." In *Putin as Celebrity and Cultural Icon*, edited by Helena Goscilo, 104–132. London: Routledge, 2013.

Rybko, Sergii. "Igumen Sergii (Rybko) o razgone gei-kluba." October 12, 2012. http://www.pravmir.ru/igumen-sergij-rybko-o-razgone-gej-kluba-sozhaleyu-chto-kak-svyashhennik-ne-mogu-prinyat-uchastie-v-akcii/.

Sadcrixivan. "Esli by u muzhchin byla menstruatsiia. . . . " February 5, 2005. http://feministki.livejournal.com/373.html.

Salmenniemi, Suvi. *Democratization and Gender in Contemporary Russia*. London: Routledge, 2008.

Samarina, Aleksandra. "Prosto 'ne davat' povod dlia ubiistva'—Prostota argumentatsii rukovoditel'nitsy Tsentra razvitiia molodezhnykh SMI shokirovala." *Nezavisimaia Gazeta*, November 10, 2010. http://www.ng.ru/politics/2010-11-10/1_kashin.html.

Samofalova, Ol'ga. "Samye gromkie seks-skandaly 2010 goda." December 20, 2010. http://www.rb.ru/topstory/entertainment/2010/12/20/090147.html.

Sanger, David E. "Putin Is Target of the Pecan Pie Tactic." *New York Times*, November 15, 2001. http://www.nytimes.com/2001/11/15/international/15RANC.html.

Savenkov, Viktor. "Interview with Effective Policy Foundation President Gleb Pavlovskiy." *Svobodnaya Pressa*, December 6, 2011.

"Scantily-Clad Girls in Putin's 'Army' Wash Russian-Made Cars" [video], July 21, 2011. http://www.youtube.com/watch?v=aOe4JRry5j8&feature=player_embedded.

Schippers, Mimi. "Recovering the Feminine Other: Masculinity, Femininity, and Gender Hegemony." *Theory and Society* 36 (2007): 85–106.

Schoenfeld, Gabriel. "Boris Yeltsin's Ambiguous Legacy." *Commentary*, April 24, 2007. http://www.commentarymagazine.com/2007/04/24/boris-yeltsins-ambiguous-legacy/.

Schwirtz, Michael. "Putin in Martial Arts Video." *New York Times*, October 8, 2008. http://www.nytimes.com/2008/10/08/world/europe/08iht-putin.1.16776325.html.

Schwirtz, Michael. "In Russia, a Watch Vanishes Up Kirill's Sleeve." *New York Times*, April 5, 2012. http://www.nytimes.com/2012/04/06/world/europe/in-russia-a-watch-vanishes-up-orthodox-leaders-sleeve.html?_r=0.

Schwirtz, Michael, and David Herszenhorn. "Voters Watch Polls in Russia, and Fraud Is What They See." *New York Times*, December 5, 2011. http://nyti.ms/Tuo0wJ.

"Section 28." http://en.wikipedia.org/w/index.php?title=Section_28&oldid=552693762, accessed May 3, 2013.

Seitz-Wald, Adam. "Assault Rifle Company Issues 'Man Cards,'" December 17, 2012. http://www.salon.com/2012/12/17/bushmasters_horrible_ad_campaign/.

Seldner, Mimi. "Still Using the Old Model for Sexist Car Advertisements." *Ms. Magazine*, August 29, 2011. http://msmagazine.com/blog/blog/2011/08/29/still-using-the-old-model-for-sexist-car-advertisements/.

"Seliger 2009: Honour Watch" [video], August 4, 2009. http://www.youtube.com/watch?v=rNcXqRYWX_4.

"Seliger 2009: Putin-Medvedev Disco" [video], August 4, 2009. http://www.youtube.com/watch?v=6Ii8cJdRqO4&feature=related.

"Seliger 2011" [video], March 20, 2011. http://www.youtube.com/watch?v=97yQVXRgdMo.

"seliKhER. mnogo foto." July 28, 2010. http://tapirr.livejournal.com/2516191.html.

"Semenova, Galina Vladimirovna." *Vikipediia*, http://bit.ly/1kCVSlQ, accessed March 24, 2014.

Sergeyyugov. "feminizm po-russki?" [video], March 11, 2012. http://www.youtube.com/play list?list=PLAB65D4BD49285A0A.

Shagirt. "Feministskii miting ili kak ia provela 8 marta." March 10, 2013. http://feministki. livejournal.com/2592697.html#comments.

Shakirov, Mumin, and Aleksandr Kulygin. "Game Show Shocker Raises Questions About Holocaust Education." May 2, 2012. http://www.rferl.org/content/game_show_shocker_raises_questions_holocaust_education_russia/24531474.html.

"Shapovalova." http://www.shapovalova.ru/, accessed November 21, 2012.

Shchitov, Kirill. "Devushki porvut za Putina." July 17, 2011. http://kirillschitov.livejournal. com/211912.html.

Shenderovich, Viktor. "Opasnost' dlia obshchestva." March 6, 2012. http://www.svobo-danews.ru/content/article/24507039.html.

"Shkola feminizma" [audio], February 5, 2012. http://www.feminismru.org/load/audio/ shkola_feminizma/2-1-0-57.

"Shou: Bezumno krasivye." http://www.vokrug.tv/product/show/Bezumno_krasivye/, accessed January 17, 2013.

Showstack Sassoon, Anne. *Gramsci's Politics*. 2nd ed. Minneapolis: University of Minnesota Press, 1988.

Shuster, Simon. "The Managed Democracy: A How-to-Manual from Putin's Russia." *Time*, October 15, 2012. http://world.time.com/2012/10/15/the-managed-democracy-a-how-to-manual-from-putins-russia/.

Shvedova, Nadezhda. "Zhenskoe dvizhenie v Rossii: Problemy sovremennogo etapa." In *Zhenskoe dvizhenie v Rossii: Vchera, segodnia, zavtra: Materialy konferentsii*, edited by Galina Mikhaleva, 35–48. Moscow: RODP "Yabloko" and KMK Publishers, 2010.

Sindelar, Daisy. "How Many Demonstrated for the Kremlin? And How Willing Were They?" December 13, 2011. http://www.rferl.org/content/how_many_and_how_willing/ 24420674.html.

"Singing PM: 'Fats' Putin over the Top of 'Blueberry Hill' with Piano Solo" [video], December 11, 2010. http://www.youtube.com/watch?v=IV4IjHz2yIo.

"Skandal v efire: Dobrokhotov vs Kurginian" [video], December 17, 2008. http://www.you tube.com/watch?v=-tw_yd9srGQ.

"Smeshenie Neba i preispodnei." *Vzgliad*, February 21, 2012. http://www.vz.ru/ opinions/2012/2/21/563022.html.

Smith, David. "South African Court Finds ANC's Julius Malema Guilty of Hate Speech." *The Guardian*, March 15, 2010, http://www.guardian.co.uk/world/2010/mar/15/anc-julius-malema-guilty-hate-speech.

Smith, James F. "But Chilean Leader Slips in Polls: Combative Gen. Pinochet: Defeat Is Not in His Blood." *Los Angeles Times*, October 4, 1988. http://articles.latimes.com/1988-1910-04/news/mn-3481_1_augusto-pinochet/2.

Snow, David A., and Robert D. Benford. "Ideology, Frame Resonance and Participant Mobilization." *International Social Movement Research* 1, no. 1 (1988): 197–218.

solar2000. "Medvedev Girls" [video], August 3, 2011. http://www.youtube.com/ watch?v=mLdoJb4mOXM.

"Sovet po konsolidatsii Zhenskogo Dvizheniia Rossii." January 4, 2013. http://on.fb. me/11Hpd5p.

Sperling, Valerie. "Making the Public Patriotic: Militarism and Anti-Militarism in Russia." In *Russian Nationalism and the National Reassertion of Russia*, edited by Marlene Laruelle, 218–271. London: Routledge, 2009.

———. "Nashi Devushki: Gender and Political Youth Activism in Putin's and Medvedev's Russia." *Post-Soviet Affairs* 28, no. 2 (June 2012): 232–261.

———. *Organizing Women in Contemporary Russia: Engendering Transition.* Cambridge: Cambridge University Press, 1999.

———. "The Last Refuge of a Scoundrel: Patriotism, Militarism, and the Russian National Idea." *Nations and Nationalism* 9, no. 2 (2003): 235–253.

"St. Petersburg 'Gay Propaganda' Law Author Defiant after Milan Snub." RIA Novosti, November 28, 2012. http://en.rian.ru/russia/20121128/177798647.html.

"Stal' 'nasiluet' Nemtsova" [video], January 9, 2011. http://www.youtube.com/watch?v=5iEMZ7bHJfg [video removed by user].

"State Symbols of the Russian Federation." http://www.montreal.mid.ru/inf_symb_e.html, accessed October 19, 2012.

Stcukov. "Namedni—99. Skuratov" [video], October 13, 2009. http://www.youtube.com/watch?v=4icOg44nRWQ&feature=related.

Steinem, Gloria. "If Men Could Menstruate." *Ms. Magazine*, October 1978.

Stewart, Will. "The Portrait of Vladimir Putin as a Woman Which Got Artist Arrested by Secret Service." *MailOnline*, June 17, 2009. http://www.dailymail.co.uk/news/article-1193430/Artist-arrested-secret-service-portraying-Vladimir-Putin-woman.html.

Stites, Richard. *The Women's Liberation Movement in Russia: Feminism, Nihilism, and Bolshevism, 1860-1930.* Princeton, NJ: Princeton University Press, 1978.

Stobart, Janet. "British Admit Using 'Embarrassing' Fake Rock to Spy on Russians." *Los Angeles Times*, January 20, 2012. http://articles.latimes.com/2012/jan/20/world/la-fg-britain-spy-rock-20120120.

Stoltenberg, John. *Refusing to Be a Man: Essays on Sex and Justice.* New York: Penguin Books, 1989.

Stolyarova, Galina. "Not a Pretty Picture." January 31, 2013. http://www.tol.org/client/article/23576-russia-prison-women.html.

StreetFem. "Listovka k mitingu 8 marta." March 8, 2013. http://radical-fem-msk.livejournal.com/16382.html.

———. "Segodnia v Moskve proshel edinstvennyi feministkii miting." March 8, 2013. http://radical-fem-msk.livejournal.com/15881.html.

Strukov, Vlad. "Russian Internet Stars: Gizmos, geeks, and glory." In *Celebrity and Glamour in Contemporary Russia: Shocking Chic*, edited by Helena Goscilo and Vlad Strukov, 144–169. London: Routledge, 2011.

"Studenty SPbGU sdelali pervoaprel'skii kalendar' dlia Matvienko (foto)." April 1, 2011. http://www.rosbalt.ru/piter/2011/04/01/834965.html.

Sturdee, Nick. "Don't Raise the Bridge: Voina, Russia's Art Terrorists." *The Guardian*, April 12, 2011. http://www.guardian.co.uk/artanddesign/2011/apr/12/voina-art-terrorism.

Sukhareva, Tat'iana, and Olgerta Ostrov. "Miting 8 marta—Feminizm eto osvobozhdenie." March 8, 2013. https://www.facebook.com/events/218586968279328/.

Sulimina, Anna. "Occupy Seliger." *The Moscow News*, July 19, 2012. http://themoscownews.com/politics/20120719/189979244.html.

Sundstrom, Lisa McIntosh. *Funding Civil Society: Foreign Assistance and NGO Development in Russia.* Stanford, CA: Stanford University Press, 2006.

———. "Russian Women's Activism: Two Steps Forward, One Step Back." In *Women's Movements in the Global Era: The Power of Local Feminisms*, edited by Amrita Basu, 219–244. Boulder, CO: Westview Press, 2010.

"Takogo kak Putin/One Like Putin, English Subs" [video], December 6, 2008. http://www.youtube.com/watch?v=zk_VszbZa_s&feature=related.

Tayler, Jeffrey. "Femen, Ukraine's Topless Warriors." *The Atlantic*, November 28, 2012. http://www.theatlantic.com/international/archive/2012/11/femen-ukraines-topless-warriors/265624/.

Taylor, Alan. "Vladimir Putin, Action Man." *The Atlantic*, September 13, 2011. http://www.theatlantic.com/infocus/2011/09/vladimir-putin-action-man/100147/.

Taylor, Brian D. *State Building in Putin's Russia: Policing and Coercion after Communism.* Cambridge: Cambridge University Press, 2011.

Tcsbank. "Obysk-2 u Ksenii Sobchak" [video], July 11, 2012. http://www.youtube.com/watch?v=wqdSLXCyCwA.

Temkina, Anna. "Gendernyi vopros v sovremennoi Rossii." June 16, 2012. http://polit.ru/article/2012/06/16/gender/.

Ternovskii, Dmitrii. "Seliger 2012. Reportazh s otkrytiia." July 3, 2012. http://www.ridus.ru/news/38565/.

Timchenko, V. *Putin i novaia Rossiia.* Rostov-na-donu, Russia: Feniks, 2005.

Tolokno, Nadia. "Nelegal'nye feministskie kontserty v Moskve." November 7, 2011. http://feministki.livejournal.com/1857679.html.

Tripp, Aili Mari. "Toward a Comparative Politics of Gender Research in Which Women Matter." *Perspectives on Politics* 8, no. 1 (March 2010): 191–197.

"Tsentral'noe televidenie. Vypusk ot 7 oktiabria 2012 goda" [video]. NTV, October 7, 2012. http://www.ntv.ru/peredacha/CT/m23400/o113999/comments/.

Tsentral'nyi vybornyi komitet. "Spisok kandidatov." October 2, 2012. http://compass.cvk2012.org/candidates/.

UN Office on Drugs and Crime. *2011 Global Study on Homicide.* Vienna: UN Office on Drugs and Crime, 2011.

Uskov, Nikolai. "Pro menia." 2013. http://www.snob.ru/profile/24889.

Utkin, Sasha. "Kalendar'." October 7, 2010. http://sasha-utkin.livejournal.com/147833.html.

"V godovshchinu kazni dekabristov iablochniki obideli Andropova." July 29, 2004. http://novayagazeta.ru/data/2004/54/06.html.

"V Moskve proshla aktsiia 'S putinistami ne spim!'" February 14, 2009. http://www.grani.ru/Politics/Russia/activism/m.147569.html.

"V Moskve proshla teatralizovannaia aktsiia 'Odin den' iz zhizni rossiianki.'" *Yabloko,* November 29, 2011. http://www.yabloko.ru/regnews/Moscow/2011/11/29.

"V Voronezhe arestovan khudozhnik, napisavshii portret Putina v zhenskom plat'e." June 16, 2009. http://www.newsru.com/russia/16jun2009/shurik.html.

Varlamov, Il'ya. "'Kogda sleduiushchii terakt?'—Kalendar' dlia prem'era/Kommentarii." October 7, 2010. http://www.echo.msk.ru/blog/varlamov_i/716443-echo/.

———. "Nashi protiv NAShIkh." December 7, 2011. http://echo.msk.ru/blog/varlamov_i/836960-echo/.

Varlamov, Ilya. "Besporiadki v Moskve." December 11, 2010. http://zyalt.livejournal.com/330396.html.

———. "Fotoputeshestviia i eshche.—Chto-to ne tak? Rozhaite!" May 18, 2011. http://zyalt.livejournal.com/399790.html.

———. "Fotoputeshestviia i eshche.—Seliger." August 2, 2011. http://zyalt.livejournal.com/432712.html#cutid1.

Vasilyeva, Maria, and Nikolai Isayev. "Amnestied Russian Punk Band Pair Criticize "Putin after Release." *Chicago Tribune,* December 23, 2013. http://www.chicagotribune.com/news/sns-rt-us-russia-pussyriot-release-20131222,0,5817915.story.

Vershinina, Kseniia. "Artemii Troitskii: Mitingi dolzhny privesti k perenosu prezidentskikh vyborov i smene TsIK." December 26, 2011. http://www.1tvnet.ru/content/show/artemii-trocikii-mitingi-doljni-privesti-k-perenosu-prezidentskih-viborov-i-smene-cik_07202.html.

Vinnik, Nikolai. "Zhenskoe dvizhenie i runet: Naiti drug druga." In *Zhenskoe dvizhenie v Rossii: Vchera, segodnia, zavtra: Materialy konferentsii,* edited by Galina Mikhaleva, 94–96. Moscow: RODP "Yabloko" and KMK Publishers, 2010.

Vinogradova, Elena, Irina Kozina, and Linda Cook. "Russian Labor: Quiescence and Conflict." *Communist and Post-Communist Studies* 45, nos. 3–4 (December 2012): 219–231.

"'Vinzavodu' ob"iavili boikot za podderzhku khudozhnika Trushevskogo." June 7, 2010. http://lenta.ru/news/2010/06/07/vinzavod/.

Viola, Lynne. *Peasant Rebels under Stalin: Collectivization and the Culture of Peasant Resistance.* New York: Oxford University Press, 1996.

Viroli, Maurizio. *The Liberty of Servants: Berlusconi's Italy.* Princeton, NJ: Princeton University Press, 2010.

"Visit to Russia Today Television Channel." June 11, 2013. http://eng.kremlin.ru/news/5571.

"Vladimir Putin pozdravil sograzhdan s Voskreseniem Khristovym." May 5, 2013. http://www.pravoslavie.ru/news/61349.htm.

"Vladimir Putin promenial Iuliu na Iru (foto)." 2007. http://www.mosstroy.su/news-word/various/Vladimir-Putin10/.

"Vladimir Putin Rides Harley-Davidson with Russian Biker Gang" [video]. *Huffington Post,* August 30, 2011. http://www.huffingtonpost.com/2011/08/30/putin-motorcycle-russia-_n_941963.html.

"Vladimir Putin Says Pussy Riot Should Not Be Treated Too Harshly." *The Telegraph,* August 2, 2012. http://www.telegraph.co.uk/news/worldnews/vladimir-putin/9448370/Vladimir-Putin-says-Pussy-Riot-should-not-be-treated-too-harshly.html.

"Vladimir Putin: F1 Driver." *The Telegraph,* November 8, 2010. http://www.telegraph.co.uk/news/worldnews/europe/russia/8116882/Vladimir-Putin-F1-driver.html.

"Voina ebetsia za naslednika Medvezhonka (ren-tv)" [video], April 18, 2008. https://www.youtube.com/watch?v=BstpfQuQzuw.

Von Twickel, Nikolaus. "Punk Band's Legal Team Reveals Full Performance." *The Moscow Times,* June 6, 2012. http://www.themoscowtimes.com/news/article/punk-bands-legal-team-reveals-full-performance/459967.html#ixzz1x2CNf5X4.

"Vova Putin pidoras" [video], February 16, 2011. https://www.youtube.com/watch?v=3JvVeFjm0jo.

"Vsemirnyi den' kontratseptsii: aktsiia v Moskve—28 Sentiabria 2010—Za feminizm." September 28, 2010. http://www.zafeminizm.ucoz.ru/news/vsemirnyj_den_kontracepcii_akcija_v_moskve/2010-09-28-1.

"Vserossiiskii molodezhnyi forum Seliger 2012." http://www.forumseliger.ru/, accessed December 4, 2012.

VTsIOM: Vserossiiskii Tsentr Izucheniia Obshchestvennogo Mneniia. "Domashnie khlopoty: Kto i chto delaet v rossiiskoi sem'e." May 23, 2011. http://wciom.ru/index.php?id=459&uid=111631.

———. "Gomoseksualistami ne rozhdaiutsia?" May 17, 2012. http://wciom.ru/index.php?id=459&uid=112769.

———. "Muzhchiny i zhenshchiny ravny, no kto iz nikh 'ravnee'?" June 3, 2007. http://wciom.ru/index.php?id=459&uid=4120.

———. "Odnopolaia liubov'—Normal'no, braki—Rano." February 15, 2005. http://wciom.ru/index.php?id=459&uid=1084.

———. "Zhenshchiny i vlast': Kak garantirovat' ravenstvo polov v politike?" March 6, 2009. http://wciom.ru/index.php?id=459&uid=11527.

"Vybory! Vybory! Kandidaty—pidory!" [video], October 11, 2007. http://www.youtube.com/watch?v=1CLBANCVHTw.

Wahl-Jorgensen, Karin. "Constructing Masculinities in U.S. Presidential Campaigns: The Case of 1992." In *Gender, Politics, and Communication,* edited by Annabelle Sreberny and Liesbet Van Zoonen, 53–77. Cresskill, NJ: Hampton Press, 2000.

Wander Woman. "Fotoreportazh s mitinga 8 marta 2012 g. v Moskve." March 9, 2012. http://www.zafeminizm.ru/137-fotoreportazh-s-mitinga-8-marta-2012-g-v-moskve.html.

———. "Predstavitel' RPTs v popytkakh diskreditirovat' idei gendernogo ravenstva." February 15, 2012. http://www.zafeminizm.ru/115-predstavitel-rpc-v-popytkah-diskreditirovat-idei-gendernogo-ravenstva.html.

———. "Seksist Goda-2011: Itogi." March 6, 2012. http://www.zafeminizm.ru/2012/03/06/seksist-goda-2011-itogi.html.

———. "Seksist goda-2012. Golosovanie." February 13, 2013. http://www.zafeminizm.ru/180-seksist-goda-2012-golosovanie.html.

———. "The 100th Anniversary of International Women's Day in Russia: Details of the Forcibly Dispersed Feminist Meeting at Novopushkinsky Park on 8th March." March 9, 2013. http://www.zafeminizm.ru/186-the-100th-anniversary-of-international-womens-day-in-russia-details-of-the-forcibly-dispersed-feminist-meeting-at-novopushkinsky-park-on-8th-march.html.

Washington, Tom. "Puckering Up for Russia's President." *The Moscow News*, July 7, 2011. http://themoscownews.com/politics/20110707/188818857.html.

———. "Shorts Stunt Gives Putin a Sharp Shock." *Moscow News*, May 31, 2011.

———. "Voina come back for kisses." *TheMoscowNews.com*, March 1, 2011. http://www.themoscownews.com/local/20110301/188458300.html.

Weir, Fred. "Putin Eyes Trip to Antarctica, Shuns Elder Image." *Christian Science Monitor*, January 29, 2013. http://www.csmonitor.com/World/Global-News/2013/0129/Putin-eyes-trip-to-Antarctica-shuns-elder-image.

West, Candace, and Don H. Zimmerman. "Doing Gender." *Gender and Society* 1, no. 2 (June 1987): 125–151.

White, Gregory. "Russia after Putin." *Wall Street Journal*, February 25, 2012. http://online.wsj.com/article/SB10001424052970203960804577241392587109400.html?mod=WSJ_hpp_RIGHTTopCarousel_1.

White, Gregory L. "Having Vowed Reform, Kremlin Said to Dilute It." *Wall Street Journal*, April 18, 2012. http://online.wsj.com/article/SB100014240527023035134045773517741370360480.html?mod=googlenews_wsj.

White, Stephen, and Ian McAllister. "The Putin Phenomenon." *Journal of Communist Studies and Transition Politics* 24, no. 4 (2008): 604–628.

Whitmore, Brian. "The Pavlovsky Affair." April 29, 2011. http://www.rferl.org/content/the_pavlovsky_affair/16798268.html.

Williams, Christine L. *Gender Differences at Work: Women and Men in Nontraditional Occupations*. Berkeley: University of California Press, 1989.

Williams, Kimberly A. *Imagining Russia: Making Feminist Sense of American Nationalism in U.S.–Russian Relations*. Albany: State University of New York Press, 2012.

Wood, Elizabeth. "Performing Memory: Vladimir Putin and the Celebration of WWII in Russia." *The Soviet and Post-Soviet Review* 38 (2011): 172–200.

———. "Russia's Anti-Putin Protests Are More Than Just a Generational Temper Tantrum." *Boston Globe*, January 18, 2012. http://www.boston.com/bostonglobe/editorial_opinion/blogs/the_angle/2012/01/putins_failures.html.

———. "The New Façade of Autocracy: Vladimir Putin and Hypermasculinity, 1999 to the Present." Keynote Speech, Modern European Lunch, American Historical Association, 2011.

Wood, Elizabeth A. *The Baba and the Comrade: Gender and Politics in Revolutionary Russia*. Bloomington: Indiana University Press, 1997.

Woodward, Bob, and Carl Bernstein. *All the President's Men*. 2nd ed. New York: Simon & Schuster, 1994.

Woolf, Virginia. *Three Guineas*. Adelaide, Australia: University of Adelaide, 2014. (originally published 1938)

Yashin. "Putin i politicheskaia pedofiliia" [video], May 3, 2011. http://yashin.livejournal.com/1027773.html.

———. "Ulybaites.' Vas snimaet skrytaia kamera." March 23, 2010. http://yashin.livejournal.com/894296.html.

"'You Don't Own Me' PSA Official" [video], 2012. http://vimeo.com/51940856.

"Youths Take Aim at Russian Foes." *Calgary Herald*, October 25, 2007.

Yuval-Davis, Nira. *Gender and Nation*. London: Sage Publications, 1997.

"Za spravedlivost'!" March 27, 2012. http://kro-rodina.ru/all-news/207-za-spravedlivost.

"Za svobodnoe materinstvo." https://sites.google.com/site/protivabortov2011/, accessed February 19, 2013.

Zagvozdnina, Dar'ia. "Delo Pussy Riot—V interv'iu 'Gazete.Ru' Ekaterina Samutsevich rasskazala o patriarkhe, feminizme i zhizni v tiur'me." October 17, 2012. http://www.gazeta.ru/social/2012/10/17/4815193.shtml.

Zaitseva, Valentina. "National, Cultural, and Gender Identity in the Russian Language." In *Gender and National Identity in Twentieth-Century Russian Culture*, edited by Helena Goscilo and Andrea Lanoux, 30–54. DeKalb: Northern Illinois University Press, 2006.

Zamyatin, Yevgeny. *We*. New York: Harper Voyager, 2001.

Zdravomyslova, Elena, and Anna Temkina. "The Crisis of Masculinity in Late Soviet Discourse." *Russian Studies in History* 51, no. 2 (Fall 2012): 13–34.

Zhirinovskii, Vladimir, and Vladimir Iurovitskii. *Azbuka seksa: Ocherki seksual'noi kul'tury v rynochnom mire*. Moscow: Politbiuro, 1998.

Zhokhov, Egor. "Pro Seliger, nashistov i Putina." February 11, 2013. http://yagrazhdanin.ru/post1230.

Zubov, Mikhail. "Lift Iakemenko." *Moskovskii Komsomolets*, December 1, 2010. http://www.mk.ru/politics/article/2010/11/30/548359-lift-yakemenko.html.

Zychowicz, Jessica. "Two Bad Words: Femen and Feminism in Independent Ukraine." *Anthropology of East Europe Review* 29, no. 2 (Fall 2011): 215–227.

Interviews

Vera Akulova, Moskovskaia Feministskaia Gruppa, interview by author, Moscow, June 6, 2012.

Alena Arshinova, Molodaia Gvardiia, interview by author, Moscow, June 14, 2011.

Natal'ia Bitten, Initsiativnaia Gruppa "Za Feminizm," interview by author, Moscow, June 4, 2012.

Nikita Borovikov, Nashi, interview by author, Moscow, June 9, 2011.

Nikita Borovikov, Nashi, interview by author, Moscow, June 19, 2012.

Frau Derrida, Moskovskaia Feministskaia Gruppa, interview by author, Moscow, June 7, 2012.

Roman Dobrokhotov, My, interview by author, Moscow, June 9, 2011.

Tat'iana E., FemInfoteka, interview by author, St. Petersburg, June 14, 2012.

Irina Fetkulova, Molodezhnoe Dvizhenie "Ostanovim Nasilie," interview by author, Moscow, June 18, 2012.

Kirill Goncharov, Molodezhnoe Yabloko, interview by author, Moscow, June 10, 2011.

Tat'iana Grigor'eva, Initsiativnaia Gruppa "Za Feminizm," interview by author, Moscow, June 18, 2012.

Igor' Iakovlev, Molodezhnoe Yabloko, interview by author, Moscow, June 14, 2011.

Aleksandra Kachko, Drugaia Rossiia, interview by author, St. Petersburg, June 15, 2012.

Anastasiia Khodyreva, Krizisnyi Tsentr dlia Zhenshchin, interview by author, St. Petersburg, June 15, 2012.

Vera Kichanova, Libertarianskaia partiia, interview by author, Moscow, June 16, 2011.

Irina Kosterina, interview by author, Moscow, June 18, 2011.

Irina Kosterina, interview by author, Moscow, June 8, 2012.

Oleg Kozlovskii, Oborona, interview by author, Moscow, June 8, 2011.

Elena Maksimova, Moskovskie Radikal'nye Feministki, interview by author, Moscow, June 22, 2012.

Galina Mikhaleva, Chair, Gendernaia Fraktsiia Partii Yabloko, interview by author, Moscow, June 8, 2012.

Mariia Mokhova, Sestry, interview by author, Moscow, June 9, 2012.

Elizaveta Morozova, Moskovskaia Feministskaia Gruppa, interview by author, Moscow, June 20, 2012.

Zhenia Otto, Komitet za Rabochii Internatsional, Kampaniia protiv ekspluatatsii i diskrimi-
    natsii zhenshchin, interview by author, Moscow, June 18, 2012.
Irina Pleshcheva, Nashi, interview by author, Moscow, June 16, 2011.
Nadia Plungian, Moskovskaia Feministskaia Gruppa, interview by author, Moscow, June 20,
    2012.
Mariia Savel'eva, interview by author, via Skype, June 22, 2012.
Mariia Savel'eva, Oborona, interview by author, Moscow, June 8, 2011.
Tivur Shaginurov, Oborona, interview by author, Moscow, June 20, 2012.
Tivur Shaginurov, Oborona, interview by author, Moscow, June 11, 2011.
Anton Smirnov, Stal'/Nashi, interview by author, Moscow, June 17, 2011.
Anna Temkina, interview by author, St. Petersburg, June 14, 2012.
Mariia Tronova, Molodezhnoe Dvizhenie "Ostanovim Nasilie," interview by author, Moscow,
    June 18, 2012.
Ol'ga Vlasova, Molodezhnoe Yabloko, interview by author, Moscow, June 14, 2011.
Oksana Zamoiskaia, Rossiiskoe Sotsialisticheskoe Dvizhenie, interview by author, St. Peters-
    burg, June 16, 2012.
Polina Zaslavskaia, Verkhotura, interview by author, St. Petersburg, June 14, 2012.
Nikolai Zboroshenko, Oborona, interview by author, Moscow, June 6, 2011.

INDEX

The ABCs of Sex (Zhirinovskii), 65
Abdulaeva, Mariia, 164
abortion: Orthodox Church and, 74, 149, 252,
    256–257, 261, 274, 276, 281–282;
    protests against, 152; protests and support
    for legal right to, 194, 240, 244, 253,
    256–257, 261–262, 265, 267, 291–292;
    Russian legal restrictions on, 149, 154,
    197, 219, 245, 252–253, 255–257, 267,
    274, 276, 281–282, 291, 300; in the Soviet
    Union, 252–253; Sterligov's media
    campaign against, 286; in Ukraine, 240
Action in Memory of Raped Women (2010),
    265
activism. *See also specific organizations*:
    abortion rights and, 194, 240, 244, 253,
    256–257, 261–262, 265, 291–292; anti-
    conscription protests and, 141, 143–148,
    168; anti-corruption protests and, 92;
    anti-Putin protests and, 43, 46–47,
    85–86, 93–94, 108–109, 113–116,
    119–122, 204–206, 226–227, 231, 240,
    245, 260, 263, 302; for feminist causes,
    215, 218, 245, 249–267, 285–286, 293,
    300–303, 309; gendered framing of, 2–3,
    5–6, 27, 47, 91, 123, 136, 141–148, 151,
    168, 174, 191–192, 194, 197, 213–214,
    241, 278, 290; LGBT rights and, 75,
    106–107, 109–110, 169, 202–206, 255,
    258–263, 265–266, 292, 299–300, 308,
    312; Orange Revolutions' impact on,
    83–84; patriotism and, 136; post-election
    protests (2011–2012) and, 46–47,
    113–116, 119–122, 163–164, 204, 206,
    226–227, 231, 245, 258–265, 276;
    protests against pro-natalism and,
    154–155; suppression of, 56, 86, 93–94,
    115–116, 207–208, 258, 263, 265, 276,
    278–282, 287–290, 292–293, 298–304,
    308–309

Adagamov, Rustam, 292
Aeroflot, 57
AIDS, 116–118
Aivazova, Svetlana, 305
Akin, Todd, 49
Akulova, Vera: on abortion rights campaign,
    257; on feminism in Russia, 51–52; on
    gendered notions of protest, 192; on
    "Happy Birthday, Mr. Putin" calendar,
    268, 270; on homophobia in Russia,
    205–206; on "March of Burning Hearts"
    protest, 262; on Pussy Riot, 237–238,
    280–281; on Putin and Medvedev, 111; on
    rape, 189; on sex discrimination in Russia,
    186, 300
Alekhina, Mariia, 223, 260
Alekseeva, Liudmila, 86, 155
Alexander, Jeffrey, 13–15
Alexei II (patriarch of Russian Orthodox
    Church), 75
Andropov, Yuri, 85
ANNA (anti–domestic violence organization),
    183, 216, 253
Arab Spring (2011), 225
Arbatova, Mariia, 218, 260
Argentina, 14–16
Arshinova, Alena: on gender stereotypes in
    Russia, 173–174; on "Happy Birthday,
    Mr. Putin" calendar, 81; on
    homosexuality, 201–202; on LGBT
    rights, 204; on military service,
    127–128; Molodaia Gvardiia leadership
    and, 139
Astakhov, Pavel, 305
Avianova, 57–58
Azhgikhina, Nadezhda, 209, 214, 219

"baba" (derogatory term for woman), 36, 230
Banksy, 165
Barandova, Tatiana, 70, 220